MISSING LINKS

John Reader

MISSING LINKS

In search of human origins

OXFORD
UNIVERSITY PRESS

OXFORD
UNIVERSITY PRESS

Great Clarendon Street, Oxford OX2 6DP

Oxford University Press is a department of the University of Oxford.
It furthers the University's objective of excellence in research, scholarship,
and education by publishing worldwide in

Oxford New York

Auckland Cape Town Dar es Salaam Hong Kong Karachi
Kuala Lumpur Madrid Melbourne Mexico City Nairobi
New Delhi Shanghai Taipei Toronto

With offices in

Argentina Austria Brazil Chile Czech Republic France Greece
Guatemala Hungary Italy Japan Poland Portugal Singapore
South Korea Switzerland Thailand Turkey Ukraine Vietnam

Oxford is a registered trade mark of Oxford University Press
in the UK and in certain other countries

Published in the United States
by Oxford University Press Inc., New York

© John Reader 2011

British Library Cataloguing in Publication Data
Data available

Library of Congress Cataloging in Publication Data
Data available

Typeset by SPI Publisher Services, Pondicherry, India
Printed in China
on acid-free paper by
C C Offset

ISBN 978–0–19–927685–1

1 3 5 7 9 10 8 6 4 2

HOMO nofce Te ipfum.

Carolus Linnaeus
Systema Naturae, 1735

———————————

MAN know Yourself

An enlarged and fully updated edition of a
definitive work on the study of human origins.

First published thirty years ago, *Missing Links*
was described in *Nature* as 'the best popular account of
palaeoanthropology I have ever read, [which also] makes a
original and stimulating contribution to the science'.

FOREWORD

FRESH FINDS of fossil humans are exciting and interesting. New discoveries attract the notice of journalists and an attentive public, apparently eager to acquire information about our human evolution, about our remote ancestors and relatives, and where we might have come from. This is a natural enough impulse attesting to a deep-seated fascination with our origins. Many cultures around the world, past and present, have ideas and myths about their remote history, and where they might be going. Often these involve the notion that people were once not as they are now, and that they have changed to get to where they are at present. However, as a science, the study of human evolution is a relatively recent one, having really only been inaugurated by Darwin and Huxley around 150 years ago. When Charles Darwin wrote *On the Origin of Species*, published in 1859, he knew of no fossil remains of our lineage—although a few existed—but specimens came to notice fairly rapidly in the coming years.

In this splendid book John Reader gives an account of human evolution not by explicitly describing the state of the science just at the present time, but by recounting the history of discovery and the changes of thought that these discoveries have provoked. And in doing this he incidentally introduces us to some rather striking and odd characters. They are perhaps odd partly because as a science palaeoanthropology itself is a rather odd one. Most sciences are contemporary, in that they study aspects of the present world. The things that concern them are happening now, or can be made to happen experimentally. They mostly study processes and events that happen repeatedly, or the events of interest can be replicated in the laboratory. Ideas can be tested, and rejected or provisionally supported. Also in most sciences the nature of the data collected is in some sense controlled by and is part of the subject we are interested in. Where you find information about aspects of contemporary ecology, for instance, is somehow part of ecology itself. The most obvious distinctive feature of palaeoanthropology is that, like a few other historical sciences, it deals with the past.

And in palaeoanthropology some of the most interesting incidents in our history have probably only happened once—the move to a curious and unique bipedal form of locomotion, for example; the acquisition of an incomprehensibly large brain. Also the information is not controlled by aspects of the subject itself, but mainly by vagaries of geological accident influencing the preservation of fossils and other relevant data; where on Earth we find them, and what time periods they represent. So, for example, if some theory would benefit from discovering what our hominid ancestors were like in Arabia two million years ago, we cannot simply go there and guarantee being able to collect fossils of them. There may be no fossil sites at all dating to that time in Arabia—none are so far known—and if there are, they may not preserve fossil hominids even if hominids were actually even living in the region at the time. Things are not so bad for us humans as for gorillas though. Even though the gorilla lineage diverged from other apes about eight and half million years ago, so far we have not a single fossil of one of them. And as for our nearest living relatives, chimpanzees, the total fossil evidence consists only of around half a dozen teeth from a single site dated to about half a million years ago.

Because of these factors, and others like them, information about the past and about single events is not easy to get. Consequently in palaeoanthropology there are great difficulties with testing ideas. In most sciences people have ideas and theories about how or why something came about. Subsequently, researchers can make certain crucial observations by which they can try to falsify these ideas and theories, or in various ways provisionally assess the likelihood of them being true. This is how science works, by eliminating possibilities. But in data-difficult, data-impoverished palaeoanthropology there is more freedom for extravagant notions, which can persist for longer, as it is harder to challenge them. Consequently almost every fossil discoverer's new specimen is affirmed to be the best ever found, the site it comes from is the finest in the World, and no matter how like existing specimens the new one is, we are led to believe it is in fact completely different, perhaps deserving a new scientific name, and solving all scientific problems.

However, not all is simply relative; I do not want to give the impression that the history of the subject—or its current practice—has consisted simply of a succession of outsized embodied egos uttering random self-serving pronouncements and assertions. Amid these sometimes hyperbolic claims some turn out actually to be true. Checks and balances work, testing works, and much positive progress has been made over the last century or so. Increasingly older hominid fossils have been found, we know a good deal about the timing of various events in our evolution, about the acquisition of bipedalism, changes in teeth, expansion of the cranial capacity. We have some understanding of the diversity of hominids at different times; there were periods when at least four species of hominid lived in the same places and at the same time in the past.

Most of this knowledge has come about from the discovery of fossils, and without them we would know very little about palaeoanthropology. There is important work in molecular biology, which provides some insights about broad relationships and timing of evolutionary events. There is important work involving the context of human evolution that reveals information about the environments hominids lived in, and the climatic and environmental forces that may have influenced our evolution. But even now, when we have many thousands of ancient human remains, it is still new fossils that cause the most fundamental modification of existing ideas and lead to progress in our knowledge. And despite still being frustratingly rare, since Darwin human fossils have been found at an ever increasing rate.

John Reader has here radically revised a book he wrote over a quarter of a century ago, and which had considerable impact on a number of people at the time—myself included. Like that first one, this edition treats the discovery of evidence for human evolution principally by focusing on the discoverers of classic remains of extinct species. The book successfully reveals the way discovery has occurred, the intellectual and philosophical preconceptions behind interpretation, and in general gives a superb insight into the way the science has worked since its beginnings. Another major and important feature of the book is John's outstanding photographs. He originated a style of photography in this subject which combines the original fossils with memorabilia and portraits of the discoverers, to present a very telling visual statement. The original work has long been out of print, and much has happened in the subject since its first publication. In that time about seven or eight new, and plausibly acceptable, species of extinct hominid have been discovered and described. As well as these, important new specimens have been found of already known kinds of hominid, which provide more detailed information about them and their lives. And the time scale of the physical evidence of our ancestry has been doubled, being pushed back from around three and a half million years to nearer seven million years ago. Much has happened, driven by intense and dedicated exploration, mostly in fairly remote regions of the world, principally in Africa but also elsewhere, by a small number of ongoing expeditions.

Most other books on human evolution have been written by the discoverers of specimens and other significant practitioners, and it is understandable that they have a particular personal opinion and point of view. But John has no apparent personal agenda, and his keen and enquiring intelligence, coupled with decades of mingling on easy terms with palaeoanthropologists and other relevant scientists, has I think provided him with insights into the subject, its development and practice, that others perhaps recognize less. The study of human evolution remains an exciting field, not only for those of us who actively participate in it professionally, but also apparently to people in general. John Reader in this volume captures much of that enthusiasm and excitement, provides us with the history leading to the state of the subject at this point in time, and also establishes a valuable background and critical perspective for appreciating, evaluating, and understanding the many important discoveries that will no doubt be made in future years.

Andrew Hill

Yale University
11 *November* 2010

ACKNOWLEDGEMENTS

A GREAT DEAL has happened in the world of palaeoanthropology since the first edition of *Missing Links* was published in 1981; calls for a second edition have been persistent and I count myself very fortunate indeed to have had that motive to remain in close contact with this fascinating science and its practitioners. Even so, though leavened by insider reporting, this is still an outsider's book, based principally on the published material to which an honorary research fellowship in the department of anthropology at University College, London, gave me easy access—in its libraries and online. This is an invaluable facility for which, in the first instance, I am indebted to Leslie Aiello and offer thanks accordingly—to Leslie and to UCL.

Among the numerous scientists and commentators I have consulted on this edition, and to all of whom I offer again my sincere thanks, there are some whose contribution merits individual acknowledgement and thanks. They are Andrew Hill, Tim White and Berhane Asfaw, David Pilbeam, Chris Stringer, Rob Foley, Jean-Jacques Hublin, Svante Pääbo, Michel Brunet, Zeray Alemseged, Chris Stringer, Jean-Luis Arsuaga, Phillip Tobias, Ron Clarke, Francis Thackeray, Bob Brain, the late Hilary Deacon, Sarah Wurz, Kathy Kuman, Lyn Wadley, Sally McBrearty, Bill Kimbel, Chris Henshilwood, Meave Leakey, Fred Spoor, and Alain Beauvilain.

On the illustrative side of things, the involvement and encouragement of Rose Taylor and Science Photo Library have been invaluable. Tim White was especially helpful with images I could not otherwise have obtained, so too were Dan McCarthy, Keith Montgomery, Javier Trueba, Zeray Alemseged, Bert Sliggers, Elisabeth Daynes and Peggy, Michel Brunet, Alain Beauvilain, and Roydon Yates. The expertise of Josh Smith was crucial to the successful presentation of the images, and Chris Lovell offered helpful advice at a critical moment—my sincere thanks to all.

Caroline Dawney, Carol McArthur, and Hilary O'Shea have been especially helpful and understanding, and working with Oxford University Press has been a revelation in terms of the exceptional care, guidance, and resources that were allocated to the book. The final stages of the production process have been a joy, thanks to the efficiency and encouragement of Taryn Campbell, Tessa Eaton, and Heather Watson.

And then there is Brigitte, whom I cannot thank enough for the companionship and constancy that is fundamental to everything I do…

CONTENTS

LIST OF ILLUSTRATIONS

CHAPTER ONE

Time and Place

THE EXECUTION of Charles I on the 30 January 1649 took place on a scaffold erected alongside the Banqueting House in Whitehall. The scaffold was hung round with black; the block and the axe lay ready. The king walked directly onto the scaffold from the gallery of the Banqueting House and after a minimum of preliminaries, the executioner severed his head from his body with a single blow.

James Ussher, the frail 58-years-old Archbishop of Armagh, watched from a balcony overlooking the scene. He staggered as the axe struck and would have fallen but for the intervention of a servant. His distress was understandable: not simply for having watched the death of a king whose patronage he had enjoyed, and whom he had counselled on the crucial issues of religious conscience just weeks before, but also for the implications of the act: a repudiation of Ussher's conviction that royal authority was divinely ordained; the severing of a link between church and state.

Ussher was a devout cleric and politically astute; Irish, a Protestant born and educated in Dublin while the wounds of the Reformation were still raw. The vehement anti-Catholicism expressed in his sermons and publications was much appreciated by religious and secular authorities alike. On visits to London

Ussher had been received by the king and had preached to both houses of parliament. In 1625, Charles appointed him Archbishop of Armagh. In 1641, when the Irish uprising deprived Ussher and his family of home and income, parliament approved his move to London and granted him a pension of £400 per year.

James Ussher lived in the tumultuous times that led ultimately to civil war, but he moved easily between the opposing royal and parliamentary factions. As the dispute hardened around issues of religion, his reputation for scholarship and sound interpretation of biblical texts earned him the respect of both king and parliament. Both sought his opinion; both courted his support.

In what could be interpreted as a last attempt to find common ground, parliament allowed Ussher to visit Charles at Carisbrooke Castle on the Isle of Wight, where he was being held while they argued about what should be done with him. Ussher left London on 7 November 1648 and spent a number of days with Charles. But if parliament had hoped he would persuade the king to moderate his religious principles, thus avoiding a trial and possible execution, they were disappointed. The substance of his advice on the crucial issues of conscience is a matter of speculation, but the sermon he preached to king and congregation on the 19th is known to have been on the divine source of royal authority—hardly a message designed to persuade Charles that he should bow to parliament. Though a staunch royalist, it seems Ussher was not about to suggest that even the fate of a king could excuse any wavering from the edicts of the holy script. Charles was taken to London, tried, found guilty, sentenced, and executed.

Ussher's position at the heart of affairs during one of the most critical periods of English history is intriguing. His deployment of religious belief, biblical knowledge, and intellectual stamina sustained the respect of both royal and parliamentary factions to the end—Charles entrusted final letters to him for delivery; on Ussher's death in 1656 Oliver Cromwell accorded him a state funeral in Westminster Abbey.

In the year following the execution, Ussher oversaw the publication of the work for which he is principally remembered: the *Annales veteris testamenti, a prima mundi origine deducti* ('Annals of the Old Testament, deduced from the first origins of the world').[1] This was a typically meticulous piece of scholarship, which drew from his knowledge of ancient history, languages, and calendars those points in time that could be confidently aligned with biblical events (the reign of Nebuchadnezzar and the construction of Solomon's temple 'in the 480th year after the children of Israel were come out of Egypt' are two examples). Then, with the Bible anchored to secular events at key points he used the dates and passages of time cited in the Bible itself to construct a chronology that regressed to the creation of the world, as described in Genesis: *In the beginning God created the heaven and the earth. And the earth was without form, and void; and darkness was upon the face of the deep…*

According to Ussher's chronology, the world was created during the night preceding the twenty-third day of October, 4004 years before the birth of Christ. Precision aside, there was nothing especially novel or revelationary about this. For centuries, Peter's pronouncement (2 Peter 3. 8: *With the Lord a day is like a thousand years and a thousand years is like a day*) had been aligned with the six days of creation, as spelled out in Genesis, to conclude that the world had a six-thousand-year lifespan, with the birth of Christ occurring on the morning of the fifth day and the earth due to end two thousand years later. The General Epistle of Barnabas is even more specific:

> in six thousand years the Lord God will bring all things to an end. For with him one day is a thousand years; as he himself testifieth, saying, Behold this day shall be as a thousand years. Therefore children, in six days, that is, in six thousand years, shall all things be accomplished.

This tradition was deeply entrenched by Elizabethan times, as certain as the daily round, unquestioned and cited as fact in numerous manuscripts and books before and after Ussher. Shakespeare, in *As You Like It* (1599, Act 4, Scene 1) has Rosalind wistfully remark that 'The poor world is almost six thousand years old'. Even the countrymen's folklore contains references to the birth of Christ having freed old Adam from four thousand years of captivity,[2] The corollary, of course, was that the world would end two thousand years after the birth of Christ—but exactly how far off was that?

The passage of time since the birth was reliably documented, but establishing its position on the six-thousand-year continuum since the day of creation was a more complex matter, depending as it did upon texts that were open to a variety of interpretations. And there were worrying implications: if the earth's six-thousand-year span had begun earlier than was assumed, then the two thousand years since the birth of Christ began earlier too, and Doomsday was that much closer. This was not an issue likely to have caused widespread concern. Most people probably were content to know that the end of the earth was still many generations off. But scholars looked for greater precision. So Ussher was not alone. Indeed, an early nineteenth-century author found 156 such chronologies in the literature, variously giving dates for the day of creation that ranged from 6500 to 3500 BC. Ussher's was among the sixty-five that clustered around a peak at between 4100 and 3900 BC.[3]

But Ussher's date was supported by a massive body of evidence, computation and closely argued interpretation; furthermore, it was the work of a highly respected man whose erudition and intellectual integrity had been called upon by both the Parliamentary and Royalist factions during the years of their conflict. This should have been enough to ensure Ussher's work not only achieved precedence, but was also acknowledged when Bibles were printed with a marginal note giving the date 4004 BC alongside the opening of Genesis. But no. That practice was not initiated until 1701 and the date of creation was taken from the work of a chronologer who was alive at the time—the Bishop of Worcester, William Lloyd (1627–1717).[4]

Ussher's more comprehensively computed deduction was acknowledged in late nineteenth-century editions, the implied concern for precision probably reflecting a resurgence of interest in the beginnings of the earth that developments in natural science had provoked. Belief in the biblical version of events became especially resolute as alternatives emerged. And scientists were among the most resolute. At the 1865 meetings of the British Association for the Advancement of Science, for example, at which Darwin's theory of evolution was a contentious issue, 716 delegates signed a declaration supporting the biblical interpretation of Earth's history, claiming that: 'it is impossible for the Word of God as written in the book of Nature, and God's Word as written in Holy Scripture, to contradict one another'. Of the signatories, seventy-two were Fellows of the Royal Society, and 111 were Fellows of the Geological Society.[5]

It was during the nineteenth century that Ussher's name became so obstinately linked to 4004 BC as the date of creation—justifiably, since his was a thorough and accomplished piece of scholarship; but regrettably too, since such painstaking

FIGURE 1.1 A page from the manuscript of James Ussher's 1638 *Canon Chronicus* shows some of the computations leading to his conclusion that the Earth was created during the night preceding the 23rd October 4004 BC.

I. A Mundo condi cœpto mensis i. die 1.° (23.° sc
Octobris anni Periodi Julianæ 710.) usq ad Dilu=
vium finitum eodem ejusdem mensis die, sunt
Mundi veteris anni a

Anni. Menses. Dies.

1056. 0. 0.

.13.

II. Hinc ad profectionem Abrahami ex urbe Charam,
in terram Chanaan (unde peregrinationis Hebræ=
orum deducitur initium) mensis 7. die 15.°

426. 6. 14.

III. Hinc ad exitum Hebræorum de Ægypto, men=
sis i. (sic enim ab hoc tempore mensis 7.us
antiquorum appellatus est) die 15.° a

430. 0. 0.

10, 41.

IIII. Hinc ad jacta fundamenta Templi Salomonici
mensis 2. die 2.° anno 4.to regni Salomonis.

479. 0. 17.

V. Hinc ad ejusdem Templi conflagrationem, men=
sis 5.i die 10.° anno 19.° Nebuchadnezaris.

424. 3. 8.

.12.

VI. Hinc ad finitum Templum secundum, anno
Darij filij Hystaspis 6.° (desinente) mensis 12.
Adar die 3.° a

72. 6. 23.

VII. Hinc ad Kalendas Januarias anni primi
æræ vulgaris Christianæ sive anni Periodi
Julianæ 4714.) a

514. 9. 9.

| Summa | 4003. 2. 11. |

Ab initio Mundi ad verum Natalem Messiæ, anni sunt 3999. menses
2. et dies 4. à vero Natali Messiæ usq ad Kalendas Januarias anni
primi vulgaris æræ Christianæ, anni 4. et dies 7. Christum enim
natum supponimus 25.° die Decembris anni Periodi Julianæ 4709
desinentis; currente anno Mundi 4000.

Periodus Juliana est Cyclus postulatitius annorum 7980. Juliano=
rum: quorum singuli per 15. 19. et 28. divisi, Indictionem Ro=
manam, Cyclum Lunarem et Cyclum Solarem exhibent. Ab
ejus capite usq ad Kalendas Januarias anni primi vulga=
ris æræ Christianæ, annos 4713. decurrisse fingimus. Da=
tam hanc hypothesin pro communi omnium variantium tem=
porum mensurâ deinde assumentes.

Ex eâ hypothesi, à capite Periodi Julianæ usq ad initium Mun=
di, anni numerandi fuerint 709. menses 9. cum diebus 19. circiter.

exactitude has made him a figure of fun. Outside of specialist circles, Ussher is remembered today as the man who said the world was created during the night preceding the twenty-third day of October, 4004 years before the birth of Christ. Some accounts raise further laughter by observing how neatly the date coincided with the beginning of the academic year (mistakenly attributing the refinement to John Lightfoot (1602–75), Master of St Catherine's College, Cambridge).[6]

Quaint and amusing though Ussher's assertion may seem, it is important to see it in the context of *his* time, not ours. Ussher was a learned authority who had used the best available information and procedures to investigate an issue. He published the results, together with the data from which they were derived and the methods by which the conclusions had been reached. The work was definitive, and so long as its results were open to testing and confirmation by others, would remain valid until new data, or improved investigative procedures, disproved it. In this respect, Ussher deserves recognition as an early practitioner of methodological procedures that govern the sciences today.

Ussher, of course, lived and worked at a time when the word of God, as revealed in the scriptures, was the supreme authority. In his day, the biblical texts were an all-encompassing paradigm of knowledge and understanding upon which the ordering of society was based—much as the word of law governs modern democracies. Meanwhile, though, the savants had been, in effect, constructing a parallel understanding—a proto-scientific, secular cause-and-effect understanding—as the foremost among them showed that the nature of the Earth and its constituent features was governed by immutable, overarching, laws of nature (or, to use modern terminology, laws of physics).

During the seventeenth century, Europe became what has been aptly called a continent-wide 'republic of letters' as correspondents pursued this secular, cause-and-effect understanding, exchanging observation, speculation, and comment.[7] Soon, the exchange of personal letters was supplemented by journals specifically intended to further the dissemination of knowledge and ideas, with editorial attention focused on two broad categories of learning: scholarship of all kinds; and fields of investigation that would eventually become known as 'the sciences'.

The *Journal des Savants*, launched in Paris in 1665, was the first; Britain's Royal Society followed with the publication of its *Philosophical Transactions* the same year. Thereafter the trend grew rapidly: 330 journals were published in seven countries between 1665 and 1731.[8] Not just Paris and London, but also Rome, Berlin and

Amsterdam, Florence, Parma, Leipzig, and Rotterdam were among the centres where savants were plentiful enough to support the publication of a journal.

By adding the complexities of cause and effect to the sheer wonder of observation, the new understanding had the potential to enrich the glories of creation more than it debased them; and it must have seemed that, as in other areas of intellectual endeavour, scholars were simply using their God-given talents to affirm the supremacy of the Almighty: if immutable physical laws existed, then God must have created them too. This cosy relationship received a jolt in 1543 when the Polish astronomer and mathematician Nicholas Copernicus (1478–1543) published a work entitled *On the Revolutions of the Heavenly Bodies*, showing that the Earth was not the heart of the universe, with the Sun and the heavenly bodies revolving deferentially around it, but merely one of several planets circling the Sun.

Sigmund Freud described Copernicus's dismissal of the Earth from centre-stage to a place in the wings (thereby toppling humanity from our exalted position at the centre of the universe) as the first of 'two great outrages' which transformed our understanding of what his generation called 'Man's Place in Nature'.[9] The second was Darwin's theory of evolution, which demoted us, 'the beauty of the world, the paragon of animals', to the status of naked ape. Both 'outrages' aroused criticism in religious circles. Copernicus was already on his deathbed when his theory of the heliocentric solar system was published, so was spared personal condemnation, but those who promulgated the theory were not so fortunate—Galileo (1564–1642) foremost among them. (The outrage that Darwin aroused reverberates to this day.)

Galileo was charged and found guilty of heresy for his support of Copernican theory, and spent his last years under house-arrest. Copernicus's work was added to the Vatican's Index of Forbidden Books in 1611, and ostensibly withdrawn from circulation. But knowledge and understanding were not so easily contained. The theory spread, finding tacit acceptance if not open espousal among those on the parallel search for understanding. Copernican principles are implicit in a theory of the Earth's formation published in 1644 by the French mathematician and philosopher René Descartes (1596–1650), for instance.[10] Famous for the line, 'Cogito, ergo sum—I think, therefore I am', in his *Discourse on Method* (1637), Descartes formulated a mechanistic approach that he applied to all facets of existence: from the workings of the human body to the Universe. Everything, he showed, could be explained in mechanical terms. In mathematics he introduced the familiar square root symbol and the use of x and y in algebraic equations.

As with the revisions that Copernicus brought to contemporary understanding of the Universe, Descartes's theory of planetary formation stands as one of those important works to which generations of scholars thereafter were compelled to refer (to ignore it would be to reveal a basic lack of knowledge). The theory was original, innovative, and in some respects a seventeenth-century precursor of modern thinking on what happened immediately after the Big Bang.

According to Descartes, the planets were formed from the gaseous remnants of extinguished stars, brought together and concentrated by gravity until they condensed and cooled to become the substance of a planet. The Earth, he said, had cooled from the outside inwards, its amorphous constituents settling out into five distinct layers. Beneath the globe's solid surface crust there was a layer of liquid; then a layer of hard small accreted spheres, and beneath that two layers of coagulated sunspot material wrapped around a core of indeterminate hot matter.

As the Earth continued to cool after its initial formation, gases escaping from the hot inner layers left cavities into which sections of the surface crust collapsed, creating basins that filled with water from the subterranean layer of liquid. The basins became the oceans, while the release of surface tension triggered by the collapse of the surface crust caused the rims to spring upward, thus creating mountains. Rivers, Descartes thought, were the product of water which seeped from the oceans to the deepest layers, where it evaporated then rose as steam through mountain fissures to condense at the surface and emerge as springs.

The distinctive feature of Descartes's theory was that it described mechanical processes acting upon a variety of materials according to the laws of nature known at the time. There was a logic to the Earth's formation; no external force or deity was required. Descartes gave no clue as to how long the process might have taken—thus avoiding any suggestion that his theory contradicted the Bible's six days of creation, and leaving its mechanistic principles available, untainted, to scholars of religious bent who wished to reconcile the new understanding with the old.

Thomas Burnet (1635–1715) was not the first to attempt a reconciliation of this kind, but *The Sacred Theory of the Earth* he published in Latin in two volumes in 1681 and 1689 as *Telluris Theoria Sacra* was destined to become the best known— deservedly so, both for the captivating quality of its prose, and for Burnet's determination to leave no question unanswered. Initial interest was sufficient to warrant an English translation, which appeared in 1684 and 1689; the naturalist John Evelyn told Samuel Pepys he had read the original Latin edition 'with great delight' and found the English version 'still new, still surprising, and the whole hypothesis so ingenious and so rational, that I both admire and believe it at once'.[11] In Europe, a German translation was published in 1698, and a third Latin edition was printed in Amsterdam in 1698.

Burnet's fate, however, has been to become—like James Ussher—a figure of fun; cited, quoted, and derided for his assertions with little attempt to assess the work in the context of its time. *The Sacred Theory* was described in 1795 as 'a dream, formed upon a poetic fiction of a golden age'; a standard history of geology published in 1897 included it among the 'monstrous doctrines' that infested late seventeenth-century science; in 1911, the official history of the Geological Society of London called it a work of 'romantic and unprofitable labour[s]', and a popular work of 1952 dismissed it as a 'series of queer ideas about the earth's development'. Its reputation is aptly summed up by Stephen Jay Gould: 'Burnet emerges from our textbooks as the archetype of a biblical idolatry that reined the progress of science'.[12]

As a man of God, Burnet based *The Sacred Theory* on the assumption that the Bible is unerringly true; as a man of the world, he used the new understanding of mechanistic principles to explain how events described in the Bible had come about. From his point of view, this was not so much a matter of reconciling the Scriptures with the new understanding, for he saw no conflict there; rather, he was using the new understanding to amplify and illustrate them. Illustrations were an important aspect of the work, beginning with the frontispiece, which lays out the essence of Burnet's *Sacred Theory* in visual terms, clearly and simply.

With clusters of cherubim adorning its four corners, the frontispiece shows a ring of seven globes, each depicting a key phase in the Earth's past, present and future, as revealed in the Scriptures. Jesus stands above, his left foot on the Earth at the beginning of its history and his right on its final phase. Above his head is the definitive statement from the Book of Revelation: I am Alpha and Omega (the beginning and the ending, the first and the last). The first globe, under Christ's left foot, shows the original Earth as a chaotic jumble of particles and darkness; next, with the chaos settled into a series of smooth concentric layers, comes the perfect Earth, Eden's Paradise; then the Flood, with the Earth submerged and a tiny Noah's Ark floating on the troubled waters. The waters retreat, and the fourth globe depicts the present distribution of continents and oceans. The last three globes represent the future, as foretold by the prophets. Globe five is consumed by the conflagration associated with Christ's second coming; globe six is restored to its perfect state, whereon Christ will reign for a thousand years with his resurrected saints; finally, with the force of evil eliminated, the just will ascend to heaven and the Earth, no longer needed as a human abode, will become a star—the seventh globe, under Christ's right foot.

Burnet's text dealt at length with each of the seven phases, skilfully deploying the new understanding of physical principles to explain events, then confirming his explanations with witnesses and traditions from biblical and other ancient texts. He believed his theory should be granted 'more than a moral certitude',[13] but his prose probably earned as much commendation as his reasoning. Here is his introductory description of the second globe:

> In this smooth Earth were the first Scenes of the World, and the first Genera-
> tions of Mankind. It had the Beauty of Youth and blooming Nature, fresh and
> fruitful, not a Wrinkle, Scar or Fracture in all its Body; no Rocks nor Moun-
> tains, no hollow Caves, nor gaping Channels, but even and uniform all over.

In that state of perfection, the Earth's axis was vertical; there were no seasons, and the Garden of Eden was located so that its inhabitants enjoyed a perpetual spring and might live for nine hundred years and more. The Fall, and then the Flood brought an end to such privilege. Burnet acknowledged that explaining the Flood was the single greatest challenge hindering acceptance of biblical history: where had all the water come from? Where had it gone afterwards? One might suppose that, as a man of God, he would resort to the notion that a divine miracle had been responsible, and it is a measure of his attachment to the principles of the new understanding that he did not. No, *The Sacred Theory* had to present a rational, logical explanation.

Rejecting the idea that only part of the globe had been flooded (in that case the inhabitants would have saved themselves by migrating to the unaffected regions), Burnet pursued the mechanistic approach. He estimated the volume

---

FIGURE 1.2 In the title page illustration from Thomas Burnet's *Sacred Theory of the Earth*, Noah's Ark floats on the troubled waters of the third globe.

The
Sacred Theory
of the
EARTH.

of water required to flood the earth to a given depth and showed that the volume in the existing basins would have been sufficient—*if* the Earth had been perfectly smooth, lacking the continents, mountains, valleys and ocean basins of its present condition. Thus, what was required to explain the flooded state of the third globe, neatly confirmed the pristine state of the second. But he still had to explain where the water had come from.

With echoes of Descartes, he invoked a scenario in which the Earth's crust had split and water from the interior had escaped to the surface. With the crust weakened, huge segments had subsequently collapsed into the abyss, which in due course left the Earth transformed, as the flood waters drained away, into its fourth state: the 'hideous ruin' (in Burnet's words) of continents and ocean basins we inhabit today. The disruptions which created the fourth state were so violent, Burnet said, that the Earth's axis was jolted from the vertical to its current tilt, creating seasons and hardship. And so, according to Burnet, we live on a 'dirty little planet', with lifespans just a fraction of those enjoyed by our ancestors in Paradise, awaiting the transformation promised by the Scriptures: at a time foretold, the Earth's volcanoes will erupt in unison, and the global conflagration will begin.

Isaac Newton (1642-1727) was among those who gave *The Sacred Theory of the Earth* serious attention.[14] He and Burnet exchanged a series of long letters on the subject, and here we find the founding figure of modern physics insisting that God must have been responsible for certain aspects of the Earth's history, while the man of God is adamant that a combination of natural laws and historical narrative has to suffice. In particular, Burnet resisted Newton's suggestion that the Earth had rotated much more slowly to begin with, which would have lengthened the days enormously and given plenty of time for the creation of all the Earth's features and inhabitants. In reply, Burnet argued that one could not even speak of days until the sun had been created, and besides, what natural cause could have speeded up the rotation to produce the current 24-hour day? Here Newton called upon divine power:

> Where natural causes are at hand God uses them as instruments in his works, but I do not think them alone sufficient for the creation and therefore may be allowed to suppose that amongst other things God gave the Earth its motion by such degrees and at such times as was most suitable to the creatures.

Burnet did not explore the question of time explicitly in his *Sacred Theory*, but he did argue that God and nature operate in a cyclical fashion, in an eternal cycle of events that recovers what was lost and decayed, and restores it to its original pristine condition. Day follows night, spring follows winter, and in the greatest cycle of all the Earth itself would be restored to its state of heavenly perfection. How long would that take? Burnet admitted that he did not know the exact age of the Earth, but suggested that it was not more than 6,000 years.[15] This was good enough for the late seventeenth century, when science had yet to discover the facts and methodology that would contradict Archbishop Ussher's still widely accepted pronouncements; it would not fare so well in the eighteenth, however, as the physical laws responsible for natural phenomena were described and seemed to suggest that much more time was required for the creation of the Earth than the Bible allowed.

A brilliant French scientist and mathematician, Georges-Louis Leclerc, Comte de Buffon (1707–88) brought new insight to the issue. Buffon has achieved fame among mathematicians for a pioneering work on geometric probability theory, now known as 'Buffon's Needle problem'; among botanists and zoologists he was renowned as author of an encyclopaedic *Histoire Naturelle*, which ran to forty-four volumes, the first published in 1749.

The *Histoire Naturelle* introduced the wonders of the world to a wide academic and popular readership; it was an outstanding success, with some fifty editions in France, wide distribution throughout Europe and North America, and translations into English, German, Italian, Spanish, and Dutch.

Buffon wrote on the origin of the Earth in the first volume of his *Histoire Naturelle*, proposing that the planets were formed of debris thrown out when a comet had crashed into the Sun. He accepted that the Earth had a cyclical history but believed it was far longer than the biblical accounts allowed. France's academic establishment took exception to this and demanded an apology. An apology duly appeared in subsequent editions, but the offending remarks were not withdrawn and in the 1760s Buffon returned to the problem of the Earth's origin and early history, his interest stimulated by the phenomenon of heat transfer—thermodynamics.

Isaac Newton, in his *Philosophiae Naturalis Principia Mathematica* published in 1687, had speculated that the Earth had originally been molten and was slowly cooling down; he suggested that 'a red hot iron equal to our earth, that is, about 40,000,000 feet in diameter, would scarcely cool...in above 50,000 years'. He suspected the rate of cooling would vary according to the size of the body losing heat and hoped someone would investigate the issue experimentally.

Buffon had a forge and furnace built on his estate near Dijon, specifically to conduct the experiment Newton had hoped for. There were deposits of iron ore near by, forests to provide timber for fuel, and a tributary of the Armançon River was diverted to waterwheels driving bellows that pumped air into the furnace. The facility was built on a grand scale (and is still standing); a 'Vulcan's cave', with facilities for prestigious visitors to observe operations, lodgings for the permanent workers, a fine dwelling for the manager, and a pavilion reserved for Buffon's comfort during his visits.[16] The forge produced the best iron in the region, Buffon claimed, some of which was sold, though its most valuable output was the series of iron spheres that Newton's experiment required.

Buffon had sets of ten spheres made of forged and beaten iron, ranging in diameter from half an inch to five inches at half-inch intervals. The spheres were heated to white-hot, just below the melting point of iron (1,537 degrees centigrade), then allowed to cool under controlled conditions, while the time required for them to reach ambient temperature was recorded. Extrapolating from these results, Buffon calculated that an iron sphere the size of the Earth would take 86,667 years and 132 days to cool. But the Earth did not consist solely of iron; it was formed of layers with different characteristics and these variations would affect cooling times. Accordingly, Buffon repeated the experiment with spheres of copper, tin, gold, lead, marble, stone, and sundry other materials.

Analysing his data, Buffon concluded that 74,832 years had elapsed from the Earth's formation to the year of his experiments. This was bold, and again provoked the anger of the academic establishment, but in fact was far less than he believed was required. Manuscript drafts of *Nature's Epochs* (1778), in which Buffon constructed a timescale for the formation of the Earth's stratigraphic layers, give figures of about three million years for the whole sequence, and some estimates range up to ten million years.[17] These figures did not appear in the published work—perhaps in deference to the establishment, but more probably in respect for scientific method: there was experimental evidence for an age of 74,832 years, but only an informed guess to support the other figures.

Nature's great workman, Buffon wrote,[18] is time...We do not pay any consideration that, though the time of our existence is very limited, nature proceeds in her regular course. We would condense into our momentary existence the transactions of ages past and to come, without reflecting that this instant of time, nay, even human life itself, is only a single fact in the history of the acts of the Almighty.

Buffon was not alone in his beliefs (others shared them, though few expressed them quite so openly). By the end of the eighteenth century, the Earth's structure had been described in some detail; the subject was taught in universities and the growth of the mining industry and canal building had created a demand for practical knowledge and professional expertise (the word 'geology' was coined around then).[19] Fellow-thinkers shared a general sense of the vast extent of time required to account for the deposition of sedimentary layers, the erosion of deep valleys, and the accumulation of lava around volcanoes. They could see that even a major landslide shifted only a tiny fraction of a mountainside and some rough mental arithmetic would quickly show that, given the infrequency of landslides, gouging out the valley would take far more time than Archbishop Ussher had provided. Deep time: a concept whose novelty must have provoked shivers of awe—just as modern minds baulk at the concept of light-years and the infinite expanse of the astronomers' deep space.

Time without end: 'no vestige of a beginning—no prospect of an end'. The phrase is familiar to generations of geology students; it resonates with the awe and wonder of fantastic discovery: an eternal truth, ever-present but until then hidden behind the flimsy curtain of unawareness. The author was James Hutton (1726–1797), whose *Theory of the Earth* (1795) was but one of many such works published in Europe during the late eighteenth and early nineteenth centuries, but distinguished from them all by Hutton's concept of the Earth as a dynamic entity: a 'machine', constructed by an unidentified 'author of nature', its parts working together in beautiful synchrony for the benefit of humanity, for all time.

James Hutton was born in Edinburgh to a merchant family. As a young man he studied the humanities in Edinburgh, chemistry and anatomy in Paris, and gained the degree of Doctor of Medicine from Leiden University; then—at the age of 24—he turned to farming land he had inherited from his father, fifty miles east of Edinburgh. Agriculture exposed Hutton to a fundamental link between

the Earth and human life: soil. The experience showed him that soil was a diminishing asset, exhausted by cultivation and the elements; he saw that the land-
masses on which plant, animal, and human life depended were slowly wasting
away, eroded by wind and rain, carried by rivers to the sea and ultimately deposited on the ocean floor; he realized that the only source of replenishment was
the Earth itself, and here faced a disturbing paradox: that the land's continuing
habitability depended upon its disintegration, and could only be guaranteed if
the wasting continents were somehow replaced.[20]

Hutton gave up farming in 1768 because, a biographer recounts, once he had
established good farming methods, 'the management of it became more easy
[and] less interesting'.[21] He moved permanently to Edinburgh where, as a man of
independent means, he moved easily among the luminaries of what was then the
'thinking capital of Europe'. He joined the Philosophical Society. David Hume,
Adam Smith, and James Watt were among those he joined at informal gather-
ings in the city's dining clubs. They belonged to what is now an extinct breed:
the polymaths who delved into all fields of contemporary knowledge, sharing
observations, discussing ideas, and recognizing no distinction between philosophy and science. Hutton's attention, however, was increasingly focused on developing a theory of the Earth that would resolve the paradox of its renewal being
dependent upon its disintegration. He found it in the analogy of the machine.

Machines were the pioneering phenomenon of Hutton's day, but not as we
know them. For Hutton and his contemporaries, 'machine' meant one device
above all others: the steam engine. The improved steam engine devised by his
friend James Watt was destined to set the industrial revolution in motion, and
behind the power of the piston, the crank wheel, and the oscillating beam Hutton discerned a power that could also move continents: heat.

Hutton's self-renewing Earth machine worked on a three-stroke cycle. First,
the Earth's surface decayed as the rocks were broken down to form soils which
then eroded and were washed into the oceans. Second, the fragments of old continents were deposited as horizontal layers in the ocean basins, where the weight
of accumulating layers generated enough pressure and heat to melt those at the

---

FIGURE 1.3 Contemporary sketches illustrate geological features James Hutton presented
as evidence for his theory of the earth. The engraving of an unconformity exposed at Jedburgh
is matched with a modern photograph of the same location.

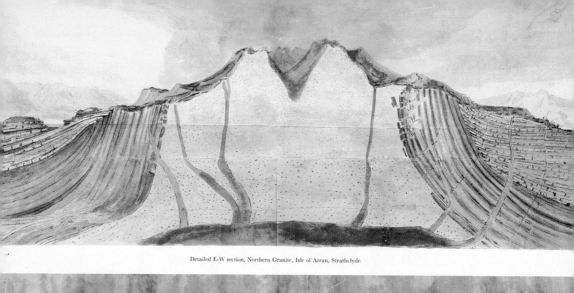

Detailed E-W section, Northern Granite, Isle of Arran, Strathclyde

bottom. Third, the heat of those melting sediments caused matter to expand
'with amazing force', generating extensive uplift and building new continents at
the sites of old oceans; leaving new oceans where old continents eroded away.

In the last edition of the *Theory of the Earth* published during Hutton's lifetime,
proofs and illustrations were added as evidence of the theory's contentions. In
effect they were intended to show how the Earth had told its own story, which
Hutton had merely observed and transcribed as a coherent system, so that the
Earth became, as it were, its own interpreter. This sealed his reputation as a paragon of empirical science and the founding father of geology in the Anglophone
world. An influential textbook, Sir Archibald Geikie's *The Founders of Geology* (first
published 1897), claimed Hutton had:

> vigorously guarded himself against the admission of any principle which
> could not be founded on observation. He made no assumptions. Every step in
> his deductions was based upon actual fact, and the facts were so arranged as to
> yield naturally and inevitably the conclusions which he drew from them.[22]

This is not entirely true. Hutton's key pronouncements were made years before
he saw the features that were said to have inspired the theory. Hutton himself
tells of observations he had made specifically to confirm—rather than test—it.
A chapter in the final edition of the *Theory of the Earth* is entitled: 'The theory
confirmed from observations made on purpose to elucidate the subject'.[23]

It would be churlish to rebuke Hutton when it was Geikie who presented him
as a paragon of empirical science. Strict adherence to the principle of collecting facts and only then postulating a theory is not always possible, particularly
where facts are few and hard to find. Investigators have often dreamed up a
theory then gone in search of facts that substantiate it (this is especially true
of palaeoanthropology, as we shall see). In any case, Hutton's appointment as
founder of geological science doubtless derived more from Victorian conceits
of superiority than from an assessment of eligible candidates.

As mentioned above, Hutton's *Theory of the Earth* was but one of many such
works published in Europe around that time (indeed, nearly half the *Theory* itself
consisted of long untranslated quotations from French sources). Theories of the
Earth were ubiquitous enough to be described as a scientific *genre*, just as painting, music, and novels are artistic genres,[24] but a new generation of investigators

was finding reason to reject them. The idea that anyone could construct a single theory of the Earth from the facts then available had begun to seem misconceived, premature and faintly ridiculous. As Georges Cuvier, at the leading edge of the new wave, remarked in 1807, 'it has become almost impossible to mention its [geology's] name without provoking laughter'.[25]

The new generation recognized that the Earth was even more wonderful than had been supposed, that the facts being uncovered simply would not fit in a single overarching theory of the old style; nor were they yet plentiful enough to allow the formulation of a valid and durable new one. Nonetheless, Hutton deserves credit for having laid down a benchmark for the concept of deep time. His *Theory of the Earth* represents the culmination of inquiries by generations of savants trying to construct a theory that would explain everything. The available facts and procedures of their day allowed them to do that, but science had moved on, leaving James Hutton as not so much the founding father of a science, but the quintessence of a venerable tradition.

The Geological Society of London formalized the new approach in procedures drawn up on its foundation in 1807. As befits an organization established to promote investigations of the Earth's physical properties at a time when the industrial revolution was beginning to make unprecedented demands for iron and coal, utility and verifiability were the watchwords of the Geological Society. The primary task of geology was defined as unravelling the sequence of the earth's accessible strata. Interpretation was to be shunned, and discussion restricted to facts alone.[26] It is appropriate then, that the next major development stemmed principally from the work of a man who *did* things (a technologist, in modern terms) rather than one who *knew* things (an academic): William Smith (1769–1839).[27]

William Smith worked for his living; first as a land and canal surveyor and engineer; then as a drainage and irrigation engineer; a sea erosion and harbour engineer, and finally a prospector or mineral surveyor. His father was the blacksmith for an Oxfordshire village who died when William was 7 (which probably spared the boy from a lifetime at the forge).

Beginning his career as pupil and assistant to a land surveyor based in Stow-on-the-Wold, Gloucestershire in 1787, within a few years Smith had acquired the skills and experience from which his hugely important contributions to geological science were derived. He learned to observe the land, not simply measure it; to note the relevance of distinctive features, not simply their presence. In 1791, while surveying an estate near Bath where coal was mined, the 22-year-old went underground to make sections and plans of the collieries and was struck by the definitive character of the strata through which the mineshafts had been sunk. Above ground, on other surveys, he noted the surface indicators of different soils: the Chalk escarpments near London, the Cotswold limestones, the red soils of Worcestershire, and the gravels of the New Forest.[28] Smith also developed a habit of collecting any fossils he came across, which he then labelled and saved according to the location and strata they had come from.

Meanwhile, the landowners whose collieries he had surveyed were becoming frustrated by the difficulties of transporting their coal to points of sale. Landlocked, their prices uncompetitive, they were missing out on one of the greatest moneymaking opportunities ever. A canal, linking the coalfields to the Kennet and Avon Canal, which in turn formed a direct east–west link with Bristol and Bath on the Avon, and Reading on the Kennet would answer their need. Bristol was on the Severn estuary; the Kennet was a tributary of the Thames; with access to such a network their coal would be available to half of England. Smith was called in to make preliminary surveys for what would be the Somerset Coal Canal.

Cutting a canal through the undulating countryside involved some deep surgery; uniquely, much of the ten-mile waterway was to run along two parallel valleys, following the course of brooks which, it was found, would provide an abundance of water even in the driest summers. Excavations began in 1794 and Smith soon realized that the regular stratification he had noted inside the coal mines was repeated outside. Furthermore, as excavation proceeded he was able to compare the strata exposed in one valley with those exposed in the other, a few miles away. This was crucial to Smith's mounting interest and understanding of stratification.

Until the advent of railways a few decades later, waterways were the most efficient means of transporting goods in bulk. With the growing demands of industry, canals were being cut throughout the country and Smith was encouraged to go on a fact-finding tour, looking out for new technology. He was away for two months, observing canal construction but also noting the repetitious nature of strata and other geological features across the country. He began mapping their distribution, beginning with the area around Bath, and in 1799 produced a hand-coloured geological map of that region, accompanied by a table of

twenty-three strata, from The Chalk, No. 1, down to The Coal, No. 23. The detail
was unprecedented, differentiating as it did between widely separated but often
very similar strata. Two different 'Freestones' occurred at 7 and 12, for instance,
while at least four separate blue clays were identified: Clunch or Oxford Clay at
3; Forest Marble Clay at 5; Fullers Earth Clay at 8-11, and Marl Clay at 14.[29] Two
years later he produced a rough geological map of England and Wales.

1799 was an important year in Smith's career. It had been exceptionally wet 'as
ungenial to the productions of the earth and to the animal creation as any upon
record, and the inclemency extended over a great part of Europe...On 18 March
great land floods had overflowed the river at Bath and from July 8 an extremely
wet summer [led to] a very bad harvest.'[30] But farmers' woe was Smith's gain. An
intimate knowledge of geological strata combined with the practical experience
of cutting canals made him an expert in land drainage whose services were in
demand long after the floods had subsided, all across the country. At the peak,
he was travelling 10,000 miles a year, and so busy that although his numerous
consultancies added to his knowledge of stratigraphy, he had precious little time
to work on the detailed geological map of England and Wales he planned.

Getting the money to pay for it was also a problem. In 1801 he published a
prospectus for the map, an ambitious project that would plot 'the natural order
of the various Strata' and their outcrops across the entire country. In 1802 his
patron Sir Joseph Banks, then president of the Royal Society, exhibited a manuscript version of the map, already 'in a very considerable state of forwardness' at
various locations, but practical and financial difficulties delayed its publication
for another thirteen years.[31]

Smith's 1815 map is one of the most important geological publications ever
produced: massive, masterful. Entitled *A Delineation of the Strata of England and
Wales, with Parts of Scotland*, it was drawn at the scale of five miles to an inch.
Subsequently, Smith published cross-sections illustrating the underlaying and
thus three-dimensional geology of the 1815 map, and a series on the geology of
twenty-one English counties.

The scale of Smith's achievements is remarkable enough, but the detail is staggering. Quite apart from its overall description of the country's geology, the map
defined the order of formations in numerous specific regions; large numbers of
separate formations were identified and their outcroppings plotted with great
precision. Each outcrop was coloured in gradations of intensity, which brought

out the three-dimensional structure of the formations and made the map particularly informative.[32] But Smith had to wait years for the credit his work deserved. He was spurned by the geological establishment (though this did not stop the Geological Society of London from publishing a plagiarized version of his map in 1819);[33] a disastrous property investment led to debts that eventually saw him imprisoned for ten weeks.[34]

Recognition was eventually forthcoming: in 1831, the Geological Society of London awarded him the Wollaston Medal, its highest prize; and in 1835, Trinity College Dublin conferred upon him an honorary degree in law. By then, Smith's map had triggered a revolution in geological investigations. Geologists everywhere were using his methods to identify formations and define the order in which strata had been laid down. Broadscale identification of stratigraphic sequence had been going on for centuries, but Smith had found a way of achieving much finer resolution: the fossils he had been collecting.

The fossils were mostly shells of one sort or another; as the collection grew, Smith saw that certain types of shell were found in certain strata only, and the respective strata always occurred in the same order, from the bottom layer to the top. Across the country, he encountered the same phenomenon time and again: strata with characteristic fossils occurring in the same order he had seen elsewhere. He realized that each suite of fossils must have had a widespread existence while their particular stratum of rock was being laid down, and it was this insight that enabled him to map the order in which rocks had been formed at numerous points across England and Wales. Correlating the evidence was a formidable task. The Cornbrash Limestone, for instance, was one of the thinnest formations that Smith identified, but it contained an assortment of nine characteristic shells and these enabled him to trace its occurrence across England for more than 200 miles.[35]

Fossils had enabled William Smith to follow geological formations across the landscape, leaping valleys, subsuming uplands and ultimately producing a fine and verifiable picture of the Earth's structure as it had built up, layer upon layer, over an immeasurable expanse of time. Conversely, he had also shown that the ascending strata were a natural archive of facts from the deep past: if fossils were the petrified remains of living creatures (as was already widely accepted in

FIGURE 1.4 An original copy of William Smith's geological map of England, Wales, and parts of Scotland.

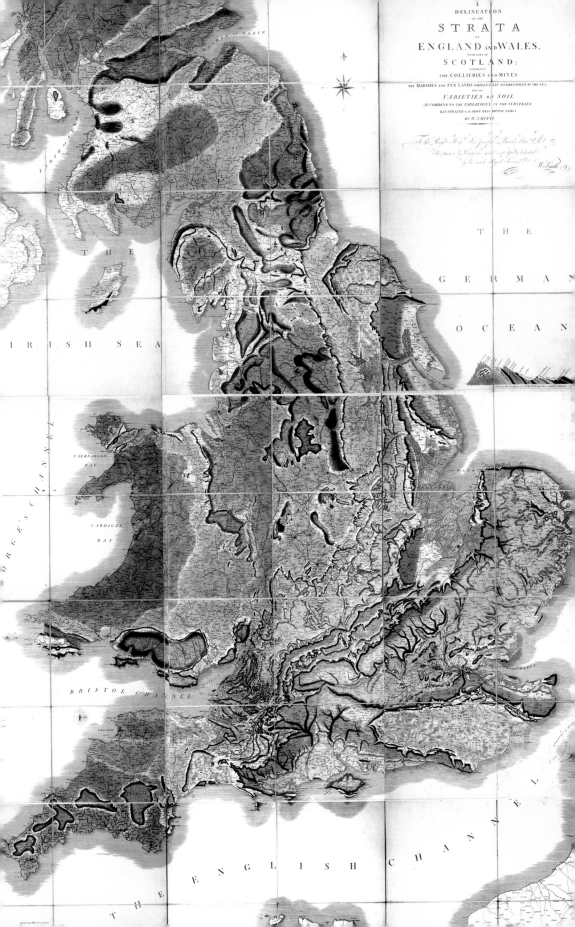

A
DELINEATION
OF THE
STRATA
OF
ENGLAND AND WALES,
WITH PART OF
SCOTLAND;
EXHIBITING
THE COLLIERIES AND MINES,
THE MARSHES AND FEN LANDS ORIGINALLY OVERFLOWED BY THE SEA,
AND THE
VARIETIES OF SOIL
ACCORDING TO THE VARIATIONS IN THE SUBSTRATA,
ILLUSTRATED BY THE MOST DESCRIPTIVE NAMES
BY W. SMITH

THE GERMAN OCEAN

THE IRISH SEA

CAERNARVON BAY

CARDIGAN BAY

BRISTOL CHANNEL

THE ENGLISH CHANNEL

FIRTH OF FORTH

SEA OF FORTH

CARDIGAN BAY

Smith's time), they were clues to the history of life through time. Smith did not himself take much interest in this potential of his work (he was a practical man) but others did, and it was here that geology developed a subsidiary discipline: palaeontology (the study of life in prehistoric times from fossil evidence).

Subsequently, palaeontologists have used fossils and the principles Smith established to organize the history of life into a series of geological chapters, from the Cambrian strata at the base, where only invertebrates are found, to the dinosaurs of the Jurassic, the Crustacea of the Cretaceous, and the mammals of more recent times.

CHAPTER TWO

The Meaning of Fossils[1]

THE WORD fossil, from the Latin *fossus* (past participle of *fodere*, to dig), referred originally to any object that has been dug from the ground. The practice of using it exclusively for the petrified remains of living plants and creatures, as we do today, began only in the nineteenth century. For centuries—indeed millennia—it was a generic term applied to everything from gems to utilitarian metals, from stones with alleged medicinal properties to items collected simply for the wonder of it.

Picking up odd, useful, or beautiful objects is something we all do—a whimsical pastime which probably derives from the innate curiosity that has been a formative feature of our evolution. Certainly it goes back a long way: over two million years in the case of the cobbles our ancestors in East Africa used as tools, and tens of thousands of years in the case of items used for adornment. A cluster of pierced shells found in a coastal cave at Blombos in South Africa, for instance, was probably a necklace and dates back seventy thousand years.

Writing about them goes back a long way too.[2] There is a scattering of classical texts on the subject; one of the earliest—written around 315 BC—is noted for classifying the stones as either male or female (which was subsequently interpreted as indicating that they were able to breed within the earth). Characteristics and properties are described. One second-century BC writer claims that diamonds rendered the bearer undefeatable, and repelled 'the appearance of ghosts, and poisons and law suits'. Sapphires were said to keep a man from envy. The stones were also believed to have medicinal properties, and a principle of sympathetic magic or *similia similibus curantur*—like cures like—is evident: most typically in the case of haematite, a powdering of which was prescribed, predictably, to staunch profuse bleeding.

The practice continued into medieval times, acquiring wider distribution from the advances in printing that Gutenberg's invention of moveable type brought about, and attracting the interest of savants with a rational, investigative approach to the subject; of whom Georg Bauer, better known by the Latin version of his name, Georgius Agricola (1494–1555), was an early and influential example. Born in the Saxony province of what is now Germany, Agricola studied classics and then medicine; first at Leipzig, subsequently at Bologna and Padua. In 1527 he was appointed City Physician in the flourishing mining town of Joachimsthal in Bohemia, where he practised for six years before moving to Chemnitz, another important centre of mining. Agricola remained in Chemnitz for the rest of his life, as City Physician and public figure: he was elected Burgomaster in 1546 and held several public and diplomatic posts under the Duke of Saxony.

Agricola was thus in close contact with the mining industry in what was then Europe's greatest mining region. He never ceased practising medicine, but also managed to devote a great deal of time to the study of rocks and minerals, mines and mining technology. His book, *De Re Metallica* (On the Nature of Metals) was published posthumously in 1556 and remained the standard text on mining for two centuries.

De Re Metallica covered everything then known about mining: prospecting; surveying and digging shafts; assaying and smelting ores; mine management and even the occupational diseases of miners. Agricola described ores and the rocks in which they were found; he noted that the layers of rock (strata) occurred in a consistent order and could be traced over a wide area. In this respect, Agricola made an early contribution to the field of study (stratigraphic geology) that would culminate in William Smith's work 250 years later—but without realizing that fossils could be an identifying feature.

Fossils, in fact, were the subject of an entire book Agricola had published in 1546, *De Natura Fossilium* (On the Nature of Fossils). Here, Agricola described all kinds of minerals, gemstones (and even gallstones), as well as several specimens that we would recognize today as true fossils. He summarized ancient Greek and Roman writings on the subject; gave a list of the hundred classical authors whose work he had consulted, but abandoned the practice of classifying the rocks and minerals by their alleged medicinal or magical powers; he even declined to group them alphabetically, but instead listed them according to the distinctive physical properties that would enable readers to identify them easily:

> minerals have differences, which we observe by colour, taste, odour, place of origin, natural strength and weakness, shape, form, and size...*Lapis judaicus* [the Jew's Stone]...usually occurs in the form of symmetrical acorns. Prominent lines run from the blunt to the pointed end and these are so regular they appear to have been made in a lathe and resemble the striae on a shell. The people who call this mineral *pyren* liken these lines to the bones of a fish that extend from the back down to the belly...[3]

Agricola's *De Natura Fossilium* established the first principles of palaeontology—classifying specimens under a series of standardized names, recording the localities in which they could be found, and giving a full description of their appearance. Conrad Gesner (1516–65) added greater precision to the science when his *De Rerum Fossilium, Lapidum et Gemmarum* (On Fossils, Stones and Gems) was published in 1565. This was the first book of its kind to include numerous illustrations of the objects under discussion—an important and pioneering development. There had been illustrations in earlier works, but generally these were of scenes showing the alleged origin, or use, of a fossil: 'tongue-stones' falling from the sky; afflictions being cured.[4] Only rarely was a single fossil illustrated,[5] but Gesner showed every one in isolation and with as much detail as the technology of the day (woodcuts) allowed.

This was an innovation of immense significance. Even the best sixteenth-century naturalists might fail to find the words that described a fossil clearly and unmistakably. Illustrations bypassed this problem by allowing instant non-verbal communication between author and reader, and thereby reducing the risk of confusion. Agricola had provided an authoritative text, but ambiguity could lurk in even the best descriptive writing; Gesner had produced what we might call a handbook, with illustrations facilitating identification where a verbal description might be ambiguous.

Gesner was born to a Protestant family in Zurich.[6] Religious conviction and the work ethic were deeply instilled. After graduating in the classics he studied medicine and qualified as a physician but then devoted the rest of his life to the study of natural science. Gesner spoke Latin, Greek, Hebrew, German, French, Italian, Dutch (probably English too)—and could read Arabic. He wrote and published seventy-two books during his lifetime and left about eighteen in manuscript form when he died—painfully and lingeringly, of the plague, at the age of 49.

Gesner's books covered a wide range of subjects, including important contributions to medicine and theology, but it was to natural history that his interest was most devotedly applied. On botany, he wrote three large volumes, while an even more comprehensive treatment of the subject remained unfinished at the time of his death. On zoology he published five massive folio volumes (two on quadrupeds, and the others on birds, fishes, and serpents respectively), as well as two folio volumes of illustrations and notes on the various classes of animal. In this scheme of things, his *On Fossils* might seem to have been an afterthought: a small octavo volume consisting of just 169 pages. In a sense it was, bringing together his thoughts (and those of others) in a concise and accessible manner. It was written rapidly as a pleasure and recreation, he said, and was intended to encourage students and anyone interested in fossils to continue their studies. He hoped the illustrations would be helpful, and asked to be informed of any observations or contentions that might arise. He had hoped to include such communications in a supplementary volume, but death denied him the opportunity.

Like Agricola, Gesner did not present his fossils in alphabetical order. Nor did he classify them on the basis of substance, or in accordance with the alleged 'virtues' and miraculous properties that were so important to the earliest writers. He wanted the book to reflect the delight he personally experienced when contemplating the 'forms and shapes in which the Creatress Nature had expressed herself'. Aided by the illustrations, his classification was therefore based on shapes and forms found in Nature.

Gesner sorted his fossils into fifteen classes. First were those of the simplest form, resembling lines, angles, and circles, as seen in the heavens; then came those which bore a resemblance to more complex forms, descending by degrees from the heavens and celestial phenomena to the earth and the forms of life it nourishes, including fossils which resembled plants or animals, or parts of them. Thus, for example, Class 2 groups together forms that resemble the stars; Class 6 includes made objects of metal or stone; the fossils in Class 7 resemble plants or herbs, and those in Class 14 are like things in the sea.

A glance at the illustrations for Class 14 immediately reveals to the modern eye that the subjects did not merely *resemble* things in the sea—they *were* the fossil remains of molluscs and ammonites. But if Gesner ever wondered if this meant they were actually the remains of once-living creatures, it was not an issue he pursued. To us it might seem inconceivable that a fine naturalist like Gesner could have failed to make the connection; from a sixteenth-century savant's point of view, however, questions of origin were not a cause for concern. Divine creation ultimately explained everything, of course, but even those puzzled by the oddities of the Almighty's plan could take comfort in explanations that had yet to be disproved. The theory of spontaneous generation could account for the origin of living things, for example, and in the case of non-living specimens a belief in the Earth's moulding force or 'plastic virtue' could be called upon.

This is not to say that the resemblance of fossil and living creatures, and questions of origin, had not been remarked upon. Writers in classical antiquity alluded to it and, more than fifty years before Gesner wrote *On Fossils*, Leonardo da Vinci (1452–1519) had recorded his belief that fossil shells were organic in origin. In notebooks dating from 1508–9 Leonardo described the similarities between living and fossil molluscs so precisely that the causal link was inescapable. He noticed that the fossils were similar to their living counterparts not only in general form but also in incidental features: they were preserved in various stages of growth, for example, and sometimes with other organisms stuck to them, or bored into them.[7]

If Leonardo, Agricola, and Gesner are typical, their work suggests that the study of fossils was principally a passive and expository undertaking in the sixteenth century. Subjects were clarified and specimens classified, but the question of origin was not pursued. It was the enquiring minds in the seventeenth century that initiated the search for a rational explanation of how the fossils had been formed.

Three main schools of thought emerged: one group refuted every suggestion of organic origin, arguing instead that nature, in some mysterious way, had produced rocks with an uncanny resemblance to living organisms. The fossils were *lusus naturae* (sports or tricks of nature), they said, or *lapides sui generis* (rocks of a unique kind) produced by a *vis plastica* (plastic force, or virtue). A second group claimed the fossils had grown *in situ* within the rocks, not as mere imitations of organisms, but from the same 'seed' as the living organism they resembled, the 'seed' having been washed into position through crevices in the rocks. The third group stated, unequivocally, that fossils were the remains of living organisms which had been drowned in the Flood.[8] Johann Scheuchzer (1672–1733), a Swiss physician and ardent collector of fossils, summarizes the three positions in the introduction to a book on the subject he published in 1708:

> The learned and the unlearned World is full of opinion about the petrified shells, snails, crabs and plants which are dug up here and there and exhibited in cabinets of curiosities. One says that these stones are but a whim of nature, the next has different ideas, as the origin should be a sort of brood oven in the earth's insides. I thought at one time that they were brought forth by nature according to her own laws, without any male-female help. However, after collecting a great number of such fossil, my eyes were opened and now I see their origin in the Biblical Deluge…[The fossils], which are found here and there in quarries and mines, are not bastards of nature but belong to the animal kingdom.[9]

Argument and counter-argument flowed freely via the personal correspondence and the journals that began to be published in centres across Europe.[10] From among the voluminous literature, the naturalist John Ray (1627–1705) emerges as an exemplary commentator on the question of fossils and their origin—a man willing to consider the arguments dispassionately, but unwilling to adopt any position that was not supported by irrefutable evidence.

The son of a blacksmith, Ray studied and taught at Cambridge. He was ordained as a minister of the Church at the age of 23 and throughout his life held unquestioningly to the belief that the Universe, the Earth and all its parts

---

FIGURE 2.1 Conrad Gesner's 1565 work, *On Fossils*, was the first to include detailed illustrations of the as yet unidentified remains of living creatures.

est, ita vt margines placentarum, rotu
la coquinaria vel placenta diffecti.
Videtur quidem fimilitudinem ali-
quam habere primo afpectu cum cor
nu Ammonis, fimiliter ferè ftriata &
reuoluta fuperficie: plurimum verò
differt. nam huius exterior ambitus,
non tereti figura vt Cornu fpectatur,
fed in angufto margine tortofe col-
ligit: & tum foris ferro fimilior eft, tũ
intus lapis durior: totaq́ figura lati-
or, planior, compreffior. Sed neq́ fœ-
tet in ore mandentis, vt illud. Media
pars, qua reuolutio definit, caua eft
ab vno latere: ab altero protuberat,
nec apparent reuolutiones. Ad ferrũ
ignem emittit.

tis exhibit. Primo & alium fimilem
pharmacopolæ quidam vocant Aga-
pen nefcio qua ratione. est autem exi-
lior, & magis in acutũ fuis fpiris exit.

1. Pecten lapideus. Subftãtia intus
...llida albicans, ceu luti in lapi-

...us lapideus, Strombites.

lapidi eundẽ, aut cognatũ facit, fiffi-
lé, nigrũ, bituminofum, ærofum, &c.

Lapilli è pifciũ
quorundã O-
ceani, Afello-
rũ præfertim
generis, talibus, tan-
tiq́.

A

B

-3   -2   -1

C

In tribus hifce formulis, quæ notã-
tur literis A.B.C. lapid...
quos Gloffopetr...
Lamiarum dente...
des, Germani Na...
tricũ linguas. Glo...
inquit Agricola, ...
lingua dicitur: cui ...
magis linguæ Pici. ...
aluminofa. Sic ille. ...
gro, fed albicante in ...
re & fplendido reper...
terdum inclufi. Vene...
dare in menfa credunt...
vaporem alij quoq́ læ...
lapides fudant. Differu...
gnitudine. figura. Alij ...
ratis marginibus funt, a...
eo qui in A. formula exp...
ra leges in Volumine Aq...
ftro, vbi de Cane carchar...
agimus, pag. 210. In form...
merum primum expreffus...
lis eft cæteris, fubftãtia, du...
Y

CONRADVS GESNERVS TIGVRINVS MEDICVS ET
PHILOSOPHIÆ INTERPRES AÑO ÆTATIS SVÆ XLVIII
AÑO SALVTIS M·D·LXIIII NONIS MARTIIS

...
totus folidus: a...
dicã cauitatẽ habet, e rufo a...

2. Alius maiufculus, fufci coloris:
fuperiùs tantùm in cochleam retor-
tus: inferiori parte planus & pilæ feu
columnæ rotũdæ ferè fimilis, nifi pau-
lò anguftior effet in imo.

3. Porcellana minima, alba: nõ mu-
tata quidem in lapidem: fed fuapte natura, vt reliquæ etiam porcellanæ, fer-
mè lapidea.

1.2. Lapides funt folidi, pugno mi-
nores, miro naturæ artificio depicti.
Pondus eis mediocre, crufta ambiés
filicea, alba, craffiufcula, & prædura
eft in

dabimus,) contra. idem verò & at ta
bula quædam habet, hi duo nõ habent.

Pagurus lapideus, parte
fupina expref
fus.

Ein fteininer
Meerkrebſſ o-
der Täfchen-
krebſſ.

1. Lapis caudæ Cancri, fiue Aftaci
fluuiatilis potiùs, perfimilis, Ombriæ
nomine ad me miffus. Ego fuprà cap.
2. Ombriam alium exhibui.

2. Idem, parte altera. Totus pau-
lò breuior eft fuperiore pollicis arti-

were a divine creation. He accepted the Bible as an ultimate authority on the creation and ordering of the natural world, though he could not always reconcile its pronouncements with the implications of his observations.

Botany was John Ray's first love and indeed he occupies a revered position in the history of the science. The *Catalogus Cantabrigiam* he published in 1659 is not just a catalogue of plants, but also a critical review of everything that had been published on botany to that date, as well as compendium of new information derived from his own investigations. Furthermore, it glows with wisdom, enthusiasm, humility and, characteristically, is not dedicated to an establishment figure as might be expected, or to a wealthy patron, but 'in accordance with God's glory' to those:

> whose concern is not so much to know what authors think as to gaze with their own eyes on the nature of things and to listen with their own ears to her voice; who prefer quality to quantity, and usefulness to pretension...[11]

In the Spring of 1663 Ray left England for a tour of Europe that would give him first-hand experience of fossils and questions of their origin. He was away for three years, travelling through the Low Countries, Germany, Austria, Italy, and France. Botany was his principal interest, but he also spent time examining fossil collections and sites. In Bruges he gazed at petrified trees and reasoned that 'before all records of antiquity' a living forest must have been overwhelmed by the sea, then buried beneath 'the sediments of those great rivers which there emptied themselves into the sea' before being exposed on dry land once again. But that would take so much time...'which yet is a strange thing considering the novity of the world, the age whereof, according to the usual account, is not yet 5600 years'.[12]

Petrified wood was as common as fossil shells, and also a puzzle. In an early application of the microscope to science, Robert Hooke (1635–1703), the Royal Society's 'Curator of Experiments', found a convincing resemblance in thin sections of fossil and extant wood (he also attempted some experimental petrification and although he failed to petrify a wooden stick 'throughout', claimed a degree of success).[13] Hooke was among those who believed in the organic origin of fossils, arguing that any other explanation of their existence would contradict 'the infinite prudence of Nature' which, as the ancients had said, 'does nothing in vain'. What could have been the purpose of a fossil shell, if not to protect a living animal as its modern counterpart does?

Ray addressed the issue in an essay of 1673, setting out the arguments for and against both the organic and inorganic origin of fossils. His own functionalist approach to biology predisposed him to the organic theory. He agreed that the functional similarity of fossil and living shells could not be simply fortuitous: if fossil bivalve shells were hinged like living bivalves it was absurd to suggest they had not functioned identically in both cases. But why were they not *exactly* identical? A general resemblance was common enough, and the functional similarities indisputable, but as more specimens were found and described it became increasingly clear that the fossils had no living counterparts. Could it be that some living representatives of the divine creation had subsequently been allowed to vanish from the face of the Earth? Extinction? No! That was impossible. Struggling to reconcile belief and rational deduction, Ray suggested that since they were creatures of the oceans, a vast and largely unknown territory, it was reasonable to assume that living specimens awaited discovery in some distant parts.

But what about the fossil plants that coal miners were bringing to light? Their resemblance to living terrestrial plants was unmistakable, but like the shells they had no exact counterparts. Edward Lhwyd (1660–1709), Keeper of the Ashmolean Museum in Oxford and a distinguished naturalist, had assembled and described a representative collection but was uncertain of their origin. Like Hooke and Ray, he rejected the idea that they were 'sports of nature' or the product of the Earth's 'plastic force', but also refused to believe they could be organic in origin. Instead, he proposed the theory that they had grown *in situ* from the seed of the living plants they resembled. In correspondence, Ray offered constructive criticism of Lhwyd's theory but still could not accept the conclusion to which his reasoning led…Yes, the plants 'had once grown', he wrote, no other explanation could suffice, but:

> there follows such a train of consequences as seem to shock the Scripture-history of the novity of the world; at least they overthrow the opinion generally received, and not without good reason, among Divines and Philosophers, that since the first Creation there have been no species of Animals or Vegetables lost, no new ones produced.[14]

John Ray had glimpsed the conundrum of extinction and it offended the tenets of his faith; ultimately, he turned away from the prospect that the logic of observation and deduction had revealed to him and retreated into the comfort of belief:

> There is a Phenomenon in Nature, which rather somewhat puzzles me to reconcile with the Prudence observable in all its Works, and seems strongly to prove that Nature doth sometimes *ludere* [amuse itself], and delineate Figures, for no other End, but for the Ornament of some Stones, and to entertain and gratify our Curiosity, or exercise our Wits; that is, those Elegant impressions of the Leaves of Plants upon Coal-Slate.

Extinction. In our day, when it is common knowledge that of all the species ever to have existed on Earth, more than 99 per cent are extinct; when the media bombards us with bleak news of how many species are currently threatened with extinction as a consequence of our plundering of the Earth's resources; when it is not unrealistic to conclude that our own extinction is a serious possibility—in these circumstances it requires a leap of imagination to appreciate what extinction can have meant to anyone in the seventeenth century, when the concept was wholly new, undreamt of, and a contradiction of Divine perfection.

Life in Europe was very different then. Nine of every ten people worked on the land, producing food. Every essential item of everyday life was but the skill of a craftsman away from the providing Earth: stone, wood, leather, wool, linen. The daily chores, the round of seasons, the flow of generations, the social bonds—all sustained by self-affirming belief and stories told around the fire. No power, other than in the wind, rivers, and the muscle of oxen, horses, and men; no light, other than the sun and a flame; no entertainment, other than that which people made themselves. Life was hard for the most part, and longevity uncommon, but there can have been no uncertainty: though individuals were born and died, Earth and life were eternal. As it was in the beginning, is now and ever shall be.

There was no place in this arrangement for the concept of extinction; few will have heard of it to begin with, and most who did will probably have rejected it

FIGURE 2.2 Though Edward Lhwyd drew attention to the resemblance between fossils from the coal measures and living plants, he refused to believe the fossils were organic in origin.

out of hand. But intellectual discipline obliged the savants to take it seriously, to consider the evidence dispassionately, objectively, and accept the conclusion to which rational deduction might lead them. That a man of John Ray's calibre could do this and to his life's end deny the fact of extinction is a measure of its impact. And not only could it cause personal anguish—there were social considerations too. Accepting the fact of extinction was regarded as a nasty, deviant trait to which only the bravest would confess. John Ray was among those who preferred to dissemble.

So long as the majority of fossils providing evidence for extinction were clearly of marine origin, it was still possible to argue that extinction was not the only viable explanation for the lack of living counterparts. As Ray believed, living specimens might yet be lurking in distant oceans. The fossilized remains of terrestrial animals were another matter. Bones had been found—enough to be collected and commented upon as oddities, but not sufficiently complete or plentiful enough to merit serious analysis. This state of affairs changed in 1669, with the publication of a thesis by Nicholaus Steno (1638–86).

Born Niels Stensen (but in professional life better known by his Latin name), Steno was a Danish physician and anatomist brought to Florence by the Duke of Tuscany in 1665. A hospital post provided a living, but also left plenty of time for research under the auspices of the *Accademia del Cimento* (Experimental Academy) which the Duke's brother, Leopold de' Medici had founded expressly to further Galileo's experimental and mathematical approach to science. In anatomy Steno solved the mystery of muscle function by showing that they swelled because the muscle fibres contracted, without any increase in volume, not as the result of some insensible cause; in palaeontology he struck an early blow for the theory of organic origin by demonstrating that teeth taken from a rare shark caught off Livorno in October 1666 were identical to the hundreds of so-called 'tongue-stones' found in deposits around the Mediterranean.

At the time, Steno was also engaged on the work for which he is better known and justly famous: the *Prodomus* (1669), effectively a theory of the Earth as revealed by the geology of Tuscany. Analysis of the rocks revealed distinct strata which, he said, must have been deposited in horizontal layers that were subsequently distorted to their present formation. He distinguished six periods of deposition and (with prescient anticipation of William Smith's far more thorough work, see p. 21) correlated them according to the fossils they contained. The lowest layers contained no fossils at all; the uppermost contained (among other things) the 'tongue-stones' which he had shown to be of organic origin. The evidence was unequivocal, but Steno was careful to disavow any certainty, claiming only that he was making the case for their organic origin available to whosoever might have wished to contest it.[15]

Steno shared with his contemporaries the assumption that the Earth was only about six thousand years old; therefore it was obvious to him that the skeleton of an elephant found (as well as tongue-stones) in the youngest strata could only be a relic of the animals which had accompanied Hannibal's army. After all, there were historical records of the invasion and no evidence at all for elephants in Italy at any other time. But such reasoning was not good enough for Wilhelm Ernst Tentzel (1659–1707), a German scholar to whom farmers from near Gotha in Thüringen had brought an assortment of strange bones in 1695. Tentzel recognized them as petrifications—fossils—and details such as the hollows that formerly contained marrow convinced him they were the remains of an animal which must have lived in some prehistoric age. An elephant, he concluded after making comparisons with a living specimen, but definitely not one of Hannibal's, whose invasion had not reached Thüringen; nor could it have come with the Roman legions that did penetrate the region, he said, for the Romans surely would not have buried its valuable tusks (contemporaries were particularly impressed with this point).[16]

Tentzel published his conclusions in 1696, and discussed their implications in a lengthy exchange of letters with Gottfried Leibnitz (1646–1714). The renowned philosopher and mathematician agreed that the remains were most likely those of an elephant or at least an elephant-like animal, but was adamant this did not imply that it had become extinct:

> I do not assert that *any species have died out*, although I am not prepared to say that it is absurd. But I think we must distinguish between extinct species and those that have greatly changed. Thus the dog and wolf, cat and tiger can be seen as being of the same species. The same can be said about the amphibious animals or marine oxen [hippopotamus] once analogous to the elephant.[17]

There is a hint of evolutionary theory in Leibnitz's contention—one hundred and fifty years before the publication of Darwin's work—which suggests that the theory's earliest glimmerings were as much inspired by a determination to deny the extinction of species, as by an urge to explain the origin of new ones.

More and more large fossil bones were being discovered throughout Europe, however, and while many could be readily described as the recent remains of elephants (raising only the question of how they came to be where they were found), some clearly were not. The contemporary literature is enlivened with an imaginative parade of large animals—giant horses and oxen, giant hippopotami and even human giants—among which a fossil bone described in Plot's *Natural History of Oxfordshire* (1677) is especially relevant.

Robert Plot (1640–96), Oxford University's first Professor of Chemistry, and first Keeper of the Ashmolean Museum (Edward Lhwyd was Plot's assistant and succeeded him as Keeper), was an assiduous collector of formed stones. He rejected the idea that fossils had ever been living organisms and was among those who believed they were formed in the rock, chemically. Their resemblance to living creatures was entirely coincidental, he claimed, like stalactites and snow-flakes (and, one imagines, like the potatoes and carrots occasionally found in the likeness of something or other). But then he was confronted with teeth and bone which defied such categorization— especially the bone:

> I have one dug out of a quarry in the Parish of Cornwell [in Oxfordshire, not the county of Cornwall]…that has exactly the Figure of the lowermost part of the Thigh-Bone of a Man or at least some other Animal…

The bone was huge, twenty-four inches in circumference at the widest point and, though only a short length of the whole thigh-bone, almost twenty pounds in weight. Given that the anatomical detail and the internal structure were pre-served, Plot could hardly deny that it was, indeed, a petrified animal bone, but what animal could have been so large? Fortuitously, there was a travelling circus in Oxford at the time, with a living elephant among its attractions. Plot compared the animal's teeth and legs with the fossils and found that they were 'incompara-bly different'. Therefore, he concluded, if the fossils belonged to neither elephant, horse, nor oxen:

> it remains, that (notwithstanding their extravagant Magnitude) they must have been the bones of Men or Women: Nor doth any thing hinder but they

may have been so, provided it be clearly made out, that there have been Men and Women of proportionable Stature in all Ages of the World, down even to our own Days.[18]

He then gives an entertaining list of giants to prove the point. Goliath, he writes, 'was for certain nine foot nine inches high'. The sons of the Titans were also of great stature; a Giant found standing in a rock cleft by an earthquake measured 46 cubits (twenty-one metres!)…and so on, until:

> There was one Gabbara, brought out of Arabia, in the days of Claudius the Emperor, exactly the height of Goliath, viz. nine foot nine inches high; which being a size very proportionable to our bone found at Cornwall, I am rather inclined to believe that Claudius brought this Gabbara into Britain with him, who possibly might die and lay his bones here, than that they belonged to any elephant…

In fact, the origin of the bone was more fantastic than even Robert Plot could have imagined. He was correct in his anatomical identification—it was the distal end of a femur—but its owner definitely had not been an elephant, nor a human giant. Gigantic, certainly—we now know that the living creature was six metres long, had stood three metres tall and was fearsome in the extreme: indeed, it was one of the most ferocious creatures ever to have lived—a carnivorous dinosaur. *Megalosaurus*, to be exact, which had hunted across the landscape of what is now Britain throughout the Jurassic Period, 193 to 136 million years ago. Historically, this was the first dinosaur bone ever discovered, though by the time it was named *Megalosaurus* (huge lizard) in 1824, a bewildering assortment of fossils from similar creatures had also been found. In 1841 they were grouped together as the *Dinosauria*, the 'terrible lizards'.[19]

Animal fossils aplenty were collected as the seventeenth century advanced, from across Europe to Russia and the far reaches of Siberia; from both South and North America. That they were the petrified remains of living creatures was no longer in doubt—the question now was: what were they, and what had happened to them? Mammoths from the permafrost regions of Russia and Siberia were distinctive enough to be identified as relatives of the elephant (prompting the assumption that elephants must once have inhabited much more of the Earth than was currently the case), and some fossil finds were similar enough to be classified among them; other assemblages were a jumble of disarticulated bones and teeth, which could have belonged to one species or several, one individual or many—no one could tell. The largest, and therefore potentially the most useful, of these assemblages had come from Big Bone Lick, Kentucky, in the United States.[20]

Actually, the famous fossil site (now 'Tomb of the Mammoths', a Kentucky State Park) was recognized as such before even the United States was founded. In 1739 a French military party travelling down the Ohio river to strengthen forces in one of the Indian wars being fought in that barely explored region, had come across masses of fossil bones, teeth, and tusks at a salt lick near the banks of the Ohio.[21] A large collection of representative specimens was assembled and shipped to Paris.

In Paris, the fossils were delivered to George-Louis LecLerc, Comte de Buffon, director of the Jardin du Roi (later to become France's National Museum of Natural History), who was then compiling his massive *Histoire Naturelle* (see p. 13). The first section of the *Histoire Naturelle* was to have detailed descriptions of the 182 quadrupeds which had been dissected by Buffon's colleague, the naturalist Louis-Jean-Marie Daubenton (1716–1800). Daubenton was invited to apply his anatomical expertise to a study of the fossils from Big Bone Lick.

Buffon initially wanted to classify them with the mammoths from Siberia, claiming they proved that the species had been common to both the Old and New Worlds (but changed his mind later). Daubenton found more complexity in the assemblage. His study, published in 1764, showed that although the bones and the tusks from Ohio were indeed very similar to those of living elephants and fossils from Siberia, some of the teeth were quite different: instead of the elephant's flat convoluted grinding surface, the Ohio teeth in question had a knobbly configuration, more like the teeth of a living hippopotamus. Apart from raising questions of identification, this also implied that more than one species were represented in the consignment from Big Bone Lick. And raised yet more questions: How many individuals were there in the assemblage? What species did they belong to? Which bones belonged to which species? Sorting the bones and reaching definitive

---

FIGURE 2.3 In his *Natural History of Oxfordshire*, 1689, Robert Plot proposed that the fourth specimen opposite had belonged to a gigantic human. In fact it was the lower end of a dinosaur's femur.

where) about 15 inches; in weight, though representing so short a part of the *thigh-bone*, almost 20 pounds.

156. Which are *dimensions*, and a *weight*, so much exceeding the ordinary course of *nature*, that by *Agricola*[c], *Cæsalpinus*[f], and *Kircher*[g], such *stones* have been rather thought to be formed either in hollows of Rocks casually of this *figure*, and filled with *materials* fit for *petrification*; or by some other sportive *plastic power* of the Earth, than ever to have been real *bones*, now *petrified*.

157. And that indeed there are *stones* thus naturally fashioned, must by no means be doubted, since no question the stony *teeth* of which there are Cart-loads to be had in a *Cave* near *Palermo*, beside others in the shape of *leg* and *thigh-bones*, and of the *Vertebræ* of the back, are no others than such[h]. None of ... *Charles* Marquess of *Ventimiglia* well ob- ... of the *marrow*,

the *body* to be changed, as indeed it ... instance of our *petrified bone*: for w... picted *Fig. 5.* in its exact bigness, ... not at all *petrified* but perfect *bone* ft... thing short of it in *proportion*; whe... cluded, that there could be but ... all.

160. And if it be asked how it ... *thigh-bone* should be *petrified*, and ... swered, and that *experimentally* too... fily of any change or *petrification*, ... closely compacted *substances* than a... that we so often find them sound an... are consumed. Thus at *Bathendon*... *Badonicus* of *Nennius*) not far from ... have been Cap fulls of *teeth* picke... Plough[i], but we are told of no ot... ... med by *Fazellus*, in ...

TAB. VIII.

ad pag 142

according to which m... tioned *Species of Plan*... as each of them will co... *herbaceous Plants.*

2. By which I under... of a *succulent* and *carnous*... become *lignous*, (or ha... *Shrubs* and *Trees* de...

conclusions on these points—crucial to a proper understanding of the fossils—would be a monumental task, requiring a new kind of insight, analysis, and skill.

Meanwhile, Big Bone Lick had been attracting visitors; fossils collected at the site were being studied by experts in all the scientific centres of Europe. As an example of the confused and varied interpretation that such a mixed assemblage of fossils could inspire, the conclusions of William Hunter (1718–83), Britain's leading anatomist, are especially revealing.

Hunter was particularly impressed by a jawbone among the fossils from Big Bone Lick given to the British Museum by an Irishman who had collected them while in the vicinity for negotiations with the Indians. The jawbone was distinguished by having the molars still in place, which led Hunter to a conclusion that, in effect, combined the views of the experts in Paris: Daubenton's putative hippopotamus teeth belonged in the jaw of Buffon's putative elephant. Therefore only one large species was represented at Big Bone Lick, Hunter concluded. But, though related to living elephants, it was quite distinct from them, he said, calling it the 'American *incognitum*' or 'pseud-elephant'.

> Speculating further, Hunter thought the knobbly teeth could have belonged to a carnivore, but confessed he was not aware of such a fearsome creature ever having existed—either alive or as the subject of rumours among American hunters and their Indian informants. A fact which although 'we may as [natural] philosophers regret…,' he wrote, 'as men we cannot but thank Heaven that its whole generation is probably extinct.'[22]

The organic origin of fossils was no longer seriously disputed in the mid-seventeenth century. Extinction, however, was still more of a theory than established fact, and set to become an issue no discussion could avoid as the number of fossil sites and specimens grew. Too many of the bones defied classification as relatives of living animals, implying that they must represent something entirely different and offering only three possible explanations: either their relatives were still alive in some unexplored region to which they had migrated (possibly to escape climatic or environmental changes); or they had changed, generation by generation, into quite different forms; or they had become extinct.

Migration, transmutation, or extinction. Each explanation had its supporters, but it is clear that advocates of the first two were strongly motivated by a wish

to disprove the third. The dedicated naturalist and future President of the United
States, Thomas Jefferson (1743–1824), for example, insisted that:

> Such is the economy of nature, that no instance can be produced of her hav-
> ing permitted any one race of her animals to become extinct; of her having
> formed any link in her great work so weak as to be broken.[23]

The Ohio bones were the remains of animals related to the Siberian mammoth,
he said, and as such represented a cold-climate cousin of the tropical elephant.
It might flourish still in the vast American wilderness that lay beyond the settled coastal states, Jefferson insisted. Indeed, he urged expeditions venturing into
that unexplored territory to look out for living 'mammoths'. At the same time,
expeditions that Europe dispatched around the world were expressly intended to
seek out and bring back what was new. The era of exploration sustained a belief
that extinction could yet be disproved.

Meanwhile, Erasmus Darwin (1731-1802) in England, and Jean-Baptiste
Lamarck (1744–1820) in France were refining ideas that would give transmutation an intellectual grounding. Erasmus Darwin was, of course, Charles Darwin's grandfather and although he died seven years before Charles was born, his
work and writings were an inherited fact of life for the young scientist and an
edge, we can imagine, against which his early ideas of evolutionary theory were
sharpened. Some of the grandfather's observations certainly define a basis for
the grandson's inquiries. In the *Botanic Garden* (1791) Erasmus remarks:

> As all the families both of plants and animals appear in a state of perpetual
> improvement or degeneracy, it becomes a subject of importance to detect the
> causes of these mutations.

In *Zoonomia* (1794) he proposes that the cause lies essentially in:

> The power of acquiring new parts, attending with new propensities, directed
> by irritations, sensations, volitions, and associations; and thus possess-
> ing the faculty of continuing to improve by its own inherent activity, and of
> delivering down these improvements generation by generation to its poster-
> ity, world without end![24]

The elder Darwin's work was translated into French (and German) and it has been suggested that Lamarck was a plagiarist. But although their ideas of transmutation were broadly similar and published sequentially, there is no evidence of Lamarck having derived his theory of acquired characteristics from Darwin (it is far more likely that they both had been inspired by Buffon's monumental *Histoire Naturelle*). Where Darwin was an unashamed amateur enthusiast, Lamarck was a professional, working in Paris at what was then the world's foremost centre of scientific research in the natural sciences: France's National Museum of Natural History. In the course of his work, Lamarck coined two of the most commonly used words in the science: *biology* (in 1802) and *invertebrate* (in 1815).

Lamarck had been elected to the French Academy of Science at the age of 35. In 1793 (the year after Louis XVI and Marie Antoinette went to the guillotine) he was appointed as a professor at the museum, and on 11, May 1800 gave a lecture in which he presented his ideas on evolution (or transmutation) for the first time. These were published nine years later, in Lamarck's most famous work, *Philosophie Zoologique*, a book which the young Charles Darwin read while on the *Beagle* and which shocked much of the scientific establishment by proposing a 'tendency to perfection' and claiming that life is in a constant state of advancement and improvement that is too slow to be perceived—except in the fossil record.

Lamarck argued that organisms contained a 'nervous fluid' that enabled them to adapt to their local environments, acquiring advantageous characteristics which were then passed on to the next generation. Thus wading birds evolved long legs as they stretched to stay dry, and the giraffe's long neck was the result of succeeding generations stretching for the uppermost leaves on a tree, a proposition with which Lamarck's reputation has been tainted ever since.

Though Lamarck's model for evolution was the first testable hypothesis offering an explanation of how a species could change over time, it was rejected (and sometimes ridiculed) by his contemporaries. 'All acquired conditions of the body end with the life of the individual in whom they are produced,' an authoritative critic remarked in a paper read before the Royal Society.[25]

But the inadequacies of migration and transmutation as explanations for the fossil remains of strange, hitherto unknown creatures were not proof of extinction. In contrast to the ponderings of Erasmus Darwin and the hypotheses of Jean-Baptiste Lamarck, the proof of extinction called for hard evidence, and an astute analysis of verifiable facts. Enter Georges Cuvier (1769–1832), another who survived the social and political upheavals of the French Revolution and, as a younger man, was better able to thrive in the avant-garde milieu of its aftermath, when the old dogma and institutions of learning were pushed aside to make room for a fresh, vibrant, evidence-based search for knowledge. In science, the effect was as though the lid had been lifted from a boiling pot. The French National Museum of Natural History quickly became the envy of the world's scientific community. Nowhere else was such a brilliant group of scientists gathered together, working in an integrated research centre, supported so liberally by the state.

Georges Cuvier and his work epitomize the fresh and vigorous approach to science in the new Republic. As a boy, he had read and re-read his treasured set of Buffon's *Histoire Naturelle* (and painstakingly coloured its engraved animal illustrations).[26] With a sound education in the sciences bolstering his passion for natural history, a good measure of personal energy and ambition, Cuvier joined the Museum's scientific community in 1795, at the age of 25, and sprang up through its ranks 'like a mushroom'—but a good one, his colleague Jean-Marie Daubenton later remarked.[27]

Cuvier's exceptional aptitudes became apparent within months of his Museum appointment. Towards the end of 1795 he took over a senior colleague's public lectures on comparative anatomy and made them his own by speaking of animals as complex but functionally integrated machines. This innovative concept was fundamental to his life's work: all vertebrates are functional variations on one basic skeletal theme, parts of which are modified to suit particular ways of life—the bird's wing, the horse's foreleg, and the monkey's arm, for example. Furthermore, the form of certain anatomical parts is invariably related to the form of other parts: hoofs and horns are always associated with the large grinding molars of herbivores; claws with the fangs of carnivores. In short, there is always a 'correlation of parts', which Cuvier, more than anyone else, established as the basic principle of comparative anatomy.

Cuvier confidently expected that the correlation of parts would enable him to sort individuals from a random collection of fossils and then, by comparing them with the modern counterparts, reconstruct the complete or partial skeletons of previously unknown creatures. 'We will take what we have learned from the comparative anatomy of the living', he said, 'and we will use it as a ladder to descend into the past'.[28] This was the task Cuvier had been set, with the Museum's unparalleled collection of vertebrate skeletons (which included practically everything from aardvark to zebra) and its correspondingly extensive collection of fossils.

'I found myself as if placed in a charnel house,' Cuvier later wrote,[29]

> surrounded by mutilated fragments of many hundred skeletons of more than twenty kinds of animals, piled confusedly around me. The task assigned me was to restore them all to their original positions. At the voice of comparative anatomy every bone and fragment resumed its place.

Cuvier had scarcely begun these studies when news arrived of a skeleton on display in Madrid which had been reconstructed from fossil bones found in Spanish South America. Nothing so complete had been known hitherto, and although Cuvier had only a short description and five engravings to work from, he soon published a report on the skeleton.[30] It was twelve feet long, six feet high and complete except for the tail and some paired bones which had been imitated in wood. Applying the principles of comparative anatomy, Cuvier concluded that the animal was an ancient relative of the three-toed sloth but limited himself to a more general name: *Megatherium fossile*, huge fossil beast (in the published paper the name was changed to huge American beast: *Megatherium americanum*). This was the first time a prominent naturalist had named a fossil animal according to the Linnaean system of taxonomy and it was provocative, for if the animal was distinct from any living species it must be extinct. But Cuvier claimed only that *Megatherium*:

> adds to the numerous facts that tell us that the animals of the ancient world all differ from those we see on earth today; for it is scarcely probable that, if this animal still existed, such a remarkable species could hitherto have escaped the researches of naturalists.

No mention of extinction. Such reticence in a man not known for his modesty seems out of character, but it is no more than an example of good science.

FIGURE 2.4 Anatomical principles enabled Cuvier to reconstruct the extinct *Megatherium* (top). The tiny jaw was found in deposits which also contained a dinosaur's toe-bone (foreground); Buckland recognized its mammalian affinities, which Cuvier subsequently confirmed.

PHASCOLOTHERIUM BUCKLANDI.

Nat. size.

Without having studied the actual bones of the specimen and compared them directly with analogues from modern animals, Cuvier could not make a defensible case for *Megatherium* having become extinct. This is important in respect of scientific procedure, but academic as regards proof of extinction. In fact, Cuvier had already announced that extinction was a phenomenon which had occurred in the history of life. The occasion was a lecture 'On the species of living and fossil elephants' given in Paris 21 January 1796. The evidence was the anatomy of modern Indian and African elephants and fossil analogues from Europe and Siberia. Cuvier began by showing that the living species were as different from one another as the horse from the ass or the goat from the sheep—far more than could be attributed to natural variation. Similar comparisons established that the fossil specimens were different again, subtly but unequivocally, and therefore extinct.[31]

So, although *Megatherium* was the first individual extinct animal to be described, the case for extinction was first made with Cuvier's lecture on living and fossil elephant skulls. 'In retrospect, and even at the time, it was an occasion of outstanding importance for the history of palaeontology,' writes Martin Rudwick, a leading authority on the history of science. '[F]or the first time the world of science was presented with detailed and almost irrefutable evidence of the reality of extinction.'[32]

Two years later, Cuvier had identified twelve animals from among the fossil bones in the 'charnel house' which were sufficiently different from their living analogues to be distinct species. To the megatherium and mammoth of 1796 were added a fossil rhinoceros, a cave bear, the Ohio animal (from among the Big Bone Lick fossils), the Irish 'elk', and a fossil hippopotamus as well as some smaller creatures. This was an impressive range of animals, demonstrating considerable variation in size and form, and Cuvier now claimed explicitly that all the species were truly *extinct*.[33]

In November 1800, Cuvier described twenty-three species he had reconstructed, 'all quite certainly unknown today, and which all appear to have been destroyed, but whose existence in remote centuries is attested by their remains', and in 1812 published a major work on a total of seventy-eight quadruped species which he had identified among the bones of the charnel house—including mammals and marsupials, hoofed animals, both ruminant and non-ruminant, carnivores, sloths, amphibians, and rodents. Forty-nine of the seventy-eight species were definitely extinct, Cuvier wrote, and the remainder uncertain to a greater or lesser degree. Among the extinct species, twenty-seven belonged to seven entirely new genera. Thirty-six genera and sub-genera were identified in all.[34]

In the course of this work, the fact of extinction had brought Cuvier to another significant observation: the fossilized manifestations of life became more complex and varied through the ascending strata. The oldest rocks, devoid of fossils, showed that life itself 'had not always existed', he told audiences at a series of public lectures given in 1805, and the earth had experienced a series of 'different ages, producing different kinds of fossils'. Molluscs had preceded fish, fish had preceded mammals...[35]

These ideas were more fully expressed in his *Essay on the Theory of the Earth*, published in 1815: 'There is a determinate order observable in the disposition of these bones in regard to each, which indicates a very remarkable succession in the appearance of the different species'.[36] The rocks revealed a gradual advance in the complexity of life through the several 'revolutions' which the Earth had experienced, he said, and the most recent rocks contained the remains of animals most similar to living kinds.

But the most complex creature of all—'the paragon of animals' which many believed to be the ultimate purpose of life on Earth, 'infinite in faculty'—was missing from the rocks: no human fossils had been found. Cuvier said this was because the last revolution, which in effect had prepared the way for humanity's arrival, was too recent for human bones to have been preserved as fossils since then. But man, he concluded,

> to whom has been accorded only an instant on earth, would have the glory of reconstructing the history of the thousands of centuries that preceded his existence, and of the thousands of beings that have not been his contemporaries![37]

CHAPTER THREE

Nothing so Rare

I T WAS not for lack of enquiry that no human fossils had been found at the time of Georges Cuvier's authoritative pronouncement on the issue. After all, for those who claimed that fossils were a consequence and evidence of the Flood, the fossilized remains of some poor sinner would be the ultimate proof of their contentions. And such 'evidence' had been found: the 'stone teeth of giants' were on display in many museums (though even in the early 1700s they were thought more likely to have been elephant teeth); the Royal Society Museum in London possessed what resembled 'two bones of a human leg' encased in a vein of iron; there was a 'stony human foot' and a 'stone knee' in Verona's Calceolarian Museum and the Worms Museum had an entire 'Granite Man'.[1]

Though the general public might have accepted that these curiosities were indeed the remains of people, many of the intrepid amateurs whose fossicking so enlivens the early history of palaeontology considered them to be 'sports of nature'—nothing more than odd-shaped stones; but they did wonder why no remains of men drowned in the Flood had been found. Could it be, mused Johann Scheuchzer (1672–1733), a leading believer in the Diluvial Theory, that the remains of:

such innocent creatures as plants, testacea [molluscs], fishes and even lowly insects are more abundant because these are more deserving of remembrance than men—all of whom, except some (though not all) of Noah's family, had taken to paths of infernal, as well as physical corruption, and had richly deserved to be consigned to eternal oblivion.

Born in Zurich and a qualified physician, Scheuchzer was a typical savant of his day—erudite, active in many fields of inquiry, fluent in several languages, and a contributing member of the 'republic of letters' through which observation and conjecture flowed freely across Europe. He conducted geological, mineralogical, climatological, and meteorological observations (in the course of which he became the first to record barometrical altitude measurements in the Alps); he lectured in the natural sciences at university and published extensively on Swiss history and literature as well as on science. His detailed map of Switzerland (1712) remained authoritative for two hundred years.

As a young man, Scheuchzer had belonged to a group that met weekly to discuss puzzling issues: are comets the omens of divine punishment or world catastrophes? Where do storks and swallows go for the winter? Does a creature born with two heads have two souls? Why are Moors black? Where did Christ find the clothes he wore for his Ascension? Were mountains created in the beginning, or had they been formed during the deluge? Later, he sent a list of 200 questions to authoritative figures across Switzerland, seeking detailed information on topography, geology, climate, vegetation, and animal life: everything from the annual range of temperature variation to the length, width, and depth of rivers and lakes.

Scheuchzer's thirst for knowledge was nothing if not comprehensive. But fossils were a primary interest and in 1708 the search for specimens took him to Altorf, on the Lower Rhine in north-eastern France. Altorf was a small town, but large enough to have its own gallows, standing grim and bleak in a walled enclosure outside the town. Scheuchzer entered the enclosure, and it must have seemed prophetic that in the shadow of the gallows—that terrible instrument of human condemnation—he found what he took to be the relics of a sinner who had died in the Flood: a pair of petrified, human dorsal vertebrae.

Their substance is almost wholly stone, shiny black, and the structure of the bony fibres is beautifully preserved. In their entire form and in the arrangement of their processes, they have the exact specification of vertebrae of the human back.

Though undoubtedly fossils and organic in origin, the two vertebrae were no more impressive than the curiosities on display in Verona, Worms, and London. Indeed, but for 'a remarkable favour of Providence' Dr Scheuchzer might never have attracted the attention that has earned him a mention in most histories of palaeontology. In 1725 'a new guest' arrived at Dr Scheuchzer's museum:

> the dearer that is the rarest, dearer still that it has no need of clothing or provisions, coming well supplied with all such, and surpassing the former specimen[s] in size, age and intriguing features. Here, immersed in…fissile stone, we have…an adult human skeleton.

The specimen had come from a quarry at Oeningen in Germany, and had been partially excavated from the stone to reveal a spine, a head, and some disarticulated bone. Scheuchzer named it *Homo diluvii testis* (Man who witnessed the Flood). His report, published in the Royal Society's *Philosophical Transactions* (1726, vol. 34 pp. 38–9) and elsewhere, gave anatomical details (along with an engraving of the specimen) and spelled out its affinities with the human skeleton, boldly concluding that:

> no-one who would direct even a passing glance, not to say an attentive study, upon this stone would fail to recognise it as a real and authentic relic of the Flood, for this most unusual handiwork of Nature will meet even the exactions of the Anatomist.

In fact, attentive study would soon convince a modern anatomist that *Homo diluvii testis* was a fossil salamander, not human; and a passing glance would be enough to persuade even the uninitiated that the fossil was more reptile than man.

FIGURE 3.1 The original fossil that Johan Scheucher described in 1726 as the remains of a man who had witnessed the Flood (*Homo diluvii testis*) currently resides in Teylers Museum, Haarlem. The specimen is about one metre long.

Scheuchzer's 'ancient sinner' was celebrated in its day nonetheless, the illustration appearing in numerous publications and the specimen itself eventually being purchased by Teylers Museum in Haarlem, where it became a popular exhibit. Doubts concerning its human affinities were expressed, but no formal exposure of Scheuchzer's error was made until Georges Cuvier examined the specimen and published his conclusions in 1812. Cuvier had of course seen the illustration and made a preliminary judgement before visiting Haarlem to examine it personally in May 1811.

Boldly, he removed more of the stone in which the fossil was set, with a sketch of a salamander skeleton alongside for guidance and comparison, and 'with no little pleasure, noted that with each bit of stone ejected by the chisel, there appeared a bone to match one that was already in the sketch'. Exactly as predicted, the well-preserved forelimbs of the fossil were revealed, thereby confirming Cuvier's earlier conclusion that it was a giant salamander. *Homo diluvii testis* was in no way related to any human being, and the fossil's preservation had nothing to do with any biblical Flood.

Cuvier's report gave descriptions and measurements of the specimen's diagnostic anatomical features, prefaced by an expression of disdain for the scientific acumen of its finder:

> Nothing less than total blindness on the scientific level can explain how a man of Scheuchzer's rank, a man who was a physician and must have seen human skeletons, could embrace such a gross self-deception. For this fragment, which he propagated so sententiously, and which has been sustained for so long on the prestige of his word, cannot withstand the most cursory examination.

It is a salutary tale. Johann Scheuchzer was a man of 'indefatigable industry and extensive knowledge', but also was driven by preconceived notions of what must be found. His unquestioning belief in the Noachian Flood obscured the true nature of the fossils he was describing (which were interesting enough in their own right). In the fashion of his time, he was not so much trying to broaden understanding of the earth and life history as he was trying to confirm his beliefs.

Today, with hindsight, the failing seems obvious and easy to avoid, but it is surprising how often the tendency (perhaps temptation is a better word) has been apparent in palaeontology—especially in the study of fossil humans (palaeoanthropology). In this discipline, where evidence is sparse and often inconclusive, even leading figures have made claims their evidence was too weak to support; proposing, unabashedly, that their latest discovery—a leg bone perhaps, skull fragments, or a single tooth—was proof of the beliefs that inspired them to search for it.

Some months before Cuvier was revealing the true identity of Dr Scheuchzer's drowned sinner, a British force under the command of Sir Alexander Cochrane captured the Caribbean island of Guadeloupe from the French. Close to six hundred French soldiers were killed and another 1,309 taken prisoner.[2] Among the booty found at headquarters was a block of stone from which was emerging a partially excavated human skeleton. The block, eighteen inches thick and measuring eight by two-and-a-half feet, weighed two tons and had been quarried from a site on the north-eastern corner of Guadeloupe where the presence of human fossils embedded in solid rock had been noted in 1805. The specimen was awaiting shipment to France and delivery to Cuvier's laboratory when Cochrane arrived, and so was diverted to the British Museum instead.[3]

This trophy of ongoing British–French hostilities (the Rosetta stone captured in Egypt was another) aroused considerable excitement in England. Popular accounts contradicted Cuvier's account of its acquisition, claiming instead that it was a prized item of cargo taken from an enemy vessel captured in battle at sea, and a suspicion of jingoism taints the fact that British naturalists had acquired France's 'opportunity of investigating the nature and age of this first known example of the bones of man in a fossil state'.[4] At the British Museum the specimen received the personal attention of Charles König, curator of the natural history collections, who delivered his findings in a paper read to the Royal Society in 1814.[5]

The Guadeloupe specimen was indubitably human, König announced, but not a fossil; chemical analysis by Humphry Davy (inventor of the eponymous miners' lamp) having shown that the bone still contained organic material. Nor was the rock limestone, or marble, as had been supposed, but a cementation of gravel, sands, and calcareous materials that were still friable when the body was interred some centuries before. Though perhaps a disappointment for British prestige, König's pronouncements demonstrated two fundamental difficulties of palaeontology very clearly. First, that the rock containing a putative fossil—no matter how hard—need not be very old (concrete sets in days); second, distinguishing fossils from the bones of animals that died in the recent past is not always a simple matter—especially in the case of human remains.

The effect of the fossilization process is that instead of breaking down into their chemical components, the bones of dead creatures (or plants, or insects) are buried away from the agents of decomposition, and infiltrated by minerals which replace them, molecule by molecule, until, where organic material existed before, stone remains, exactly preserving the form of the original.

The fossil remains of marine creatures, extinct elephants, and so forth, are unmistakable. Human fossils, on the other hand, are found only in geologically recent (and therefore comparatively shallow) deposits, where they may easily be confused with historically recent burials. So how can fossilized and unfossilized bone be distinguished one from the other? In the early nineteenth century the 'tongue test' was a method commonly used; the idea being that bone or fossil adhered to the tongue to a greater or lesser extent depending upon the amount of collagen it contained. However, the tongue test was occasionally contradicted by the hydrochloric acid test, which sometimes revealed large quantities of collagen where the tongue test had suggested it was absent.[6] In view of these factors, geological circumstances were always the best indication of antiquity: were the remains found above, below, or among the bones of extinct animals? But even where such indications existed, the evidence of early man was often overlooked or disregarded.

The first discovery of fossil remains now thought to have been human actually pre-dates Scheuchzer's drowned sinner: a skull fragment found in southern Germany. The provenance of the specimen is obscure, but a 'huge heap' of mammoth bones is said to have been found in the banks of the river Neckar, near Cannstadt, in April 1700. The discovery inspired a local Duke to order the systematic digging of the area and within months, at least sixty mammoth tusks had been unearthed, along with the many bones of other large animals—and a single human calotte (skullcap). The tusks and bones were ground up and sold as medicines. The skullcap, being rather more of a curiosity, was preserved and eventually consigned

FIGURE 3.2 Georges Cuvier's comparison of Scheucher's *Homo diluvii testis* with a fossil giant salamander left no doubt of the former's reptilian origin.

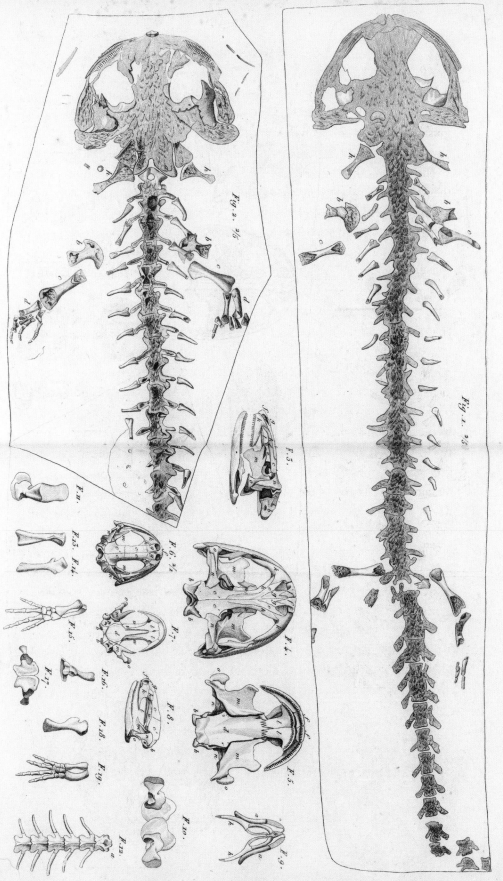

Pl. XXVI.

to the Stuttgart Museum where it languished, hardly noticed, until being called upon to serve as a prototype of an 'early fossil race' in an 1882 publication. Today, it is recognized as having been a genuine fossil human.[7]

The significance of human bones found by Baron von Schlottheim in 1820 near Koestritz, Upper Saxony, nearly two metres below the remains of extinct hyenas and rhinoceros, was also overlooked, even though the nature of the deposition indicated that they could not have been buried there, nor could they have 'fallen into fissures during battles of ancient times'. But then, the Baron himself had expressed some uncertainty about their provenance; which suggests that Cuvier's opinion and example were encouraging lesser mortals to be cautious with their claims.[8]

Georges Cuvier died in 1832 at the age of 63, still unpersuaded that the human species could have existed when the fossils of extinct quadrupeds were formed. His reputation and convictions lived on, potentially an unyielding measure against which finds and claims were to be assessed. But it was not religious dogma that framed Cuvier's views—simply a refusal to accept assertions that were not supported by good evidence. He is quoted as having claimed, emphatically, 'L'homme fossile n'existe pas',[9] when his actual words on the subject were much more circumspect: '[the evidence] leads us to believe that the human species did not exist in the countries where fossil bones are found, at the time of the revolutions that buried those bones'.[10]

Such circumspection surely would have characterized Cuvier's conclusions had he been invited to assess the fossil human bones reported by Paul Schmerling in 1833. They had been found among the remains of animals which Cuvier himself had identified as extinct. Would he have recognized them for what they were? We will never know. Death intervened and the finds were assessed more by what was becoming the dogma of Cuvier's opinions, than by the example of his science: their significance was overlooked.

Schmerling (1791–1836), Belgium's leading palaeontologist, had devoted many years to the exploration of caves along the valleys of the Meuse, near Liége. This was no easy undertaking, as the English geologist, Charles Lyell, subsequently noted:

> To be let down, as Schmerling was, day after day, by a rope tied to a tree so as to
> slide to the foot of the first opening of the Engis cave, where the best-preserved

human skulls were found; and, after thus gaining access to the first subterranean gallery, to creep on all fours through a contracted passage leading to
larger chambers, there to superintend by torchlight, week after week and year
after year, the workmen who were breaking through the stalagmite underlying bone breccia nearly as hard; to stand for hours with one's feet in the mud
and with water dripping from the roof on one's head, in order to mark the
position and guard against the loss of each single bone of a skeleton, and at
length after finding leisure, strength and courage for all these operations, to
look forward, as the fruits of one's labour, to the publication of unwelcome
intelligence, opposed to the prepossessions of the scientific and as well as the
unscientific public—when these circumstances are taken into account, we
need scarcely wonder, not only that a passing traveller failed to stop and scru-
tinise the evidence, but that a quarter of a century should have elapsed before
even the neighbouring professors of the University of Liége came forth to vindicate the truthfulness of their indefatigable and clear-sighted countryman[11]

In the Engis cave, Schmerling had found the remains of at least three human
individuals preserved in deposits that also contained extinct rhinoceros and
mammoth remains. 'There can be no doubt that the human bones were buried
at the same time and by the same cause as the other extinct species', he wrote.[12]
Furthermore, he not only demonstrated the coexistence of humans with the rhinoceros, bear, hyena, and other animals, but also described some 'relics worked
by the hand of man': shaped bones, flint arrow-heads, and tools.

> Everything considered, it must be admitted that these flints have been cut by
> the hand of Man, and that they have been used to make arrows or knives...Even
> if we had not found human bones in circumstances strongly supporting the
> assumption that they belonged to the antediluvian period, proof would have
> been furnished by the worked bones and shaped flints.[13]

Yes, but it could not be so readily acknowledged while preconceived notions
derived from the Cuvier dogma persisted. Schmerling pointed out the absurdity
of denying the contemporaneity of the human and extinct quadruped fossils
while accepting the coexistence of the other living species (including deer, wild
cat, boar, rabbit, and shrew) whose bones had also been found alongside extinct

quadrupeds in the cave.[14] But to no avail. Schmerling would be dead twenty-five years before his discoveries were given the attention they deserved. And what if Cuvier himself had been able to examine them? Perhaps he would have repeated the words he once addressed one day to a colleague: 'My dear friend, we have been mistaken.'[15]

It was not only in continental Europe that the early evidence of man's prehistoric existence was passed over; in England too, significant finds were given scant attention. Kent's cavern, near Torquay, supplied evidence of flint tools together with extinct animals in 1829, but did not arouse serious scientific interest.[16] The significance of a skull found in Gibraltar sometime before 1848 was similarly overlooked.

Respect for the sanctity of human remains was another factor militating against the collection of evidence. In 1852, for instance, a man chasing rabbits near Aurignac, in the foothills of the Pyrenees, thrust his arm down a hole after his prey and, instead of a rabbit, drew out a large bone. He dug deeper and discovered a cave almost filled with bones, among which were two complete skulls—indisputably human. The people of Aurignac, astonished to hear of so many human relics in so lonely a spot, flocked to the cave. The mayor and town physician, Dr Amiel, ordered all the bones to be taken out and, having employed his anatomical knowledge to establish that they had belonged to seventeen individuals of both sexes and all ages, arranged for their Christian burial in the parish cemetery. Eight years later the sexton professed complete ignorance of the burial site when the paleontologist Édouard Lartet inquired after them.[17]

Industrialization and the expansion of railway networks were mutually supportive in the first half of the nineteenth century, changing forever the economic, social, and physical landscapes of Europe. Towns which hitherto had existed to serve local communities became centres of commercial activity attracting people from across a much wider area. The first West German line, completed in 1841, linked Elberfeld (now Wuppertal) and Düsseldorf as a structural element of what would become the industrial complex of the Ruhr. Wealth was generated; the urban middle-class expanded and increasingly found its leisure in escaping from the grimy reality that industrialization had brought.

Those who lived in Düsseldorf were fortunate to have near by the bizarre rocky landscape and forested slopes of the Neander Valley. Known simply as 'Im Gesteins' (In the Rocks) until 1850, when it was given the name of the poet Joachim Neander (1650–80), a resident of Düsseldorf who had often visited the valley, the cliffs and caves of the valley (actually more a gorge) were popular with nature-lovers from far and wide. Indeed, it was compared with the Via Mala gorge in Switzerland. Numerous pictures of the gorge were painted by members of Düsseldorf's Art Academy; colourful names were given to prominent features: Angel's Chamber, Shining Castle, Lion's Pit, Devil's Chamber, Horse Stall, Raven Rock, Neander Cave, and while artists set up their easels overlooking attractive views, the caves became a popular destination for picnics and parties:

> We agreed to take a large excursion with horse and cart to the Neander Cave. The horses and carts were ordered for the riders and drivers, and…[W]e arrived without accident around 1 o'clock. A small barrel of wine, as well as a cold buffet, were taken in wheelbarrows into the largest of the caves, the Neander Cave, while the colourful company toured and enlivened the lonely wooded gorge with hearty singing.[18]

Today, the Neander Valley in its pristine state, with its spectacular cliffs, woods, and caves, would be seen as a natural monument worthy of protection; in the mid-nineteenth century those in control of its destiny regarded it as a natural resource worthy of exploitation. The region's growing heavy industry required huge amounts of limestone as an aggregate for iron-smelting and for building. The Neander Valley cut through deep beds of limestone—previously worthless but now of great value—and by the 1850s quarrymen were steadily blasting away the beautiful face of the valley. Whenever a cave was exposed, the thick deposits of compacted loam which covered its floor was laboriously broken up with pick-axes, shovelled into wheelbarrows and tipped into the valley below.

In early August 1856, two workmen clearing the floor of a cave that less destructive visitors had known as the Kleine Feldhofer Grotte noticed some bones among the debris they were shovelling into their wheelbarrows. To the eternal gratitude of palaeoanthropological science, one of the quarry owners, Wilhelm Becker-shoff, was checking operations at that precise moment and decided the bones were sufficiently interesting to merit saving. He even sent the men down to look for any that might have been among the debris they had already tipped into the valley. Sixteen pieces of what might have been an entire skeleton were recovered in all—both thigh bones, most of the right arm and shoulder blade, the right collar-bone, portions of the left arm, a piece of the pelvis, five ribs and a calotte (skull cap). Most were damaged to some degree by the rough handling of excavation, but still, this was a discovery to match the significance of the Rosetta Stone: primary evidence and substantial enough to illuminate a hitherto obscure—not to say fraught—area of investigation: did fossil man exist? Had humans once shared the earth with creatures which are now extinct?

The calotte, with its large eyebrow ridges and shallow profile, was so unlike anything human that Beckershoff and his partner Friedrich Pieper are said to have thought they had saved the remains of a cave bear, such as had been found elsewhere along the valley. They gave the bones to Johann Carl Fuhlrott (1803–77), a teacher from Elberfeld who was known for his interest in fossils. Fuhlrott recognized them as human, and in due course showed them to Hermann Schaaff-hausen (1816–93), professor of anatomy at the University of Bonn, who in turn presented them to the world of science at a meeting of the Lower Rhine Medical and Natural History Society held in Bonn on 2 February 1857.[19]

Schaaffhausen was convinced that the remains were ancient and human. The strange shape of the skull was natural, he said, and though definitely not affected by disease or injury was quite different from that of any modern race, even the most barbarous. The limb bones were exceptionally thick, he pointed out, with pronounced muscle attachments denoting an extremely powerful individual. The prominent eyebrow ridges—'characteristic of the facial conformation of the large apes'—must have been typical of the race, he suggested, giving them a savage and brutal aspect. He concluded that the remains had belonged to one of the original wild races of north-western Europe; a barbarous lot whose 'aspect and flashing of their eyes' had terrified even the Roman armies.[20]

Schaaffhausen was the first of many to offer an opinion on the bones from the Neander Valley. Over the past one hundred and fifty years observation and interpretation have been profuse, ranging from the outlandish to the elegantly scientific, and Neanderthal Man has become the iconic figure of our prehistoric existence. Neanderthal Man: named after a valley that was given the name of a poet who started life as Joachim Neumann but, in the fashion of his time, had preferred to use the classical Greek version as an adult: Neander...Neumann...which of course means New Man—an apt title for a specimen that not only closed the argument as to whether fossil man existed, but also opened a new chapter in the story of palaeoanthropology.

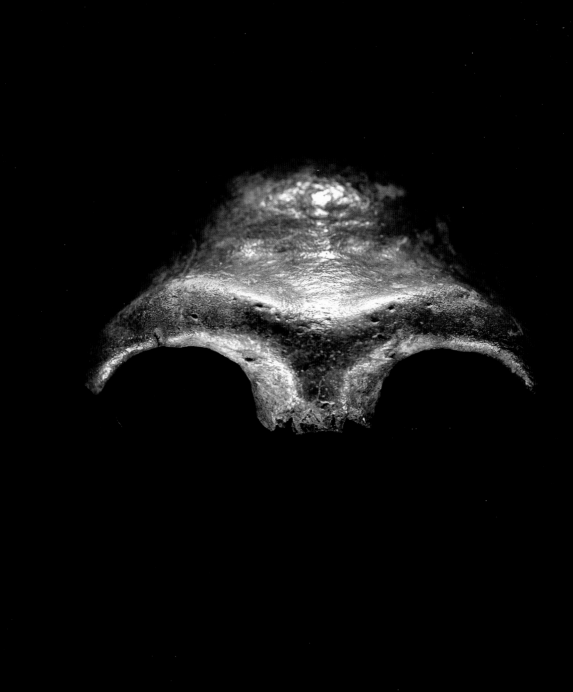

CHAPTER FOUR

Neanderthal Man
(1857)

I F THE extinction of species had been a major focus of debate in the late eighteenth century (awaiting the definitive work Georges Cuvier published in 1796), the origin of species became the centre of attention during the early nineteenth century (with Charles Darwin poised to publish his definitive work on the subject in 1859). As arguments about extinction cooled down, debates about the origin of species warmed up. Darwin, born 1809, had grown up with the idea that species had mutated from one to another through time—not least from the writings of his own grandfather Erasmus, and those of Jean-Baptiste Lamarck (see p. 43)—as well as from discussions among the naturalists with whom he studied while at university in Edinburgh and Cambridge. But while exposed to a wealth of informed opinion and advocacy on transmutation (the term 'evolution' was not yet in general use), Darwin was not persuaded. Indeed, in a letter of 1871 he admitted that 'When I was on board the *Beagle* I believed in the permanence of species'. When back in England and preparing his journal of

FIGURE 4.1 The calotte (skullcap) of *Homo neanderthalensis*, the first putative ancestor to be given formal zoological distinction.

the voyage for publication, however, he began to see 'how many facts indicated the common descent of species'.[1]

With hindsight, the facts seem so obvious, but for Darwin's generation of naturalists and scientists the origin of species was a puzzle that simply would not fit into any existing paradigm. The *Beagle* voyage primed Darwin with a wealth of data and observation from which to draw conclusions on the issue; he took the first deliberate step in that direction soon after, as his diary records: 'In July [1837] opened first note-book on *transmutation of species*.' There would be several more, in which he recorded a veritable 'flurry of ideas' that stretched as far as his imagination would take him. Meanwhile, he had been observing how selective breeding enabled farmers to improve their crops and livestock, generation by generation. Species did change, and selection for desirable traits was the key, he concluded. In agriculture the selection was made by farmers but 'how selection could be applied to organisms living in a state of nature remained for some time a mystery', he wrote.

The solution struck him in September 1838 while reading 'for amusement' Thomas Malthus's *Essay on the Principle of Population*. Malthus (1766–1834) claimed that since populations tended to increase faster than their food supply, only some kind of restraint on a population's growth could ensure its continued existence. Some kind of restraint. In nature that could only be the environment:

> it at once struck me that under [certain] circumstances favourable variations would tend to be preserved, and unfavourable ones to be destroyed. Here, then, I had at last got a theory by which to work.[2]

Among organisms living in a state of nature, with no human interference, *natural* selection restrained their population growth. The mutations that arose in some individuals enabled them to prosper more than others if environmental circumstances changed; nature, in other words, selected for advantageous mutations, so that fortuitously endowed populations would thrive, and as the generations passed, could potentially evolve into a new species. So simple; not just a theory but, like gravity, an inevitable feature of the universe we inhabit; there to be observed.

Even so, it was not until 1842 that Darwin allowed himself 'the satisfaction of writing a very brief abstract' (thirty-five pages) of his theory. An expanded version of some 230 pages followed two years later. Then, in 1846, Darwin put the theory to one side and devoted himself to a study of barnacles (which was published in four monographs). In 1856, urged on by friends, Darwin finally settled down to write his book on evolution, to be entitled *Natural Selection*. Two years later, 18 June 1858, with ten chapters complete, Darwin's orderly progress was rudely interrupted by a package from the naturalist Alfred Russell Wallace, then exploring the Malay Archipelago.[3]

Wallace had also been thinking about how species arose. He had also read Malthus, which together with his observations on the profuse plant and animal life in the Dutch East Indies, had stirred him to the same conclusion that Darwin had reached: natural selection was responsible. This was the news that reached Darwin that morning—accompanied by a twelve-page summary of Wallace's ideas on evolution that duplicated Darwin's, and a request to forward the essay for publication if its ideas were deemed worthy. Shaken, Darwin wrote that evening to his mentors, the geologist Charles Lyell and botanist Joseph Hooker:

> I have never seen a more striking coincidence…if Wallace had my MS sketch written out in 1842 he could not have made a better short abstract!

Darwin was in a difficult position. He did not want to lose his scientific priority for a theory on which he had been working for many years. At the same time he wanted to behave honourably towards Wallace. Lyell and Hooker felt the Wallace paper deserved to be published without delay, and persuaded Darwin to allow a chapter from his manuscript to be presented at the same time. Accordingly, less than two weeks after its arrival, Wallace's essay and Darwin's chapter were read at a meeting of the Linnaean Society, and published in the Society's journal a few months later. Neither author attended. Wallace because he was still on the other side of the globe (and received news of the event only three or four months later); Darwin because his tenth child, still a baby, was dangerously ill with scarlet fever and died on 28 June, only two days before the Society meeting.

Much has been made of the fact that this action was taken without Wallace's knowledge or consent, that Darwin's items were read before Wallace's and that Darwin then quickly went on to complete and publish his *Origin of Species*. These facts have led some to believe Darwin has been unfairly credited with developing the theory of evolution by natural selection, when Wallace was the first to put the idea to paper. Others say Darwin wanted to take the credit. However, the pair corresponded frequently over the following years and held each other in high regard, crediting and complimenting each other's work. There is no indication that Wallace felt Darwin had acted dishonourably. In fact he seemed very flattered that Darwin had forwarded his essay for presentation at the Linnaean Society. The relationship between the two men was undoubtedly complex, but always gentlemanly. Darwin was the country squire, living off inherited wealth and sound investments. Wallace was a committed socialist whom Darwin and his colleagues ultimately saved from abject poverty by arranging a Crown pension.

The low-key and high-brow nature of Linnaean Society meetings ensured that the theory of evolution which the Wallace and Darwin papers introduced to the world on 1 July 1858 did not attract much attention beyond the rooms in which they were read. There, 'the interest excited was intense', Joseph Hooker later recalled,[4] 'but the subject was too novel and too ominous for the old school to enter the lists before armouring. After the meeting it was talked over with bated breath.' There was no semblance of a discussion.

This will have been welcome news to Darwin, who was still mourning the death of a child and was always concerned about the reaction his theory might provoke. In March 1859, as the long-delayed book was nearing completion he wrote to Charles Lyell:

> Would you advise me to tell Murray [publisher] that my book is not more *un*orthodox than the subject makes inevitable. That I do not discuss the origin of man. That I do not bring in any discussion about Genesis, etc. etc, and only give facts, and such conclusions from them as seem to me fair.
>
> Or had I better say *nothing* to Murray, and assume that he cannot object to this much unorthodoxy, which in fact is not more than any Geological Treatise which runs slap counter to Genesis.[5]

Though the vexed question of how species originated had swirled through the community of naturalists with mounting vigour in the early nineteenth century, polarizing opinion, hardening conviction, and encouraging advocates

FIGURE 4.2 Charles Darwin's theory of evolution derived much of its substance from his observations of birds and flowers, especially during the voyage of the *Beagle* (notebooks, bottom right). The magnolia resembles the earliest of the flowering plants.

CHARLES DARWIN.

for and against transmutation to gather a body of fact and support around them, it probably did not reach many of the broader public in any comprehensive, or even comprehensible form, until 1844 when it appeared as a package that was available to all—blockbuster style—in a book called *Vestiges of the Natural History of Creation*, written by Robert Chambers (1802–71), a journalist of scientific bent. The book was very successful, selling out four editions in seven months, more than 20,000 copies by the time Darwin's *Origin of Species* appeared fifteen years later, and nearly 40,000 by 1890.[6]

Vestiges was published anonymously to protect Chambers' business interests (he and his brother published the *Chambers' Edinburgh Journal*, a successful weekly magazine covering the arts and sciences, manners and morals) and thus, writing for a popular audience and free from the constraints of precise scientific presentation, he could afford to be bold in presenting what he called 'the first attempt to connect the natural sciences into a history of creation'. He drew together all available scientific evidence and hypothesis to describe how the universe is arranged, and how the earth is composed of matter condensed from 'vaporiform chaos'. Calling upon (and occasionally misinterpreting) the evidence of biology and palaeontology he told how organic creation and the proliferation of life was the result of natural law, rather than divine intent. 'The simplest and the most primitive type…gave birth to the type next above it,…this again produced the next higher, and so on to the very highest.'[7] There was a principle of *development* involved, he said, that had operated over a vast space of time. All animals were variations of the same basic skeletal plan; they were, in fact, 'merely modifications of that plan to suit particular conditions' and 'the whole train of animated beings, from the simplest and oldest, up to the highest and most recent [should] be regarded as a series of advances of the principle of development'.[8]

Chambers did not stress the point, but his development hypothesis clearly made man an immediate descendant of the apes, retaining a 'strong affinity' to the preceding form, just like every other animal. And, of course, 'the development hypothesis would demand…that the original seat of the human race should be in a region where the quadrumana [the four-handed species, apes and monkeys] are rife'.[9]

It is tempting to think of *Vestiges* as a brilliant forerunner of Darwin's evolutionary theory, lacking only the principle of Natural Selection to make the hypothesis complete. But it lacked other elements too. Darwin's geology pro-

fessor at Cambridge, Adam Sedgwick, accused 'Mr Vestiges' of making philosophy out of moonshine. The book was so uninformed, inaccurate, contentious,
and lacking a basis of fact, he said, that it could have been written by a woman.
Darwin himself was more circumspect, remarking that the book displayed 'little
accurate knowledge and a great want of scientific caution'; the geology was bad,
he said, and the zoology far worse.[10] Even so, he praised the book's 'powerful
and brilliant style', and considered that it had 'done excellent service…in calling
attention to the subject, in removing prejudice, and in thus preparing the ground
for the reception of analogous views'.[11]

A charitable thought. It is possible that with *Vestiges* having drawn the fire, so
to speak, the attack on Darwin's work was less fierce than it might have been.
But it is equally possible that *Vestiges* awakened a broader spectrum of prejudice
than would otherwise have been the case and, furthermore, that the book was
regarded as a popular version of evolutionary theory upon the basis of which
Darwin's work could be attacked without the necessity of reading his more
knowledgeable and rigorously scientific book.

On the Origin of Species by Means of Natural Selection was published on 24 November 1859—the book of the year (even the book of the century), though it faced
stiff competition. Dickens' *Tale of Two Cities* and George Eliot's *Adam Bede* were
also published in 1859, as well as the first in Tennyson's long cycle of Arthurian
poems and John Stuart Mills's *On Liberty*. But such was the level of interest in the
topic of evolution by then, and the reputation of its author, that *Origin of Species*
was an instant bestseller. The first edition of 1,250 copies sold out on publication day. Another 3,000 copies were printed to meet immediate demand and the
book has remained in print, in a multitude of languages, ever since. Darwin published six editions during his lifetime, totalling 18,000 copies. Altogether, 56,000
copies in the original format were sold before the copyright expired in 1901, plus
another 48,000 copies of a less expensive edition, it has been reported.

The timing could hardly have been more fortuitous. Not only in that *Vestiges*
had already introduced evolution to a popular readership, or that scholarly
interest in the subject was by then approaching critical mass, but also because
mid-century Victorian Britain was enjoying an unparalleled measure of peace
and prosperity, political stability, and imperial expansion. The achievements
and rewards of the Industrial Revolution had awakened an interest in science
that was diverse, widespread, and well served by a growing publishing industry

and new review journals. Local scientific societies and lending libraries; public lectures and practical demonstrations created a demand for information of all kinds—including, of course, the origins of life and humankind.

As awareness of Darwin's theory spread beyond scholarly circles, however, the implication that man was an animal who shared a common ancestor with the apes, and was not a divine creation, caused understandable concern in some quarters. The Bishop of Worcester's wife, on hearing the news, is said to have exclaimed: 'My dear, descended from the apes! Let us hope it is not true, but if it is, let us pray that it will not become generally known.'[12] Of course, the man-descended-from-ape image was a gift to commentators and cartoonists, allowing them to introduce the controversy surrounding Darwin's scholarly proposition with a note of levity their readers were certain to appreciate.

Inevitably, such treatment reduced debate to a stand-off between science and religion; ape ancestor or divine creation. 'Is it on his grandfather's or his grand-mother's side that the ape ancestry comes in?' the Bishop of Oxford asked of Thomas Huxley at a meeting of the British Association held in June 1860. Hux-ley replied to the effect that he would rather have an ape in his ancestry than an ignorant bishop and although no verbatim report exists,[13] that exchange is probably the most frequently repeated anecdote from the widespread debate that Darwin's theory stimulated. Its humour gives the banter a sportsmanlike touch—but laughter cuts many ways. Darwin himself was the butt of endless jokes—cruel as well as funny—and although the debate may have appeared frivolous to a popular audience, in science it was deadly serious. The pulpit was a source of much outspoken, ill-considered, and inflammatory opposition to which direct response was impossible, but scientists who disagreed were obliged to engage in debate, and to use science in support of their arguments—whatever their religious beliefs. At this level Darwin's theory inspired a great deal of ear-nest endeavour as scientists who did not accept its conclusions attempted to demolish the challenging new paradigm.

In Britain the scientific opposition was led by Richard Owen (1804–92), a bril-liant anatomist, palaeontologist, and administrator who is remembered today as much for his arrogance and conniving behaviour as for his achievements—considerable though they were. Among much else he coined the word dinosaur, identified the dodo, showed that the duck-billed platypus was a mammal, pub-lished over 600 papers and founded the magnificent Natural History Museum in London. But 'this is not to say he was a nice character', said the organizer of an exhibition commemorating the 200th anniversary of his birth held at the museum in July 2004, 'because we know he wasn't. He was a brilliant man, but he was also very competitive, very arrogant and he didn't want anybody taking his crown away from him.'[14]

From a merchant family in Lancaster, talent, toil, and determined networking took Owen to the heights of Victorian science and society. He was knighted, gave lectures to the royal family at Buckingham Palace, received an income from the Civil List, and spent the last years of his life occupying a grace-and-favour Crown property in Richmond Park.

Owen studied anatomy in Edinburgh, specialized in comparative anatomy at the Royal College of Surgeons in London, and by the age of 30 was hailed as 'Britain's Cuvier' and had been elected a fellow of the Royal Society. In 1856, he became the first superintendent of the British Museum's natural history collections—a priceless assortment of dried plants, pickled fishes and reptiles, fossils, skeletons, skins, and stuffed animals brought home by Captain Cook and other adventurers. The collections were growing and deteriorating simultaneously. Owen initiated a campaign to deal with the problem that culminated—twenty-five years later—with the opening of the magnificent 'cathedral of nature' in South Kensington in 1881. 'That's the main thing we must acknowledge and thank Owen for,' the organizer said. 'If he hadn't been the forceful and persistent advocate he was, we would never have had this museum.'

Owen went to his grave believing that Darwin was wrong to argue that natural selection was responsible for the origins of species. His opinions were often immoderately expressed, most notoriously in a long review of Darwin's *Origin* published (anonymously) in the *Edinburgh Review*,[15] but there was also an element of aggrieved frustration here, for Owen had been working on the problem of species for a long time too. He had even sought Darwin's advice, and Darwin's use of morphology as an argument for common descent owes a lot to Owen's work.[16] But though identical in aim, the two men's approach and conclusions were very different.

As might be expected of a comparative anatomist educated as Cuvier's work gained ascendancy and respect, Owen took a mechanistic approach. He believed the key to explaining 'the successive introduction of specific forms of living beings into this planet' lay in the structural modifications which differentiated one from another. To demonstrate how this might have worked, he developed the concept of the Vertebrate Archetype—a skeleton not intended to represent any creature that ever existed, but a structural idea, he said, of which all actual vertebrates were functionally diverse embodiments. In a series of detailed drawings, each bone of the fishes, reptiles, birds, mammals, and man was related by numbers to those of the Archetype. This impressive piece of work was published in 1848;[17] it clearly demonstrated a progression of structural adaptation that was evolutionary in effect, but lacked an essential ingredient: cause.

> 'To what natural laws or secondary causes the orderly succession and progression of such organic phenomena may have been committed we are as yet ignorant', he admitted in a later paper. 'But if without derogation of the Divine power, we may conceive the existence of such ministers, and personify them by the term "Nature", we learn from the past history of our globe that she has advanced with slow and stately steps, guided by the archetypal light, amidst the wreck of worlds, from the first embodiment of the Vertebrate idea under its old Ichthyic [fish-like] vestment, until it became arrayed in the glorious garb of the Human form...For the Divine mind which planned the Archetype also foreknew all its modifications, [and the] Exemplar for the Vertebrated animals proves that the knowledge of such a being as Man must have existed before Man appeared.'[18]

These pronouncements, authoritative, and from a man whom society respected, will have comforted the Bishop of Worcester's wife and strengthened belief in the Divine creation of the world and humanity. There was no suggestion of descent from the apes in Owen's work. Indeed, as though to demolish the idea once and for all, he subsequently presented a paper claiming to disprove the theory of evolution at its most controversial point—man's link with the apes.

The occasion was an evening meeting of the Royal Institution of Great Britain. Owen discussed the structure of the apes as compared to man, referring in particular to 'the last link in the chain of changes—from Quadrumana to

FIGURE 4.3 The 400,000 year-old fossils found in the Sima de los Huesos (Pit of Bones) in Sierra de Atapuerca, Spain are said to represent the remote ancestors of the Neanderthals.

Bimana [four-handed to two-handed] proposed in the hypothesis that specific characters can be so far modified by external influences, operating on successive generations, as to produce a new and higher species of animal, and that thus there had been a gradual progression from the monad up to man'.[19]

Beginning and ending with disparaging remarks about those who supported the evolutionary theory, Owen endeavoured to show that although ape and man are structurally very similar, the differences between them are much more relevant. He mentioned especially the differences that are not subject to external influences, and therefore should be passed from generation to generation without modification, appearing exactly alike in ancestor and descendant. Owen cited the gorilla's prominent eyebrow ridge as an example of such a feature. There is no muscle attached to it, he pointed out, nor is there any aspect of the gorilla's behaviour which suggests that the prominent ridge could be lost or gained by external causes operating on successive generations. Therefore the ridges must have occurred in the gorilla's ancestors, said Owen, and should occur in all that ancestor's descendants. It followed that if man and gorilla shared a common ancestor, they should also share the prominent eyebrow ridge. But ridges rarely—and then only feebly—occur in man, he pointed out; therefore man and gorilla could not have an ancestor in common. Thus, Owen concluded, the notion that man had evolved from the apes was disproved.

The gorilla's eyebrow ridges were not the only evidence Owen offered in support of his contentions that evening, nor was it the only occasion on which he argued against the common ancestry of man and ape. Nonetheless, it is an extraordinary coincidence that the first fossil to be accepted as evidence of early man's physical form, Neanderthal Man, should have presented prominent eyebrow ridges as its most distinctive feature. Since 1857, when the Neanderthal remains were found, the prominent ridges above its eyes, which Owen claimed were an exclusively ape-like feature, have become symbolic of the prehistoric human form.

When Hermann Schaaffhausen introduced Neanderthal Man to the world of science at a meeting of the Lower Rhine Medical and Natural History Society held in Bonn on 4 February 1857 (see p. 62) reaction was muted. Some listeners challenged Schaaffhausen's views (mostly contending that the remains were not human at all), but controversy did not assume significant proportions until his paper appeared in English in the *Natural History Review* of April 1861. It was translated by George Busk (1807–86), then Professor of Anatomy at the Royal College of Surgeons, who appended some remarks of his own, drawing particular attention to the Neanderthal skull's overall resemblance to that of the gorilla and chimpanzee. Shortly thereafter the recently knighted geologist, Sir Charles Lyell, acquired a plaster cast and some photographs of the original specimen which were examined and described by the biologist Thomas Huxley (1825–95), and before very long Neanderthal Man became the nub of an argument that was distinguished by its vigour, imagination, and unintended humour.

Broadly speaking, there were two points of view. The physical peculiarities of Neanderthal Man represented either an early stage of human evolution linking people to an ape-like ancestor, or pathological deformities of modern humans more gross than any medical science had ever encountered. Quarrying had continued in the Neander Valley, so that within a few years the cliff face in which the Feldhofer Grotte had been set was gone, and along with it every prospect of finding more specimens in the cave or recording more detail of its provenance. No more bones, extinct or otherwise, had been found. The evidence for the antiquity of the specimen lay solely in its physical appearance.

Because the fossils' antiquity could be neither proved nor disproved, assessment of them was conditioned by preconceptions concerning the theory of evolution. Those willing to accept the theory believed the remains were very old and freely discussed their primitive, 'barbarous' and ape-like characteristics in evolutionary terms. Those opposed to the theory of evolution, on the other hand, believed the remains were of a modern human and sought a modern, medical explanation for their peculiarities.

As it happened, the first thorough descriptions of the fossils were compiled by evolutionists and, so long as the fossils and casts remained unavailable for general inspection, these reports constituted the evidence itself. Which no doubt added the suspicion of bias and misrepresentation to any anti-evolutionist stance. Add the clashing personalities of ambitious individuals to this already volatile mixture of inconclusive evidence and preconceived belief, and the result is a very lively brew. The protagonists were 'in danger of allowing the wanderings of imagination to take the place of scientific deduction, and to lead us far away from sober fact', as the *Medical Times and Gazette*, Britain's leading medical journal of the day, commented in an editorial reviewing the evidence of '*Homo Antiquus*'.[20]

Taken out of context, this remark seems the essence of moderation and good sense, but the context reveals how preconceptions may rule in the absence of conclusive evidence. Schaaffhausen's description of the Neanderthal fossils 'strongly reminds one of Sir Walter Scott's Black Dwarf,' wrote the editors, 'a theory of rickets and idiocy would…go some way towards unravelling the mystery,' they said, and concluded that '…this skull belonged to some poor idiotic hermit whose remains were found in the cave where he died'.

There is a salutary observation to be made here, which applies to virtually every discovery that has added new knowledge to the story of human evolution. Where the evidence is not sufficient to prove interpretations based on current beliefs right or wrong, any speculation is permissible. Furthermore, the acceptance that speculation achieves is more a measure of the proposer's standing than of its validity. Some speculation of course turns out to be correct, but corroborative evidence is always required and, until that evidence is forthcoming, speculative argument continues.

For many years idiocy and rickets remained the anti-evolutionists' best explanation of Neanderthal Man's physical peculiarities.[21] The theme was developed and expounded most forcefully by F. Mayer, Professor of Anatomy at Bonn University. Mayer had the advantage of having examined the original fossils. He dismissed the significance of the prominent eyebrow ridges and remarked instead upon the absence of a sagittal crest (the ridge of bone running along the top of an ape's skull to which the chewing muscles are affixed). 'Show me a human fossil skull with a sagittal crest, and I will acknowledge the descent of man from an ape-like ancestor,' he said.[22]

Mayer was convinced that the remains had belonged to a modern individual. In the skull he saw similarities with some Mongolian, and even some Caucasian specimens he had examined. Nevertheless, Neanderthal Man had been a degraded creature in his view, and had probably suffered from rickets as a child, the disease being common, he pointed out, among those who lived in wet houses and ate nothing but potatoes. Thus rickets might explain the distinctly bent legs of Neanderthal Man. But bow-legs are also common among those who spend a lifetime in the saddle, Mayer observed. And so turning to the evidence of history, the anatomist offered his interpretation of Neanderthal Man: a Cossack army under General Tchernitcheff had camped in the vicinity prior to their advance across the Rhine on 14 January 1814, and he believed that the bones in the Neanderthal cave must have belonged to an ailing Cossack deserter who had hidden and died there.

Thomas Huxley, the evolutionists' most ardent champion, dismissed Mayer's conclusions as a work 'laden with numerous jocosities of small size, but great ponderosity, directed against Mr Darwin and his doctrine…'. He also noted that Professor Mayer had failed to explain how the dying man had managed to climb a precipice twenty metres high and bury himself after death; and wondered why the man would have removed all his clothes and equipment before performing these wonderful feats.[23]

On a more serious level, Huxley meanwhile had defined the evolutionist view concisely in three essays published together under the title Man's Place in Nature in 1863. Here he described the natural history of the apes, defined humanity's relationship with the lower animals, and presented the first thorough and detailed comparative description of the Neanderthal remains. Huxley concluded that although the cranium was the most ape-like yet known, it did not represent a being that was intermediate between the apes and humans; at most it showed some reversion from the modern human form towards that of an ape-like ancestor. The determining factor, Huxley said, was the size of the brain. The capacity of the Neanderthal cranium was well within the modern human range and twice that of the largest ape. And so, with these remarks, Huxley effectively set brain size as the definitive characteristic of the genus Homo—a status that has been central to interpretations of the fossil evidence of human evolution ever since. In the same work Huxley discussed the remains Paul Schmerling had recovered from the Engis cave, near Liége, thirty years earlier (see p. 59). The specimen, he said, was 'a fair average human skull, which might have belonged to a philosopher, or might have contained the thoughtless brains of a savage'.[24]

The assessment of Neanderthal Man's brain size also raised the interesting question of his mental abilities. Could a creature of such ape-like appearance think as humans do? The anti-evolutionists, of course, said no, it had been an idiot; and even some evolutionists were unwilling to accept the creature as sapient. William King, for instance, Professor of Geology at Queen's College Galway, believed that Neanderthal Man had stood next to 'benightedness' with 'thoughts and desires…which never soared beyond those of the brute'. In fact, King felt so strongly about Neanderthal Man's mental deficiencies that he proposed his exclusion from the human species (Homo sapiens). He would have liked to exclude him from the genus *Homo* altogether, he said, but in the absence of facial bones and the base of the skull he appreciated that this 'would be clearly overstepping the limits of inductive reasoning'. So King settled for a new species: *Homo neanderthalensis*.[25] This was a startling development, suggesting for the first time that formal zoological distinction could be given to the fossils of human ancestors—which in turn implied that more than one species of *Homo* could have existed. Since then naming new species on humanity's evolutionary path has become common practice, as we shall see.

Given the liveliness of the Neanderthal debate it was inevitable that corroborative, or dismissive, evidence would eventually be found. It arrived just a matter of weeks after King had created the new species: the remains of a skull which, though missing some parts, possessed features that the Neanderthal cranium had lacked—the face, and the upper jaw with most of the teeth in place.[26] The new specimen had been found during the construction of military fortifications in Gibraltar. When and by whom is not known. The first mention of the relic appears in the minutes of the Gibraltar Scientific Society for 3 March 1848, where it is recorded that the secretary 'presented a human skull from the Forbes Quarry, North front'. In other words, the discovery predated Neanderthal by at least eight years. Furthermore, it was strikingly similar to the Neanderthal specimen, especially in respect of the eyebrow ridges. In short, the new skull was just what King had required to complete his inductive reasoning; but it would not have helped him relegate Neanderthal from the genus *Homo*. On the contrary, it might well have persuaded him that the specimen did not deserve specific distinction, for its general aspect confirmed Huxley's assessment.

But the Gibraltar specimen did not attract attention until much later. Meanwhile, it was consigned to the 'small museum of natural curiosities which at one time existed in Gibraltar', where it languished while the museum was 'allowed to fall into a state of confusion and neglect' until 1863 when 'its extraordinary peculiarities fortunately struck the notice of Dr Hodgkin', an ethnologist on a visit to Gibraltar who then arranged for its dispatch to George Busk.[27]

FIGURE 4.4 George Busk and the Gibraltar skull.

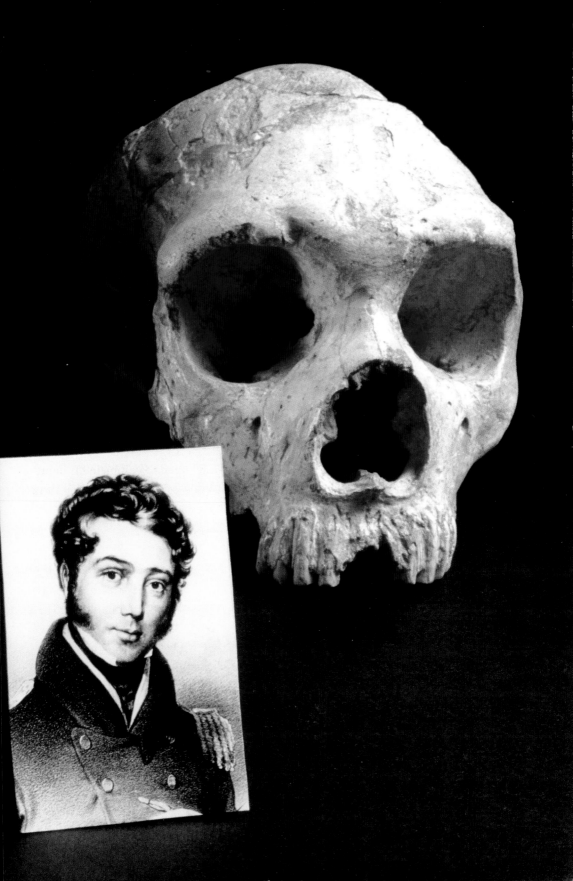

Busk, of course, was the man who translated Schaaffhausen's Neanderthal paper, and he immediately recognized the importance of the new and more complete specimen, not only in its own right, but also for the corroborative evidence it brought to the Neanderthal case. The Gibraltar skull 'adds immensely to the scientific value of the Neanderthal specimen', he wrote in the *Reader* a few days after receiving the skull, 'showing that the latter does not represent…a mere individual peculiarity, but that it may have been characteristic of a race extending from the Rhine to the Pillars of Hercules; for…even Professor Mayer will hardly suppose that a ricketty Cossack engaged in the campaign of 1814 had crept into a sealed fissure in the Rock of Gibraltar'.[28]

Busk exhibited the skull at the meeting of the British Association for the Advancement of Science held in Bath during September 1864. He spoke of its general appearance and compared it with the skulls of modern races, but primarily stressed how it matched and complemented the Neanderthal specimen. In a letter discussing the forthcoming meeting, the palaeontologist Hugh Falconer had suggested that Busk should name the fossil *Homo calpicus*, from Calpe, the ancient name for the Rock of Gibraltar. Falconer also composed an advertisement that would introduce the new species to science: 'Walk up: and see Professor Busk's Grand Priscan, Pithecoid, Mesocephalous, Prognathous, Agrioblemmatous, Platycnemic, wild *Homo calpicus* of Gibraltar'. Falconer was particularly pleased with Agrioblemmatous, feeling that the Greek combination happily united 'the truculence of the eye and the savagery of the face' which he was certain must have characterized the man on the Rock of Gibraltar.[29]

But the Gibraltar skull inspired little or no comment—despite its undoubted significance. After its formal description[30] the specimen virtually disappeared from the literature, and its corroborative evidence was missed (or ignored) by the pathologist Rudolf Virchow in 1872, when he added his views to the Neanderthal debate. Virchow (1821–1902) was a highly respected medical academician. He had been the first to describe the breakdown of the cell that marks the onset of disease, and the science of pathology was built upon his discoveries. He was also the founder and president of Germany's Institute of Anthropology; and, while his fierce opposition to the theory of evolution predicated his conclusions on the Neanderthal remains, his twin interests—pathology and anthropology—characterized their substance.

On the evidence of pathology Virchow decided that the bones had belonged to a very old man who had suffered from rickets as a child, severe head injuries in middle age, and from crippling arthritis for many years before he died. Thus the physical peculiarities were accounted for. To show that Neanderthal Man had died in the recent past and was not, therefore, a human ancestor, Virchow called upon the evidence of anthropology. Such an ill and crippled individual could not have survived to old age in one of the nomadic hunter-gatherer groups that characterized the earliest stages of human social development, he said; therefore he must have lived in an agricultural society of much more recent times, when people were settled and able to care for their sick and aged relatives.[31]

Virchow's pronouncements on the Neanderthal remains were the last to be made by a scientist reared and educated in the years before Darwin presented his comprehensive theory of evolution; in effect they were the last words of the pre-evolutionists, and they present yet another example of science struggling to reconcile new evidence with old beliefs. But of course the debate concerning human evolution did not end with Virchow. Subsequently the search for more conclusive fossil evidence became intense and some spectacular discoveries were made. Two complete skeletons were found in a cave near Spy in Belgium during 1887; another was found near La Chapelle-aux-Saints in France during 1908 and several more came from La Ferrassie in 1909, and from La Quina in 1911. The most striking feature of these remarkably complete finds was their overall similarity to the original Neanderthal specimens; clearly they all represented a race that had populated Europe from Belgium to Gibraltar.

Had he seen the new evidence, Virchow might have felt obliged to revise his diagnosis of head injuries and arthritis. But now the discoveries were examined by a new generation of investigators: a generation born and educated in the post-Darwinian era, but one which was nonetheless subject to preconceptions of its own. And it is ironic that although fundamental beliefs had changed so radically, the conclusions of Virchow and the new investigators were essentially the same: both excluded Neanderthal from the story of human ancestry.

Marcellin Boule (1861–1942) was perhaps the most authoritative of the post-Darwinian investigators. He was destined to become Director of Human Palae-ontology at the French National Museum of Natural History, and for more than fifty years commanded the respect of both science and the interested public, especially after the First World War had cast German science into disfavour and disarray. Boule wrote extensively on the fossils of early humans.[32] His views and preconceptions are largely responsible for the image—which lingers today—of Neanderthal Man as a shambling, frowning brute of low intelligence.

By the turn of the century, most scientists accepted the great antiquity of the Earth, the theory of evolution, and the inevitable conclusion that humans had evolved from an ancestor in common with the apes. There was no question that Neanderthal Man *had* evolved from some primitive stock—but could such a creature represent the ancestor of modern humans? This was a question that Boule and his fellow thinkers barely deigned to contemplate.

Boule's judgement was based on his thorough studies of the skeleton from La Chapelle-aux-Saints.[33] Neanderthal Man, he pointed out, was quite different from modern humans in physical form, yet very close in time; and he concluded that the process of evolution could not have effected so much change in so few generations. Neanderthal Man had divergent toes like the apes, Boule said; he had walked on the outer edges of his feet like the orang-utan; he could not have straightened his knees; he lacked the convex spine essential for upright posture; he had the head slung forward with jutting jaw; and possessed only the most rudimentary psychic nature and articulate language.

Of those who endorsed Boule's conclusions, Grafton Elliott Smith (1871–1937), Professor of Anatomy at the University of London, was among the most influential English-speaking scientists. In his book *The Evolution of Man*, published in 1924, Elliott Smith described Boule's reconstruction of the La Chapelle-aux-Saints skeleton as:

> a clear-cut picture of the uncouth and repellent Neanderthal Man. His short, thick-set and coarsely built body was carried in a half-stooping slouch upon short, powerful and half-flexed legs of peculiarly ungraceful form. His thick neck sloped forward from the broad shoulders to support the massive flattened head, which protruded forward, so as to form an unbroken curve of neck and back, in place of the alternation of curves which is one of the graces of the truly erect *Homo sapiens*. The heavy overhanging eyebrow-ridges and retreating forehead, the great coarse face with its large eye-sockets, broad

FIGURE 4.5 The bent limbs and arthritic spine of this fossil skeleton from La Chapelle-aux-Saints led Marcellin Boule to conclude that the Neanderthals had been a degenerate race.

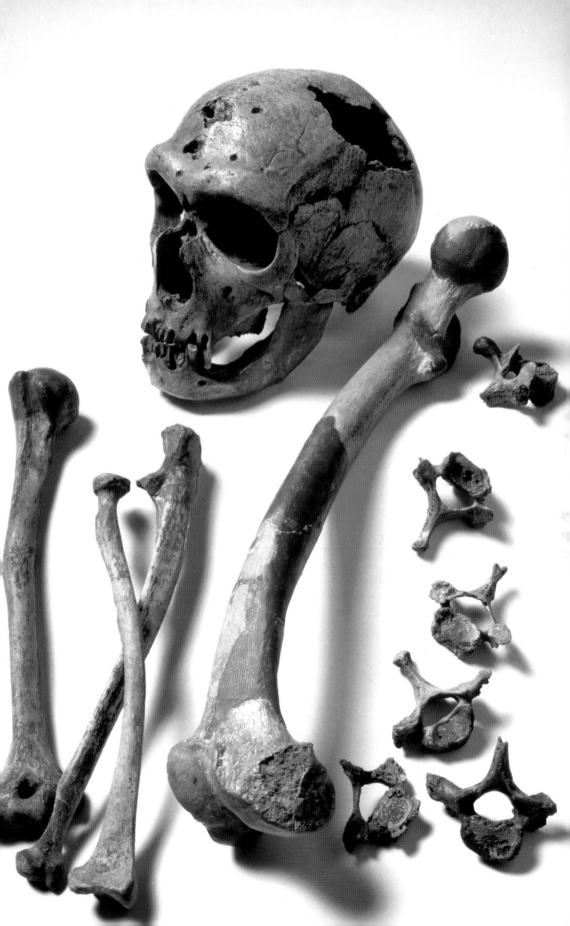

nose, and receding chin, combined to complete the picture of unattractive-
ness, which it is more probable than not was still further emphasized by a
shaggy covering of hair over most of the body. The arms were relatively short,
and the exceptionally large hands lacked the delicacy and the nicely balanced
co-operation of thumb and fingers which is regarded as one of the most distinctive of human characteristics.... The contemplation of all these features
emphasizes the reality of the fact that the Neanderthal Man belongs to some
other species than *Homo sapiens*.[34]

The views of Boule and Elliott Smith are a mirror image of those expressed
fifty years before—the same evidence called to support diametrically opposed
conclusions. Mayer and Virchow had claimed that the Neanderthal fossils were
the remains of a modern human who was not related to the apes; now Boule and
Elliott Smith claimed that Neanderthal Man was a descendant of the apes who
was not related to modern humans. In both cases the evidence lay in the physical peculiarities of the fossils and, in the interpretation of this evidence, Boule
and Elliott Smith were no less guilty than their predecessors of allowing preconception to cloud conclusion. Mayer and Virchow had stressed the pathological
aspects that supported the conclusions they preferred; Boule and Elliott Smith
ignored the pathological aspects that would have refuted their conclusions. In
fact, the pathological evidence was the same in both cases: severe arthritis.

This was first noted by Camille Arambourg in 1955 and precisely defined by
Cave and Straus in 1957.[35] These critical reassessments questioned Boule's reconstruction of the La Chapelle-aux-Saints skeleton (he placed the centre of gravity
so far forward that the man would have fallen flat on his face before taking a
step). Cave and Straus expressed surprise that Boule had not noticed the 'severity
of the osteo-arthritis deformens affecting the vertebral column'. In conclusion,
they found 'no valid reason for assuming that the posture of Neanderthal Man
differed significantly from that of present day man'. Given a bath, haircut, collar
and tie, he would have passed unnoticed in a New York subway, they said.

Suggesting a Neanderthal might have mingled unnoticed among the com-
muters of New York was not unreasonable in 1957, given the information then
available, but the succeeding half-century has produced many more fossils for
inspection and developed a far more extensive suite of investigative procedures.
There are now hundreds of Neanderthal fossils available for researchers to work

on, and the distinctive characteristics of the Neanderthals are no longer questioned. Full grown, they were short, stocky, and *strange*. Clothes might have
hidden their thickset, barrel-chested body and short muscular limbs, but the
disproportionately large and elongated head, with its beetle-brow, enormous
nose, and lack of a chin would have been certain to attract attention. Indeed, a
study comparing diagnostic cranial features of Neanderthals, modern humans,
apes, and monkeys found that the difference between Neanderthals and modern
humans is greater than between chimpanzees and gorillas.[36]

Neanderthals were unique in appearance and the sole human presence in
Europe for a very long time. Their origin is still something of a mystery (as is
their fate—both issues to be addressed in the next chapter), but by 700,000
years ago they, or their immediate ancestors, had already extended to their
northernmost limit and were occupying a swathe of floodplain in what is now
East Anglia. Britain was then still joined to continental Europe, 'at the edge of
the inhabited world, at the edge of human occupation and human capabilities',
says Chris Stringer, head of human origins at the Natural History Museum and
director of the Ancient Human Occupation of Britain (AHOB) project which
completed the first phase of its investigations at Pakefield, near the North Sea
coast of Suffolk, in 2006. No human remains were found, but stone tools indicated that people had occupied the site and analysis of material collected during
the excavations—ranging from microscopic pollen grains, to hyena droppings,
the teeth of tiny extinct voles and the curious straight tusks of an enormous
elephant—has produced a wealth of information on the kind of environmental
conditions under which they lived.[37]

   Seven hundred thousand years ago, Britain was as warm as the Mediterranean today. The Pakefield residents inhabited a marshy landscape of extensive
reed-beds and alder trees adjacent to a meandering river with shallow riffles and
deeper pools. Oak woodland grew on drier ground, with open grassland near by.
This mosaic of habitats supported a variety of animals: beaver, boar, deer, moose,
bison, horses, hippos, rhinos, elephants, and mammoths. There were lions too,
and hyenas, wolves, bears, and the spectacular sabre-toothed cat. The presence
of humans was clearly evident in the assortment of flint artefacts that was found,
each bearing the unmistakable signs of having been worked by human hands
(some were actual tools, others were debris from the process of making one).

The ultimate prize eluded the investigators, however: no skulls, no human bones of any sort were found.

But then, Pakefield was an open site, not a cave, and humans were always rare figures in the ancient landscape. And even without fossils, their tools and knowledge of the environment they occupied are valuable additions to what is known of the earliest human colonization of Europe. Pakefield provides a context in which to place the somewhat enigmatic human remains which have been found in Britain hitherto—skull fragments recovered in 1935 from a gravel pit near Swanscombe in Kent, dating from around 400,000 years old; a 700,000-year-old shinbone found in 1993 at Boxgrove in Sussex; a jaw fragment and nineteen teeth found in a cave near Pontnewydd (Newbridge, in Wales) in 1981, dated at 225,000 years old. This is humanity at the edge, pressing to the limits of what is possible—not just once, but eight times, as the Ice Age glaciers advanced and retreated.[38]

The Pontnewydd remains are the most north-westerly evidence of Neanderthals or their putative ancestors who have, at various times, been present in a region that extended from Wales across Europe and the Mediterranean basin to Israel and Iraq; from Portugal to Uzbekistan. More than fifty locations are known. Apart from the classic sites in Germany, France, and Belgium, human fossils and / or archaeological evidence has been found in Italy, Spain, Croatia, the Czech Republic, Turkey, Ukraine, Russia, Syria, Slovakia, and Slovenia. This wealth of evidence, combined with climatic records, provided the basis for an 'ebb and flow' hypothesis, which proposed that human populations had expanded northwards with the advance of temperate conditions, and retreated southwards as conditions deteriorated again. This implied that humans could only survive in the higher latitudes of Europe when a Mediterranean-type climate prevailed, and that early colonization of the continent was confined to areas south of the Pyrenees and the Alps.[39]

Thus, the fact that so much evidence was found in the south, while in the north what little evidence there was came only from deposits dating to warmer times, was interpreted as a measure of the early human capacity for adaptation and survival—prompting the conclusion that they could only live in temperate conditions, moving back and forth with the vegetation and animals upon which they depended for food. This generally accepted view was shaken in 2010, however, with the announcement that evidence of a human presence in north-west Europe had been found in deposits dating from not less than 780,000 years ago, and up to 950,000 years ago, when the prevailing climate of the region was distinctly chilly—more Scandinavian than Mediterranean.

The AHOB team had moved some 50 kilometres or so northwards from Pakefield, and opened a site just above the high water line near the small village of Happisburgh, on the north-east coast of East Anglia. This was a region through which the ancestral River Thames had flowed into the sea 150 kilometres north of its modern estuary, when a wide seabridge joined Britain to the continent, 900,000 years ago. The Thames (and the now-extinct Bytham river) had laid extensive deposits of sands and gravels across the region and a band of sediments uncovered a few metres down in the Happisburgh excavations contained the telltale signs of a human presence: stone tools. Seventy-eight pieces of flint, shaped by human hands into primitive cutting and piercing tools.

The deposits also contained minerals which enabled geochronologists to establish that humans had occupied the site between 990,000 and 780,000 years ago. Furthermore, organic remains were exceptionally well preserved. No human bones, but evidence of red deer and primitive horses, mammoths, sabre-toothed cats and hyenas, together with the remains of beetles, shellfish, and barnacles; pine cones, wood, and pollen grains were plentiful.

The rare combination of terrestrial and marine remains at Happisburgh enabled researchers to create a snapshot of environmental and climatic conditions 200,000 years before those which were revealed at Pakefield. The differences were dramatic. Whereas oak woods and open grasslands characterized the landscape at Pakefield, forest and woodlands consisting primarily of conifers dominated at Happisburgh—similar to that which is found in southern Scandinavia today. This was a challenging environment for early human settlement, with winter temperatures falling several degrees below those which prevailed at Pakefield. And, while lower temperatures increased the need for food—especially carbohydrates, short winter days limited the time that could be spent foraging.

But the Happisburgh population had settled on the forest-fringed estuary of the ancestral Thames, where they had access to the varied resource-rich habitats of a large tidal river with freshwater pools and marsh on its floodplain, with salt marsh and a seashore near by. This mosaic of habitats could provide a range of critically important winter resources, such as tubers and rhizomes, edible seaweeds and shellfish, to supplement whatever the forest had to offer. Indeed, the presence of humans so far north during what were previously thought to have been uncongenial times can be explained entirely by where they chose to live.

The Happisburgh evidence shows that the first Europeans were not trapped in the ebb and flow of climatic change, staying with the warmth, moving back and forth with the availability of their food resources, as was previously believed. No, if Happisburgh is correct, humans were already capable of adapting their survival strategies and behaviour as the world changed around them, 900,000 years ago. This is a major advance in knowledge. No less important, it reveals how abruptly and completely a deeply entrenched view of early human history can be overturned by a single discovery.

Pakefield and Happisburgh were open sites where there was only the remotest chance of human remains being preserved. Indeed, the majority of human fossils known from this critical period have come from caves—but not, thankfully, caves that were in the process of being destroyed, as in the Neander Valley. Where fossils have been found they have lain, largely undisturbed, in the deep sediments that accumulate in every cave system.

Caves and tunnels that extend like a warren through the limestone uplands of what is now the Sierra de Atapuerca region of northern Spain are a case in point. Set in the gently rolling landscape of oak and chestnut forest to the east of Burgos, this complex system of large limestone caverns had been known to the local people for centuries. Those brave enough to explore their dark recesses had found numerous cave bear teeth and other animal fossils, but the caves had received little serious scientific attention until 1976, when a palaeontology student searching for cave bear fossils found a lower jaw that definitely had not belonged to a bear. It was human and, judging from the kind of animal bones found in the same deposit, was probably around 400,000 years old. This was remarkable enough to merit further investigation—and there was much more to be discovered.[40]

Early surveys found that when a railway line had been laid through the landscape during the 1890s, it had cut open a slice of prehistory. Moving down the face of some cuttings was like travelling more than one million years back into

FIGURE 4.6 Top: the Gran Dolina site in the Sierra de Atapuerca. Left: excavation of a skull from Sima de los Huesos (Pit of Bones). Right: Juan Luis Arsuaga (centre) and his team with fossils found at Sima de los Huesos.

the past, traversing layer upon layer of sediments rich with animal fossils. At a site called Gran Dolina they found human fossils and stone tools too—evidence of the first western Europeans, the pioneers of human migrations into western Europe during and between the Ice Ages.

Not far from Gran Dolina, lay one of the most remarkable sites in all of palaeoanthropology. It is located 500 metres from the main entrance of the cave system, and could be reached either through a labyrinth of tunnels and caverns or via a 14-metre shaft which provided direct access (and air) from the surface. Excavations revealed the bones of animals such as cave bears, lions, foxes, and wolves crammed into a pit dating from between 300,000 and 600,000 years ago which, unsurprisingly, soon became known as Sima de los Huesos (Pit of the Bones). But the excavations produced quality as well as quantity. More than 4,000 human fossils were found, including several well-preserved skulls, jaws, teeth, and skeletal parts of at least twenty-eight individuals, most of them teenagers and young adults.[41]

All together, the fossils from Sima de los Huesos comprise the world's largest collection of human fossils from a single site—indeed, they represent more than 80 per cent of all fossil hominids known from that time period, worldwide. They have enabled scientists to create a remarkably complete story of the people who lived on the Atapuerca hills around 400,000 years ago. In physique they were similar to the far-younger Neanderthals from other sites, but certain features of the skull, jaws, and teeth were different enough for the research team to conclude that they represented a population that was possibly ancestral to the classic Neanderthal. Accordingly, they described the Atapuerca hominids as a new species: Homo antecessor—'pioneer man'.[42]

But despite the wealth of information that has come from the Pit of Bones, a crucial question remains unanswered—a question which touches upon the social behaviour of the Atapuerca population: how did their bones end up in the cave? There is nothing to show that they actually lived there—no evidence of fire, or tools. They might have fallen in accidentally, but in that case you would expect a wider range of ages to be represented. In their preliminary assessment, the research team favoured an explanation involving the people themselves: the bodies were dropped into the chamber as part of an early mortuary practice.[43]

Atapuerca was designated a UNESCO World Heritage site in 2000 in recognition of its contribution to palaeoanthropology. Perhaps more than any other sites, Atapuerca demonstrates that the science is no longer so dominated by the 'treasure-hunt' syndrome. Fossils are wonderful in themselves, as the tangible relics of beings who lived and died so long ago, but unearthing the oldest skull, or discovering a link perceived to have been missing from the evolutionary sequence, is no longer the ultimate prize. With the accumulation of so much evidence since the 1950s (when all the known fossils would not have covered a billiard table), palaeoanthropology has become a multi-disciplinary affair, with a host of scientists deploying their skills not simply in the quest to find fossils, but as contributions to the emerging picture of humanity's evolution and existence over millions of years.

So while it was once enough for earlier generations to conclude that Neanderthal Man was (or was not) an idiot, an arthritic cripple, or even the ancestor of modern humans, modern inquiries are more circumspect. Assumptions are tested and occasionally overturned. The Neanderthals' adaptation to the cold conditions they must have experienced for lengthy periods during their occupation of northern Europe, for example, turns out not to be as great as was believed.

The assumption had seemed to be justified, since the Neanderthals' cylindrical, stocky bodies and short muscular limbs matched those of cold-adapted arctic dwellers in modern times. The ratio between surface area and body volume was the key here: the stouter the body the smaller the surface area to volume ratio and the greater the efficiency in retaining heat. But in fact, analysis has demonstrated that the Neanderthals' stature conferred only a modest advantage—even with their greater muscle mass and if they had a layer of fat. Without still more insulation, they would have had difficulty under the increasingly harsh conditions that prevailed in northern Europe from around 37,000 years ago.[44] As would today's Inuit without their sealskin suits.

So did the Neanderthals make clothes? There is no direct evidence; but the evolution of lice provides an indirect clue. Humans support two species: the head louse which lives and feeds exclusively on the scalp, and the body louse which feeds on the body but lives in clothing. Dating derived from comparative DNA analysis has shown that they diverged to become separate species only around 72,000 years ago. The inference seems clear: since body lice live exclusively in clothing, people probably began wearing clothes around 72,000 years ago, when body lice became a distinct species.[45]

Clothes certainly would have had a beneficial effect on the Neanderthals' dietary requirements. Even to maintain basic levels of activity in a cold climate, an adult male of average Neanderthal stature would have needed close to 5,000 calories a day—approaching what a cyclist in the Tour de France burns each day. This level of consumption, year-round, in locations where vegetative sources of carbohydrate were limited, could only have been satisfied by eating meat—and meat with about 10 per cent body fat at that. This implies a good deal of hunting; indeed, a study of Neanderthal bioenergetics has calculated that a social group of ten Neanderthals, comprising three adult males, three adult females and four juveniles would have required the equivalent of two 80 kg deer per week. If all the adults hunted, their return rates would have needed to be some 3.8 kg per hunter per day. If only the males hunted, they would have each needed to bring back 7.6 kg per day—which exceeds by a considerable margin the rate that wolves average (between 5.4 and 5.6 kg per hunting wolf per day).[46]

It sounds improbable that Neanderthals could have been such successful hunters and devoted consumers of meat, but the probability is confirmed by studies from yet another branch of science that lends its expertise to modern palaeoanthropology: stable isotope analysis. The ratios of the stable isotopes of carbon and nitrogen in mammal bone collagen are a record of the sources from which an animal derived the majority of its protein during the last years of life—plants or meat. In 2000, collagen from two Croatian Neanderthals was analysed at Oxford University's Radiocarbon Accelerator Unit and showed that they had obtained almost all their dietary protein from animals.[47] This was confirmed in 2005 by a French study which analysed the carbon and nitrogen isotopic signature of collagen from twelve Neanderthals. Again, the results showed an overwhelming dependence on meat as a source of protein and could even detect what class of animal the meat had come from. Astonishingly, from among the prey available to them, the Neanderthals had consumed much less reindeer than might be expected, and much more rhinoceros and mammoth than hyenas from the same location and period whose bone collagen was also analysed.

Unequivocally, these studies conclude that Neanderthals were 'top predator in an open environment, with little variation through time and space'.[48] Highly successful hunters—indeed, 'top level carnivores' as another paper puts it,[49] 'occupying that spot with other large carnivores such as wolves and lions'.

The hunting prowess which brought such success has proved more difficult to confirm than its results. Stone-tipped and wooden spears have been found—including rare examples of such weapons in the remains of prey animals and the miraculously preserved wooden throwing spears discovered in 1997 in the course of operations at the Schöningen opencast lignite mine in northern Germany.[50] The eight spears average around two metres in length and were made from individual spruce or pine trees which must have been deliberately felled, debranched, and debarked. The growth rings are close together, implying slow growth in a cool environment.

With an age of 400,000 years old, the Schöningen spears are the world's oldest complete hunting weapons. To prove the point, subsequent archaeological excavations at the site have yielded more than 20,000 well-preserved animal fossils—mainly of horses. There can be little doubt that the site had been a hunting camp, indicating that people were already specializing in systematic big game hunting 400,000 years ago, and were also skilled in woodworking.[51]

Hunting is a dangerous activity and almost every well-preserved adult Neanderthal skeleton has lesions indicating that the individual suffered some significant injury or stress during his or her lifetime which could have resulted from hunting strategies that required getting close to large prey animals. Of course, fighting within or between groups could be a factor too—but whatever the case, there is no doubt that injury contributed to the short life expectancy and very low population densities that studies of the Neanderthal collections have revealed.

A study of 206 Neanderthal skeletons from across Europe and the Near East, ranging in age from 100,000 to 30,000 years ago, found that very few survived beyond their prime reproductive years; indeed, between 70 and 80 per cent of individuals died before the age of 40. Mortality was especially high among infants and young adults. Furthermore, patterns of tooth development and wear implied 'that periods of poor nutritional quality and/or famine must have been relatively common', all of which indicates that they were able to maintain only very low population densities, with survival barely keeping pace with mortality, and may well have experienced frequent periods of local extinction and recolonizations. Nutrition would have been a factor too, for it is not the quantity of food consumed that matters most, but the diversity of foodstuffs. If the Neanderthals were eating meat excessively, mothers and infants would have missed essential nutrients that only a diverse diet provides, threatening survival and thus hindering recruitment to the population.[52]

Dental hygiene is an unknown aspect of Neanderthal life; they probably used fibrous twigs to brush their teeth, much as do present-day inhabitants of regions where toothbrushes are not available, and most fossil teeth are in commendably good condition. Signs of decay are rare but dental plaque is often present, fossilized along with the teeth to which it adhered, and plaque is an accumulation of food residues (and bacteria) that builds up over a period of time.

With this simple, but hitherto overlooked fact in mind, three researchers from the Smithsonian Institution in Washington DC scraped minute quantities of fossilized plaque from seven Neanderthal teeth, which they examined under a high-magnification microscope. The results, published in 2010,[53] have obliged scientists to revise their opinion of Neanderthal cuisine. It was broader and more sophisticated than they had supposed. Not quite meat and two veg, but containing a substantial quantity (and variety) of vegetable foods. This does not contradict the evidence of meat consumption revealed by isotopic studies[54] (the Neanderthals were not vegetarians!), but it does correct the bias resulting from the fact that nitrogen isotopes record only the consumption of meat and protein-rich plant foods.

The Smithsonian researchers found residues of date palms, seeds, and legumes (the family which includes peas and beans). Most unexpectedly, the plaque on the Neanderthal teeth contained particles of starch from a barley-like cereal, and from water lilies, that bore the tell-tale signs of having been cooked. The starch grains were gelatinized, and that can only be caused by the heat associated with cooking, said Dolores Piperno, who led the study.[55]

The teeth had belonged to a 36,000-year-old Neanderthal unearthed from the Spy cave in Belgium, and a 46,000-year-old specimen found in a cave at Shanidar in Iraq. Thus they represented both the warm eastern Mediterranean and cold north-western European climates, and covered a timespan of 10,000 years, indicating that throughout a wide range of time and space, Neanderthals were making good use of the diverse plants foods available in their local environment.

The Neanderthal sites contained no evidence of intensification (such as grinding tools or storage features) in the use of plant foods, but cooking and the fact that several of the plants identified would have required moderate to high levels of preparation (husking seeds, for example) indicate that Neanderthals were investing time and labour in activites that increased the edibility and nutritional value of plant foods. This in turn suggests that Neanderthals may have organized themselves like early hunter-gatherer groups.

'When you start routinely to exploit plants in your diet,' Piperno explained,[56] 'you can arrange your settlements according to the season. In two months' time you want to be where the cereals are maturing, and later where the dates are ready to pick. It sounds simplistic, but this is important in terms of your overall cognitive abilities.

'In early human groups, women typically collected plants and turned them into food while men hunted. To us, and this is just a suggestion, this brings up the possibility that there was some sexual division of labour in the Neanderthals and that is something most people did not think existed.'

Meanwhile, advances in the extraction and sequencing of DNA from fossil bones and teeth (the development of which is covered in the next chapter), had enabled researchers working on Neanderthal remains from the El Sidrón cave site in northern Spain to add evidence of their mating behaviour to the broadening picture of Neanderthal life.[57] The remains of twelve individuals had been recovered from the cave, consisting of three male and three female adults, three adolescents, two juveniles, and one infant. Geological, palaeontological, and archaeological evidence indicated that they represented all or part of a contemporaneous social group, possibly a family, who had died around 49,000 years ago, and were subsequently buried together when the cave system collapsed.

The mitochondrial DNA (mtDNA) from teeth and bone fragments was sequenced and analysed with a view to discovering how the group members were related. The researchers infer from the results that the infant and two juveniles were indeed the offspring (or close matrilineal relatives) of two of the adult females; furthermore, it appears that while the three adult males were close relatives, each of the three adult females carried a different mtDNA lineage.

The El Sidrón Neanderthals thus provide 'tantalizing clues about the demography and behavior of the species', the researchers conclude,[58] suggesting the twelve individuals were a social unit based on patrilocality, in which females and their offspring live with the adult male's family.

New discoveries and advances in investigative procedures promised a fuller and more empathetic understanding of the Neanderthals, but the general impression remained one of people having a hard time: shivering as the ice ages set in; sharing the landscape with huge herbivores and dangerous carnivores; starving as food resources diminish then vanishing, pityingly, as the last child-bearing woman dies. But of course, the duration and distribution of the Neanderthal presence were far more entensive than such images allow. Overall, enough infants were born and raised to adulthood for the population to sustain itself for several thousand generations.

The advance of the glaciers took centuries and however hard a Neanderthal's day-to-day existence may seem to us, it was perfectly normal to them. The species was destined for extinction, but individual lives cannot have been all bad; in fact, evidence from the time closest to the Neanderthals' final demise presents an image of them living in idyllic luxury.

Gorham's Cave, on the eastern face of the Rock of Gibraltar at the southernmost tip of Europe, where the carbon dating of charcoal fragments excavated alongside spear points and basic cutting tools indicates the presence of twelve to fifteen Neanderthals some 28,000 years ago (and possibly as recent as 24,000 years ago), is the youngest site known.[59] The cave was a comfortable home; large enough for natural light to penetrate deeply, and commodious enough for natural ventilation to disperse the smoke of fires. A freshwater stream ran near by. From the cave rim, its occupants could watch the sun rise over the Mediterranean, then nearly five kilometres away and 100 metres lower than at present. The research project's director, Clive Finlayson, abandoning the exactitude of scientific language for a moment, describes the landscape they gazed upon as a 'Mediterranean Serengeti' of scrub savanna and undulating dunes capped with stands of cork oak and stone pine, scented with rosemary and thyme, graced with wild asparagus, and supporting healthy populations of deer and their predators.

Vultures roosted on the cliffs above the cave and as they soared aloft each morning, circling to locate the carcasses of animals killed during the night, Finlayson imagines the Neanderthals would have watched closely, noting where the birds descended and then hurrying down to chase them off what was left. They ate meat, but enjoyed a far more varied diet than Neanderthals elsewhere. Heaps of tortoise shells and mussels have been found in the cave, along with dolphin and seal remains, and such evidence of plant foods as was preserved. Add some rice and they could have made a fine paella, jokes Finlayson.[60]

The archaeological deposits preserved in Gorham's cave are 18 metres thick, indicating that it was a favoured location, used repeatedly over many thousands of years. Like a medieval cathedral when the congregation leaves, it retains a palpable sense of ancient purpose: 'It can be very powerful being in the cave', Finlayson said.

> You can get that feeling that a Neanderthal was sitting in exactly the same spot, that the only thing separating us is time. It's like a connection over tens of thousands of years and it makes you want to know more. We're humans studying humans.[61]

CHAPTER FIVE

Neanderthals and Modern Humans

THOUGH NEANDERTHAL fossils are more numerous than the remains of any other hominid, even the interpretation of their story depends very heavily upon the contributions of other disciplines—as the last chapter showed. To recap briefly: geology establishes a context of *relative* age, according to the strata in which the fossils were found (and these days, sophisticated dating techniques enable geochronologists to establish the *absolute* age); palaeontology reveals the environmental and climatic context, as determined by the nature and variety of other fossil organisms found in the same deposit; and archaeology sets the context of cultural status by defining the levels of technical expertise (toolmaking, for instance) and social behaviour (such as cave painting, carvings, and personal adornment) that had been achieved.

The archaeological scheme of Stone Age, Bronze Age, and Iron Age to which archaeologists refer was established early in the nineteenth century by collectors and curators of antiquities in Denmark, who, lacking the succession of Celtic, Anglo-Saxon, and Roman influence that dominated so much of European history, were obliged to find other terms under which to classify and describe their numerous pre-Christian artefacts. The first person to set out clearly the notion of the three ages was the historian Vedel-Simonsen, in his *Udsigt over*

Nationalhistoriens oeldste og maerkeligste Perioder, the first volume of which was published in 1813:

> The weapons and implements of the earliest inhabitants of Scandinavia were at first of stone and wood, wrote Vedel-Simonsen. These folks later learned the use of copper...and only latterly, it would appear, iron. Therefore, from this point of view, the history of their civilisation can be divided into an age of stone, an age of copper, and an age of iron.[1]

These categories were used in 1819 by Christian Jurgensen Thomsen, first curator of Denmark's National Museum, as the arrangement under which to display the National collection of antiquities. Separate rooms were allotted for the Stone Age, the Bronze Age, and the Iron Age. This was the first step in the transformation of antiquarianism—the magpie-like collection of objects for the curiosity value alone—into the science of archaeology.

The three-age system appeared in print in 1836, was translated into English[2] and other languages, and so became the fundamental system of classification of prehistory. Stone Age, Bronze Age, Iron Age: a chronological succession of increasing sophistication and—it implied—improvement. By the 1860s, however, it was clear that the term Stone Age was too narrow a classification for all the numerous and varied stone artefacts that archaeologists were discovering, particularly in France. A division into the *période de la pierre taillée* and the *période de la pierre polie* was proposed by the French and given an air of scientific respectability by the English archaeologist, John Lubbock (also known as Lord Avebury), in 1865 with the Latin terms *Palaeolithic*—the Old Stone Age, 'when man shared the possession of Europe with the Mammoth, the Cave Bear, the Woolly-haired rhinoceros, and other extinct animals', and the *Neolithic*—the New Stone Age, 'the later or polished stone age; a period characterised by beautiful weapons and instruments of flint and other kinds of stone'.[3]

Stone Age archaeology received its greatest impetus during this time from the work of Édouard Lartet (1801-71), a magistrate who gave up law to pursue palaeontology. After investigating sites at Aurignac (see p. 60) and in the Pyrenees, Lartet moved to the Dordogne in 1863, where, financed and helped by an English banker, Henry Christy, he began excavations at a number of now-famous sites along the valley of the river Vézere: Les Eyzies, Le Moustier, La Madeleine, Gorge d'Enfer...

Among the artefacts they uncovered in the caves of the Dordogne, Lartet and Christy found carved bone and images of animals engraved on stone. These were the earliest known manifestations of art and, as such, represented the culmination of what Lartet and Christy saw as a succession of cultural phases through time. In their *Reliquiae Aquitanicae* (1866-75), Lartet set the chronological sequence of successive cultural phases during the Palaeolithic in an ecological context, according to the species of animal remains most prevalent in each. Refined in the light of subsequent discoveries, he named the phases: the Age of the Hippopotamus, the Age of Cave Bear and Mammoth, and the Age of the Reindeer.

In palaeontological terms, Lartet's three ecological phases represented the Lower, Middle, and Upper levels of Lubbock's Palaeolithic Age, and an archaeological correlation was added in 1869 by Lartet's pupil, Gabriel de Mortillet (1821-98), who proposed a system of classification which named the successive phases of human cultural endeavour according to the sites at which the various stone industries proliferated. In this scheme of things, the Age of the Hippopotamus became the Chellean epoch, named for the simple chipped-flint tools found at Chelles, near Paris; the Age of the Cave Bear and Mammoth was divided into two parts, the lower and older portion became the Mousterian, after the rock shelter at Le Moustier, where flaked-flint tools (but no worked bone) had been found, and the upper portion the Aurignacian, characterized by the worked bone and stag horn found together with flint tools at Aurignac and similar sites. The Age of the Reindeer was similarly divided into two: the Laugerian and the Magdalenian—the latter characterized by a profusion of worked bone and the development of artistic endeavour.

While these systems of Stone Age classification were discussed (and sometimes dismissed) by the authorities of the day, the evidence of human activity in the Stone Age was expanded considerably in 1868, when Édouard Lartet's son, Louis, uncovered the remains of five people in a rock shelter at Cro-Magnon, also in the Vézere valley. The bodies appeared to have been deliberately buried, with flint tools and ornaments alongside.[4] Four years later, a skeleton covered with red ochre and decorated with pierced seashells and the canine teeth of red deer was excavated from the Grimaldi caves, near Menton. Later, the skeletons of two children were found in another cave at Grimaldi, both wearing belts of perforated seashells.[5]

The human remains at Cro-Magnon and Grimaldi were the first to be recovered from sites of the Upper Palaeolithic, or Aurignacian period. Anatomically, the remains were virtually indistinguishable from modern *Homo sapiens*; their flint tool technology was well established, they also used tools of bone, their artistry was beautifully expressed, and the deliberate manner of their burial indicated, as Glyn Daniel implied in his review of these developments, that people in Upper Palaeolithic times were not merely sophisticated toolmakers and artists, but also had an awareness of death and, if not the concept of an afterlife, certainly a primitive philosophy of life.[6]

Thus archaeology suggested that Upper Palaeolithic people had lived in a manner which any modern civilized person might find acceptable—quite different from the seemingly more crude lifestyle of the Neanderthals. While the people of the Upper Palaeolithic had produced fine flint and bone tools of the Aurignacian industry and displayed a sense of artistry, the Neanderthals had employed only Mousterian stone-tool technology—no bone tools, and no sign of any artistic endeavour. Subsequent discoveries (and the re-examination of earlier finds) confirmed the distinction. Remains from Engis, Gibraltar, Neanderthal itself, Spy, Krapina, Le Moustier, La Chapelle-aux-Saints, La Quina, Ehringsdorf, La Ferrassie, all showed that although the Neanderthals had populated Europe widely, and for a considerable period of time, they remained essentially different from the people of later times, both physically and culturally. Another very obvious difference between the two groups was that the Neanderthals had become extinct, while the anatomically modern humans lived on. Why? And what had been the relationship between them—if any?

The Neanderthal Problem, as it became known, was identified over a century ago and has generated intense debate for much of the time since then. Logically, there were only three possible explanations: (1) the Neanderthals evolved into modern humans; (2) they were overrun and replaced by modern humans who moved into Europe from some other point of origination, or (3) they interbred

---

FIGURE 5.1 Modern humans represented by the Cro-Magnon remains (bottom right) co-existed with Neanderthals (left and top right). 90,000 year-old fossils from Skhul, Israel (top left), may represent the ancestral population of modern humans.

with the modern human immigrants, losing their distinctive Neanderthal characteristics in the process. All three explanations have had their advocates. Arguments and counter-arguments have been pursued at length—often with some heat—and the history of the case is a very good example of how the intensity of argument in palaeoanthropology almost always indicates a lack of evidence strong enough to settle the case one way or the other.

Following the dramatic pronouncements of Professor Schaaffhausen, the 'numerous jocosities' of Professor Mayer, and the solemn appraisal of Virchow among others, the first serious attempts to set Neanderthal in the context of human evolution were undertaken by K. Gorjanovic-Kramberger, and Gustav Schwalbe in the early 1900s. Both believed that human evolution had proceeded through distinct stages of development, with the Neanderthals representing the immediate ancestors of modern humans. Gorjanovic-Kramberger's views developed from the evidence of Neanderthal remains he had dug personally from a rock shelter near the small town of Krapina in Yugoslavia,[7] but Schwalbe's experience was less direct, his views inspired primarily by the heightened interest in human evolution which the discovery of a so-called 'missing link'—*Pithecanthropus* (meaning 'ape-man')—in 1891 had aroused (see Chapter 6).

Over a period of years, Schwalbe made a thorough study of all the then known Neanderthal remains, enumerating a series of anatomical features which he described as intermediate between those of *Pithecanthropus* and modern humans, and concluding that the Neanderthals were the penultimate stage in an evolutionary progression that led stage-by-stage from an ape-like ancestor to modern humans.[8]

Schwalbe's scheme set the entire history of human evolution in a single line of development, along which were arranged the three or four types of fossil hominids then known. This satisfyingly simple idea found support in some quarters, but the ancestral status it bestowed on Neanderthal Man was firmly contradicted by Marcellin Boule (see above, p. 84), whose studies of the remains unearthed at La Chapelle-aux-Saints in 1908 concluded that the Neanderthals were a degenerate and archaic race which had diverged from the line leading to modern humans, and then disappeared without issue. 'This species is fossil in a double sense,' he wrote, 'Because it dates from a geological period prior to the present day, and because we are aware of no descendants.'[9]

The first decades of the twentieth century were a time when France was becoming established as the cradle of palaeoanthropology. Boule was a major part of that development, and his pronouncements on the Neanderthals, occupying extensive portions of the *Annales de Paléontologie* and published as a large monograph in 1913, were weighty enough to convert many authorities to his point of view. But removing the Neanderthals from Schwalbe's single-line view of human evolution raised another problem: if the Neanderthals were not the ancestors of modern humans, who was? Boule could only acknowledge the absence of a candidate for the position when he summarized his views on human evolution at a Congress held in 1912, but, just two months later, the discovery of alleged fossil human remains near the small village of Piltdown in England (see Chapter 7) provided a large-brained, ape-jawed specimen that pre-dated the Neanderthals and thus filled the gap perfectly. 'The Piltdown race seems to us the probable ancestor in the direct line of recent species of man, *Homo sapiens*', he wrote.[10]

The consensus of opinion now turned against the single-line view of human evolution incorporating Neanderthal Man as our immediate ancestors, and embraced the idea that two races had existed in Stone Age times—one that became extinct with the Neanderthals and was probably descended from earlier forms represented by Dubois' *Pithecanthropus* and remains found at Heidelberg in 1907, and the other descended from Piltdown (and earlier forms as yet undiscovered) which had overwhelmed the Neanderthals and were the true ancestors of *Homo sapiens*. By the 1920s, this view of human evolution was firmly entrenched (even Schwalbe had been partially converted), and was at the core of every argument and discussion on the subject.

Ales Hrdlicka (1869-1943), who did as much to establish palaeoanthropology in the United States as Boule had done in France, was one of a small minority that did not accept the consensus view. Hrdlicka was of Czech and German origin and had studied anthropology in Paris under Léonce Manouvier (1850-1927), who promoted a rather more gradualist view of evolution than Boule. Manouvier preferred to see human evolution in terms of a progressive transformation to the modern form, and from this background Hrdlicka developed the idea of the Neanderthals as a distinct *phase* in the evolution of modern humans, rather than a *species* standing apart from it. 'My conviction that the Neanderthal type is merely one phase in the more or less gradual process of evolution of man to his present form, is steadily growing stronger', he wrote in 1916.[11]

In 1927 Hrdlicka was invited to give The Royal Anthropological Institute's annual Huxley Memorial Lecture and used the prestigious moment to spell out his view of human evolution in Europe. Entitling his talk 'The Neanderthal Phase of Man', he described the highly variable morphology of Neanderthal anatomy as an indication of 'instability, evidently, of evolutionary nature, leading from old forms to more modern'. Moving from the anatomy of the Neanderthals to the environment of the Mousterian period, he pointed out that the Neanderthals had lived towards the end of a warm phase in the global climate, when Ice Age glaciers were advancing south again. Increasingly severe winters would have demanded more shelter, more clothing, more food, more fire, more storage of provisions, he said. Such demands intensified natural selection; populations declined as the less able perished, and from among the highly variable, evolutionarily unstable Neanderthals, modern humans emerged. 'Here seems to be a relatively simple, natural explanation of the progressive evolution of Neanderthal Man, and such evolution would inevitably carry his most advanced forms to those of primitive *H. sapiens*,' he said.'[12]

Though Hrdlicka's Huxley lecture has often been cited as a definitive attempt to establish the Neanderthal ancestry of modern humans, it made little impact in its day—or, indeed, for many years thereafter. Two German authorities, Hans Weinert (1877–1967), and Franz Weidenreich (1873–1948, who had studied under Schwalbe) subsequently supported the single-line hypothesis of human evolution in their publications, but even they had reservations about the Neanderthal ancestry of modern humans, and the influence of Hrdlicka's Neanderthal Phase hypothesis may be judged from the fact that it was hardly deemed worthy of refutation until 1954—by which time Hrdlicka had been dead for eleven years and further discoveries had expanded the evidence relating to the argument.

Much had changed by 1954, when a prominent figure in the new generation of palaeoanthropologists, Henri Vallois (1889–1981), was invited to give the Huxley Memorial Lecture and used the occasion to argue against the Neanderthal phase in human evolution that Hrdlicka had presented at the same venue twenty-seven years before. The discovery of partial skulls at Swanscombe in England,[13] and Fontéchevade in France[14] presented new evidence of early humans in Europe. Fossil remains found by a joint British–American archaeological expedition in caves on Mount Carmel, near Haifa in what is now Israel, included some specimens with

Neanderthal affinities, and others more similar to modern humans—though all appeared to have lived before their European counterparts.[15] Discoveries in the Far East (see Chapters 6 and 9) had established *Homo erectus* as a candidate for the ancestry of *Homo sapiens* who appeared to pre-date both the Neanderthal and the anatomically modern remains from Europe. In Africa, Raymond Dart had discovered and described *Australopithecus* (see Chapter 8), and Robert Broom had found enough specimens to make the australopithecines prime candidates for a position close to the beginning of the human line, and Africa its cradle of origin (see Chapter 10).

Marcellin Boule had died in 1942, and Henri Vallois was the successor, both in spirit and status, of the position that Boule had held in French palaeoanthropology. In his 1954 Huxley Memorial Lecture Vallois brought Boule's views up to date and argued against Hrdlicka's Neanderthal phase of human evolution with the proposition that a group he termed the *Praesapiens* were the true ancestors of modern man, while the Neanderthals were 'a retarded form extinguished without issue'.[16] There was no evidence of continuity between the Neanderthals and modern humans, he claimed. The Neanderthals were a highly specialized group, he said, which even the selective pressures of severe climatic change could not have transformed into a modern human form in the relatively short period of time available. On the other hand, the *Praesapiens* were represented by fossils from Swanscombe and Fontéchevade (the latter discovered and described by Vallois himself), which pre-dated the Neanderthals and bore strong affinities with modern humans. Vallois concluded his lecture:

> One fact at all events seems now to be established: the European *Homo sapiens* is not derived from the Neanderthal men who preceded him. His stock was long distinct from, and, under the name of Praesapiens, had evolved in a parallel direction to, theirs. Long-debated, the Praesapiens forms are thus not a myth. They did exist. The few remains of them we possess are the tangible evidence of the great antiquity of the phylum that culminates in modern man.[17]

Vallois's 1954 Huxley lecture became a definitive statement of the belief that the Neanderthals were not our ancestors, just as Hrdlicka's 1927 Huxley lecture had stood as a definitive statement of the belief that they were. These two opposing and mutually exclusive hypotheses—Neanderthal Phase and Praesapiens—were the reference points for decades of discussion and argument on the Neanderthal Problem.

The Praesapiens hypothesis was challenged in 1955 and 1957 by observations that Boule had made some serious errors of interpretation in his reconstructions of the Neanderthals from La Chapelle-aux-Saints; correction of these errors (though possibly an over-correction) turned Neanderthal Man into a New York commuter. This rekindled interest in the Neanderthals as possible ancestors of modern humans. In the 1950s, Ralph Solecki of the Smithsonian Institution recovered Neanderthal remains from caves at Shanidar in northern Iraq; subsequent studies suggested that some remains dating from about 60,000 years ago had been buried with bunches of wild flowers collected from the surrounding grassland (the flowers were identified by pollen analysis). This information evoked poignant images of spiritual awareness denied the Neanderthals until then,[18] though Solecki's interpretation of their significance is open to question.[19] Meanwhile, the torch that Hrdlicka had held aloft in 1927 was taken up by a number of academics who continued to argue strongly in favour of a unilineal scheme of human evolution that included the Neanderthals.[20] And by the 1970s, the concept of a Neanderthal phase in human evolution had spilled over into popular knowledge: 'it now seems unlikely that the outcome [of further research] will ever demote the Neanderthals from the mainstream of human evolution...We stand on their burly shoulders', wrote the author of a Time-Life book, The Neanderthals.[21]

But argument persisted, becoming lengthier and more convoluted as point and counterpoint were raised and disputed. In 1976 it drew what amounted to an appeal for moderation from William Howells of Harvard University, who called attention to a question too often neglected by those participating in a protracted argument of interpretation, though it may be obvious to bystanders: is the available evidence capable of settling the argument one way or the other?

Howells published a paper[22] which stripped the arguments to their basic contentions: 'My interest here lies not in elegance of data or analysis but in the actual contribution to solving the main problem.' He defined the Neanderthal Phase hypothesis as one which derives modern humans directly from archaic

---

FIGURE 5.2 The numerous Neanderthal fossils found at La Ferrassie rock shelter in the Dordogne region included the remains of an unborn child.

Neanderthals already present in the area; and the Presapiens hypothesis (renaming it the Noah's Ark hypothesis), as one which assumes a single origin, with populations migrating outward and diverging genetically. 'The two hypotheses are irreconcilable', he stated at the outset and, having reviewed the available fossil and genetic evidence, concluded that both were faulty and neither could be proved right. Nor could either be proved wrong, he added. 'Paucity of fossils and infirmity of dates remains a central problem', Howells wrote at the conclusion of his paper, 'the base for most attempts at reconstructing recent human history is weaker than we like to recognize.'

In the 1960s and 1970s, the main thrust of palaeoanthropological research shifted to Africa, with a series of outstanding discoveries which pushed human origins back to putative ancestors who lived one, two, and more than three million years ago. Furthermore, advances in analytical techniques shifted the emphasis of the science from field to laboratory, from discovery to analysis, thereby introducing a greater degree of intellectual rigour to the process of interpretation. A new breed of palaeoanthropologists emerged during the golden years of discovery in Africa, and when their attention turned back to Europe and the origin of modern humans, in the 1980s, the standards they applied were more demanding than those of their predecessors.

Meanwhile, the evidence in Europe had been extended too. Especially by Neanderthal remains recovered from a deep rock shelter at Saint-Césaire, in the Charente-Maritime region of France in 1979, which were found in association with tools of an early Aurignacian industry (previously associated only with anatomically modern humans).[23] 'The discovery of a Neanderthal with an Upper Palaeolithic industry has considerably modified our ideas about the extinction of Neanderthals in western Europe and their replacement by anatomically modern hominids', a commentary reported.[24]

The evidence from Saint-Césaire, indicating that populations of Neanderthals and modern humans had existed in the same region during the same period, ruled out the possibility of modern humans having evolved from Neanderthals in that area;[25] leaving only the certainty that the Neanderthals were either absorbed into, or overrun by an immigrant population of modern humans. Supporters of the Neanderthal Phase hypothesis continued to argue for the evolutionary transformation of Neanderthals into modern humans in Europe, but they were lone voices. More central to discussions were the questions of where the Neanderthal and modern human populations had come from, and when? The emerging answer was: Africa.

Beginning in the 1920s, a host of fossils with predominantly modern anatomical characteristics were discovered at dozens of sites spanning Africa from north to south—Libya, Morocco, Algeria, Sudan, Ethiopia, Kenya, Tanzania, Zambia, South Africa. The specimens were numerous; some retained features of an archaic nature, others were entirely modern; they dated from over 600,000 years ago to less than 30,000. Analysing the detail and implications of this extensive evidence led Gunter Bräuer of the University of Hamburg to formulate what he called the Afro-European *sapiens* hypothesis.

'There are no longer any real reasons to assume the existence of two parallel lines in Europe, one leading to the Neanderthals, and one via Fontéchevade, to Cro-Magnon Man', wrote Bräuer.[26] Anatomically modern humans evolved in eastern and southern Africa during the late middle and/or early Upper Pleistocene, he concluded, from hominid stock which had probably given rise to a number of diverging early human populations (one of whom migrated from Africa around 700,000 years ago to found the populations from which Neanderthals of Europe and western Asia evolved). According to Bräuer's hypothesis, the ancestors of modern humans spread from their cradle of origin in east and southern Africa to range across the continent from north to south by about 50 thousand years ago and then moved into the Near East and Europe, replacing the indigenous Neanderthals over a period of several thousand years.

While the fossil evidence of our African origin was accumulating in museums and university departments, awaiting a synthesis such as Bräuer eventually supplied, evidence of a more immediate and intimate nature existed in the cells of every living human being: the DNA molecules that carry the code of life itself.

Evolution leaves a record of its progression in the genetic structure of every living organism. The modifications that create new species arise in the DNA sequence which directs the assembly of every individual. With each generation a reshuffling of the DNA sequence occurs, and as evolution carries diverging species away from their common ancestor, the degree of difference separating them can be measured in their DNA, thus giving an indication of the number of generations that have passed. The basis of this knowledge was established in 1901 by George Nuttall, a professor of biology at Cambridge University whose analysis of blood proteins from a wide variety of different species demonstrated the close affinity of man and the African apes.[27] Proteins differ because the DNA ordering their assembly differs, and thus Nuttall's work touched on a fundamental fact of life, even though DNA and its function were unknown at the time, and would remain so for another forty years.

A timescale was applied to the evolutionary divergence of apes and humans in the 1960s by Vincent Sarich and Allan Wilson, anthropologist and molecular biologist respectively, at the University of California, Berkeley. Noting that the degree of difference found in the proteins of different species must be directly related to the period of time that has passed since the species split from a common stock, Sarich and Wilson were able to interpret the differences as a measure of time, and thus established what has become known as the molecular clock.[28]

The molecular clock set the time at which the human and ape lines diverged from a common ancestor at 5 million years ago, which in the 1960s contradicted current interpretations of the fossil evidence and was largely dismissed. Such a timescale could not accommodate *Ramapithecus* or *Kenyapithecus*, specimens found in deposits of the Miocene period (7 to 27 million years ago) in Pakistan and Kenya and proposed as the link between early hominids and the common ancestor, which was believed to have existed about 30 million years ago.[29]

Developments during the 1970s and 1980s resolved the contradiction between the molecular clock and palaeoanthropology, however. First, fossils discovered in Turkey and Pakistan dismissed *Ramapithecus* from the hominid line;[30] and an extensive collection of new fossils from East Africa firmly established the presence of distinctly ape-like and potentially ancestral hominid species in Africa between three and four million years ago. Second, as this new fossil evidence brought palaeoanthropology in line with the broad outline of human evolution as delineated by the molecular clock, research led by Allan Wilson at the University of California at Berkeley on DNA in living cells was revealing the detail of its final stages. Thus, where proteins had enabled geneticists to establish the evolutionary distance *between* species, Wilson's team could measure the evolutionary distance *within* species and *between* populations. This in turn would throw light on the recent origin and dispersal of modern humans—the question at the root of the Neanderthal Problem which the fossil evidence had been unable to resolve.

Wilson's research exploited the unique qualities of mitochondria—the components of every cell which play a vital role in the energy production systems of living organisms. In effect, mitochondria are the 'powerhouses' of the cell, and such a basic function has endowed them with a very stable basic structure: throughout the animal kingdom, the DNA which orders their function (mito-chondrial DNA, abbreviated to mtDNA) is remarkably uniform: the same 37 genes specify the same sets of molecules in all multicellular animals, Wilson had found, and the genes themselves are arranged along the mtDNA strand in a very consistent manner. Furthermore, mtDNA molecules are identical in every cell of an individual (they reproduce clonally, by division) and are inherited only from the female parent because the mitochondria in sperm cells disintegrate at fertilization.[31]

Clonal reproduction and female inheritance leave mtDNA unaffected by the recombination of genes which occurs in the reproduction of nuclear DNA, which means their mutations pass intact from generation to generation. 'Each mtDNA molecule carries in its sequence the history of its lineage, not complicated by recombination',[32] which makes mtDNA a wonderful tool for determining the evolutionary distance between closely related species and populations.

Studies of the mtDNA of people in Papua New Guinea, who are known (from archaeological evidence) to have been isolated since the previously unpopu-lated island was first colonized between 40,000 and 50,000 years ago, enabled researchers to measure the rate at which mtDNA mutations accumulated in the population.[33] From these data, they calculated that the average rate of evolution-ary divergence in human populations is about 3 per cent per million years.

Subsequent analysis of mutations in the mtDNA of 147 people from different populations around the world revealed a very low degree of variation among them (only a fraction of that found in the great apes and other vertebrates), which can only mean that these populations diverged recently (in evolutionary terms).[34] The greatest degree of mtDNA variation was found among indigenous people in Africa, which implies that modern humans have existed there longest. Significantly less mtDNA variation is found among non-African populations around the world, which means that they are all the descendants of a relatively small group of people who left Africa relatively recently, and spread rapidly around the world. (In fact, the mtDNA of an individual born in England and another born in New Guinea was more alike than the mtDNA of two individuals born in Nigeria.)

Setting these data against the timescale of divergence, the geneticists put the origin of all modern humans at between 140 and 290 thousand years ago, in

Africa. Furthermore, the scientists concluded that every human being alive today carries the mtDNA of just one African mother who lived more than 10,000 generations ago. 'Our common mother', the geneticists have dubbed this ancestor, though she soon became more popularly known as 'the African Eve'.[35] This does not mean that she was the only woman alive at that time (along with Adam, as Creationists might like to believe). On the contrary, she was one of thousands, but her mtDNA became dominant. How could this happen? Allan Wilson explains:

> Imagine a human population containing 10,000 mothers, with each mother contributing an average of two children to the next generation. The size of the population remains stable through time. In each succeeding generation, however, some maternal lineages disappear, simply because not every mother produces a daughter. The mathematics of random walks indicate that after about 10,000 generations, all but one of the founding maternal lineages will have become extinct. Hence, all the descendants will bear mtDNA derived from only one of the 10,000 mothers who founded the population.[36]

The genetic research supported the 'Afro-European sapiens hypothesis' that Bräuer had formulated on the basis of the fossil evidence. The results were disputed by statisticians, who found inaccuracies in the computing procedures by which the single African origin of human populations had been derived. However, while these objections drew attention to inadequacies of statistical method they did not invalidate the evidence. The greater genetic diversity of African lineages remained unchallenged.[37] Indeed, it was reinforced in 1991 by the results of another worldwide study conducted by geneticists from Stanford and Yale universities, led by Luigi Cavalli-Sforza.[38]

Cavalli-Sforza and his team analysed an entirely different set of DNA data, but also concluded that the 'result is exactly what one would expect if the African separation was the first and oldest in the human family tree'. Furthermore, they found that the distribution of genes among human populations correlated surprisingly well with that of languages. A genetic tree showing the evolutionary

FIGURE 5.3 Fossil remains of anatomically modern humans recovered from the Klaasie's River Mouth cave site date from up to 125,000 years ago.

origins of forty-two populations from around the world closely matched their linguistic affiliations: the most recent language differences, such as had arisen among Pacific islanders, for instance, replicated the extent of their genetic differences. And in both the genetic and linguistic evidence, the largest and therefore the oldest differences occurred between the African group and the rest of the world population.

Thus, language correlated with genetic evidence for the African origins of modern man which in turn accorded with fossil evidence indicating that modern humans had arrived in Europe before the most recent known Neanderthal. And the picture became clearer still in the 1990s when geneticists at the Max Planck Institute for Evolutionary Anthropology in Leipzig succeeded in extracting DNA from a piece of bone taken from the original Neanderthal specimen that the limestone quarry workers had discovered in 1856. This was 'a fantastic achievement— the equivalent of landing a spacecraft on Mars', said Professor Chris Stringer of the Natural History Museum in London, 'and just as important'. Now it would be possible to compare Neanderthals and modern humans at the very core of their identity—their DNA, and this would reveal, perhaps once and for all, whether or not the Neanderthals were our ancestors; or related to us in any way.

The man leading this ground-breaking research was Svante Pääbo, who at the age of 26 had achieved the singular distinction of having *Nature* make a cover story[39] of research he had done in his 'hobby time' (as he describes it), while busy on a Ph.D. in molecular immunology at the University of Uppsala. Prompted by a longstanding interest in ancient Egypt, and aided by cooperative Egyptology professors, Pääbo had obtained specimens from twenty-three mummies and succeeded in extracting and analysing a short segment of DNA from the 2,400-year-old remains of an infant boy. Nothing like this had been done before, and although Pääbo thought its most likely consequence would be in population studies, revealing, for instance, whether the conquests of Alexander the Great and the Assyrians had introduced new genes to Egypt, the *Nature* cover story attracted much wider attention. Allan Wilson, the molecular biologist who had pioneered the application of mtDNA analysis to evolutionary studies, wrote to ask if he could spend a sabbatical in Professor Pääbo's lab. Pääbo replied to the effect that he was not a professor, did not have a lab, nor even a Ph.D., but would welcome an invitation to work with Wilson's team at Berkeley. He was invited by return.

At Berkeley Pääbo continued working on mummies for a while, then switched to animals such as the extinct moa from New Zealand, the marsupial wolf from Australia, ground sloths…all the time refining the technology, overcoming the problems of contamination, reducing margins of error. In 1990 he moved to the University of Munich, where he resumed his work on ancient human DNA, and was part of the team that sequenced DNA from the 'Ice Man' who was frozen in an alpine glacier for more than 5,000 years before being discovered in 1991. Meanwhile, technical advances, hands-on experience, and theoretical considerations had led Pääbo to the conclusion that it might be possible to retrieve DNA from fossils less than 100,000 years old—from a Neanderthal fossil, for instance.

But obtaining a suitable piece of Neanderthal fossil in which to look for DNA was no simple matter. The search would necessitate grinding up irreplaceable fossil material and dissolving it in chemicals; something no curator could be expected to permit—least of all those at the Rhineland Museum in Bonn, where the original Neanderthal Man (and Pääbo's first choice) had resided for nearly 150 years. But Pääbo persisted and the curators finally agreed. A piece of fossil weighing 3.5 grams was taken from the upper right arm of the type specimen and subjected to the meticulous process of extraction and amplification. To everyone's delight (and considerable relief), the bold experiment proved to have been justified: a short sequence of mtDNA, 328 nucleotides long, was retrieved for comparison with an average modern human sample.

The results showed that whereas individuals in a modern human population differ at an average of only eight positions on the mtDNA sequence, the Neanderthal sample differed at twenty-seven positions. This nearly fourfold difference is so wide that it proves modern humans are not the descendants of Neanderthals. 'I don't know of any reasonable interpretation of these data, other than that Neanderthals were not ancestral to modern humans. They had nothing to do with our history. We are all Africans in disguise', Pääbo told a press conference in London.[40]

The first pioneering study was followed by a programme of research directed by Svante Pääbo at the Max Planck Institute for Evolutionary Anthropology in Leipzig, culminating with publication of the entire Neanderthal genome.[41] This outstanding achievement (which cost 6.4 million US dollars and took three years to complete) showed that although modern humans are not directly descended from the Neanderthals, there is a little of them in nearly all of us.

In this first-ever comparison of the entire Neanderthal and human genomes, the researchers found that we share between 1 per cent and 4 per cent of our DNA with the Neanderthals, inherited from a common ancestor who lived up to 440,000 years ago. But the affiliation is not universal, being absent from present-day Africans while occurring widely among populations in Europe and Asia. This means that the two groups must have interbred after modern humans began leaving Africa (80,000 to 100,000 years ago), as they migrated into regions occupied by the Neanderthals. How this came about is a matter of conjecture—and could have been an extremely rare event: just two Neanderthal females in a group of about 100 humans would have been enough to leave such a trace in our genome.[42]

'How these peoples interacted culturally is not something we can speculate on in any meaningful way,' Richard E. Green, senior author of the study remarked.[43] 'We found the genetic signal of Neanderthals in all the non-African genomes, meaning that the admixture occurred early on, probably in the Middle East, and is shared with all descendants of the early humans who migrated out of Africa.'

And there were more surprises to come from the genetics department of the Max Planck Institute in Leipzig. In the summer of 2008, Russian researchers excavating in the isolated Denisova Cave, in southern Siberia, had found a fragment of human finger bone. The team stored it away, assuming that the unprepossessing specimen came from one of the Neanderthals who had also left a profusion of tools in the cave some 30,000 to 40,000 years ago. Nothing about the bone seemed exceptional but its genetic material told another story.

The Russian group had asked Svante Pääbo for assistance in determining whether or not the finger bone had belonged to a Neanderthal, as they assumed (they had helped the geneticist when he needed material from ice-age humans). The bone went to Leipzig, but when its DNA was extracted and sequenced Pääbo's team found that it did not match that of the Neanderthals—or, indeed, that of modern humans, who were also living near by at the time. The differences were significant and pointed to a most unexpected conclusion: the bone had belonged to a previously unrecognized extinct human species that migrated out of Africa long before our known relatives.

'This really surpassed our hopes,' Pääbo said in a preliminary announcement of the findings that was published in *Nature*. 'I almost could not believe it. It sounded too fantastic to be true.'[44]

Some colleagues were inclined to agree—applauding the work but cautioning against drawing radical conclusions from a single study. But further analysis of the sequencing did nothing to invalidate the initial interpretations. A tooth found in the cave in 2000 was added to the study, and the Denisova genome (now including mtDNA sequencing as well) was compared with all available Neanderthal genomes, and that of 938 present-day humans from 53 populations around the world—Europe, Africa, Asia, Melanesia.

The results published in 2010[45] showed that the Denisova DNA fell into a class of its own. Not only did it lack the traces indicating that there is a little of the Neanderthals in most of us, it was significantly different from that of present-day humans too. Setting the genetic differences on a timescale of divergence, the results implied that the Denisova ancestor branched off from the human family tree 804,000 years ago and split from the Neanderthals 640,000 years ago. If so, the Denisovans (as the Leipzig team chose to call them) must have left Africa in a previously unknown migration, between that of *Home erectus* 1.9 million years ago and that of the Neanderthal ancestor, 300,000 to 500,000 years ago.

No less surprising, the team found that the Denisovans shared a distinct fraction of genetic material with modern populations in Papua New Guinea, indicating that at some time in the distant past the ancestors of the Denisovans and the Melanesians had interbred. 'The story now gets a bit more complicated,' said co-author Richard E. Green. 'Instead of the clean story we used to have of modern humans migrating out of Africa and replacing Neanderthals, we now see these very intertwined story lines with more players and more interactions than we knew before.'[46]

After the discovery in 2004 of *Homo floresiensis*, the Hobbit from the island of Flores in Indonesia (more detail in the next chapter), the arrival of the Denisovans means that in the comparatively recent past there were at least four different human beings in existence, probably simultaneously: Neanderthals, Denisovans, Hobbits, and, of course, ourselves, *Homo sapiens*. The notion that human evolution had progressed in a simple single line from ancestral ape to humans is comprehensively dismissed.

Then, just as genetics research in Leipzig added complexity to the story of human evolution *out of* Africa, the discovery of an impressive suite of fossil hominid skulls in Ethiopia promised to clarify the story of modern human origins *in* Africa.[47] The fossils were found in deposits that were from 150,000 to 200,000 years old; their affinities were unambiguous, and the proposal that they represented the link between an 'African Eve' and the human population that shared Europe with the Neanderthals was therefore perfectly reasonable—all of which simplified the Neanderthal problem, and directed attention towards another pressing question: who was the common ancestor from which Neanderthals and modern humans evolved? Could it have been *Homo erectus*, the archetypal Missing Link?

FIGURE 5.4 The anatomy and antiquity of 160,000 year-old fossil skulls from Herto, in the Afar region of Ethiopia, constitute powerful evidence for the African origin of modern humans.

12 June 2003

nature

International weekly journal of science

£4.95

www.nature.com/nature

African origins

Ethiopian fossils are the earliest *Homo sapiens*

Solar System evolution
All mixed up

Functional proteomics
Into the unknown

X-ray astronomy
Lonesome neutron stars

naturejobs epidemiologists in demand

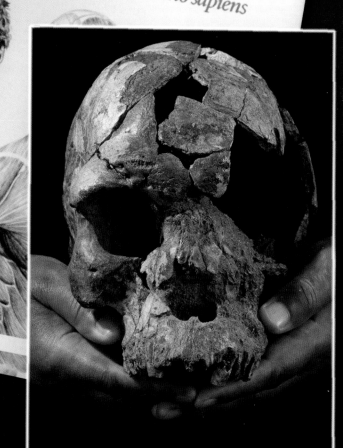

Skul
sapi

Tim Radford Sc

The fossil skull
and a child wh
160,000 years
region of Ethi
est represent
sapiens, scier
today.

The finds s
that moder
in Africa
years ago
coexisted
other hun

An Ame
reports in
unearthe
lake on t
the first
prehum
300,00
vious r
remain

"Th

CHAPTER SIX

Java Man
(1891)

I N 1865, six years after Darwin published *The Origin of Species*, and six years before *The Descent of Man* appeared, a German zoologist, Ernst Haeckel, published his *Generelle Morphologie*, in which he presented evolution as established fact and ventured to speculate upon the yet deeper mysteries of life and natural order to which Darwin's theory might be applied. Haeckel subsequently expanded and developed his ideas in *The History of Creation*, an extremely popular book which caused Darwin to write:

> if *History of Creation* had appeared before my essay [*The Descent of Man*] had been
> written, I should probably never have completed it. Almost all the conclusions
> at which I have arrived I find confirmed by the naturalist, whose knowledge on
> many points is much fuller than mine.[1]

Ernst Haeckel (1834–1919) was a perceptive and innovative scientist who created several of the words and images now central to the natural sciences ('ecology' is one worthy of mention). He was the first to depict the evolution of life in the form of the now commonplace ancestral tree, though his was more complex than most, showing how animal life had evolved from 'living creatures of the simplest kind imaginable, organisms without organs',[2] through twenty-one stages of development to modern man—the twenty-second and final stage. Within this general scheme of things, Haeckel created the concept of the *phylum*, that is the 'stem', to accommodate all organisms descended from a common form, and the word *phylogeny* to describe their evolutionary development from common form to distinct species. Within each species, Haeckel suggested that *ontogeny* should describe the development of the individual from conception to maturity and, recognizing the parallels that exist between the evolution of a species and the development of an individual, proposed his 'fundamental biogenetic law'—ontogeny recapitulates phylogeny.[3]

In principle, Haeckel's law synthesized the observation that an organism seemed to pass through all the stages of its species' evolution as it grew from egg to mature individual. During nine months in the womb the human embryo could be said to recapitulate man's entire evolutionary history, and as it grew the important stages of development could be recognized. To begin with, the foetus had only the internal organs of the simplest creatures. Later the gill-arches of the fish appeared (and subsequently disappeared), followed by the backbone of the vertebrates and finally the placenta of the mammals. An important corollary of Haeckel's observation was that, at certain stages, the embryos of quite different creatures should reveal the identical form of their common ancestor. And indeed, in *The History of Creation* Haeckel presented illustrations which showed that at four weeks, for example, there was little to differentiate the embryos of man, dog, and tortoise.[4]

Thus Haeckel found the theory of evolution proved to his satisfaction in the science of embryology. There were several awkward anomalies, it is true—some organs appeared in the embryo out of the evolutionary sequence, for instance, and some vestigial features were retained while other, once important features scarcely showed at all. But Haeckel created a new term for each anomaly—*caenogenesis, dysteleology, heterochronism*—and regarded them as mysterious puzzles rather than negative evidence. A similarly creative attitude characterized much of Haeckel's work. Where no scientific evidence was available he used his own persuasive logic to fill the gap. The 'Chain of the Animal Ancestors of Man' he devised is a case in point, particularly relevant here because its twenty-first link inspired the discovery of some important fossil human remains.

Haeckel's chain began with 'structureless and formless little lumps of mucous or albuminous matter' or protoplasm, and proceeded via the sack worms (eighth stage), the mud fish (twelfth stage), the tailed amphibians (fourteenth stage), to the tailed ape (nineteenth stage). The twentieth stage in the chain comprised the man-like apes (Anthropoides)—the orang-utan, the gibbon, chimpanzee, and gorilla. But were the man-like apes the ancestors of modern humans? 'There do not exist direct human ancestors among the Anthropoides of the present day,' reasoned Haeckel, 'but they certainly existed among the unknown extinct Human Apes of the Miocene period.' And how did he know? 'The certain proof of their former existence is furnished by the comparative anatomy of Manlike Apes and Man,' he wrote.[5]

In fact, Haeckel considered the apes to be so much like humans that his chain hardly required an intermediate stage connecting the two. But there was one behavioural characteristic that merited distinction in Haeckel's opinion—articulate speech. This important human attribute was not shared by the apes, and could not have been acquired in just one stage of the Chain, he reasoned, so there must have been some sort of speechless primeval stage between the apes and people. He proposed *Pithecanthropus* (Ape-man) as this intermediate link and twenty-first stage of his Chain of the Animal Ancestors of Man. 'The certain proof that such Primeval Man without the power of speech, or Ape-like Man, must have preceded men possessing speech is the result arrived at by an inquiring mind':

> We as yet know of no fossil remains of the hypothetical primeval man who developed out of the anthropoid apes, but considering the extraordinary resemblance between the lowest woolly-haired men, and the highest man-like apes, which still exists at the present day it requires but a slight stretch of the imagination to conceive an intermediate form connecting the two, and to see in it an approximate likeness to the supposed primeval men, or ape-like men. The form of their skull was probably very long, with slanting teeth...their arms comparatively longer and stronger...their legs, on the other hand, knock-kneed, shorter and thinner, with entirely undeveloped calves; their walk but half erect.[6]

FIGURE 6.1 Ancestral tree devised by Ernst Haeckel, from his *History of Creation*, 1876.

PEDIGREE OF MAN.

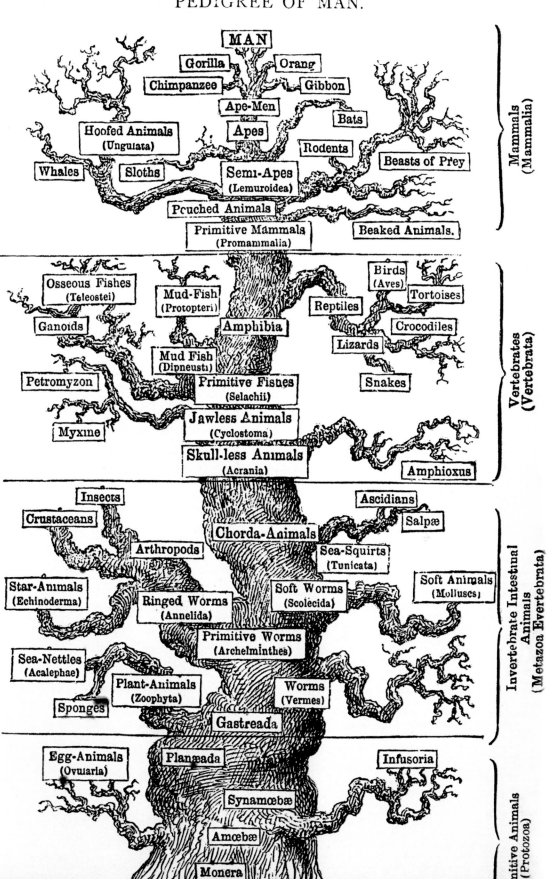

And where might this chain of man's ancestry have been wrought? Haeckel said a continent now sunk below the Indian Ocean was the most likely place. Such a landmass had been postulated by other scientists on the basis of plant and animal distributions; it was called Lemuria, after the ancestral primates (the lemurs) that would have characterized the fauna of the ancient continent. In Haeckel's scheme, Lemuria embraced what is now Madagascar (where lemurs are found today) and India, and extended from Africa across the Indian Ocean to Indonesia and the Philippines. From this 'so-called Paradise, the cradle of the human race',[7] the ancestor Haeckel called *Pithecanthropus alalus* (speechless ape-man) would have spread and populated the world. Westward to Africa, north-westward to the Middle East and Europe, northward to Asia and over the landbridge to the Americas, eastward via Java to Australasia and Polynesia.

Of course, the best proof of Haeckel's contentions would be a series of fossils representing each of the links in his chain, but Haeckel was fully aware that fossil collecting was an imprecise affair—it is 'ridiculous to expect palaeontology to furnish an unbroken series of positive data', he once wrote.[8] And besides, for Haeckel, logic and reason supplied ample proof of evolutionary theory. In his view the descent of man from an extinct series of primates was not a vague hypothesis to be proved, but an historical fact, and therefore as incapable of exact scientific proof as the fact that Aristotle, Caesar, and King Alfred once lived.[9]

The History of Creation was translated into a dozen languages and remained in print for many years. Haeckel's ideas were well known among students of the immediate post-Darwinian era, and among those whom they inspired was Eugene Dubois (1858–1940), the eldest son of a devout Dutch Catholic family who collected fossils as a boy and entered medical school in 1877 at the age of 19.

The impressionable, formative years of Dubois's generation of medical students coincided with the period during which evolutionary thinking suffused the biological sciences with new vigour. Scientists were exploring the new horizons revealed by Darwin's work, formulating new hypotheses to answer old questions—and thus creating new beliefs. It was a period of consolidation, but while medical school introduced Dubois to the persuasive excitement of a revolutionary discipline, at home he was subject to the intractability of the old faith. And from these irreconcilable influences of his youth, Dubois emerged as an unwavering, even stubborn, believer in evolution.

Dubois completed his medical studies in 1884 and seemed poised for a successful academic career. He taught anatomy at the University of Amsterdam, and might have succeeded Max Furbringer as Professor of the Department had he not angered the professor in 1886 by publishing, under his own name, a paper on the larynx of the platypus which Furbringer felt should have carried *his* name. This may have been only a contributory factor, but in any event, the matter of his status became the subject of increasingly heated conversations with senior colleagues thereafter, and Dubois finally decided that he would much rather look for fossil evidence of the human ancestor than become a professor of anatomy. In 1887 he resigned his lectureship, leaving behind only the rumour that he had promised to return with the 'Missing Link'.

As an anatomist acquainted with both geology and palaeontology, Dubois was well equipped for the search. And, indeed, the circumstances of the day were especially auspicious: Darwin's theory was established; Huxley and Haeckel had shown that human ancestry lay among the extinct apes; Haeckel had proposed *Pithecanthropus* as a likely link, and the East Indies as an early stage in their dispersal from Lemuria, 'the cradle of mankind'. Furthermore, Emil Selenka had recently described certain features of the human embryo as closer to those of the orang-utan and gibbon than to those of the African apes. This suggested an evolutionary connection between humans and the orang or the gibbon. Orangs and gibbons lived only in the East Indies, and the East Indies were a Dutch colony. Where better could a Dutchman search for fossil evidence of early human evolution? Getting there, however, was another matter. Attempts to raise finance for a private expedition failed completely so, as a last resort, Eugene Dubois signed on for eight years in the Medical Corps of the Dutch East Indian Army. With wife and infant daughter, he sailed for Sumatra in the autumn of 1887.

Such a long spell of military service might seem a desperate choice for a medical man in search of human ancestors, but if Dubois had not arranged a degree of official connivance with his real ambition before leaving Holland, he certainly managed to do so within a few months of arriving in the East Indies. First his immediate colleagues, then his commanding officer, then some senior administrators were all persuaded to lighten his duties and allow him to explore the fossil-bearing deposits as often as possible. Later, Dubois honoured two of the gentlemen concerned by naming a fossil antelope and a fossil tiger after them.

Finally, Dubois won the support of the Dutch East Indian Government itself. During 1889 he persuaded the relevant officials that a comprehensive palaeontological survey should be conducted under his full-time supervision. Second Lieutenant Eugene Dubois was placed on active reserve, inactive duty, with instructions to pursue scientific investigations as he saw fit. In March 1890 he moved to Java, where convict labour awaited his deployment under the direction of sergeants Kriele and de Winter.

Dubois made his base at Tulungagung, in the south of eastern Java. Immediately to the north stood Mount Willis, one of the many volcanoes that form the spine of the Malay Archipelago (another is Krakatoa, which had killed 36,417 people seven years before). The region was well endowed with promising limestone caves and volcanic sedimentary deposits. Dubois had a predilection for the former, not only because of boyhood discoveries in such places, but also because all the hominid remains known in Europe had been found in caves and rock shelters. So his Java search began near Wadjak where, in fact, some fossil human skull bones had been found the previous year by a Dutchman looking for workable marble deposits. By May 1890 Dubois's team had recovered a skull, some teeth, and other fragments from the same site but, like the earlier find, they all proved to be of recent origin. Soon thereafter Dubois abandoned the caves and turned to the sediments.

Dubois's proposal to the Government had called for a systematic, widespread survey and indeed he did travel extensively on his preliminary explorations; but before long his attention was almost exclusively devoted to the Kendeng deposits at the foot of Mount Lawu, an occasionally active volcano standing about thirty-two kilometres west of Mount Willis. In trial excavations throughout the Kendeng deposits his workmen found many vertebrate fossils, some in quite large accumulations, which led Dubois to believe that the animals had been killed simultaneously by volcanic action, and their bodies and bones swept together by flood waters down ancient rivers, to be deposited in calm pools and on sharp bends. The quantity and variety of the fossil fauna were impressive. It included fish and reptiles, elephants, rhinoceros, hippopotamus and tapir, deer, cats, and a giant pangolin. In all more than 12,000 fossils were collected, filling more than 400 cases when they were shipped back to Holland and holding a wealth of information on the fauna and environment of prehistoric Java. But Dubois's consuming interest was fossils that would shed light on human ancestry, and these remains were very few.

The first appeared in November 1890. It was a fragment of a primate's chin unearthed at Kedung Brubus. The first right pre-molar was still in place, and the socket of the canine tooth next to it could be seen. Dubois mentioned the specimen in his regular quarterly report.[10] It was human-like, he said, but 'of another and probably lower type than those existing and the extinct diluvial species'. His judgement was based on the manner by which the digastric muscle appeared to have been attached to the bone; Dubois felt the attachment was incompatible with the functioning of the tongue for normal articulate speech—echoing Haeckel's prediction.

The Kendeng deposits were transected by the Solo river. On a bend in the river near a village called Trinil, a sequence of sandstone and volcanic deposits fifteen metres thick attracted Dubois's attention. He decided to concentrate his efforts there for a while, and began excavations in August 1891, less than three months before the seasonal rains would flood the Solo.

Once Dubois had outlined how excavations should proceed, he left day-to-day management to Kriele and de Winter while he continued to reconnoitre, or returned to Tulungagung. Every few weeks the sergeants packed the newly-found fossils in teak leaves and sent them to Dubois, together with progress reports which often were little more than complaints about the weather and the workmen. The fossils accumulated on Dubois's veranda as he endeavoured to discover their affinities with fossils from other parts of the world. Ultimately he concluded that the Kendeng fauna corresponded in age with some from the Siwalik deposits in India. While not exactly confirming the existence of Lemuria, this certainly affirmed the existence of a landbridge between India and Java across which animals could have mingled.

The Trinil excavation was roughly circular, about twelve metres in diameter. Up to fifty convicts laboured in the pit, each of them assigned a specific portion of the deposit to remove each day. Fossils characteristic of the Kendeng fauna were frequently encountered as the excavation floor progressed below the high-water mark. Within a month the workers had reached the low-water mark, fifteen metres below the surface, and here they struck a lapilli formation—a bed of compacted tuff containing numerous fragments of volcanic rock. The lapilli bed was a metre or so thick; under it was a layer of conglomerate and beneath that a bedrock of marine origin extending beneath the river itself. Fossils were most numerous in the lapilli bed, and removing them from the hard material was arduous, especially as the approaching monsoon heightened humidity. The rains finally brought excavations to a halt sometime around the end of October.

During the course of these excavations, two very important fossils were discovered. It is generally assumed that Dubois personally witnessed the discoveries, but there is no evidence of this. Indeed, the absence of any such assertion from his reports on the discoveries, and the lack of dates and precise detail, make it more likely that he first encountered the fossils on his veranda at Tulungagung. This point subsequently became very important when the position of one fossil in relation to another became crucial to its interpretation. Then Dubois found himself most embarrassed: if he had been present at the time of discovery, he was guilty of not recording the details carefully enough; if he had not been present, then he had to admit that the sergeants' reports were open to question.

The fossils were a tooth, found in September, and a skullcap found in October. It was immediately clear that both specimens had belonged to a primate, but which genus and species of primate was far from clear, and Eugene Dubois was the first to demonstrate the uncertainty of their affinities. He did so not by indecision, nor by emphasizing the ambiguous and inconclusive nature of the evidence they offered—on the contrary, Dubois consistently expressed the most confident opinions on his discoveries; but they changed with his needs. In the beginning Dubois decided that the tooth and skullcap had both belonged to a chimpanzee. In the *Mining Bulletin* for the fourth quarter of 1891 he wrote, 'The Pleistocene fauna of Java which in September of this year was augmented by a molar of a chimpanzee, was much further enriched a month later. Close to the site on the left bank where the molar had been found, a beautiful skullcap was excavated which without any doubt, like the molar belongs to the genus *Anthropopithecus* (troglodytes)'.[11] (*Anthropopithecus* was the scientific name of the chimpanzee then in use and means 'man-like ape'.) However, a fossil found the following year caused him to revise this assessment.

Weather and water level did not permit the resumption of excavations at Trinil until May 1892. Then the convicts began digging a trench twenty-four metres long and eight metres wide upstream from the 1891 excavations. In August a fossil thighbone was discovered, human-like in every respect. The fossil was found in the same lapilli bed that had held the 'chimpanzee' tooth and skullcap, but some distance away. No accurate record was made at the time, though on different occasions Dubois later claimed that the femur had been found ten, twelve, and fifteen metres away from the skull. In any event, Dubois was convinced that thighbone, skullcap, and tooth had all belonged to the same individual. But was it a chimpanzee? The thighbone suggested not, because it quite obviously had belonged to a creature with an habitual upright stance. Dubois resolved the problem by blending his evidence into a new species of upright chimpanzee, which he called *Anthropopithecus erectus* ('upright man-like ape') . The new species was announced in the *Mining Bulletin* for the third quarter of 1892, where Dubois claimed 'through each of the three recovered skeletal parts, and especially by the thighbone, the *Anthropopithecus erectus* (Eugene Dubois) approaches closer to man than any other anthropoid'.[12]

In October 1892 another tooth was picked up two or three metres from the spot where the skullcap had been found. No more primate remains were discovered that year, nor during 1893 when the excavations were doubled, nor during subsequent years when more than ten thousand cubic metres of sediments were removed from around the site of the original discoveries. With the exception of a few thighbone fragments found among the four hundred cases of vertebrate fossils when they were examined during 1932, Dubois's collection was complete at the end of the 1892 season: a scrap of jawbone, two teeth, one skullcap, and one thighbone.

While preparing a monograph[13] on the fossils, Dubois revised their attribution once again. In this he was entirely justified, for *Anthropopithecus erectus* would have been very difficult to support with the inconclusive evidence he held. In fact, the evidence was too scanty, and the current state of knowledge too slight, for any specific attribution at all. But not for the first (or last) time in the search for human origins, an absence of evidence encouraged speculation; leaving Dubois free to reach the conclusion which became a point of faith (and argument) dominating the rest of his life. He decided the bones had belonged to an ape-like human. In other words, he reversed the earlier attribution and *Anthropopithecus* (man-like ape) became *Pithecanthropus*, (ape-like man), though he retained the species name. *Pithecanthropus erectus*—upright ape-man. The generic name, *Pithecanthropus*, acknowledges the hypothetical form Haeckel had created for the twenty-first stage on the Chain of the Animal Ancestors of Man.

On the basis of the chin fragment which Dubois had earlier described as having belonged to a 'speechless lower type of man', we may ask why Dubois did not call the Trinil fossils *Pithecanthropus alalus*—the speechless ape-man that Haeckel had proposed. But, of course, the chin fragment afforded only weak evidence of an inability to speak, while the thighbone presented strong evidence of an erect posture, and Dubois needed to emphasize the stronger elements of his evidence rather than draw attention to the less substantial. Later he wrote:

> this was the man-like animal which clearly forms such a link between man and his nearest known mammalian relatives as the theory of development supposes…the transition form which in accordance with the teachings of evolution must have existed between man and the anthropoids.[14]

Dubois believed he had discovered the Missing Link, and telegraphed the news to Holland. He followed in August 1895, eight years of military service completed. *Pithecanthropus erectus* was presented at the Third International Congress of Zoology held in Leiden that same year, at a meeting presided over by Rudolf Virchow. The fossils were greeted with unanimous recognition of their great importance but Dubois's interpretation was questioned. Virchow did not believe the fossils had belonged to one individual; others felt they were more ape than human, while another group said they were more human than ape. Only a minority shared Dubois's view that the creature represented an intermediate stage. Among them was Ernst Haeckel, certain that the fossils confirmed his prediction of a Missing Link, but astute enough to remark: 'Unfortunately, the fossil remains of the creature are very scanty: the skullcap, a femur, and two teeth. It is obviously impossible to form from these scanty remains a complete and satisfactory reconstruction of this remarkable Pliocene Primate.'[15]

The reaction at Leiden was repeated at meetings in Liége, Brussels, Paris, London, Dublin, Edinburgh, Berlin, Jena. Everywhere, Dubois's discoveries were applauded and his interpretations doubted. Dubois became increasingly impatient and angry with his critics; as the British anatomist Arthur Keith wrote, 'he

FIGURE 6.2 The original calotte (skullcap) of *Pithecanthropus erectus* rests on Dubois's own photographs of the specimen, beside photographs of Dubois as a young man, in middle age and shortly before he died.

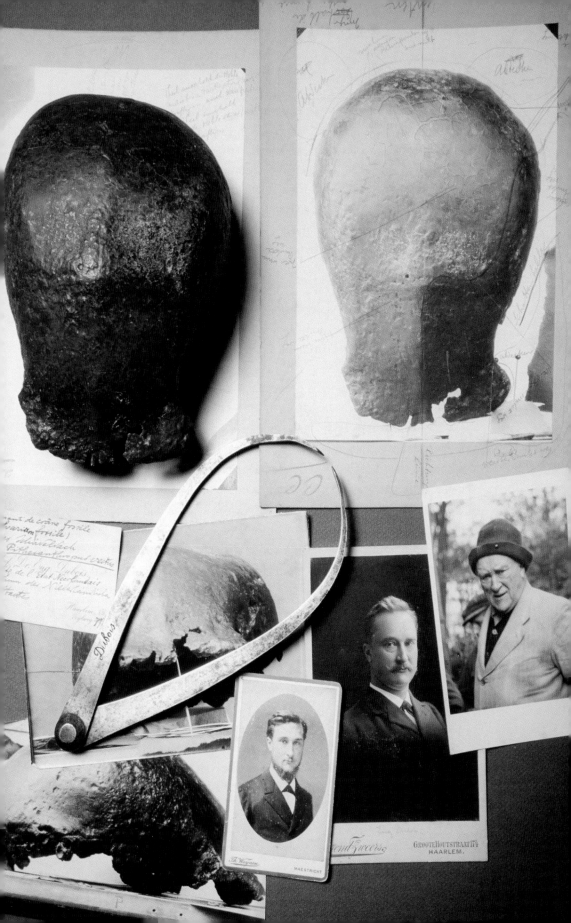

attributed their opposition to ignorance, or to personal animosity, rather than to a desire to reach the truth'.[16]

The points of contention were quite straightforward. If the remains had belonged to one individual, as Dubois claimed, then they represented an ape, a human, or the intermediate form that Dubois proposed. But not everyone agreed that the fossils had belonged to one individual, which increased the number of possible interpretations; and the question could never be proved one way or the other. It was more a matter of probability than of fact, and in considering it, the protagonists were free to choose the facts they thought most applicable. Dubois, for example, ignored his own assertion that the Kendeng fossil accumulations were the jumbled remains of many volcano victims, while his critics ignored the observation that the four fossils were the only primate remains among thousands of fossils recovered from the lapilli bed, which Dubois felt was enough to prove their association.

But, while the question of provenance could never be proved, Dubois was certain that the proof of status lay in the fossils themselves, and he thoroughly re-examined the scanty evidence they presented. He compared the thighbone with more than one thousand modern specimens. He removed the compacted sediment from the interior of the skullcap, made a cast of the braincase and estimated the cranial capacity. He could do no more, but from this limited amount of information Dubois drew conclusions he believed should convince everyone that his *Pithecanthropus erectus* was, indeed, the 'Missing Link'.

Presenting his conclusions at the Fourth International Congress of Zoology, held at Cambridge in August 1898, Dubois announced that the thighbone was significantly different from that of modern humans, suggesting that although *Pithecanthropus* had stood erect and walked on two legs, it retained some ape-like characteristics. And turning to the evidence of the braincast, Dubois produced an 'index of cephalization' and attempted to prove the intermediate status of *Pithecanthropus* by disproving the contentions that it was either ape or human. Applying the brain-size to body-weight ratio of modern apes to the fossils, Dubois pointed out that an ape with the cranial capacity of *Pithecanthropus* (854 cubic centimetres) would have weighed 230 kilograms, while a human with so small a brain would have weighed only nineteen kilograms. Both propositions failed the test of logic in Dubois's view and he concluded his Cambridge address: 'From all these considerations it follows that *Pithecanthropus erectus* undoubtedly is an intermediate form between man and the apes...a most venerable ape-man, representing a stage in our phylogeny.'[17]

Approaching the issue from another direction, it could have been shown that a modern human with a thighbone the size of the Java specimen would have weighed about seventy kilograms and, with a cranial capacity of 854 cubic centimetres, would have made a perfect candidate for immediate ancestry. In other words, not an ape, or 'a most venerable ape-man', but a slightly less brainy human; and there the arguments might have ended. But Dubois was absolutely committed to his belief. He is not known to have made any converts at the Cambridge congress, though he may have earned an apologist or two; nonetheless, his conclusions invited comment and scientists travelled to Holland to examine the fossils and discuss their interpretation. But Dubois found these visits increasingly tiresome, especially as so few of the visitors shared his views. Science honoured him with gold medals, diplomas, and honorary degrees, but would not give him what he most wanted—agreement with his belief that *Pithecanthropus erectus* was neither ape nor human but a link between the two. Finally, Dubois retaliated by severely restricting access to the fossils.

By thus alienating sympathizers as well as the critics, and by withdrawing himself, as well as the fossils, from the international scientific community, Dubois harmed himself more than he affected scientific opinion. If he had been able to change his mind instead of closing it with the fossils, the remaining forty years of his life might have been less difficult.

In the event, scientists everywhere rejected his views, and at home in Holland his work was even less appreciated. The Church reviled him from the pulpit and the academic establishment showed him very little respect. In 1898 he was appointed Assistant Professor of Crystallography, Mineralogy, Geology, and Palaeontology at the University of Amsterdam, but it was not a prestigious post. The salary was less than he had earned as a lecturer in anatomy little more than a decade before.

During the years of seclusion Dubois described the Wadjak skulls found in 1889 and 1890 as representing the recent ancestors of Australia's aboriginal population,[18] and published a number of papers on the geology and hydrology of Holland. He also refined his Law of Phylogenetic Cephalization, postulating a 'coefficient of cephalization' and publishing a series of papers which culminated in a formula whereby all mammals could be placed in an evolutionary sequence in respect of brain size and body weight. The sequence was a geometric progression, with one convenient gap. 'Putting the cephalization of Man equal to 1,' wrote Dubois,[19] 'we find exactly 1/4 for the *Anthropomorphae*; about 1/8 for the majority of our large Mammals: Ruminants, Cats, Dogs, etc.; about 1/16 for Kanchils, Civet-Cats, Hares, Large Bats (*Megachiroptera*), etc.; about 1/32 for Mice, Moles, Leaf-nosed Bats (*Phyllostomidae*), etc.; about 1/64 for Shrews, common Small Bats (*Microchiroptera*), etc.

'The only real void space in the series,' Dubois observed, 'is between Man and the anthropomorphous Apes. This void marks the place of *Pithecanthropus*,' he concluded, the fossil having twice the cephalization of the apes and half that of humans—according to Dubois's computations.

The fossil itself reappeared in 1923, when discreet representations finally found favour with Dubois and he invited some scientists to examine them. Ales Hrdlicka of the Smithsonian Institution and H. H. McGregor of Columbia University were among the first. They were given every facility and courtesy, but their conclusions still differed from Dubois's. The Java fossils had belonged to an early form of human, they said, not an ape or an ape-man.

By now it must have been abundantly clear to everyone except Dubois that the amount of controversy surrounding his fossils reflected a severe lack of definitive evidence. He had spent the greater part of his life trying to wring from those few scraps of bone the proof they could never provide—not simply because their evidence was too fragmentary, but also because the judgement Dubois wished to impose upon them was wrong. It is a sad tale. If the fossils had been more complete Dubois could not have avoided the truth; less complete and he could not have built any serious claims upon them.

The argument lingered on, while others searched for the more complete fossils that would either corroborate or confound the theories and beliefs of its protagonists. Eventually new evidence was found, the first in 1929, when Dubois was over 70 years old. It was a skull from Peking, with undeniable similarities to the Java specimen, but Dubois dismissed its significance out of hand—simply because it contradicted his own views on human evolution. The Peking skull was just another example of the Neanderthal race, he said.[20]

Then came a stream of discoveries from Java—a skull from the banks of the Solo River at Ngandong, not far from Trinil, and others from Sangiran, about seventy-five kilometres away. In all, a dozen fine Java specimens were recovered, most of them under the direction of the German palaeontologist Ralph von Koenigswald, who called the Sangiran specimens *Pithecanthropus.*

As the evidence of affinity between Dubois's fossils and the new specimens became increasingly difficult to resist, so Dubois's effort became more desperate. In 1935 he attempted to show that von Koenigswald's *Pithecanthropus* was in fact a very large ape of gibbon-like appearance, weighing about 104 kilograms.[21] In 1940 he claimed the new skulls variously resembled the Neanderthals of Europe and the Proto-Australians he had discovered from Wadjak.[22] But by then events had overtaken Dubois and his interpretation.

In 1938 von Koenigswald described a superb skull from Sangiran as *Pithecanthropus*, and in 1939 he collaborated with Franz Weidenreich, then working in Peking, to define the precise relationship between the Java and the Peking fossils.[23] The similarities far exceeded the differences that Dubois would have stressed. The new specimens matched what there was of Dubois's fossils, and supplied enough of what was missing to satisfy everyone that the Java and Peking fossils all represented an early form of human, with almost nothing of the ape about him. *Pithecanthropus erectus* was not an ape-man. (Subsequently, in fact, the name was changed to *Homo erectus.*[24]) Needless to say, these conclusions did not satisfy Dubois. In his eighty-third year he embarked on a tedious attempt to challenge the evidence von Koenigswald and Weidenreich had presented. These papers were the last he published, and they reflect the acrimony of a weary old man. There is a touch of irony too, in his very last paragraph:

> It is most regrettable, that for the interpretation of the important discoveries of human fossils in China and Java, Weidenreich, von Koenigswald and Weinert were thus guided by preconceived opinions, and consequently did not contribute to, on the contrary they impeded, the advance of knowledge of man's place in nature...Real advance appears to depend on obtaining material data in an unbiased way, such as the *Pithecanthropus* fossil remains...[25]

Eugene Dubois suffered a heart attack and died on 16 December 1940, little more than two weeks after delivering those words. In an obituary, Arthur Keith wrote: 'He was an idealist, his ideas being so firmly held that his mind tended to bend facts rather than alter his ideas to fit them.'[26]

By 1940, palaeoanthropology was facing a crisis of classification. During the eighty years that had passed since William King attached the name *Homo nean-derthalensis* to the fossils recovered from the cave in the Neander Valley and thus initiated the practice of applying formal zoological distinction to the evidence of human ancestry, no less than 29 genera and 100 species had been created around the various hominid fossils recovered in different parts of the world.[27] Like Dubois's *Pithecanthropus erectus*, many of the descriptions were primarily a means of accommodating new (or reconsidered) discoveries within a favoured scheme of human evolution. The literature was filled with 'missing links', their putative ancestral status and relationships so confused that it was virtually impossible to reconstruct a plausible scheme of human evolution from the fossil evidence as then presented.[28]

This confusion appalled many observers, but appealed to the biologist Ernst Mayr as an opportunity to test an approach then gaining favour in studies of evolutionary biology: systematics, which classified organisms strictly according to the features they had in common. Could systematics simplify the classification of hominid fossils? Adopting a dictum of fourteenth-century philosophy known as Occam's Razor: 'it is vain to do with more what can be done with fewer', Mayr looked for the simplest arrangement of hominid taxa that could be reconciled with the plethora of names, and produced a startling result: one genus and only three species.[29] Subsequent developments have rendered the scheme something of an oversimplification, as Mayr himself noted, but its significance in the study of early man remains undiminished.

In the new classification, Mayr described our upright posture as the defining characteristic of hominids at the genus level, and grouped all known fossils in a single genus: *Homo*. Species within the genus could be most readily distinguished by characteristics derived from their upright posture, he said, such as the freeing of the hands for new functions, and the evolution of the brain. Mayr defined three species of *Homo* on these grounds, and distributed the fossils among them accordingly. The most ancient, *Homo africanus*, included the small-brained australopithecines (who will feature in later chapters); the most recent brought the Neanderthals and Cro-Magnon together as *Homo sapiens*, immediately antecedent to modern humans; and between the most ancient and most recent he put the Java and Peking hominids, calling them *Homo erectus*.

Mayr's classification made *Homo erectus* an archetypal 'missing link': poised between ancestral and descendant groups, affined to both, but separated from each by an expanse of time broad enough to accommodate the notion that one had gradually evolved into the other. The simple logic and intellectual authority of this unilineal scheme was persuasive. Subsequently, it was conflated into the single species hypothesis,[30] a view of human evolution which looked upon the development of the brain as the primary human adaptation, and the evolving culture it inspired as a process which could not have tolerated the existence of more than one hominid species at any one time. In this scheme of things, human evolution was a gradual ascent to the modern form and, while the fossil record remained sparse enough to define only a few well-marked stages along the route, it seemed a reasonable hypothesis. Since then, however, fossil discoveries have complicated the issue at every stage—and *Homo erectus* has been no exception.

The problem was that palaeoanthropology lacked a recognized and universally applied method of analysis. Different experts used different methods on the same fossils and, not surprisingly, came up with different results. During a discussion on *Homo erectus* held in New York in 1984, for example, an 'old hand' spoke of how the preliminary analysis of any fossil evidence should be conducted: 'You've got to have "green fingers" for them,' he said, 'I only need to look at a skull, and hold it, to know if it is *Homo erectus* or not…'. It was a polarizing moment, a participant observed. Though the speaker carried on, unaware of the effect of his words on his audience, the meeting paused intellectually, alerted to the intuitive method of analysis which has been responsible for many problems of interpretation in palaeoanthropology. Glances were exchanged among the listeners, and then the meeting relaxed again, confident that a majority of the palaeoanthropologists present favoured a more rigorous method of analysis.

During the late 1970s a new approach to the analysis and classification of fossil hominids had begun to challenge even the method of evolutionary systematics that Mayr had tidied up and made respectable. Called cladistics, the new approach was devised in the 1950s by the German entomologist Willi Hennig (1913–76), as a means of classifying living species according to their evolutionary relationships.[31] By the 1980s the cladistic approach was firmly established as the preferred means of establishing, and defining, the presence or absence of evolutionary relationships among fossil hominids.

Briefly, cladistic classification groups specimens according to the features they share. Some shared features may be unique to the group, others may be derived from an earlier form, and the evolutionary relationship between groups can be defined on the basis of their unique and/or derived features. The capacity of cladistics to impose a new perspective on evolutionary classification is demonstrated very clearly by an exchange of views on the topic reported in the pages of *Nature*.[32] At a meeting held at Reading University, one exasperated advocate of evolutionary systematics had exclaimed that he supposed cladists would say a lungfish is more closely related to a cow than to a salmon. 'Yes', a cladist replied, 'I cannot see what is wrong in that.'

The evolutionary systematists subsequently accused the cladists of 'religious fervour'; to which the cladists replied with charges of 'McCarthyism and a witch-hunt', but the difference of opinion seems to have centred around the meaning of the term 'relationship' in evolutionary classification. As the cladists pointed out, it was Ernst Mayr—the architect of modern systematic classification—who summarized Hennig's definition of relationship in evolution as 'the relative recency of common ancestry'. In terms of this definition, behavioural similarities are irrelevant; the lungfish and the cow share derived characters not found in salmon, and therefore must share a more recent common ancestor than that shared by the lungfish and the salmon.

'The power of cladistic analysis lies in its clarity', said a leading proponent of the method in palaeoanthropology.[33] It is not the only way of analysing the affinities of fossil hominids and classifying them, but it does impose logic and rigour on the process. Unlike results reached intuitively, the cladistic method obliges scientists to validate each stage by which an interpretation is reached—it is not enough to say 'I have green fingers and know this or that to be true'; assumptions unsupported by demonstrable facts must be explicitly stated, and their consequences examined. The aim of the cladistic method is to produce unequivocal conclusions. Sometimes the conclusions are themselves inconclusive, but an identified lack of knowledge can be more useful than subjective claims based on intuition. As the experienced (and very successful) Kenyan fossil hunter, Kamoya Kimeu, replied when asked if the fossils spoke to him: 'Yes, but you can't understand them!'[34]

FIGURE 6.3 Otto Schoetensack had the discovery of Heidelberg Man notarized. His extensive monograph on the specimen featured x-ray images—a novelty in 1908.

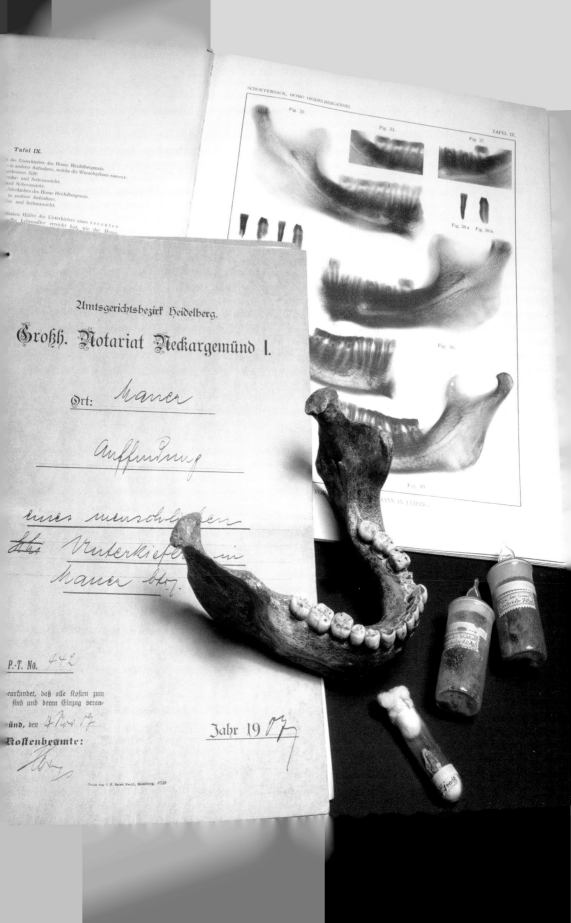

When Eugene Dubois announced in 1895 that he had retrieved the Missing Link from its resting place in Indonesia, there was little or no evidence to dispute his claim that the human line had originated in South East Asia—then, and for years after, very few other specimens were known. Heidelberg Man[35] was recovered in 1907 from a sandpit at Mauer, near Heidelberg, Germany, but since the specimen consisted solely of a massive, chinless mandible its status was enigmatic. Even its discoverer, the palaeontologist Otto Schoetensack, who had been scouring the Mauer sands for twenty years in pursuit of his conviction that hominid fossils would be found among the many fossil elephant, rhino, bear, bison, deer, and horse already recovered—even he admitted that 'an expert could not be blamed if he hesitated to accept it as human'.[36] Experts agreed, noting that although the teeth were entirely human, the size and robust nature of the jaw itself made it more likely to represent an ancestor of the Neanderthals.

Dubois was far from pleased when von Koenigswald and Weidenreich combined his *Pithecanthropus* with Peking Man and changed the name to *Homo erectus*, but the Chinese fossils actually strengthened his case for the South East Asian origin of humans and, perversely perhaps, even the skull recovered in 1921 during mining operations at Broken Hill, in what was then Northern Rhodesia (now Zambia) could be seen as further evidence. Described as a new species in the *Nature* announcement of its discovery,[37] *Homo rhodesiensis*, or Rhodesian Man, was the first fossil hominid to be found in Africa and, given the poor state of prevailing knowledge and sentiment concerning the continent at the time, implicitly more likely to have been a migrant from Asia than a resident ancestor of humanity.

By the 1980s, however, it was clear that Africa had indeed been the home of humanity's earliest ancestors. The earliest evidence known has been recovered there, as will be seen in forthcoming chapters. Furthermore, fossils with strong affinities to *Homo erectus* from Java and China had been found across the length and breadth of Africa—at Swartkrans, near Pretoria in the south; at Olduvai Gorge in Tanzania; at Lake Turkana in Kenya; in Uganda, Ethiopia, and Eritrea in the east; in Algeria and Morocco to the north. Across the Mediterranean, they are known from Spain, Italy, Greece, France, Germany, and, at the northern limit of their range, England. Yet more fossils with *Homo erectus* affinities have been found around the eastern Mediterranean, in the Jordan Valley of Israel, and to the east of the Black Sea, on the southern slopes of the Caucasus Mountains at Dmanisi, in the Republic of Georgia. The oldest are the African specimens, which date from close to 2 million years ago. From the species' probable origin in the sedimentary basins of the eastern Rift Valley they had extended their range to the far northern and southern margins of the continent by 1.8 million years ago, and then spilled out around the eastern end of the Mediterranean, or across the Straits of Hormuz, then eastward to China and Indonesia, and westward into Europe.[38]

It was a massive expansion, the scale and awesome nature of which tends to be overlooked as palaeoanthropologists struggle to classify the discoveries. But perhaps the fossil evidence of *Homo erectus* stands beyond the scope of classification. It is, after all, the most widely distributed and longest-surviving hominid species, spanning two million years and three of the world's major masses. Even though hundreds of specimens are known, they represent a minute sample of the numbers that were born and died across the species' range of time and space. Of course scientists want to label and classify them according to procedures that will eventually, it is hoped, reveal the evolutionary history of our species. But is it possible to assess the detail of such fragmentary evidence in this way? Researchers themselves admit that in the case of the specimens discussed here, it is difficult, if not impossible, to identify species boundaries among them. On the other hand, if all were described as belonging to a single species the amount of variation it encompassed would exceed that found in any other higher primate species, fossil or living.[39]

Perhaps then, so far as fossils are concerned, there is a superfluity of fragmentary evidence which clouds, rather than clarifies, the issue. The evidence that adds something new is always going to be rare—and instantly, unquestionably, recognizable, requiring no more than 'old hand'-style analysis. Alan Walker, an anatomist closely associated with many outstanding hominid fossils from the Lake Turkana basin in Kenya, remembers his first encounter with a skull from the Koobi Fora exposures discovered in 1975. It was 'exquisite', he writes, and complete enough for its affinities to be immediately apparent: 'It looked startlingly like...Peking Man',[40] ergo: *Homo erectus*.

The worldwide collection of *Homo erectus* remains consists mostly of skulls and teeth; fossils representing other parts of the skeleton were virtually unknown until the 1980s, when a team excavating on the western shore of Lake Turkana in Kenya under the leadership of Richard Leakey and Alan Walker unearthed an almost complete *Homo erectus* skeleton, the first discovered of such antiquity—1.6 million years old. The story had begun in late August 1984 when, amid the black lava pebbles, dried leaves and twigs littering the banks of a sand river, Kamoya Kimeu picked up a small piece of fossil bone; it measured only about two by one inches, but Kamoya recognized it as part of a hominid skull even before he picked it up, he says, and on turning it over in his hand could tell from the thickness of the bone that it must be *Homo erectus*.

From that simple beginning stemmed a programme of excavations that continued until 1986. Around 1,500 tons of sediment were dug out and sieved—by hand—and most of an entire skeleton was recovered, including the skull and mandible, the vertebral column, sacrum, ribs, collar-bones, and shoulder-blades; the principal bones of both legs, most of the right arm, the radius of the left arm…and the pelvis. For Alan Walker, the discovery of the pelvis was particularly memorable:

> When we saw that pelvis, we *knew*. We had more than just a cranium, more even than a skull with a few ragtag bits and pieces of other parts of the body. *It was a skeleton*, the only one of *Homo erectus* that anyone had ever seen. Nearly one hundred years had passed since the species was first discovered. Our scientific ancestors had spent their lives, expended their funds, risked their health, built and sometimes derailed their careers, all in the frustrating search for the missing link—and we had found it. The moment of realization was sweet.[41]

Apart from its iconic status, the shape of the pelvis indicated that the individual was male, and analysis of tooth and bone development showed that he had been no more than 12 years old when he died. The boy's height was about 1.6 m (5 ft 5 in), tall for a 12-year-old, and if the growth pattern of *Homo erectus* matched that of modern humans he would have stood 1.8 m (6 ft) high as an adult. The head showed characteristic *H. erectus* features in the lack of a chin, the large flat but jutting face and broad nose, the heavy brows and a brain capacity of about 900 ml (compared with a modern male average of about 1,350 ml).

FIGURE 6.4 The Human Evolution gallery of The Swedish Museum of Natural History features a replica of the Turkana Boy skeleton and a reconstruction of how he may have looked in life.

The cause of death was not apparent—it rarely is with fossils—but the preservation of so much of the skeleton showed that he had died in unusual circumstances: lying face down in a swampy pool, Walker believed, where his body was missed by crocodiles and other scavengers as the flesh decomposed and the bones sank into the soft mud. Except for parts of the hands and feet, some vertebrae and fragile ribs, everything was preserved—awaiting its rebirth 1.6 million years later, by which time over fifty thousand generations of his kind had lived and died, dispersed through Africa and migrated to establish their presence thousands of miles away in Europe, China, Indonesia, and doubtless other places where evidence has not survived or has yet to be found.

The Turkana Boy is unique—an object of wonder, a tangible remnant of ancient history and, most of all, a presence that strikes chords of empathetic enquiry: how had he lived? what did he know? what did he feel?—but, with all that, is he a missing link? The answer must be no. Not as a being who stood halfway between the apes and modern humans—the skeleton is too human-like for that. But yes, perhaps, in the sense that *Homo erectus* stands between the more ancient australopithecines and the more recent modern humans and Neanderthals. The australopithecines were principally herbivores, its seems, whose low-quality diet required them to devote most of their activities to eating, whereas a comparatively large brain relative to body size indicates that *H. erectus* had crossed (or was in the process of crossing) the cognitive Rubicon that turned later hominids from eating machines into thinking machines. Subsequently, the discovery of an adult female *H. erectus* pelvis with a capacious birth canal from 1.8 million-year-old deposits in Ethiopia confirmed that the pelvic shape was evolving in response to increasing brain size by that time.[42]

By the late 1970s, when Ernst Mayr and the cladists introduced the systematic method of classifying fossil evidence, it was already clear that where Dubois had proposed a single 'missing link' between an ape-like ancestor and modern humans there was a sizeable 'muddle in the middle'.[43] Valiant attempts were made to put the existing evidence in some sort of order (typically with *Homo erectus* arising in Africa then splitting into two branches, one of which left the continent and migrated through Eurasia to China and Java at an early stage, while the other moved into Europe at a later date and subsequently evolved into the Neanderthals[44]), but the quantity and variety of fossil remains discovered in the 1980s and '90s brought as much complexity as clarity to the scenario and there was more and startling evidence to come: *Homo floresiensis*, the Hobbit.

The discovery was published in *Nature* in October 2004 and made front page news around the world.[45] On a remote island, a hitherto unknown species of human being had survived until about 18,000 years ago, it seemed. They were small, little more than 1 metre tall, and walked upright. They had tiny brains, even for their size, but had made stone tools and shared the island with dwarf elephants, giant carnivorous storks and komodo dragons. This was the stuff of fairy tales. The third film of the *Lords of the Rings* trilogy had been filmed in New Zealand and released the previous year. Public attention was focused on Australasia and Tolkien's much-loved character to such an extent that *Homo hobbitus* was considered as a name for the new species. (*H. floresianus* was also considered, but rejected for fear that generations of students would refer to it as 'flowery anus').

The Hobbit captured attention at all levels. Acres of newsprints were devoted to the discovery; commentators pondered the philosophical implications of knowing that another species of our kind had survived until relatively recent times; Damian Hirst, a leading world figure in contemporary art, produced a painstakingly realistic painting of the Hobbit skull alongside that of a modern human[46] (the canvas measures 2.74 m by 3.50 m, sale price undisclosed). Among the luminaries called upon for an opinion, Richard Dawkins described the discovery as 'one giant leap for our sense of wonder'. He pleaded for 'these wonderful little creatures' not to be called hobbits—for this was a case, he said, in which the facts really were much stranger than fiction.[47]

The facts were unearthed, recorded and published in exemplary fashion[48]— and they were indeed strange. At first, it seemed reasonable to assume that *H. floresiensis* represented descendants of Eugene Dubois's Java Man (*Homo erectus* or, more correctly, *Pithecanthropus erectus*) who had made their way along the chain of islands from Java to Flores. Once there, the phenomenon of island-dwarfing had caused the isolated population to become progressively smaller (this can happen relatively quickly where there is a restricted food supply and an absence of predators renders large size unnecessary: the one-metre-high fossil elephants found on Malta and Sicily, for instance, are believed to have dwarfed from a 4 metre high ancestor in less than 5,000 years[49]). Stone tools dating from nearly one million years ago had been found on another part of the island, presumably made by the hobbits' earlier ancestors, leaving plenty of time for their descendants to have shrunk in size from *H. erectus* to *H. floresiensis*.

Further analysis revealed problems with these early assumptions. Though the skull was basically similar in shape to *Homo erectus*, in some critical features it was more primitive. The limb-bones, shoulder and pelvis also possessed primitive features; the hands were more like apes than those of evolving humans. And the feet were unlike anything previously encountered in the fossil record: 20 cm long, though their owner was little more than a metre tall (a 5:1 ratio, which would give today's 1.8 m tall male a foot of 36 cm in length). The species was bipedal, but long flappy feet and relatively short legs would have produced a curious high-stepping gait. Walking long distances would have been a struggle, and running was pretty much out of the question.

And then there was the question of the brain. Small animals are expected to have small brains and the *Encephalisation Quotient* (a modern version of Dubois's coefficient of cephalization) is a measure of how much bigger (or smaller) a brain is than it 'ought to be' for its size. Modern humans have an EQ of 6 (which means our brains are about six times bigger than they 'ought to be' for our size); the EQ of *Homo erectus* is about 4; *Homo floresiensis* comes in at around half that. Thus, the hobbit's brain was far smaller than even that of an island-dwarfed Java Man should be. Indeed, in terms of the body to brain-size ratio, a critic calculated that if *Homo erectus* had shrunk as much in height as its brain had shrunk in volume, *Homo floresiensis* would stand only 30 cm tall, less than one-third of its already diminutive height.[50]

But if the hobbit, *Homo floresiensis*, was not a descendant of Dubois's Java Man, *Homo erectus*, what was it? Extensive comparative analysis of the fossils produced a result that confounded all expectations. Researchers found that *H. floresiensis* most closely resembles apelike ancestors that had lived in Africa more than two million years ago—the australopithecines and, most especially, *Homo habilis* (the story of these species is covered in later chapters). These findings contradicted the favoured paradigm of the day: namely that the australopithecines and the habilines were the ancestors of *Homo erectus*, whose first migrants had left Africa around 1.8 million years ago.

The idea that some ancestors of *Homo erectus* had moved out of Africa before their descendants, and migrated across Asia to found a population which survived on a remote Indonesian island until the relatively recent past—any such idea qualified as preposterous until 2009, when the definitive research was published in a special edition of the *Journal of Human Evolution*. The evidence presented was sound—facts (certainly not fiction, however strange) which, from a palaeoanthropological point of view, allowed for no alternative interpretation. The very points which dismissed the possibility that *H. floresiensis* could have been a descendant of *H. erectus* also confirmed the new species' affinities with the pre-*erectus* hominids from which *H. erectus* was said to have evolved.

The implications for palaeoanthropological theory were profound. If the fossils had been found in Africa in deposits dating from two million years ago, they would have aroused little comment. But they were found in Indonesia, in 18,000 year-old deposits. The cosy consensus view of human origins and global colonization was rudely shaken. 'If something this primitive left Africa and got to Flores so long ago, it shows how screwed up the hominid fossil record really is,' one insider expostulated. 'Absolutely anything could be going on. Where are the equivalent hominids in the rest of Asia, for example? All is fucked,' he concluded.

'We are still grappling with what this has done for our thinking and our conventional scenarios', said Professor Chris Stringer, a foremost advocate of the standard Out of Africa hypothesis.

Inevitably, there were objections to the creation of a new species and all it implied, based principally on the contention that its distinctive features were the consequence of disease or abnormal development. A pathological explanation of the specimen's small stature, tiny brain and skeletal peculiarities would invalidate the idea that it was descended from hominids who lived in Africa more than 2 million years ago, and leave conventional scenarios of human evolution unaffected. But, interestingly, it was not the palaeoanthropologists who were most persistent in their rejection of the new species (though it had shaken their science to its roots); it was scientists with broad experience of modern human variation—geneticists, clinicians and human biologists. They argued that the pathological explanation could not be rejected until medically informed scientists had eliminated all possible pathological explanations.[51]

The possible explanations they put forward have included syndromes that caused the brain not to reach full size (microcephaly); cretinism, in which the lack of a functioning thyroid restricts development and Laron's syndrome, a genetic disorder that causes insensitivity to growth hormones. But none of them accounted for the totality of conditions found in *H. floresiensis* and all have been countered by further discoveries (bones representing an estimated fourteen individuals have been recovered from the site) and analysis. The new species hypothesis cannot be rejected, its advocates say, until a pathological explanation can account for the morphology observed in *H. floresiensis*.

The debate matches the controversies that were provoked by the discoveries of Neanderthal Man, Dubois's Java Man (*Pithecanthropus erectus*) and the Taung child (*Australopithecus*, see Chapter 8). As in those cases, *Homo floresiensis* is fundamentally inconsistent with prevailing notions about the course of human evolution. Does the new material represent a paradigm-changing discovery, or is it just a diseased modern human (or an ape in the case of Taung)?

In a comprehensive review[52], paleoanthropologist Leslie Aiello concludes that although a pathological explanation for *H. floresiensis* would be the simplest and most comfortable solution to the questions it raised, the evidence supports the hypothesis that *Homo floresiensis* is a late-surviving species of early *Homo* with its closest affinities to early African pre-*erectus* hominids. We may be on the threshold of a major transformation in our understanding of human evolution, she writes, that will have profound and far-reaching implications.

By 2010, five years after the initial announcement of the new species, there was little its critics could add to their objections. Medical science offered few pathological explanations for its condition and the repeated assertion that they were enough was becoming less and less convincing. Meanwhile, the researchers were back in the field, confident that answers would be found. For or against, only more evidence could settle the argument, but it would need to be as convincing as that which settled the Neanderthal, Java and Taung controversies.

FIGURE 6.5 Anthropologist William L. Jungers, who has participated in the excavation, analysis and description of the Floresiensis fossils, stands behind a life-size reconstruction of the hobbit. He is 1.93m tall.

CHAPTER SEVEN

Piltdown Man
(1912)

ARTHUR KEITH (1866–1955), anatomist, was one of a British scientific triumvirate whose beliefs and work profoundly affected investigations into the evolution of man for nearly fifty years. His associates were Arthur Smith Woodward (1864–1944), palaeontologist and Keeper of Geology at the British Museum of Natural History, and Grafton Elliot Smith (1871–1937), an anatomist whose speciality was the study of the brain. All three gentlemen were knighted for their contributions to science, and their talents were memorably displayed in discussions concerned with the significance of alleged fossil human remains found at Piltdown, Sussex, between 1908 and 1915.

In an autobiography written late in life, Keith remarked that 'the ideas which a man devotes his life to exploring are, for the greater part, those which come to him in the first tide of his inquiries'.[1] The observation is certainly sustained by the facts of his own career. In the first year of his medical studies, Keith was awarded a copy of *The Origin of Species* for his work in the anatomy class. While working as medical officer to a mining company in Thailand immediately after he qualified, Keith dissected monkeys in the hope of determining whether or not the animals shared the affliction of malaria that plagued the human population and discovered an absorbing interest in comparative anatomy as the means of elucidating the evolutionary development of humans. Within a year he dissected thirty-two assorted primates, and on returning to England in 1892 arranged to receive and dissect primate carcasses from the London Zoo.

He dissected human foetuses as well, and the comparative anatomy of the ligamentous structure of the feet and hands of monkeys and human babies became both the subject of his doctoral dissertation and the basis of his views on the evolution of our erect posture.[2] At home in Scotland Keith performed cerebral dissections on farmyard cats of all ages to clarify his understanding of the development of the individual brain; in London he studied primate skulls at the Royal College of Surgeons and at the British Museum of Natural History, carefully noting about 150 observations on each of over 200 skulls. It was during the course of these studies, in the winter of 1894, Keith later wrote,[3] that he learned 'the alphabet by which we spell out the long-past history of man and ape' from the evidence of fragmentary fossils.

In 1895 Keith met Dubois; he made a reconstruction of the Java skull and wrote an article on the specimen for a popular journal (concluding that the specimen was essentially human, but of a lowly kind). Thereafter he wrote frequently on the subject of human ancestry and, on his appointment as Hunterian Professor of Anatomy at the Royal College of Surgeons in 1908, vowed to uncover and write 'the anthropological history of the British'.[4]

In *The Descent of Man* (1871), Charles Darwin had implied that the early forerunners of humans probably retained some characteristics of the ancestor they shared with the apes. Males were probably furnished with great canine teeth at one time, he said, but as they acquired the habit of using stones, clubs, and other weapons for fighting they would have used their jaws less and less, with consequent decrease in the size of the canines and some restructuring of the jaw. Scientists drew several important conclusions from Darwin's observation. Reshaping the jaw would have provided the space essential for the movement of the tongue in articulate speech; the ability to handle stones and clubs presumed an erect posture; both speech and erect posture require a considerable development of the mental abilities. Thus the crucial developments on our evolutionary path were clearly defined. But which came first? Development of the brain? The erect posture? Or the ability to speak? Darwin hardly commented upon the question but, as the slowly accumulating fossil remains inspired competing interpretations of their imprecise evidence, it was clear that some idea of the manner in which human evolution had proceeded would help by suggesting the features that fossils ought to possess. If people had walked before they could talk, then fossils could be expected to demonstrate the fact.

As a result of his work on the feet and hands of apes and human babies, Arthur Keith believed erect posture was an ancient attribute and the large brain our most recent acquisition.[5] An opposing view was championed by Grafton Elliot Smith, whose pioneering work on the function and evolution of the vertebrate brain had convinced him that 'the brain led the way'. At its most primitive, the brain had discerned little more than the sensation of smell, he said. Later, vision had been acquired and then 'an arboreal mode of life started man's ancestors on the way to pre-eminence' for, while they avoided the fierce competition for size and supremacy waged among the terrestrial carnivores and ungulates, 'the specialization of the higher parts of the brain gave them [the primates] the seeing eye, and in the course of time also the understanding ear;…all the rest followed in the train of this high development of vision working on a brain which controlled ever-increasingly agile limbs'. Thus 'the Primates found in the branches the asylum and protection necessary for the cultivation of brain and limbs,' he said, and the erect posture developed when they had become 'powerful enough to hold their own and wax great'. It was 'not the real cause of man's emergence from the Simian stage, but…one of the factors made use of by the expanding brain as a prop still further to extend its growing dominion'.[6]

Arthur Smith Woodward appears to have contributed little to the early stages of the debate. In 1885 he remarked upon the preponderance of 'Missing Links' in the fossil record.[7] In 1913 he told his audience at the annual British Association meetings that 'we have looked for a creature with an overgrown brain and ape-like face',[8] who was missing from the chain connecting the human and primate ancestors, although he personally had not given the subject much attention until then. In fact, by far the greater part of Woodward's career was devoted to the study of fossil fish. In all he published more than six hundred papers on the subject and related palaeontological issues—more than three hundred before he became Keeper of Geology at the British Museum in 1901—and only thirty or so on fossil hominids. These figures, of course, also reflect the relative abundance of the fossils in question.

The hominid fossil evidence discovered by the beginning of the twentieth century was slight—but nonetheless significant. Specimens from France and

Belgium had confirmed the existence of a Neanderthal race; there was the Heidelberg mandible and Eugene Dubois's enigmatic Java Man—which at the very least indicated that the late Pleistocene ancestors bore a receding chin as evidence of their simian associations and had existed across the globe from Europe to South East Asia. These specimens added a measure of information to the story of human evolution in general, but of the British anthropological history that Arthur Keith had vowed to write there was no indisputable evidence whatsoever. The state of affairs was slightly more advanced in France, where a belief that the New and Old Stone Ages (the Neolithic and Palaeolithic) had been preceded by the Eolithic, or Dawn Stone Age, was at least supported by some putative archaeological evidence.

The term Eolithic had been coined in 1883 by the archaeologist Gabriel de Mortillet (1821–98)[9] as a category under which to classify the crudely worked flint implements which had been found in deposits that were demonstrably older than the Palaeolithic. Mortillet was convinced that the development of culture and technology was a reflection of biological evolution. Therefore, he reasoned, it was logical to assume that just as the Neolithic and Palaeolithic industries documented the gradual emergence of modern humanity in the Quaternary Period, so the crude tools of the preceding Tertiary Period must be the work of a transitional creature—a missing link—who had stood between humans and the apes. He even had a name for his Tertiary Man: *Anthropopithecus*.

Even in France, support for Mortillet's Tertiary Man was by no means unanimous, principally because the tools upon which it was based were so crude that they could have been formed naturally, in the rough and tumble that waterborne flints inevitably undergo before coming to rest—especially when Ice Age glaciers were churning over the landscape. There was also serious doubt as to whether humans could have existed in Europe *before* the Ice Age, as Mortillet's idea of Tertiary Man required.

In Britain the idea met with strong resistance, but found support with a few authoritative figures. In particular, the influential geologists Joseph Prestwich (1821–98) and James Geikie (1839–1915) were firmly committed—the latter convinced that the remains of 'Preglacial Man', as he preferred to call it, would be found in England and 'will cause the hairs of cautious archaeologists to rise on end'.[10] Such enthusiasm failed to stir their professional colleagues, but it was more than enough to excite Britain's venturesome band of amateur fossil and artefact hunters. Even if they failed to find the ultimate prize—the remains of Tertiary Man himself—an eolith or two would establish his presence in Britain just as effectively. Furthermore, since the chalk Downs of south-east England were known to be part of the formations that extended across the Channel to north-west France, where Mortillet's eoliths had been recovered, there was surely a good chance of finding similar treasures in England—and with a bonus: the sequence of geological deposition and erosion over the millennia was such that the flint-bearing deposits exposed in England were older than in France; therefore, England's eoliths and Tertiary Man would pre-date any French evidence of his existence. England would have the world's Oldest Man—treasure indeed.

A leader of eolith-hunting operations on the North Downs was Benjamin Harrison (1837–1921), who owned a grocery shop in the small village of Ightham, about twenty-five miles south-east of London. Poised about 300 feet above sea-level on the southern slope of the Downs, Ightham overlooked the Weald of Kent and Sussex. To the north, the Downs rose steadily for another 450 feet to form the northern rim of the Chalk Plateau, which ran from east to west across the breadth of Kent and at its western end was punctuated by several rivers, which flowed northwards into the Thames estuary.

Harrison's interest in archaeology had been little more than an adjunct to walks on the Downs, picking up any odd-looking flint that might be poking from the chalk, until 1879, when he paid a visit to Joseph Prestwich, who had retired to live in Shoreham, another small village about seven miles from Ightham. He took along some of the flints he had found. They spoke of geology, eoliths, and Tertiary Man. Harrison knew that the implement-bearing formations of northern France extended across the Channel to south-east England, so asked the geologist where they might occur on the Downs. Prestwich is said to have turned to his study window, and pointed across the valley of the river Darwent, 'If we take the Darwent to be the Somme,' he said, 'the implement-bearing gravels would lie at about the level of the railway station'.[11] This was exciting news, for many of the flints then spread across Prestwich's desk had been found some distance above the level of the Shoreham railway station.

The news spread. During the 1880s bands of dedicated enthusiasts regularly congregated in Ightham to join Harrison for a weekend of tramping across the North Downs in search of Tertiary Man and the implements he made. No human remains were found, but by 1894 England's putative eoliths were numerous enough for the British Association to decide that only a properly organized excavation could settle the question of their authenticity. A committee was formed. Harrison was assigned to direct operations at two sites. A number of what were described as Plateau palaeoliths and 'rudes' were found five foot down in one excavation, and a few 'worked' objects at a depth of eight feet in the other. Prestwich said the finds were convincing, but another prominent Committee member, the antiquarian John Evans (1823–1908), was unimpressed: 'Has the absolute uselessness of such flints as tools never struck you ... ?', he asked in a letter to Harrison.[12]

Meanwhile, though, the eolith debate had re-ignited interest in a fossil skull and human bones that another amateur collector, Robert Elliot, had discovered along with crude putative implements in 1888 in a chalk pit on the northern rim of the plateau at Galley Hill in Kent. The collection was presented to the Geological Society of London in 1895, where experts concluded that although no geologists had been present when they were found, and the exact site had since been destroyed, the primitive implements were sufficiently similar to those from Harrison's excavations near Ightham for the skull to represent a pre-Stone Age race.[13] The argument was favourably received, but the question of the skull's provenance remained and that—combined with uncertainties concerning its relationship with the Neanderthals—was enough for it to be consigned to a 'suspense account'. Where it remained until 1910, when Arthur Keith decided that reappraisal was merited.

Over a period of months Keith confirmed the skeleton's affinities with *Homo sapiens* and concluded that the remains had been buried in ancient deposits but, whereas these factors had caused earlier investigators to question the claims of great antiquity, Keith deduced from them that Galley Hill Man was as ancient as the deposits in which he had been buried, and the burial was not recent, but ancient. 'We hardly do justice to the men who shaped the [artefacts],' he wrote, 'if we hold them incapable of showing respect for their dead.'[14] The implications of these deductions were considerable: if large-brained, walking *Homo sapiens* had existed at the beginning of the Pleistocene, as Keith now claimed, then all the crucial evolutionary development of *Homo sapiens* must have taken place long before; people had remained unchanged for a very long time, and the Neanderthal and Java fossils represented not our ancestors, but a 'degenerate cousin'.

Geologists, in particular, did not accept that *Homo sapiens* could be so ancient. But Keith said this was because they had grown up with a belief in the recent origin of the species and therefore expected to see a sequence of anatomical change marking the course of our evolution. In fact the geologists' views simply conformed with the rationale of their palaeontological training, which taught that the long and absolute lack of evolutionary change Keith proposed would be unique among the higher vertebrates, and therefore unlikely. But Keith, the anatomist, was untroubled by the niceties of palaeontology and quite prepared to believe that our species is unique. Thereafter his claims for the exceptional antiquity of *Homo sapiens* became a point of faith. He called upon it to explain the anomaly of apparently modern human remains found beneath ancient deposits at Ipswich.[15] At a meeting of the British Association for the Advancement of Science held at Dundee in 1912, Keith offered perhaps the first full and authoritative exposition of the claim that *Homo sapiens* acquired both large brain and erect stature a very long time ago and has remained relatively unchanged ever since.

Remarking upon the Neanderthal and Java fossils, Keith told his audience: 'thus we have a knowledge—a very imperfect knowledge—of only two human individuals near the beginning of the Pleistocene period. The one was brutal in aspect, the other certainly low in intellect.' If these are the ancestors of our species, he said, then we have to accept 'that in the early part of the Pleistocene, within a comparatively short space of time, the human brain developed at an astounding and almost incredible rate'. To Keith it seemed more reasonable to reject Neanderthal and Java from human ancestry and assume they were simply contemporaries and cousins of our large-brained ancestor, whose evolutionary development had occurred long before. 'Is it then possible,' he asked, 'that a human being, shaped and endowed as we are, may have existed so early as the Pliocene?' Briefly reviewing the evidence he had presented, Keith concluded that it was. 'The picture I wish to leave in your minds,' he said, 'is that in the distant past there was not one kind but a number of very different kinds of men in existence, all of which have become extinct except that branch which has given origin to modern man. On the imperfect knowledge at present at our disposal it seems highly probable that man as we know him now took on his human characters near the beginning of the Pliocene period.'[16]

FIGURE 7.1 Arthur Keith and the Galley Hill specimen.

At the same meetings, Grafton Elliot Smith confidently extended the ancestral pedigree back still further, to the Eocene, explaining how the 'steady and uniform development of the brain along a well-defined course throughout the Primates right up to Man…gives us the fundamental reason for "Man's emergence and ascent"'.[17]

Thus the leading anatomists of the day expounded the theories of human evolution that they hoped palaeontologists might one day substantiate with the evidence of human fossil remains. Just a few months later, in December 1912, Arthur Smith Woodward, the leading palaeontologist of the day, unveiled Piltdown Man and thus presented the anatomists with a conundrum in which the expectation of theory and the logic of observed fact were wonderfully counterpoised.

Though he was responsible for the reconstruction and presentation of Piltdown Man, Woodward had not discovered the remains. The first pieces of fossil skull bone were brought to him by Charles Dawson, an amateur geologist who had already contributed important palaeontological specimens to the British Museum collections. Dawson (1864–1916) was a solicitor practising at Uckfield in Sussex, a position which left time for a wide range of other activities (in 1909 he published *A History of Hastings Castle* in two volumes and at the onset of his terminal illness was investigating a case of incipient horns on the head of a carthorse) but geology and palaeontology were the interests he pursued most energetically. In 1885—at the age of 21—Dawson was elected a fellow of the Geological Society for his contributions to the science, though little appeared in the literature under his own name. 'He preferred to hand over his specimens to experts who have made a special study of the groups to which they belonged,' an obituary recounts,[18] rather than describe them himself, and Smith Woodward was surely rewarding this respectful deference to greater knowledge when he named Piltdown Man *Eoanthropus dawsoni* (Dawson's Dawn Man), and made Dawson principal author of their joint paper.[19]

At a crowded meeting of the Geological Society held in London on 18 December 1912, Dawson presented the geological and archaeological evidence of the discovery, following which Woodward the palaeontologist described the specimen at some length, drawing attention to anatomical features which appeared to support his claims for its antiquity and status as the Earliest Englishman; only then did he speak on the palaeontology of the site, a subject to which his qualifications might have been more justifiably applied.

The details of Dawson's initial discovery are imprecise; not even the exact year is known. Dawson told the meeting how he had been attracted to the site 'several years' before when he traced some unusual brown flints found on a farm near Fletching to a small gravel pit on a farm adjacent to Piltdown Common, Sussex. He asked the labourers who occasionally worked there to keep any fossils they might encounter, and on a subsequent visit, they presented him with a small, concave, tabular object. It was part of a coconut shell, the men said, which they had found and broken in the course of their digging. They had kept one piece for Dawson and discarded the rest. Dawson, however, realized that the object was part of a fossil human skull. Thereafter he visited the site frequently and 'some years later—in the autumn of 1911', he found another fragment of the same skull among the spoil heaps.

Believing the pieces might match the proportions of the Heidelberg jaw, in May 1912 Dawson took his finds to the British Museum for more accurate assessment. Woodward was impressed and joined Dawson in the search for more remains that summer—though only as a private, weekend holiday affair, and without the involvement of any of the British Museum's resources. Apparently they wished to keep the discovery wholly to themselves. At first, just one labourer was employed to do the heavy digging in the small pit, but later they were joined by Father Teilhard de Chardin and another French priest who were studying at the Jesuit College near Hastings. Teilhard de Chardin shared Dawson's amateur interest in fossils and geology (they had met by chance in their rambles about the Sussex countryside) and in later years Chardin was to become a recognized authority on the fossil evidence of human evolution.

During the summer of 1912 solicitor, palaeontologist, and priests scrutinized every spadeful dug from the pit and sifted through all the spoil heaps of previous years. In one heap they found three pieces of the right parietal bone from the skull—one piece on each of three successive days—and later Woodward found another fragment which fitted the broken edge of the occipital and connected with the left parietal found by Dawson. 'Finally, on a warm summer evening after an afternoon's vain search,' Woodward recounts,[20] 'Mr Dawson was exploring some untouched remnants of the original gravel at the bottom of the pit, when we both saw half of the human lower jaw fly out in front of the pick-shaped end of the hammer he was using. Thus was recovered the most remarkable portion of the fossil which we were collecting.' In addition the pit supplied three 'undoubted' flint implements, several eoliths, fragments of an elephant tooth, some beaver teeth, and one much-rolled fragment of a mastodon tooth, while on the surface of an adjacent field the party found a piece of red deer antler and a horse's tooth—both fossilized and both presumed to have been thrown over the hedge by the workmen. In all, a remarkably comprehensive haul.

According to Dawson's assessment of the site's geology, the Piltdown gravel bed lay about eighty feet above the level of the River Ouse, deposited there before the river began excising the valley through which it presently flows. The gravel bed could be divided into four distinct strata, he said, and the fossils had come from the third, which lay about three and a half feet below the land surface and was distinguished by a dark ferruginous appearance and the presence of iron-stone. The fossil fauna from the pit were of early Pleistocene—even Pliocene—age, he concluded, and the flint artefacts appeared to be similarly ancient—all of which strongly implied that the human remains found in the same deposit represented the earliest known example of a human ancestor.

Woodward was not known to be a secretive man, but he went to some lengths to keep the Piltdown material to himself until it was unveiled at the Geological Society meeting in December 1912. He made an anatomical reconstruction of the skull he would present, but worked alone without seeking the assistance or even the advice of Museum colleagues who knew more about anatomy than he did (they were surprised and dismayed when they saw the reconstruction, feeling that more caution would have been advisable).[21] Woodward made a cast of the interior of the reconstructed skull and invited Grafton Elliot Smith to comment upon the brain of Piltdown Man when the specimen was unveiled at the Geological Society in December, but Elliot Smith has made it clear that he did not help with the reconstruction of the skull itself.[22]

Despite Woodward's attempt to keep the Piltdown discovery secret until the Geological Society meeting, the news was leaked to the *Manchester Guardian*, in whose pages a prominent report appeared on 21 November, concluding:

> There seems to be no doubt whatever of its genuineness, and more than a possibility of its being the oldest remnant of a human frame yet discovered on this planet.

Within hours, Fleet Street's best gathered at the Natural History Museum, waiting to be ushered through the steepled galleries into Woodward's presence.

He confirmed the *Guardian* story, but declined to give details of the find, for fear of the site becoming haunted by enthusiasts hoping to dig more relics. 'Be patient', he urged, but when pressed on the age of the specimen replied without hesitation: 'Yes, it is the earliest that has ever been found...and might possibly be found to supply a link between the ape and man.'[23]

Woodward's coy suggestion that Piltdown was the missing link 'stirred the smouldering embers of scientific and public interest into an excited flame of anticipation', as one commentator puts it.[24]

The audience that packed the Geological Society's lecture room on 18 December 1912 was larger than any before, and the Piltdown skull they had come to see perfectly fulfilled the expectations of many who attended. Smith Woodward's reconstruction had produced a creature with the jaw of an ape, the skull of a human and a cranial capacity (1070 cubic centimetres) appropriate to an intermediate stage between human and ape. A small minority thought the combination of ape and human characteristics was just a little too good to be true, and Woodward himself accurately defined the point when he told the meeting: 'while the skull, indeed, is essentially human, only approaching a lower grade in certain characters of the brain [as described in Elliot Smith's contribution to the same meeting]...the mandible appears to be almost precisely that of the ape'.[25]

Elliot Smith, however, did not find the combination at all unreasonable. The Piltdown brain was the most primitive and the most simian so far recorded, he said, and its association with an ape-like jaw was not surprising to anyone familiar with recent research into the process by which the human brain had evolved from the brain of the ape.[26]

Arthur Keith, on the other hand, was among those who had misgivings. He was jealous that the remains had been given to a palaeontologist at the British Museum and not him, an anatomist known to be specially interested in the anthropological history of the British. But then he knew Woodward regarded his belief in the antiquity of *Homo sapiens* as 'an amusing evolutionary heresy'.[27] At the Geological Society meeting, Keith hailed Piltdown as the most important discovery of fossil human remains ever made, at home or abroad, but took exception to some aspects of the reconstruction. The chin region and the form of the front teeth were too much like the chimpanzee, he said.[28]

The arguments concerning the association of jaw and skull, and the form of the reconstruction, would never have arisen if the remains had been more complete. But the anatomical features capable of proving or confounding the association of jaw and skull were exactly the ones that were missing: the chin region of the jaw, which would have clearly demonstrated the human or ape-like shape of the canines; and the knob on the end of the jawbone, which would have shown the form of the joint in which the jaw articulated with the skull.

In May 1913 Arthur Keith acquired casts of the remains and immediately began work on his own reconstruction of the Piltdown skull, one which assembled the available parts in accordance with anatomical principles and supplied the missing parts in accordance with his belief in the antiquity of *Homo sapiens*. The chin and front teeth were entirely human and the cranial capacity was 1500 cubic centimetres—greater than the average for the modern form. A few weeks later the conflicting interpretations of anatomist and palaeontologist were reviewed by the participants at an International Congress of Medicine held in London. At the Natural History Museum, the visiting experts viewed Woodward's anatomical reconstruction of the original remains, and at the Royal College of Surgeons Arthur Keith showed them where the palaeontologist had gone wrong.

Because of a misconception concerning the jaws and teeth, Woodward had fitted a chimpanzee palate and jaw on a skull that could not possibly carry them, Keith said, with the result that the upper vertebrae were so close to the palate that there was no room for windpipe or gullet and Piltdown Man would have been unable to eat or breathe. The Woodward reconstruction was anatomically impossible, he said.[29] If skull and jaw truly belonged together then the skull must be large enough to accommodate the massive jaw and the front teeth must be human enough to match the form of the skull.

The two reconstructions were widely discussed, with the third member of the triumvirate, anatomist Grafton Elliot Smith, lending his support to the palaeontologist's version, but Woodward himself did not respond publicly to Keith's claims until 16 September 1913, when he told a meeting of the British Association for the Advancement of Science assembled in Birmingham of further discoveries at Piltdown:

> Fortunately, Mr Dawson has continued his diggings during the past summer and, on August 30, Father P. Teilhard, who was working with him, picked up

FIGURE 7.2 Original Piltdown specimens with some of Dawson's many letters to Smith Woodward.

the canine tooth which obviously belong to the half of the mandible originally discovered. In shape it corresponds exactly with that of an ape, and its
worn face shows that it worked upon the upper canine in the true ape-fashion.
It only differs from the canine of my published restoration in being slightly
smaller, more pointed, and a little more upright in the mouth. Hence, we have
now definite proof that the front teeth of *Eoanthropus* resembled those of an
ape, and my original determination is justified.[30]

The Piltdown canine settled the argument about the chin so conclusively in
Woodward's favour that Arthur Keith was forced to concede an important point
of his belief in the antiquity of the modern form of *Homo sapiens*. Despite the
evidence of Galley Hill and Ipswich, it seemed that some ancestors in the early
Pleistocene had displayed distinctly ape-like characteristics after all. But the argument about the size of the Piltdown brain-case was still unresolved. Woodward
believed it must have been relatively small because, in his view, the association
of the primitive jaw with a *large* brain-case would be a most improbable combination of primitive and modern features. Keith, on the other hand, insisted that
the brain must have been large because the association of a large jaw with a *small*
brain-case was anatomically impossible. The difference between the estimates
of anatomist and palaeontologist soon became a subject of heated debate in the
pages of *Nature* and elsewhere.

But Woodward was not directly involved; in his stead, Grafton Elliot Smith
promoted the smaller estimate and thus the palaeontologist was able to remain
a passive observer while the merits of his Piltdown reconstruction were argued
by two anatomists. In Keith's view the anatomical errors responsible for the
small brain-case were manifest and glaringly obvious; he was surprised and
irritated by Smith's refusal to acknowledge them. Acrimony developed between
the two men and, although Keith eventually came to terms with most of the
colleagues with whom he argued during his career, he and Smith were never
on good terms again.

The difference in the estimates of the Piltdown brain size resulted solely from
the manner in which the existing fragments were assembled and their curves
projected to delineate the parts missing in between. A large area of the forehead,
and the roof of the skull were among the important missing pieces, as Keith
pointed out in a letter to *Nature*,[31] but he believed it was possible to reconstruct a

complete skull from what remained of it by applying the principle of symmetry. 'The right and left halves of the mammalian head and skull are approximately alike,' he continued, but Woodward's reconstruction showed a 'great discrepancy between the right and left halves', the extent of which was largely responsible for his low estimate of brain size; if the symmetry of the palaeontologist's reconstruction was restored by adding to the right side of the skull, then the cranial capacity was substantially increased.

In reply, Smith stressed the position of the middle line of the skull as the most important factor in reconstructing a skull, and attributed Keith's alleged misplacement of this feature to his having worked from casts of the Piltdown fragments without reference to the original specimens.[32] He made little mention of the asymmetry of the skull, though it is interesting to note that such a feature was fundamental to his subsequent theory that the left- or right-handedness of a person is shown in the relative sizes of certain parts of the left and right hemispheres of the brain.[33] A few weeks later Keith pointed out that Smith's remarks did less than justice to F. O. Barlow, who had made the casts, and even reflected badly upon the conduct of Woodward who, he wrote, had permitted 'the freest access to the specimens', even to those who like himself 'regarded the original reconstruction of the skull and brain cast as fundamentally erroneous'.[34]

Keith championed his views in *The Times* and challenged Grafton Elliot Smith's conclusion at a noisy meeting of the Royal Society where he claims to have earned the reputation of a brawler; but behind the public controversy he was, by his own admission,[35] beginning to have private doubts about the validity of the argument. The problem he saw was quite simple: the quality of the evidence. Can a skull *ever* be reconstructed accurately from just a few fragments of the original? Such skills obviously were essential to anyone aspiring to study the progress of human evolution because most of the evidence was contained in fragmentary fossil remains. Several authorities claimed to possess the skills needed to reassemble such fragments, but in the case of Piltdown Man, their differing results begged the question: is it possible to reconstruct a skull from such scant evidence?

To test his own skills, Keith arranged that some colleagues should cut fragments exactly duplicating the Piltdown remains from a modern skull in their possession, which he would then reconstruct according to his anatomical principles and afterwards compare with a cast of the original. The results were close enough to restore Keith's confidence in his skills and re-confirm his belief that Piltdown Man had possessed a large brain; the experiment was described at a meeting of the Royal Anthropological Institute and published accordingly.[36] Nevertheless, the reconstruction was wrong in one important respect: Keith failed to reproduce the proper form of the forehead, of which there was almost no evidence at all among the Piltdown remains.

While these deliberations concerning the form and size of the Piltdown skull were exercising the skills of the experts in London, Charles Dawson continued the search for more remains. The gravel pit having been worked out, he wandered further afield, examining newly ploughed land and heaps of stones raked from the fields. His endeavours were attended by extraordinary good fortune. Sometime before 20 January 1915, in a field about two miles from the site of the original discovery, Dawson found a fragment of fossil bone which, he was certain, had belonged to a second Piltdown Man. The fragment was a piece of the forehead, retaining a portion of the eyebrow ridge and the root of the nose. In July 1915 he found a molar tooth at the same site; and on another occasion a piece of the back of the skull.

Unhappily, Dawson became seriously ill with anaemia in the autumn of 1915. The condition worsened and turned to septicaemia, of which he died in August 1916. His last discoveries were presented before the Geological Society by Arthur Smith Woodward in February 1917, where it was concluded that the new evidence must support the contention that *Eoanthropus dawsoni* was a definite and distinct form of early human, as originally supposed, for, as Woodward pointed out, the occurrence of the same type of bone with the same type of molars in two separate localities must add to the probability that they belonged to one and the same species.[37] The frontal bone revealed the form of only a small area of the interior surface, and one devoid of obtrusive features, but nonetheless Grafton Elliot Smith found that its evidence corroborated his opinion that the Piltdown skull presented features 'more distinctly primitive and ape-like than those of any other member of the human family at present available for examination'.[38]

Arthur Keith attended the meeting too, and in the ensuing discussion effectively abandoned his opposition to the specimen. He never accepted the small brain Smith Woodward postulated, but he succumbed to the persuasive logic of the amazing discoveries and their presentation. The new Piltdown finds 'established beyond any doubt that *Eoanthropus* was a very clearly differentiated type of being', Keith said; adding that the frontal bone was particularly valuable because it cleared up any doubt as to the contour of the forehead.[39]

The triumvirate of British palaeoanthropological science was now united in believing that the Piltdown remains represented the earliest known ancestor of *Homo sapiens*, a unique link between humans and the ape-like creatures from which they had evolved. And doubtless their knighthoods (Sir Arthur Keith 1921; Sir Arthur Smith Woodward 1924; Sir Grafton Elliot Smith 1934) were bestowed with an element of patriotic pride for their having shown that the ancestor of *Homo sapiens* was an Englishman.

But while Piltdown Man bolstered English pride, he was still under attack. And the attacks were concerned not simply with the size of the skull, but with the more fundamental question of whether or not the jaw and skull belonged together. Arthur Smith Woodward, it will be remembered, had drawn attention to this question when the remains were first presented to science; and, at that same meeting, David Waterston, professor of anatomy at King's College, had remarked that it was very difficult to believe that the two specimens could have come from the same individual. Later Waterston reiterated his opinion; in a letter to *Nature* he wrote: 'it seems to me to be as inconsequent to refer the mandible and the cranium to the same individual as it would be to articulate a chimpanzee foot with the bones of an essentially human thigh and leg'.[40]

Similar views were voiced elsewhere. In France, Marcellin Boule approached 'the paradoxical association of an essentially human skull with an essentially simian jaw' with the question: 'Is *Eoanthropus* an Artificial and Composite Creature?' Boule considered the evidence and concluded that Piltdown Man was at least composite (if not artificial). The jaw had come from a chimpanzee, he said, and the skull was human but had belonged to a race quite distinct from the Neanderthals and closely related to the ancestry of modern humans.[41] Objections to the paradoxical association of ape jaw and human skull were also raised in Italy and Germany, but the most serious consideration of the issue came from America.

At the Smithsonian Institution in Washington DC, the mammalogist Gerrit Miller (1869–1956) compared casts of the Piltdown fossils with the corresponding parts of twenty-two chimpanzees, twenty-three gorillas, seventy-five orangutans and a series of human skulls, concluding that 'a single individual cannot be supposed to have carried this jaw and skull' without assuming 'the existence of a primate combining brain-case and nasal bones possessing the exact characters of a genus belonging to one family, with a mandible, two lower molars, and an upper canine possessing the exact characters of another' without any blending of their distinctive characteristics. Miller concluded that the remains must represent two individuals despite the amazing coincidence of their discovery in such close proximity, and created a completely new species of chimpanzee (*Pan vetus*) to accommodate the peculiarities of the Piltdown jaw.[42]

Miller's study was a detailed piece of work, and thorough enough to convince America's leading palaeontologists, anthropologists, and anatomists that the English had made a serious mistake—even though several of them had previously supported the contention that jaw and skull belonged together. George Grant MacCurdy from the Yale Peabody Museum recanted in the pages of *Science*: 'The prehistoric archaeologist sometimes uncovers strange bedfellows', he wrote '...Nature has set many a trap for the scientist; but here at Piltdown she outdid herself in the concatenation of pitfalls left behind.'[43]

Miller and his colleagues had expected the English reaction to be less than welcoming, but were surprised when none at all was forthcoming. Woodward was simply 'not inclined to reply' they learned from an inside source at the Natural History Museum, while the man to whom Miller wrote directly asking for a response, Museum zoologist William P. Pycraft, at first excused himself as about to leave 'for a much needed holiday', and in a reply written many months later implied that Miller's study was misconceived and poorly carried out. Miller has endeavoured throughout, he concluded, 'to confirm a preconceived theory; a course of action which has unfortunately warped his judgement and sense of proportion...'[44]

If anyone deserved to be accused of allowing preconceptions to rule over facts, it was of course the English. The anatomical evidence was indisputable. If the jaw and skull had been discovered in separate excavations no expert would have dreamt of suggesting they belonged to the same species, but at Piltdown the scientific evidence of anatomy collapsed against the circumstantial evidence of palaeontology. The remains had lain within feet of each other on the same geological level (or so it was said) and therefore *must* belong together; and the discovery of matching remains some distance away supported the conclusion.

FIGURE 7.3 The Piltdown canine and an *Illustrated London News* illustration of Dawson (left) and Smith Woodward at the Piltdown site.

Right Lower Canine of
Eoanthropus
.... dawsoni, A.S.W.
Form............yel.

Loc.y P............................ssex.
...........................Soc.
Des.y & fig............................igs. 2, 3
vol. 70 (1914), p. 8/1
Presented by
Charles Dawson, Esq.
Sept. 1915.   E.611
Brit. Mus. Geol. Dept.................

As Grafton Elliot Smith wrote: there was no reason to assume 'that Nature had played the amazing trick of depositing in the same bed of gravel the brain-case (*without* the jaw) of a hitherto unknown type of early Pleistocene Man displaying unique, simian traits, alongside the jaw (*without* the brain-case) of an equally unknown Pleistocene Ape displaying human traits unknown in any Ape'.[45] Rational minds found it much more likely that jaw and skull belonged together—especially since the creature thus formed so closely resembled the form that many authorities believed must have existed at that stage of human evolution.

In 1922 Smith, in conjunction with a colleague, made another reconstruction of the skull, supplementing those by Keith and Woodward. The cranial capacity was 1200 cubic centimetres, its form was more in keeping with the structure of the jaw and Marcellin Boule, for example, found Smith's contribution persuasive. The new facts should eliminate or at least lessen the 'anatomical paradox', he wrote, expressing the view that the balance of the argument now inclined more towards Woodward's interpretation. Boule was glad of this, he said, for he esteemed 'both the knowledge and the personal attributes of this scientist'.[46] Another sceptic, Henry Fairfield Osborn, President of the American Museum of Natural History, spent two hours after church examining the Piltdown remains at the invitation of Woodward. He concluded that 'paradoxical as it had appeared to the sceptical comparative anatomists, the chinless Piltdown jaw, shaped exactly like that of a chimpanzee…does belong with the Piltdown skull, with its relatively high, well-formed forehead and relatively capacious brain case.'[47]

There can be no doubt that the character and prestige of Arthur Smith Woodward were very largely responsible for the degree of acceptance that Piltdown Man achieved. His pronouncements on the fossils constituted a very small part of his work, but they carried the weight of authority. Arthur Keith remarked that Woodward liked to set a puzzling specimen on a table where the light from a window caught it at all hours of the day, so that as he passed and repassed it in the course of his work, a chance glance might reveal aspects he had not seen before and the significance of the fossil would gradually become clear. The Piltdown specimens were afforded this treatment,[48] so we must assume the palaeontologist was satisfied with what he saw.

Although expert opinion differed on the provenance and anatomical compatibility of Piltdown Man, there was unanimous agreement on a point which would have a most pervasive effect, particularly in respect of the beliefs and predispositions that were presented to a generation of anthropology students. The experts may have disputed the association of the Piltdown jaw and skull, they may have argued about the absolute size of the brain, but of one thing they were all certain: the Piltdown remains proved that the human ancestor had already developed a remarkably large brain by the beginning of the Pleistocene. The implications of this were very important: first, a brain so large at that time must have begun its development long before, which meant the human line must be very ancient indeed; and second, since the Piltdown remains of this 'true man' were older (as it was believed) than the Java and Neanderthal fossils, they firmly consigned those 'brutish' creatures to the status of 'aberrant offshoots', evolutionary experiments that led to extinction—cousins of mankind perhaps, but not ancestors.

Thus Piltdown Man contributed to a consensus view in the 1920s and 1930s which led to the neglect of some significant discoveries because they did not conform with accepted beliefs, while others, less accurately founded, were welcomed because they conformed only too well. Regardless of the continuing controversy over their details, the Piltdown remains had to be taken into account in every paper on the subject of human evolution, and were a measure against which subsequent discoveries had to be compared. This Piltdown effect, as it might be called, is well demonstrated in the work of Louis Leakey (1903–72), who studied anthropology at Cambridge during the 1920s and was an admiring disciple of Arthur Keith.

In 1934 Leakey published a popular book called *Adam's Ancestors*. Here, he supported Keith's appraisal of the Galley Hill remains and described Piltdown Man as a good candidate for the ancestry of our species. 'The Piltdown skull is probably very much more nearly related to *Homo sapiens* than to any other yet known type,' Leakey wrote, and would have granted the specimen full ancestral status if it had been 'vastly more ancient' than the Kanam mandible he had recently found in East Africa and which, he believed, must represent the oldest ancestor of modern humans.[49]

We have concentrated so far on the anatomists' and palaeontologists' views of Piltdown Man, but a third approach was available to science: geology, and it was from this direction that resolution of the conundrum would eventually emerge. Charles Dawson had said that the remains were found in a gravel bed lying about eighty feet above the level of the River Ouse. This implied an antiquity not much less than that of other river terraces in Britain and Europe; indeed, on the evidence of the extinct fauna they were said to contain, the Piltdown grav-els could hardly have been younger. Thereafter Dawson's estimate was repeated as fact by other authorities and, in particular, gained considerable respect from the support of W. J. Sollas, Professor of Geology at Oxford—who even improved upon the Dawson estimate.

In his book, *Ancient Hunters* (1924), Sollas converted eighty feet to twenty-five metres, bracketed twenty-five with thirty and thus correlated the Piltdown grav-els with those lying on terraces thirty metres above other rivers (the Thames for instance), concluding that the Piltdown remains must, therefore, date from the early Pleistocene. Thereafter, Sollas's assessment became the most authorita-tive reference on the geology and age of the Piltdown deposits. 'Thirty metres' was frequently converted to 'one hundred feet' and in turn offered to support a contention that the fossils might be even older than originally thought, perhaps even of Pliocene age—though the only Pliocene deposits known from that part of England were of marine origin and above the five-hundred-foot contour. All of which undoubtedly helped to obscure the fact that Dawson's original estimate was based on an erroneous assumption.

Dawson had claimed the Piltdown gravels were part of a plateau lying above the one-hundred-foot contour line, and he had calculated their height in rela-tion to that feature. But the gravels were actually part of a larger, well-defined terrace which maintained a constant height of fifty feet above the River Ouse throughout its extent. The portion in which the fossils were found is no excep-tion, as was clearly revealed on the six inch to one mile Ordnance Survey map of the district published in 1911. If this had been noted in 1913, and the stratigra-phy of the area accurately ascertained, it would have seemed more correct to correlate the Piltdown gravels with the fifty-foot terraces of the River Thames rather than with anything older, in which case the Piltdown fossils could only have been of Late, not Early Pleistocene. Had this been pointed out, interest in the remains probably would have evaporated very quickly—the fossils might have seemed odd and anomalous, but no one could have claimed any great antiquity for them, especially since Smith Woodward had always said that the skull was the same age as the deposit in which it had been found.

But the error was not noted in 1913; and it drew no comment in 1926 when a map giving the correct elevation appeared in a Geological Survey publication with text repeating Dawson's estimate.[50] In fact, the error and its significance was first mentioned only in 1935, when the attributes of the Piltdown skull seemed difficult to reconcile with those of the skull found at Swanscombe. The Swanscombe specimen came from gravels of the one-hundred-foot terrace of the River Thames itself, and when the problem of its correlation with the Pilt-down remains arose at a meeting of the British Association at Norwich, Kenneth Oakley, a geologist at the British Museum, challenged Sollas's assertion that the Piltdown gravels were part of the thirty-metre terrace. He drew attention to the 1926 map of the area and its author's observation that the deposits more satis-factorily corresponded with those of the fifty-foot terrace.

The Swanscombe remains were found by Alvan T. Marston, a dentist with an interest in fossils, in a gravel pit not far from the site of the Galley Hill discovery. They comprised the rear half of a skull; there was no clue whatsoever to the form of the face, the jaw, or the forehead. The cranial capacity was estimated to be 1325 cubic centimetres and comparative anatomists could find little to distinguish the specimen from *Homo sapiens*. Yet the Swanscombe skull had come from deposits no younger than those at Piltdown, and the Piltdown skull was held to be so old and so distinct from *Homo sapiens* as to merit the creation of a new genus, *Eoan-thropus*. Clearly something was amiss.

The geology at Swanscombe was well documented, and the Swanscombe skull's affinities were well defined, so Marston concluded that the fault must lie with the Piltdown specimen. The jaw must have belonged to an ape, he said, and the skull must have belonged to a human more recent than even the Swans-combe remains—whatever the circumstances of the discovery. Marston sum-marized the problem in 1937:

> that the Swanscombe skull had to be considered in its relations to the Piltdown was inevitable, and once this was embarked upon the gross inconsistencies of the large-brained, Pliocene, ape-jawed, Eolithic medley became apparent. The relegation of the Piltdown skull to a later date will remove the disharmony which has occasioned so much difficulty for those who have tried to describe it as an early Pleistocene type.[51]

By the 1930s, fossil evidence from other parts of the world was beginning to suggest that the brain had not led the way in the evolution of mankind. Fossils of no less antiquity than was proposed for Piltdown Man revealed distinctly man-like jaws and teeth, while the brain remained relatively small, so that it became increasingly difficult to reconcile the large brain and ape-like jaw of Piltdown Man with a reasonable interpretation of hominid evolution as suggested by the new evidence. Scientific papers repeatedly drew attention to the differences rather than the similarities between Piltdown and the new fossils. The triumvirate of British anthropology (they became two with the death of Grafton Elliot Smith in 1937) remained convinced of the specimen's validity, and regarded the new evidence as proof of the theory that two lines (at least) of hominid evolution had once coexisted, the surviving line represented by modern man, Piltdown, and little else, while all the new discoveries represented lines that had led to extinction. To other authorities, however, Piltdown simply did not fit; the specimen was a chimera, a once-intriguing riddle about which there seemed little more to be said.

But the truth—if discernible at all—must be contained in the evidence. The question was: could it ever be extracted? Oakley actually had begun to answer this question in 1935 when he had referred to the observation that Dawson had estimated the height of the Piltdown gravels incorrectly. The implications of Dawson's error were clear: the age of Piltdown Man was derived solely from its association with extinct fauna of the early Pleistocene found in the same pit; but if the deposits were younger than had been claimed, then the older fossils must have come from somewhere else and there could be no compelling reason to believe that *all* the Piltdown fossils were of equal antiquity. The extinct fauna was indisputably older than the deposit, but Piltdown Man could be the same age or even younger. Was there some way of determining whether or not bones found close together in a single deposit are actually the same age? This question became a subject of Kenneth Oakley's research programme after the war, and although the solution of the Piltdown riddle was not his specific interest, that was an important result of his endeavours.

Fossils absorb fluorine from the soil in which they are buried, and Oakley's research explored the observation that the amount of fluorine in a fossil steadily increases with time and therefore might give some indication of its geological age. The phenomenon had been noted by J. Middleton in 1844, who remarked that the 'accumulation of fluorine seems to involve the element of time, so interesting to geological investigations',[52] and attempted to establish a timescale based on fluorine content by which the absolute age of fossils could be determined.

Taking the quantity of fluorine in a bone of an ancient Greek known to be 2,000 years old as his standard, Middleton dated fossils from the Siwalik Hill in Pakistan (then India) at 7,700 years, and an extinct pachyderm at 24,200 years—age estimates which even then must have seemed a trifle ungenerous. Furthermore, Middleton had overlooked the fact that, because the soil's fluorine content varies considerably from place to place, fossils found in different deposits are likely to have absorbed quite different amounts and therefore cannot be dated one against the other reliably on this basis.

Middleton's observations were not pursued, and the significance of fluorine in fossil bones slipped into obscurity until it was discovered anew by Adolf Carnot, a French mineralogist. In 1892 Carnot published tables showing the increasing amounts of fluorine in fossil bones from progressively more ancient deposits; the following year he reported on the fluorine contents of a fossil mammoth bone and a human bone from the same deposit—they were different, he said, and therefore the bones must be of different ages.[53] This observation was fundamental to the potential of fluorine content as a means of dating fossil bones. It could never provide an absolute timescale, such as Middleton had sought, but it could provide a useful relative scale and, furthermore, a means of assessing whether or not bones found together in a deposit had all been there for the same length of time. But even Carnot's work passed unnoticed; the principle of fluorine dating again slipped into obscurity, and there it remained for fifty years until it was rediscovered by Kenneth Oakley.

In 1943, while Oakley was assessing Britain's wartime phosphate resources, a colleague showed him Carnot's 1892 tables giving the fluorine content of fossil bones. Oakley realized that Carnot's work suggested a means of comparing the age of fossils within a single deposit, and for several years thereafter believed this primary observation on fluorine dating was his alone. Only after he had refined and tested his methods did he learn of Carnot's 1893 paper, and later still of Middleton's work.

The quantity of fluorine absorbed by a fossil is never large, even in the oldest bone, and measurement involves complicated chemical analysis. At the instigation of Oakley and the British Museum, preliminary trials were conducted by the Government Chemist during 1948 to establish the most satisfactory procedure, and the perfected fluorine dating method was used to assess the relative age of a fossil assemblage that same year. For this first ever test, Oakley and his colleague

M. F. A. Montagu selected the Galley Hill skeleton.[54] The results profoundly contradicted Arthur Keith's belief in the great antiquity of the specimen.

Briefly, Oakley and Montagu showed that the fossil fauna from the Middle Pleistocene gravels contained about two per cent fluorine, those from Upper Pleistocene deposits in the same sequence about one per cent, and the post-Pleistocene bones not more than 0.3 per cent. The Galley Hill skeleton (which had been found in the oldest gravels) contained only about 0.3 per cent fluorine. Therefore it matched the post-Pleistocene bones and could not have been older; the skeleton must have been of recent origin, entombed in the ancient deposits by man, not nature, despite Keith's assertions to the contrary. The antiquity of the Swanscombe skull, on the other hand, was confirmed by the fluorine test; the bones contained two per cent fluorine, perfectly matching the Middle Pleistocene fauna with which it was associated.

So the antiquity of Galley Hill Man was dismissed, and of Swanscombe Man confirmed; where did that leave Piltdown Man, with his combination of 'ancient' ape-like jaw and 'recent' large brain? In October 1948 Kenneth Oakley was authorized to apply his fluorine dating method to the Piltdown material, the Keeper of Geology at the British Museum having deemed it likely that the results might help resolve the riddle of its age and association. Every available bone and tooth from the assemblage was analysed, thirty-six specimens in all, including ten pieces of the *Eoanthropus* material, and six of the extinct fauna from which the Lower Pleistocene age of *Eoanthropus* had been derived. The fluorine content of the entire assemblage ranged from a minimum of less than 0.1 per cent to a maximum of 3.1 per cent. The higher levels were found in the extinct fauna only, confirming their antiquity; while the remains of Piltdown Man contained an average of only 0.2 per cent, clearly showing that he was not as old as the Lower Pleistocene fauna with which he was supposed to have been associated. *Eoanthropus dawsoni*—Dawson's Dawn Man—was no older than *Homo sapiens* from Galley Hill, it seemed.

Oakley's results were published in March 1950.[55] 'That the figures scarcely provide any differentiation between *Eoanthropus* and the recent bones requires some explanation,' he remarked, but the deeper implication of his observation was not fully realized until three years later.

Meanwhile, Oakley had added another twist to the riddle. The combination of jaw and skull was puzzling enough when both were believed to be of great antiquity, but if both stemmed from the recent past further problems arose. The skull was reasonable enough, it matched the modern form. But what about the jaw? No one could have possessed such an ape-like form at so late a stage in human evolution. This might seem to have vindicated the contention that jaw and skull represented different individuals, but this in itself presented another problem: if the jaw did not belong to the skull, obviously it came from somewhere else. But where? The great apes do not occur in the fossil record of Britain and Europe, and are highly unlikely to have inhabited the region during the upheavals of the Ice Age. So Oakley provided no comfort for either side of the Piltdown controversy.

With the ageing and passing of its protagonists, the controversy had lost much of its impetus by 1950. Although Piltdown Man so completely contradicted the evidence of the small-brained hominid fossils with human-like jaws subsequently found in Africa and the Far East, most anthropologists were content to consign the riddle to a 'suspense account' and await clarification, rather than actively search for it.

But one evening towards the end of July 1953 a chance remark by Kenneth Oakley prompted Joseph Weiner, an anatomist working with Le Gros Clark at Oxford, to ponder the problem again as he drove home. In the early hours of the morning he found the key to the riddle. If Piltdown Man was not as old as had been claimed, if the strange jaw with man-like features matched no apes living or extinct, if it belonged neither to the skull nor to the deposit in which the specimens were found, then all 'natural' explanations of the Piltdown phenomenon were eliminated. Which left only an 'unnatural' alternative, reasoned Weiner.[56] Could it be that the man-like features of the jaw were artificial, and the whole assemblage was deposited in the Piltdown gravels with the express intention of suggesting to its discoverers that a human ancestor in the early Pleistocene had possessed an ape-like jaw and a large brain?

The proposition seemed outrageous, but as Weiner weighed the evidence, the case for a deliberate hoax gained strength on several counts. That the discovery of the second Piltdown remains so precisely echoed the first considerably lessened the likelihood of either or both being an accident. The fact that the chin region and the articular knob were missing strongly suggested that these critical diagnostic features had been deliberately removed. The pieces of the puzzle began to fall into place.

Next day, Weiner examined the casts of the Piltdown remains in the collection of the Department of Anatomy at Oxford and discussed his theory with Le Gros Clark. Even on the casts, the wear of the molar teeth seemed more compatible with artificial abrasion than natural wear; and similarly on the canine, where artificial abrasion would also explain the apparent paradox—first noted by a dentist in 1916[57]—of so much wear on such an immature tooth.

Weiner and Le Gros Clark took their case to the British Museum, and during the autumn of 1953 the riddle of Piltdown Man was finally resolved—forty-one years after it had arisen. The teeth confirmed Weiner and Le Gros Clark's preliminary observations. Further fluorine testing revealed that the jaw was not only recent, but not long dead; the skull was slightly more ancient. The remains were all stained to match the Piltdown deposit, so too were the mammalian fossils with which they were associated. The hoax had been ingeniously planned, carefully carried out, and totally unsuspected.

When the news was released in November 1953 it excited comment from many quarters. In the House of Commons a motion was put forward proposing a lack of confidence in the trustees of the British Museum 'because of the tardiness of their discovery that the skull of the Piltdown Man is partially a fake'. The proposers were angry at the 'sycophantic servility' of the museum tradition which had itself been playing a hoax on the public with this 'so-called Missing Link', they said, but the motion aroused more laughter than serious debate: Speaker—'not sure how serious the motion is (laughter), but sure [we] have many other things to do besides examining the authenticity of a lot of old bones' (loud laughter). Lord Privy Seal—'the government had found so many skeletons to examine when they came into office that there had not yet been time to extend the researches into skulls' (laughter).[58]

A letter to *The Times* asked: 'Sir, May we now regard the Piltdown Man as the first human being to have false teeth ?'[59]

Piltdown Man had become a joke, but for science he remained a very serious matter. Those most affected by the forgery were aware that it could not have been simply a light-hearted practical joke, or hoax, that went too far. It had required knowledge, technical skill, planning, and ingenuity of Machiavellian proportions. The perpetrator, in effect, demonstrated that he (no female has yet been implicated) knew more about the sciences involved than the distinguished figures he deluded. As a columnist noted when the forgery was revealed, not only must he have been a well-trained, though misguided *anthropologist*, he was also a *geologist*, who could reconstruct clues so that his colleagues were foxed. He was an *anatomist* skilled in the bones of man and animals; a *dentist* who could make modern teeth look like prehistoric teeth; and a *chemist* who could take specimens and make them look genuinely ancient.[60]

Gerrit Miller had come closer to the truth than he could have known with a remark in his 1915 paper on the Piltdown fossils that was reiterated in a 1929 review entitled 'The controversy over human "missing links"':

> Deliberate malice could hardly have been more successful than the hazards of deposition and recovery in so breaking the Piltdown fossils and losing the most essential parts of the original skull as to allow free scope to individual judgement in fitting the pieces together…According to the different reconstructions the form of the cranium may be completely human in striking contrast to the apelike jaw, or it may have partially simian features which cause this contrast to become less.[61]

Deliberate malice. Perhaps that was exactly what Miller had concluded, but could not mention without proof. As author of the most thorough assessment of Piltdown and the claims made for its significance, Miller might have expected his objections to be taken seriously, and the implications investigated. After all, as Joseph Weiner would eventually note, once all natural explanations are eliminated, only the unnatural remain. But malice was unthinkable. Even a hint that it was suspected could have been enough to ensure that Miller's paper would not get the attention it deserved—especially if the perpetrator was among the authors whose interpretations it criticized.

No. Science depends on trust. As veteran palaeoanthropologist Phillip Tobias has written in a brief introduction to the Piltdown affair, 'the assumption of truthfulness in science is the very *leitmotif*, almost the religion, of the scientist. We may think our colleagues have been mistaken, foolish, ill-advised, pigheaded or simple-minded, but the very last thing we tend to suspect them of is dishonesty.'[62]

But here was a blatant case of dishonesty, and an inside job at that—for no amateur could have carried it off so successfully. So who was responsible? It is at this point that the Piltdown affair tumbles into the realm of the popular detective novel. And it is a wonderful story, a whodunit with a prehistoric corpse and a colourful collection of wing-collared suspects from the upper reaches of society. At least twenty-five men have been implicated, including Charles Dawson, all three of the triumvirate, and even the creator of Sherlock Holmes, Sir Arthur Conan Doyle.

As in all good detective stories, there is a case to be made against every suspect, but not enough evidence to prove any of them guilty beyond reasonable doubt. Most of the outsiders can be cleared on the grounds of inadequate technical knowledge, lack of opportunity or motive—though the Conan Doyle case is intriguing. He lived just eight miles from Piltdown and regularly played golf near the site. Dawson found the first scraps of Piltdown Man just around the time that Conan Doyle was writing his novel, *The Lost World*, which contains numerous alleged allusions to Piltdown, including cryptic references to local road maps and monkey puzzle trees which, it so happens, grew close to the site.[63]

And the insiders? Well, they were busy men, and high profile. Did they have the time and the nerve to risk their reputations and future prospects on a complex hoax that would certainly bring disaster if it went wrong? And what was to be gained? On balance, it seems unlikely that Arthur Keith could have been responsible—even though the fact that he burned all his notes and correspondence on the subject of Piltdown is suspicious. And would Arthur Smith Woodward have returned to dig at Piltdown every summer except one for more than twenty years after Dawson's death, hoping to find more pieces of the puzzle, if he had put them there in the first place? The case against Grafton Elliot Smith is sustained principally by his brash and dogmatic manner. Charles Dawson has rather more to answer for.

Indeed, circumstantial evidence makes Dawson the most obvious culprit— and his case is not helped by revelations suggesting that he was not the straightforward solicitor and honest amateur scientist he portrayed himself to be. A biography alleges that he was involved in a series of actual or probable forgeries, at least one suspect property deal, and gross plagiarism of the work of others. But Dawson is often excused on the grounds that he is just *too* obvious and had

---

FIGURE 7.4 Reconstructed skull of Piltdown Man. The brown pieces represent the fragments found at Piltdown; the remainder is plaster.

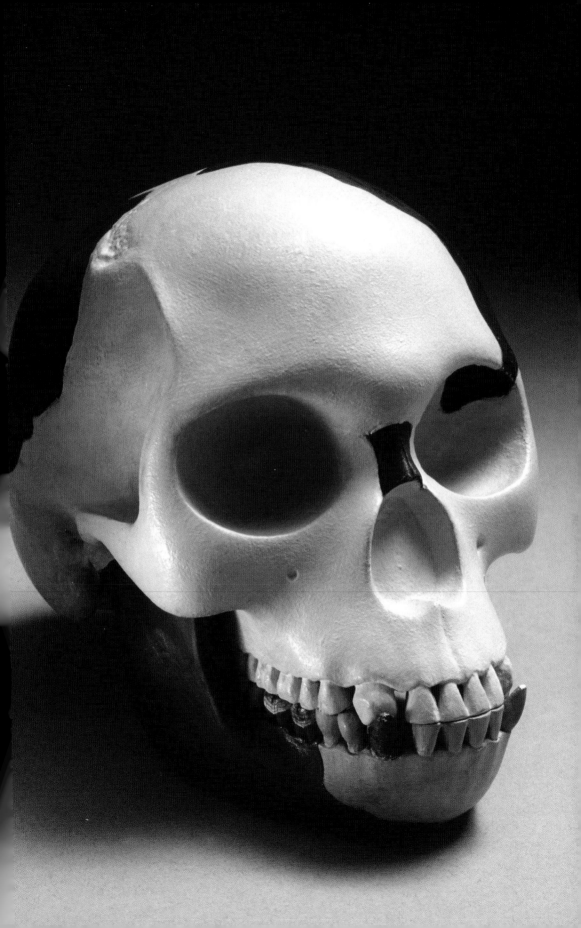

too much to lose, given his profession and his ambitions of election to the Royal Society and perhaps even a knighthood. In any case, the accusatory spotlight moved off Charles Dawson in 1996 and focused on Martin Hinton (1883–1961), who had worked in the Geology and Zoology departments of the Natural History Museum throughout the Piltdown affair.

As palaeontologist Brian Gardiner reported in his Presidential Address to the Linnaean Society that year, the case against Hinton comes from a trunk stored in an attic in the west tower of the Museum. A departmental assistant had been given the unenviable task of cleaning out the long-neglected attic. In the trunk, under a pile of bank statements and boxes filled with sundry palaeontological specimens, right at the bottom, he found a set of ten mammalian bones and teeth stained chocolate brown, just like the Piltdown material.[64]

Subsequently, chemical analysis showed that the Piltdown bones had been stained in exactly the same manner as Hinton's, while biographical investigation revealed that Hinton had published (in 1899, at the age of 16) a paper showing that fossils in river gravels would be impregnated with iron and manganese oxides, staining them a characteristic chocolate-brown colour. Furthermore, Hinton had been an active member of Benjamin Harrison's Ightham Circle, whose members devoted much of their leisure time to tramping across the Downs in search of the eoliths that would prove their belief in the distant antiquity of mankind.[65] In 1954 he had written what could be read as an admission of some involvement to the then Director of the Natural History Museum, Gavin de Beer:

> The temptation to invent such a 'discovery' of an ape-like man associated with late Pliocene Mammals in a Wealden gravel might well have proved irresistible to some unbalanced member of old Ben Harrison's circle at Ightham. He and his friends (of whom I was one) were always talking of the possibility of finding a late Pliocene deposit in the Weald...I spent the long vacation of 1902 and the Easter and part of the long vacation of 1906 in searching the water partings in the Weald near Ightham...But I was not successful; at least I found nothing that would give any clear evidence of such remote antiquity. Old Ben and I had many a walk to likely spots ...[66]

The case against Hinton is strong. After all, the condition of the bones in the trunk implies that he was experimenting on how to fake fossils. But was it to make forgeries, or to show how Piltdown was done? And what about motive? Hinton could have made the forgery to defame Woodward, with whom he did not always get along. But, although he told a BBC producer in 1954 that the perpetrator had been working at the Natural History Museum at the time of the hoax, he also refused to name the man because he was still alive[67]—which excludes Arthur Smith Woodward, who died in 1944. So, was Hinton referring to himself? We do not know. Martin Hinton died in 1961, without leaving any further clues—at least, none has been found yet. The story will run and run...

The inconclusive nature of the Piltdown affair virtually guarantees that its fascination will endure far longer than if it had been an open and shut case—simply because a complex unsolved mystery leaves plenty to think about after the last page has been turned. But while the story continues to entertain, it is important that its relevance to palaeoanthropology is not allowed to fade into the past as just a bizarre aberration. Piltdown exposes a fundamental and persistent problem of the science: the fossil evidence of human evolution rarely offers just one clear interpretation. At the same time, the hoax emphasizes two vital points: first, accurate geological and stratigraphical determinations are essential. And second, when preconception is so clearly defined, so straightforwardly reproduced, so enthusiastically welcomed, and so long accommodated as in the case of Piltdown Man, palaeoanthropology reveals a disturbing predisposition towards belief before investigation—as perhaps the hoaxer was eager to demonstrate.

CHAPTER EIGHT

Australopithecus africanus (1925)

RAFTON ELLIOT Smith's contribution to the Piltdown affair was largely inspired by his belief that the imprint of the brain's fissures and convolutions on the interior of a fossil skull permitted some comparative assessment of the owner's intellectual development. His researches had suggested to him that the significant differences in the brain development of apes and humans could be recognized on casts taken from the interior of their skulls; so, if the form of the ape's 'primitive' brain, and of the human 'evolved' brain was known, Smith reasoned that it should be possible to define and recognize the intermediate stages on casts taken from the fossil skulls.

The idea was not universally accepted by any means, but among those with whom it found favour was Raymond Dart, a fellow Australian and senior demonstrator in anatomy at University College London, under Smith, from 1919 to 1922 while the latter was still busy with the problems of the Piltdown reconstruction. The evolution of the brain and the nervous system was Dart's own special interest, which Elliot Smith helped to supplement with an interest in human evolution so that Dart was especially well-equipped to recognize the significance of certain hominid fossils that came his way a few years later.

Raymond Dart (1893–1988) was born in a suburb of Brisbane, one of nine children. He graduated from medical school in 1917, served with the Medical Corps in France during the final years of the First World War and, after a spell in London, was appointed Professor of Anatomy at the Witwatersrand University, Johannesburg, in 1922—largely at the instigation of Grafton Elliot Smith and Arthur Keith.

Many might have found it flattering to be appointed a full professor at the age of 29 but, all in all, the Witwatersrand Medical School in 1922 was not the most attractive proposition for a young anatomist with interests in neurological research and human evolution. Johannesburg was still a pioneer town of tin-roofed houses and impermanent appearance. Barely fifty years old, founded on a gold-rush by the kind of people such events attract, the city was struggling to establish identity and respectability. The University had received its charter only three years before and the Chair of Anatomy was vacant only because its incumbent had been forced to resign in disgrace following his divorce. Dart was hardly a welcome replacement. He was an Australian, and the University Board did not approve of Australians much more than it approved of divorce. The Principal himself wrote expressing regret that an Australian was appointed, but realized the choice was limited.

The medical school awaiting the new professor was an unprepossessing place—a double-storeyed building standing among weeds behind an old garrison wall. The anatomy department comprised just three or four small rooms and a dissecting hall whose walls bore signs of its customary use by students for practising tennis (and a confidant has disclosed that the balls were unorthodox and the bats similarly a by-product of the anatomy course). The department was devoid of electricity, water, or gas and, apart from a few scraps of cadavers remaining from the previous course, almost entirely lacking in essential facilities. No library, no museum, no specimens, an abysmal lack of equipment. 'There wasn't a bloody thing,' Dart complained, 'except what I happened to carry out with me from England.'[1] He had arrived feeling more like an exile than an academic elevated to a professorship and for the greater part of the first two years in Johannesburg he was a very unhappy man.

The events which changed the course of Dart's life and introduced an important new dimension to the study of fossil man began in the early part of 1924 when Dart's sole female student, Josephine Salmons, noticed a fossil baboon skull gracing the mantelpiece of a friend's living room. She told the professor of it and he, then unaware of any fossil primates from anywhere south of the Fayoum deposits in Egypt, asked her to borrow the specimen if she could and bring it to him for examination. The skull was indeed that of a baboon, Dart confirmed the next day, possibly of a new and primitive species. It had been found in the course of lime-quarrying operations near a place called Taung, one among many such items discovered there (in fact, unbeknown to Dart, a new species of fossil baboon had already been reported from the deposit by a government geologist).[2] Dart wanted more specimens if they were available, and immediately sought the advice of R. B. Young, a colleague in the university's geology department. Young knew the Taung quarry and, as it happened, was due to visit the area. He agreed to look for primate fossils while he was there and to ask the quarry managers to preserve any that might be discovered.

The Taung fossils had been preserved in cave deposits that typically occur along valleys cut through the dolomitic rock of South Africa's inland plateau. These deposits are completely different to those in which the Neanderthals and early humans had been found in Europe; they are very much older, and not necessarily caves that had been occupied by the creatures whose bones were found in them. So how were the South African cave deposits formed, and how did fossils accumulate in them?

Dolomite is a limestone, in which caverns had formed when the water table of the region was so high that it covered the rock entirely. The water percolated through cracks in the rock, leaching away the soluble calcium salts and thus carving out caves and tunnels. As the rivers cut valleys through the dolomite, the water table dropped with the level of the surface water. At last the caves and tunnels were left high and dry. Rain continued to percolate through rock fissures, of course, and this water leached out the soluble calcium salts as before. But instead of being washed away, these substances now accumulated within the cave system—in the form of stalagmites and stalactites.

Eventually this slow but inexorable process of deposition could fill entire caves, but frequently a rockfall or erosion would open them to the surface before that happened; then external debris would fall in and mingle with the purer chemical deposition; animals could enter or perhaps fall in and die there, leaving their bones to fossilize among the accumulating debris as the caves gradually filled. It was a continuous process of erosion and deposition that over millions of years has left the Dolomite plateau of South Africa dotted with caves and cave deposits containing fossils.[3]

Stalagmites and stalactites and such primary cave deposits consist of pure lime. Lime is an important constituent of cement and, as the South African building boom gathered momentum after the First World War, every workable deposit in the country became a valuable resource. The purer the better of course, but even those where the pure lime was surrounded and interfingered by a secondary deposit were worth exploiting. The secondary deposits comprised the earth and debris that had fallen in once the cave had opened to the surface; they were mixed with varying proportions of lime and compacted to rock hardness. The fossils lay within this rock, and were revealed as the lime-workers blasted and quarried the deposits. The Taung quarry was an extensive operation, and it is certain that large quantities of fossil bone were shovelled into the limekilns before Dart's pronouncements on a fossil found there in 1924 brought worldwide attention to the significance of the deposits.

A 1974 publication commemorating the fiftieth anniversary of the discovery,[4] reports that Young first saw the fossil in question on the desk of the quarry manager where it served as a paperweight, having been brought into the office sometime before by a workman convinced he had found the fossilized remains of a bushman. In an account given to newspapers at the time, however, Young himself says that he found it on arriving at the Taung quarry just after blasting operations had taken place. 'One large piece of rock had apparently been split in two,' he told reporters, 'embedded in the one fragment was the "Missing Link" fossil, the face itself hidden in the rock. The brain portion was found quite loose, but it fitted exactly into position in the skull, each fracture corresponding.' He packed the find carefully and after returning to Johannesburg, handed it to Dart.[5]

In his popular book *Adventures with the Missing Link*, Dart gave yet another version of the fossil's discovery. Two large boxes of rocks, mailed to him from the Taung lime-works on Young's instructions, arrived while he was donning white tie and tails for a wedding to be held at his house. With collar unfixed, the guests arriving and the groom waiting, he hurriedly wrenched open the boxes. The contents of the first were disappointing, but in the second he immediately recognized a fossil brain cast with distinctly hominid features and, further ransacking the boxes, also found the back of the forehead and face into which the cast fitted. He recalled the moment:

I stood in the shade holding the brain as greedily as any miser hugs his gold, my mind racing ahead. Here, I was certain, was one of the most significant finds ever made in the history of anthropology. Darwin's largely discredited theory that man's early progenitors probably lived in Africa came back to me. Was I to be the instrument by which his 'missing link' was found? These pleasant daydreams were interrupted by the bridegroom himself tugging at my sleeve. 'My God, Ray,' he said, striving to keep the nervous urgency out of his voice, "You've got to finish dressing immediately—or I'll have to find another best man. The bridal car should be here any moment."[6]

A fossil brain cast, or more correctly, an endocranial cast, is formed when the cranial cavity of the dead creature, lying undisturbed in a cave, fills with debris— for instance, bat droppings, sand, lime—which subsequently fossilizes along with the bone. In the case of the Taung specimen, only a little more than half the skull cavity was filled, giving a cast of the right side only and a flat surface on the left, covered with glistening white crystals. Endocranial casts are extremely rare. Five are known from South Africa; the Taung specimen was the first ever to be recognized. That it was formed in the first place is remarkable enough; that it was recovered in the course of a mining operation which, by its very nature, is destructive, is even more remarkable—but, following such a fortuitous chain of circumstances, that it should have found its way into the hands of one of the three or four men in the entire world capable of recognizing its significance, is most remarkable of all. And there was more to come.

In the course of his pioneering work on the brain and endocranial casts, Dart's professor at University College, Grafton Elliot Smith, had identified the lunate sulcus, (a fissure between two convolutions towards the rear of the brain) and suggested that the gap between the lunate and the parallel sulcus (another fissure close by), is an important indication of evolutionary development. In apes the sulci are close together, in humans they are farther apart. Dart, of course, was familiar with this work and that first glance at the Taung endocranial cast told him that the gap between its lunate and parallel sulci was about three times greater than in the living apes. In terms of cranial capacity, the cast was large for an ape, but still far smaller than then thought possible for an ancestral hominid,

FIGURE 8.1 The original Taung fossil, type specimen of *Australopithecus africanus.*

thirty years before Piltdown was debunked. Even so, Dart felt that 'by the sheer-est good luck', the fossil had brought him 'the opportunity to provide what would probably be the ultimate answer in the comparatively modern study of the evolution of man'.[7]

Seventy-three days later (during which Dart worked in his spare time with a variety of tools, including his wife's knitting needles, sharpened for the fine work), the matrix was removed from the rock into which the cast fitted, and the face of the Taung specimen exposed. There were no great eyebrow ridges, nor did the jaws jut forward, as in the apes. The brain had not belonged to a large adult ape, it was revealed, but to an infant with rounded forehead, a full set of milk teeth and the first molars just emerging.

The Taung fossil had reached Dart in mid-October; by Christmas he had uncovered most of its detail; by mid-January he had written a preliminary paper on the discovery and posted it, with photographs, to *Nature* in London. During this period Dart's resources were limited. He had worked on the fossil entirely alone, there were no colleagues with whom to discuss it; no library to provide references, or museum specimens with which to compare it. His most useful aid had been a book he had brought from England which had some drawings of infant chimpanzee and gorilla skulls. In comparing these drawings with the Taung specimen, however, Dart saw enough to convince him that the fossil dif-fered from both the chimpanzee and the gorilla as much as they differed from each other. In the *Nature* paper, Dart drew some precocious conclusions from his unavoidably limited observations.[8]

The Taung specimen represented a creature that was advanced beyond the apes in two distinctly human characteristics, he said: its teeth were more human than ape-like and the 'improved quality' of its brain indicated that the creature could appre-ciate colour, weight, and form; it knew the significance of sounds and had already passed important milestones along the road towards the acquisition of articulate speech, he claimed. Furthermore, the forward position of the foramen magnum (the hole in the base of the skull through which the spinal cord passes) suggested to Dart that the Taung skull must have balanced on the top of the vertebral column in a manner approximating that of modern humans. Therefore, the creature had walked upright, he concluded, with hands free to become manipulative organs and available for offence and defence—a proposal rendered all the more probable, Dart reasoned, by the absence of 'massive canines and hideous features'.

As regards the evolutionary pressures that may have given rise to this 'Missing Link', Dart pointed out that the creature had lived on the fringe of the Kalahari desert, two thousand miles from the easy picking of the tropical forests, at a time when, geologists proclaimed, the climate was no less harsh than in modern times. Compared with the luxuriant forests of the tropical belts, where 'nature was supplying with profligate and lavish hand an easy and sluggish solution, by adaptive specialization, of the problem of existence', Dart suggested that the relative scarcity of water and 'fierce and bitter mammalian competition' for food and with predators, made Southern Africa the perfect laboratory for sharpening the wits and quickening the intellect during the 'penultimate phase of human evolution'. Of the other candidates then proposed for human ancestry, Dart alluded to the chimpanzee-like features of the Piltdown jaw; and referred to Dubois's Java Man as 'a caricature of precocious hominid failure', an ape-like curiosity destined for extinction while the Taung specimen represented 'our troglodytic forefathers' intermediate between the apes and humans. He proposed a new zoological family to accommodate the phenomenon—the *Homo-simiadae*—and named the Taung child *Australopithecus africanus* as the first known genus and species of the group.

There can have been few instances, in any science, where somewhere so isolated has been presented with so important and unambiguous a piece of evidence—so new, so unlike anything found before as to seem incredible. The Missing Link? In Africa? The significant features that Dart had recognized in the Taung child, and their implication, should have been immediately obvious to any expert with his training and interests, but if it had turned up on the desk of the experts in Europe it almost certainly would have been squeezed into some existing category. Isolation, and a measure of academic belligerence emboldened Dart.

He has said that he prepared his preliminary report 'proudly' and with 'a sense of history'. When it was sent off to *Nature*, he fully expected some scepticism from the British scientific community, but hoped that he would be taken seriously at least. Considering the woefully inadequate facilities in Johannesburg, Dart had assembled a paper of commendable perspicacity. In some respects it tended more towards inspirational interpretation than cool scientific appraisal, and occasionally Dart lapsed into a florid style not normally encountered in *Nature*; nonetheless, the editors deemed the report important enough to merit immediate attention (no mean compliment in itself) and pre-publication review by four of Britain's most distinguished anthropologists: Arthur Keith, Arthur

Smith Woodward, Grafton Elliot Smith, and W. L. H. Duckworth—the triumvirate of the Piltdown affair and one other.

The reviewers received proofs of the report on 3 February 1925, but they hardly had time to collect their thoughts before Fleet Street descended upon them for comment on that morning's cables from Johannesburg announcing that the Missing Link had been found in South Africa by Professor Dart. The next day, and indeed for several days thereafter, the news occupied much space in the papers. Sir Arthur Keith endeavoured to instil a note of scientific calm with the comment that 'we have a rumour of this kind three or four times a year', but his efforts had little effect. 'Missing Link 5,000,000 years old', 'Ape-Man of African had commonsense', 'Missing Link that could speak', 'Birth of Mankind', 'Missing Link 500,000 years old',...ran headlines around the world above stories in which Dart expounded variously and at length upon the nature and talents of the ancestor he believed was represented by the fossil from Taung.

In the first days of his thirty-third year, Raymond Dart became a celebrity. He was inundated with press enquiries and congratulatory cables; publishers called to offer book contracts; General Smuts and the University Principal (who disliked Australians) both sent personal congratulations; then, on 14 February, the first serious scientific comment appeared, when *Nature* published the reports of the four experts they had asked to review the paper.[9] Although all four saw more immediate affinities with the apes than with humans, the reports were sympathetic. They all emphasized the difficulty of assessing a fossil—especially a juvenile fossil—from a preliminary report and a few photographs. To judge the claims Dart had made they needed more material, and looked forward to receiving full-size photographs, casts of the fossils, and the monograph Dart had promised. Of the four, Sir Arthur Smith Woodward was the least complimentary. He concluded his report with an expression of regret that Dart had chosen such a 'barbarous' combination of Latin and Greek in naming the specimen *Australopithecus africanus*.

The name *Australopithecus africanus* was intended to be descriptive. It means 'the southern ape of Africa' and its form follows the precedent set in 1922 by *Hesperopithecus*, the 'western ape' (see p. 215). Of course, *Australopithecus* is also

FIGURE 8.2 A page from Raymond Dart's personal album of newspaper reports of his discovery.

IS SEEN WITH A COLLECTION OF SKULLS. HE HAS THE TAUNGS SKULL IN HIS HAN... RIGHT SIDE IS A HUMAN SKULL AND ON THE OTHER THE SKULLS OF A CHIMPANZ... AND A BABOON.—(T. Brittain.)

4

AFRICAN BAPTIST.

March 25, 1925

... just been on a visit to the Anatomy ... of the Medical School, Johannes- ... the already world-famous Taungs ... fessor Dart's explanation of the ... es of the skull was extremely in- ... what struck us as being perhaps ... ant was the fact that Professor ... cally asserted that no one can ... olutionary theory without discard-

We agree with him. Bishop ... ady stated that the recent findings ... xplode the "Genesis Myth." ... the main thesis in Paul's argu- ... th Chapter of I. Corinthians, ... is dissertation upon the priority ... n to that of woman? There is ... s in evolution. We have not ... y of reconciling evolution with ... the Bible, whatever be our ... inspiration. The modern ... dges that he can give no ... asserts that the believer in ... no proof. Truly, the things ... from the wise and prudent ... babes. Material things ... roof and spiritual things ... the scientist will never ex- ... proof until he becomes as ...

Extract from
DAILY PROVINCE
VANCOUVER, B.C.
ate 22 FEB 1925

TAUNGS SKULL IS THAT OF MAN-APE

Photos Give British Scientists More Exact Idea of Discovery.

Are Unable to Find Trace of Canine Teeth of Apes.

In Many Respects Fossil Remains Greatly Resemble Human

Anthropologis...
Are Incline...
Dec...

(By Cable
(Copyright, 1925,
LONDON, Feb...
of the Taungs ...
London, giving ...
more exact ide...
of the fossil tha...
cabled descript...

Professor G. ...
ing to the Lond...
the cabled acco...
that the evide...
with the huma...
been more obv...
ally are. Yet...
definitely a ma...
man.

Suggesting ...
study of the ...
though the m...
unobtrusive th...
Smith proceed...

"It must no...
fossil ape is a...
only three or ...
at such a stag...
is a much cl... ...keness of apes
one to the other, as well as to
human child, than there is later,
when differentiated characteristics
dinstinctive of several adults manifest themselves.

HUMAN
CHARACTERIS...

... ha
... are
... ha
... sim
... ma
... fac
... in ...
... fore
... that
... the ...

"A ...
diffe...
lectiv...
robo...
austr...
manl...
know...

The ...
ery ac...
sor Da...
betwe...
ape, is ...
by lea...

Sir ...
describ...
poid a...

SCIEN...
NOT S...

Sir ...
writes:
knowled...
satisfied ...
more."

Both ...
warm ...
Dart's di...
of great i...
they are ...
as the "n...

Keith, ...
ian, says:...
Taungs sk...
the "miss...
based too ...
reports, ...
greater ...
gorilla of ...
creature, th...
anthropoid ...
cousin to the ...
but more ...
them. He ...
likely to ha...
man than a ...

CANINE
TEETH MIS...

"The disco...
because the ...
headed, whic...
sibly be du...
limestone, ...
in the shape ...
which has si...
is more hun...
chimpanzee, ...
some respect ...
being no sig...
teeth of apes.

But the fo...
Keith was w...
self:

"The impor...
in the light i...
and the vari...
anthropolds.
thropoids as n...
common stock ...
along different ...
ment, we may ...
the type of anth...
off from the s...
developed hum...
ways hitherto u...

akin to the name of Dart's homeland; but he always expressed the utmost surprise if anyone should suggest he had chosen the name as an acknowledgement of his own origins.

Such factors apart, the most important requirement during the months following the announcement of the discovery was that Dart should publish a thorough description of the remains, and make casts of it available with the same dispatch as he had prepared and sent off his preliminary description. The scientific establishment was not impressed with his extravagant speculations in the popular press, nor by the popular acclaim he had achieved—not all of it complimentary. 'Hammer and Taungs' was a popular headline, and among the frivolous comment, ditties, and music hall jokes, Dart had also to endure the wrath of those who believed evolution offended religious belief. His discovery contributed to the anti-evolutionist sentiment that culminated in America with the Scopes trial,[10] following which the State of Tennessee banned the teaching of evolution in schools. Promises that he would 'roast in the fire of Hell' were commonplace; he was accused of betraying his Creator, helping Satan and—horribly cruel—threatened that he would be 'unblessed with a hideous family which looks like this monster with the hideous name'.[11]

On the academic front, Dart may have been disappointed that the reviewers' reaction was 'criticism rather than adoration of their potential ancestry',[12] but that was to be expected. After all, constructive criticism is a key element of the process by which interpretative science proceeds. Dart should have responded by quickly providing the additional material reviewers were expecting, but his attention seems to have been more directly applied to the promotion of his views in the popular press. Meanwhile, and perhaps inevitably, expert opinion was steadily hardening towards the conclusion that *Australopithecus* was a form of chimpanzee, its human-like attributes due to the phenomenon of parallel evolution.

It is widely supposed that Dart and the Taung specimen were unfairly attacked by the scientific establishment of the day. The Fiftieth Anniversary publication mentioned above says the fossil had caused 'sensation and argument' wherever it was mentioned and brought 'an avalanche of scorn' upon Dart. But was the scientific reaction really so extreme, or unfair, given the time and the circumstances?

In the first place, Dart's reputation did not inspire confidence. According to Oxford's Professor of Anatomy, Wilfred Le Gros Clark,[13] the memory of an unorthodox theory Dart had once proposed about the evolution of the nervous system still lingered in some minds, suggesting a readiness to draw far-reaching conclusions from limited evidence. Secondly, significant portions of the Taung report depended upon the interpretation of an endocranial cast, while such interpretations in general were still regarded with scepticism. And then there was 'the extraordinary repetitious coincidence between Dart's discovery and that of Dubois in Java', as Le Gros Clark puts it.

Both Dart and Dubois were anatomists with an interest in human evolution. Both went to outlandish places and both found a 'Missing Link' within a few years of arrival. The coincidence of Dubois's discovery was remarkable enough. That Dart should now come along with an almost identical second coincidence 'seemed almost too much of a good thing', said Le Gros Clark. 'At any rate,' he continued, 'combined with the few awkward features of Dart's preliminary article..., it seems to have alerted the minds of anthropologists generally to the possibility that in his too enthusiastic zeal Dart had claimed far more for his *Australopithecus* skull than was warranted by the evidence.'

Eventually some casts of *Australopithecus* were made, and Dart produced a head and shoulders representation of the creature, but the manner of their subsequent display in London did little to improve his standing. The casts, in fact, were not intended for appraisal by senior colleagues; on the contrary they were intended to edify the general public—from a showcase in the South African pavilion at the British Empire Exhibition which opened at Wembley in the summer of 1925. When Arthur Keith wished to inspect the cast he had to peer at it through a glass case, jostled by other visitors, standing beneath a banner proclaiming 'Africa: The Cradle of Humanity', set before a chart alleging that all mankind had evolved from the ancestor represented by the Taung child.

Once again Dart had flouted convention and Arthur Keith, for one, was not amused. He wrote to *Nature* complaining that students of fossil man had not been given an opportunity of purchasing casts of *Australopithecus* but must visit the Wembley exhibition if they wished to study the specimen.[14] But despite the limited facilities for calm scientific appraisal at Wembley, Keith was able to conclude that the Taung skull had belonged to a young anthropoid ape 'showing so many points of affinity with...the gorilla and the chimpanzee that there cannot be a moment's hesitation in placing the fossil in this living group'. Any claim of Missing Link status was preposterous, he said, and as for it being the ancestor of mankind, well, that was like claiming 'a modern Sussex peasant as the ancestor of William the Conqueror'. The last remark referred to Dart's apparent inability to provide data contradicting suggestions that the skull was younger than he claimed, younger even than Piltdown or Heidelberg, to which he had claimed it was ancestral.

Dart attempted to make light of these remarks, but he had nothing substantial to add and fared badly, the more so when his letter appeared in *Nature* together with another cold rejoinder from Keith on the same page.[15] Thereafter, Dart and the Taung child were hardly more than a music-hall joke, while in the study of human evolution Dubois's release of the Java material, and the discovery of hominid fossils in China, diverted attention. In South Africa, Dart concentrated on building up the Witwatersrand Medical School. He did not instigate any exploration of cave deposits around the country, or actively seek more remains of *Australopithecus*, but he did complete the monograph on the Taung specimen.

In 1930 he sent the manuscript to London for consideration by the Royal Society, and he himself followed a year later, hoping to convince everyone that *Australopithecus africanus* really was all he claimed it to be. He arrived in London with the fossil six years to the day after the initial *Nature* announcement. Finally Dart had bowed to convention, but he was too late to be persuasive.

The triumvirate, Grafton Elliot Smith, Arthur Smith Woodward, and Arthur Keith welcomed him warmly enough, but they were all much more interested in telling him about the skull recently discovered in China than in hearing the Taung tale all over again. Smith had just returned from Peking and was to address the Zoological Society on his visit; he invited Dart to accompany him to the meeting, suggesting that he might like to tell the audience of the Taung child. Dart readily agreed, for it seemed a splendid opportunity to present his case properly; but the result was otherwise. 'This was no setting in which to vindicate claims once daring but now trite,' he later wrote:[16]

> I stood in that austere and chilly room, my heart bounding with the hope that the expressions of polite attention on the four score faces before me might change to vivid interest as I spoke. I realized that my offering was an anti-climax but with undiminished optimism launched into my story....What a pitiful difference between this fumbling account and Elliot Smith's skilful demonstration: I had no plaster casts to pass round, no lantern slides to

throw on the screen to emphasize my points. I could only stand there with the tiny skull in my hand, telling the audience what I saw as I looked at it—all of which had been previously published, with illustrations...My address became increasingly diffident as I realized the inadequacy of my material and took in the unchanging expressions of my audience...

Dart found little joy in London that year. Just before sailing back to South Africa he was told that the Royal Society would only publish the section of his monograph concerned with the teeth of *Australopithecus*. Meanwhile, Keith had acquired a cast of the specimen and was preparing to publish nearly one hundred pages on the Taung skull in the revised edition of his text book, *New Discoveries Relating to The Antiquity of Man* (1931); and the Austrian anatomist Wolfgang Abel published another one hundred pages on the fossil in a European journal.[17] Both these authors dismissed Dart's interpretation of the fossil. Keith aligned it with the chimpanzee, while Abel chose the gorilla. A third author, Louis Leakey, similarly cast doubt upon the validity of Dart's claims by omitting all mention of *Australopithecus* from his book *Adam's Ancestors*, published in 1934.

The trouble was that although Dart had drawn the right conclusions from the Taung skull, the evidence was not strong enough to invalidate all other interpretations. The fossil could be ancestral to humans, but it had ape-like characteristics too. Moreover, it was a juvenile specimen, which made diagnosis even more difficult because juveniles and adults differ greatly in all primate species, and the juveniles of different species are remarkably alike, the specific differences becoming apparent only as they grow into adults. Dart needed more evidence— fossil evidence—to support his contentions, and it surely existed in the South African cave deposits; but he chose not to look for it.

In 1925 Dart refused the Witwatersrand Education Department's offer of money and time to travel abroad and write his monograph with access to comparative collections and good libraries. Recalling this decision more than fifty years later, he explained that he had not wanted to leave his anatomy department and his home for so long, and was unwilling to be bound by the condition that he should donate the Taung fossil to the University.[18] Subsequently, the fossil became part of the University's permanent collection anyway, and Dart wondered if it might have been wiser to have toured the world in search of support for his *Australopithecus*. 'It's no good being in front if you're going to be lonely,' he said.[19] And equally regrettable is the fact that while Dart was lonely, for ten years and more, cave deposits that could have been checked for *Australopithecus* remains were consigned to the lime-kilns without a thought. At the time, the world of palaeoanthropology was much more interested in the discovery of Peking Man.

FIGURE 8.3 Raymond Dart, photographed in 1978 with the original Taung fossil and the issue of *Nature* that announced its discovery.

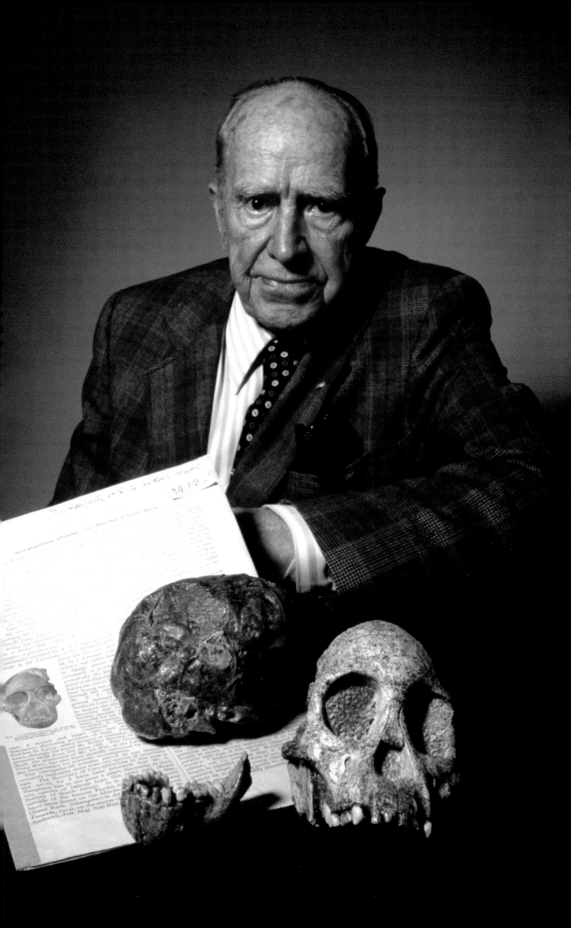

CHAPTER NINE

Peking Man
(1926)

THE STORY of Peking Man is an intriguing tale with an unhappy ending, and as befits a good story it begins with the improbable: dragons. Not the malignant, fire-breathing dragons of Western mythology whose destiny is fulfilled on the end of Saint George's lance; no, in Chinese mythology dragons are benign creatures—all-powerful, but well-disposed towards mankind. Emperors were born of dragons who had attended their mothers on stormy nights; beautiful azure dragons descended from the skies to be present at the birth of wise men like Confucius. Dragons rule the seas, the rivers and the rain; when dragons quarrel above the clouds, thunder and rain result; when dragons are thirsty they suck the land dry before retiring to palaces beneath the sea. Thus they were believed to control the seasons and dragon worship therefore pervaded the life of the rural Chinese. Rubies were petrified drops of dragon's blood; perfume was dragon's saliva; and, more down to earth, dragon bones and teeth, pulverized and mixed in strange potions could cure a multitude of ills. This particular belief still persists: ethnic Chinese drugstores (in London and San Francisco as well as Shanghai and Hong Kong) still dispense Lung Ku—dragon's bones—and Lung Ya—dragon's teeth. These dragon relics are, in fact, fossil bones and teeth, found in the ancient sedimentary deposits of China and purchased from peasants who 'mine' them during the dry season, when the dragons are in their watery palaces and there is little profit in agriculture.

'Dragon bones' were first brought to the attention of palaeontologists and anthropology by K. A. Haberer, a German naturalist who travelled to China in 1899, hoping to explore the hinterland. Unhappily, the disturbances of the Boxer Rebellion restricted his movements severely; he was confined to the ports, so explored the drugstores instead of the hinterland and returned to Europe with a collection of 'dragon' bones representing no less than ninety species, with not a single reptile among them—dragon or otherwise. Haberer's collection was described by Max Schlosser in a monograph entitled *The fossil Mammals of China* (1903). Schlosser gave details of fossil elephants and camels, bears, hyenas, rhinoceros, giraffe, horses—and a solitary primate, represented by an upper molar tooth that Schlosser felt could be either human or ape. The tooth's affinities were no more certain than that, he said, while adding the tantalizing observation that China might be a good place to search for the missing link. Nowadays that particular tooth is regarded as representing an ape, but in the first decades of the century Schlosser's observations accorded well with a growing conviction that mammalian life had originated in Asia and from there had dispersed to populate the world. Any tooth of the higher primates was enough to suggest the birthplace of humans. Schlosser's monograph aroused a good deal of interest among palaeontologists and anthropologists.

These specialists were not the first westerners to find China interesting. Following the footsteps of Marco Polo, enterprising 'foreign devils' travelled extensively through the country during the late nineteenth and early twentieth centuries. Some were naturalists, others were adventurers, but none travelled without an eye for some kind of foreign profit and exploitation. By the time of the First World War, however, the Chinese authorities believed that foreign exploration should be directed primarily towards the greater benefit of Chinese interests. Thus it was that Johan Gunnar Andersson, a Swedish mining expert appointed as adviser to the Chinese Government, discovered large deposits of iron ore that were exploited by Chinese entrepreneurs most profitably while war raged in Europe. Demand fell with the advent of peace however; so did the incentive to pay Andersson's salary as regularly as he expected, and Andersson therefore sought an income elsewhere.

Andersson's hobby was collecting fossils. Perhaps prodded by Professor Wiman of Uppsala University, who was certainly aware of China's potential as a repository of palaeontological treasures, and no doubt using the salary default to full advantage, Andersson negotiated an arrangement with the National Geological Survey of China whereby he would collect Chinese fossils for Swedish institutions. Expenses (including Andersson's salary) would be met by the Swedish China Research Committee, established expressly for that purpose and its chairman, His Royal Highness the Crown Prince of Sweden, personally attended to the diplomatic aspects of the negotiations. In return for the collecting privileges, the Chinese would receive a duplicate set of fossils. As Andersson later wrote,[1] it was an arrangement 'both beneficial to Chinese science and generous to Swedish museums'. It was also a coup that gave Sweden considerable control over palaeontological investigations in China for a decade and restricted American expeditions to the further reaches of the Gobi Desert when they searched for early man in Asia during the 1920s.

One might imagine that after centuries of medicinal exploitation 'dragon bones' would have been scarce in China. But not so: Andersson's endeavours met with immediate and considerable success. Soon he was excavating several sites at once and, when his first collections were lost in a steamer sunk by a typhoon, he was able to replace them all during the following year.

It is difficult to assess exactly how much material Andersson collected, but it is hardly an exaggeration to say that Professor Wiman built Uppsala's Palaeontological Institute around the fossils he received from China; even today, the material is still not fully described.

By 1921 Wiman had chosen a select band of scientists and students to assist with the preparation and description of the Chinese material, but he was becoming concerned about the manner in which the fossils were collected. Andersson was not a palaeontologist; furthermore, he left the excavating to his Chinese labourers, who were not as careful as was desirable. Wiman felt there should be an expert in charge and persuaded Otto Zdansky, a young Austrian palaeontologist, to spend three years in China ensuring that the excavations were handled 'in a more businesslike way'.[2] Zdansky had recently completed a doctoral thesis on fossil turtles and was willing to go to China but, because Wiman offered no

---

FIGURE 9.1 'Dragons' teeth, bought from a traditional Chinese drugstore, with a recipe for their preparation.

remuneration beyond travel and living expenses, only on condition that he was given the right to describe his finds himself. 'After all,' Zdansky explains, 'the publications would be all I got out of my stay in China.' Wiman accepted the condition and so, with Schlosser's monograph prominent among his baggage, Zdansky set off for China in the summer of 1921.

Zdansky quarrelled with Andersson very soon after arrival, and threatened to return to Europe immediately. Andersson placated him, but thereafter the relationship between the two men was decidedly cool.

To familiarize himself with Chinese conditions before venturing into more remote regions, Zdansky went first to a disused lime quarry about fifty kilometres from Peking known as Ji Gu Shan (now written Chikushan). There, he established headquarters in the neighbouring town called Chou K'ou Tien (now Zhoukoudian) and began work on a column of secondary infill which the limeworkers had left standing in the quarry. The column was packed with fossils, mostly rodents and small predators, which the local people assumed to be bones of animals they knew—principally chickens. Hence the name they had given the location: Chicken Bone Hill.

Not long after Zdansky had begun work on the deposits, Andersson paid a visit, bringing with him Walter Granger, chief palaeontologist on an expedition organized by the American Museum of Natural History which was going to look for the missing link in China. Coincidently, a local resident arrived that day with word of bigger and better 'dragon bones' in another quarry, about 150 metres from the Chou K'ou Tien railway station. In a matter of hours the new site provided fossils of rhinoceros, hyena, and bovids (of the Bovidae family, which includes cattle, antelope, sheep, and deer), and that evening a 'happy trio' raised their glasses to the prospect of further discoveries. Zdansky agreed to spend two or three weeks at the site.

When Zdansky published his report, he named the site after the nearby town, Chou K'ou Tien, by which name it has been known in scientific circles ever since. But in fact, the deposit had been known to the local people for centuries as Long Ku Shan, Dragon Bone Hill, now written Longgushan.

Andersson had noticed fragments of quartz dotted through the deposit; he became convinced they were the primitive tools of an early human population and on a subsequent visit said to Zdansky: 'I have a feeling that there lie here the remains of one of our ancestors and it is only a question of your finding him.

Take your time and stick to it until the cave is emptied, if need be.'³ Zdansky, however, did not agree that the quartz fragments might be tools. He felt they were just splinters fallen from the veins of quartz that traversed the limestone.

Nonetheless, Zdansky did find evidence of early humans at Zhoukoudian during the late summer of 1921: a single molar tooth that could only have come from an ancient human jaw. 'I recognized it at once,' Zdansky recalled later, 'but I said nothing. You see, hominid material is always in the limelight and I was afraid that if it came out there would be such a stir, and I would be forced to hand over material I had a promise to publish. So I said nothing about it.'⁴ The fossil tooth Zdansky had found was, in fact, the first evidence of Peking Man.

Andersson's interest in looking for the missing link may have been awakened by Schlosser's monograph, but it was surely encouraged by Walter Granger, and the scale of the American Museum of Natural History expedition that became evident when its experts and equipment began arriving in Peking. The expeditions were inspired by the 'brilliant prediction' of Fairfield Osborn, then President of the Museum, that 'Asia would prove to have been a great dispersal center for northern terrestrial mammalian life'.⁵ The avowed intention was 'to seek and discover the ancestry of man'—hence the popular title: 'The Missing Link Expeditions'. They were conducted over a period of seven years, from 1921 to 1928, with a scale of expenditure, organization, and flamboyance that might have seemed to guarantee success, but they were hampered by one important consideration— namely a formal undertaking with the Chinese National Geological Survey (and a 'gentleman's agreement' with Andersson) that 'the expeditions would not enter upon geological, palaeontological or archaeological explorations in Northern China'.⁶ Which effectively restricted the Americans to the wastes of Mongolia, an area of deposits so ancient they could never contain the remains of man. As cynics suggested, they might as well have looked for fossils in the Pacific Ocean.

Nonetheless, the Americans were provided with ample resources; $600,000 to be precise, with undertakings of more to follow. Their leader, Roy Chapman Andrews, a colourful zoologist and explorer, envisaged ten years of exploration in China. The problems he faced were enormous, but Andrews found a solution for many of them in motorized transport. Cars and trucks could travel one hundred miles a day, ten times faster than a camel, and thus should enable the Americans 'to do approximately ten years' work in one season', Andrews reasoned; and he claims to have achieved that ratio. But for all their benefits, motor vehicles brought problems peculiar to themselves. Accidents were frequent, with 'many people killed and injured'; and fuel was a constant headache.

The fleet of five cars and two trucks required a total of 4,000 gallons of fuel each season, which weighed twelve tons and would have left little space for the expedition's personnel, equipment, and discoveries if carried in the vehicles themselves. So Andrews resorted to camels, employing several score as a fuel train. Forty-four-gallon drums could not be packed on a camel's back, and had to be returned after use, so disposable five-gallon cans were used instead. Each camel carried twelve of these, weighing 400 pounds—a heavy load, but one that quickly lessened as the cans expanded, rubbed and leaked when subjected to a camel's rolling gait under a desert sun. Fifty per cent of the fuel was lost in this way the first year, but Andrews reported that better packing reduced leakage to twenty-five per cent by 1925.

Logistical problems notwithstanding, the American expeditions achieved remarkable results. They found a fossilized redwood forest, and the graves of a shovel-tusked mastodon with jaws five feet long; they sent over 26,000 specimens back to America and described more than one thousand fossil and living forms new to science. In all they collected enough data for hundreds of scientific articles and for twelve volumes of final reports. But in respect of the missing link, the expeditions were a complete failure. As Andrews wrote in a paragraph of his report headed 'The Unfinished Task': 'we have not been successful in one object of our search—the "Dawn Man". It is a scientific tragedy that Chinese opposition to foreign investigations should end our work when that goal might be attained. Still, we have shown the way, broken trail as it were. Later, others will reap a rich harvest. We are more than ever convinced that Central Asia was a palaeontological Garden of Eden.'[7]

The 'Chinese opposition' that Andrews mentioned in his report led ultimately to the expulsion of the American Museum team from their newfound 'Garden of Eden' and stemmed principally from Chinese objections to the manner in which the Americans had disposed of some fossilized dinosaur eggs found in 1923.

The expedition found twenty-five dinosaur eggs in all, the first known to science,[8] and the discovery aroused widespread excitement. When Andrews returned to America, newspapers clamoured for exclusive rights to the story, some offering thousands of dollars. But Andrews refused all in favour of *Asia* magazine, to whom he was contracted for popular articles. Eventually the story and pictures were made available to the press free of charge, but Andrews and his colleagues at the American Museum determined to cash in on the enormous interest aroused by auctioning one egg to the highest bidder. Not only would the sale contribute directly towards expedition expenses the following year, they reasoned, it would also publicize the value of the expeditions and perhaps encourage private donations.

The egg went to Colonel Austin Colgate (of toothpaste fame) for $5,000 and Andrews raised $284,000 that winter, but he soon had reason to wish the publicity campaign had not been quite so successful. The Chinese, Mongolian, and Russian authorities assumed that every egg was worth $5,000 and, not surprisingly drew the conclusion that the fossil collection Andrews and his team had removed from Central Asia was of enormous commercial value. They never could be persuaded otherwise, and, with a change of government and civil strife not helping, co-operation gradually turned to direct opposition. The American Museum was forced to withdraw, pending 'the dawn of a more tolerant era of sympathy and co-operation with foreign scientific endeavour', as Andrews wrote in his report, *The New Conquest of China*.

While the Americans were having difficulties with the Chinese, a Swede by the name of Sven Hedin was enjoying considerably more success—though he had not the slightest interest in the search for the missing link. Born in 1865, educated with royalty and the last man in Sweden to be knighted, Hedin was a romantic figure who spent the greater part of his life in the Far East. He wrote several books on his travels and achieved popular fame with one in which he claimed to have rediscovered Marco Polo's Silk Road, which even the Chinese had been unable to find. Hedin was an adventurer more than a scientist or a businessman. He managed to allay Chinese suspicions that he was removing valuable treasures from the country, but his expeditions often had a commercial application: in 1925, for instance, his travels through Tibet, Mongolia, and China were financed by Lufthansa, the airline which was then seeking topographical details for its proposed air route to Peking.

The strength of Hedin's position in China was that he knew how to manipulate the Chinese authorities to his own ends, and he knew how to raise money in Sweden and elsewhere. As such he was a threat to both the American and the Swedish explorers: even though he declared no interest in the search for the missing link, his presence in the country compounded the uncertainties of an already complicated situation.

Meanwhile, Andersson's expeditions were achieving a commendable degree of success. Apart from the fact that Zdansky had found a fossil hominid tooth within weeks of arriving in China (which he had decided to keep to himself), he and Andersson had also uncovered the beginnings of deciduous vegetation among the fossils of Southern Manchuria; in Central China they found a rich field of fossil plants including many new to science. Fossil fish, turtles, cockroaches, and dragonflies came from eastern China—from there too came some strange dinosaurs. One of them was fully ten metres long; Zdansky and his men cut out the near-complete skeleton in great blocks of sandstone and, in Sweden, four men spent a year preparing and reassembling the bones. From the structure of the bone and the form of the skeleton, Wiman deduced that the creature had lived in the water rather like a very large, long-necked hippopotamus. He called it *Helopus zdanskyi*, which means marsh-footed and acknowledges its discoverer. Wiman regarded *Helopus* as a most important discovery.

But despite the success of the expeditions' palaeontological endeavours, it was a recurrent disappointment to Andersson that all the sites they investigated were far too old to contain the remains of a human ancestor. In fact the only site they had encountered with fauna recent enough to have been contemporary was the very first they had visited—Chou K'ou Tien. And there, of course, he had seen the quartz fragments. 'I could never forget the thought of hominid remains in this cave,' he wrote later; and in 1923 he persuaded Zdansky to return to the site. Of course, Zdansky already had in his pocket, so to speak, the very thing Andersson most wanted, the hominid tooth found two years earlier. He was aware of the world-wide interest in the search for the missing link. But still he said nothing of the tooth to Andersson. The fact that he disliked the man eased any qualms and, in any case: 'I wasn't interested in what Andersson wanted,' Zdansky later recalled, 'I wanted only the fauna of the cave'.[9]

Zdansky returned to Sweden in 1923 to study and describe his discoveries and later that year published a preliminary paper on the Zhoukoudian deposits, with Andersson as co-author.[10] The hominid tooth was not mentioned, and indeed its existence might have remained a secret until Zdansky finally published his monograph[11] if the Crown Prince of Sweden had not made a visit to Peking in 1926, while on a world tour. It will be recalled that the Crown Prince was Chairman of the Swedish China Research Committee which had funded Andersson's work. To mark the Prince's visit, Andersson arranged a scientific meeting and wrote to Professor Wiman, asking for details of any important discoveries that could be announced to coincide with the event. Wiman responded with a description of the magnificent *Helopus zdanskyi* and asked Zdansky if he had anything to contribute that might 'give an additional spice to the meeting'. 'Yes I have,' replied Zdansky and promptly dispatched a description of two hominid teeth from Zhoukoudian (he had found a second while sorting the material), together with photographs and lantern slides.

Andersson's response to the revelation that Zdansky had found the ultimate prize and kept it to himself is not recorded (but can be imagined). Later he wrote that Zdansky had thought the first tooth was an ape's when he found it, but in October 1926 he kept his counsel and saved the 'spice' for the very end of the meeting. As Zdansky had expected, the announcement caused a sensation: the teeth were immediately labelled 'Peking Man' and reported as 'The oldest human type whose remains have been found in the strata of the earth'.[12]

But the boldness of such grand conclusions was also remarked upon—could a few teeth reveal so much? 'How are things just now with the Peking man?' Andersson was asked at a dinner party, 'is it a man or a carnivore?' 'The news from Chou K'ou Tien is that our old friend is neither a man nor a carnivore,' Andersson replied, 'but rather something half-way between the two. It is a lady.'[13]

As a palaeontologist of uncompromising determination, Zdansky had deliberately avoided the glamour of the search for the missing link; he sought the broad picture of ancient life, in which humanity was an insignificant detail. But in the audience at the Peking meeting sat an anatomist with an interest in fossils for whom early hominids filled the entire canvas. His name was Davidson Black, a Canadian who was Professor of Anatomy at the Peking Union Medical College—an establishment generously endowed by the Rockefeller Foundation of New York.

Black was inspired by the Chou K'ou Tien teeth. With only the photographs and a written description to hand (reports that Black worked from the originals are erroneous, according to Zdansky), Black compiled a report on the discovery which he submitted to *Nature* and *Science*.[14] The teeth are 'two specimens of extraordinary interest', he wrote 'which cannot otherwise be named than *Homo? sp.* [an unidentified species of the genus *Homo*]…the actual presence of early man in Eastern Asia is no longer a matter of conjecture,' he said and, recalling Schlosser's prediction, concluded that 'the Chou K'ou Tien discovery…furnishes one more link in the already strong chain of evidence supporting the hypothesis of the central Asiatic origin of the Hominidae.' Thus wrote the anatomist.

A few months later Zdansky published the more cautious view of the palaeontologist.[15] Noting that the discovery was 'decidedly interesting but not of epoch-making importance', he wrote:

> I am very sceptical towards a great deal of prehistoric-anthropological literature, and convinced that the existing material provides a wholly inadequate foundation for many of the various theories based upon it. As every fresh discovery of what may be human remains is of such great interest not only to the scientist but also to the layman, it follows only too naturally that it becomes at once the object of the most detailed—and, in my opinion, too detailed— investigation. I decline absolutely to venture any far-reaching conclusions regarding the extremely meagre material described here, and which cannot be more closely identified than as ? *Homo sp.*

With this honest and accurate assessment of the evidence and ideas then prevailing in the search for fossil evidence of human origins, Otto Zdansky retired from the story of Peking Man. He completed his monographs in 1928 and thereafter was appointed professor at Cairo University. And with his retirement, the Swedish option on hominids in China effectively lapsed. The two teeth Zdansky found at Chou K'ou Tien (plus a third found later in among the collection in Uppsala) still reside in the Palaeontological Institute at Uppsala, but the subsequent discoveries they inspired were destined for a much less satisfactory resting place.

Within days of the sensational announcement of the fossil teeth at the Peking meeting, Black convened a smaller, more select gathering in his office. With the Crown Prince in the chair, representatives of the Geological Survey of China, and of the Rockefeller Foundation in attendance, Black and Andersson gained unanimous approval for a joint Chinese/Swedish/American expedition to

FIGURE 9.2 Hominid teeth found by Otto Zdansky at Chou K'ou Tien, 1921–3, with a third tooth found later among the Chou K'ou Tien material at the Palaeontogical Institute, Uppsala.

Chinese Turkestan two years hence. But while he was negotiating this cooperative endeavour (which in fact never came to fruition), Black was also applying to
the Rockefeller Foundation for money to conduct a systematic two-year research
project on the Chou K'ou Tien deposits. The Foundation responded generously.
Black arranged that the project would be conducted in conjunction with the
Geological Survey of China and undertook that any hominid fossils recovered
would be studied in the Peking laboratory.

The second round of excavations at Chou K'ou Tien began on Good Friday
1927. Otto Zdansky had been invited to take charge but declined in favour of
the Cairo appointment. In his stead Professor Wiman sent one of his current
graduate students, Birger Bohlin, who had recently completed his doctorate on
the fossil giraffes Andersson had sent from China. Like Zdansky, Bohlin was primarily interested in the broadest aspects of palaeontology but, unlike Zdansky,
his work in China was narrowly circumscribed from the start. 'I went to China
chiefly because I wanted to go somewhere,' said Bohlin, 'but I was ordered to find
man. You could see from a distance that Davidson Black wanted fossil man. The
rest was just by-product. He gave me some directions of how to work at Zhoukoudian: he said I should remove the whole deposit in six weeks and take it back
to Peking. In the first few days I saw that this was impossible'.[16]

Even so, with the help of five thousand dollars' worth of explosive, a small
army of Chinese labourers, and the able assistance of C. Li, a Chinese geologist, Bohlin managed to blast and examine 3,000 cubic metres of deposits in
six months. He uncovered the plan of the cave, revealing a deposit about 800
metres square and between eleven and seventeen metres thick. But for all that,
evidence of any hominid presence eluded him until three days before work was
to finish for the year. Then, on 16 October, Bohlin found a single hominid tooth
poking from a corner of the cave. 'Here you are,' he told Li triumphantly, 'we
can go home now.'

'Do you think one is enough ?' Li replied.

Not long after Bohlin's return to Peking, Davidson Black identified the single
tooth as a child's, matching the second tooth that Zdansky had discovered in Uppsala. On reflection, he decided that both must come from the same jaw, and both
must have been related to the adult represented by the third tooth—remarkably
fortuitous discoveries among such a vast quantity of excavated deposit. Then,
comparing the Bohlin tooth with corresponding teeth from a chimpanzee and a

10-year-old child, Black concluded that 'the newly discovered specimen displays in the details of its morphology a number of interesting and unique characters, sufficient it is believed, to justify the proposal of a new hominid genus'.[17] He called the creature *Sinanthropus pekinensis* Black and Zdansky, 'Peking Chinese Man'. And so, despite Zdansky's caution, the 'extremely meagre material' he had found was used in a manner he abhorred, with his name attached in honour of the discovery.

In the light of subsequent finds at Zhoukoudian, Davidson Black's creation of a new genus on the basis of one tooth is often viewed as a bold and inspired move. At the beginning, though, many authorities considered the announcement irresponsible. The first announcement produced no correspondence in the journals and little comment in the newspapers—though the indifference which greeted *Sinanthropus* was probably not unrelated to almost simultaneous dethroning of *Hesperopithecus haroldcooki*, another solitary molar hailed as a human ancestor and, in view of its relation to the story of Peking Man, worthy of a brief digression.

Hesperopithecus had been presented to the world in April 1922 by the palaeontologist Henry Fairfield Osborn (who as Director was responsible for the American Museum of Natural History expeditions to China). The specimen comprised a small water-worn tooth found in the Snake Creek fossil beds of Nebraska by Harold J. Cook, geologist. Cook sent the tooth to Osborn who, on receipt, replied: 'The instant your package arrived I sat down with the tooth, in my window, and I said to myself: "It looks one hundred per cent anthropoid... we may cool down tomorrow, but it looks to me as if the first anthropoid ape of America had been found."'[18]

This was an event that American anthropologists had been 'eagerly anticipating' for some time. *Hesperopithecus* means 'ape of the land where the sun sets', but in the London *Times* on 20 May 1922 Grafton Elliot Smith extended the description somewhat and welcomed the tiny tooth as 'the earliest and most primitive member of the human family yet discovered... One would regard so momentous a conclusion with suspicion,' he continued, 'if it were not for the fact that the American savants' authority in such matters is unquestionable.' The shape and structure is like a palimpsest to the anatomist, he said, revealing the ancestry of the creature that once owned it.

The palaeontologist Arthur Smith Woodward took a rather less favourable view of *Hesperopithecus*—if the tooth were set differently in its hypothetical jaw, he remarked, its owner could just as well have been an extinct form of bear as an early kind of man.[19]

As with most palaeoathropological issues of this kind, the differences of opinion concerning *Hesperopithecus* were as much concerned with detail absent from the specimen as with detail present on it; by 1925 the issue was still unresolved, inspiring Osborn to write: 'In the whole history of anthropology no tooth has ever been subjected to such severe cross-examination as this now world-famous tooth of *Hesperopithecus*. Every suggestion made by scientific sceptics was weighed and found wanting.'[20] Subsequently, however, a Mr Thompson of the American Museum of Natural History looked for more specimens of *Hesperopithecus* in the Snake Creek deposits. Lo and behold, he found a number of teeth, some quite unworn, among which there was sufficient resemblance to the original tooth to establish their overall affinity beyond doubt, and sufficient detail on the unworn specimens to show quite clearly that all the teeth had come from the jaw of an extinct pig.

'An ancient and honourable pig no doubt, a pig with a distinguished Greek name,' commented a London *Times* leader when the news was released, 'but indubitably porcine'. *The Times* wondered whether the worshippers who had so eagerly proclaimed themselves made in the image of *Hesperopithecus* were now left desolate; and concluded: 'If there is a place where the spirits of forsaken gods congregate…to condole with one another on ruined temples and smokeless altars, there also, aloft in the branches of a monkey puzzle tree overlooking the asphodel meadow,…conscious of his own distinction as one who has received the offering of unsuperstitious science, should sit the spirit of the Evening Ape.'[21] Palaeontologists had been badly bitten by the Nebraska tooth, said Grafton Elliot Smith.[22]

As this salutary lesson on the dangers of applying bold and inspired interpretations to limited evidence was rumbling to its climax, in Peking Birger Bohlin had painted a charming portrait of Peking Man among the flowers of Chou K'ou Tien (which he photographed and made tinted copies of throughout his life), and Davidson Black set off for America and Europe with the tooth of *Sinanthropus pekinensis* in a specially made brass capsule that was variously suspended from his

FIGURE 9.3 Birger Bohlin in 1978, with his paintings of Peking Man (and Woman), all based, he claimed, on the evidence of the single tooth he found at Chou K'ou Tien.

watch chain, or about his neck. Ostensibly he was on holiday, but he also toured the world of anthropology to present *Sinanthropus*. The trip was not marked with much success. Some colleagues were critical, some indifferent, and others plain rude. But Black was unmoved; according to Grafton Elliot Smith, rejection had no effect on Black 'beyond awakening his sympathies for anthropologists who are unfairly criticized and to make him redouble his efforts to establish the proof of his claim'.[23]

A little more of that proof awaited Black on his return to Peking in December 1928—half a lower jaw with three teeth in place. Again, Bohlin had found the fossil, and again it was found a few days before excavations ceased—the only hominid specimen among over 400 large boxfuls of fossils recovered that year. The teeth matched *Sinanthropus*, and the shape of the jaw seemed to show ape-like characteristics, so Black felt his earlier claims were vindicated, but even so, the evidence recovered from Chou K'ou Tien during his years of expert, expensive, and extensive excavations was not impressive: four teeth and a fragment of jaw.

The Rockefeller Foundation grant had been for two years' work; now that the money was spent, could these meagre hominid finds convince the trustees in New York that further investment was justified? On the face of it, probably not, and it is therefore quite likely that but for the collapse of his other plans, Black would not even have asked. As already mentioned, Black and Andersson had planned a joint Chinese–Swedish–American expedition to explore Chinese Turkestan for two or three years from the beginning of 1929. Naïvely, they had sought the advice of Sven Hedin at an early stage, telling him everything: destination, objectives, and expectations. So, when Hedin returned to Sweden soon after hearing their plans, he organized an expedition of his own to fulfil them instead, thereby absorbing all the Swedish money available for such an undertaking. The Swedes would not support a second expedition; the Americans (that is, the Rockefeller Foundation) would not foot the entire bill to duplicate what was, in effect, Sweden's unilateral action, and the Chinese had no money at all, so the Black and Andersson enterprise was abandoned.

Black had already arranged a three-year release from his duties at the Medical College and was sorely disappointed that his plans for the exploration of a little-known region of China could not proceed. But he quickly saw that the collapse of one project could be turned to the advantage of another: Hedin's devious behaviour could help the search for more evidence of human origins in

China. Black knew the Rockefeller trustees were sympathetic to his plight; and as money had already been budgeted for the expedition (Black had requested $20,000 per year), perhaps it could be diverted to the search for hominid fossils. Black applied to the Foundation accordingly. But the proposal that reached the New York offices in January 1929 was not simply for funds to continue excavations at Zhoukoudian; it was much more ambitious.

Black proposed that the Rockefeller Foundation should establish a laboratory specifically to investigate cenozoic geology and palaeontology throughout China (cenozoic means 'recent life' and is the name of the geological era extending from the present to about sixty-five million years ago). The Cenozoic Research Laboratory should be a special department of the Geological Survey of China (then in dire financial straits and kept afloat by private mining interests), Black proposed, though it would be housed in the Anatomy Department of the Rockefeller-funded Medical College in Peking. Eventually the laboratory would deal with all aspects of geology and palaeontology throughout China, including prehistoric archaeology, but Chou K'ou Tien would be of particular concern from the start. An important condition was that all fossils and artefacts must remain in China—research material would never again be sent abroad for study and preparation. Black presented an impressively bold and inspired plan, and the Rockefeller Foundation responded with a grant of $80,000 to cover its initial establishment. Black's mood changed from depression to jubilation— 'things have turned out very differently than I…supposed possible,' he wrote to Sir Arthur Keith, 'it's better to be born lucky than rich'.[24]

At the conclusion of the first Chou K'ou Tien excavations Birger Bohlin had joined Sven Hedin's expedition (where an early task was to purchase equipment abandoned by the American Museum of Natural History expedition on their expulsion from China), but Black did not look again to Sweden or to America for a replacement. Instead he relied on Chinese geologists and palaeontologists to manage the excavations (under his direction), with the further help of occasional visitors like Teilhard de Chardin, the Jesuit priest and expert on fossil hominids who subsequently contributed extensively to the study of the geology and the fossil fauna of the Chou K'ou Tien deposits.

By 1929, a total of 8,800 cubic metres of fossil-bearing deposit had been removed from the site and 1,485 cases of fossils packed off to Peking. There were a few more hominid teeth among them, but nothing substantial enough to underpin the shaky foundations of *Sinanthropus pekinensis.* Black appeared to remain confident throughout, but not until December 1929—once again at the very end of the season—did the combination of Rockefeller dollars and Black's confidence finally pay a significant dividend.

The weather had turned bitterly cold towards the end of November; the first snows had fallen around Zhoukoudian; pails of water froze overnight. Work had been halted forty-two metres below the highest point of the deposit by rock that could be breached only by extensive quarrying; the palaeontologist in charge of operations, Wenzhong Pei, found two caves opening away from the southern extremity of a fissure low in the deposit. He was lowered into one of them on a rope and explored it 'with great difficulty', finding only a few hyena vertebrae.

The other cave was less deep, and since it opened horizontally, Pei was able to crawl in and explore the interior on 29 November. On 1 December his team began removing the uppermost part of the material filling the cave. Only three men could fit in at the bottom of this narrow, dark, and cold hole. They dug by candlelight, pick in one hand, candle in the other, and worked longer than usual because Wenzhong Pei had a hunch...

> On the afternoon of 2 December, Pei's pick pulled away a piece of consolidated sandy and pebbly cave sediment that revealed a tantalizingly interesting round surface of bone...There were no antlers or horns. There was no long snout. There were no extended crests of bone. Just the rounded, beautiful simplicity of a hominid skull. The realization dawned that he had found it—the long-sought-after skull of Peking Man.[25]

Pei worked on into the night to remove the skull from the cave and spent the next few days preparing it for the journey to Peking. He left Chou K'ou Tien by train early in the morning of 6 December, and delivered the specimen to the Cenozoic Laboratory in Peking by noon the same day.[26]

The skull Pei had found was the culmination of Davidson Black's work in China, substantiating his claim that fossil evidence of human origins would be found in Peking, and presenting scientists with the first hint in many years of evidence that was both new and credible. The specimen diverted attention from the Piltdown riddle and eclipsed the significance of Raymond Dart's *Australopithecus.* Once all the matrix had been removed from the skull, however, it became clear that *Sinanthropus pekinensis* was not unique after all. Despite the slight dental distinctions Black had emphasized when proposing the new genus and species on the basis of teeth alone, the new specimen was very similar to the *Pithecanthropus erectus* fossils that Eugene Dubois had found in Java.[27] Subsequent discoveries at both sites confirmed the association, and the Java and Peking fossils were grouped together as *Homo erectus*. But Davidson Black did not live to see this. He died suddenly, aged 49, of a heart complaint while working at his bench in the Cenozoic Research Laboratory during the night of 15 March 1934.

After Black's death, Teilhard de Chardin took charge of the Chou K'ou Tien excavations, and in 1935 Franz Weidenreich (1873–1948) arrived in Peking to take over as head of the Cenozoic Research Laboratory. Weidenreich was one of the world's foremost anatomists, an authority on human evolution and fossil hominids, but also a victim of Germany's anti-Jewish iniquities. He had been forced to resign as Professor of Anatomy at Frankfurt University in 1934, and welcomed the opportunity of working at the Cenozoic Research Laboratory—now a renowned centre for hominid research. But leaving Germany was difficult for a Jewish professor and his family. Weidenreich managed to get his wife and one daughter out of the country with him, but two other daughters and his mother-in-law were sent to concentration camps. He worked ceaselessly for their release and did eventually succeed in reuniting with his daughters in the United States, but his mother-in-law did not survive the camps.[28] A pall of anxiety hung over Weidenreich's personal life in China.

By 1937, a huge section of hillside had been removed in the search for early man at Zhoukoudian. During a total of 1,873 days worked on the site, the excavators had blasted and sifted through the equivalent of a twelve-storey building about twenty-three metres long and fifteen metres broad. Of course, such effort pales into insignificance against the tons of rock that are mined from holes kilometres deep to produce every ounce of gold, but the remains of Peking Man were no less of a treasure. In all, fourteen skulls in varying degrees of completeness were found, together with eleven mandibles, 147 teeth, portions of seven thighbones, two upper armbones, one collarbone (of doubtful attribution), and one wristbone.[29] Then work at the site was brought to an abrupt halt, as the tension which had been growing ever since Japanese forces occupied Manchuria in 1931 erupted into full-scale war.

On 7 July 1937, the Imperial Japanese Army fired on Chinese civilians at the strategically important Marco Polo Bridge, on the road between Peking and Chou K'ou Tien. The incident signalled Japanese determination to take over more of China (and the beginning of the second Sino-Japanese War). Excavations ceased as Japanese forces swiftly advanced over all of northern China around Peking—including Chou K'ou Tien. But the occupying army was thinly spread, allowing Communist guerrillas to establish secret operational bases across the country. One group became ensconced at Chou K'ou Tien, virtually under the noses of the Japanese High Command in Peking, and three excavation workers were among the local people who surreptitiously supported the guerrilla cause. They were also among several dozen who were rounded up, interrogated, tortured, and bayoneted to death when the Japanese took action against the Chou K'ou Tien guerrillas in 1938.[30]

It was in these circumstances, surrounded by terror in China and fearing for his family in Germany, that Franz Weidenreich retired to the laboratory when excavations ceased at Chou K'ou Tien. While the chaos of war threatened the world, he devoted himself to imposing order on the remains of some of its earliest inhabitants. He studied and recorded the fossils' anatomical structure. Casts and drawings were made, photographs were taken, and Weidenreich issued a stream of authoritative monographs on the mandibles, the teeth, the brain casts, the long bones, and finally, a truly monumental work on the skull. No fossils had ever been so assiduously documented.[31]

Because of its American connections, the Cenozoic Research Laboratory was regarded as a pocket of foreign interest during the early stages of the Japanese incursion, and was not molested. But with the beginning of the Second World War in September 1939, the growing danger of conflict between Japan and America posed a serious threat to the laboratory and the fossils it housed. The official understanding remained precisely as Davidson Black had stipulated: the Chou K'ou Tien fossils must remain in China. But the Chinese seem to have overlooked their responsibilities in this respect when the government moved from Peking. In January 1941, the director of the Geological Survey, Dr Wong, suggested from his refuge in South West China that Weidenreich should take the fossils with him on his planned return to America. Weidenreich declined. He feared the fossils would be confiscated if customs officials found them among his personal baggage and, in any case, considered them much too valuable to expose to an unprotected voyage in so dangerous a time. The diplomatic pouch was the obvious alternative and apparently Weidenreich suggested to the American Ambassador that the fossils should be sent to the United States in official baggage not subject to customs examination. But his suggestion was rejected and so, while Weidenreich travelled safely to America in April 1941 with a complete set of casts, photographs, drawings, data, and his research notes, the original fossils remained in the safe at the Cenozoic Research Laboratory.[32]

Peking Man has never been seen again and his disappearance has generated almost as much speculation and popular interest as the appearance of Piltdown Man had done. A review of the circumstances published in 1974 concluded that the fossils were packed in two large boxes and taken to the United States Embassy in July 1941, with a request that they should be shipped to America. For some unexplained reason, three months passed before the appropriate authorities were informed. By then it was mid-November 1941. The fossils are believed to have left Peking early in December in the care of a US Marines contingent due to sail for America in the SS *President Harrison*, but the Japanese attack on the American naval base at Pearl Harbour occurred before they reached the port. War was declared between Japan and America. The *President Harrison* ran aground trying to evade a Japanese warship and never docked. The marines were held by Japanese troops, and no one knows what happened to the fossils in their care.[33]

This version of events is plausible enough to have become the basis of most accounts, but doubt is cast on its veracity by a lack of any agreement on how—or even whether—the fossils actually got as far as the American Embassy. An extensive survey of the issues conducted by Chinese journalists and published in Chinese in 2000 could confirm only that the fossils were packed for shipment and delivered to the office of the Controller at Peking Union Medical College. Beyond that, 'none of the Chinese knew what happened to them'.[34] Nor did anyone else, while the behaviour of the Japanese military police who moved their headquarters to the Medical College in May 1942 is not encouraging. Sixty-seven boxes of non-primate fossils and stone artefacts from Chou K'ou Tien, ten boxes of fossil reptiles from another site, and thirty boxes of publications were thrown out, scattered, smashed, and burned.[35]

It was wartime. Hopes that Peking Man might have survived the chaos and destruction persist only because there is no absolute proof that he did not. Perhaps he was buried in a secret place, which was how Ralph von Koenigswald saved the remains of Java Man when Indonesia was invaded; if so, the time for them to be disinterred is long past, the hero responsible is almost certainly dead, and the chances of finding the site minimal. No, as a review published in 2004 concludes, it is most likely that soon after leaving the safety of a scientific laboratory the remains of Peking Man became dragon bones once more. Perhaps they were sold and consumed as medicine so that like the bones of Davidson Black, whose grave was razed in the post-war reconstruction of Beijing, the bones of Peking Man are now commingled with the earth of China.[36]

After the war, work on the Chinese fossils that Roy Chapman Andrews collected in such vast numbers continued in America. In Sweden, Berger Bohlin continued his work on the fossils Andersson had sent back, and on those he had collected himself on the Hedin expedition. The teeth Zdansky found are still at Uppsala, the only surviving original remains of Peking Man. It is ironic to reflect that had Otto Zdansky been a less determined scientist, and more concerned with the romance of finding the missing link, if he had told Andersson of that first tooth and spent the next two years in the Chou K'ou Tien cave, he probably would have found the fossils that Black's excavations later uncovered. Then Peking Man too would be safe in Sweden.

In 1949 Chinese researchers resumed excavations at Chou K'ou Tien (soon to be known as Zhoukoudian). Five hominid teeth were found in that year, two limb fragments in 1951, a female mandible in 1958 and, in 1966, two skull fragments which fitted the casts of others found in 1934 to form a complete skull.[37] Excavation and research has also been conducted at other sites in China.[38] A skull fragment of ancient but ill-defined date was found at Maba in 1958.[39] A skull and mandible, dating from over 500,000 years ago and assigned to *Homo erectus*, were recovered from two separate excavations at Lantian in 1963–4.[40] Other *Homo erectus* skulls were found at Dali in 1978,[41] and at Hexian in 1980.[42] Fossil apes and hominoids have also been recovered from sites around China, and the abundance of material has given palaeoanthropology in China a distinctly Chinese bias: the study of early humans is the study of early China.

FIGURE 9.4 A photograph of Franz Wiedenreich, with drawings, memorabilia, and casts of the reconstructions he took to New York in 1941.

The Institute of Vertebrate Palaeontology and Palaeoanthropology of the Chinese Academy of Sciences instigated a comprehensive five-year study of the Zhoukoudian cave site in 1978, involving 120 Chinese scientists from 17 Chinese universities and research institutions.[43] This work convinced its participants that evidence from the cave traces 'the development of a single community over a period that spans a significant fraction of the evolution of the genus *Homo*',[44] and has inspired almost continuous investigation since then. The site has yielded 17,000 stone artefacts and fossil evidence for more than fifty *H. erectus* individuals, variously dated to between 400,000 and 600,000 years ago, with the results (published in 2009) of a new dating method,[45] which exploits the formation of unstable aluminium and beryl isotopes in quartz grains exposed to cosmic radiation, pushing the age of the lowest occupation levels at Zhoukoudian back to 780,000 years.

Other sites in north-east Asia date back to more than 1.2 million years ago, showing that human occupation of the region began around 1.3 million years ago and continued to at least 400,000 years ago (the age of the youngest occurrence of *H. erectus* at Zhoukoudian).

Hominids were using fire throughout their occupation of the Zhoukoudian cave, the Chinese researchers believe, and the stone tools they left behind are said to reflect increasing technological skill through time. Vertebrate fossil remains from the cave show that deer were the commonest prey, which in turn suggests they were skilled and efficient hunters. Because successful hunting demands the cooperation of many individuals, they are presumed to have lived in groups, and the discovery of stone tools at locations about 150 kilometres north-west of Zhoukoudian indicates the long-term presence of a widespread and successful hominid population. The tools are not unlike those of a similar age from East Africa, which suggests the people making them may have been of African ancestry.[46]

Hitherto, palaeoanthropologists have assumed that the hominid populations in China and Indonesia which Weidenreich and von Koenigswald united as *H. erectus* originated from a group that dispersed from a single source in Africa, settling first in south-east Asia before moving north to colonize what is now mainland China. This consensus had been questioned, however, by evidence that *H. erectus* was present in China at least as early as the species appeared in Indonesia.[47] The temperate (Chinese) and equatorial (Indonesian)

H. erectus populations were probably not connected, a review paper suggests.[48] It seems more likely, the authors say, that the two groups derived from separate dispersals and have always been independent. This scenario suggests that after leaving Africa, one group took the coastal route around the Arabian Peninsula, along the southern flanks of the Himalaya and into equatorial south-east Asia, while the other passed through central Asia and southern Mongolia into the basins and plains of north-east Asia, a temperate region. Though sharing a recent origin, the two groups existed in parallel foraging niches on either side of what is now known to have been vast and ecologically unattractive forest.

While the idea that humans originated in Africa is widely accepted as a valid interpretation of the fossil and genetic evidence, it contradicts traditional Chinese views on their origin. For millennia, the Chinese have been taught to believe they are unique. An official encyclopaedia says all Chinese are the descendants of the Emperor Wu, a mythical ruler who supposedly saved his people by taming floods that threatened to ruin the country, 4,000 years ago.[49] The most accomplished Chinese palaeoanthropologists acknowledge that Africa has played a role in the early stages of human evolution and their publications in western journals reflect this premiss, but the government, other official bodies, some scientists, and the popular media still claim that although the very earliest ancestors of the human line may have originated in Africa, their descendants spread far and wide soon thereafter and established 'Man's place of origin ... in the southern part of East Asia'—China.[50]

In this scenario, fossil remains described as those of *Ramapithecus* found in Yunnan province represent the hominid ancestor, and human evolution proceeded in a direct line from *Ramapithecus* to the modern Chinese population. It is claimed that 'tool-using hominids, present in China since at least early Middle Pleistocene times (one million years ago) and perhaps much earlier, constitute the basal stock from which the various Chinese national minorities ultimately emerged'. Analytical research was said to indicate 'substantial continuity in the development of the mongoloid physical type as well as in the phylogenetic relationships among the various stages of hominid development ... [so that] ... although the modern mongoloid race seems to be a product of only the past few tens of thousands of years of evolution, its origins may be traced into the earlier Pleistocene ...'.[51] A 1990 publication even set 'the birthplace of the human being' on what is now the barren Tibet plateau, but was then the congenial slopes of the Himalayas (only 1,000 metres above sea level at the time), moistened by the warm and humid monsoon from the Indian Ocean.[52]

A sinocentric view of human evolution has probably helped to maintain the unity of a nation that constitutes one-quarter of all people alive today. The Chinese government officially recognizes fifty-six ethnic groups, and a belief in their shared (and unique) origin perhaps makes the rule of the Han people (93.3% of the population) more acceptable—but the foundations of this belief were shaken in 1998 by a team of Chinese geneticists who analysed the genetic profiles of twenty-eight sample populations in China and found that the 'evidence does not support an independent origin of *Homo sapiens* in China'.[53] Interestingly, the results showed that the closest living relative of the Chinese are Native Americans, followed by Australian aborigines and New Guineans, which confirms that people settled in Australia before reaching the Americas and therefore had more time to differentiate.[54] Their most distant relatives, however, were most definitely from Africa. In their discussion of the results the researchers wrote: 'It is now probably safe to conclude that modern humans originating in Africa constitute the majority of the current gene pool in East Asia.'

One might have expected these results to have aroused some interest if not outrage in China, but they were largely ignored. 'Do not expect Beijing's textbooks to be revised in a hurry,' wrote a commentator. 'That Chinese civilisation is unique is an idea deeply embedded in its political culture.[55] Indeed, while contradictory genetic evidence passed without notice, evidence supporting the traditional view received maximum attention. A skull found at Xuchang in 2008, Henan province, was hailed by government officials as 'the greatest discovery in China after the Peking Man... [which] will shed light on a critical period of human evolution'. *China Daily* welcomed the 80,000- to 100,000-year-old skull as a 'stirring' find that will:

> pose a challenge to one of the prevailing theories regarding the origins of modern man in China. The 'out of Africa' hypothesis contends that anatomically modern man first arose in eastern Africa about 150,000 years ago, then radiated outwards until the species eventually conquered the planet. The discovery at Xuchang supports the theory that modern Chinese man originated in what is present-day Chinese territory rather than Africa.

The oldest human fossils found in China so far are those of the 1.7 million-year-old Yuanmou Hominid. All ancient human fossils unearthed in China share a common morphology…which indicate[s] that ancient man living in China evolved continuously along an uninterrupted evolutionary chain for 1.7 million years.

Extraordinary archaeological discoveries are critical to maintaining our national identity as well as the history of our ancient civilization.[56]

Chinese reports on Xuchang Man (and other finds) highlight an important difference between western and Chinese attitudes regarding the role and purpose of palaeoanthropological science. In the West, the Chinese evidence is regarded as part of the broad picture of human evolution that is emerging worldwide; in China, it is a part of national history—an ancient and fragmentary part, it is true, but nonetheless one that is called upon to promote a unifying concept of unique origin and continuity within the Chinese nation.

CHAPTER TEN

Australopithecus substantiated (1936)

WHILE THE scientific establishment argued over the conundrum of Piltdown Man and was diverted by the discoveries from Peking, the significance of the South African fossil that Raymond Dart had named *Australopithecus africanus* in 1925 was neglected. After his skirmish with fame and controversy Dart applied himself wholly to the creation of a creditable anatomy department at the Witwatersrand Medical School. Meanwhile, lime-quarrying kept pace with the country's development and the cave deposits, together with the fossils they undoubtedly contained, were shovelled into the kilns without a thought for palaeontological considerations. That the potential Dart had identified was left unexploited, even wasted, was the result of circumstance and temperament unhappily combined. That it was exploited twelve years later, and Dart's claims subsequently vindicated, was entirely due to the initiative and effort of one man—Robert Broom.

The biologist J. B. S. Haldane once described Broom as a man of genius, fit to stand beside Shaw, Beethoven, and Titian;[1] and his biographer, George Findlay, offers the observation that Broom was about as honest as a good poker player.[2] On reflection, these remarks may not seem wholly complimentary when applied to a dedicated scientist, but the evidence of Broom's life and work indicates that both are true and neither is a discredit to the man or science.

Robert Broom was born in Scotland on St Andrew's Day 1866. Poor health and his family's lack of money permitted him only four years of unbroken schooling. Nonetheless, he entered Glasgow University at the age of 16 and emerged a Bachelor of Medicine and Master of Surgery at 23. At Glasgow he was introduced to the natural sciences while they were still freshly inspired by the work of Darwin, Lyell, Huxley, and Haeckel. He was a great believer in 'Missing Links' and searched for them assiduously in later life, but in effect he was a link himself—between the eccentric, idiosyncratic methods of Victorian science, among which he was reared, and the mechanistic, statistical investigations of the mid-twentieth century among which he died in 1951.

Broom held firm beliefs that were often provocatively displayed. He liked to remove all his clothes while fossil-hunting in remote hot places (he once misplaced them altogether), so that he might enjoy more fully the sunshine he considered so beneficial to health. To demonstrate the benefits of sunshine and fresh air in the treatment of flu, he once encouraged an African victim to leave his hut and sit in the sun outside while another stayed inside the murky hut. Next day, sunshine had cured one, and the other in the hut was dead.[3] To further his studies in physical anthropology, he buried dead prisoners and Bushmen in his garden, to be exhumed when decomposition was complete, and boiled their skulls clean on a kitchen stove. He sent a Bushman skeleton collected in this manner to colleagues in Paris, proudly claiming that it was 'probably the most perfect pure Bushman skeleton in the world'.[4]

The racist undertone of these actions (recorded in a biography that purports to be an 'appreciation') is chilling, but horribly typical of a time when science saw no shame in treating Africans and native Australians as the living representatives of an early, inferior, stage of human evolution.

In the field of palaeontology, Broom found and described key fossil evidence of the evolutionary link between the reptiles and the mammals but, although he accepted the theory of evolution, he rejected Darwin's proposal of Natural Selection as the driving force.[5] In Broom's view the process was too complicated and the results much too wonderful to be the product of mere chance. He believed that life on earth was the work and concern of a divine creative force.[6]

To a casual eye, a predilection for the odd and quirky is immediately evident in the bibliography of 456 papers, books, and monographs that Broom published during his lifetime.[7] But a closer look suggests that the explanation of the odd and the quirky was in itself a central theme of his scientific inquiries. Robert Broom's first paper, published in 1885 when he was 19, was 'On the volume of mixed liquids' and showed that two and two did not add up to four in the case of some chemical solutions—when mixed together the whole became less than the sum of its parts. His second paper (1888) was on 'a monstrosity of the common earthworm' and described a worm with two tails, each 'furnished with a perfect anus'. In 1895 he described the anatomy of a four-winged chick, and the Organ of Jacobson in the duck-billed platypus.

The Organ of Jacobson, a tiny accessory sense organ in the nose of many mammals, was one of Broom's lifelong interests. As a student he collected a specimen from a kitten and the comparative anatomy of the organ later became the subject of his doctoral thesis. Subsequently he described its anatomy in ant-eaters, squirrels, moles, horses, bats, shrews, and marsupials and, during the First World War, his collection was enhanced by the addition of a rare and fully developed specimen taken from the nose of an unsuspecting woman on whom he was operating for a quite different purpose.

Broom's interest in the Organ of Jacobson developed into a reasoned belief that since the organ was not affected by habit, its varying structure and form should provide clues to the zoological distinction between mammals whose appearance was otherwise very similar. This has echoes of the argument Richard Owen had deployed against the idea of evolution that was gaining support in the 1840s (see p. 76), but Broom's objective was to verify evolution, not disprove it. He divided a group of the Insectivores into three different orders on the basis of such evidence.[8] And in Australia, where he practised general medicine from 1892 to 1896, Broom found that the Organ of Jacobson in the duck-billed platypus is supported by a structure remarkably similar to that found in the snakes and lizards. The platypus is a mammal that lays eggs, and Broom's work on the Organ of Jacobson in its snout provided further proof of the mammals having evolved from egg-laying reptiles.

—————————

FIGURE 10.1 Robert Broom, some of his writings and drawings, an australopithecine fossil from Sterkfontein and an article on its discovery.

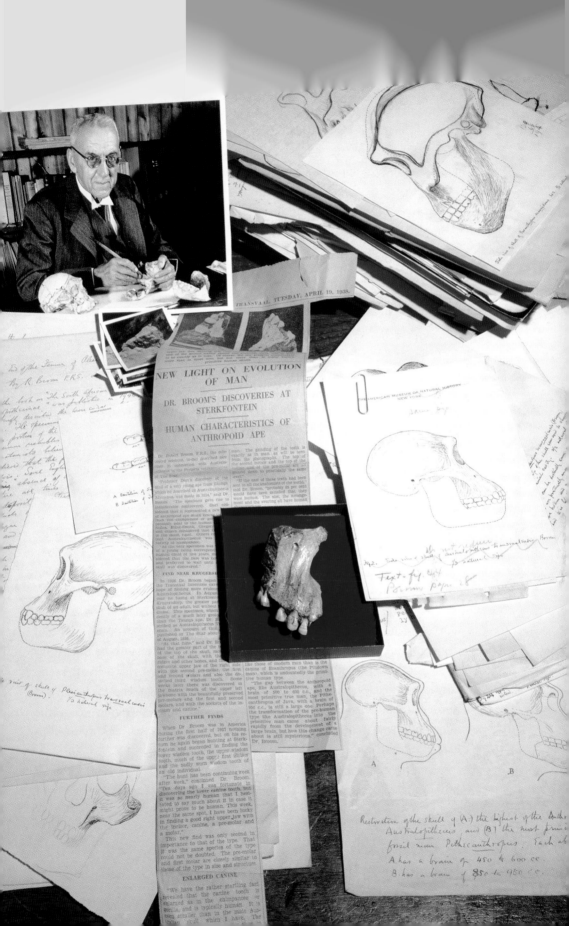

Broom moved to South Africa in 1897 and, turning from living creatures to the evidence of fossil remains, sought clues to the origin of the mammals among the fossil reptiles preserved in the ancient sediments of that country. He identified several important mammalian features in fossil reptilian skeletons and ultimately assembled a series of fossil forms that demonstrated, he said, the progressive stages by which a group of reptiles had evolved into mammals.

In 1920 Broom was elected a Fellow of the Royal Society; in 1928 he received the Society's Royal Medal for his work on the origin of the mammals. The citation read:

> At the time he went to South Africa thirty-five genera and sixty-five species (of fossil reptiles) had been identified. Little was known of their structure and the classification was hopelessly confused. He trebled the number of genera, quadrupled the number of species and worked out the details of the anatomy of most groups and established a classification that is universally accepted.[9]

In South Africa, however, Broom's work on the fossil reptiles was not quite so well received. Throughout his life Broom earned a living from medical practice; but for many years he also ran what amounted to a wholesale fossil business from his consulting rooms, paying collectors to bring him fossils, and selling them to museums abroad. In this manner a number of important specimens had gone to the American Museum of Natural History, who paid rather better than other establishments. Of course, this flow of fossils aided Broom's research as well as his pocket—as the Royal Society Medal amply demonstrated—but the South African museum authorities did not recognize such distinctions. The fossils belonged to South Africa, they said, and Broom had no right to sell them abroad for his personal gain. His behaviour was held to be reprehensible and dishonest. In the early 1920s Broom was forbidden all access to the collections of the South African Museum and his reputation in South Africa thereafter sank very low indeed, despite accumulating acclaim from abroad. The position eased a little with the death of the Museum Director, and was further improved by the interventions of General Smuts, Raymond Dart, and the discovery of *Australopithecus africanus*.

When the first reports of *Australopithecus* were published in February 1925, Broom immediately wrote to Dart, congratulating him on such an important discovery and noting that although he (Broom) had achieved so much, still he had not been 'so blessed by fortune' as Dart. 'The missing link is really glorious,' he wrote, 'perhaps I'll run up to Johannesburg for the day and pay my respects to my distinguished ancestor...what a new chapter you will be able to add [to the story of human evolution]. Possibly an adult skull or perhaps a whole skeleton will yet turn up'.[10]

Two weeks later Broom visited Dart's laboratory. Unannounced, and ignoring both professor and staff, he strode over to the bench on which the skull reposed and dropped to his knees 'in adoration of our ancestor', Dart recalled.[11] Broom spent a weekend examining the fossil and found nothing to contradict Dart's contentions. Although probably no older than the Pleistocene, the specimen was undoubtedly a 'Missing Link', he reported to Nature in April 1925,[12] connecting the higher apes with the lowest human types. Australopithecus was surprisingly similar to Java Man, he wrote, and probably the forerunner of Piltdown Man. Broom illustrated these affinities with a drawing of the adult Australopithecus skull he envisaged (and in which jaw and dentition almost precisely duplicated those parts in Piltdown Man); concluding his report with a reference to the 'considerable probability' that adult specimens would be found.

In common with Dart's critical reviewers, Broom knew that a proper evaluation of Dart's claims for the juvenile Australopithecus from Taung required adult specimens. But no adult specimens were found, or even sought, in the years immediately following the 1925 announcements. They were still undiscovered in 1934, when Robert Broom finally gave up medical practice and, at the instigation of General Smuts, accepted the post of palaeontologist at the Transvaal Museum in Pretoria. For nearly two years he worked on the collection of fossil reptiles, writing sixteen papers on twenty-three new genera and forty-four new species until, in May 1936, he decided to look for what he called 'an adult Taung ape', as he put it.[13] By then the cave deposits had been neglected for nearly twelve years and Dr Robert Broom was 69 years old. He already considered himself the greatest palaeontologist that ever lived, Broom later remarked, and saw no reason why he should not become the greatest anthropologist as well.[14]

It is never unreasonable to suppose that where one of a kind has been found there may be more, but in the case of Australopithecus the problem confronting Robert Broom in 1936 was not so much whether the fossils existed as whether there were any left. Dart's Taung fossil owed its initial discovery to the activities of lime workers; twelve years later, in a country short of lime, there were likely to be more scenes of devastation than discovery. Broom deplored the fact that the deposits had been ignored for so long. 'Dart was not much of a fighter,' he said, and had been too easily discouraged by criticism of his pronouncements.[15] But Broom found some consolation in the thought that even if he did not find the remains of *Australopithecus* he was certain to find some interesting Pleistocene mammals. He could not afford to travel to Taung, so he began his investigations on some old lime workings around Pretoria. Within a few weeks he had discovered half a dozen new species of rats and moles, a small sabre-toothed tiger, and a giant baboon.

Cave deposits and lime workings similar to those on which Broom was first engaged are common features of the dolomitic region to the north and west of Pretoria and Johannesburg. There are some near Krugersdorp, and if circumstances had taken Robert Broom to that small market town about sixty kilometres west of Pretoria, he probably would have noted Mr Cooper's general store on the main street where a sign beside a small display of fossils invited his customers to 'Buy Bat Guano from Sterkfontein and find the Missing Link'. Prodigious quantities of bat guano are frequently deposited in caves; it is a very good fertilizer and, as such, was a profitable adjunct to Mr Cooper's sale of agricultural and building lime from lime works at Sterkfontein, ten kilometres away.

The man in charge of the Sterkfontein quarry was a Mr Barlow, who had been manager at Taung when the first *Australopithecus* was found. No doubt Mr Barlow's interest in fossils had inspired Mr Cooper's window display, but it was one of Dart's graduate students, Trevor Jones, who eventually brought Sterkfontein and its fossils to Broom's attention.[16] Some of Jones's colleagues regretted Broom's intervention,[17] feeling that the subsequent discoveries ought to have been reserved for Dart, but there can be no doubt that Broom had more time and enthusiasm for the quest than Dart had shown. Broom pursued the investigation most energetically and found an adult *Australopithecus* skull at Sterkfontein on 17 August 1936, nine days after his first visit to the site and just three months after he had decided to look for one.

The discovery was almost an exact repetition of events at Taung twelve years before (if R. B. Young's account of those events is accepted—see p. 189). An endocranial cast was found after blasting in the morning, and rocks containing associated pieces of skull and face recovered from the rubble during the afternoon and the next day. The cast was undistorted and lacked only its rear portion, but the face and side of the head were badly crushed and, furthermore, the fossil bone was extremely friable and therefore very difficult to remove from the much harder rock in which it was embedded. Four upper teeth were also preserved, however, and one of these, together with the braincast, were in fact the only useful diagnostic features available in the new specimen. Broom acknowledged the inherent difficulty of comparing such fragmentary evidence of an adult with more complete juvenile remains, but reported to *Nature* that the 'newly found primate probably agrees fairly closely with the Taung ape', despite 'certain distinctive details' in its teeth.[18] Broom was no less confident of the fossil's human affinities and, in the *Illustrated London News*, described his find as 'A New Ancestral Link between Ape and Man'.[19]

The skull was first described as *Australopithecus transvaalensis*, Broom proposing specific distinction from the Taung specimen on the grounds of his belief that the Sterkfontein deposit was appreciably younger. Subsequently, however, he decided that the differences he had noted in the teeth merited generic distinction and renamed the creature *Plesianthropus transvaalensis*, which means 'near-man' of the Transvaal and defined Robert Broom's opinion of its position in human evolution rather more precisely than *Australopithecus*—'southern ape'. Since then, the generic distinction has been dropped and the specimen assigned to its initial genus: *Australopithecus*.

In November 1936 Robert Broom celebrated his seventieth birthday; in February 1937 he showed casts of the new discovery at a Congress of Early Man held in Philadelphia; in June he received an honorary doctorate from Columbia University—during a six-month tour abroad he was enthusiastically applauded wherever he went. But the acclaim was for Robert Broom more than for the fossil of which he spoke. The Sterkfontein discovery was notable, but hardly conclusive enough to persuade everyone that Raymond Dart had been right after all. Interest in the South African claims had dwindled considerably by 1937; the works of Keith and Abel (see p. 199) were widely regarded as the definitive appraisals of *Australopithecus*, and, although disagreement may have persisted on the question of whether the creature was related to the gorilla or the chimpanzee, there was general agreement with the contention that *Australopithecus* was not an ancestor of mankind. Polite scepticism characterized the majority view that Broom encountered abroad, but his belief in the ancestral status of *Australopithecus* was undiminished and, on returning to South Africa in August 1937, he immediately resumed the search for more substantial evidence.

In fact, Broom's investigations were dependent upon the financial arrangements he made with Barlow, who was encouraged to look out for interesting specimens exposed by the quarrying operations but expected to be paid for fossils of merit. Between August 1937 and May 1938 Broom bought from Barlow a wrist bone, a facial fragment, the lower end of a thigh bone and a nice piece of upper jaw with four teeth in place. All were undoubtedly remains of *Australopithecus* but none matched the significance of the first skull. And then on 8 June, Barlow produced a palate with one molar still in place that Broom knew to be worth considerably more than the two pounds he gave for it. Perhaps Barlow knew too, for he would not reveal precisely where the fossil had come from, and nor would the workmen when Broom returned to question them in Barlow's absence a day or two later.

Broom then tried a more straightforward approach: the specimen was very important, he told Barlow, it had belonged to a large ape-man quite different from those previously found at Sterkfontein. But some teeth had been freshly broken off, he said, and in the interests of science Barlow should assist the search for the missing teeth and more remains of the creature. Where had the fossil come from?

Relenting, Barlow directed Broom to Gert Terblanche, a young boy whom Broom found at school some five or six kilometres away. In the presence of his headmaster, Gert 'drew from the pocket of his trousers four of the most wonderful teeth ever seen in the world's history', Broom recounts.[20] They were the teeth missing from the palate; Broom promptly bought them, transferred them to his own pocket and, after enthralling pupils and staff with an impromptu lecture on cave formations and fossils, walked with Gert to the hillside where the palate had been found in an outcrop of eroded cave deposit. The place was called Kromdraai; it was but three kilometres from the Sterkfontein site and, as Broom had suspected, the deposit contained more remains belonging with the palate. Within

---

FIGURE 10.2 Fossil endocranial casts and facial remains of an adult austraopithecine (right) that Broom found at Sterkfontein in 1936, with other endocranial casts from the Transvaal cave deposits.

a few days Broom assembled a specimen comprising practically the entire left side of the skull, the palate and a large portion of the right lower jaw.

The face of the Kromdraai skull was flatter, the jaw more powerful and the teeth larger than in the Sterkfontein specimen. The whole aspect of the specimen was larger, more robust and, Broom believed, more man-like than either the Taung or the Sterkfontein skulls, so he gave the new specimen generic distinction from both of them and called it *Paranthropus robustus*, which means 'robust equal of man'.

In *Nature* Broom described the anatomical features of the new fossil and in the *Illustrated London News* his find was heralded as 'The Missing Link No Longer Missing'.[21] The scientific establishment responded predictably—chiding Broom for creating new genera on 'extremely slender grounds' (as with *Plesianthropus*, this specimen was subsequently assigned to the *Australopithecus* genus), advising greater caution and remaining unmoved by the new evidence.[22] Broom was equally unmoved by the criticism and continued the search for more remains.

Lime quarrying at Sterkfontein ceased in 1939 and the advent of the Second World War curtailed explorations at Kromdraai, so Broom continued his investigations in the laboratory at the Transvaal Museum, where he worked on the blocks of fossil-bearing rock he had previously removed from the Kromdraai deposit. From the block in which the *Paranthropus* skull had been embedded he recovered much of an elbow joint, an ankle bone and some hand and finger bones. Their close proximity to the skull implied that the bones belonged to the same individual and, although they hardly comprised the adult skull and skeleton Broom had hoped Dart would seek and discover, the scant collection did substantially vindicate Dart's claim that a small-brained, bipedal man-like ape with manipulative skills had once inhabited Southern Africa. The ankle bone was quite unlike that of either the gorilla or the chimpanzee, for instance, and more closely resembled the human form, strongly suggesting a habitual upright bipedal gait. The hand bones were slender and more suited to manipulative dexterity than to walking on all fours, and the elbow joint was similarly man-like. If the bones had been found separately no anatomist would have doubted their human affinities, but at Kromdraai they were associated with a small-brained ape-like skull which many scientists believed to be more closely related to the gorilla or the chimpanzee than to man. Was Broom's new evidence substantial enough to overcome the negative predispositions this association aroused?

Proper presentation of the evidence was vital. Preliminary reports appeared in *Nature*,[23] and casts of the Kromdraai remains were sent to interested parties, but the war undoubtedly diverted attention and judgement was effectively suspended while Broom gathered together all the evidence of the South African fossil ape-men for publication in a comprehensive monograph.[24] He worked on the volume during much of 1944 and 1945, describing the Taung, Sterkfontein, and Kromdraai fossils in turn; attributing them all to one subfamily, the Australopithecinae, while describing the basis for the generic distinctions he made between them. Broom's text filled 133 pages and was illustrated with well over one hundred anatomical drawings, all his own work. A further hundred pages of the monograph, reviewing the evidence of the endocranial casts, was the work of the Johannesburg anatomist G. W. H. Schepers.

In discussing the affinities of the Australopithecinae Broom concluded that 'these primates agreed closely with man in many characters. They were almost certainly bipedal and they probably used their hands for the manipulation of implements...The dentition...agrees remarkably closely with the dentition of man,' he said, and the brain, though smaller, was of the human type. 'What appears certain,' wrote Broom, 'is that the group, if not quite worthy of being called men, were nearly men, and were certainly closely allied to mankind, and not at all nearly related to the living anthropoids. And we may regard it as almost certain,' he wrote, 'that man arose from a Pliocene member of the australopithecinae probably very near to *Australopithecus* itself'.[25]

The monograph was published in Pretoria on 31 January 1946, a little more than two months after Robert Broom's seventy-ninth birthday, and its authoritative and comprehensive presentation won a large measure of support for *Australopithecus*. The scientific establishment began to suspect that Raymond Dart's bold assertions—made more than twenty years before—might have been correct after all. Sir Arthur Keith acknowledged the man-like attributes of *Australopithecus* but continued to doubt its ancestral status. Wilfred Le Gros Clark, the Oxford anatomist, on the other hand, was more wholly impressed by Broom's work. He wrote a favourable review for *Nature*[26] and subsequently visited South Africa to examine the original fossils. He found good anatomical reasons to support the contention that *Australopithecus* represented the stock from which mankind had evolved.

Though over 80, Robert Broom continued to search for *Australopithecus* remains in 1947; but, while his work and the South African cave deposits were achieving international recognition, some local authorities were becoming concerned about Broom's apparent lack of regard for geological evidence and the recording of stratigraphic detail. Now that important fossils had been found, this information was essential if the relative ages of the discoveries were to be established—especially at Sterkfontein, where the cave entrances had eroded away and lime workers had removed most of the interior.

Exercising its rights, the Historical Monuments Commission issued a ruling which expressly forbade Robert Broom to excavate without the assistance of a 'competent field geologist'. The ruling was intended to do no more than correct a deficiency, but its effect was threefold. First, it insulted Broom; after all, he had been a medallist in geology at Glasgow University, and had held the Chair of Geology at Stellenbosch University for seven years. Second, the ruling prompted Broom to begin excavations at Sterkfontein on 1 April in direct contravention of the Commission, believing, as he wrote later, 'that a bad law ought to be deliberately broken'.[27] And third, the ruling thus led to the discovery of a superb *Australopithecus* skull on 18 April. The specimen was undistorted and complete but for the teeth and the lower jaw. Broom, with his usual enthusiasm, described it as 'the most important fossil skull ever found in the world's history'; and indeed, its significance was readily acknowledged by scientists in Europe and America. In South Africa, however, Broom was unanimously condemned at a meeting of the Historical Monuments Commission and once more banned from the Sterkfontein site.

The irony of a world-renowned scientist being banned from the site of his investigations immediately following an important discovery did not escape the press and their cartoonists. Public and private pressure mounted and the ban was lifted a few weeks later. Broom triumphantly resumed work at Sterkfontein, with continuing good fortune. At the end of June 1947 he discovered a lower jaw, complete with teeth, which confirmed the man-like, rather than ape-like, attributes of the adult *Australopithecus* dentition. In August, he unearthed the ultimate prize: a nearly complete pelvis and vertebral column with associated leg bone fragments, part of a shoulder blade and upper arm. At last, twenty-two years after

---

FIGURE 10.3 Partial fossil skeleton from Sterkfontein: the first conclusive evidence that the australopithecines were bipedal.

Raymond Dart announced the new species, Robert Broom had assembled teeth, skulls, and skeleton of the adult *Australopithecus*, and the assemblage presented unequivocal evidence of the creature's man-like affinities. 'Congratulations on brilliant discoveries. Proof now complete and incontestable,' cabled Wilfred Le Gros Clark. 'All my landmarks have gone,' wrote Sir Arthur Keith, 'you have found what I never thought could be found': a man-like jaw associated with an ape-like skull, the exact opposite of Piltdown.

Keith's conversion to the belief in the ancestral status of *Australopithecus* was absolute. 'Professor Dart was right and I was wrong,' he conceded in a letter to *Nature*. In *A New Theory of Human Evolution*, written in his eighty-second year and published in 1948, Keith agreed that 'of all the fossil forms known to us, the australopithecinae are the nearest akin to man and the most likely to stand in the direct line of man's ascent'. They represented the pre-human stock from which the various divisions of mankind had evolved in the late Pliocene, he said; adding the suggestion that for the sake of brevity, if not contrition, they should be renamed 'Dartians'.[28]

With *Australopithecus* presenting such convincing evidence that the enlargement of the brain was the final stage of mankind's evolution from an ancestor shared with the apes, Keith now attempted to define the point at which the man-like ape could be said to have become man. In *A New Theory of Human Evolution* he proposed brain size as the measure, suggesting that just as the eruption of the first permanent molar provides a convenient mark for determining the end of infancy and the beginning of childhood in the individual, so the acquisition of a certain brain size could mark the species' evolutionary transition from apehood to manhood. Taking the largest known brain size in the gorilla (650 cubic centimetres), and the smallest known in man (855 cubic centimetres) as the most valid determinants, Keith proposed a cranial volume of 750 cubic centimetres as the 'cerebral Rubicon' to be crossed before the ancestors of mankind may be called truly human. By this measure, Java Man (with an estimated mean cranial capacity of 850 cubic centimetres) and Peking (ranging from 915 to 1225 cubic centimetres) were justifiably assigned to the genus Homo, while Australopithecus (435 to about 650 cubic centimetres) had not yet crossed the Rubicon.[29]

Of course, Keith's *New Theory of Human Evolution* in part reaffirmed views he had expressed thirty-six years before when he described the erect posture as

mankind's most ancient attribute and the large brain as a relatively recent acquisition (see p. 154). But the evidence of the large-brained, early Pleistocene Piltdown Man he had championed for so long was not so easily accommodated in
the new theory. 'If we could get rid of the Piltdown fossil fragments, then we
should greatly simplify the problem of human evolution,' he wrote,[30] but 'getting
rid of facts which do not fit into a preconceived theory' is not the manner usually
pursued by men of science, he continued, and proposed instead that Piltdown
Man should be regarded as an 'aberrant' type who found lonely refuge, and then
extinction, in England sometime after the late Pliocene.

Meanwhile Broom continued to search for australopithecine remains. In
September 1948 a site was opened under his direction at Swartkrans, another
disused lime quarry across the valley from Sterkfontein. *Australopithecus* fossils
were found within days, and many more have been found there since. In 1950
Broom was the principal author of a monograph on the Sterkfontein hominids[31]
and by then felt that the impact of his discoveries and publications was such that
only two eminent scientists remained unconvinced that the australopithecines
represented the ancestors of mankind. The dissidents were W. L. Straus and
S. Zuckerman, both of whom still maintained that the fossils were related to
the apes, not to man. Zuckerman, a zoologist, bothered Broom most; he had
made a pioneering behaviour study of the monkeys in the London Zoo and was
a scientist of standing and repute.

Zuckerman believed in figures and statistical method and would not accept
findings that did not demonstrate some metrical consistency. So, as Broom produced the fossils and his collaborator, Le Gros Clark, published reports defining
their man-like affinities, Zuckerman (aided by E. H. Ashton) checked their assertions by comparing the dental dimensions of the fossils with the corresponding dimensions of assorted apes. In all, he checked a total of forty-eight overall
dimensions in the fossils with those of eighty chimpanzees, ninety gorillas, and
sixty orang-utans.[32] The results, said Zuckerman, showed that the fossils were
more like the apes than like man.

Broom had little respect for mathematical method and scoffed at the findings. 'I suppose that because the molar teeth of horse and cow are often identical, Zuckerman would conclude that a horse is a cow,' he said. Le Gros Clark
was similarly sceptical, once remarking that measurements of length, breadth,
and height would proclaim a cube, a sphere, and a pointed star identical.[33]

Nonetheless, Le Gros Clark felt obliged to respond in kind and, using even more diagnostic measurements than Zuckerman, compared the fossils with the adult dentition of 238 gorillas, 276 chimpanzees, and 39 orang-utans, as well as with the juvenile dentitions of 39 gorillas, 105 chimpanzees, and 29 orang-utans.[34] These results directly contradicted Zuckerman's findings.

Some lively correspondence ensued, in the course of which a statistician revealed that the Zuckerman team had neglected to divide by the square root of two in some vital computation.[35] But 'the mistake was due to a misunderstanding in the interpretation of the analysis of variance', replied Zuckerman,[36] and made no difference at all to the overall result. Clark disagreed, but contrary to some claims,[37] the square root factor did not conclusively settle the argument either way. Indeed, the argument shows very clearly that the addition of complex detail can sometimes confuse an issue more than it clarifies it. In this respect, there is more to approve in the idiosyncratic, qualitative approach of an earlier age that Broom employed, than in the statistical quantitative methods that Zuckerman introduced in the mid-twentieth century.

Robert Broom died on 6 April 1951 at the age of 84. More than any scientist or discovery, Broom's work on *Australopithecus* fundamentally and unequivocally revised the study of fossil man. At first glance he may seem to have confused the story of mankind's evolution with a profusion of complicated names, new genera, and new species, not all of them warranted (and several introduced as 'Missing Links'). But the significant point is that Broom assigned all except one of the taxa to a single zoological subfamily, the Australopithecinae, and showed that these habitually erect and bipedal hominids, with their human-like dentition and relatively small brains were good candidates for the ancestry of mankind.

Today, palaeoanthropologists recognize two broad groups within Broom's Australopithecinae: the heavily built 'robust' australopithecines, which include Broom's *Paranthropus* from the 1930s,[38] as well as specimens unearthed in East Africa since the 1960s; and the lightly built 'gracile' australopithecines, which include both the Taung child and Broom's *Plesianthropus*, as well as the famous 'Lucy' and other *Australopithecus afarensis* fossils found in Ethiopia and Tanzania.

In 1945, while Broom was still busily collecting australopithecines from Sterkfontein and Kromdraai, another rich source of fossil material was found in the Makapansgat Valley, about 300 kilometres north of Johannesburg, by a team of students from Witwatersrand University under the leadership of Phillip Tobias, who was studying anatomy under Raymond Dart at the time. Tobias later succeeded to Dart's position at the Medical School, and has become a leading figure in modern palaeoanthropology. His work has broadened the subject in several dimensions (not least on library shelves), and its predispositions may be judged by the effort he has made to establish a personal connection with the original discovery of Australopithecus: 'My boy,' he exclaimed when queried on the point, 'I was conceived on the very day that Dart's announcement of *Australopithecus africanus* was published in *Nature*.'[39]

Tobias returned from that first visit to Makapansgat with the skull of a fossil baboon which suggested that the site might be as old as Sterkfontein and therefore a potential source of hominid remains. According to Dart, Tobias reawakened his interest in palaeoanthropology with this evidence.[40] Thereafter, excavations at Makapansgat provided Dart with the foundations of a theory which profoundly influenced the study of human origins, and lingered on in the popular consciousness for decades.

Australopithecine fossils were indeed recovered from Makapansgat, but Dart was more impressed by the evidence of australopithecine lifestyle that he believed was preserved at the site. He attributed the hominid fossils to a new species, *Australopithecus prometheus*,[41] on slight evidence that they had used fire (since refuted), and drew far-reaching conclusions from the variety of animal species and body parts found among the fossil remains, and their fractured condition.

A preponderance of certain bones persuaded Dart that the australopithecines had been using them as tools and weapons—long bones as clubs and bludgeons; shoulder blades as cleavers; horn-cores and split bones as daggers; mandibles as scrapers and saws. Examination of forty-two baboon skulls (from Taung and Sterkfontein as well as from Makapansgat) convinced him that twenty-seven (64 per cent) of them died from a violent blow to the head. Further investigation along these lines appeared to show that some australopithecines had been killed in a similar fashion, and Dart concluded that the australopithecines had been violent carnivores who indulged in cannibalism from time to time.

In 1957 Dart published a monograph entitled 'The Osteodontokeric Culture of Australopithecus prometheus', in which he presented the evidence of australopithecine lifestyle he claimed to have discovered among the fossil collections, but the conclusions he drew from that evidence were published four years earlier, in a paper entitled 'The Predatory Transition from Ape to Man'.[42] Herein, Dart described the australopithecine ancestors of mankind as essentially 'human in their cave life, in their love of flesh, in hunting wild game to secure meat…[who]…seized living quarries by violence, battered them to death, tore apart their broken bodies, dismembered them limb from limb, slaking their ravenous thirst with the hot blood of victims and greedily devouring livid writhing flesh'.[43]

Dart believed that the evidence of ancestral violence he perceived among the fossils explained what he saw as the predominantly aggressive nature of modern man. 'The loathsome cruelty of mankind to man forms one of his inescapable, characteristic and differentiative features; and it is explicable only in terms of his carnivorous, and cannibalistic origin', he wrote. 'The blood-bespattered, slaughter-gutted archives of history from the earliest Egyptian and Sumerian records to the most recent atrocities of the Second World War…[proclaim]…this mark of Cain that separates man dietically from his anthropoidal relatives and allies him rather with the deadliest of Carnivora.'[44]

Though Dart's theory of mankind's bloody ancestry evoked little positive response in academic circles, it found wide popular support—perhaps because its evolutionary perspective was a salving context in which to set painful memories of the recent war. The Hollywood dramatist Robert Ardrey spelled out the Dart version of human evolution in *African Genesis* (1961), a best-seller whose attitude towards man's early ancestors may be summarized by an index entry for 'tools' which instructs the reader to '*see* weapons'. The theme of ancestral violence was pursued in other notable books,[45] and found memorable expression in the opening sequence of Stanley Kubrick's film, *2001*, wherein the killer man-apes are seen eliminating their less able brethren. A rumour that Phillip Tobias had advised Kubrick on this sequence is untrue. 'It would have been fun to be involved,' he says, though 'a tremendous set-to over the issue of violence or gentleness' would have been hard to avoid. Tobias has been strongly opposed to the killer Ape theory for decades, he explains, and more inclined 'to see the early ape-like hominids as gentle creatures'.[46]

As Kubrick's film helped to etch an image of mankind's ancestors as violent (and hairy) little humans on the popular imagination, where the most deplored aspects of modern human behaviour were explained as a legacy of our evolutionary past, scientists were completing the circle with research and interpretations which explained the ancestral status of the australopithecines in terms of their human characteristics and behaviour patterns.

In general, archaeologists, anthropologists, and palaeoanthropologists tended to confirm the assumption that early man had been primarily a hunter. Stone tools and postulated living sites dating from millions of years ago were discovered in East Africa. The modern-day !Kung San (Bushmen) of the Kalahari provided a model of a way of life, seemingly based on hunting, that might have characterized that of early man in Africa. Hypotheses concerning the evolution of hunting were proposed;[47] conclusions about the social structure of early hominids were drawn;[48] and the 'home base' concept was established.[49] Early man went out hunting for food, it was said, while early woman stayed home and cared for the children—a style of living strikingly similar to that of suburban man in the post-war decades.

Meanwhile, a long-term observational study of chimpanzees conducted from Jane Goodall's research station in Tanzania's Gombe National Park was developing an alternative view of the apes themselves. The Gombe chimpanzees were observed hunting in organized bands and eating meat whenever the opportunity arose. They were predators too, the study showed, who killed and ate monkeys, bushpigs, buck—and occasionally their own kind.[50] People everywhere were shocked to learn that chimpanzees were not the innocent vegetarians whose behaviour Dart had compared so favourably with that of our bloodthirsty ancestors. Conversely, an intensive study of the !Kung San showed that people living as they did were more vegetarian than carnivorous, far more dependent on plants than on meat for their sustenance—gatherers more than hunters.[51] And as a final upset, Dart's proposal of a predatory transition from ape to man was directly contradicted by a definitive study of the fossil evidence upon which it was based.

More than a decade of research by C. K. Brain of the Transvaal Museum in Pretoria showed that fossil bones preserved at Makapansgat and in other South African cave deposits had accumulated naturally, over hundreds of thousands of years, without hominid intervention. They were the remains of animals who either had died in the caves, or had been carried there by predators—or even by porcupines, whose habit of dragging large bones back to their dens to gnaw (leaving tell-tale marks on the bones) is well documented. Brain showed that the bones were broken in rockfalls and under the sheer weight of the deposits accumulating above them, not by the action of hominid ancestors. Furthermore, the australopithecines found in the caves, far from being the bloodthirsty hunters of Dart's interpretation, were most probably the prey of leopards, Brain concluded. In short, the evidence gave every reason to believe they were the hunted, not the hunters, as the title of Brain's monograph suggests: *The Hunters or the Hunted? An Introduction to African Cave Taphonomy.*[52]

Taphonomy, the study of how and why fossils accumulate where and when they do, contributes important information to the story of human evolution. At Taung, for instance, reassessment of fossils recovered from the mining debris revealed a preponderance of small mammals (and no more hominids). This is very different to the state of affairs at other South African cave sites (where both hominids and large mammals are found), but very similar to what is found today beneath the nests of large eagles. Palaeontologists Lee Berger and Ronald Clarke examined the fossils more closely and saw that the manner in which the fossil baboon skulls from Taung had been broken matched those that eagles had discarded. There were typical bill and talon marks on the fossils too.

Turning to the feeding behaviour of South Africa's crowned, black, and martial eagles, they found that these raptors—with wingspans of up to two metres—commonly took monkeys, baboons, and even small antelope, along with the hyraxes, hares, rodents, and reptiles that form the greater part of their diet. In Zambia, crowned eagles were reported to have attacked and almost killed a 7-year-old child who weighed nearly 20 kg, and there were numerous reports of adults being attacked near eagle nests. Could the Taung child have been the victim of an eagle? Lee and Clarke believed this was a valid inference to be drawn from the taphonomic data. The Taung child would have weighed no more than 10–12 kg, they pointed out, well within a large eagle's capability and approximately the size of the baboons whose fossil skulls were found at Taung. The birds might have nested in a cave or rock shelter, leaving feeding debris to accumulate near by, as they do today; or their nest could have been in a tree growing above a pothole, into which the bones fell and eventually fossilized.[53]

While working on the Taung child fauna, Ronald Clarke was also supervising operations at Sterkfontein, a site destined to become the focus of ever-greater

---

FIGURE 10.4 Dr C. K. Brain in the Swartkrans cave (1978); two holes in the australopithecine skull (left) precisely fit the canines of the fossil leopard jaw on which it rests.

attention with its listing as a UNESCO World Heritage Site—the Cradle of Human-kind—and the opening of a multimillion dollar visitors' centre near by. While visitors were being taken on conducted tours through the caves, where they gazed in awe at the majesty of the caves and perhaps could imagine the sheer improbability of finding a fossil in their labyrinthine depths, the palaeontological work went on. Much of it above ground, where preparators were continuously working on promising blocks of breccia (the geological term for the fossil-bearing sedimentary rock that typically forms in caves) selected from among the mining debris dumped around the site. With air scribes they chiselled the concrete-hard matrix, millimetre by millimetre, from around the much softer fossils. The fossils they extracted were stored in boxes, identified by the species they were thought to represent, the dump from which the breccia had come and its location in the cave.

In late 1994, Clarke was looking through the boxes of fossils that had come from Dump 20 in 1980. His interest had been stirred by an apparent excess of carnivores and shortage of bovids [antelopes etc.] from that dump but was abruptly diverted when a hominid anklebone tumbled out. Clearly it had been missed. So had another three bones from the same foot, all of which fitted together—but with one very distinctive feature: the foot had a divergent big toe, indicating, Clarke said, that its owner possessed 'a degree of adaptation intermediate between the hominoid [ape-like] arboreal foot and the human foot adapted for habitual bipedalism'. A Missing Link, as it were, between the ape and human modes of locomotion at an early stage of human evolution.

Clarke's report (with co-author Phillip Tobias) appeared in *Science*[54] while the fossils were consigned to the Palaeoanthropology Research Unit's safe in the University of the Witwatersrand Medical School. It was there, two years later, that Clarke just happened, he says, to notice a box labelled D18 Cercopithecoids [Old World monkeys]. There was no reason for the D18 box to attract more of his attention than anything else in the safe, Clarke insists, and only a twinge of curiosity that caused him to take it out and have a look inside. The first thing he saw was a plastic bag labelled D20. A misplaced bag was annoying but also, given the consequences of his last encounter with D20, good reason to look through the box more thoroughly. He emptied the bag onto the table and found—yes!—the lower end of a hominid leg bone. That it would fit the foot bones seemed too much to hope for, and indeed it did not fit, but only because it was from the other leg. Further rummaging produced more leg and foot bones. Evidence of two legs and feet, all clearly from the same individual, whose entire skeleton might be awaiting excavation—if the spot from which the fossils had come could be located.

A big if… but there was reason to hope. One of the bones had a clean break, which could have happened when the miners were dynamiting the cave. If so, the matching face of the break should be exposed on the rock surface and the rest of the skeleton would be close by. But to look for the broken end of a legbone, about 2 cm across, on the expanse of a jagged and dirty quarry wall, roughly 20 metres underground, would be like trying to find a postage stamp down a coalmine. 'It was a chance in a million,' admits Clarke, but worth a try. At least they knew which of the several vast caverns the D20 breccia had come from. Clarke had casts made of the broken fossil and asked two of the Sterkfontein preparators, Stephen Motsumi and Nkwane Molefe, to go down and see if they could find its counterpart.

Clarke had other matters on his mind when he next returned to the site a few days later, and was completely unprepared when Motsumi and Molefe casually sidled up to him. 'You know that piece you asked us to look for? We've found it,' they announced. 'Good grief!' said Clarke, never one to over-emote. But indeed they had found it, and over the next days and weeks careful chiselling away of the breccia surrounding the exposed piece revealed more bones, and uncovered the left side of a complete skull. The state of preservation and position of the bones indicated that the rest of the skeleton was definitely still in the rock.[55] A year later, the bones of an almost complete left arm and hand had been exposed.

Excavation was a slow and tedious process—even though an electric cable had been run down to provide light and an awning erected to deflect the water constantly dripping from the cave vault. Also, the scattered and unpredictable distribution of bone within the breccia meant that the work had to proceed very slowly, removing the matrix, millimetre by millimetre, with infinite care. By 2003 Clarke had located and uncovered some ribs, the left and right femurs, tibiae, the left foot, part of the pelvis, and vertebral column. He could now say conclusively that the skeleton was lying on its back, with the left leg crossed over the right, its head facing down to its right side, and its left arm stretched out above its head. The body had probably rolled down the slope, he said, and the fact that so much was still joined together indicated that it was at least partially mummified before being covered with cave infill and, ultimately, fossilized.

The work proceeded steadily, though Clarke would not even hazard a guess as to how long it would take to free this unique and extraordinary specimen from the breccia. But the observations he felt able to make on the basis of what was already exposed gave an indication of the contribution the skeleton would make to science. For the first time, it was possible to determine the actual ratio of arm length to leg length in a single individual (all previous estimations were based on incomplete bones or those from different individuals). The hand bones were almost exactly human, Clarke wrote in a 2002 progress report, with a long thumb, a short palm and fingers and lacking both the long strong fingers used by chimp and gorillas for knuckle walking, and the elongated hand of the more arboreal gibbons and orang-utans. However, the finger bones were curved, indicating they were probably used for climbing.

The morphology of the foot and the hand, plus the limb proportions, showed that the Sterkfontein individual was a climber in the trees (using its powerful thumb in a vice-like grip) and bipedal on the ground, Clarke wrote, which implied that the strong opposable thumb evolved in the human ancestral stock for grasping branches and only later, when their descendants had adopted a mainly terrestrial way of life, was it to prove useful for tool-making and manipulation. He concluded:

> The suggestion in reconstructions and in the scientific literature that human ancestors were transformed into an upright position from a knuckle-walking ancestor is not supported by this new and important addition to the fossil record.[56]

'It's very exciting,' Rick Potts, director of human origins at the Smithsonian Institution remarked when the discovery was first announced, 'if in fact we do have a complete or nearly complete skeleton, we're going to learn an awful lot more by studying it rather than reconstructing *Australopithecus* from fragments'.[57] Quite so, for the Sterkfontein individual makes the paucity of conclusive evidence in the science painfully obvious (even Potts's remark could be read as an implicit warning against the danger of saying too much about too little). The skeleton is unlikely to have been a missing link in human evolution, but it is certainly a link that was hitherto missing from the science of palaeoanthropology.

FIGURE 10.5 Ronald Clarke with the australopithecine skeleton during its excavation from the rock deep in the Sterkfontein cave. Hand and lower arm (left); skull and humerus (right).

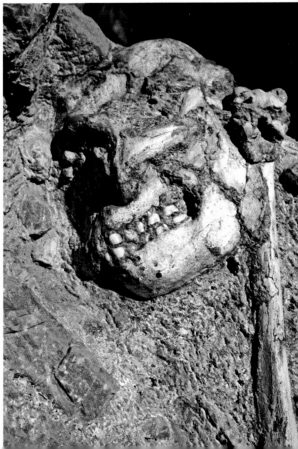

CHAPTER ELEVEN

Zinjanthropus boisei
(1959)

Louis Leakey (1903–72) often expressed affection and admiration for Raymond Dart and Robert Broom, but he never accepted their contention that *Australopithecus* was a direct ancestor. Leakey believed that human evolution has been a long slow affair, and that humans—in common with the rhinoceros and the flamingo, for instance—were shaped millions of years ago and have remained relatively unchanged ever since. The fossil record shows, he said, that most, if not all, vertebrate lineages have their dead branches along which related forms have evolved to extinction, and he saw no reason why the *Homo* lineage should be any different.

In Leakey's view, the hominid line leading to humans, and the line leading to the African great apes, branched away from their common ancestral stock about twenty million years ago,[1] and he believed there have been many more branches since then. *Australopithecus*, for instance, left the *Homo* line about six or seven million years ago, he said, and virtually every fossil mentioned in the preceding chapters similarly was no more than an 'aberrant offshoot' from the human stem. Neanderthal, Java, Peking, and *Australopithecus* were all, in Leakey's view, evolutionary experiments that ended in extinction. They were 'rather brutish creatures', who may have existed at the same time as the true human ancestor, but played no direct part in the story of human evolution.

These views echo the early pronouncements of Arthur Keith, Leakey's mentor; but whether they were wholly the product of his learning, or whether an upbringing as a missionary's son had predisposed Louis Leakey towards a belief in the antiquity of the human lineage, it is only certain that the views were formed early in his career and never changed. Throughout his professional life Leakey expressed the belief that human ancestry is a long direct line on which the enlargement of the brain was a decisive feature, thin skull bones a distinctive characteristic, and the ability to make stone tools a crucial development.

Stone tools are the key to the story of Louis Leakey, his wife Mary, and their discoveries at Olduvai Gorge. They are also perhaps the most evocative relics of our ancestors. Fossil bones may reveal the physical characteristics of the creatures whose flesh once clothed them—their height, their weight, the relative proportions of their bodies—but the tools they have left behind add an unexpected dimension of understanding. A stone tool may have lain undisturbed for more than a million years, but we can be certain that the hand that made it differs hardly at all from the hand that picks it up today. We heft it, consider using it, perhaps even imagine our lives depending upon it. That we are here to wonder is in itself proof of the evolutionary success of the lifestyle adopted by the early toolmakers. The cutting edge was the beginning of culture and technology. The crude stone tool is a tangible link with those origins.

Louis Leakey perceived the magic of this connection as a boy and undoubtedly it heightened his sensitivity to the subject, predicating his important discoveries and underscoring his success in print and the lecture hall. Louis Leakey could envisage and communicate the predicament of early man more eloquently than most; and his public audiences were probably unaware that the bold and inspiring story he told was as much the product of his intellectual and emotional preconceptions as it was a reflection of the evidence and the facts.

Young Louis' earliest ambition was to become a missionary like his father.[2] He was born on 7 August 1903 in a mud and wattle house that his parents occupied on the mission station established by the Church Missionary Society among the Kikuyu people at Kabete, fifteen kilometres from Nairobi. When he was 12 years old, Louis received a book on the Stone Age as a Christmas gift from a cousin in England and was immediately inspired to search for flint arrowheads and axeheads in the vicinity of Kabete. He had no clear idea of what he was looking for, or even of what flint was, but this deficiency was probably an advantage, for there is no flint in East Africa and if the young enthusiast had searched for what was not there he might have overlooked the obsidian flakes that were quite common in the road cuttings and exposed ground of the region. Assuming the shiny black material to be flint (actually it is volcanic glass), Louis collected every scrap he encountered. Subsequently he learned from Arthur Loveridge, the curator of the Nairobi Museum and Leakey's childhood hero, that his collection, though obsidian not flint, included some pieces that were undoubtedly Stone Age implements. The boy's delight can be imagined. Loveridge encouraged him to make a record of his finds and at the age of 13, Louis Leakey embarked upon a study of the Stone Age in East Africa, determined to continue until he knew all there was to know about it.

Many years later Leakey learned that in 1912 two American archaeologists had visited Kenya in search of human origins, intending to initiate extensive investigations if they found any worthwhile evidence. But, trained in the European tradition, they were looking for flint tools and of course found none. Leakey was convinced that had they not searched under this misconception they would have recognized the obsidian implements, discovered the archaeological potential of East Africa and pre-empted his entire career.

An upbringing among the Kikuyu hardly prepared the 16-year-old Leakey for life in the English public school he entered in 1920 in pursuit of formal education and his ultimate ambition: a degree in anthropology from Cambridge. He had gained a fair knowledge of French, Latin, and mathematics from his father and the tutors brought to Kabete, but he had no knowledge of the English academic system. He did not know the meaning of the word 'essay', understood nothing of Greek or cricket, made few friends, and by his own account was very unhappy. But it appears he was an extremely bright pupil in whom pride produced a fierce determination.

He caught up in most things (including cricket) and at Cambridge his upbringing proved to be a distinct advantage, enabling him to gain acceptance for the anthropology course by offering Kikuyu for the Modern Languages Tripos. In his autobiography Leakey says that although the university authorities were perplexed by the proposition, there was no regulation by which Kikuyu could be disallowed; it was spoken by a large living population, the Bible (translated by

Leakey's father) was evidence of its written form, and Leakey could produce two certificates of competent knowledge, one from a missionary and the other bearing the thumb-print signature of a tribal chief. The only problem was to find an instructor. The university wrote to the School of Oriental and African Studies in London, asking if examiners in Kikuyu could be found. The SOAS registrar replied in the affirmative and at a later date sent along their names: Mr G. Gordon Dennis, a retired missionary, and Mr L. S. B. Leakey; in other words himself.[3]

At the beginning of his second year Leakey suffered concussion on the rugby field. Severe headaches ensued whenever he attempted any reading and his doctor recommended a year's absence from all academic work. This was a serious setback to his ambitions, but Leakey solved the pressing problem of financing a year's enforced holiday by joining a British Museum of Natural History expedition to Tanganyika, where its leader, W. E. Cutler, hoped to recover the fossil remains of dinosaurs from some excavations at Tendaguru begun by German archaeologists before the war.

Cutler had collected fossil reptiles in America, but he had never been to Africa. Leakey's knowledge of the continent and its people was undoubtedly useful to Cutler, but Leakey himself appears to have been the major beneficiary of the expedition. He gained invaluable practical experience in excavating and preserving fossils, although the fossils they found were of minor significance. Leakey celebrated his twenty-first birthday at Tendaguru and returned to Cambridge with over one hundred ebony walking sticks, carved by the workmen in their spare time, which he sold on commission through some Cambridge tailors and thus financed a portion of his college bills. W. E. Cutler died of blackwater fever at Tendaguru some months after Leakey had left.

With First Class examination results and sheer enthusiasm to encourage grants, stipends, and other financial support, Leakey managed to organize a series of four archaeological expeditions of his own to East Africa between 1926 and 1935. The first two of these explored caves and burial sites in Kenya. An abundance of stone tools and recent skeletal remains was recovered. The later expeditions continued the investigations in Kenya, but also explored Olduvai Gorge in Tanganyika (now Tanzania) and here set the scene for the culmination of Louis Leakey's career.

Olduvai Gorge is an unavoidable feature of the south-eastern Serengeti Plains. The popular story of its accidental discovery by Professor Kattwinkel in 1911 is hard to credit, though Louis Leakey particularly enjoyed recounting how the German lepidopterist had apparently nearly plunged to his death over the cliffs of the gorge while in absent-minded pursuit of some exotic butterfly. Recoiling from the brink, Kattwinkel descended into the gorge and noticed large quantities of fossil bone lying about the erosion slopes. He made a small collection that aroused excitement in Berlin when it was found to include some bones from a three-toed horse. This extinct creature was well known in Europe from deposits of the early Pliocene period, but the Olduvai deposits seemed much younger than that, implying that the three-toed horse had survived longer in Africa than it had in Europe. This startling scenario called for further investigations and so, with the Kaiser's personal blessing, an expedition set off in 1913 to make a thorough study of Olduvai Gorge.

Led by Dr Hans Reck of the University of Berlin, in three months the team completed a geological survey, collected more than 1,700 fossils and confirmed the geological antiquity of the Olduvai deposits, but the significance of this work was overwhelmed by the controversy that arose when Reck claimed that a human skull and skeleton found in the lower deposits of the gorge was as old as the extinct animals from the same level. Reck returned to Berlin with the skull wrapped in his personal linen, while the skeleton followed with the other fossils. He announced the discovery in March 1914, and the London *Times* of 19 April that year reported him as saying that the ribs and breast were akin to those of the ape, while the skull was unmistakably human; an observation which he subsequently claimed as proof 'that the human race more or less as it is now is of considerably greater antiquity than has been imagined'.[4]

The skeleton had lain on its side, knees drawn up in the foetal position. Sceptics suggested that it had belonged to a tribesman of the recent past, who had been buried in ancient deposits. But Reck remained firm in his belief that the skeleton was contemporary with the extinct animals among which it was found, even though they were definitely of Lower Pleistocene age, a time when the human ancestor might be expected to look a little less modern than the large-brained Olduvai specimen.

To resolve the problem, Reck planned another expedition to Olduvai. Quite independently, but presumably attracted by the controversy, three other German expeditions to the gorge were planned as well; all four were actually on their way when war was declared in August 1914. None reached their destination. Reck stayed in Tanganyika as a government geologist and became a prisoner of war when the British took the Territory in 1916. After the war, Tanganyika became a British Mandated Territory, no longer so readily available to German science, with the result that the problem of the Olduvai skeleton was still unresolved when the first of Leakey's East Africa archaeological expeditions returned to England in 1927.

Some fossilized human remains that the expedition had recovered from a burial site near Lake Elmenteita in Kenya resembled Olduvai Man, Leakey thought, but the fossil fauna seemed very different; so he went to Germany to examine the Olduvai collections and discuss the matter with Reck, now returned to the University of Berlin. Reck still believed in the great antiquity of the Olduvai skeleton, but Leakey could not agree; he found the state of preservation very different from that of the extinct animal fossils and this, combined with the faunal disparity between Olduvai and Elmenteita, convinced him that the skeleton was younger than Reck believed, though not as young as the critics had suggested.

In this conclusion Leakey was essentially correct, but he was to change his mind before the problem of Reck's Olduvai skeleton was finally resolved. Meanwhile, his second East Africa archaeological expedition (1928–9) added another twist to the mystery. Skulls were discovered in a cave near Elmenteita which were even more like the Olduvai skull than the specimens found in 1927, yet the associated fauna was very much younger. And then there was the question of tools: why had none been found at Olduvai? At Kariandusi in Kenya, Leakey and his colleagues had collected impressive numbers of handaxes from deposits that Leakey was certain were the same age as Olduvai, yet Reck insisted that despite a most diligent search he had found no stone implements of any kind, anywhere in the gorge. But could he have overlooked them? Leakey suspected there was a good chance that he had. Quite apart from the circumstantial evidence, he recalled noticing a rock among Reck's geological specimens in Berlin which strongly resembled the handaxes from Kariandusi.[5]

With further investigations patently necessary, Leakey included Olduvai Gorge in the itinerary of his third expedition to East Africa and invited Hans Reck to join the party. He was so confident that there must be some evidence of Stone Age culture in the Gorge that he bet Reck ten pounds he would find a stone tool within twenty-four hours of arriving there. Reck was equally confident he would not. The party arrived at Olduvai Gorge just before 10 a.m. on 26 September 1931 and spent the rest of the day establishing their camp and water supply. Reck was up for most of the night as well. He had difficulty locating the spring he had used eighteen years before and, having awaited the rise of the full moon to light his way back to camp, was frustrated by the occasion of a total lunar eclipse that night. No doubt he had intended to sleep late the next morning, but that plan was frustrated, too, by the excited Louis Leakey who had left camp at dawn and found a perfect handaxe very soon thereafter. 'I was nearly mad with delight,' he writes, 'I rushed back with it into camp and rudely awakened the sleepers so that they should share in my joy'.[6] One of the principal objects of the expedition was thus achieved within twenty-four hours of arrival and Reck had lost ten pounds as well as a night's rest.

Subsequently, thousands of stone tools have been found at Olduvai, and doubtless thousands remain. Why had Reck not seen them on his first visit? It transpired that like the young Leakey at Kabete, Reck had been looking for flint tools but, unlike Leakey, he knew flint very well. Of course there is no more flint at Olduvai than there is at Kabete; the tools that litter the gorge are made from a variety of volcanic lavas, chert, and quartz, and Reck simply did not notice them (though apparently he took at least one back to Berlin as a rock sample). It is another example of how training can create preconception.

It was at this point, at the age of 28, with virtually the whole of East African prehistory laid before him, that Leakey's own preconceptions began to colour his interpretations, particularly those concerning the antiquity of large-brained *Homo sapiens*. This was revealed when Leakey and Reck reassessed the contention that Olduvai Man was as old as the Pleistocene fossil fauna found at the same level. Within four days of their arrival at the Gorge Leakey abandoned the evidence of the physical and faunal inconsistencies he had found so persuasive while examining the fossils in Berlin, and accepted instead his senior colleague's interpretation of the geology, concluding that the large-brained skeleton was as old as Reck had claimed.

Within a week of arrival, the expedition leaders sent a note to *Nature* claiming that the problem of the Olduvai skeleton was solved.[7] Stone tools reinforced Leakey's conviction. In marked contrast to Reck's previous visit, the 1931 expedition found tools in each of the five geological beds; and among them Leakey claimed to see an evolutionary sequence of manufacturing skills, from

FIGURE 11.1 Stone tools in a variety of materials collected from a single site in Bed IV, Olduvai Gorge date from about 700,000 years ago.

the simplest pebble tools of Bed I to the advanced handaxes of Bed IV. Later he claimed these discoveries were important enough 'to startle the scientific world and lead palaeontologists to revise their concepts of the age of *Homo sapiens*'. Reck's Olduvai skeleton was probably the maker of an intermediate pebble tool culture, he wrote in *The Times* of 3 December 1931, suggesting that '*Homo sapiens* goes back in East Africa to an age in the evolution of modern man far more remote than the evidence found anywhere else in the world suggests.'

A few weeks later tools and apparent traces of fire attributable to Peking Man were found in the Chou K'ou Tien (now Zhoukoudian) cave and, in a revealing comment, Leakey told readers of *The Times* that although Peking Man was probably the same age as Olduvai Man he represented a cousin, not an ancestor, of *Homo sapiens*. Further excavations at Chou K'ou Tien would probably show that *Homo sapiens* had lived there too, Leakey suggested, and had made the tools and the fire, while the remains of Peking Man were 'the relics of his meat feasts'.[8]

After the Olduvai interlude Reck returned to Europe while Leakey and the rest of the party set off to explore some deposits near a village called Kanjera in the vicinity of Lake Victoria. Fossils had been found there in 1913 and Leakey was anxious to see if the deposits matched the age of those at Olduvai. In a matter of weeks the contemporaneity was confirmed to Leakey's satisfaction—not least by the discovery of two fragmentary skulls as large as those of modern humans and his alleged ancestor from Olduvai Gorge, and then by a scrap of hominid mandible from another site (Kanam West) which Leakey claimed also represented *Homo sapiens* and was even older than Olduvai Man. 'The world's earliest *Homo sapiens*,' he called it, 'one step further back than even Olduvai.'[9]

Neither the Kanjera skulls nor the Kanam mandible were particularly impressive fossils, nor was the evidence for the antiquity of Olduvai Man very convincing; but such was Leakey's reputation in the early 1930s that he persuaded a number of important people to agreement on all counts. Arthur Keith for instance, who had rejected Reck's claim in 1914, wrote: 'In the light of the discoveries made by Mr Leakey in the Rift Valley, there can no longer be any doubt as to the antiquity of Oldoway [*sic*] man…I have had to reconsider my opinion and acknowledge that Dr Reck was in the right when he claimed Oldoway man as a representative of the Pleistocene inhabitants of East Africa.'[10]

At Cambridge in March 1933 a conference organized by the Royal Anthropological Institute expressly to examine all aspects of the Kanjera and Kanam finds unanimously agreed with Leakey's interpretations and congratulated him 'on the exceptional significance of his discoveries'.[11]

Leakey had achieved considerable success at a relatively young age, but how much of it was due to the fact that his views so closely echoed those of his mentors? Is it simply ironic that Sir Arthur Keith, Professor Elliot Smith, Sir Arthur Smith Woodward, and Dr W. L. H. Duckworth (the triumvirate of British anthropology plus one), who all congratulated the 30-year-old Louis Leakey in 1933, were the very same gentlemen who had cast doubt upon the announcement of *Australopithecus* by the 32-year-old Raymond Dart seven years before? Or does the irony reveal the predispositions of those involved ? *Australopithecus* was an ape, they had said; but Leakey's fossils differed hardly at all from *Homo sapiens*, despite their apparent antiquity. 'A most startling discovery,' commented Arthur Smith Woodward.[12] However, while Dart's pronouncements were corroborated by later discoveries, Leakey's were soon discounted.

Leakey's moment of acclaimed success was brief. It was first tainted by the findings of independent geologists reconsidering the antiquity of Olduvai Man. They showed that the body had been buried comparatively recently in an ancient Bed II surface exposed by faulting that was subsequently covered again during the deposition of Bed V. Reck and Leakey had to agree.[13] Olduvai Man was not the oldest *Homo sapiens* after all. Reck had been wrong and Leakey was left with only the dubious comfort of learning that his first interpretation of the evidence had been correct. But even that comfort evaporated when a voice of dissension was raised concerning the provenance of the Kanam and Kanjera fossils. It came from the Professor of Geology at Imperial College London, Percy Boswell, who suggested that more evidence of the geology and palaeontology ought to be collected before definite conclusions could be drawn.

Boswell was a Senior Fellow of the Royal Society, a most important figure, and it is a measure of Leakey's conviction and straightforwardness that his response to the implied criticism was an invitation for Boswell to join the fourth expedition to East Africa then being planned. If the Royal Society would finance Boswell's trip, Leakey would be happy to accompany him to Kanam and Kanjera so that Boswell might assess the evidence for himself and science. However, commendable though this action was, it did nothing to strengthen Leakey's case; in fact, Boswell's assessment virtually destroyed it.

The first essential was that Leakey should prove to Boswell that the Kanam and Kanjera remains had been found in the deposits precisely as claimed, and not washed in or carried there from somewhere else. For reasons unexplained, Leakey had not made a map recording the position of each discovery in 1932, an omission which became doubly unfortunate when, on returning with Boswell nearly three years later, he found that local tribesmen had removed all the iron pegs he had hammered into the ground to mark the spots. Furthermore, a camera fault had rendered all Leakey's photographs of the sites useless, and those of another expedition member proved to have been incorrectly labelled when he attempted to locate the sites from them. In short, it was impossible to show Boswell the precise location of the finds. This did not entirely disprove Leakey's claims, but Boswell would not accept them on trust. 'It is regrettable that the records are not more precise,' he commented in *Nature*, and 'disappointing, after the failure to establish any considerable geological age for Olduvai Man…that uncertain conditions of discovery should also force me to place Kanam and Kanjera man in a "suspense account"'.[14]

Louis Leakey's attempts to explain the debacle were not persuasive, although his own belief in the conclusions remained unshaken.[15] Boswell's conclusions did little to enhance the reputation of either Leakey or Kanam and Kanjera, but did not deter a succeeding generation of palaeontologists looking for sites to explore. Expeditions to the area fifty years later recovered many fossils and artefacts from the Acheulian, Middle and Late Stone Ages. Major programmes of investigation at Kanjera have shown that while Leakey's site management was poor, his conclusions were essentially correct: ancestral hominids had used the site during the Pleistocene, and into the Pliocene. The new evidence came from over 200 square metres of excavation, a one-metre-deep section of which yielded approximately 4,000 artefacts and 3,000 fossils. Laser technology was used to record the three-dimensional coordinates of each of the thousands of objects recovered directly from the dig, and the provenance of thousands more recovered by sieving is known to square metre and 5 cm depth.[16] Such finesse was not available to Louis Leakey, but even a modicum of care would have supported his case.

No hominid fossils were found, but the association of tools and animal bones (some with the cut marks that typically occur when fresh meat is cut from the

FIGURE 11.2 Louis Leakey on an early expedition; the Kanjera fragments and a reconstruction; the Kanam jaw fragment in the foreground.

bone) made the presence of hominids irrefutable. The studies also showed that Leakey's Kanjera hominids were decidedly recent, and thus 'probably irrelevant to theories of the origins of modern humans'.[17]

After the Kanam and Kanjera debacle, Boswell returned to England and the Fourth East African Archaeological Expedition spent several months at Olduvai Gorge, where Leakey's research team comprised himself, a geologist, a zoologist, a surveyor, and a young archaeologist named Mary Nicol. The expedition concentrated its attention on sections of the Gorge which had not been fully explored on previous visits, noting geological evidence and collecting palaeontological specimens. Large numbers of Stone Age implements were recovered, from horizons throughout the sequence, which enabled Leakey to substantiate (to his satisfaction at any rate) the evolution of the stone tool culture at Olduvai he had proposed in 1931. He described the simple pebble tools of Bed I as the Oldowan Culture, and traced the growth of manufacturing skill from the Oldowan, through eleven stages, to the relatively sophisticated tools of Bed IV, which he compared to the Acheulean flint handaxes of Europe.[18]

In all, the potential for prehistoric research at Olduvai was confirmed. Altogether, Leakey's 1931 and 1935 expeditions explored about 300 kilometres of fossiliferous exposures up and down the Gorge, ranging in depth from seventeen to one hundred metres of cliff and slope face. They discovered more than thirty promising sites, identifying them with the initials of expedition members followed by the letter 'k' for 'korongo', which is the Swahili word for 'gully'.

The stone tool Louis Leakey had found when he first visited the Gorge with Hans Reck in September 1931 signified the beginning of his work at Olduvai; he named the site FLK for his wife, Frida. Towards the close of the 1935 season, Mary Nicol found two fragments of a fossilized human skull among remains of antelopes and pigs and a scattering of stone tools at a site they named MNK. The pieces were small and isolated but undeniably hominid. In effect they marked the end of the first stage of Leakey's Olduvai investigations with a hint that Olduvai held the sort of evidence that no critic could dispute: the campsites of early humans, on which their fossilized bones were preserved, along with their stone tools and the remains of their meals. And if the Gorge held hominid fossils in each of its geological levels, then Leakey would be able to show the process of human evolution from the Lower Pleistocene to recent times—a prehistorian's dream.

In 1936 Louis Leakey was divorced by his wife and married Mary Nicol, bringing down upon themselves the opprobrium such behaviour attracted at that time. Leakey's biographer implies that the divorce precipitated their move to Kenya once Leakey came to realize that, in conjunction with the Kanam and Kanjera affair, the divorce rendered him unsuitable in some eyes for the academic posts he would have liked to fill at Cambridge.[19] Perhaps; in any event, it was not until 1951 that stage two of his Olduvai investigations seriously commenced.

For many years academic and government institutions were Leakey's main source of funds, supplemented from his own pocket and the proceeds of his popular writings. In 1948, however, his financial problems were eased by the generosity of an American-born London businessman with an interest in prehistory, Charles Boise. Early in 1948 *The Times* had published a letter from Louis Leakey, describing the problems of conducting such research in Kenya. This caught the attention of Boise and prompted him to contribute £1,000 towards Leakey's research. Subsequently Boise visited the Leakeys in Kenya, travelled with them to Olduvai Gorge and became the major contributor towards the cost of the excavations that began there in 1951; first in the form of direct financial aid, and later through the Boise Fund which he established at Oxford University expressly for the purpose.

Leakey's early Olduvai investigations had been limited to surface explorations, with very little excavation, mainly because of the expense of the petrol that would have been needed to maintain an adequate water supply for a large workforce. Boise solved the money problem, but now time was the limiting factor. Olduvai Gorge was in Tanganyika; Leakey was a Kenya government employee and could hardly explore the prehistoric site of another country on official time, so work there was restricted to his holidays and unpaid leave.

Accordingly, the Leakeys concentrated attention on the most promising of the sites that the surveys had revealed; in particular BK (Bell's Korongo) and SHK (Sam Howard's Korongo). Both were in Upper Bed II, both were what the Leakeys took to be living floors and both provided large accumulations of stone implements and the fossilized remains of the animals the occupants might be presumed to have eaten there. At SHK there were over two thousand stone implements and evidence of a unique and extensive mammalian fauna. BK proved to be a veritable 'slaughter house', with more than three thousand stone tools littered among numerous animal bones. Remains of the extinct *Pelorovis* were especially prevalent: prompting Louis Leakey to suggest that a group of hominids had driven a herd of the massive herbivores into a bog there, dragging out the smaller individuals for the slaughter while the largest became inextricably stuck in the mud, where they died. One skeleton was found standing upright.[20]

A remarkable feature of the Upper Bed II fauna was the presence of several giant herbivore species. Louis Leakey suggested that optimum feeding conditions were responsible for their development.[21] The giants included a pig the size of a hippo (whose tusk was at first mistaken for that of a primitive elephant); *Pelorovis*, with a horn span in excess of two metres (first classified as a sheep but later shown to be a relation of the buffalo) and a baboon the size of a gorilla. The size aspect was seized upon by the *Illustrated London News* which published a review of the latest discoveries from Olduvai Gorge in 1954, with an artist's impression of the prehistoric creatures looming above their modern counterparts. Olduvai had been the hunting ground of prehistoric humans, the headline implied and, at the conclusion of his accompanying article, Louis Leakey wrote: 'the remains of the men themselves still elude us, and it is interesting to wonder whether, when found, they will be giants like the animals they hunted, or of normal stature.'[22]

Leakey himself provided an answer of sorts four years later, with the description of two hominid teeth found at the BK site in 1955. One was a canine and the other a molar. The canine attracted little attention, but the molar was unusual enough to fall into the category of uncertainty that inevitably attracts controversy, not least because Louis Leakey suggested that, though huge, it had come from the lower jaw of a 3- to 5-year-old human, which meant the child would have been a giant. Leakey's judgement was based upon the cusp pattern of the tooth. In *Nature* he remarked that although the pattern was the most unusual he had ever seen in a deciduous (milk) molar, the tooth nonetheless had more affinities with fossil and modern humans than with the australopithecines. 'We are, therefore, possibly dealing with a very large true hominid which is not of australopithecine type. The teeth, in fact, suggest we are dealing with a human.'[23] The *Illustrated London News* reported the discovery more colourfully: 'A giant child among the giant animals of Olduvai?…a really gigantic human milk tooth has been found at Olduvai Gorge…which suggests that [prehistoric] Man in Tanganyika may have been gigantic'.[24]

The tooth was certainly a puzzle, but many believed that an anatomist, John Robinson, had given a more likely explanation of its size. It was not a milk tooth from the lower jaw of a human child, Robinson said in his *Nature* paper, but a permanent tooth from the upper jaw of an australopithecine adult.[25] Robinson had excavated australopithecines with Robert Broom and written a monograph on their dentition; his word carried weight, but before Louis Leakey's reply pleading uncertainty appeared in print,[26] events were overtaken by an even more contentious discovery.

By the end of the 1958 season, the Leakeys were beginning to feel they had exhausted the immediate potential of Bed II and decided that in 1959 they would first of all look for living sites among the Laetoli deposits south of Olduvai. Three weeks at Laetoli proved totally unrewarding, but soon after their return to Olduvai a hominid tooth was found at MK I, a Bed I site that had yielded many Oldowan tools since its discovery in 1931. The tooth obviously rendered MK I worthy of immediate excavation, but research funds for the year were finished.

Leakey returned to Nairobi and managed to arrange an overdraft on his research account sufficient to cover three weeks' excavations at MK I. He also arranged for the operation to be filmed by Des Bartlett for Armand and Michaela Denis's *On Safari* British television series. Bartlett was to arrive on 17 July, bringing with him the Leakey's 14-year-old son Richard. Louis and Mary travelled down a few days in advance. On the morning of the 17th Louis remained in camp, recovering from a bout of influenza. Mary took the dogs and walked across to the FLK site where the first stone tools had been found in 1931 and where she and Louis suspected there might be an Oldowan living floor.

At about 11 a.m. she noticed a skull just breaking the surface of a slope about seven metres from the top of the bed. At first glance it was not at all like a hominid, for the exposed bone was not solid as in human skulls, but permeated with air cells like the skulls of very large animals where compensation must be made for excessive weight. She brushed away some of the covering soil and two teeth were revealed, unquestionably hominid, but suspiciously australopithecine.'I was tremendously excited by my discovery and quickly went back to camp to fetch Louis,' Mary Leakey wrote, but Louis did not share her excitement. 'When he saw the teeth he was disappointed,' she continued, 'since he had hoped the skull would be *Homo* and not *Australopithecus*.'[27]

Nonetheless, FLK proved to be a site of unique significance. In terms of what was known at the time, it was an occupation site, but older, less disturbed, and more informative than any that had been found before, anywhere in the world. Many thousands of years before, a group of hominids had camped at FLK, which was then located beside a lake whose waters rose and fell periodically. As the site became littered with their debris, the hominids moved away and shortly thereafter the rising lake waters combined with a fortuitous shower of volcanic ash to preserve the clues of their presence and lifestyle. Organic matter such as skins, wood, and the like soon rotted away, but the bones of the animals they had consumed, many of them broken to extract the marrow, were covered over before the weathering effects of sun and rain could fragment them further. Among the bones, the hominids left many stone tools of the Oldowan culture; and on the same living floor, in direct association with the animal remains and the tools, lay the impressively complete skull that Mary Leakey discovered that July morning.

If the skull had been *Homo* it would have vindicated Leakey's claims for the Kanam and Kanjera fossils, but the new skull had obvious australopithecine affinities and this was far more discomforting than its failure to settle an old argument. At FLK the Leakeys had discovered, for the first time ever, hominid remains of great antiquity and indisputably associated with stone tools. By the accepted definition of the time, a toolmaker *was* man,[28] but the skull that lay among the tools was clearly an australopithecine, who supposedly had been incapable of making tools, and whom Louis Leakey had repeatedly excluded from his version of human evolution.

By 1959, Louis Leakey was one of only a few that still refused to accept Dart's and Broom's assertion that *Australopithecus* was an ancestor of man, but he was one of many still unwilling to believe that the creatures had been capable of making tools. Simple tools of the Oldowan type were known to have been made during australopithecine times, but who made them was another question. The evidence against *Australopithecus* was entirely negative: the brain was not large enough, there was no proof that he had made tools. A few chipped pebbles had been found together with australopithecine fossils in one of the gravel levels of the Makapan caves in South Africa, it was true, and Dart claimed they were tools made by *Australopithecus*,[29] but other authorities were sceptical. The chipping could have been natural, they said, and the specimens were too heavily weathered to be conclusive.

A large collection of more acceptable tools had been recovered from the Sterkfontein caves between 1956 and 1958, though not associated with any fossils. Who had made these? The site had produced large numbers of australopithecine fossils, but John Robinson thought it more likely that the tools had been made by a more advanced hominid from the Swartkrans site, a mile or so away.[30] In this conclusion Robinson was congratulated by Louis Leakey for 'proving...that these "near-men" [australopithecines] were contemporary with a type of early man who made these stone tools and that the australopithecines were probably among the victims which he killed and ate'.[31]

This remark echoed Leakey's comment on the occurrence of tools with the *Sinanthropus* fossils at Peking, made twenty-seven years before; indeed, it expressed his long-standing and vigorously expounded belief that the pedigree of Man the Toolmaker was a line of great length and exceptional purity, from which most of the hominid fossils found theretofore were but 'aberrant offshoots'. How extraordinary then, that it should fall to Leakey to discover the most 'aberrant' of those 'offshoots' lying among some of the earliest known examples of stone tools on what was then regarded as the world's oldest and best preserved living floor of early humans.

Research does on occasion uncover evidence that directly contradicts pre-conception, but rarely is the confrontation as stark as Louis Leakey faced at FLK. The evidence of skull and tools in direct association implied that a group of australopithecines had made the tools, where one of their number had died. But if the australopithecines had made the tools then they qualified as human ancestors, a corollary which contradicted Leakey's notion of human evolution. In these uncomfortable circumstances, he might have been expected to cling to his preconceptions and suggest that, as with Peking and Sterkfontein, FLK had been the campsite of another hominid species, the true ancestor of humans, who made tools and ate australopithecines along with all the other animals whose bones littered the living floor, but was still unknown in the fossil record. In the long term, his preconceptions have proved closer to the truth than the implications of the evidence; but in the short term Leakey took the pragmatic view and resolved the dilemma with a blend of interpretation and preconception that revealed the extent of his faith in both and brought extensive publicity.

Because the skull was virtually intact he concluded that it represented the occupants of the campsite rather than their victims; because of direct association he concluded that the occupants of the site had made the tools with which it was strewn; because the occupants had made tools he concluded that the skull represented a human ancestor; but because he did not believe the australopithecines had played any part in the *evolution of modern humans* he concluded that the

Olduvai specimen was not an australopithecine, and created a new genus to accommodate the phenomenon: *Zinjanthropus boisei*. *Zinj* is the ancient name for East Africa, *anthropus* means man, and *boisei* of course honours Leakey's benefactor: *Zinjanthropus boisei*: Boise's East African Man.

Though the recovery of the skull and the subsequent reconstruction of the specimen might have been expected to take some time, Leakey's announcement of the new genus was written and ready to appear in an edition of *Nature* less than a month after the discovery,[32] but although dated 15 August 1959, a printers' strike delayed actual publication until September.[33] The skull showed no sign of having been broken before fossilization, Leakey said, so there was no good reason to suppose that its owner had been 'the victim of a cannibalistic feast by some hypothetical more advanced type of man'. It was much more likely that the fellow and his kind had themselves made the tools among which he was found. But, whereas for some this might have proved that *Australopithecus* was a toolmaker after all, for Leakey it meant that the Olduvai toolmaker was not an australopithecine. He conceded general affinities but claimed the new skull differed from both *Australopithecus* and *Paranthropus* much more than the two genera differed from each other; he listed twenty points that he felt supported the call for generic distinction and concluded: 'the new find represents one of the earliest Hominidae, with the Olduvai skull as the oldest yet discovered maker of stone tools'.

In the *Illustrated London News* he was bolder: 'Zinj was a close relative of the "near-men" of South Africa and yet he was a man in the sense that he was a maker of stone tools "to a set and regular pattern"…Zinj, moreover, shows a number of morphological characters which are definitely man-like, far more so than any of the South African "near-men" and so he can be regarded almost certainly as being in the direct line of our ancestry'.[34] And in the *National Geographic* magazine he described 'Finding the World's Earliest Man…who lived in East Africa more than 600,000 years ago'.[35]

It is unlikely that Leakey persuaded any but the uninitiated with his claim that Zinj was an ancestor of man and the australopithecines were not. John Robinson called the new genus 'unwarranted and biologically unmeaningful', and claimed that the characteristics Leakey saw as distinctive of *Zinjanthropus* were, in his view,

---

FIGURE 11.3 *Zinjanthropus boisei*, the original specimen set against the Castle, a distinctive feature of the Olduvai landscape.

either related to the greater size of the specimen, or were not real differences at all.[36] But a questionable new genus could not detract from the significance of the specimen itself. The skull was more complete and less distorted than any of the South African forms and its discovery at such an ancient level, along with pebble tools marking the beginnings of human technology, was a major event in the progress of the science. It could hardly have been more appropriate in the centenary year of *The Origin of Species.*

In the one hundred years since Darwin had provided a theoretical basis, zoologists had been striving to establish the path of man's evolution from primal origins. At the same time, archaeologists and prehistorians, encouraged by Joseph Prestwich's confirmation of the geological antiquity of stone tools, also published in 1859, were delving ever deeper for the origins of culture. The two lines of inquiry, both seeking the roots of humanity, appeared to have met when skull and tools were found together at the FLK site in Bed I of Olduvai Gorge. 'It is now clear that tools ante-date man,' wrote anthropologist Sherwood Washburn.[37]

The skull's evolutionary significance and the tools' relationship to the origin of humans were matters of interpretation, quite distinct from the fact of their antiquity. Whatever those interpretations may be, and no matter how varied, the new evidence from Olduvai Gorge was a milestone of the science—a reference point against which earlier and subsequent discoveries would be assessed. The certainty of antiquity stemmed from the geological circumstances of the Gorge which, though not uncomplicated, could be discerned more easily than most. The Gorge slices through a 'layer cake' of deposits, revealing a sequence of remarkable clarity. Furthermore, it is packed with fossils, and the advent of new species, combined with the extinction of others through the ascending strata, enables palaeontologists to determine the relative age of Olduvai fossils with unusual accuracy.

Zinj and the tools had accumulated at FLK during Lower Pleistocene times. That much was certain, and no one was inclined to dispute Leakey's claim in *The Times* that 'the Olduvai skull represents the *oldest* well-established stone toolmaker ever found anywhere'.[38] But relative age determinations are of limited value, particularly in attempts to discern the detail of hominid evolution, all of which is packed within the relatively recent geological past. Something more precise was called for: an absolute timescale that would give ages in years rather than in geological eras.

The actual age of this or that fossil was frequently given in books and articles, it is true, but these were very rough estimates based on guesses of how fast evolution proceeds, or how long sedimentary deposits take to accumulate. In the science, these estimates had little value—everyone knew they were produced primarily for the media (where their inconsistency might have confused as many as were enlightened). So the suggestion that Zinj was over 600,000 years old would not have disturbed Leakey's colleagues too much, even if they were unaware that the suggestion had originally come from a science writer, G. Mortelmans, who should have known better.[39] However, not many months later Leakey himself claimed that Zinj was not just 600,000, but 1.75 million years old; and this claim did startle his colleagues, not only because of the great age, but also because Leakey and his co-authors claimed that this was the *absolute* age of the fossils.[40] This announcement introduced the potassium–argon dating procedures to palaeoanthropology, a development that matched the importance of the fossils themselves.

During the 1950s, as the inquiries of palaeontologists and archaeologists approached their rendezvous with Zinj and stone tools at FLK, a group of geologists and physicists in the laboratories of the University of California at Berkeley were working out how to determine the age of sedimentary deposits with far greater precision than the geological timescale allowed. The principle upon which the Berkeley group's work was based is simple enough: certain chemical elements are unstable in that spontaneous disintegration occurs within their atoms; as this disintegration proceeds radioactivity is emitted and different chemical elements are formed successively until a stable state is reached. Uranium, for instance, eventually becomes lead. The rate of disintegration is consistent and can be determined, so that if the relative amounts of unstable and stable elements in a given quantity of material are measured, it is possible to calculate how much time has passed since all the material was in its pristine unstable state, and that of course is a measure of how long ago the element was formed and gives the age of the rocks in which it was found.

The uranium–lead decay was actually used to date rocks as long ago as 1913, but since uranium decays very slowly indeed (a given quantity loses half its radioactivity in 4,500,000,000 years) the amount of decay material in a sample accumulates very slowly too; in fact it is infinitesimally small and impossible to measure in all but the very oldest rocks. For more recent rocks a radioactive material with

a faster decay rate was called for, and the Berkeley group turned to potassium. But even here they faced problems of daunting proportions. Many rocks contain potassium, but only about one per cent of natural potassium comes in the radioactive form called K40. K40 decays into an inert gas called argon (Ar40), losing half its radioactivity in 1,310,000,000 years—which is considerably faster than uranium but still means that in two or three million years only some 0.1 per cent of the K40 will have turned into Ar40.

The quantities were still extremely small, but once the Berkeley group had perfected their extraction methods, and succeeded in developing a mass spectrometer capable of measuring billionths of a gram with consistent accuracy, then potassium–argon dating was available to science. Since its application to the Zinj deposits at Olduvai it has become an integral part of palaeoanthropological research. Of course, it is not the fossil itself that is dated, but the deposits with which the fossil is associated, which is both a limitation and a problem: a limitation because potassium-bearing rocks do not occur at every fossil site; and a problem because collecting undisturbed, uncontaminated rock samples of known and indisputable association with the fossils has proved, in some cases, to be difficult.

The skull that had lain undisturbed beneath the Olduvai sediments for 1.75 million years travelled extensively in the months following its rebirth as *Zinjanthropus boisei*. First to Kinshasa, where the specimen was introduced to science by Louis Leakey at the Pan African Congress on Prehistory which opened there on 22 August, and earned the sobriquet 'Nutcracker Man' in acknowledgement of its enormous teeth. Then to London in October, where it was presented at the British Academy and achieved popular fame as the oldest human ancestor, though several scientists contested the claim. And in November, Leakey and his charge joined Sir Charles Darwin and Sir Julian Huxley (grandsons respectively) as guests at the University of Chicago's Darwin Centennial celebrations. Zinj was an unexpected guest; not surprisingly the specimen was welcomed as the archetypal Missing Link—found at last.

While in America, Leakey made an extensive lecture tour. He also told the tale of Olduvai Gorge to the research committee of the National Geographic Society where, like a magician saving his best trick for the end of the show, he casually drew Zinj from cotton wool wrappings in his briefcase as he concluded a plea for funds to extend the excavations in the Gorge.[41] The NGS responded with a grant of over $20,000.

After America, Zinj travelled to Johannesburg, where he resided for several years in Phillip Tobias's anatomy department, and was subjected to extensive examination, measurement, and comparison. Tobias published the results as volume II of the Olduvai Gorge series of monographs, according *Zinjanthropus* only subgeneric rank, with the australopithecine affinities firmly asserted by the name *Australopithecus (Zinjanthropus) boisei*. In January 1965 Zinj made another journey, this time to Dar es Salaam, where the specimen resides in a sealed glass case, within a small locked box, inside a locked steel cupboard in the air-conditioned strongroom of the Tanzania National Museum.

During the early 1960s Louis Leakey arranged for an expedition, combining researchers and resources from France, the United States, and Kenya, to explore the fossil beds widely exposed along the Omo river as it drained into the northern end of Lake Turkana (then known as Lake Rudolf). The region lay just across the Ethiopian border from Kenya, and access was best gained from Nairobi, in Kenya.

The Omo Research Expedition was the first to be planned as a multi-disciplinary international operation involving geologists, palaeontologists, anatomists, and archaeologists whose investigations would ensure that fossil hominid discoveries could be assessed and interpreted in the fullest scientific context. Initially, it was composed of three groups: a French-funded group under the overall direction of Camille Arambourg (1885–1969) from the French National Museum of Natural History, with Yves Coppens directing field operations (Coppens assumed overall direction of the French group with the death of Arambourg in 1969); a group funded by the United States National Science Foundation under the direction of F. Clark Howell (1925–2007), and a group supported by the National Geographic Society under the overall direction of Louis Leakey and led by his 22-year-old son, Richard, who was then in the business of running tourist safaris.

In 1967 the Kenyan team explored the youngest deposits in the succession and discovered two skulls, an early suggestion that modern humans had lived in Africa as much as 100,000 years ago whose significance would be more fully appreciated decades later in the context of the transition from *Homo erectus* to *H. sapiens*[42] and the Out of Africa debates (see p. 111). The French and American teams explored older deposits (dating from between 1 and 3 million years old), where they recovered a total of 231 hominid specimens from ninety-four separate localities. The specimens included 208 teeth, four incomplete skulls, nine

mandibles, one complete ulna (lower arm bone), and seven other pieces of post-
cranial skeleton; preliminary assessment indicated that they represented four
taxa: *Homo erectus* and *H. habilis* (see Chapter 13); *Australopithecus africanus* and the
robust *A. boisei*.[43] This was an impressive haul, which might have been expected
to ensure that expeditions to the Omo would continue for years to come. But
not so. Attention was diverted elsewhere.

During that first season at the Omo, Richard Leakey chartered the helicopter
leased by the American group for some exploration of his own. He directed the
pilot to land close to a promising-looking ridge of sediments along the north-
eastern shores of Lake Turkana in Kenya, and the helicopter's rotor had scarcely
stopped before he found a primitive stone tool very similar to the earliest known
from Olduvai Gorge.[44] This encouraging find persuaded Leakey junior to with-
draw from his father's international Omo expedition: 'I already knew how to
organise an expedition and find fossils. I wanted to have my own show', he
explained later.[45] Moving swiftly, he made a personal application to the National
Geographic Society for funding, gained their support, and led his own expedition to East Turkana in 1968 and 1969. This was the beginning of a research
project which soon eclipsed endeavours at the Omo and has gone on to yield an
immense body of information on early hominid evolution.

Leakey's first major discovery at East Turkana was a complete hominid skull, a
magnificent specimen found in August 1969, unmistakably a robust australopithecine, with distinct similarities to *A. boisei* (Zinj) from Olduvai. This find, together
with those from the Omo, extended the range of the species from South Africa,
where Robert Broom had discovered the first *A. robustus* specimen, through Tanzania to southern Ethiopia. Many more robust australopithecine specimens have
been unearthed subsequently, indicating that they inhabited a wide expanse of
southern and eastern Africa from about 2.7 until 1.2 million years ago.[46]

The robust australopithecines were acknowledged to have been an integral part
of the African landscape for a million years, but their status in the saga of human
evolution was ill defined. Because they became extinct, it has been tempting to
think of them as inferior relatives, but worth remembering that they existed a
good deal longer than *H. sapiens* has so far and no species has existed forever, all
will become extinct, eventually. In any event, because all known robust australopithecines are more recent than any known gracile australopithecine and they
have a good deal in common, it has seemed reasonable to conclude that one had

evolved from the other, with the oldest *A.africanus* representing the beginning of a line on which the increasingly specialized characteristics of *A. robustus* and *A. boisei* had evolved.

In 1979 the description of *Australopithecus afarensis* (see Chapter 15) added weight to this scheme by providing a three- to four-million-year-old ancestor from whom the australopithecine line could have diverged and evolved, while the *Homo* line proceeded through *H. habilis* and *H. erectus* to modern man. And in 1983 the scheme was furthered strengthened by a study which explained the increasing bulkiness of the face in the australopithecines as an evolutionary process of gradual reinforcement and strengthening through time, in response to a diet calling for increased chewing forces which in turn placed increased stress on the facial architecture.[47]

But while the existing evidence persuasively indicated that an evolutionary trend had led the australopithecine line from gracile to robust, the fossils had another lesson in store. In 1985 a robust australopithecine skull was found by Leakey's team on the western shore of Lake Turkana that was no less robust than any previously known, but nearly half a million years older than all of them.

The Black Skull, as it became known (the uptake of manganese during fossilization had given the skull a rich blue-black colour), was similar to robust specimens from Olduvai and East Turkana and was initially assigned to the *Australopithecus boisei* taxon;[48] subsequently, however, it has been described as a different species, *Australopithecus aethiopicus*, in acknowledgement of its affinities with similarly aged specimens found by the Omo expedition of 1967. The new skull was found in sediments 2.5 million years old, and therefore invalidated the scheme wherein *A. africanus* was said to be the earliest representative of a lineage which led to *A. robustus* and *A. boisei*: clearly, *A. boisei* could not be the end of an *A. africanus–robustus–boisei* evolutionary line if it was already present at the beginning.

The response to the new discovery was a flurry of discussion and publications,[49] during which the majority view of early hominid evolution sprouted an extra branch with impressive alacrity. Instead of two branches diverging from *A. afarensis*, three were now postulated: one leading to *A. robustus*, a second to *A. boisei*, and a third leading to modern humans.[50]

The story of the robust australopithecines (or *Paranthropus* species, as much as the scientific community prefers to call them)[51] demonstrates how chronology and morphology interact in the study of hominid evolution: the long stretches of time that lay between specimens in the fossil record can be bridged with hypothetical schemes of evolutionary development, but in the final analysis it is 'morphology and not time that reveals which taxa (or samples) are most closely related'.[52]

But even as morphological evidence accumulates (in the form of more fossils) the picture does not necessarily become clearer. Indeed, although specialists may generally agree on the number of species and the differences that distinguish one from another they continue to argue about which similarities are derived from a common ancestor, and which may reflect only parallel adaptation to similar circumstances. Without clarity on this point it is impossible to be certain about their evolutionary relationship: which was ancestral to which? But a broad picture emerges from the known fossil record that is widely regarded as the most parsimonious interpretation of the evidence:[53]

The earliest clearly documented hominids, the Kenyan and Ethiopian finds dating from between 4.5 and 2.9 million years ago, bear the stamp of ape ancestry. They were agile tree climbers and proficient bipeds. By 2.5 million years ago, at least two separate hominid lineages had emerged, both with teeth that were human in form, and both retaining ape-like limb proportions and the ability to climb trees. Then one lineage, the *Paranthropus* species, developed dramatically enlarged teeth with the skull structure and musculature that facilitated powerful grinding between the upper and lower tooth rows. This lineage experienced only minimal brain expansion and became extinct about 1 million years ago. Meanwhile, by 1.8 to 1.7 million years ago the other lineage had developed body proportions and behavioural features that indicated commitment to a fully terrestrial lifestyle; teeth and associated chewing apparatus were progressively reduced, and the size of the brain increased significantly. This lineage, which includes the ancestors of living people, became increasingly reliant on technology as a preference for high-quality diets (indicated by smaller teeth and chewing muscles) interacted with the increased cognitive capacity of a larger brain: the representatives of this lineage probably made the flaked stone tools that also appear in the palaeontological record from about 2.5 million years ago.

FIGURE 11.4 Fossil remains found in contemporaneous deposits at East Turkana, Kenya, during the 1970s show that three distinct species of hominid lived in the region 1.8 million years ago.

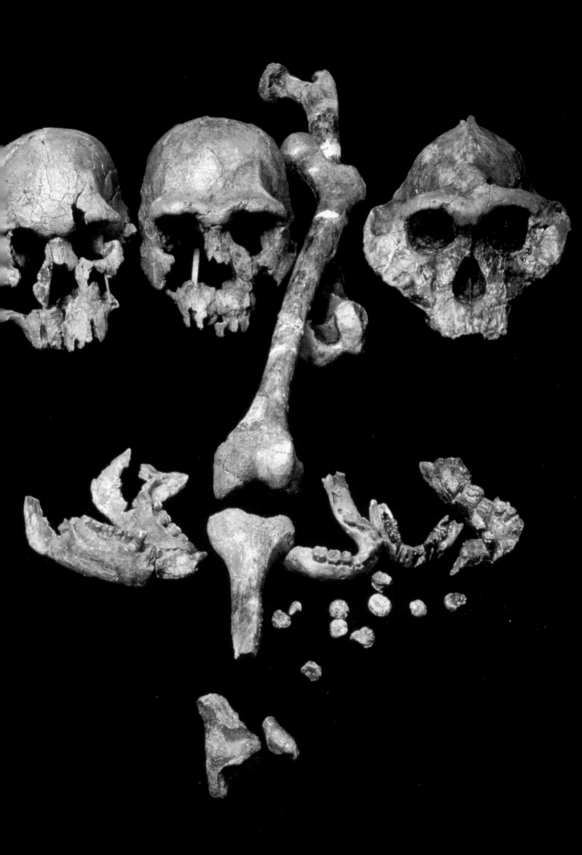

CHAPTER TWELVE

Tools

WHEN MARY Nicol joined Louis Leakey's archaeological expedition to Olduvai Gorge in 1935 she was just 22 years old and her two most important interests in life were archaeology and Louis Leakey. The conventionally minded might have whispered that it was not quite proper for a young lady to join four young gentlemen on an extended visit to the wilds of Africa, unchaperoned, especially as her heart was taken by the leader of the expedition, who was married and had two small children. But Mary Nicol was an unconventional young lady who smoked cigarettes, wore trousers, and could pilot a glider. Her background and upbringing were unconventional too, and from them she had emerged as determined and ambitious as Louis Leakey himself, with an independence of spirit that perfectly complemented his.

Mary was an only child, born in 1913 when her father was 45 and her mother ten years younger. Her mother's maiden name was Frere. In 1797 her great-great-great-grandfather, John Frere, had been the first man ever to recognize that the curiously shaped flints found in gravel pits and the like were actually implements 'fabricated and used by a people who had not the use of metals', who lived at a time 'even beyond that of the present world'.[1] Her father, Erskine Nicol, was a landscape painter, successful enough in the aftermath of the First World

War to maintain an enviable way of life. In the autumn, winter, and spring, he travelled about Italy and southern France with his wife and daughter, painting stylish pellucid watercolours that sold well at the exhibitions he held in London during the summer and financing the next trip to Europe. There was never any regular schooling for Mary. The family was always on the move while they were in Europe, and the schools in England were closed whenever they were there. Nonetheless, she picked up French as they travelled, her father taught her the elements of arithmetic, and the excitement of *Robinson Crusoe* read aloud by her parents encouraged her to read the book herself at the age of 7.

Erskine Nicol painted during the mornings only, strictly alone, and devoted the afternoons to his family. Mary recalled a series of afternoons when they were at Les Eyzies in France, near the famous caves where Cro-Magnon Man and the La Ferrassie remains had been discovered not many years before. Excavations were still going on and Mary visited the sites with her father. They talked to the archaeologists, and rummaged through the debris from the caves—looking for stone tools. Not as a kind of child's treasure hunt, Mary would insist when talking of those times, but because of her father's interest. He was intrigued by the tools' aesthetic qualities, and by the images they evoked of the men who had made and used them. Mary was 11 then, and doubtless the magic of those moments touched her too.

Erskine Nicol died unexpectedly of cancer in 1926. With the end of her father's life, Mary's idyllic childhood came to an abrupt end too. Her mother settled them in London, where Mary became an unhappy and rebellious teenager, quite unwilling to follow the path of formal education her mother planned. She persistently ran away from the convents she was supposed to attend, never completed a school course, never sat for an examination, and never gained the slightest of academic qualifications. But this did not deter Mary Nicol from pursuing the only subject that really interested her—archaeology and the Stone Age.

At some point—she could not recall how, where, or when—Mary was told that she could attend lectures at University College, London without entrance qualifications and without having to endure the tedium of a full undergraduate course. This discovery she said, marked her 'return to sanity'. Such informal study could never qualify for a degree, but Mary was more interested in information than accolades and followed lectures in geology and archaeology as closely as any enrolled student.

In the summer of 1930 she was invited to join the excavations of an Iron Age fort at Hembury, Devon, under Dorothy Liddell, whose brother-in-law, Alexander Keiller, had excavated the Avebury site (1924–39) and pioneered modern archaeological methods. In 1931 she worked under Dorothy Liddell again, at Stockbridge in Wiltshire, and she returned there in 1932 and 1933. The following year she ventured forth on her own and, with Kenneth Oakley handling the geological aspects, excavated a Stone Age site at Jaywick Sands near Clacton-on-Sea in Essex. Jaywick proved to be an important site which resolved some puzzling anomalies concerning the development of stone tool technology.[2] Mary was only 21, but already she was becoming an accomplished archaeologist.

Not surprisingly, Mary Nicol inherited a degree of artistic talent from her father. It lay dormant throughout her childhood and adolescence, but blossomed in 1932 at the instigation of a family friend who, possibly sympathetic to both the daughter's ambition and the mother's low income, introduced Mary to the archaeologist Gertrude Caton-Thompson just when that lady needed some drawings of implements for her book on *The Desert Fayoum*. Mary was given the task and thus earned some money of her own for the first time. The drawings turned out splendidly. Then, whether by accident or design is not clear, Caton-Thompson introduced Mary to Louis Leakey just when he was in need of some drawings of stone tools for his book *Adam's Ancestors* (1934). The occasion was an informal dinner in London, and Caton-Thompson arranged that Louis should sit beside Mary. According to Mary the attraction was immediate and mutual, and given their shared interests that was perhaps not surprising.

Mary drew the tools for *Adam's Ancestors*; Louis visited the excavations at Jaywick. There was always a plausible platonic reason for their meetings, but Mary's mother never approved of Louis. Perhaps in an attempt to forestall the inevitable she took her daughter to South Africa during the winter of 1934–5, but if her intention was that visits to the country's prehistoric sites should erase thoughts of Louis from Mary's mind, she was disappointed. Mary left her mother at Victoria Falls, flew to Tanganyika to join Louis on his fourth expedition to East Africa, and together they spent three months in Olduvai Gorge, searching for stone tools and the remains of the people who made them.

Over the next fifty years, their investigations made Olduvai Gorge the longest, fullest, and most revealing record of early man and his 'predicament' known to that date. Evidence was recorded from no fewer than 127 sites ranged along the length and breadth of the Gorge and throughout its geological sequence. From the base of Bed I up to the most recent deposits, the sites span nearly two million years. Artefacts, and the fossilized remains of hominid meals, have been collected in tens of thousands. Among them are stone anvils that have lain undisturbed since they were last used, and tiny fish scales so perfectly fossilized that even their transparency is preserved. The sheer quantity is impressive enough, but the quality of the Olduvai evidence lies in the glimpse it affords of early cultural activity and development at a single location during a known period of time.

Mary Leakey began the post-Zinj investigations at Olduvai in February 1960, with a full-time work force of sixteen Kenyan labourers and the part-time assistance of visiting scientists, students, and family. The first phase of the work, dealing primarily with the oldest deposits, was brought to a close at the beginning of 1964. In forty-six months only thirteen sites had been excavated, but they spanned 700,000 years from the base of Bed I (1.9 million years) to the top of Bed II (1.2 million years). Forty-three distinct levels, strewn with the evidence of hominid occupation, had been uncovered. The total area of the occupation levels amounted to over 55,000 square feet and every square inch of it was mapped. The position, size, and shape of every artefact, every stone, every fossil was plotted before its removal for study and analysis. In all, 37,127 artefacts and 32,378 fossils were recorded; and the latter figure does not include all the remains of birds, rodents, frogs, and the like which occurred in prodigious quantities but were generally very small and fragmentary: 14,000 rodent fossils from one site, for instance, weighed less than fifteen pounds.[3]

The series of monographs published on the Olduvai excavations show that the work done at the Gorge was roughly equivalent to recording the precise position and physical form of each stone and object encountered while digging a trench ten feet wide, ten feet deep, and one mile long. Excavating procedures were simple enough. After the over-burden had been removed with pick and shovel the fossil-bearing levels were marked in a grid of one-metre squares, each of which was excavated in ten-centimetre spits with a home-made chisel-like instrument. The matrix surrounding the fossils was removed with a dental probe and paint brush before the specimen was coated with a preservative (many fossils were extremely friable). All the debris removed from the grid was sieved through a mesh one-sixteenth of an inch wide, and this is how most of the very small fossils came to light. Every artefact, fossil, and stone was plotted on a map of the grid, numbered and recorded. But, though the procedures were simple, circumstances were not always favourable. At some sites the deposits were rock-hard when dry and slushy mud when wet; at others the sides threatened to crumble and had to be bolstered with sandbags; at yet others the overlying deposit tore away the fossil level beneath unless it was first thoroughly moistened to separate the two.

The work was tedious for the labourers, and stressful for Mary Leakey. It fell upon her to manage the investigations in general and oversee the work at every site—ensuring, for instance, that the excavations proceeded vertically, that measurements were taken in every plane, that the relationship of different levels and any stratigraphic change were all recorded, and every find plotted on the map of the site. These things were all crucial and if they were not recorded at the time of excavation, there would be no chance of doing so later on. Supervision, in fact, determined the speed of the investigations. Many more men could have been employed, but experience had shown that excavations were difficult to control when more than about half a dozen people were working on the site at one time: detail was often neglected as speed increased, and detail was everything.

But to interpret the fine detail being revealed at every site, the picture of their context had to be properly focused too. This task was performed by geologist Richard Hay from the University of California at Berkeley, who undertook a geological survey of the entire Olduvai basin.[4] Hay collected substantial amounts of detailed data in the field, but no less effort was expended in the laboratory, where he analysed the rock samples and the data he had collected.

Hay's conclusions are a fascinating insight into both the process of geological inquiry and the evolution of a natural landscape, quite apart from the importance of the evidence they lent to the archaeological investigations. In this latter respect Hay's prime objective was to correlate the deposits throughout the Gorge and determine the exact temporal sequence in which the sites occurred. This would be simple if each lay directly above the other in a neat geological sequence, but such is rarely the case. At Olduvai the sites are widely distributed in the horizontal plane, and the geological strata in which they occur are not always at the same height in the vertical plane; this may be because the thickness of the beds varies from point to point, or because they have been disturbed by erosion or by geological faulting. Five major faults associated with the formation of the Rift Valley are known at Olduvai, and there are many smaller ones that further complicate the picture.

FIGURE 12.1 Olduvai Gorge, and Mary Leakey with members of the National Geographic Society's Research and Exploration Committee at the site of the *Zinjanthropus* discovery.

THE SKULL OF
AUSTRALOPITHECUS BOISEI
(ZINJANTHROPUS)
WAS FOUND HERE BY
M. D. LEAKEY
... LY 17TH, 1959

Physical exploration and examination of the gorge was essential but complete understanding of its geology was finally achieved in the laboratory, where chemical and microscopic examination of the samples he had collected enabled Hay to determine the characteristics of each deposit and thus relate them to one another at all points along the Gorge. This in turn made it possible to state with certainty the sequence in which the archaeological sites had been occupied by early man, and build up a picture of the physical environments at Olduvai during those times.

Hay's study showed that numerous small rivers and streams from the southeastern highlands had maintained a sizeable lake in the Olduvai basin during Bed I and lower Bed II times. It had measured roughly ten by five kilometres and persisted for several hundred thousand years, despite periodic inundation by showers of ash from the erupting Kerimasi and Olmoti volcanoes (Ngorongoro and Lemagrut, which dominate the scene today, were extinct before Bed I was laid down). The ash, of course, created the Olduvai deposits and preserved all the artefacts and fossil remains that are found in them.

Helped by the accumulative effect of rapid evaporation in a lake with no regular outflow, the ash was also responsible for the high alkalinity of the Olduvai lake, creating a perfect environment for both the microscopic algae which flourish in such alkaline waters and the fish and birds which feed on them—tilapia and flamingos, for instance. That such creatures lived in and around the Olduvai lake in large numbers is confirmed by their fossil remains, as indeed is the presence of their predators—crocodiles and hominids among them. Thus the volcanic ash not only created the ecological circumstances that enabled the early Olduvai inhabitants to congregate in large numbers, it also preserved their remains.

At about 1.6 million years ago the lake shrank to a third of its former size. By 1.2 million years ago it was reduced to a series of seasonal pans dotted about an alluvial plain. One might imagine that volcanic ashes had filled the basin and lake they had previously made so productive, but there were other factors at work too. Foremost was geological faulting which would have drained the lake very rapidly and was certainly responsible for the eastward movement of the drainage sump until about 400,000 years ago, when it reached the Olbalbal depression, where it rests today.

At the same time as the faulting, dramatic changes in climate also occurred. In Lower Bed I times, Olduvai was very wet, with perhaps even a groundwater forest standing around parts of the lake shore. By Upper Bed I times, however, a much drier climate prevailed, but this reverted to wetter conditions again in Lower Bed II. These climatic changes are revealed by the fossil remains of animals that live exclusively in wet or dry habitats, by the evidence of microscopic fossil pollens that identify the vegetation, and by the nature of the windblown and waterborne minerals that Hay found in the sediments.

The distribution of the ancient stream channels in Beds I and II indicated that the drainage pattern of the basin also had been altered by the faulting and climatic changes. Streams and rivers from the highlands had merged into a single large stream that flowed westward. With time, as the volcanoes continued to puff ash into the basin, laying down Bed III, drainage from the west joined this main stream. Ultimately it turned about, and flowed eastward, as it does today. The stream began cutting the Gorge about half a million years ago, while the deposition of volcanic ashes and lake sediments continued until about 15,000 years ago, so that some of the younger deposits overlie earlier excisions, which makes the geology difficult to interpret in some places. The spot where Reck's Olduvai Man was found is a case in point.

Correlating geology of the Olduvai basin with the archaeology of the fossil offered a view of our ancestors as an integral part of the ecological landscape. Evidence of hominid activity was found principally in association with evidence of perennial freshwater, relatively abundant vegetation, and the presence of animals that could be hunted, and eaten. There was not much sign of anything happening out on the savannah and barren floodplains. All of the twenty sites in Bed I were situated around the lake margin, eighteen of them on the eastern side where most of the streams had flowed into the lake.

Subsequently, a long-term study of the ecological framework in which hominids had lived at Olduvai was instigated. Called the Olduvai Landscape Paleoanthropology Project, it began work in the late 1980s with the excavation of Bed 1 deposits located on the western margin of the lake. These have produced not only a hominid fossil, stone tools, and animal bones showing signs of butchery, but also evidence of hominid land-use in the region, more than 1.8 million years ago.[5] The environmental setting of the hominid locality was a stream in a small valley cut into the western lake margin during a period of low lake levels. The stream could have supported a gallery forest, and the broader landscape was generally more moist than had previously been thought, constituting a mosaic of grassy woodland and wooded grassland. It was possible that the region had supported a local population of hominids, the researchers concluded, but more likely that it had been used irregularly on seasonal forays from the ecologically more productive south-eastern basin.

During the depositions of Bed II, when the lake dwindled away to nothing, hominid activity became much more widespread: of the sixty-three known Bed II sites, fifty were to the east of the lake basin and many were situated on the banks of watercourses. In Beds III and IV, the site pattern followed the change in drainage, forty out of forty-three sites were to the west of the basin.

Apart from establishing the geological and environmental circumstances of the sites, Hay's study was also a source of information on the Olduvai tools and toolmakers. The source-points of nearly all the stone used for making tools were identified. This is yet another pioneering point that made Olduvai unique at the time, for nowhere else were the sources of raw material so thoroughly researched, and recent work has built upon this.[6] This kind of knowledge is particularly illuminating, in that it offered clues to a growing awareness that some materials made better tools than others, and indicated a willingness to travel ever greater distances in search of the best. In Beds I and II, most tools were made of lava obtainable within two kilometres of the campsite; other materials were used too, but rarely was the source more than four kilometres away. Higher in the sequence, however, the variety of material increased and more and more of it came from further afield. Bed III assemblages include many tools made from rock found eight and ten kilometres away and by Bed IV times the basin is criss-crossed with a veritable network of supply routes. Different rocks have different properties, and they seem to have been collected and used selectively.

Trachyte (a coarse-grained lava) was brought in from the Olmoti foothills, fifteen kilometres away; green phonolite (a fine-grained lava) was carried twenty kilometres from its source on Engelosen; Kelogi gneiss was found thirteen kilometres to the east. These are distances as the crow flies; on foot, across the undulating landscape, they would have been greater, and certainly difficult to cover there and back in less than a day when carrying a load of stone. So the toolmakers must have been planning ahead, and the rewards must have made

FIGURE 12.2 In the first stages of making a handaxe, flakes fly from a block of quartzite.

the effort worthwhile. Indeed, the raw materials may not have been carried over the entire distance by members of a single group; the apparently random distribution throughout the basin could indicate that some form of barter was taking place among the groups camped closest to the sources of the various rocks—a kind of 'trade' in raw materials, Mary Leakey suggested, that was operating in Africa more than half a million years before its first known appearance in Europe's archaeological record.[7]

The 1960 Olduvai excavations began at FLK, where Zinj had been found. Given that the cranium was relatively intact, there was some hope that the jaw might also be recovered, but it was not. This was regrettable, for the jaw would have helped to resolve the nagging question of Zinj's australopithecine affinities (Louis thought the jaw might also reveal whether or not Zinj could talk), but in the event, its absence was amply compensated for by a wealth of information on the activities of people at the site.

The site at which Zinj had been found extended over an area of 3,384 square feet. In the forty feet of deposits excavated from the hillside directly above, there were another twenty-one levels at which some evidence of hominid activity was found. On the Zinj floor itself (which seems likely to have been in use for five to ten years or more),[8] 2,470 artefacts, 3,510 fairly large fossils, and literally thousands of bone fragments too small to be numbered were found. The material was remarkably well preserved, and showed little or no sign of disturbance or weathering, probably because the site had been covered by a shower of ash soon after it was abandoned.

The excavations at FLK were significant for their extent, the quantity of material, its fine preservation, and the Zinj skull—but beyond all that, it was important for offering the first suggestion that our ancestors were operating from something like a 'home base' nearly two million years ago. Until then experts had doubted this could be possible, but the evidence at Olduvai 'proved conclusively', said Mary Leakey, that by then 'man had already reached a stage of social structure which included communal centres where groups gathered together, built shelters and ate food'.[9]

The published plan of the FLK site shows a scattering of artefacts and faunal remains over the entire area, with a densely concentrated patch on one side surrounded by a narrow, barren zone. The bones within the concentrated area were almost exclusively those of the meat- and marrow-bearing variety, while those outside were mostly jawbones, shoulder blades, hipbones, vertebrae, ribs, and the like—all devoid of marrow. Therefore it seemed most probable, Mary Leakey suggested in a preliminary review of the evidence,[10] that the concentrated remains marked a place where hominids had gathered to consume animals they had caught, slicing meat from the carcass with small flake tools, then smashing the bones to get at the marrow. The large unbroken fossils scattered about the surrounding area represented the rejects from their meals, she suggested, and the barren zone between the two assemblages was precisely where a brushwood shelter might have been erected to break a prevailing south-east wind (the skull of *Zinjanthropus*, incidentally, had lain about fifteen feet from the patch of concentrated remains, on the lee side).

Excavations at two other sites revealed a similar distribution of cultural and faunal material, though each had not one, but two patches of concentrated material. Both were roughly circular and lay quite close together, reminiscent of how the modern !Kung San hunter-gatherers arrange their camps in the Kalahari. At all three excavations the evidence for there having been a brushwood windbreak was entirely circumstantial, with only the bare ground on which it might have stood to proclaim its existence. At a fourth site, however, a group of hominids appeared to have camped where there was little or no soil into which branches could be thrust. Here, there was no strategically situated patch of bare ground; instead, excavations revealed a circle of small lava rocks, such as might have supported a windbreak.

Mary Leakey has claimed she was at first reluctant to believe the circle had been artificially arranged, but the evidence from FLK and the other sites, plus the 'almost unanimous' opinion of visiting geologists and prehistorians, eventually persuaded her that the circle was not a natural feature. Later, she was proud to claim that it was the world's oldest man-made structure.[11]

The site was dubbed DK (Donald McInnes Korongo), and lay immediately above a lava flow dated at 1.9 million years. A profusion of flamingo bones and some fish remains indicated its proximity to the lake, and fossilized roots suggested that a bed of reeds or papyrus once grew there. The circle was little more than a ring of loosely piled lava blocks, about thirteen feet across, with six small heaps spaced along the northern rim where it was best preserved; maximum height was about twelve inches. It stood on a small hummock at a spot that could have been chosen because it was conveniently close to the lake and the creatures that congregated there, but drier than the surrounding areas; it might have been a small promontory.

The widespread publicity given to claims that the Leakeys had discovered lakeside living sites at Olduvai Gorge, nearly two million years old and littered with stone tools and animal bones, contributed to a significant shift of opinion on what might be called the moral calibre of our earliest ancestors. The image of Man the Killer-Ape promoted by Raymond Dart (see Chapter 10) was replaced by the rather more appealing image of Man the Noble Hunter, and the dimensions of the new image were well demonstrated at a symposium on Man the Hunter held in 1966:

> in contrast to carnivores, human hunting…is based on a division of labour and is a social and technical adaptation quite different from that of other mammals. Human hunting is made possible by tools, but it is far more than a technique or even a variety of techniques. It is a way of life, and the success of this adaptation (in its total social, technical, and psychological dimensions) has dominated the course of human evolution for hundreds of thousands of years. In a very real sense our intellect, interests, emotions, and basic social life—all are evolutionary products of the success of the hunting adaptation[12].

The emphasis had moved from the killing aspect of hunting, to the sharing aspects of social behaviour that underpinned the system. Studies of the !Kung San in the Kalahari showed that cooperative behaviour and altruism were essential aspects of the modern hunter-gatherer lifestyle, and the archaeological evidence from Olduvai Gorge appeared to confirm the presence of a similar hunter-gatherer lifestyle at a very early stage of human evolution. Before then, the ancestral hominids had been largely vegetarian, it was believed, and as uncooperative among themselves as modern primates.

The addition of meat to the diet had fuelled both the enlargement of the brain and the development of the skills needed to catch meat—an interactive process that called for the establishment of home bases, and an increasing degree of cooperation among the individuals occupying them. The sharing hypothesis was founded on these observations, its basic premiss being that, although tools and hunting had facilitated access to a highly nutritious food source, it was the willingness to share labour and share food which had set our ancestors on the road to humanity.[13]

Working under the auspices of the Leakeys' Olduvai research projects, the archaeologist Glynn Isaac (1938–85) made the study of what was thought to be a Pleistocene living site at Olorgesailie in Kenya the subject of his doctoral dissertation, and subsequently became a leading advocate of the sharing hypothesis.

The idea of a 'home base' was a vital component of the sharing hypothesis, but Isaac acknowledged that home bases were not the only feasible explanation of the fossil and stone tools assemblages uncovered at Olduvai, Olorgesailie, and (subsequently) East Turkana. The bones and stones could have been washed together by water currents; they could have accumulated independently at different times, or they could have been brought together by other agencies. During the last years of his life Glynn Isaac was involved with a number of research projects that were specifically designed to test the validity of the sharing/home base hypothesis, and the results of these studies began to suggest that the hypothesis might not be valid.[14]

In fact, the widening field of investigations at East Turkana was beginning to show that early hominids employed 'an opportunistic, least-effort strategy' of stone tool manufacture and use, and in 1981 Isaac acknowledged that evidence of sites used for only brief periods, rather than as home bases, would radically alter the pattern of early hominid lifestyle he had proposed.[15]

In 1982 a Ph.D. student from Harvard University, Richard Potts, completed a re-evaluation of the evidence from Olduvai Gorge which led him to conclude (1984) that the assemblages of fossils and tools found in the Gorge did not represent home bases, but at best were evidence of some other hominid activity. Potts suggested that even the famous stone circle at the DK site was likely to be the product of some natural phenomenon. Water flow could have been responsible for its accumulation of fossils and tools, and the stone circle itself could have been produced by the roots of a large tree—which are known to be capable of penetrating and breaking up bedrock. Other assemblages at Olduvai could be interpreted as 'stone caches', he said, representing an energy-saving strategy of leaving a supply of stone tools and raw materials at convenient locations in the foraging area, to which the hominids would carry meat (and other foods) for further processing, away from the attention of competing carnivores.[16]

And while Potts was working on the Olduvai fossils in Nairobi, a taphonomist, Pat Shipman, was also examining the collection, trying to establish a method of

distinguishing between the bones which hominids had eaten from, and those
which had been gnawed on by other carnivores, tumbled in rivers, or otherwise
damaged. In the course of this work, she noticed what looked like cutmarks on
one bone, and then on another. Alerted by Shipman, Potts found similar marks on
the fossils he was studying, and another researcher, Henry Bunn, found them on
fossils from East Turkana. Subsequent analysis convinced all three workers that the
marks on the Olduvai and East Turkana fossils had been made by hominids cutting
meat from the bones with stone tools.[17] 'This direct evidence of early hominid diet
allows us to dismiss models of human evolution which do not incorporate meat-
eating as a significant component of early hominid behaviour...[and]...lends
strong support to the food-sharing model proposed by Isaac', concluded Bunn.

When Shipman came to analyse the body parts represented by the cut-
marked bones, however, she discovered that more than 50 per cent were
non-meat-bearing—lower limb bones, for instance, which have virtually no
meat on them, only skin and tendon. Shipman was also surprised to find that
there was no evidence of cuts indicating that the hominids had dismembered
carcasses and cut meat from the bone for carrying and distribution as the home
base/food-sharing hypothesis would demand.[18] These observations might seem
to discredit the suggestion that the cuts had been made by hominids, but Shipman drew other conclusions.

The prevalence of non-meat-bearing bones among the cut-marked specimens
indicated that hominids must have indulged in skinning and tendon-removal as
well as meat-eating, she observed, recalling an earlier suggestion that tendons
would be useful for tying bundles.[19] And if the hominids were not dismembering
carcasses and carrying meat back to a home base, they must have been eating it on
the spot—scavenging, in other words. In this way, a lack of evidence confirming
the home base hypothesis actually became the basis of a scavenging hypothesis
that found much favour in the early 1980s.[20] But, while Shipman expanded this
idea into the proposition that scavenging was the ecological niche from which the
ancestral hominids evolved,[21] evidence suggesting an alternative explanation of
the cutmarks on the fossil bones from East Africa was accumulating at the base
of a small limestone cliff near Cheddar Gorge in Somerset, England.

A young cow had fallen over the cliff and died in January 1977. Being value-
less and lying on an unfrequented track, the dead animal was abandoned by its
owner and thus provided two anthropologists with an opportunity to record

the details of its progressive disintegration over a period of seven years.[22] The carcass was only minimally utilized by foxes, badgers, dogs, and crows but, as it broke up, bones were kicked about and trampled by cows using the rough track. Subsequent examination of these bones under a scanning electron microscope revealed scratches no different from the 'cutmarks' found on fossil bones from Olduvai and East Turkana, though in this case, of course, no stone tools had been involved—only trampling.

Further affirmation of the significance of trampling in bone marking has also resulted from controlled experiments in the United States.[23] Clearly, trampling is just as likely to produce interesting marks on bones as stone tools, or any other agency. Indeed, experimental work published in 2005 has shown that even mould and bacteria can produce effects on bone surfaces that are not easy to distinguish from the marks made by carnivores, or hominids.[24]

The home base, food-sharing, cutmarks, and scavenging episodes are important examples of palaeoanthropological science in progress. And the contribution that Olduvai has made to the science continues, both at the Gorge and in its vicinity, and in laboratories, where the material that was collected so assiduously and documented so meticulously is re-examined and re-evaluated by a stream of scientists who have new techniques, new insights (and occasionally, it must be said, new preconceptions) to apply to the old evidence. Some of the early interpretations have been shown to be mistaken: the living floor concept is one and, of particular significance here, the Leakeys' exhaustive work on the stone tools is another.

Deliberately turning a stone into a usable tool requires a surprising amount of skill. Even with our high level of general knowledge concerning technical and mechanical matters, very few people today could decide by themselves which stone is best and precisely where it should be struck to achieve the desired result. We know it can be done: there are many examples of beautiful and sophisticated stone tools to remind us that the effort is worth while. But the first toolmakers lacked this incentive. They acquired their skills in pursuit of an end, driven by a need—which means they had reached the conceptual threshold enabling them to identify a problem and appreciate the benefits of solving it. The beginnings of culture.

Louis Leakey coined the term Oldowan Culture to describe the stage of human evolution at which the oldest tools found at Olduvai had been made. Its most common form was 'a crude chopper varying in size from about the dimensions of a ping-pong ball to that of a croquet ball', he said.[25] Leakey believed that the evolution of toolmaking skills at Olduvai could be traced in a direct line from the simple chop-pers at the base of Bed I to the fine handaxes at the top of Bed IV. Given the length of time spanned by the deposits it was almost certain that some progress must have occurred, but further excavation and analysis have shown that it was by no means as straightforward as he supposed. But then, Leakey's pronouncements were derived from investigations in Europe, where it was obvious that the fine feather-flaking of an Acheulean handaxe (named after the town St Acheul in France, near where they were found) required far more skill than the crudely flaked Chellean pebble tools (from St Chelles). In the latter, flakes were removed with a hammerstone; in the former a soft, broader hammer was used, of wood, bone, or horn.

By making tools themselves, European experts had assessed the degree of skill needed to make each kind, and had established a stone tool chronology based on the number and form of the flake scars. This enabled them to rank sites in chronological order, but could never be confirmed because no European deposits spanned enough time to demonstrate the acquisition of skills from one type of tool to another through ascending levels. But Olduvai spanned many ages. There were no flint tools in the Gorge, but understandable that Louis Leakey approached those made of other materials with the same ideas that were held in Europe. And reasonable that as he collected and studied specimens from levels throughout the deposits he should seek the continuity and technical development which Europe's experts had said ought to be there. And he found it, or at least he believed he had found it. On the evidence of flake scars and presumptions of technique Leakey carefully documented eleven stages by which, in his opinion, the skills used in the manufacture of Oldowan tools had evolved into those required for making Acheulean tools. The findings were well received at the time, but diminished in significance as his wife studied the material with greater diligence.

With the benefit of finance, time, and patience not available to Louis, Mary Leakey recorded the physical characteristics of all the 37,127 artefacts collected from Beds I and II at Olduvai; noting the material of which each was made, the number of flake scars it bore, and, where visible, the angle of the striking plat-form, which determines the depth of the flake that is detached.

It was obvious from the start that the collection would be easier to describe if it could be divided into a variety of tool categories (which may or may not provide clues to evolving skills). Twenty distinct categories were eventually identified.

Some described the form of the tool: spheroids, discoids, bifacial points, proto-bifaces, laterally trimmed flakes, polyhedrons, outils écaillés ('scaled tools'), and débitage (flakes produced during manufacture of other tools but showing some sign of use themselves). Other terms indicated the probable function of the tool: awls, anvils, choppers, chisels, hammerstones and handaxes, cleavers, picks, scrapers, and punches.[26] In addition she describes manuports (rocks foreign to the site but lacking any sign of modification), and utilized material (artefacts which defy closer description).

In the analysis of these data, the relative proportions of the various raw materials and categories of tool occurring at each site was calculated. This was only one line of inquiry but, relating the results to the position of the sites in the geological sequence, significant trends did emerge. As already noted, raw materials appeared to be more specifically selected at sites in the higher (and younger) levels. This could reflect an increasingly complicated lifestyle, while the variety of materials, together with developing manufacturing skills, could indicate a growing ability to perceive and solve the problems of that lifestyle.

So what conclusions were drawn from the evidence? The toolkit on relevant Bed I living floors contains an average of only six different tools, but in Bed II the average had risen to just over ten different types. During the same period, the ratio of artefacts to faunal remains changed too: there were fewer but larger bones on the younger sites, and more tools. People were catching larger animals than their predecessors, it seems. Throughout the upper levels of Bed II the remains of giraffe, hippopotamus, and rhinoceros were far more common than lower down. At each of two butchery sites, for instance, the bones of an elephant were found strewn among a profusion of tools. Obviously, one elephant would feed as many people as would a herd of antelope.

So, among the wealth of detail provided there were ample grounds for suggesting that technical skills developed considerably during the period of time spanned by the Olduvai deposits. The Oldowan Culture evolved into what Mary Leakey described as the Developed Oldowan Culture. Tools became more refined, she said, the toolkit was enlarged, and a wider range of raw materials was used. Even so, overall, the Oldowan assemblage was distinguished more by continuity than by change. In fact, after its advance from Bed I technology, the Developed Oldowan persisted virtually unchanged through Beds II, III, and IV. In other words, the use of stone tools remained at the same level for over a million years at Olduvai—from 1.8 million years to 700,000 years. Clearly, toolmakers throughout that period were doing enough to sustain viable populations and experienced nothing to prompt any dramatic change.

Mary Leakey's work on the Olduvai stone tools was a considerable advance on that of her husband, in terms of both its diligence and the conclusions she drew from the evidence. But it too has been superseded, with re-evaluations of the material and her documentation in many instances replacing what she would have agreed was largely conjecture with more soundly based conclusions.[27] Many of the categories she described have been discounted, while the material she dismissed as débitage has been found to include many flakes which had been deliberately fashioned and used as tools. In fact, many of the oldest and simplest tools she described, the choppers (which have an edge formed by removing flakes alternately from either face around one end), are now said to have been cores from which small sharp flakes had been knapped. Similarly, the polyhedrons and other such categories as she described are also deemed to have been cores left over from the manufacture of really useful tools—the small razor-sharp flakes that could slice through skin and meat in seconds.

But however much the Leakeys' work is reinterpreted, nothing can distract from the fact that the Oldowan Culture they described provides the earliest concrete evidence of hominid material culture, as well as documenting the butchery of an enormous range of animals, from hedgehogs to elephants. Thus, the advent of Oldowan technology reflects one of the most important adaptive shifts in human evolution[28]. Stone tool manufacture, and the greater consumption of meat that it facilitated, set the scene for significant changes in the physical and cultural realms of hominid existence.

It has been dubbed 'The Dawn of Technology', and attracts a good deal of attention—not only at Olduvai Gorge, where the oldest deposits date from 1.8 million years ago, but also in other parts of East Africa, where Oldowan tools have been found in even older deposits. Archaeological exposures along the Omo river in Ethiopia and around Lake Turkana in Kenya have yielded stone tools dated to 2.3 million years, but the oldest of all have come from Gona, in the Hadar region of the Awash Valley, Ethiopia. These occurrences are securely

---

FIGURE 12.3 Though initially described as a polyhedron 'tool', this specimen is more likely to have been a core from which small sharp flakes were knapped.

dated to between 2.6 and 2.5 million years. They are the oldest known artefacts from anywhere in the world, found more than 1,000 miles from Olduvai but similar enough to be classed as examples of the Oldowan Industrial Complex.[29]

The Gona tools have been subjected to intense study, aimed at understanding the mode of manufacture, and the degree of skill required, rather than simply assigning them to categories. The results reveal a surprising degree of technological sophistication. The Late Pliocene toolmakers who made them were not simply hammering cobbles, they had mastered the skills of basic stone knapping. The working edges of the majority of the Gona tools are still very fresh and sharp. Many of the cores show signs of having been used as hammerstones and for other pounding activities, as well as being the source of sharp-edged flakes. The large number of well-struck flakes in the assemblage, with conspicuous bulbs of percussion, indicates that the toolmakers had a clear understanding of what the researchers call 'conchoidal fracture mechanics': they knew all about the principle of striking a sequence of flakes from a core, a procedure which requires expert selection of core stones and a thorough knowledge of where to strike them, what to strike them with, and how hard.

Such knowledge and expertise can be learned, of course, and passed on to succeeding generations; which in itself implies that the toolmakers lived in groups that stayed together, had good communicative skills and had made learning an integral part of their culture—at least 2.5 million years ago. The age is remarkable, but the most extraordinary aspect of the Gona tools, is the revelation that the Oldowan industrial complex had existed, and remained technologically unchanged, for even longer than had been supposed. The Gona tools are 700,000 years older than the oldest examples from Olduvai, which means that unchanging Oldowan technology had sustained the toolmakers for 1.8 million years. Furthermore, the sophisticated understanding of conchoidal fracture evident at Gona implies that the hominids who lived there about 2.5 million years ago were not novices to lithic technology. Gona does not represent the beginning of stone tool manufacture. The research team confidently predicts that even older artefacts will be found.[30]

But who were these people? So far, no hominid remains have been found in direct association with the 2.5 million-year-old tools. By default, therefore, the debate focuses attention on behaviour rather than fossils: on what people do rather than what they are. Hold a fossil ancestral skull and you have in your hands the actual remains of a being who lived more than a million, or even four-and-a-half million years ago. It is an experience charged with feeling, but ultimately sterile, because it is such a stark reminder that death brings all experience to an end. But hold a stone tool, heft it, and imagine what you could do with it—there is a true sense of connection here, an unmissable link between them and us, continuity. As Louis Leakey once remarked: 'Stone tools are fossilized human behaviour'.[31]

Fossilized human behaviour, but persisting even to modern times. When Glynn Isaac (1937–85) and his colleagues were surveying the East Turkana deposits soon after dawn one morning in 1968, they encountered a young Shangilla boy tending a herd of goats. In their presence, the herdboy came across the carcass of an antelope that had been killed during the night and abandoned—but not yet found by scavengers. 'Spontaneously,' Isaac reported, 'he tapped off a very small flake from a lava cobble and proceeded to slit the skin covering a cannon bone, which he then peeled and cracked open to obtain marrow.'[32] A freshly knapped stone flake can be as sharp as a steel blade and, as the Shangilla herdboy demonstrated, the basic knowledge of how to produce them has been serving humanity for a very long time. The herdboy needed nothing more; nor, presumably, did the hominids who made the Oldowan toolkits. But something else happened about 1.6 million years ago, when an entirely new form of tool begins to occur in the deposits: the Acheulean handaxe.

At Olduvai the new technology arrives abruptly and fully fledged in the middle of Bed II, dating from about 1.4 million years ago (it is slightly older at sites elsewhere). Thereafter the Oldowan and the Acheulean are contemporary. In one part of the Gorge two cultures are found within a few hundred metres of each other, on the same geological horizon. But there is no mingling. They remain distinct for one million years, despite such close proximity. One can imagine that although they shared a basic talent, they lived entirely separate lives. As different, perhaps, as two species of antelope, exploiting the same environment, derived from a common ancestor, but very different in terms of their behaviour. Only an insurmountable degree of separation could explain why the technologies did not intermingle.

Aptitude would have been a contributing factor, for handaxe manufacture requires a new order of technical skill. The Oldowan understanding of conchoidal fracture was sophisticated and impressive, but still very basic in that it consisted of knocking flakes from a core and making best use of whatever might result. The Acheulean toolmakers, by contrast, were making bifacial cutting tools according to a predetermined pattern. Having selected a suitable piece of stone, they struck flakes from both sides to produce a tool that was longer than it was broad, pointed at one end and rounded at the other; it had a sharp edge all around, was perfectly symmetrical, and curved from end to end and from edge to edge on both sides. There was nothing arbitrary about this manufacturing process. The long axis, the cutting edge, the point, and the symmetry of the carefully controlled curves were imposed upon the stone, they did not occur by chance. Each blow struck on the stone opened up too many possibilities for that. The process could be performed only by constantly comparing the work in hand with a mental image of the finished product.

Experts have puzzled over the function of the Acheulean handaxes. They are inefficient butchery tools (flakes are generally sharper and more quickly made); undeniably cutting tools—but for cutting what? An answer has been provided by the analysis of plant residue on Acheulean handaxes from the 1.4 million-year-old site at Peninj, Tanzania. The residue consisted of phytoliths (meaning 'plant stones'), which are rigid and durable microscopic bodies that occur in many plants. Most are made of silica and vary in size and shape, according to the plant they were a part of. Those found on the Peninj handaxes were identified as having come from acacia trees, and the fact that many such tools were found in close association at one site is seen as indicating that wood was being worked there. Furthermore, the mineralized remains of string-like plant fibres were found on some handaxes, which suggests that they had been hafted in some way. In any event, the study shows that Acheulean toolmakers were producing some kind of wooden implements 1.5 million years ago that have not been preserved in the archaeological record. Rudimentary spears perhaps, which certainly would have enhanced their adaptation as hunters in open environments.[33]

Since there is no sign of the Acheulean having been developed at Olduvai, its sudden appearance is generally credited to the arrival of technically more adept outsiders (though the innovation and perfection of the new technology could easily have been achieved at Olduvai. It need only have taken a few months; but even if it had taken years, or decades, the time involved was still too brief to have left any evidence of its development in the archaeological record). It could have been developed by Oldowans who split away from the main group; it could have been brought in by a different group that migrated into the region. But this is just speculation. All that is known for certain is that the Acheulean industry appears around 1.6 million years ago, almost simultaneously, at a number of sites across

East Africa and Ethiopia—and its arrival coincides with a change in climate. The lake at Olduvai disappeared and the landscape became drier and more open, supporting a different suite of plants and animals. The hominids may have adapted their food acquisition strategies in response to these changes. If so, handaxes were among those adaptations.

Homo erectus is a plausible candidate for the introduction of Acheulean technology. The species appears in the fossil record at about the same time; furthermore, *H. erectus* had a brain that was about twice the size of the australopithecines (averaging 1,000 cc to theirs of about 500 cc) and was therefore more likely to have been capable of the cognitive feats that inspired handaxe technology. Brain size is not an absolute measure of cognitive ability, or intelligence, but with a brain measuring roughly three-quarters the modern average (1,330 cc), *Homo erectus* surely marks the point at which the further existence of the human ancestor—an animal with very generalized physical characteristics up to that point—was entrusted to a single highly specialized organ: the brain. The species' survival would be increasingly dependent upon the brain's capacity to find ways of satisfying the body's needs. No other animal possesses the human capacity for reasoned action. Only humans depend for their survival upon elaborate systems of culture and social interaction; only the human brain could organize and sustain such complex systems.

The appearance of Acheulean handaxes in the archaeological record, about 1.6 million years ago, probably marks a point at which the trend towards a dependence on brain power became irreversible—though *Homo erectus* was not destined to be the species that took the trend through to where we are today. They were the longest surviving and most widely dispersed of the ancestral toolmakers, but disappeared from the fossil record around 200,000 years ago; coincidentally, Acheulean handaxes cease to dominate the archaeological record at roughly the same time,[34] and another form of technology takes over: these were small, carefully fashioned blades. Flake tools had of course been in use since Oldowan times, but these blades introduced a new order of sophistication, employing skills previously thought to have evolved only with the Late Stone Age in Europe, about 40,000 years ago. The oldest known African examples are around half-a-million years older, dating back to between 509,000 and 543,000 years ago.[35]

Though present alongside the Acheulean for some time previously, by about 120,000 years ago the new tools dominated assemblages throughout Africa and had assumed a form which represented a major advance in manufacturing technology. Most characteristic were long narrow blades which had been struck from a carefully prepared block (the Levallois technique), but all the new tools indicated a heightened degree of technological insight and the adaptation of existing techniques to fresh perceptions of need. Handaxe-style tools were still being made, but they were smaller, heart-shaped or triangular with carefully flaked butts, suggesting they were used as adzes. There were fine slivers of stone, which could have been used for scraping and piercing skins; and single-edged blades which seemed designed for cutting and sawing. In a word, the new tool kit suggested refinement. It was as though the toolmakers had looked beyond the basic imperatives of life and had seen a multitude of secondary needs. Animals were no longer simply food, but also a source of skins that could be fashioned into bags and clothing, and of sinews for sewing them together; plants supplied fibres that could be twisted into string and rope; trees oozed gum for fixing stone blades to wooden shafts.

The new technology has been found at hundreds of sites down the length of Africa; in caves along the southern shores of the continent, and along the Mediterranean coast of Algeria and Libya. Most sites are concentrated in the eastern half of the continent, notably along the length of the Rift Valley; there are some in the Sahara, the Namib, and the Kalahari and at the few places in equatorial West Africa that have been investigated. The arrival of the new technology was a continent-wide phenomenon, but not a revolution—more a dissemination that spread across tens of thousands of years. The earliest evidence comes from the Kapthurin Formation near Lake Baringo in Kenya, where blades demonstrating the presence of fully conceptualized, well-executed methods of production, and high levels of technical competence, date back to between 509,000 and 543,000 years ago.[36]

Hafting appears to have become routine over a period of time, as blades were deliberately modified to facilitate the procedure, either by thinning the butt (or even making a tang). In a rare instance, traces of the mastic used to attach them to the shaft has been found on a blade. The blades themselves were carefully made, thin and symmetrical—just right for use as projectiles. Some were deliberately shaped to create equal distribution of mass around the

FIGURE 12.4 Finely knapped blades such as these 70,000 year-old examples from the Blombos Cave, indicate that this advanced technology was practised in Africa long before it appeared in Europe.

midline, suggesting an awareness of aerodynamic principles. The points could have been fitted to throwing or stabbing spears, though the small size of some suggests they were delivered by bow and arrow. Such points have been found embedded in the bones of prey animals.

The toolmakers apparently became very specific in their choice of raw material, and would go to great lengths to obtain the best—quite literally. Obsidian, a form of volcanic glass, is a highly valued material that produces blades as sharp as razors. The sources were few and far between, but artefacts made of obsidian have been found at sites widely distributed across East Africa. By analysing the elemental and chemical composition of the obsidian, scientists have been able to link source with site—with some surprising results. For instance: two specimens from a site in western Kenya came from two different sources, 185 kilometres and 190 kilometres away, journeys that involved not only a long walk but also a challenging 1,000 m climb over the western shoulder of the Gregory Rift. Further south, in Tanzania, the obsidian found at a site near Lake Eyasi came from a source 240 km to the north. Another Tanzanian site, dating from between 100 to 130 thousand years ago, had obsidian which had come from an outcrop that lay 320 km away.

It is unlikely that individual toolmakers themselves travelled such distances to collect their obsidian; far more likely that the widespread distribution indicates increased interaction and exchange among groups roaming across the landscape. This in turn suggests that people were becoming more numerous. Certainly there are more young sites than old ones, which implies not only a real increase in numbers but also more people per area of available resources—more mouths to feed. As the undesirable aspects of crowding and a diminishing food supply became apparent there was a heightened need for greater intellectual ability, and for the technical sophistication that is found in tools at the younger sites.

In the 1980s, a team of archaeologists working at Katanda, just north of Lake Edward in the Western Rift Valley, uncovered evidence which demonstrated how the need for food and the intellectual potential for acquiring it had interacted to produce a distinctive pattern of behaviour by around 90,000 thousand years ago.[37] There were no handaxes or large core tools of the Early Stone Age in the assemblage, nor any of the blades or refined tools that would indicate Late Stone Age origin. No, the sites were clearly from the Middle Stone Age and the most remarkable aspect of the assemblage was a number of highly formalized worked bone tools—50,000 years before anything like it appears in the European record, which hitherto was the oldest known.

The bone tools included seven well-made barbed points, two unbarbed points, and a large dagger-shaped implement of unknown function. All had been made from rib fragments or long bone splinters of large mammals; they were designed for fixing to a shaft, which in turn suggests they were made and used for catching fish. Indeed, catfish bones are so prevalent that the site could have been not just a toolmaking workshop, but also the equivalent of a works canteen. The catfish these people were catching weighed up to and in some instances more than 35 kg. All the remains were of adult fish, which indicates that fishing occurred only at the beginning of the rainy season, when the fish came inshore to spawn. This in turn suggests that the fishing was a regular, organized seasonal activity, not something that happened on an *ad hoc* basis.

Clearly, the people who frequented the Katanda sites 90,000 years ago were competent hunters and fishers who planned their movements around the seasonal availability of meat and fish. What's more, their behaviour could have made a crucial contribution to the evolution of modern humans.

The Katanda fishers never knew that their catches were especially rich in omega-3 long-chain polyunsaturated fatty acids, or that these fats were essential for the growth of the brain in young mammals, but the practice of eating fish probably contributed significantly to the development of the modern human brain. Omega-3 fats are not present in many plants and only minimally present in terrestrial animals (except for the brain), so eating fish was a change with fortuitous advantages. Especially when it was eaten by women during pregnancy and lactation, the times when the greatest amount of omega-3 fatty acids is required for the growth of an infant's brain.

Some authorities argue that eating fish, with its potential for improved infant nutrition, survival, and population growth, was a major evolutionary stimulus. 'The evolution of *Homo sapiens* took place at the land–water interface,' they say.[38] Well, if the earliest-known evidence for this contention comes from the Rift Valley, its most powerful support is to be found around the coast of the south-western Cape Province in South Africa. Here, the soils are generally poor and acidic, but nevertheless covered with a dense profusion of tough, long-lived plant species. The fynbos (meaning 'fine bush' in Afrikaans), is the most varied and concentrated area of vegetation of Earth. Extending over more than 90,000 square kilometres of the coast and hinterland to the north and east of Cape Town, it supports over 8,600 different plant species, nearly 5,800 of which are found nowhere else. The fynbos (also known as the Cape Floral Kingdom) is unique, and has been named as one of the world's six botanical kingdoms, but it is not well-endowed with the kind of plants on which animals and people could feed. Browsing antelope cropped the fynbos vegetation, but their population density was always low. For people, the best option the fynbos had to offer were the tubers, roots, and corms of plants which store an edible portion of their biomass underground—geophytes.

Geophytes are a characteristic feature of the fynbos, but they grow and regenerate very slowly under natural conditions. However, people learned to hasten the process by deliberately setting fire to the plants, which cleared the ground and caused seed-cases to burst, thus bringing about the germination of seeds that might otherwise have lain dormant for decades.[39] This environmental manipulation marks the beginnings of agriculture, in Africa 70,000 years ago, which in turn denotes another significant development in human behaviour. Indeed, 'fields' of geophytes are said to match the distribution of occupation sites in the region. Geophytes doubtless were a dependable source of carbohydrates in the fynbos; but for protein and essential fats people made extensive use of what the sea coast had to offer.

The land was poor, but the coastal waters were extremely rich in seafoods—especially shellfish, which nourished the evolving brain both in terms of the nutrients it supplied, and the intellectually testing demands of systematic collection. Huge shell middens are heaped above the highwater line at many points around the Cape coast where shellfish are plentiful on offshore rocks, and human occupations sites are never far away. But apart from availability and proximity, there was a social aspect here that added another level of relevance: gender. In terms of what shellfish and omega-3 could contribute to the evolution of the large human brain it was important that they should have been available to women who were pregnant or breastfeeding. But the women's capacity to move around was limited at such times, and they probably did not share much the brains and marrow that came from successful hunts (these do not keep and were likely to have been eaten at the scene of the kill—hunters' rewards). At the coast, however, women could feast on mussels and limpets, both exceptionally rich in omega-3 fats, on every low tide; and on the spring tides, twice a month, they had hours of access to the largest specimens.

The link between shellfish and women is a persuasive explanation for the evolved brain of modern humans.[40] Shellfish was a food source that not only nourished the infants' developing brain but also challenged their mothers' intelligence, since the systematic collection of intertidal shellfish required an understanding of the complex cycles of tides and seasons, which in turn affected settlement mobility and resource scheduling. In other words: it created a need for planning. At Katanda there were seasonal peaks in catfish availability to be planned for; around the Cape coast it was the daily and monthly tidal cycles that imposed an intellectual challenge. In both scenarios, nutrition was cause and effect of the shift towards a more complex way of life, one in which intelligence and nutrition were linked.

It must have been at this stage in our evolution that people began to think perhaps there is more to life than the problems of finding food. The brain was turning out to be an excellent survival tool—with capacity to spare. And so the evidence for behaviour that goes beyond the mere functional begins to appear in the archaeological record. Archaeologists call it symbolic behaviour—the creative urge that lies at the root of all art, music, and literature—though a creative act can also be functional, of course, in establishing identity, or ownership, or in building reciprocal relationships within and between groups.

Early manifestations of symbolic behaviour are well known in the cave paintings and decorative artefacts that were being made in Europe around 35,000 years ago. But in Africa it occurs much earlier—long before *Homo sapiens* first painted a cave wall in France. At a site near Lake Baringo in Kenya, in levels dated to at least 285,000 years ago, archaeologists have found large quantities of red ochre (haematite, an iron ore), along with grindstones, which indicates that people were using the pigment to decorate themselves, or for other symbolic purposes, just as is done today.[41] Tiny ostrich eggshell beads from a cave site in central Kenya, 43,000 years old,[42] are virtually identical to the ones that are strung together and exchanged as gifts (and sold to tourists) by the !Kung San people of the Kalahari. More prosaically, archaeologists have identified symbolic behaviour in tools from around 70,000 years ago that seem to have been made more with aesthetic or traditional considerations in mind, than for mere functional efficiency. The toolmakers need not have gone to so much trouble, so this could be an early case of manufacturers adding value to their product.[43]

Archaeologists have also found significant evidence of symbolic behaviour in a small cave overlooking the Indian Ocean, at Blombos, about 300 kilometres east of Cape Town.[44] Hearths indicate that generations of people had lived there; the fossil bones of deep-sea fish weighing 30 kg or more show they were highly proficient fishermen; a shell-necklace, incised bone and large quantities of worked ochre—including a remarkable rectangular slab decorated with an engraved geometric pattern—are poignant testimony to patterns of human behaviour we can empathize with, present in a cave at the southern tip of Africa, 75,000 years ago.

The necklace is especially revealing. The cord had long since gone, but the forty-one pierced shells lay together; smoothed from wear and marked with red ochre. Not the familiar ostrich eggshell beads, as might be expected, but the shells of *Nassarius kraussianus*, a small freshwater mollusc, the closest present-day source of which is about twenty kilometres away. To have made such a necklace implies a desire to make something distinctive. Of course, the necklace need not have been made at Blombos, its owner could simply have left it there, but even that denotes behaviour beyond the functional—exchange, for instance, or social interaction (or carelessness).

'Blombos presents absolute evidence for the earliest storage of information outside the human brain,' said Christopher Henshilwood, director of the excavations. 'Personal adornments such as beads incontrovertibly represent symbolically mediated modern behaviour. The discovery..., accurately dated at 75,000 years old, provides important new evidence for early symbolically organised behaviour in Africa.'[45]

Behind the claims that are made for the significance of individual discoveries lies an important overall point that deserves to be emphasized. Namely, that the acquisition of modern human behaviour was not a sudden event that occurred around 40,000 years ago, in Europe, when increased cognitive sophistication is said to have inspired a dramatic alteration in human behaviour. This long-standing Eurocentric scenario is invalidated by the evidence from Africa. In fact, all the innovations which mark the arrival of the

FIGURE 12.5 Stone Age sites in Africa often contain quantities of ochre, an iron ore used to make body or decorative paints. The pattern engraved on a block from 75,000 year-old deposits at Blombos could be an early example of symbolic behaviour.

so-called 'human revolution'—finely-knapped blades, pigment processing, long-distance exchange, fishing, bone tools, mining, incised pieces, beads and images—all occurred first in Africa. Furthermore, as archaeologists Sally McBrearty and Alison Brooks make clear:[46] there was no revolution of the 'Big Bang' genre, but rather an incongruent 'evolution' which occurred in response to local conditions in different places across a wide expanse of space, at different times, over a very long period.

CHAPTER THIRTEEN

Homo habilis
(1964)

W HEN LOUIS Leakey squeezed *Zinjanthropus boisei* into his scheme of
human evolution, he subjected both the interpretation of the evidence and his own preconceptions to some distortion. He claimed
the specimen resembled modern humans more closely than it resembled the
South African australopithecines—which even the most casual observer might
have disputed; and he accepted the unseemly creature as a direct ancestor—which
must have offended his notion of the antiquity of the pure *Homo sapiens* line. How
ironic, then, that not many months after Leakey had claimed that Zinj was our
earliest ancestor, the excavations funded by the media's generous response to his
discovery should produce a more worthy candidate: a series of fossils that could be
accommodated much more readily than Zinj within the Leakey concept of human
evolution. The fossils in question were found together with tools, some of them
in deposits even older than those in which Zinj had been found. They were more
lightly built in tooth and bones, and estimates of cranial capacity suggested that
the fossils represented a hominid whose brain was large relative to body size.

With no apparent embarrassment, Louis Leakey embraced the new evidence
and returned to the comfort of his former beliefs. He demoted *Zinjanthropus boisei* to
the status of non-toolmaking aberrant offshoot from the human line and hailed

the new discovery as the true maker of the Oldowan tools—an entirely new species of human being from whom *Homo sapiens* had evolved in Africa (by way of Kanjera Man) before migrating to Europe. The discovery pushed human origins back another 1.25 million years, he said, and would require many experts to rewrite their textbooks because it proved that *Australopithecus* was not an ancestor, but simply another hominid lineage that had existed at the same time, just as he had said all along. The new species was called *Homo habilis*—'handy man'.[1]

Of the fossils attributed to the new species, the first to be discovered were a tibia and a fibula (the bones of the lower leg) found at the Zinj FLK site. Like Zinj, they lay outside the area of concentrated remains and were unbroken. They were found some distance from the skull, several yards apart. At first it was presumed they had belonged to Zinj himself, even though they seemed too lightly constructed for a creature with a skull of such large proportions. And indeed, the presumption had to be revised when remains of similarly light construction were found at other sites.

The first came from FLK NN, a few hundred metres north of FLK (another site, FLK N, lay in between). The site was discovered quite fortuitously by the Leakey's eldest son, Jonathan, then 19, who had just finished school and was helping at Olduvai. Wandering away from the main Zinj site excavations on a fossil hunt of his own one day in May 1960, Jonathan saw an unusual mandible poking from a nearby slope. Since what could be seen of it was not unlike the jaw of a sabre-toothed cat (a rare find), the specimen was deemed interesting enough to warrant a search for more remains of the creature. The surface soil of the slope was sieved. The jaw had indeed belonged to a sabre-toothed cat; nothing more of it turned up, but a solitary hominid tooth and a single fingerbone were compensation with far greater promise. To locate the level from which the tooth and fingerbone had eroded, a step trench 1.53 metres wide and six metres long was cut into the slope. On 13 June Jonathan found a hominid collarbone, followed a few days later by several fragments of a very thin hominid skull.

As the excavations were extended to left and right (an area of more than 200 square metres was eventually uncovered), an interesting collection of hominid remains, artefacts, and debris was revealed. Most of the fossil-bearing layer appeared to have eroded away some time before Jonathan chanced upon the cat's

FIGURE 13.1 From top: *National Geographic* tribute, Louis Leakey's personal copy of the *Zinjanthropus* paper, and the type specimen of *Homo habilis* with the original *Nature* publication.

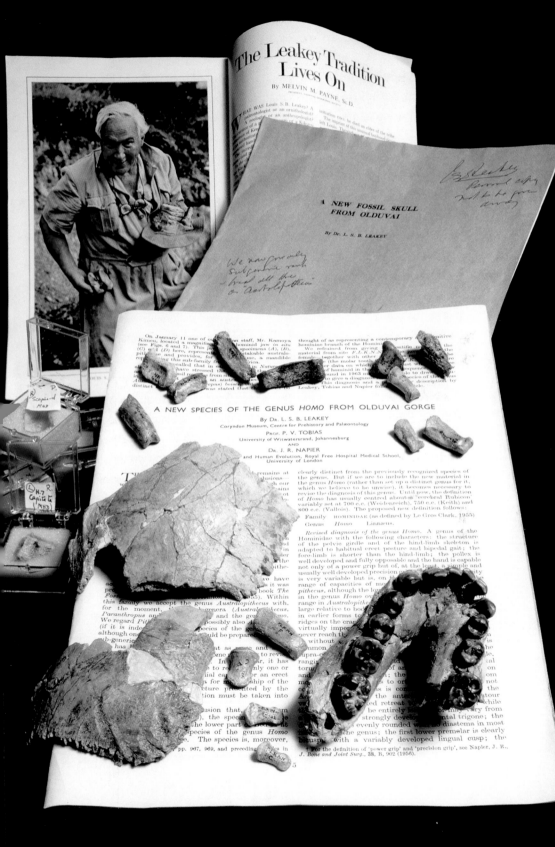

jaw; only the outer limits were left and, as with the area surrounding the alleged 'windbreak' at the Zinj site, the remains were mainly of the non-marrow-bearing variety. Among a total of 2,158 fossils, there were the ribs, vertebrae, shoulder blades and jawbones of pig and bovid; six catfish skulls and seventeen tortoise shells. Artefacts were not plentiful (only forty-eight are recorded), but hominid remains were scattered about the entire floor.

They comprised a curious assortment, curiously distributed. Twelve associated foot bones, for example, were found among a variety of non-hominid ribs, vertebrae, and the sundry remains of horse and bird. Six metres away, twenty-one hand bones lay beside a pig's skull; and nine metres from the hand bones, a piece of lower arm bone lay beside a pig's jaw. Towards the south-western edge of the site, one toe bone and one finger bone lay in splendid isolation more than six metres from both the hand and the foot to which they may—or may not—have belonged. In the vicinity of the trial trench from which the collarbone and skull fragments already mentioned had been retrieved, Jonathan found more skull fragments scattered over a wide area: more than four metres separated the most widespread; a left and right parietal, which together formed the central arch of a skull, lay three metres apart. A solitary mandible completed the hominid collection: this important specimen was found about two and a half metres from the left parietal, where it lay with an unidentified rib between two tortoise shells.

The assemblage posed several intriguing questions. Why such a strange assortment of bones? Why were they spread across the floor in such a curiously random fashion? There are no conclusive answers but the evidence, as assessed and interpreted by experts in the applicable disciplines, stands as a good example of palaeoanthropological procedure in the 1960s. Geologists identified the stratigraphic level of the fossil deposits, and geochronologists gave them an age of 1.7 million years. Archaeologists found the distribution of fossils similar to that pertaining at the Zinj site, and felt it likely that the *H. habilis* site had also borne evidence of a crude shelter. Palaeontologists identified animals the occupants were believed to have killed and eaten. Anatomists concluded that three individuals were represented among the hominid remains: they found parts of two adult left feet, and decided that the parietals, hand bones, and mandible all had come from a single young individual—though this could not be proved.

The hominids had died of natural causes, anthropologists believed, suggesting the bodies had been left at the site when the rest of the group moved on—a practice that has been recorded among modern nomadic people. Taphonomists, who study the processes affecting the nature of fossil assemblages, believed the corpses were almost entirely devoured by scavengers. Some skull fragments and some foot bones bore characteristic teeth marks, and the widespread scattering of the few remains was typical of hyena activity, for instance.

Though the hominid fossils may have seemed ill-assorted, and unlikely to reveal much of early human physical form and behaviour, together with the leg bones from the Zinj site, they supplied a good deal of new information—just about all of which lent strength to Louis Leakey's belief that the remains represented the earliest ancestor of *Homo sapiens*. Among the hand bones, anatomist John Napier found evidence of at least two hands (one juvenile and one adult), an opposable thumb and the physical capacity to manufacture the Oldowan tools found on the living floor.[2] From the foot bones another anatomist, Michael Day, reconstructed an almost complete adult left foot; it was entirely human, with no sign of the ape's divergent big toe and every indication that its owner had stood erect and walked with a bipedal and free-striding gait[3]—a view which a third anatomist, Peter Davis, confirmed in an independent study of the tibia and fibula from the Zinj site.[4] In the mandible, Leakey found the front teeth relatively large and the cheek teeth relatively small; this was quite different from the australopithecines, he said, and quite appropriate for a new and distinct type of early hominid.[5] From the parietals and other fragments yet another anatomist, Phillip Tobias, reconstructed a skull and estimated its cranial capacity as 680 cubic centimetres; which was nicely beyond the australopithecine average and approaching the *Homo* range.[6]

So the scanty remains appeared to represent a hominid with a relatively large brain, thin human-like skull bones, *Homo*-like teeth, manipulative hands, and the ability to make stone tools—evidence which, together with the age of the site, invited the conclusion that the new fossils must represent the earliest known ancestor of *Homo sapiens*. Contrary to Leakey's earlier contentions, it seemed certain that Zinj had been an intruder—or a victim—after all. The evidence was more compelling than much that Louis Leakey had used to support his theories in the past, but this time he did not rush to publish his conclusions.

Brief descriptive announcements appeared, but none assigned the fossils to any particular genus or species. The new species, *Homo habilis*, was finally announced in April 1964,[7] by which time several more specimens had been found at Olduvai. Among them, the end joint of a big toe added little, but two skulls and two isolated jaws (one upper and one lower) offered valuable corroboration. The skulls were broken, but the bone was indisputably as thin as in the new species and the cranial capacity appeared equally large. The dentition of the new and earlier finds was also very similar. Even more important, the finds ranged from the base of Bed I to the middle of Bed II, a span of about three-quarters of a million years during which there appeared to have been very little change in physical form—implying that *Homo habilis* had been a successful and enduring species.

Furthermore, to add to the significance of the *H. habilis* fossils, classic *Homo erectus* remains had been found in Upper Bed II (about 1.2 million years old) in December 1960. The first of these was a skull found by Louis Leakey himself, the only hominid fossil he ever found. Only the top of the skull was exposed which, at a distance, Leakey had assumed would turn out to be a modern tortoise carapace—something that had raised hopes many times before.[8]

For many palaeoanthropologists, Leakey's *Homo erectus* skull was the link that had been missing from the story of human evolution at Olduvai Gorge: it completed the *Homo habilis–Homo erectus–Homo sapiens* sequence at a single site. But not for Louis Leakey. He had described *Homo erectus* as an aberrant offshoot from the human line long before he found a representative of the species at Olduvai and was not about to change his mind now. In his view, the apparently conflicting evidence of the new skull (which was especially thick-boned) simply proved that three hominid lineages had existed at Olduvai: the robust australopithecines (now that he had assigned Zinj to that group), *Homo erectus*, as represented by his find, and the species he regarded as the true human ancestor, *Homo habilis*.

The advent of *Homo habilis* marked the first time that an assortment of fossil bones was used to define a new hominid species. Until then, species had been founded on the evidence of skulls or teeth demonstrably belonging to just one individual. The mandible on its own could have supported the definition, but Leakey and his co-authors Napier and Tobias decided that the skull and hand bones should be included, since they believed that the fossils all represented the same individual (something which could never be substantiated). So the remains 'of a single juvenile individual from Olduvai, Bed I' were presented as the holotype, or defining specimen, of the new species. The foot bones and other fossils were listed as paratypes—examples of the same species included in the reference sample.

Leakey and his co-authors believed that *Homo habilis* represented a hitherto unknown stage in the course of human evolution, so they felt entitled to revise the standing definition of the genus *Homo* in accordance with their new evidence. This may seem an audacious step, but in fact the genus had never been more than provisionally defined.[9] Linnaeus had given a succinct definition in his *Systema Naturae* of 1735: *Homo* nosce te ipsum (*Man* know yourself)—a term that is open to more than one interpretation and certainly does not preclude a fuller description of the genus.

At the time, it was generally believed that the distinguishing feature of the evolving *Homo* genus was brain size, and cranial capacities ranging from 700 to 800 cubic centimetres had been proposed as the size beyond which a hominid brain could be termed human. Leakey and his co-authors scrapped this notion. The *Homo* brain was highly variable in size, they said, and proposed *relative* brain size as a more accurate indication of generic status. The most important factor, in their view, was that the evolving *Homo* brain was large in relation to body size. In respect of the other evidence, skull shape, facial form, and bipedal gait were described as distinguishing features of the genus, plus a list of dental characteristics and the opposable thumb.

Following the announcement of *Homo habilis* in *Nature* in April 1964, the new species was subjected to frequent reappraisal. It was suggested that one of the type specimen's hand bones was in fact a vertebral fragment; that two others may have come from the hands of an arboreal monkey, and that six had belonged an unspecified non-hominid.[10] Even so, the evidence remained inherently valid; its significance never doubted. *Homo habilis* was accepted as further proof that Olduvai Gorge was 'the finest prehistoric site on earth…geologically and archaeologically sensational'; the 'immense value of [Leakey's] discoveries' was not disputed, but his interpretations were questioned[11]—mainly because he had chosen to stress differences rather than similarities and had created a new species rather than assign the specimens to one that already existed. And then, most provocatively of all, he had reinforced his own conception of human evolution by calling the new specimen *Homo* instead of *Australopithecus*, which most believed had stood on the path of human evolution at that point.

Critics complained that the conventions of classification had been flouted;[12] they said that the distinctiveness of the new species had been inadequately demonstrated,[13] and claimed there was simply not enough 'morphological space' for another species between *Australopithecus* and *Homo erectus*.[14] But at the same time, critics and supporters alike accepted the association of stone tools as evidence that the hominid Leakey had discovered was responsible for the Oldowan culture and therefore qualified as a human ancestor; and all agreed that the enlarged brain was a significant step in the direction of *Homo sapiens*.

In essence, then, it was agreed that *Homo habilis* was an ancestor of humans and, for those who believed *Australopithecus* had stood on the human line, the controversy had more to do with name than status. Was *habilis* the most advanced *Australopithecus* or the lowliest *Homo*, they asked? Given the difficulty of determining when one species becomes another on a lineage where evolution is presumed to be gradual, this purely academic question could never be answered. As the debate reached the correspondence columns of *The Times* even the anatomists Tobias and Napier confessed that the association of stone tools was the most convincing evidence of *habilis's* affinities with the genus *Homo*.[15] But such an assertion was hardly adequate. Classification is determined by morphology, not by inferred behaviour.[16] And besides, Leakey had offered exactly the same argument as evidence that *Zinjanthropus* was a human ancestor, and that claim had proved to be incorrect.

Acknowledging that the fossils needed a label, most authorities would probably have accepted *Australopithecus habilis*. Indeed, that label was applied.[17] But for Louis Leakey, of course, such a name was a contradiction in terms: he had never believed that *Australopithecus* was a human ancestor, while he had known since a boy that stone tools were made by the ancestor of humans, who was called *Homo*. Therefore in his view *Homo habilis* was the only name that could be applied.

Meanwhile, Phillip Tobias embarked upon the task of writing the definitive monograph of the species. It was published as volume 4 of the Olduvai Gorge series in 1991, three decades after the fossils had been found. By then, Tobias had published more than fifty papers examining the nature, validity, and evolutionary significance of a creature which, he believed, was the 'last missing link'.

FIGURE 13.2 Phillip Tobias, with a cast of *Zinjanthropus* and other mementoes of an illustrious career.

He was convinced that these 'gracile Olduvai pygmies had stridden manfully across a generic boundary—from *Australopithecus* to *Homo*' and in the monograph he went to prodigious lengths to make the case: two volumes, four kilograms of paper, 921 pages of text, 104 pages of photographs (and a superfluity of exclamation marks). No fossils have been reported in such detail—not even the Peking material. This was not so much a monograph as a monument to *Homo habilis*—or a monumental plinth on which he might stand. Does it support him, or does it make him a more visible target?

In the opening pages of the monograph, Tobias makes an enlightening, light-hearted, comment on the process by which he and his co-authors had initially arrived at the conclusion that the fossils recently recovered from Olduvai Gorge should be assigned to a new species of the genus *Homo*. Louis Leakey's method was 'intuitive, arbitrary, prescient, inspirational', he writes, while he and John Napier employed methods that were 'dogged, statistical, functional, anatomical—and perspirational!'[18]

It has often been said that the anatomists were reluctant to accept that the new specimen was anything other than a relative of *Australopithecus africanus*, and had to be persuaded by Louis Leakey to change their minds. Leakey of course had no such doubts. The enlarged brain, manipulative hand, and bipedal foot accorded perfectly with his theories of *Homo* having evolved during the earlier Pleistocene. This had to be *Homo*. And so, Leakey's wife, Mary, writes in her autobiography,[19] 'he directed his considerable powers of eloquent persuasion towards Phillip Tobias and John Napier,...'.

Not so, Tobias protests. He admits that at first he was 'most hesitant to recognise the single specimen OH 7 [its accession number] as being different from *A. africanus*'.[20] The teeth fell outside the range of measurement and indices observed in the australopithecines, he said, but that could be just an aberration occurring in just one individual. But then the continuing excavations at Olduvai produced another 'handful' of upper and lower teeth. These showed the same kinds of departure from the *A. africanus* dental pattern as the first specimens. It was clear, Tobias writes, that several individuals were represented, all with the same distinctive dental patterns. That, together with the *Homo*-like characteristics of the hand and foot were enough to convince him that Louis Leakey's intuitive and inspirational assessment had indeed been prescient.

The pursuit of distinctive characteristics in the teeth carried Tobias into a realm of detail that would be easy to mock were it not the work of palaeoanthropology's most distinguished practitioner. More than 300 words, for instance, are devoted to a description of the lingual (inner) surface of a canine tooth from the upper jaw, where we learn that 'The tubercle below the distal marginal ridge is the more strongly developed and constitutes a virtual *distal cusplet* (though it does not reach the occusal margin). Within the lingual fossa the relief differs…',[21] and so on. Tobias presents similar detail on the 343 distinctive morphological traits he has identified in the fossils. Numerous tables provide a wealth of supporting metrical data, and the distinctive features of each trait are compared with corresponding data (wherever possible or available) from six other hominid species.

In the final chapters of the monograph, Tobias considered the cultural and behavioural status of *Homo habilis*. On the basis of the detailed analysis he has presented he concluded that the species 'had the anatomical structure, both cerebral and vocal, which made speech possible,…possessed a culture which was of an advanced degree of complexity and embraced concepts beyond those attained by living apes'.

> *Homo habilis* was the first hominid who substantially distanced himself from his animality; who developed a whole new tool-kit for survival; who at last employed those emancipated hands to wrest a variety of implements from tough and intractable materials; who built a shelter behind rock walling; and who spoke about what he was doing. That moment of transmutation deserves, perhaps demands, to be rated as a transcendence…By taking this great step forward, *Homo habilis* was enabled by its cerebral revolution to attain a new mode of evolution, as an articulate, language-bound, culture-dependent hominid.[22]

Tobias described the twenty-one years that passed between the discovery of the fossils and the publication of the *Homo habilis* monograph as 'an aloneness' of striving to establish the taxon as a good species of hominid. He likened 'this time of conceptual solitude, the habiline pre-revolution, to the terrible and unutterable solitariness that Darwin faced after he published [*On*] *The Origin of Species* or that Dart confronted when, for decades after the discovery of the Taung skull, he was virtually alone in his belief that *Australopithecus africanus* had stood on the threshold of humanity'.[23]

No doubt aloneness and conceptual solitude are partly responsible for the monograph's crusading tone of righteous determination. It is a formidable, even daunting, piece of work whose proportions alone are enough to deter criticism. But, with such a plethora of fact, figures, and interpretation derived from such a small body of evidence, the objective reviewer might just begin to wonder if the professor with the eloquent pen doth protest too much. Was the Olduvai sample comprehensive enough to support one conclusion and refute all others? Or is this another case in which the depth, duration, and intensity of an argument is inversely proportional to the quantity and quality of the evidence that inspired it? Ultimately, as the story of palaeoanthropology repeatedly demonstrates, it is evidence, not eloquence that settles the argument.

More than a dozen specimens from Olduvai Gorge were attributed to *Homo habilis* in the decades following the initial description of the species in 1964, and others were described from Sterkfontein and Swartkrans in South Africa, from the Omo in Ethiopia, and from the excavations directed by Louis's son, Richard, at East Turkana in Kenya. The expanding collection did not resolve the issue of the species' status, however. Commentators felt that *Homo habilis*, as originally defined, was too variable to be a sound species. There were also differences of opinion concerning its functional abilities. Morphological analysis of the leg, foot, and hand bones from Olduvai, convinced Randall Susman and Jack Stern of the University of New York at Stony Brook, for instance, that although *Homo habilis* shared modern man's ability to walk upright and make stone tools, the species also shared the apes' ability to climb trees.[24] This interpretation was greeted with some scepticism (not least because it was questionable that the hand and the foot they examined had come from the same individual), but the combination of ancient and modern features they defined was ideally suited to a species postulated as the link between the generalized morphology of an ancestor and the more specialized characteristics of a descendant.

The discovery of *Australopithecus afarensis* (more popularly known as 'Lucy', see Chapter 15) in 1979 had pushed hominid ancestry back to more than three million years ago, well beyond *A. africanus* and opening up a temporal gap that was more than large enough for a species such as *Homo habilis* to have arrived and subsequently evolved to become *Homo erectus* (then still regarded as the best candidate for the recent ancestry of modern humans). In other words, *H. habilis* could have been a link in the evolutionary sequence that led from the australopithecines to modern humans. A hominid that made tools and walked upright but still climbed trees to sleep, feed, and escape from predators, as Susman and Stern conjectured, fitted this scheme of things perfectly: a classic case of speculation filling a stretch of time from which morphological evidence was absent.

Mary Leakey continued to live and work at Olduvai Gorge through the 1970s and into the 1980s, but by 1984 life at the Gorge had become a battle for survival. Provisions were difficult to obtain, and petrol supplies erratic; at the age of 71 she handed over the camp and its facilities to the Tanzanian Department of Antiquities and moved permanently to the house she had kept in Nairobi.[25]

Barely one year later, the Olduvai camp was occupied by a team of Tanzanian and United States researchers led by Donald Johanson and Tim White, two protagonists in the *Australopithecus afarensis* debate for whom Mary Leakey had very little sympathy indeed. The irony of Johanson and White taking over the Olduvai excavations from the Leakeys needs no more than a mention here, though it generated plenty of comment in private. The team returned for the 1986 season, and on the third day of surface survey, Tim White picked up a piece of hominid armbone just off the track leading to the Zinj site. Subsequent excavations and sifting recovered nearly 18,000 fragments of fossil bone and tooth, including antelope, giraffe, hippopotamus, pigs, baboons, reptiles, birds, and hominid.

In total, 302 pieces of hominid fossil were recovered: fragments of skull, jaw and limbs representing a single individual who had died about 1.8 million years ago. In their announcement of the discovery (identified by its accession number, OH 62),[26] the authors attributed the partial skeleton to *Homo habilis* on the basis of its skull and teeth, but pointed out that its postcranial anatomy was strikingly similar to that of *Australopithecus afarensis*. 'There's no doubt that it is *Homo habilis*', Johanson remarked.[27] 'This is the first time that limb bones and cranial material of *Homo habilis* have been found in definite association', he went on. 'The result is a big surprise.'

The surprise was that the hominid represented by the new find, though indisputably adult (and female), stood only 36 inches high, with hands hanging to the knees—just like apes and the famous Lucy Johanson and his team in Ethiopia had discovered thirteen years before. But Lucy and her kind dated back to more than 3 million years ago, while the remains of *Homo habilis* at Olduvai were only about 1.8 million years old. This meant that the ape-like characteristics of *Australopithecus afarensis* must have remained a distinctive and unchanging feature of the ancestral hominid for a very long time. The earliest humans were more like apes than had been supposed, it seemed, and if they had remained unchanged for so long, the subsequent adaptation to *Homo erectus* must have been completed between the time of the youngest *Homo habilis* and the oldest *Homo erectus*—a gap of no more than about 200,000 years.

White interpreted this implication of long-term stasis and abrupt change as evidence of stability in the *Australopithecus afarensis* adaptation. '*Australopithecus afarensis* was not poised on a razor edge between apes and humans', he said; 'this adaptation lasted at least 2 million years, right up to the origin of *Homo erectus*'. According to White, the new find from Olduvai raised problems of interpretation only because 'people have viewed human evolution through the glasses of gradualistic change'. 'Well', he said, 'this fossil has smashed those glasses. The change was obviously abrupt, with a big modification in body form between *Homo habilis* and *Homo erectus*.'[28]

Susman and Stern welcomed the new find from Olduvai as proof of their contention that *Homo habilis* had been an accomplished tree-climber but, whatever OH 62 might do for the arboreal status of the habilines, its arrival did not clarify the concept of *Homo habilis* as a link in the saga of human evolution; indeed, it introduced more confusion. Phillip Tobias, the foremost authority from whom comment might have been expected, was uncharacteristically silent on the subject. In the *H. habilis* monograph he listed OH 62 among the Olduvai hominids that were relevant to the study, but made no further mention of the specimen. A reviewer excused this omission on the grounds of the discovery having come too late for inclusion, even though it had been announced and described four years before the monograph was published.[29]

In a commentary published in 1987 when the OH 62 discovery was first announced, the anatomist Bernard Wood concluded that the new specimen 'rudely expose[d] how little we know about the early evolution of *Homo*'. There was 'compelling evidence' for it not being a robust australopithecine, he said, but despite claims that it consolidated the taxonomic unity of *H. habilis*, it also suggested that the range of variation within material assigned to early *Homo* was

FIGURE 13.3 Original fossils of the OH62 specimen, laid out where they were excavated from a 1.8 million-year-old locality at Olduvai Gorge.

too great to be encompassed within one taxon. 'Who is the "real" *Homo habilis?*' Wood asked.[30]

Who indeed? Bernard Wood returned to the question in a paper on the history of the genus *Homo* published in 2000, and found it no easier to answer. *Homo habilis* was a 'problem' species, he wrote. The original fossils were believed to have represented an animal that was habitually upright and bipedal, and dextrous enough to make the Oldowan stone tools. However, functional studies of the relevant fossils made since those initial announcements had shown that they had most probably belonged to an animal that was not a committed biped, but one in which bipedalism was combined with the ability to climb. Likewise, there was nothing about the hand morphology of *Homo habilis* to distinguish it functionally from hand fossils attributed to *Australopithecus*. Thus there were no anatomical grounds for claiming that only *Homo habilis* could have made the Olduvai Bed I stone tools, and, in any case, stone tools had since been found in Ethiopia that were older than the fossil evidence of *Homo habilis*. All this meant that *Homo habilis* no longer matched the functional criteria that Leakey, Tobias, and Napier had set out. The species was insufficiently advanced in terms of its adaptations to justify inclusion in *Homo*, Wood concluded, and should either be transferred to *Australopithecus* or placed in a new genus.[31]

Nearly half a century of accumulating evidence and discussion has left *Homo habilis* more open to question, more insecure than it ever was. While the species stood alone, a box of fossils separated from their putative ancestors and descendants by respectable distances in both time and morphology, its intermediate status seemed perfectly safe. Further evidence has filled the temporal gaps and intensified discussion of the species' morphological characteristics, but has not supplied the foundation of unequivocal evidence on which a valid new species could stand, safe and unassailed. *Homo habilis* remains more of an evolutionary idea than an example of anatomical fact linking one species to another.

CHAPTER FOURTEEN

1470 (1972)
and the Oldest Man

W HILE THE scarcity of evidence blights palaeoanthropology and the dangers of saying too much about too little are repeatedly exposed, it is worth noting just how rare the fossils are. These treasured but intrinsically worthless relics of our past are less common than diamonds, and more difficult to find than gold—or just about any other fraction of the Earth's bounty that we value. In Africa, for instance, all the known deposits of an appropriate age that might contain fossils add up to an area that in total is about 0.1 per cent of the continent's land surface,[1] and their whereabouts is not easy to predict in the way that geologists can say where a gold seam might be.

Sizeable exposures of fossil-bearing deposits occur down the length of the Rift Valley and smaller sites are dotted about elsewhere, but nearly all of them are in regions that are difficult to reach and hard to work in. At every location, the deposits cover isolated periods of time—but identifying those of an age that makes them worth exploring is just a small part of the gamble that palaeoanthropologists take on. Even at the most promising sites they confront the sheer improbability of any hominids having died and their skeletal remains having fossilized in that precise location. The chances are extremely low. It has been calculated that hominid fossils found in ten years of work at

East Turkana in Kenya (an exceptional collection spanning over one million years), represent only one individual for every 100 million that lived during the course of that timespan.[2] One seasoned practitioner described attempts to decipher the course of human evolution from the fossil evidence as rather like trying to follow the story of *War and Peace* from a few pages torn at random from the book.

If fossils are rare, the ability to find them is even more uncommon—requiring not only the hawk-eyed talent to recognize a scrap of bone poking from the dirt as having belonged to a hominid, not a pig, an antelope, or a tortoise, but also an aptitude for finding the resources and time that make it possible to look for them in the first place. Single-minded determination is a common characteristic of the palaeoanthropologists who return each year to spend weeks roaming the exposures, eyes to the ground, alone, silent, sustained by the knowledge that miracles do happen; fossils are found—almost always by those who just keep on looking.

As a science, palaeoanthropology came of age in the 1970s, a decade when the advances in geological investigation, dating technology, and archaeological methods began to produce results. During the previous 100 years, fewer than a dozen fossils which added something new to what was already known of human evolution were found. Now the rate of accumulation increased dramatically—with much of the credit due to the efforts of the Leakey family, and their discoveries at Olduvai Gorge. With Zinj, the australopithecine found in 1959, Louis Leakey had laid the groundwork for a new and more dynamic approach to fossil hunting. He tapped into public interest and the media as a source of funds, which certainly enabled him to recruit the best scientists but also moved the investigations away slightly from the primarily scientific motivation that had powered them hitherto, and created a demand for discoveries that could be announced in a blaze of publicity.

Louis became a superstar of the lecture circuit, especially in the United States. His talks were packed with enthusiastic audiences; he was a frequent guest on radio and television shows; he revelled in the adulation and hospitality that was showered on him…America simply loved this witty, gruff, and iconoclastic old colonial, and in the final years of his life he tried very hard to give his admirers something they would very much like to have: an Early Man of their very own.

At the time, most authorities believed that humans had crossed the Bering Straits into north America around 12,000 years ago, when sea levels were low enough for a land bridge to have provided access from Asia. Stone spearheads found near the town of Clovis, New Mexico, and elsewhere in deposits dating back to around 11,200 years ago supported the consensus. But, in typically idiosyncratic manner, Louis did not agree. Ever since his Cambridge days, a biographer reports, Louis had had a hunch that humans had reached America much earlier than was generally accepted.[3] In 1963, while a visiting professor at the University of California's Riverside campus, he was presented with an opportunity to pursue that hunch.

Ruth DeEtte Simpson (better known as Dee Simpson, 1918–2000), an archaeologist and Associate Curator at the Southwest Museum in Los Angeles, told him of primitive-looking artefacts which had been found in 1942 at a site to the east of the Calico Mountains where, in Pleistocene times (10,000 to 2 million years ago) there had been a lake. Louis accompanied her to the site, and soon identified a location which, he was certain, would have been ideal for early human settlement during the Pleistocene. It was on an alluvial fan, formed by a river flowing towards the ancient lake, to which geologists and geomorphologists had given a probable age of between 50,000 and 80,000 years. There had been fresh water available and out in front, as Louis himself put it, 'a great plain which must have been verdant green, with animals and plants suitable for food'. All he had to do now was find some tools *in situ*.

Miss Simpson recounts how he then went striding over the hills until he saw some scraps of a flint-like material, sticking out from the face of a cutting made by a mechanical excavator. The material was chalcedony, and it just *might* have been worked by human hands. That was enough for Louis Leakey. 'This is where we are going to excavate', he told the delighted Miss Simpson, who was a firm believer in Louis Leakey and early man in North America.

But first they needed funding. Louis rushed off to the National Geographic Society in Washington, where, understandably, the prospect of finding early humans in America aroused even more interest than their presence in Africa had done. Inspired by Leakey's enthusiasm, the Society gave money for excavations to begin immediately and the San Bernardino Museum County Museum forthwith agreed with Leakey's suggestion that Miss Simpson should be appointed County Archaeologist and field director of the Calico excavations.

From November 1964, Dee Simpson and her teams of volunteers worked tire-lessly at the site for the next six years. Among the volunteers one Christmas vaca-tion were two 17-years-olds, Tim White and Wes Reeder. As boys growing up in the vicinity of the San Bernardino Mountains, the pair had been collecting artefacts from ancient Indian campsites since they were 10. They presented their collections to the San Bernardino Museum County Museum in 1967 and were rewarded with invitations to join the hunt for evidence of America's earliest inhabitants.

At Calico, they joined the team working under Dee Simpson. The site was divided into five-foot squares, each of which was excavated to a depth of three inches at a time, using only small hand tools: linoleum knives, shoemakers' awls, and dental picks. The position of every likely artefact was plotted in three dimen-sions and photographed. The 'good' specimens were left in situ on a pedestal of soil for Louis to inspect if he arrived before the excavations got too deep and they had to be moved. If he did not, the piece was formally witnessed by at least three people before it was lifted.

Nothing very convincing was found during the first season and Louis was shown only a very small proportion of the thousands of stone pieces that had been unearthed. 'Those specimens which I particularly like are separated and marked "special"', Dee Simpson wrote in a museum report. 'I see them again and again,' she said, 'and select from those the ones that Dr Leakey sees.' Of the hand-picked specimens there were only about half a dozen that Louis approved of, but with his encouragement, these were enough to persuade the National Geo-graphic Society to provide more funding. Control pits were dug across the site to see if comparable finds turned up at random. They did not, and this appeared to prove that the main excavations had—providentially—struck a concentration of 'artefacts', a working-floor, of which there was no evidence elsewhere.

A second master pit was opened, and nine feet down the team found forty-three specimens which Louis accepted as artefacts. Then came something really exciting: a circle of nine fairly large rocks with smaller one in between. A boy scout visitor recognized their significance at once: 'Ma'am,' he said to Dee Simpson, 'I don't mean to tell you your business, but that looks just like where

FIGURE 14-1 Artefacts and publications relating to Louis Leakey's involvement with the Calico Hills excavations.

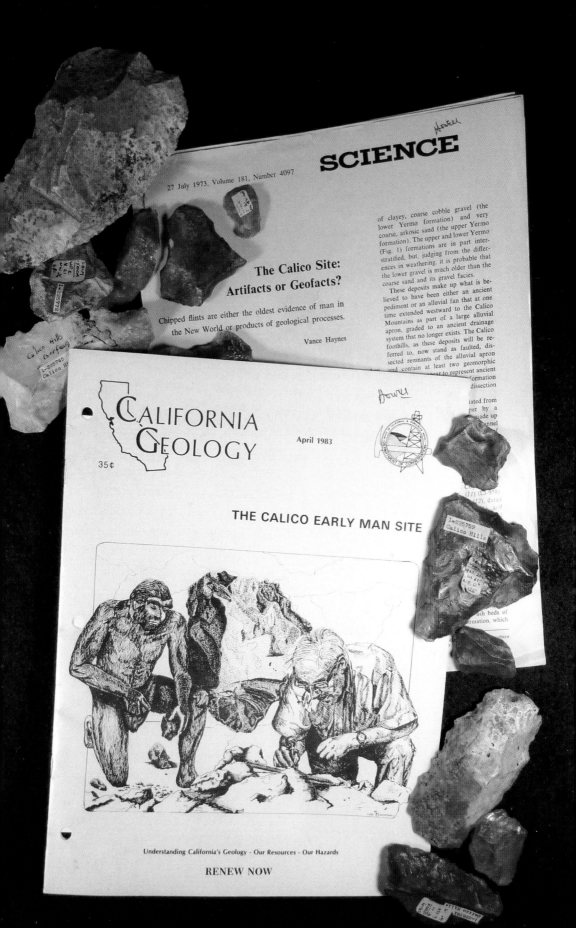

I cooked dinner last week.' Samples of the rock were independently analysed by scientists in Los Angeles and Czechoslovakia and both confirmed the boy's judgement. 'It would appear,' one of them said, 'that in that circular arrangement of stones there must have burned a fire.' And where there was a fireplace there must have been people.

By 1968, Leakey felt confident enough to publish a preliminary report on the Calico excavations in *Science*, with co-authors Dee Simpson and a University of South California geologist, Thomas Clements. The site is probably between 50,000 and 80,000 years old, the report declared, and had yielded more than 170 specimens which were considered 'to be unquestionably the result of human activity. In addition, there [were] several hundred other specimens which, in view of their close association with the first group, must also be regarded as possibly of human workmanship.'[4] Among the 'artefacts' they identified many large flakes with bulbs of percussion, which is usually—but not exclusively—the hallmark of human workmanship; also a few scrapers and simple tools apparently worked on both faces.

Casts of typical specimens were made for distribution to archaeologists and prehistorians. For the most part, the recipients were not impressed by the casts, nor, for that matter, by the actual specimens which some of them saw when they visited Calico. One of the severest critics was Louis's wife, Mary, who, if anyone, knew a genuine stone tool when she saw one. For her, Calico revealed how much Louis had changed since the discoveries at Olduvai. He had always been a showman, but science had come first. Not any more.

'However meticulous the excavation, he was arguing in a completely unscientific way, by not considering all the processes that might have produced the pieces he regarded as artefacts,' Mary Leakey wrote in an account of the Calico affair.[5] And then there was the matter of selection. 'In the dark ages of prehistory it is true that only *belles pieces* were retained by the excavators. Waste material and artefacts that did not catch the eye were discarded. At Calico, this process was carried even further,' she wrote. From among the thousands of pieces excavated, Dee Simpson selected the pieces she thought Louis might like, and then he winnowed her selection down to the few that he declared were artefacts. The proportion of pieces that finally made the grade was infinitesimal.

The point here is that the alluvial fan deposit contained many rounded boulders and angular blocks of chert which, when the fan was in a mobile state, could hardly avoid coming into frequent and heavy contact with one another. In such circumstances, how could there fail to be flakes of chert in the deposit? Some of them, if found on a true working-floor, would certainly have been accepted as genuine knapping debris: the casual flakes produced by nature and by a human toolmaker can by no means always be distinguished, but on a human working-floor there will always be products which are beyond the scope of natural processes.

Louis was very upset by his wife's criticism, but too deeply committed to retract (a not unfamiliar reaction in palaeoanthropology, before and since). He convened a meeting of geologists, archaeologists, and prehistorians at the site in October 1970, by which time Louis was a sick man, still recovering from a serious heart attack. Mary Leakey was specifically asked not to attend, and among those who did there was more concern for the effect of their opinions on Louis's precarious health than for rigorous assessment of his findings. Many expressed no opinion at all, others expressed their doubts by means of questions and the session ended with what the delegates thought was a verdict of 'not proven'.

Louis took a more optimistic view and gave a press conference which prompted the next morning's papers to report—on Louis Leakey's authority—that the presence of Early Man at Calico Hills 80,000 years ago had been confirmed by international experts. His admirers were delighted; the international experts rather less so.

The saga of Early Man at Calico was a sad episode that effectively marked the end of Louis Leakey's career. It was also a salutary lesson in archaeological procedures and politics for the young Tim White, the son of a California state highway labourer, who notes in 2010 that on the desert freeway from Los Angeles to Las Vegas, just beyond the town of Barstow, there was still a large, official Caltrans road sign announcing the EARLY MAN SITE, where enthusiastic believers are still digging.[6]

Louis died of a heart attack in September 1972, just a few days after his son Richard had shown him a prize find from that season's excavations on the eastern shore of Lake Turkana (previously known as Lake Rudolf). It was a skull that had come from deposits then believed to be 2.61 million years old. The specimen was identified by its Kenya National Museum accession number as KNM-ER 1470, but Louis recognized it immediately as the best-preserved skull of *Homo habilis* to have been found anywhere. He was excited, triumphant, and sublimely happy; able to rejoice in his own son's discovery of what he himself had been seeking for most of his life: a really early example of a hominid that would have to be recognized as *Homo* rather than *Australopithecus*, thereby proving the central point of his view of human evolution.[7]

Five years after his father had died, Richard Leakey was described in *Time* magazine as 'the organizing genius of modern palaeoanthropology'.[8] The research he initiated at East Turkana in northern Kenya was carried out by a large number of invited specialists. So far as science was concerned, Leakey played only a minor role. Like his mother, he had not gone to university, so had no academic qualifications at the time (subsequently, he has been showered with doctorates, elected a Fellow of the Royal Society, and appointed Professor of Anthropology), but he directed the investigations with extraordinary success. His background (some say his birthright) may have contributed to the East Turkana project's initial impetus, but its subsequent success was entirely due to Richard Leakey's ambition, determination, and administrative talents. He has said that he wanted the East Turkana Research Project to become less his personal enterprise, and hoped to promote a more impersonal trend in the science, whereby the predispositions of a discoverer (or expedition leader) were lost, or at least diffused, while the fossils were studied by the appropriate experts.

But like his father, Richard Leakey was destined to become a public figure whose pronouncements tended to overshadow his group's scientific utterances. He expounded his views fluently in magazines, newspapers, books, and on television, so that despite the avowed intention that less public and more impersonal scientific procedures should prevail, he became a celebrity and the first call for journalists seeking a quote on the search for human origins.

Richard Leakey shared his father's belief that human evolution had been a very lengthy affair, and *Australopithecus* had played no part in it since the two lines split from the common ancestor about six or seven million years ago. Some of his contemporaries championed the opposite view, that *Australopithecus* was indeed the human ancestor, and that the *Homo* and *Australopithecus* lineages split from a common ancestor little more than two million years ago. The best evidence used to support each of the two theories was identical: fossils found at East Turkana and in Ethiopia. Each side interpreted the evidence differently, however, though the arguments were united by familiar undertones: each reflected preconception as much as interpretation, and each revealed as much of the scientist as of science.

The field base-camp of Leakey's East Turkana Research Project was established in 1969 on the shores of Lake Turkana, which lies in the hot and inhospitable landscape of northern Kenya. The lake measures more than 250 kilometres from north to south, and is about 50 kilometres across at its widest point. Rivers flow in, but none flows out of the lake; evaporation is excessive and the salts left behind have turned the lake waters into a solution that wild animals drink with impunity but which people find very unpleasant—not least on account of its laxative properties. The surrounding landscape rarely receives more than 100 mm of rain in a year; fresh water is available only at a few widely spaced natural springs; the indigenous human population is limited to small groups of nomadic pastoralists, even though there is grazing and browse enough to support large numbers of wild animals. On most days, a fierce easterly wind is drawn across the lake by thermals rising from the baking landscape, and the surface waters are whipped to a choppy froth of erratic waves.

The base-camp at Koobi Fora, on the eastern shore of the lake was an oasis of comfort in this hot and windy wilderness. Only a hundred metres or so separated the camp buildings from the lake; water extended from the shore to the horizon. The lake had to be shared with hippos and crocodiles, but it supplied excellent fish and wonderful swimming at the end of the day. The cool sandy shore stretched away in the distance; flamingos, pelicans, and plovers congregated in large numbers. Zebra, antelope, and gazelle gathered on the flats, the sun set across the lake, the wind dropped—Koobi Fora was a place of exceptional beauty.

The camp buildings were floored with flagstones from the lakeshore and kept cool by the draught that circulated beneath the low thatched roofs. In the dining area there was always squash available, large pint glasses, ice in the fridge and a canvas watercooler hanging in the breeze. Essential supplies were brought by a lorry which constantly plied the rough five-day, 800-kilometre 'road' to and from Nairobi. Leakey himself flew in for a few days whenever he could, bringing fresh meat, fruit, and vegetables.

Koobi Fora was a haven—but a base-camp. Scientists usually spent only the weekends there, a much-needed respite in which to soak up water and wash clothes after a week of working from satellite camps where conditions were far less congenial and meals tended to consist of corned beef and little else. Working conditions in the regions where the East Turkana fossils were found are among the most testing on earth. For an hour or so each morning and evening, when the shadows were long and the sky a saturated blue, conditions were comfortable—even idyllic. For the rest of the day, however, the sun and its broiling heat took their toll: bleaching the sky; whitening the vegetation; bouncing harsh reflections from burnished lava cobbles. And the wind. An easterly gale blew most of the day, most days, and the best to be said of it was that conditions were far more uncomfortable when it dropped. With everything radiating heat, tiny sweat bees and midges clustered on exposed damp skin in the still air. They whined about the ears and irritated body and mind.

In these circumstances it might be imagined that stress would arise between individuals. In fact, the sun and wind did not so much shorten tempers as they exhausted everyone, creating silences around the table and in the casual moments when people usually chatter and gossip after a day's work. Scientists working from the satellite camps often felt unusually vulnerable: one said he needed a long thick book to preserve his sanity. In fact, scientists were only on the scene for two or three months each year; most of the East Turkana hominid fossils have been found by a group of Kenyans known familiarly as the Hominid Gang. Generally there were six of them and they scoured the exposures six hours a day, six days a week, six months a year, covering virtually every square metre of 800 square kilometres.

Finding fossils at places like East Turkana is also expensive. In the first ten years Richard Leakey channelled more than $800,000 into his East Turkana Research Project. Government institutions and the more august bodies that fund scientific research do not rate the search for fossil evidence of human evolution very highly among their priorities, and initially Leakey found all his money elsewhere. The National Geographic Society gave him $25,000 in 1968; in succeeding years other foundations contributed too and, all along, participating scientists have been required to find some independent funding for their travel and research.

In some seasons a total of up to fifty specialists worked at East Turkana, demonstrating that money was available for a wide range of palaeoanthropological investigations. Most were working on independent or university research programmes. Their results contributed significantly to the overall investigations

FIGURE 14.2 Richard Leakey team crossing the Chalbi Desert on his first expedition to East Turkana(1969); fossil-hunting by camel; Richard Leakey in 1978 with the first of many major discoveries.

of the East Turkana Research Project, but dependence upon such individual research and piecemeal funding was far from ideal.

If grants totalling the $800,000 had been guaranteed when the project began, there can be no doubt that both research and results would have benefited. But such long-term planning was impossible. Grants were made irregularly and ran for just a few years; the National Geographic Society, for example, decided upon its contribution annually. Thus funding was most readily encouraged by exciting results, even though their scientific value might depend upon other, less colourful, investigations. In this respect, hominid fossils were clearly top of the list, and Richard Leakey was fortunate in having a sequence of truly impressive finds to announce, virtually year after year, as work advanced on all fronts in the Lake Turkana basin.

The 'Missing Link' had been a media favourite for as long as anyone could remember, each new candidate reminding audiences of the controversy Darwin had aroused with his theory of evolution and its implication that we are descended from the apes. But palaeoanthropologists could do better than that now. The application of potassium/argon dating procedures enabled them to give an absolute age of fossils from suitable deposits and, since they turned out to be much older than anyone had thought likely, it was not surprising that press releases stressed age before the significance of any evolutionary context. Much less was heard of Missing Links as the 'Oldest Man' took over as the most newsworthy image of achievements in palaeoanthropology.

Richard Leakey's 1968 season at Lake Turkana produced fossil remnants of extinct pigs and elephants 'about four million years old', and a few fragments of australopithecine jaw, poorly preserved but enough to strengthen his application for more funds with the suggestion that 'near-man had lived along the eastern shore of Rudolf [the name was changed to Turkana in 1974] between two and three million years ago'.[9] Further investigations 'would turn up further evidence of man's ancestry', he said, and the National Geographic Society responded with funds for another year.

The ages Leakey had given these fossil fauna were deduced from the evidence of other sites. The pigs, for instance, seemed older than those from Olduvai. Plans for the 1969 expedition included more accurate age assessments as part of a geological and stratigraphical survey of the deposits that would be undertaken by Kay Behrensmeyer, a graduate student of geology at Harvard University.

Early in her endeavours, Behrensmeyer found some stone tools. She selected samples of the volcanic ashfall in which they appeared to have been embedded and dispatched them to Cambridge University for potassium/argon dating by Frank Fitch and Jack Miller. The first results included an age of 2.4 million years, which was enthusiastically celebrated at Koobi Fora.[10] Subsequently, tests of additional samples caused Fitch and Miller to revise their first estimate to a 'more accurate date of very close to 2.6 million years, plus or minus 260,000 years.'[11]

Meanwhile Leakey had found a complete hominid skull about fifty kilometres north of the tool site, and one of his Kenyan assistants found fragments of another—but different—skull near by. According to Behrensmeyer's stratigraphic work, the hominid site lay below the geological horizon on which she had found the tools. In Leakey's estimation, the fossil fauna confirmed her correlation and so, he deduced, the tools and the hominids must all be at least 2.6 million years old. The oldest evidence of toolmaking known theretofore had come from Olduvai, as we have seen, from beds dated at close to 1.9 million years.

So, after his second season at East Turkana Richard Leakey could claim to have pushed the toolmaking phase of mankind back nearly three-quarters of a million years. Furthermore, his expedition had discovered two skulls as well—one magnificent, the other mysterious. The first was an undistorted version of Zinj, a wonderful specimen that was found, incidentally, ten years almost to the day after Richard's mother had found the original at Olduvai. There could be no doubt about its affinities: robust australopithecine. The second was incomplete, puzzling and, in the short term, more useful for that very reason.

Leakey referred to the mystery skull in *Nature* and *National Geographic*.[12] Although the skull was too fragmentary to permit conclusive interpretation, certain things, wrote Leakey, were clear. There was not much of *Australopithecus* to be seen in it, and not much of *Homo* either; but he believed the slight morphological evidence of the latter was strengthened by the associative evidence of stone tools. It was generally agreed, he pointed out, that the australopithecines had not made tools. Therefore a second hominid species must have existed at East Turkana. Was this it? If so, then as at Olduvai a decade before, *Homo habilis* might have seemed the obvious candidate for the East Turkana toolmaker as well. But Leakey could see little of *habilis* in the mystery skull either.

If not *H. habilis*, could it be a prototype of *Homo erectus*, he wondered, making tools at East Turkana over two million years before appearing in Java and Peking? Richard Leakey believed it was quite possible. 'We will find the answer, I am sure,' he told *National Geographic* readers, 'for among the strata of the East Turkana desert lies a fascinating volume of prehistory, holding untold chapters of the origin of mankind…we have scarcely turned the first page, and I am eager to get on with the reading.'

Funds flowed, fossils too. In 1970 sixteen hominids were found, followed by another twenty-six in 1971. Among these were some important mandibles, a fragmentary half-skull (subsequently described as a female of the robust australopithecine lineage), some skeletal parts, and some isolated teeth. Preliminary reports were published in *Nature*,[13] but the 'mystery skull' was described later in the pages of *Social Biology*, where it was assigned to the *Australopithecus* lineage.[14]

The next major discovery from East Turkana was the famous 1470 skull. The first scraps of it were found on 27 August 1972 by Bernard Ngeneo. Richard Leakey and Bernard Wood, an anatomist with the research project, joined the search and within days they had collected and assembled enough pieces to satisfy themselves that Ngeneo's find was the oldest, most complete hominid skull with a relatively large brain case ever found. Large brain equals *Homo*, therefore 1470 was the Oldest Man.

An extensive area surrounding the discovery site was carefully sieved to ensure that all pieces that might belong to the skull were recovered. Richard's wife, the zoologist Meave Leakey, continued the reconstruction. Later she was joined by Alan Walker, another of the three anatomists on the project, and together they built a respectably complete skull out of about 150 pieces of the pile that had been recovered. There was a great deal left over—raising a question as to whether all the pieces could have belonged to the same skull. The reconstruction confirmed the first predictions: undeniably 1470 was a large-brained hominid. But Alan Walker saw affinities with the gracile australopithecines that he found equally undeniable. Large brain, yes; *Homo*, no. As far as Walker was concerned, 1470 was a large-brained representative of the *Australopithecus* line.[15]

Richard Leakey did not agree, nor did Bernard Wood. They acknowledged the australopithecine attributes of the specimen. But 1470, Leakey told his *National Geographic* readers, represented the 'earliest suggestion of the genus *Homo*'.[16]

The meeting at which Richard showed the skull to his father was by way of a reunion that he would remember nostalgically. Relations between father and son had been strained for some time. 'He (Louis) was a sick old man at the end of his career,' Richard told a reporter,[17] 'and he found my successes very difficult. I was not old enough or mature enough to respond to that adequately.' By unspoken agreement, they had preferred not to meet. 1470 brought them together again and, indeed, showed that in science as in spirit there was never much separating them. Louis was tremendously excited by the skull. He believed it confirmed his views on the antiquity of true man, vindicated his Kanam find, and dismissed *Australopithecus* from the human line, once and for all.

If 1470 really was, as Richard claimed, about 2.6 million years old, then, together with the robust australopithecine found in 1969, it showed that at least two hominid lines had existed at East Turkana. Louis was certain there would be more. 1470 was one thing, he told Richard, the robust australopithecines were another, *Homo erectus* was yet something else and there would be others, he said, and you will find them.

But there were dissenters, notably Alan Walker, who could not accept 1470 as *Homo*. This difference of opinion raised two crucial questions. First: if both the large brain of *Homo* and demonstrable affinities with *Australopithecus* were both recognizable in a skull 2.6 million years old, did this not suggest that the two lineages were more closely linked than the Leakey theory of two distinct lines evolved from a very distant common ancestor allowed? There could have been only one line after all, along which *Australopithecus* evolved into *Homo* with 1470 representing an intermediate stage. Secondly, if *Homo* and *Australopithecus* were indeed two separate lineages, as Leakey claimed, and assuming human evolution was gradual and proceeded at a regular pace, then did not 1470's blend of *Homo* and *Australopithecus* features imply that the two genera had diverged from a common ancestor a relatively short time before, as believers in a more recent ancestry proclaimed?

1470 was an outstanding discovery, and there can be little doubt that in an earlier scientific era it would have been presented as the archetypal 'Missing Link' and not many would have disputed its credentials. By September 1973, however, when Richard Leakey called a meeting in Nairobi to discuss the formal scientific description of the fossil, he had already introduced 1470 to the world as the 'Oldest Man', bolstering his personal belief in our species' unique antiquity.

Foremost among those attending the Nairobi meeting were the three anato-mists: Bernard Wood, Alan Walker, and Michael Day. As the anatomist most closely involved with the reconstruction of the skull, Alan Walker had under-taken and already completed a detailed, technical description of the specimen when the meeting was convened. He opened the discussions with a proposal that the title and preamble of the published paper should mention the australopithe-cine affinities he saw in the skull. Although the others acknowledged that these existed (and each of the anatomists could have made a case for them), Leakey and Wood insisted that the large brain was pre-eminent. 1470 was *Homo*, they said. Day remained non-committal.

In the ensuing debate Walker detailed the australopithecine affinities[18] and insisted that they merited nomenclatural acknowledgement regardless of brain size. Furthermore, the skull had been distorted during fossilization, he said, and the configuration of the right side of the vault had been squashed into a deceptively *Homo*-like form. But for Leakey and Wood, brain size was all that counted. As the debate warmed to argument with no concession from either side, Walker resorted to persuasion of a more personal nature. If the published description of 1470 was to include *Homo* attribution, he said, then his name must be removed from the paper. This was no mean threat, given Walker's academic standing and contributions to the science, but it did not bring the capitulation he sought. Quite the contrary in fact, for the threat drew from across the table the injudicious remark that his withdrawal might be welcomed. At this Walker picked up the fossil and left the room.

After his departure, Richard Leakey decided to resolve the conflict in the follow-ing manner: if Walker stayed away, then 1470 would be attributed to *Homo* with-out qualification; if he returned, then Walker's views would be accommodated, to some degree, in the paper. Walker did return, and the paper was published with his name beneath the innocuous title: 'New Hominids from East Rudolf, Kenya'.[19] The preamble referred to the preliminary accounts in which Leakey, personally, had attributed the specimen to *Homo*, while making it clear that detailed comparative studies (which would determine what the skull should be called) were not yet com-plete. This aspect of the study was subsequently undertaken by Bernard Wood.[20]

FIGURE 14.3 The original 1470 skull surrounded by fragments left over from its recon-struction.

The worldwide adulation that greeted the 28-year-old Richard Leakey and his two-and-a-half-million-year-old 1470 was not entirely unanimous. Among scientists familiar with the work, there were serious doubts about the fossil's age. On the basis of palaeontological evidence in particular, Canadian geologist Basil Cooke suggested that 1470 was not as old as Leakey claimed; that it was probably only 1.8 million years old and therefore no more ancient than *Homo habilis* from Olduvai Gorge.[21] Cooke's suggestion was widely supported. By September 1973, when Richard Leakey convened the meeting at which the fossil's attribution was discussed, he was becoming aware that interpreting the significance of 1470 might depend more upon accurate determinations of its geological stratigraphical and geochronological status than upon its anatomical detail.

It is difficult to achieve 100 per cent accuracy when dating hominid fossil levels; mainly because the deposits in which they are found are, in geological terms, relatively young. They are therefore nearer the surface and much more likely to be contaminated with extraneous material of a quite different origin—and age.

The inherent problem of dating young deposits were further compounded at East Turkana by the manner in which the fossil beds had been formed, and reformed. The present Lake Turkana is only a few hundred thousand years old— the latest of several short-lived lakes which have formed in the basin over the past 3.5 million years. A large perennial river and its tributaries dominated the system for the greater part of that period. The inflow was primarily from the north, draining the southern Ethiopia highlands as the Omo river does today. At times the ancestral Omo flowed through the basin and east to the Indian Ocean (a connection which is confirmed by the presence of fossilized ocean fish remains, such as the teeth of stingrays, in the Turkana deposits). At other times its waters flowed down the length of the basin like tangled braids of hair, meandering through gallery forests and woodland; creating floodplains and ephemeral lakes.

The pattern of waterways was dictated by tectonic and volcanic activity associated with the formation of the Rift Valley, and the bends of the main river 'flip-flopped' back and forth across the floor of the basin as the underlying geological surface tilted, first one way and then another. This activity peaked around 1.7 million years ago; thereafter, lava, ash, and pumice accumulated along the eastern boundary of the basin, cutting off the ancestral Omo from its Indian Ocean outlet.

The sequence of deposition (the stratigraphy) in the Turkana basin was nowhere easy to determine, and relating the stratigraphy of one area to another was even more difficult. This meant that giving an accurate absolute date for the East Turkana fossils was fraught with problems: there is room for error at every turn. Especially in the case of the KBS tuff (KBS stands for Kay Behrensmeyer Site, the spot where the tools were found), a layer of solidified volcanic ash designated as a 'marker' in the stratigraphic determinations and a reference point against which many important fossils were dated, including 1470.

Fitch and Miller's tests on the first samples of the KBS tuff that Leakey sent to Cambridge actually gave an average age of 221 million years.[22] Such an age was impossible: clearly the sample must have been contaminated and Leakey was asked to send more samples. From these the scientists selected crystals that seemed fresher than others[23] and produced an age of 2.4 million years. Later they adjusted this to 2.6 million plus or minus 260,000 years.[24] But the work on the KBS tuff did not stop there. Fitch and Miller subsequently tested many more samples (including some they had collected themselves) and their results ranged from a minimum of 290,000 years to a maximum of 19.5 million years.

The geochronologists were not embarrassed by this apparent imprecision. They were perfecting a complicated technique and developing another that they hoped would give greater accuracy. They expected discrepancies and endeavoured to identify the cause; that is how experimental science proceeds. Palaeoanthropological science, on the other hand, is primarily an interpretative affair that depends upon expensive research; and in the 1970s 'Oldest Man' was an invaluable asset in the palaeoanthropologists' unending search for funds. So, when a fossil appeared to have achieved that status, the potassium/argon date upon which it was based tended to receive far greater emphasis than the experimental techniques justified.

The potassium–argon process undoubtedly is an important aid to the study of hominid fossils, but it is not a final arbiter. Its validity is very much contingent upon other factors—geology, stratigraphy, chemistry, for example. And furthermore, it is only one of several ways by which the antiquity of fossils can be assessed, and its concordance with other assessments is fundamental to the validity of any particular potassium–argon date. Where they conflict there is likely to be something wrong.

The KBS date seemed to conflict with certain palaeontological evidence, thereby casting doubt on 1470's 'Oldest Man' status. Naturally enough perhaps, the East Turkana research team was at first more concerned with defending the antiquity of the fossil than with objectively investigating the question of its age.

Palaeomagnetic investigations (relating the shifts of the earth's magnetic field as revealed by the magnetic properties of the rocks to a geochronological scale) were instigated to support the evidence for 1470's age, and the fossil thereby acquired an age of close to three million years.[25] But more objective observers were unconvinced. Opposition grew, especially among palaeontologists familiar with the faunal evidence of the region, and when Cooke presented his report on the fossil pigs of the Turkana Basin,[26] the counter-evidence became irresistible.

Cooke had studied the pig fossils from the Omo and East Turkana. The sites are only about 150 kilometres apart; the fossil fauna is generally similar, so it would be reasonable to expect that the sequence of fossils found in the beds at one site would be the same as the sequence found at the other. And indeed it was: Cooke was able to trace an identical line of evolutionary development in the pigs at both Omo and East Turkana. Now, according to the precepts of palaeontology, it should follow that identical ages could be attributed to the beds in which the identical fossils had been found. But when Cooke placed the evolving pig lineages side by side on the scale of their potassium–argon dating, he found that identical fossils seemed to differ substantially in age. For instance, the data on one of the pigs, *Mesochoerus*, suggested that the KBS tuff at East Turkana should be about the same age as the bed known as Member F at Omo, whereas the radiometric date said it was 600,000 years older. 'The discrepancy is considerable and cannot be ignored,' Cooke reported.[27]

The implications of the discrepancy were serious. If the KBS tuff was 600,000 years younger than had been deduced from the Fitch and Miller age determinations, then everything dated in relation to it was that much younger too. The tools, for instance, were no older than those found at Olduvai, and 1470 was no longer the Oldest Man but just a very well-preserved contemporary of *Homo habilis*.

Some responded to Cooke's findings with the suggestion that the Omo dating must be wrong. But this was hard to support, since the Omo sequence was particularly well defined. Furthermore, both the potassium–argon dates and the fossil fauna (including the pigs) agreed with the ages given for Olduvai Gorge, which were exemplary.

Leakey and his supporters soon realized that if their belief in the unique antiquity of 1470 and other finds associated with the KBS tuff was to stand, the incon-
venient evidence of the pigs had to be accommodated. Pig-proof helmets were an
early suggestion that raised a laugh. Some mirth also greeted the more seriously
intended suggestion that although the fossil pigs at first seemed 'an embarrass-
ing discrepancy between geophysics and palaeontology', they might turn out
to be 'an exciting glimpse of the existence of prehistoric mosaics of spatial and
ecological differentiation between the faunas of adjacent but environmentally
contrasting regions'.[28]

In plain language, this proposal suggested that perhaps the Omo and East
Turkana pigs had evolved quite independently and at different rates. Having
inherited the identical evolutionary impetus from their common ancestor, the
two populations were somehow completely isolated from one another at a crucial point and thereafter proceeded along their identical paths of evolutionary
development at quite different rates. Thus, the idea went, the East Turkana pigs
could have reached the *Mesochoerus* stage 600,000 years before their cousins
150 kilometres away at the Omo. This process would conveniently account for
the age difference between identical specimens, but the barrier that kept the pigs
apart for so long and evolving at such different rates was not so easy to envisage. The problem exercised the imaginations of several very earnest scientists.
Islands were proposed, both aquatic and ecological, which arose very suddenly
and trapped the East Turkana pigs in unique conditions that hastened their evolutionary development.

Though these attempts to explain the pigs' age discrepancy were not as frivolous as they may seem, Richard Leakey knew that something more substantial
was required. The 2.6-million-year date for the KBS tuff had meanwhile received
another blow from Garniss Curtis at the University of California, Berkeley, a
pioneer of the potassium–argon process whose tests on KBS samples confirmed
Cooke's assertions and questioned the findings of Fitch and Miller. Curtis dated
the KBS tuff at 1.8 million years.[29]

While noting that critics of the East Turkana research team's age estimates
were willing to believe a single report from Curtis before a whole series from
Fitch and Miller, and were prepared to accept the word of one geologist, Basil
Cooke, before that of an entire multi-disciplinary research team, Richard Leakey
countered the attacks with another, grander study of the fossil pigs. He hoped

the results would prove Cooke wrong, and the study was instigated with that objective in mind, but even if it dismissed the 2.6-million-year estimate for the KBS tuff, he preferred to be proved wrong by his own efforts rather than by someone else's.[30]

The new study was undertaken by palaeontologist John Harris and physical anthropologist Tim White, and amounted to a complete review of all the fossil pigs from fifty African sites south of the Sahara.[31] They reduced the number of genera from twenty-three to seven and the number of species from seventy-seven to sixteen. They recognized the evolutionary trends shown especially well in some species, and confirmed the value of these fossils in correlating geological sequences.

Then they applied their findings to the evidence of the Omo, East Turkana, and Olduvai. The results confirmed all Cooke's conclusions. The fossil pigs showed that the age assigned to the KBS tuff was 600,000 years older than the palaeontological evidence indicated. Discussing the implications of their findings on the study of fossil hominids, Harris and White concluded that the pigs showed that 1470 was 'essentially' the same age as *Homo habilis* at Olduvai.

In the light of still more age determinations from a number of laboratories using a variety of methods, Richard Leakey conceded that earlier pronouncements on the age of 1470 (and the other fossils dated by the KBS tuff) were wrong. He accepted 1.8 million years as the age of the tuff itself, and something between 1.8 and 2 million years as the age of 1470, which had been found below it. But if the earlier estimates were wrong, what caused the error? Richard Leakey blamed the dating procedures employed by Fitch and Miller;[32] Fitch, on the other hand, wondered if the material his team had dated was actually representative of the KBS tuff. Repeated tests on the samples confirmed the older dates, he said, suggesting that they might have been collected from a tuff thought to be part of the KBS, but actually part of an older level.[33] Leakey and his team denied this, arguing that the KBS tuff was unmistakable.

The KBS tuff-dating controversy showed that modern palaeoanthropologists are no less likely to cling to erroneous data that supported their preconceptions than were earlier investigators (like Dubois before him, Leakey dismissed objective assessment in favour of the notions he wanted to believe) but more significantly, perhaps, it showed that dating discrepancies are as likely to reflect errors of geology as of geochronology, and underlined the observation that accurate geological and stratigraphic determinations are crucial to the interpretation of fossil evidence. This work has since been completed at Lake Turkana. A series of reports on the geology, stratigraphy, and chronology of the Turkana basin have correlated the sequence and age of the deposits at Koobi Fora, the Omo, and West Turkana,[34] and the KBS tuff has been firmly dated at 1.88 plus or minus 0.02 million years.[35]

1470 brought Richard Leakey popular acclaim, epitomized by an appearance on the cover of *Time* magazine (in a photograph which showed him crouched beside an African who was discreetly naked but for a rubber mask intended to resemble the physiognomy of *Homo habilis*); then, from 'organizing genius of modern palaeoanthropology' he moved on to become an influential figure in Kenyan politics and the country's international relations (especially in respect of environmental issues and wildlife conservation) while his wife Meave (born 1942), and daughter Louise (born 1972), carried on the Leakey family business of finding fossils in the Turkana basin—with considerable success.

A decade or so later, Richard Leakey became involved once again, as prime mover and Chair of the Turkana Basin Institute (TBI), created under the aegis of Stony Brook, the State University of New York. This new initiative would run a 'new and exciting research program' in the Omo-Turkana basin, its prospectus promised. Drawing on research which during the previous forty years had led to international recognition of the basin's contributions to the story of human evolution, the TBI research programme would extend back in time from modern humans via the first pastoralists and pottery makers to our earliest ancestors— and beyond: 'to the origin of the apes and monkeys, including the earliest known apes, and, even to a time unknown elsewhere in Africa, when dinosaurs domi- nated the fauna', 95 to 165 million years ago.

Significantly, the initiative vowed to correct a major deficiency for which palaeoanthropologists had been repeatedly criticized. Hitherto, research in the Turkana Basin had been conducted predominantly by scientists from European and American institutions, who had access to substantial funding. There were no Africa-based research programmes for Africans keen to engage with the subject—no money, nor much in the way of institutional facilities from which research could be conducted. The TBI planned to give indigenous Africans the opportunity to be key members and leaders of its research efforts. Through pri- vate funding they would be able to develop a career in the science, based in their home continent, but with strong links to academic institutions in the rest of the world. Furthermore, local communities were promised financial and material benefits too, with the creation of permanent research stations offering employment opportunities as well as improved local infrastructure. It was hoped this would also enhance appreciation of the heritage and bring a fuller understanding of how important their local research was viewed internationally.

The fulfilment of these ambitions would not be cheap, or rapidly achieved. Four million dollars was budgeted for the capital projects and associated expenses of Phase I. The academic programmes and extension costs of Phases II and III would amount to 5 million dollars each, and an endowment of 30 million dollars was needed to provide a minimum of 1.5 million dollars for annual operation and research funding. Phase I was on track for completion during 2008, and the TBI was scheduled to be a fully-functioning entity by the end of 2015. Finally, palaeoanthropology in Africa would have the services and long-term commitment its potential deserves.

1470's reign as the Oldest Man was brief, but even if the age of 2.6 million years had not been disproved, the throne would soon have been taken by another claimant. In 1974 hominid fossils dating back to three million years ago were discovered by a joint American and French expedition working in the bleak Afar depression of central Ethiopia. The finds were announced at a press conference as 'an unparalleled breakthrough in the search for the origins of man's evolution…extending our knowledge of the genus *Homo* by nearly 1.5 million years'. The publicity and controversy these discoveries provoked will be covered in the next chapter; here they introduce the fact that an even earlier hominid fossil had been lying, virtually forgotten, in the Kenya National Museum vault since 1967.

The fossil in question was just a scrap of lower jaw with the first molar in place and the roots of four other teeth preserved, but it had come from a site at Lothagam, near the south-west shore of Lake Turkana, which radiometric dating had shown to be between 5 and 5.5 million years.[36] To be fair, the specimen was too fragmentary for anyone to say more than that it probably should be attributed to *Australopithecus*, and that affinity was only confirmed when the 1974 Afar discoveries became available for comparison: the Lothagam specimen was very similar. Subsequent re-analysis of the data corroborated this attribution and in 1992 advanced its age to 5.6 million years,[37] which at the time of discovery would have made it the Oldest Man by a considerable margin. Meanwhile, though, the title had passed to a not dissimilar piece of lower jaw found in 1984 at Tabarin in the Tugen Hills region of the northern Kenya Rift Valley, west of Lake Baringo.[38]

The Tugen Hills are a product of the tectonic uplift and fracture which created the Great Rift Valley. They extend about 100 kilometres north–south along the Rift west of Lake Baringo and expose some 3,000 m of rocks in their fault scarps and eastern foothills. Many of these exposures contain fossils, and range in age, without much significant interruption, from over 16 million years ago to the present—a time period which not only covered the entire story of human evolution, but also was otherwise unrepresented in the African fossil record. This potential did not go unnoticed as interest in human evolution was aroused by the Olduvai discoveries.

The Hills were among several regions explored in the 1960s. Richard Leakey himself excavated a complete fossil elephant from a 3.5-million-year-old Tugen Hills site in 1967 (his first independent excavation), and described an entirely new monkey from a nearby site in 1969 (his first scientific paper).[39] But that was the year the 'organizing genius of palaeoanthropology' transferred his energies and enthusiasm to East Turkana. Work in the Tugen Hills languished until the 1980s, when it was revived in the form of the Baringo Palaeontological Research Project, sponsored successively by the top two American ivy league universities: Harvard and Yale.[40]

The Project's work has been impressive, presenting a longer, more complete and more continuous record of the interactions between climate, environment, flora, and fauna than is known from anywhere else. The depth and time-span of the Ngorora Formation, for example, documents the transition from the archaic African fauna to one which more closely resembles the modern population. The archaic species dominating the lower levels are replaced in the higher levels by modern kinds of elephant, antelope, hippopotamus, pigs, and carnivores. Immigrants from Eurasia arrive. The earliest ancestral horses known in sub-Saharan Africa occur in Ngorora sediments dating from 10 million years ago—identical to specimens from deposits of a similar age in Eurasia.

The transformation of Africa's animal population from ancient to modern, as recorded in the Tugen Hills, began around 11 million years ago and was complete by 4 million years ago. Fossils that contributed directly to the pool of knowledge on human evolution during that critical period have been disproportionately few, distinguished principally by the Tabarin mandible found in 1984[41] (dated at 4.4 million years[42] in 2002) and an assortment of thirteen fossils, said to have belonged to at least five individuals, which a French-sponsored expedition recovered in 2001 from 6-million-year-old sediments at four different localities in the Lukeino Formation.[43]

The Tabarin mandible received its share of Oldest Man publicity, though no special claims were made for its status. Indeed, the conclusion that ends the formal description of the fossil is an example of commendable moderation, noting only that the specimen is very similar to some australopithecine species, is not similar to any other species yet known, but 'shows no characters of sufficient difference to justify erecting a new taxon to accommodate it'.[44] The 6-million-year-old Lukeino specimens were rather more extravagantly introduced.

The fossils, comprising the upper portions of two left thigh bones, two pieces of upper arm, two jaw fragments, a fingerbone and five isolated teeth, were found in 2000 and thus earned the title Millennium Man. The media typically claimed that he was a 'staggering' 6 million years old, 'about twice the age of what was once considered to be the oldest of our ape-like ancestors…'. Those now outdated creatures had been 'Great Aunts' on an evolutionary dead-end that led to extinction, readers were told, while Millennium Man was our 'great, great, great, grandfather', a discovery that 'would rewrite the story of human evolution'.[45]

The Millennium Man story is a prime example of the media's tendency to exaggerate and get things wrong, but the conclusions of the people who found the fossils are more to the point here. The leaders of the team, palaeontologist Brigitte Senut and geologist Martin Pickford, decided that their fossils were so unlike anything then known that not just a new species, but a new genus must be constructed to contain them. They called it *Orrorin tugenensis*. 'Orrorin' means 'original man' in the Tugen language, but also acknowledges the French contribution to the discovery, since the first two syllables are pronounced as in the French 'aurore', meaning dawn or daybreak.

The creation of a new genus was primarily based on the specimen's teeth, Senut and Pickford explained, which were smaller, less elongated, and had thicker enamel than all other genera—plus a distinctive groove on the upper canine. Their claims for its evolutionary status were based on secondary features: the skeletal remains. The thighbones were 'more human-like than those of the australopithecines or African apes…*Orrorin tugenensis* was already adapted to habitual or perhaps even obligate bipedalism when on the ground,' they said, 'but was also a good climber'.[46]

These claims made rather more of the Lukeino fossils than seemed to be warranted. *Nature* noted that 'these are exciting times in the study of human origins', the excitement stemming not so much from the fossils, as from the controversy that flared up over the circumstances of their discovery. Doubts were raised concerning the validity of the permissions under which the expedition had been working. Yale University's research group had been working at the Tugen Hills sites nearly every year since 1985, under a permit issued by the Office of the President. It was inconceivable that another team could have been granted permission without reference to the Yale group; at the very least, such uncoordinated excavations could prejudice their work. The French group had not advised Yale of their intentions because they had the permission of a local government body, Pickford insisted, claiming that no further authorization was required.

Even so, after a press conference in Nairobi called to announce the discovery of Millennium Man, Pickford was arrested on charges of collecting without a research permit. He spent five days in a Kenyan jail, but was released when the charges against him were declared *nolle prosequi* by Kenya's attorney-general.[47] He threatened to sue the parties responsible for his arrest and incarceration, citing Richard Leakey and his family's domination of palaeoanthropological research in Kenya. Writing in support of Pickford's claim, the Director of the Community Museums of Kenya, Eustace Gitonga, observed: 'No longer is palaeontology in Kenya the monopoly of a single family or institution. Kenyans have recuperated their heritage...'.

As *Nature* observed in a news feature entitled 'The battle of Tugen Hills', the controversy provided a glimpse of the bitter rivalries that can flare up between researchers, and showed how these rivalries can become intertwined with the politics of host countries. Inevitably, it drew attention to the 'unseemly side of palaeoanthropological research', the journal remarked.[48]

On more seemly aspects of the affair, commentators questioned whether the *Orrorin* fossils could really be the remains of 'Our newest oldest ancestor?' pointing out that while the specimen's age was not in doubt, its contribution to the story of human evolution was far from clear. There were alternative versions of its status that were equally defensible, they remarked, including suggestions that *Orrorin* is not a hominid at all, but more likely to represent the apes. With so much uncertainty, it was probably best to avoid constructing evolutionary trees and naming ancestors on the basis of teeth and anatomy, they cautioned.[49]

Indeed, but caution was not much in evidence the following year, 2002, when yet another unexpected fossil burst on the scene. New fossil, new genus, new species, new Oldest Man: *Sahelanthropus tchadensis*, claimed to be between 6 and 7 million years old. The response was all too predictable. The discovery featured on the cover of *Nature* and in newspapers and periodicals around the world. 'Fossil find of the century', the headlines proclaimed; 'the scientific equivalent of a small nuclear bomb', one leading academic told journalists; 'probably the most important discovery in the search for human origins in living memory', said a science editor; 'a new window on palaeoanthropology' claimed another authority.

The leading author of the *Nature* paper, and leader of the joint French–Chad expeditions which had discovered the fossil was Michel Brunet, a professor of palaeontology at the University of Poitiers.[50] Brunet was born in 1940, just a few months before German forces took Paris. His parents lived in Versailles, near Paris, but the young Brunet spent much of his first eight years living with his maternal grandmother in a small village forty kilometres south of Poitiers, and 350 kilometres from Paris. He has fond memories of those years in the country, where he was spared the disruptions of the occupation and post-war hardships of life in the capital. There is probably as much romance as reality in his description of himself as a shepherd boy observing the behaviour of domestic animals and sleeping under a blanket, looking at the stars, but early immersion in what the French refer to as *la France profonde* was doubtless a formative experience—unsullied by the strictures of the classroom.[51]

Formal education began for Brunet when he returned to live with his parents in Versailles at the age of 8. Despite the late start, his interests and aptitude ultimately earned him a Ph.D. in palaeontology from the University of Paris, having been inspired along the way, he says, by a talk Louis Leakey gave at the Muséum national d'Histoire naturelle in Paris in 1963, when he introduced the new species, *Homo habilis*.

By the age of 36, as a professor of palaeontology at the University of Poitiers, living comfortably with wife and children in the countryside near by, studying the fossil evidence of early mammalian migrations through Europe, Michel Brunet was settled for life. Except that he was restless, and keen to pursue the interest in human origins that Louis Leakey had awakened. He wanted to find the earliest hominid, the Oldest Man, he has said.

At the time, Richard Leakey and Don Johanson, then also in their thirties, were making headlines around the world with their discoveries—they were oldest hominids yet known, but still dating back to only two or three million years ago. The earliest frontier then being explored was the 8- to 9-million-year-old deposits of the Siwalik Hills in Pakistan, where a team led by David Pilbeam from Harvard had recently found more remains of *Ramapithecus*, a species first described in 1934 which many believed was the earliest known candidate for human ancestry. With a colleague from the National Centre of Scientific Research (CNRS), Brunet went looking for extinct apes in similarly ancient deposits across the border from the Siwaliks, in Afghanistan. To no avail. They found many mammals in the three annual expeditions they undertook before it became too dangerous to work in Afghanistan, including rodents and a monkey, but no apes.

Brunet then turned his attention to Iraq, but by 1980 working there had become impossible too. He joined Pilbeam's Siwalik expeditions for a couple of seasons, but that quest also came to an end when new and more complete fossils convinced Pilbeam that *Ramapithecus* was not a hominid after all, but more likely to have been an ancestor of the orang-utan.

Meanwhile, Pilbeam had been making plans to look for chimpanzee fossils in Cameroon, West Africa, and invited Brunet to join him.

The first expedition went out in 1984. They found sites of the right age, but hardly any fossil bones. In the course of nine expeditions up to 1993, the team found fossilized leaves, insects, and just one fossil mammal bone. As colleagues had warned, the deposits were too acidic for fossil bones to be preserved. The most notable discovery was a dinosaur footprint.

Pilbeam dropped out, but Brunet focused his efforts on a region he had been keen to explore while working in Cameroon: Chad—in particular, the Djurab Desert which, millions of years ago, had been the shoreline of the much larger Mega-Lake Chad. The potential of the region as a source of fossils had already been established. Indeed, Brunet's older colleague and mentor, Yves Coppens, had been there on seven expeditions in the 1960s. Thousands of fossils were found before civil war brought operations to an end in 1967, including numerous extinct mammals and a single, sand-polished hominid cranium (which Coppens described as *Tchadanthropus uxoris*—'my wife's Chad man' because, actually, it was his wife, Françoise, who had found it).

As the security situation improved in the early 1990s, Brunet received an invitation to lecture in N'Djamena, the capital of Chad, from Alain Beauvilain, a geographer posted to Chad as part of the French government's contribution to building the research infrastructure of the nation. Beauvilain was director of Chad's newly created National Centre for the Promotion of Research and, as such, authorized to invite and encourage foreign researchers to work in Chad. Brunet needed no further encouragement. Beauvilain undertook to obtain the necessary permits and handle the logistics of an expedition to the Djurab Desert. Brunet had only to secure the funding.

In January 1994, Brunet and Beauvilain set off in a convoy of four vehicles, accompanied by a small crew of scientists and a guide. They surveyed a region to the east of where *Tchadanthropus uxoris* had been found, decades earlier, and mapped eleven sites with animal fossils up to four million years old. They were in the field again the following year. On the morning of January 23 an expedition driver, Mamelbaye Tomalta, called Brunet to look at a jaw he had found. As he brushed away the sand, Brunet knew he was looking at the teeth and jaw fragment of an ancestor who had died on the shore of the ancient Lake Chad, more than three million years before.

Brunet had not handled an original hominid fossil before, only the casts of other discoveries. It was a life-transforming moment, he has said; a dream fulfilled, at last, after nineteen years of searching. He wished that a collaborator, Abel Brillanceau, who had died of drug-resistant malaria on a Cameroon expedition six years before, could have been there to share the experience. In memoriam, he dubbed the specimen Abel.

In November 1995 Abel was described in *Nature* as an australopithecine with affinities to specimens that Johanson had described from Ethiopia, *Australopithecus afarensis* (see Chapter 15). Later, in May 1996, he named it *Australopithecus bahrelghazali*, describing it as a western cousin of the famous Lucy.

Until then, most authorities had agreed that the Rift Valley probably had been the cradle of humanity—simply on the basis of the numerous hominid fossils which had been found there. And now a single small specimen, a fragment of jawbone, was enough to upset that cosy consensus. Abel had been found 2,500 kilometres to the west of the Rift Valley. 'We're not saying we know where the cradle of humanity is,' Brunet told scientists at a press conference in May 1996, 'but the cradle is much larger than we thought.'

While Abel widened the boundaries of palaeoanthropological perception, and enhanced the status of his discoverer, for Brunet himself the greater significance of the fossil was that it brought easier access to the funds that were needed for further investigations in Chad. Abel might have been the most westerly hominid, but he was not the oldest. Even Lucy was older, let alone the Lothagam, Tabarin, and Orrorin specimens. But Brunet had seen enough of the Mega-Lake Chad sediments to convince him that older hominids could be found there too. Where there are sediments containing mammals that were more than six million years old, there was no scientific reason why hominids should not be there too, he said. It was just a matter of finding them, and now he had the resources to mobilize the French–Chad Palaeoanthropological Mission (MPFT) he had formed in alliance with the University of N'Djamena and the National Centre for the Promotion of Research (the CNAR, of which Alain Beauvilain was director), for a sustained programme of exploration. But the logistics were daunting. 'The desert is a wonderful place that can turn very quickly to hell,' Brunet told a reporter.

Pallets of bottled water and every item of equipment and provisions had to be trucked in. The sun was unrelenting, there was no shade, except under canvas or beside a vehicle, but the wind was the worst of it—often whipping up so much sand that the team had to wear ski-masks as they trudged across the ancient lake-bed, looking for fossils. Violent sandstorms sometimes kept them trapped for days in their tents, which had to be dug out when the wind abated—as if out of a snowdrift.

But the wind was also their ally, driving sand dunes across the desert like ocean waves, eroding several centimetres each year from the sedimentary sandstones beneath and thus exposing the fossilized remains of animals that had lived and died in and around the lake millions of years before. In the first six years of intensified operation, the MPFT found more than 300 sites and collected more than 8,000 fossils. Among them they identified forty-two speces of fish, reptiles, and primitive mammals, including carnivores, elephants, three-toed horses, giraffes, antelopes, hippopotamuses, wild boars, rodents, and monkeys.

Combined with the geological surveys which the MPFT had undertaken, the number and diversity of animal fossils was more than enough to sustain Brunet's conviction that the team would eventually add a hominid to the collection. Clearly, what was now bleached desert was once a green and watered land—probably akin to the Okavango Delta in Botswana today: a floodplain dotted with islands, bounded by woodland and forest, teeming with animal life; the perfect habitat for the emergent human ancestor—more than six million years ago.

Brunet had a good feeling about these older sites, he has said, but as the MPFT was gearing up to explore them more fully, he had a heart attack. In Poitiers, fortunately, not while out in the Djurab Desert, but doubtless due in no small part to the efforts he had expended on the expeditions (a lifetime of smoking was another contributory factor). Emergency bypass surgery saved his life; stents would keep his coronary arteries open; convalescence obliged him to stay away from Chad and the expeditions for nearly two years.

By now, though, the MPFT had a momentum of its own, under the direction of Alain Beauvilain. Brunet's absence probably accelerated developments he should applaud, namely that the exploration and investigations became a primarily Chadian affair—inspired by Brunet's dream and sustained by his fund-raising capacities, but no longer his personal fiefdom. Brunet was in his sixties now, had had a brush with mortality, and returned to the field knowing that his time was limited. Twenty-five years had already passed since he first went looking for the oldest man; nine of them had been spent scouring the desert sands of Chad with the MPFT. After so much effort it was an unkind turn of fate that led an undergraduate, Ahounta Djimdoumalbaye, to find the ultimate prize—a 6- to 7-million-year-old skull with hominid affinities—on the morning of 19 July 2001, a few days after Michel Brunet had left for France.

Brunet did not even hear of the discovery until five days later, when he was back in his office at the University of Poitiers and received a call from the CNAR offices in N'Djamena. He was not able to fly out and see the specimen until almost a month later, by which time numerous dignitaries had viewed the skull, the French press had suggested the discovery could represent a new ancestor of man, and the world's media were pestering Brunet for comment. He was outraged by the publicity the discovery received before he had seen it, not least because such premature viewings and comment could prejudice his options for the publication of a formal description. He blamed Beauvilain for this lapse of scientific etiquette. Beauvilain protested that he was answerable to the Chadian authorities as much as to Brunet. Relations between the two men had been fractious for some time; now they were broken irrevocably.

Before he carried the skull back to France for study, Brunet (accompanied by Beauvilain) had an audience with the Chadian President, Idriss Déby, at the conclusion of which he asked the President to give the specimen a name. The President reflected, then proposed Toumaï, a name which the Goran people of Chad give to children born in the dry season, when survival is uncertain. Toumaï means 'hope of life', he explained, and thus was appropriate for an ancestor of humanity—the Oldest Man.

After Brunet had taken Toumaï on a tour of intensive consultations with palaeoanthropologists in Europe, the United States, and Africa, he and his colleagues
concluded that only a new taxon could accommodate the distinctive features of
their discovery: *Sahelanthropus tchadensis*. Accordingly, Toumaï graced the cover
of *Nature* on 11 July 2002[52] under the headline 'The earliest known hominid', with
Toumaï floating as though in space against an aerial photograph of the Djurab
Desert, with the expedition's camp and vehicles immediately below. The coating
of a blue/black manganese material which had partially covered the skull at the
time of discovery had been removed; its crushed and flattening appearance had
been corrected by the angle from which the photograph had been taken—the
skull looked remarkably complete, remarkably hominid-like, with a long flat-
tened face and prominent eyebrow ridges.

In the preamble to the first of their two papers announcing the discovery in
Nature, Brunet and his co-authors (thirty-seven in number, Alain Beauvilain
among them) pointed out that the great antiquity of the fossil confirmed that
the earliest hominids were far more widely distributed than had been thought (as
the discovery of Abel had indicated in 1995), and that the divergence between the
human and chimpanzee lineages was earlier than otherwise indicated. But was
it possible to say, with any certainty, that *Sahelanthropus* represented the human
line that came after the divergence, and not the ape? After all, the closer evidence
comes to the point at which the human and ape lines diverged, the more difficult
it will be to distinguish between the ape and human descendants, simply because
they are all likely to resemble their common ancestor.

Certainly, Toumaï presented a puzzling mix of features. From behind, the skull
looked like that of a chimpanzee (and had a brain capacity to match); from the front,
however, it could pass for a 1.75-million-year-old advanced australopithecine, with its
brow ridges, flat face, and small canine teeth. As so many times before in the history
of palaeoanthropology, a major new discovery provoked controversy. While Brunet
brandished the issue of *Nature* with Toumaï on the cover as the 'baptismal certificate'
of his oldest man,[53] others were more circumspect. In *Nature*'s introductory review
of the discovery Bernard Wood concluded: '*S. tchadensis* is a candidate for the stem
hominid, but in my view it will be impossible to prove it.'[54] Carol Ward, a palaeoanthropologist at the University of Missouri summed up the issue: 'If you define
hominids by a reduction in the canines and premolars, then it's a hominid. But if a
hominid is going to be defined by walking upright on two feet, you can't tell.'[55]

While Brunet and his team were generally given the benefit of the doubt, pending further work, and the discovery applauded, their claims were attacked head-on by Milford Wolpoff of the University of Michigan and three co-authors: Brigitte Senut, Martin Pickford, and John Hawks. 'This is the skull of a female gorilla', Senut told the press, while Pickford described the creature's canines as being typical 'of a large female monkey'. The title of their comment published in *Nature* somewhat flippantly implied that the specimen should have been named *Sahelpithecus* (ape of the Sahel), not *Sahelanthropus*.[56] It 'was an ape living in an environment that was later inhabited by australopithecines', they declared. 'A penecontemporary primate with a perfect and well-developed post-cranial adaptation to obligate bipedalism is more likely to have been an early hominid', they said. And who did they suggest that might have been? No surprise here: their very own *Orrorin tugenensis*, who had lived in the Tugen Hills 6 million years ago. In his reply, Brunet accused the authors of not only misrepresenting the specimen's morphology, but also failing to identify a single character in support of their suggestion that Toumaï was a gorilla rather than a hominid ancestor. They were guilty of ignoring the evidence of Toumaï's hominid affinities, he implied, in favour of their own belief in the ancestral status of *Orrorin tugenensis*, their Oldest Man.

The age of Brunet's oldest man, 6 to 7 million years, had been established by the company he kept. Absolute dating methods, such as had been used to determine the age of deposits at East African sites, could not be applied to the fossil beds in Chad because there was no volcanic ash layer to provide the necessary argon and potassium. Nor were the sediments suitable for magnetism-based dating methods. Instead, Brunet's team compared the mix of extinct species at the site with the equivalent record from sites in East Africa for which there were absolute dates. The best matches produced the estimate of about 6 to 7 million years for the Chad fossils.

In search of greater precision, Brunet and his team called upon a complex procedure that could determine the absolute age of the Toumaï sediments by analysing the relative quantities of two beryllium isotopes that were present in samples from the site. The results, published in the prestigous *Proceedings of the National Academy of Sciences*, gave an age of between 6.8 and 7.2 million years,[57] neatly bracketing the upper end of the comparative faunal estimate, and putting

---

FIGURE 14.4 Chad excavation scene; Michel Brunet at work; and *Sahelanthropus tchadensis* superimposed above an aerial view of the team's base camp in the Djurab Desert.

Toumaï comfortably ahead of all other candidates for Oldest Man status—not least Pickford and Senut's *Orrorin tugenensis*.

The accuracy of the beryllium dating has been questioned in some quarters, but this was not the worst criticism that Brunet's latest claims for *Sahelanthropus* provoked. Alain Beauvilain now broke ranks.

In the interests of scientific accuracy he was now compelled to state formally that the Abel and Toumaï specimens were not found in situ, he wrote in the *South African Journal of Science*. They were not found embedded in sediment with precise stratigraphic positions from which they were unearthed, as the original *Nature* and subsequent *PNAS* papers had claimed (both in the text and in stratigraphic diagrams). The best that could be said was that they were 'collected' from their respective localities.

In particular, Toumaï was picked up from a surface comprised of loose sand, wrote Beauvilain. It was clear, he said, that the sand around the fossil, and possibly the fossil itself, had been shifted by wind or erosion, a phenomenon that can happen swiftly and frequently in the desert. How many times was Toumaï exposed and reburied by shifting sands before being picked up? he asked. The implications were serious. If Toumaï had not come from the sediments selected for dating it could have come from anywhere, and may not even have been directly associated with the accompanying fauna (and the age thereof). More palaeontological work, including a systematic comparison with other sites in the vicinity, would be required to clarify this point.

Beauvilain's paper was illustrated with a photograph of the *Sahelanthropus* cranium that he claimed to have taken at the time of discovery. Unequivocally, the photograph showed the cranium lying on loose desert sand. 'By a curious choice', Beauvilain remarked, this photograph was not used by the MPFT to illustrate the field context of the discovery. Instead, they published a photograph of a resin cast, posed on a ridge of sand, that was taken in February 2004, eighteen months after the discovery.

No formal reply was forthcoming. Informally, Brunet is said to have 'gone ballistic' whenever he was asked about the *SAJS* paper and Beauvilain's photographs, though he offered no data or explanation—probably because he was not there to witness the discovery himself.

Meanwhile, Toumaï had adorned the cover of *Nature* once again, this time as a reconstructed head suspended above an aerial photograph of the waterways and islands of the Okavango Delta (now established as a valid analogue for the environment Toumaï had inhabited). With the use of high-resolution computed tomography, a three-dimensional virtual representation of the cranium had been created, and its distortions corrected according to anatomical principles. The result was a 'robust estimate' of the skull's original form, the *Nature* paper claimed which, since it did not match the form of the gorilla or the chimpanzee, must be hominid. Unequivocal evidence of bipedalism was difficult to obtain, the authors confessed. Several lines of evidence suggested that Toumaï 'might have been bipedal', but 'postcranial evidence will be necessary to test more rigorously the hypothesis that *S. tchadensis*—the earliest known hominid, found 2,600 km west of the East Africa rift valley—was a biped',[58] they noted in conclusion.

Brunet's opponents responded at length, reinforcing the views they had previously expressed with detailed analysis contradicting each point the *Nature* paper had made in favour of Toumaï's status as a bipedal hominid. Toumaï 'was an ape', they claimed again. Furthermore, various cranial details revealed in the reconstruction actually argued against an upright stance and bipedal locomotion, they said, and only a pelvis or a femur could provide compelling evidence for it.[59]

Though the arguments put forward by each group must have been robust enough to convince the editors of reputable journals of their validity, on an objective level they demonstrated that neither party had sufficient evidence to disprove the claims of the other. The pattern was familiar: the evidence was inconclusive and as the argument intensified, judging its merits became more a matter of personalities than science. Not just a question of whether *Sahelanthropus* was a hominid, or if *Orrorin* was bipedal, but a question of who most deserved to be right—Brunet and his team or Pickford and Senut. Or, more bluntly, which of them should have the prize they both claimed, the Oldest Man.

In a science not noted for its generosity of spirit, the warmth of feeling that Brunet attracted was enough to restore a sceptical observer's faith in human nature. While respect for Pickford and Senut was often grudging at best and sometimes vehemently withheld, everyone had a good word for Brunet. Much, of course, was inspired by sympathy for his personal history and bad luck—his age, his heart attack, the twenty-five years of searching, and the cruel irony of missing the discovery he had sought so avidly—but there was always deep respect for the man and his science too. He deserved the prize, they would say, even though his evidence was not complete enough to claim it.

But respect and sympathy were not universal. One man stood aside and made no secret of his criticism of Brunet and the Toumaï discovery: Alain Beauvilain. He had some reason to feel misused. While Brunet had been fêted throughout France and made a knight of the French Legion of Honour (the nation's highest award), Beauvilain had been recalled from his appointment in Chad, unwillingly obliged to move with his wife and children back to France after fourteen years in Africa.

Nine months after *Sahelanthropus tchadensis* was described in *Nature*, Beauvilain published a book giving his account of events. He complained that Brunet had not given him and his Chadian colleagues proper credit for their role in the discovery of the specimen. He was interviewed at length by the press, which revelled in what they described as a 'paternity battle' over Toumaï.

Beauvilain's hurt and resentment ran deep, bursting to the surface again when the Brunet team published their refined dating of the Toumaï sediments in 2008. As we have seen, Beauvilain responded with a paper alleging serious errors concerning the provenance of the fossil. A few months later he was in print again. With co-author Jean-Pierre Watté, an archaeologist, Beauvilain published a paper in the *Bulletin de la Société Géologique de Normandie et des Amis du Muséum du Havre* suggesting that far from being *in situ*, the skull had been put where it was found not more than a few hundred years before. 'Was Toumaï (*Sahelanthropus tchadensis*) buried?',[60] the title of their paper asked. In translation the abstract reads:[61]

> Photographs taken when the skull of Toumaï was discovered establish that the holotype of one of the earliest known hominid species was probably reburied in the recent past. Taphonomic analysis reveals the likelihood of one, perhaps two, burial(s) which seemingly occurred after the introduction of Islam in the region…

The photographs in question, published in the Bulletin, showed the skull lying alongside an assortment of about fifty other fossil bones which formed two rows running diagonally across the photograph from top left to bottom right. Beauvilain and Watté argued that this arrangement could not have been the result of natural processes. The location of the skull in relation to the two rows of long bones evoked the disposal of a body reduced to the status of a skeleton, they wrote, suggesting that someone had found the remains and given them 'the honour of a burial'.

FIGURE 14.5 Top: Alain Beauvilain's with co-workers and the *Sahelanthropus* fossils minutes after their dicovery. Below: Beauvilain's annotated photograph, for which the skull was repositioned (green arrow), displacing a fossil fragment (green). Fossils tinted yellow were found elsewere.

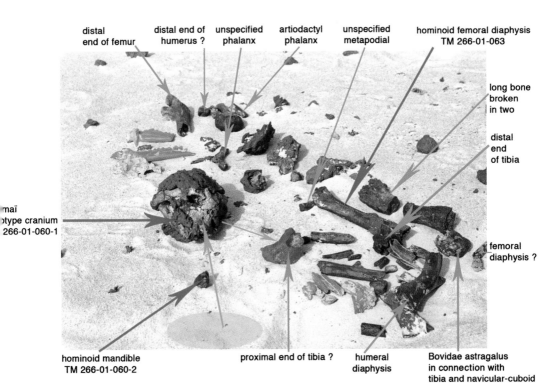

distal end of femur   distal end of humerus ?   unspecified phalanx   artiodactyl phalanx   unspecified metapodial   hominoid femoral diaphysis TM 266-01-063

long bone broken in two

distal end of tibia

...maï ...type cranium ...266-01-060-1

femoral diaphysis ?

hominoid mandible TM 266-01-060-2   proximal end of tibia ?   humeral diaphysis   Bovidae astragalus in connection with tibia and navicular-cuboid

Who could have been the authors of this burial?, Beauvilain and Watté asked. The orientation given to the 'body' was in line with the direction to Mecca, they pointed out, so it could have been buried by nomads crossing the region, who had been Muslim since the eleventh century. Their faith obliged them to bury the dead—facing Mecca.

Whether or not Beauvilain and Watté have made a valid case for Toumaï's recent burial the photographs were provocative—not least because among the bones they identified and labelled were several that could have belonged to Toumaï himself, including a femur.

This revelation came as a surprise to most of those following the saga of *Sahelanthropus*. Why hadn't the photograph been published earlier? If post-cranial remains had been found close to the skull, possibly belonging to it, wouldn't they be an important test of the specimen's hominid status? And a femur—wasn't that precisely what had been called for to settle the question of whether or not Toumaï was bipedal and therefore the earliest known hominid—oldest man?

These were questions that the French science magazine, *La Recherche* asked in its report on the Beauvilain and Watté paper. In some respects there was no mystery. Scientists were entitled to take as long as necessary to study material before publishing a description; and many had been castigated for rushing into print. On the other hand, it did seem that the evidence had been overlooked. According to *La Recherche*, the femur was still lying unidentified among sundry faunal remains in early 2004, almost three years after the discovery, when a palaeontological student brought it to the attention of her professor. 'He saw that the bone, the species of which had not yet been determined, was not the femur of an ordinary animal, but that of a hominid', *La Recherche* reported.[62] And this potentially critical piece of evidence had not been seen or heard of again until the Beauvilain and Watté paper was published in June 2009.

And Brunet's response? When *La Recherche* asked the professor for a comment, he replied:

> In Chad, we have uncovered thousands of bones, which are in the process of being studied. Perhaps there are hominid bones among them, but I only comment on those that have been published in a scientific review.

CHAPTER FIFTEEN

Australopithecus afarensis
(1978)

I F A medal were struck commemorating achievements in palaeoanthropology during the 1970s and 1980s it should have the head of Richard Leakey on one side, and that of Donald Johanson on the other. Such close proximity separated by a few millimetres of solid metal would illustrate their achievements, their affinities, and their mutual antipathy admirably. They were both ambitious, clever, and energetic men who achieved success in their late twenties and early thirties—that time of life when energy and ambition are most aggressively combined. They both directed expeditions which discovered important hominid fossils—Leakey the 1470 skull, remembered as the Oldest Man even though the dating was disproved, and Johanson the famous Lucy skeleton from Ethiopia—but held opposing views on the status of those fossils in human evolution. This difference of opinion was suffused with personal animosity which the media whipped up into a grand old scrap. *Life* magazine called it the 'Battle of the Bones'.[1]

In 1981, CBS television brought the two protagonists together for an edition of *Cronkite's Universe*, hosted by America's most avuncular television personality, Walter Cronkite. The series was an indulgent tribute to the man who had been the leading anchorman on CBS News for many years, allowing Cronkite to explore scientific issues that interested him personally. Early Man was in the news. Getting Leakey to appear on television with Johanson was a scoop that only a figure of Cronkite's stature could pull off.

'Before the discovery of Lucy made Donald Johanson a celebrity, the king of the mountain of palaeoanthropology was Richard Leakey...He was credited with finding the oldest ancestor of man—until Lucy came along,' Cronkite explained in his introduction,[2] creating the expectation that viewers were about to witness a fight for the monarchy—no realm can have two kings.

Both men had genuine claims; both had discovered important fossils; both were currently in the public eye, with television appearances and popular books to their name. Johanson had not made the cover of *Time* magazine, but a win on *Cronkite's Universe* would probably have a much wider and deeper impact—especially since the national and personal aspects of the contest would be apparent: Johanson, the cheery all-American boy who had made good, versus Leakey, the stuffy colonial Brit who had started out with the advantage of his parents' name and achievements. And what was there to win? The crown, of course, but also public endorsement of a hypothesis. Like his parents, Leakey believed that the human line went back millions of years, with no contribution from *Australopithecus*; Johanson, on the other hand, believed his discoveries showed that the Leakeys were wrong; the human line was recent and *Australopithecus* was right in the middle of it, our direct ancestors.

Johanson had brought along casts of a number of fossil skulls, laid out on the small table around which Cronkite and his guests were seated. Johanson had come prepared. Leakey had come straight from a board meeting of the Foundation for Research into the Origin of Man (FROM), an organization he had founded to raise money for research. He was tired and totally unprepared, lacking both equipment and a debating strategy. In fact, he had been well and truly set up, and could only hope the audience would have some sympathy for his discomfort as Johanson dominated proceedings. Little if any scientific debate took place, but Johanson's performance was accomplished enough to convince any non-specialist audience that his scheme of human evolution was correct, and Leakey's therefore wrong. 'I won!', he subsequently boasted. 'Unfortunate', was Leakey's assessment on the encounter.

While Richard Leakey was working at East Turkana, Donald Johanson had been joint leader on a series of international expeditions that between 1973 and 1977 found 250 hominid fossils in deposits exposed along the ravines and tributary valleys of the Hadar river in the Afar region of north-eastern Ethiopia. More fossils might have been found had the expeditions continued, but Ethiopia's internal strife made further exploration impossible for a number of years.

The age of the Afar fossils ranges from 2.3 to 3.4 million years and the extraordinary variety of bones and teeth represents a minimum of thirty-five and a maximum of sixty-five individuals. The most famous became known as 'Lucy' (because it was found while the Beatles' song, Lucy in the Sky with Diamonds was a hit) and comprised roughly 40 per cent of a complete skeleton. Another large collection of bones from a single site, known by its museum reference number 333 and sometimes referred to as 'The Family', includes seventeen adults and juveniles. This was the first discovery of fossils that might represent a hominid 'population'. In their first announcements of the discoveries, Johanson and his colleagues suggested there were three species among the Afar fossils: a small one which they thought might be *Australopithecus africanus*, a large one which could have been *Australopithecus robustus*, and a third which they thought might represent *Homo*.[3] Of course, fossil remains of *Homo* dated at three million years would also represent the 'Oldest Man'.

The fossil deposits of the Afar region were first noted by the French geologist Maurice Taieb in 1967, while he was working there on research for his doctoral dissertation. The Afar, a fractured depression in the earth's crust, is a section of the African Rift Valley of great interest to geologists because it connects with the rift systems of the Red Sea and the Gulf of Aden. It has supplied important information on plate tectonics and the origins of the continents.

Part of the Afar depression is below sea level. Here and there hot sulphur springs bubble as active reminders of the Earth's internal stirrings which about four million years ago caused lava to erupt from surface fissures and flood basalt across the Afar. The basalt subsequently became the floor of a lake basin which in turn filled with the clays, sands, gravels, and silts brought down by rivers and streams from the surrounding highlands. These sediments settled and consolidated on the lake beds at a rate of about one centimetre every ten years, filling the entire basin in the relatively short period of barely one million years, and presenting Taieb with a rugged terrain to explore in 1967. By then, the sediments had been tilted and broken by geological faulting, and rivers had sliced through them. One such river was the Hadar which, as it carried the seasonal flood from the highlands down to the larger Awash river, had gouged a meandering channel up to 140 metres deep through the sediments, exposing in its banks and ravines the fossilized remains of the many creatures which had lived and died on the shores on the ancient lake.

In 1971 Johanson worked on the joint French, American, and Kenyan expedition to the Omo from which Richard Leakey had defected to East Turkana (see p. 280). He met Maurice Taieb on a stopover in Paris; they talked of the Afar, and in 1972 Johanson went with Taieb to assess the palaeontological potential of the region. It was a brief trip, squeezed between his commitment to that year's Omo expedition but, nonetheless, they found lots of splendidly preserved fossils of extinct animals suggesting the beds were up to 3, and perhaps even 4 million years old, pre-dating Olduvai Gorge and East Turkana and therefore a likely repository of fossils representing the earlier stages of human evolution. Johanson realized immediately that the Afar presented a unique opportunity in the search for human origins. 'It was like a dream within reach,' he said. He drew up plans with Taieb for a major research expedition to explore the region in 1973.

Don Johanson was born in Chicago in 1943; his parents were immigrants from Sweden, his father a barber, his mother a cleaning lady. In 1966 he completed his undergraduate course with a distinction in anthropology and embarked upon a study of chimpanzee teeth for a master's degree. Simultaneously he began teaching anthropology and set his mind upon the search for human origins as an ultimate ambition. 'But the fossil man game is like being an astronaut,' he later recalled, 'there aren't many of them. Actually finding the fossils is only for very few, and when you're a graduate student in Chicago the prospect seems as far away as Jupiter.' And indeed, while Maurice Taieb was discovering the fossil beds of the Afar in 1967, Don Johanson was in Alaska, helping to measure teeth for someone else's anthropological study. But fossils and human evolution drew closer. He undertook an *Odontological Study of the Chimpanzee with some Implications for Hominid Evolution* for his Ph.D. and in 1970 was invited to join the Chicago group on that summer's Omo Research Expedition.

Johanson's job on the Omo expedition in 1970 (and again in 1971 and 1972) was palaeontological excavation. He and his co-workers cleared up to eight metres of overburden from over 500 square metres of fossil-bearing deposits. Most of

FIGURE 15.1 Donald Johanson with co-workers and the entire Afar collection, 1978.

the excavations were inspired by the discovery of hominid fragments on the surface, but none fulfilled the initial promise. Of the 11,781 vertebrate fossils the team found, fewer than forty were hominid.[4] There was one mandible, one lower armbone, four matching skull fragments, and twenty-four isolated teeth. Most of the Omo fossils, in fact, were of baboons, crocodiles, and ruminants. Nonetheless, Johanson gained valuable experience in the Omo.

The first International Afar Research Expedition (IARE), under the joint leadership of Yves Coppens, Donald Johanson, and Maurice Taieb, began work in the late summer of 1973. At first it seemed destined to follow the familiar pattern: weeks of mapping geology and stratigraphy; collection and cataloguing of nearly 6,000 fossils of some forty different vertebrate species—but no hominids, not even a single tooth. Until 30 October when, late in the afternoon, as Johanson's group were completing the survey of a small gully, he found four pieces of hominid leg bones, two of which belonged together and formed a perfect knee joint. The fossils came from deposits over three million years old. The individual of whom they formed a part had been a small adult, and the configuration of the joint surfaces was such that he or she must have been fully capable of walking upright. Johanson had found the earliest conclusive evidence of human bipedalism.

The promise of this discovery was confirmed the following year (1974). Within a week of the IARE establishing its camp on the banks of the Awash, Alemeyhu Asfaw (seconded from the Ethiopian Antiquities Department) found a fragment of hominid jawbone with two teeth still in place. The next day Alemeyhu found another, more complete specimen, and then another. And the day after that the site foreman, Melissa, found yet another. 'Unbelievable,' Johanson later reported, 'in three days, four hominid specimens, representing four individuals.[5] The most remarkable of these was a palate with all sixteen teeth still in place. It was remarkable not only because of its splendid preservation, but also because of its combination of primitive and modern features. The front teeth were large relative to the back teeth, like ours; but there was a gap between the canines and the incisors, as in the apes, the teeth rows were parallel rather than curved and the palate was shallow, all primitive features reminiscent of the chimpanzee, in Johanson's view. He believed that such a combination of ape- and man-like features had not been encountered before and arranged to announce the discovery at a press conference in Addis Ababa.

The fossils were introduced to representatives of the world press as 'an unparalleled breakthrough in the search for the origins of man's evolution'. In a prepared statement the IARE team claimed: 'We have in a matter of merely two days extended our knowledge of the genus *Homo* by nearly 1.5 million years. All previous theories of the origins of the lineage which leads to modern man must now be totally revised. The genus *Homo* was walking, eating meat and probably using tools to kill animals' 3 to 4 million years ago and probably already had 'some kind of social cooperation and some sort of communication system', the statement declared.[6]

The Addis announcement generated a lot of excitement and publicity, though the experts were cautious and the IARE's claim that they had discovered the Oldest Man was soon countered by Richard Leakey, who pointed out that evidence of a relatively large brain was required before fossils could be assigned to the genus *Homo*.

Johanson returned to the field. Around midday on 24 November he noticed a fragment of armbone poking from a slope he was casually exploring with a colleague, Tom Gray. At first sight he thought it was probably a monkey bone but, though small enough, it lacked the characteristic bony flange of the comparable part of a monkey. 'My pulse was quickening,' Johanson later wrote, 'suddenly I found myself saying, "It's hominid"'. There were more fragments higher up on the slope and then: 'the realization struck us both that we might have found a skeleton. An extraordinary skeleton…The searing heat was forgotten. Tom and I yelled, hugged each other, and danced, mad as any Englishman in the midday sun.'[7]

The slope was sieved extensively during the following three weeks. Many more pieces of hominid bones were recovered, including skull fragments (but not enough to reconstruct a brain case), a mandible, most of a left and right arm, several vertebrae, a number of rib fragments, the sacrum, the left pelvic bone, the left thighbone and some pieces of the right lower leg. In all, about 40 per cent of an entire skeleton. The form of the pelvic bones showed that the individual had been female, and erupted wisdom teeth suggested she had been about 20 years old, but the size of the thighbone made it clear that she had been very small—no more than 122 centimetres tall, and perhaps as little as 107 centimetres.

The Afar skeleton features in the IARE field collection specimen list as: A.L. 288-1 Partial Skeleton. But this formal title only extends to the academic journals; everywhere else—in conversation and in print—the specimen is known as Lucy, from 'Lucy in the Sky with Diamonds' which the camp tape recorder had frequently broadcast across the Afar deposits, though the name chosen by

Ethiopians working with the expedition is a better token of the fossil's status: 'Denkenesh', meaning 'you are wonderful'.

Lucy was the star of a press conference held in Addis Ababa at the end of the 1974 season. But Johanson was cautious on the question of her attribution, saying only that she was either 'a small *Homo* or a small australopithecine', which inspired a reporter from the *Herald Tribune* to comment that Johanson's team 'refused deliberately to say that the skeleton belonged to the genus *Homo*...They are trying to avoid further controversy with Richard Leakey...who has contested their claims to have found specimens of early man in the absence of crania.'[8]

Given the success of the IARE in 1973 and 1974, the following year might have been expected to be an anti-climax; but in fact 1975 was no less successful. 'I felt I was moving through a dream,' Johanson told readers of *National Geographic*, 'each day produced more remains', including 'some of the oldest remains of the genus *Homo* ever unearthed. And not just a few fragments, but enough pieces to identify men, women and children—perhaps a family—who had died together three million years ago. The find was unprecedented—the earliest group of associated individuals ever found.'[9] Treasure indeed.

In all, the trove comprised 197 hominid fossils—jaws, teeth, leg bones, scores of hand and foot bones, vertebrae, ribs, adult skull fragments and part of an infant's skull. It was a disproportionate collection, but included a minimum of thirteen individuals (another four were identified later, making seventeen in all); young and old of both sexes, appeared to have been buried together at the site. Maurice Taieb speculated that they had died together too, perhaps caught in a flash flood while sleeping in a riverbed. This explanation was repeated by Johanson on several occasions,[10] but it was never popular with other experts. Richard Leakey suggested that the band might have succumbed to a particularly virulent disease;[11] Alan Walker proposed a carnivore assemblage wherein the bones were remnants of a leopard's meals, perhaps, dropped from a tree into a waterhole below where they sank into the mud and were fossilized.[12] But however the bones had arrived where the IARE found them, Johanson was certain they represented the genus *Homo*, were over three million years old, and were conclusive evidence, therefore, that he and his team had found the 'Oldest Man'.

FIGURE 15.2 'Lucy', *Australopithecus afarensis*.

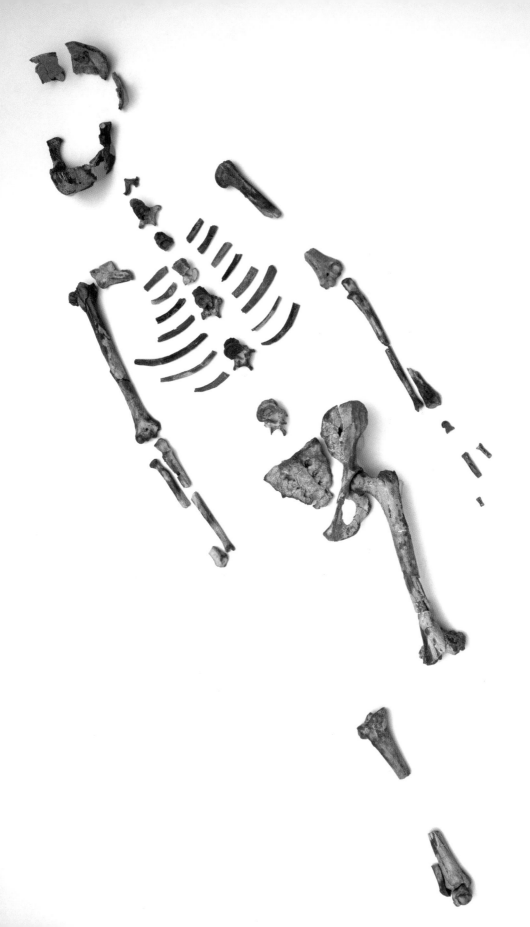

In a *National Geographic* article entitled 'Ethiopia yields first "Family" of early man', Donald Johanson described the Afar fossil hominids as 'discoveries that are writing new chapters in the annals of early man research'. He left Lucy to her australopithecine affinities, but unequivocally assigned the 'family' fossils to the genus *Homo*. What evidence was his judgement based upon? Well, there was the dental evidence already noted, and the bones were generally larger than Lucy's, said Johanson, and there were features among them that were very much like *Homo*. The foot bones, for instance, closely resembled those of modern humans, and the hand bones could be combined with modern bones to reconstruct a completely modern hand. Unhappily there were no skulls to provide the evidence of a relatively large brain that critics might call for; but among the Afar fossils Johanson did find a lower jaw that he was certain would fit 1470[13]—and thus make Leakey's 'Oldest Man' available as proof of his own claims to the title.

In 1974, while the IARE were still gathering their evidence of *Homo* in the Afar, apparent confirmation of the attribution came from a distant and unexpected source. During a Christmas picnic that year, Mary Leakey and her son Philip found a number of hominid fossils at Laetoli, fossil beds near Olduvai she and Louis had visited many years before. The new fossils were from deposits over 3.5 million years old; they included several isolated teeth, a juvenile mandible, and one adult mandible which bore a striking resemblance to the specimens found at Afar, 2,000 kilometres away and at least half a million years younger.

At an early opportunity Mary Leakey and Donald Johanson met to compare the Afar and Laetoli specimens side by side. Given the distance separating the fossils in both space and time their overall similarity was astonishing. Mary Leakey and Johanson agreed that among the larger specimens, *Homo* affinities were dominant. In a report on the Laetoli discoveries published in *Nature*,[14] Mary Leakey said that: 'preliminary assessment...suggests placement of the Laetoli specimens among the earliest dated members of this genus'. Some critics preferred to emphasize the specimens' australopithecine affinities (which undeniably were present), but Mary Leakey argued that since *Australopithecus* became extinct while *Homo* survives, any fossils with distinct *Homo* features must be assigned to the surviving lineage—*Homo*. This also implied, of course, that the title of 'Oldest Man' now belonged to the Leakey discoveries at Laetoli.

Because Mary Leakey was an archaeologist and considered herself unqualified to write a formal description of the fossils for publication, she asked Tim White to undertake the task. By then, little more than a decade after working at Louis Leakey's Calico excavations, White had progressed via a BA in biology and anthropology from the University of California, Riverside, and a Ph.D. in physical anthropology from Michigan, to be among the select group invited to work with Mary Leakey on the excavations at Laetoli. It was a fortuitous happenstance, with unfortunate consequences.

White knew Johanson, who was then busy preparing his formal description of the Afar material. Because of the similarities that had been noted between the two collections, it was obviously sensible that White and Johanson should compare and discuss the finer points of the fossils, but certainly not inevitable, or even to be expected, that they would publish a joint paper grouping the material together—the Laetoli and Afar fossils—as the remains of an entirely new australopithecine species, with the mandible Mary Leakey had said was *Homo* formally described as the type specimen of the new taxon.[15]

When she invited White to describe the Laetoli material, Mary Leakey was confident there were two species to be named. The Laetoli specimens were all *Homo* in her view, and even her critics seemed to agree that the large and small specimens from Afar must represent two distinct species. However, when Johanson, White, and their French associate, Yves Coppens, began to analyse the fossils and compare them with other collections they found themselves forced to reject conclusions that had previously seemed obvious in favour of 'exciting new possibilities', as Johanson wrote in a popular report.[16]

To cite just one among several points: although Lucy was small enough to be a representative of *Australopithecus africanus*, equally small individuals among the 'family' would stand out as anomalies if she were classified as such. Clearly it was highly unlikely that two distinct species would have existed within the confines of one family group. The anomaly disappeared, however, when Johanson, White, and Coppens concluded that only one species had existed at Afar and at Laetoli. The individuals from both sites were morphologically identical, they said, and the size variation was due entirely to sexual dimorphism—very large males and very small females—within a single species. But the degree of sexual dimorphism seemed quite exceptional, remarked other commentators; how could it be explained?

In living primates sexual dimorphism is least among the smallest species and greatest among the largest—which is the gorilla. The Afar hominids were much smaller than the larger living primates, yet their sexual dimorphism as proposed by Johanson and White appeared to exceed that of the gorilla, a point raised at an informal seminar in Nairobi when White presented the conclusions of the IARE studies to members of the East Turkana Research Project.

Alan Walker (anatomist): If the degree of sexual dimorphism is outside the modern range, then you must justify your reasoning.

Tim White (physical anthropologist): It's simplest to have only one species in the family collection, so…

Walker: Numerical simplicity is not necessarily the truth.

Richard Leakey (then Director of the Kenya National Museums): Have you done sufficient study and measurements to convince us?

White: Our scheme elucidates…

Andrew Hill (palaeontologist): Obscures!

White: We recognize a significant…

Hill: How do you know it's significant if you haven't quantified?

White: From my experience!

Walker: You need to be just a little more precise…

Leakey: It's my feeling that you are guilty of imposing what you think is right upon the fossils.

Walker: It might be nice to put the numbers down.

White: Sure! There'll be someone with red-hot water-cooled calipers to provide the measurements you want, but we're trying to understand the evolution and biology—not just catalogue the fossils.

Leakey: Well, we think the chances are that you've got it wrong.[17]

In their determination to understand the evolution and biology of the Afar and Laetoli hominids, Johanson and White concluded that if the fossils represented a single species, as they believed, then the blend of *Homo* and *Australopithecus* features they saw in them must imply that the species had been ancestral to both lineages. At the generic level they might have been inclined to call it *Homo*, as Johanson had done originally, and as Mary Leakey would have preferred. But there was no evidence of the relatively large brain that distinguishes the genus

Homo, while the fossils did have many characteristics in common with the gracile australopithecines.

The evidence, they concluded, demanded attribution to the genus *Australopithecus.* At the specific level, they felt several features (the more primitive teeth, for instance) merited distinction from the known species of *Australopithecus,* so they created a new one for their fossils: *Australopithecus afarensis.*[18]

As type specimen of the new species Johanson and White chose the adult mandible from Laetoli which, though less well preserved than a similar specimen from Afar, had already been described by White.[19] And so *Australopithecus afarensis* acquired a maximum age of about 3.7 million years (the age of the relevant Laetoli deposits) and the Johanson camp could claim that they, not the Leakeys, now had the oldest known representative of the human line.

The evolutionary scheme that Johanson and White presented with the new species was a single, straight, and slender stem with *Australopithecus afarensis* at the bottom and *Homo sapiens* at the top. One short truncated branch was provided along which *Australopithecus africanus* evolved from the main stem into *Australopithecus robustus* and subsequent extinction. Johanson and White believed that *Australopithecus* was the only hominid line for a very long time, from which the *africanus* stock diverged about 2.5 million years ago, while the genus *Homo* arose only with the advent of *Homo habilis* about 1.9 million years ago. The new scheme, though simple, was all-embracing. Within it, *Australopithecus afarensis* became not just the ancestor of *Australopithecus* and humans, but also of virtually every hominid fossil ever found. *Australopithecus* and *Homo; A. africanus* and *A. robustus; H. habilis, H. erectus,* and *H. sapiens*—all owed their origin to *Australopithecus afarensis.* Including, of course, the large-brained, 1.9-million-year-old hominid Richard Leakey had found at Lake Turkana: 1470, the Oldest Man.

Australopithecus afarensis was the first new hominid species to be created around original fossils since Louis Leakey had named *Homo habilis* fourteen years before. It was therefore an event of some significance. Johanson and White believed they would be making history, and gave careful thought to the question of where and how their new species should be announced. Johanson favoured an orchestrated campaign of media announcements and appearances designed to achieve maximum coverage and publicity. White was more cautious, concerned that the significance of the science should not be overwhelmed by Johanson's irrepressible enthusiasm for personal promotion.

In the event, however, their differences were resolved by the arrival of an invitation for Johanson to speak at the Nobel Symposium on Early Man in May 1978. The symposium was to be held in Sweden under the auspices of the Royal Swedish Academy of Sciences, in commemoration of Carolus Linnaeus, who had died 200 years before. It was, of course, Linnaeus who had formulated the binomial system of classification by which species are named. A symposium in his honour was the perfect occasion for the announcement of a new hominid species: Johanson was of Swedish descent; both he and *Australopithecus afarensis* would benefit from the Linnaean connection and the imprimatur of the Royal Swedish Academy of Sciences. Furthermore, since the Academy's interest in palaeoanthropology had been aroused by Richard Leakey's discovery of 1470, and Leakey himself had been closely involved with the conception, planning, and organization of the symposium, *A. afarensis* was bound to steal a measure of Leakey's thunder. There would be no pre-announcement. The new species would remain a secret until Johanson gave his talk at the Symposium.

'Yippee,' White wrote to Johanson in a note accompanying the final draft of their *A. afarensis* manuscript, 'tell them to start up their armchairs and fasten their seat-belts. We're on our way!'

The Nobel Symposium had a deep emotional significance for Johanson. As the son of Swedish migrants, applying Linnaean taxonomic classification to a hitherto undescribed ancestor of all humanity, he felt himself 'to be a link in the chain of scientific inquiry that led straight back to that other Swede. It was a thrill to stand up and utter the name *Australopithecus afarensis* for the first time in public.'[20] But if *Australopithecus afarensis* had been a secret until Johanson read his paper, it was not much better known by the time he had finished. The paper was long and not easily followed; the announcement of the new species merely one sentence among many. The reaction was decidedly low key.

As the assembly adjourned for tea Richard Leakey remarked that he did not like it very much, and Phillip Tobias was heard to suggest that perhaps sub-specific distinction would have been adequate—something like *Australopithecus africanus tanzanensis*. Mary Leakey later said she was incandescent with rage when she heard Johanson describing the Laetoli fossils in such proprietorial fashion, since they were to be the subject of her talk; but she said nothing at the time, and the general response was not the excited buzz of interest and discussion Johanson had been expecting. It was more the polite face of censure that snobs turn to the guest who inadvertently farts at a formal gathering. Having denied himself the fruits of orchestrated publicity, Johanson got no scientific adulation either. And then, adding yet more angst, even the formal publication of the new species did not proceed according to plan.

The International Code for Zoological Nomenclature stipulates that the first published mention of a new species shall be its defining citation, to be used subsequently whenever the species is mentioned formally (as with *Australopithecus africanus* (Dart 1925) for example). To this end, Johanson and White had prepared a full anatomical description of their new species, and had already arranged for its publication in an authoritative journal, confident that it would be cited thereafter as *Australopithecus afarensis* (Johanson *et al.* 1978). These plans were pre-empted, however, by a freelance journalist attending the Symposium. Don Hinrichsen knew very little about palaeoanthropology, and even less about the International Code for Zoological Nomenclature, but knew the announcement of *A. afarensis* was worthy of attention. His brief report appeared in *New Scientist* magazine shortly afterwards.[21] Purists complained,[22] and although the breach of ICZN rules is now hidden beneath references to the Johanson *et al.* 1978 paper (justifiably, since that is the formal description of the species), Hinrichsen 1978 remains a valid citation in terms of precedence.

In due course, though, response to the new species became robust and sustained. Comment was highly favourable at the popular level, treating the announcement as a piece of groundbreaking scientific news, accepting it as reported, and making no effort to criticize. In the United States, Johanson was invited to appear on a number of television talk shows, but the headline under which the story appeared in *The New York Times* said it all in his view: 'New-found Species Challenges Views on Human Evolution'. Only *Time* magazine demurred from the media's widespread approval of *A. afarensis*—an australopithecine—as the ancestor of humans. The fossils did not say anything new, *Time* wrote, going on to quote a 'distinguished anthropologist' who said the claims about *A. afarensis* were 'the kind of thing to expect from Johanson, who always had been a publicity hound'.[23]

'Why would they say that?' Johanson asked a former Time Inc. journalist. 'Why that crack by the unidentified "distinguished anthropologist"? Who the hell is *he*?' This was a tad disingenuous. Given that Richard Leakey had appeared on the cover of *Time* little more than a year before, and had expounded his theory of human evolution at length across the pages within, Johanson can hardly have needed a journalist to tell him that Leakey was '*Time*'s pet anthropologist'; or that the 'announcement of *A. afarensis* blows Old *Homo* right out of the water. It destroys Richard Leakey's central idea. Don't you realize that when you publish about *afarensis* you're on a collision course with Leakey?'[24]

Thus was the scene set for the *Cronkite's Universe* confrontation between Johanson and Leakey, from which Johanson was to emerge winner in the eyes of Cronkite's audience: the newly crowned 'king of the mountain of palaeoanthropology'.

As viewed from the senior common room armchairs Tim White had alluded to, the Cronkite confrontation and associated shenanigans brought more disrepute than insight to the science, but in the pages of the academic journals, serious criticism of the new species was mounting. Apart from quibbles about the flouting of ICZN convention mentioned above, the criticism centred around two points: first, the validity of grouping the Afar and Laetoli material together as one species—many felt the fossils represented at least two species; and second, the question of whether or not the material was distinctive enough to justify a new species—could it not have been assigned to existing species of *Homo* or *Australopithecus*?

After due consideration, anatomist Phillip Tobias concluded that *Australopithecus afarensis* was invalid on both counts.[25] At least fifteen cranial, mandibular, and dental features that Johanson *et al.* had cited as diagnostic of the new species were also present in *Australopithecus africanus*, he told a meeting of the Royal Society, and therefore not diagnostic at all. *Australopithecus afarensis* should be formally suppressed, Tobias demanded, and the fossils renamed with no more than sub-specific distinction based on geographic distribution: *Australopithecus africanus aethiopicus* for the Afar fossils, and *Australopithecus africanus tanzanensis* for the Laetoli specimens.[26] In the ensuing discussion, however, Tobias was reminded that the International Code of Zoological Nomenclature prohibited such suppression. Once in existence, *Australopithecus afarensis* could not be simply wished away.

Mary Leakey's reaction to the new species was vehement in private, but otherwise restrained.[27] She did not agree with the White and Johanson conclusions, and when told that the announcement of the new species would include her

FIGURE 15.3 Australopithecine mandibles and teeth from the Afar collection.

name among its authors she had demanded that it be removed. Johanson professed to be surprised by this, claiming that the inclusion of her name was a generous gesture to a deserving colleague that required no permission or advance
warning. The paper was already in the press when Leakey's demand arrived; it
had to be recalled, amended, and printed over again—which delayed publication, Johanson complained.[28]

At the Royal Society meeting, Mary Leakey questioned the wisdom of assigning specimens from localities more than 1,000 miles apart to the same species, and said that including the Laetoli hominid specimens in a new species
of *Australopithecus* did 'nothing to clarify one of the most important issues in
the study of man's evolution'.[29] Informally, she reiterated her conviction that the
Laetoli fossils and the large specimens from Afar should be assigned to *Homo*,
and expressed deep regret that 'the Laetoli fellow was now doomed to be called
Australopithecus afarensis'.

Predictably, Richard Leakey did not agree with the new species either. With Alan
Walker he attacked the scheme of hominid evolution that Johanson and White had
constructed,[30] and in his personal capacity insisted that Johanson had been correct in his very first interpretation of the Afar fossils as *Homo* and should not have
changed his mind.[31] There were two distinct species among the Afar and Laetoli
collections, Leakey said, one of them an ancestor of *Homo* and the other an ancestor of *Australopithecus*. In his view this proved that the two hominid lineages had
coexisted in the Afar basin three million years ago, just as they had at East Turkana
one and a half million years later. Richard Leakey, in fact, regarded the evidence of
Johanson's Afar fossils as proof of *his* belief that *Homo* and *Australopithecus* were no
more closely related than as the descendants of a common ancestor who had lived
in the very distant past, some six or seven million years ago.[32]

Meanwhile, Johanson was of the opinion that Leakey's 1470 and sundry other
specimens from East Turkana were compelling evidence of *his* belief that *Homo*
was of relatively recent descent from *Australopithecus*.[33] Each, it seemed, had
found the evidence to substantiate the other's hypothesis—even though the two
schemes were mutually exclusive; both could not be right.

The fact that two leading scientists could use identical evidence to support two
opposing hypotheses is primarily a measure of the quality of that evidence (and
a comment on the scientific acumen of the proposers), but it also raises another
important point: how would the science stand if, for argument's sake, Leakey

had worked at Afar as well as East Turkana? Or if Johanson had likewise worked at both sites? With the same fossils to hand, one or other of them presumably would have claimed his beliefs doubly affirmed, and the quantitative value of the fossils from two widely separated sites might have persuaded many that the evidence substantiated those beliefs.

In the event, it was scientific method and more fossils, not personalities, that settled the issue. Detailed analysis of the dental morphology of the Laetoli and Hadar material published by Tim White showed that the fossils represent one and the same species of hominid,[34] while a host of other discoveries showed that the story of hominid evolution during those crucial early stages, 6 to 2 million years ago, was more complex than anyone had supposed when Walter Cronkite brought the celebrity figures of palaeoanthropology together in 1981. There was never anything so simple as Leakey's directly ascending line, or Johanson's elegant Y. Just as today there are numerous species of monkey, often living cheek by jowl in the same stretch of forest, so there were probably several species of hominid occupying the Rift Valley environments. The remains of only a small fraction of their number had been found, and the picture was becoming more complex with each new discovery.

But while a welcome resurgence of maturity was evident in the science, things were not going so well on the popular front—especially in respect of relations with Ethiopia, where more discoveries were confidently expected. The country's civil strife had brought the first round of explorations to an end; just as they might have been expected to resume, Johanson's book, *Lucy—The Beginnings of Humankind* was published, complete with colourful episodes that risked annoying the Ethiopian authorities. Written principally by his co-author, a former Time Inc. journalist, the book was informative, racy, and entertaining—clearly pitched at the best-seller list—and Johanson allowed no sense of propriety to devalue a good story. Getting Lucy out of the country reads as a frenetic battle with bureaucracy, the success of which led him to conclude that he 'was no longer an unknown anthropology graduate, but a promising young field worker with fossils dazzling enough to match those of palaeoanthropology's certified supernova, Richard Leakey',[35] a claim which inspired a colleague to ask: 'what does that make me, a Black Dwarf?'

But worse than such derring-do and self-promotion, Johanson told how he had stolen a human thighbone from the burial mound of an Afar family—Muslims all. It happened at the end of the first field season (1973). Johanson had found a knee joint he felt sure was human but could only confirm by comparing it with a modern example. Apparently, his agreement with the Ethiopian authorities required that any fossils deemed important enough to take out of the country had to be described at a press conference before removal. Johanson was afraid that if he described it incorrectly he would have botched his first independent fossil interpretation; if he did not describe it the fossil could not be taken out of Ethiopia. There was a medical school at Addis Ababa University where a proper anatomical comparison could have been made, but Johanson opted for the more adventurous course of action: desecrating a grave of his hosts.[36]

The act was deplorable; boasting of it in a book, shameful—especially when Maurice Taieb, to whom Johanson owed his introduction to the Afar deposits, had begged him to omit the episode, arguing that it was certain to anger the Ethiopian authorities; as indeed it did. The Ethiopians were furious and responded predictably: Johanson's team, on which Taieb was geologist, were refused excavation permits for nearly a decade. Johanson finally secured permits again in 1991, but Taieb found himself dropped from the team. Johanson 'forgot to send the elevator back down', said Taieb, who as a result was never able to complete personally the work he had initiated in the Afar.[37]

However, while the pleadings of Johanson and his team achieved nothing, joint American and Ethiopian expeditions led by Tim White had been working with official permission since 1981 (with a gap between 1982 and 1990), in the Middle Awash region—which lies with its northern boundary less than 20 kilometres from the Hadar area, where Lucy had been found. Remains attributed to the same species, *Australopithecus afarensis*, dated to between 3.4 and 3.8 million years old were recovered in the early years, and something entirely new turned up in 1993 in the drainage of the Aramis river. With an age of around 4.4 million years the remains (a set of teeth, jaw fragment, upper and lower arm bones, and basal skull fragments) could not disqualify the Lothagam and Tabarin specimens from their 'Oldest Man' status, but even *Nature*'s reviewer felt they were sufficiently different from everything else to merit use of another previously fashionable term: 'The metaphor of a "Missing Link" has often been misused,' wrote the anatomist Bernard Wood, 'but it is a suitable epithet for the hominid from Aramis.'[38] Not surprisingly, this inspired a small avalanche of 'Scientists find the Missing Link' reports.

The key point, though, was that the new specimen was sufficiently older than *A. afarensis*, and younger than molecular predictions for the age of the common ancestor of apes and hominids for it to occupy the 'morphological space' in between. In recognition of the specimen's australopithecine affinities, White and his co-authors assigned it to that genus, while acknowledging its more primitive characteristics with the creation of a new species: *ramidus*, from 'ramid', which means 'root' in the language of the Afar people—*Australopithecus ramidus*.[39] A year later, in 1995, on the basis of further analysis and comparison indicating that the specimen was significantly more primitive than *Australopithecus* had been apparent initially, they assigned it to a new genus, *Ardipithecus*,[40] of which there was much more to be said, as will be discussed in the final chapter of this book.

In 1997 similar remains were found dating from between 5.8 and 5.2 million years ago—similar, but more primitive again and therefore assigned to yet another new species: *Ardipithecus kadabba*.[41] There were more new species: *Australopithecus bahrelghazali* (1996, 3.5 to 3.0 million years old); *Australopithecus garhi* (1999, about 2.5 million years old); and not only in Ethiopia: a Kenyan specimen found in 1967 was described as a new species in 1995, *Australopithecus anamensis* (dating from between 4.5 and 3.9 million years ago), *Kenyapithecus platyops* (between 3.5 and 3.3 million years old) was found in 1999; then of course there was *Orrorin tugenensis* (6.6 to 5.7 million years old), and *Sahelanthropus tchadensis* (6 to 7 million years old).

Conscious of the plethora of fossils available as evidence of human evolution, Bernard Wood and colleague Nicholas Lonergan undertook a review of the hominid fossil record in terms of the taxa which had been created and their relationships to one another.[42] Their long paper began by showing that the existing 7 genera could be lumped together in just 4, and the 22 species reduced to 8. Similarly, if the 22 species were sorted according to their perceived degree of human affinity they could all be contained in 6 groups—though none of this eliminated the uncertainties of initial identification and relationships within and between the groups. A large element of imprecision remained, which was open to resolution according to personal preference, not definable rules, Wood and Lonergan pointed out. Their paper was intended 'to provide some insight into the challenges that face those whose research focuses on [these] topics'. They concluded: 'we hope that these relatively simple explanations of the background to some of the main controversies will enable readers to apply a healthy dose of skepticism to pronouncements about the taxonomy and systematics of the hominin clade'.

All very confusing. Hitherto, hominid fossils had been recovered and discussed under the general assumption that as human evolution proceeded, a progression of time-successive species had existed which, when their fossil remains were found, would link an ancestor resembling modern chimpanzees to modern humans. While there were just a few fossils scattered through a wide expanse of time they could be linked together in imaginary chains. But no longer. That satisfying view has been falsified by the mounting evidence and, as Tim White wrote in a discussion of the issue, 'it is now abundantly clear that we will need a very large and dense fossil record in order to obtain an accurate reading of the global experiment of hominid evolution. This is a frightening realisation and a daunting challenge,' he said, 'because the terrestrial data recorders which monitored this vast experiment were so poor. We have inherited only a few fossil hominid sites that...sample deep time. We have probably already found the best of them. In working on them we have learned that their largely surface accumulations are depleted by a few years of collection, but will require millennia [of erosion] to replenish. It is therefore unlikely that a comprehensive rendering of hominid evolution lies within our immediate grasp.'[43]

But while palaeoanthropology's most erudite practitioners were composing their gloomy prognostications, in 2006 the science was reminded of its most powerful source of inspiration: discovery. An outstanding fossil was found in Ethiopia, something new and wonderful. 'Eureka, we have it!', exclaimed Tim White, speaking in terms of scientific not personal acquisition, it is true, but excited by the wonder of discovery and what it might reveal.

The specimen in question was the fossil skeleton of a 3-year-old *Australopithecus afarensis* child which the media greeted as Lucy's Baby, and Bernard Wood described in *Nature* as a 3.3-million-year-old 'precious little bundle' which promised to throw new light on the development of a human ancestor.[44] The man responsible for the discovery was Zeray Alemseged, a young Ethiopian whose interest in palaeoanthropology had been awakened during his studies for a B.Sc. in Geology at Addis Ababa University in the late 1980s. He had met Tim White, Don Johanson, and other luminaries of the science while working in the Palaeoanthropology Laboratory at the National Museum. He had seen Lucy and the fossils (they had been returned to Ethiopia by then); he had watched and listened to the experts studying them and 'had caught the bug'. A scholarship enabled him to do a Ph.D. on palaeoanthropology and palaeoenvironments in France, and on returning to Ethiopia in 1998 he made a deal with the National Museum: he would work at the Museum without pay in return for permission to pursue research interests of his choice.

With funding from the French Centre for Ethiopian Studies, he began compiling a catalogue of Ethiopia's archaeological and palaeoanthropological sites which eventually took him to Dikika, a known but hitherto unexplored location not 10 kilometres from where Lucy had been found, but older.

On that first visit to Dikika in 1999, Zeray was accompanied only by a museum representative and two armed soldiers, whose presence was intended to ensure that the local Afar tribesmen did not resort to their customary practice of attacking visitors—especially Ethiopians from the south, with whom relations were strained. He identified the potential of the location, finding the fossil remains of elephants, hippos, rhinos, pigs, and antelopes, which indicated a wooded riverine environment that hominids could have occupied too. The same team returned in November the following year. On 10 December, in the course of a routine survey along the flank of a small hill, Zeray's companion from the museum, Tilahun Gebreselassie, saw a tiny face peering from the dusty slope. Though no bigger than a monkey, with only a small portion visible, the smooth brow and small canine teeth revealed immediately that this was a hominid.

The team searched the surrounding area for more pieces of the fossil, but the marvel of this discovery was that erosion had only exposed the face, leaving almost the entire skeleton of the child hidden in the slab of sandstone behind. The fossil had been preserved in sediments that once formed the bottom of a small channel close to where a river discharged into a lake. The flow had been generally sluggish, typical of the type of braided streams that make up a river delta. The corpse of the child was buried more or less intact, and must have been covered by sediments before any predators or scavengers could get to it.[45] She (researchers have concluded that the specimen was female) probably fell into the river, or was washed away during a flash-flood, and sank into the sediments, rolled into a bundle the size of a melon, so tiny 'you want to cradle it', said a hard-bitten geologist on the team. They named her Selam, meaning Peace.

The slab containing the fossil was removed to the laboratory, where Zeray Alemseged devoted many thousands of hours to the task of extracting the child's delicate skeleton from the cement-like matrix which has entombed her for more than three million years. The patience, skill, and time this requires should not be underestimated. There are no short cuts (chemical treatments, for instance, could destroy the fossil). The sandstone is removed, virtually grain by grain, under a microscope, with dental drills and picks. Zeray spent five summers at the task before there was enough of the skeleton exposed for the child to be formally described and announced.[46]

Some parts of the specimen are still missing, but what is preserved is remarkably complete. The face, the brain case and the base of the skull, the lower jaw, all but two of the teeth (including unerupted adult teeth), both shoulder-blades and collar bones are all there. The tiny ribs lay as in life along a curving spinal column; several finger were still curled in a tiny grasp, and under her chin the hyoid bone was preserved (a rare fossil example of the bone that facilitates speech in modern humans, and therefore a clue to the evolution of the voice box); of the lower body, parts of a foot and leg bones were preserved, including a human-like knee joint and knee caps the size of dried peas.

The affinities with *Australopithecus afarensis* were unequivocal, and the specimen was assigned to that species without hesitation. Like Lucy, Selam had many ape-like features. Her brain was small, her nose flat like a chimpanzee's, and her face long and projecting. Her finger bones were curved and almost as long as a chimp's. Her shoulder blades (the first of such antiquity ever found) were similar to those of a young gorilla—which would have enabled her to climb. In these and other factors Selam's fragile bones will help researchers to understand the function and significance of the more plentiful (but individually less complete) adult fossils of her species. Already they confirm the functional dichotomy of *A. afarensis*, with a lower body adapted for walking like us and an upper body retaining features that could have enabled them to climb trees like the apes.

The advent of bipedalism was a defining moment in the story of human evolution. As we evolved from the common ancestor, was *Australopithecus afarensis* the ape that stood erect and set us walking down the road to humanity?

FIGURE 15.4 Selam, the 'world's oldest child': the fossil skull of a 3 year-old child from deposits at Dikika, Ethiopia, that date back to 3.3 million years ago.

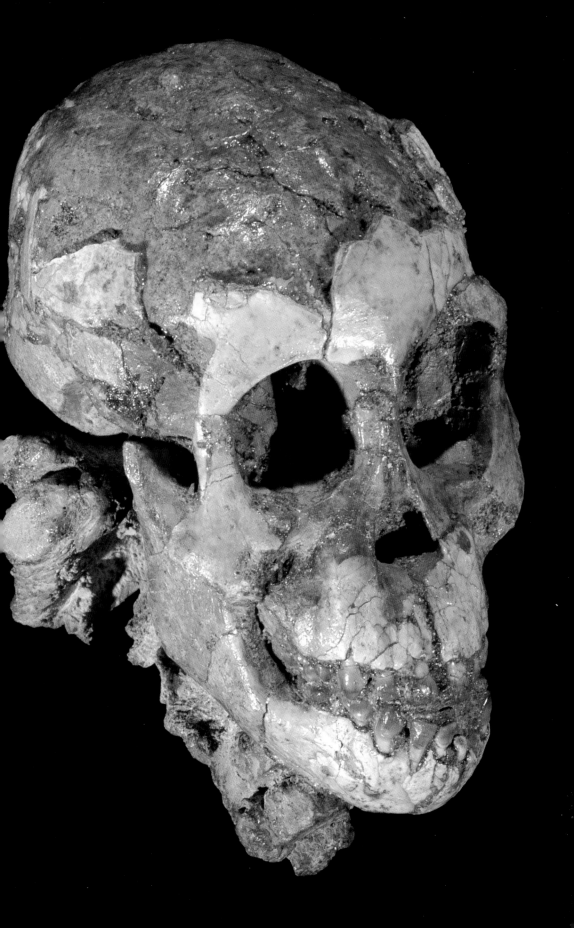

CHAPTER SIXTEEN

Footprints

E VERYTHING THAT makes humans special among the primates—indeed, special among animals—stems from our habitual bipedal gait: the ability to stand and walk erect. Questions of how, why, and when the human ancestor acquired this unique talent have been the hardy perennials of debate in the study of human evolution. Charles Darwin set out the parameters of discussion in the *Descent of Man* (1871):

> Man alone has become a biped; and we can, I think, partly see how he has come to assume his correct attitude, which forms one of his most conspicuous characters. Man could not have attained his present dominant position in the world without the use of his hands, which are so admirably adapted to act in obedience to his will…But the hands and arms could hardly have become perfect enough to have manufactured weapons, or to have hurled stones and spears with a true aim, as long as they were habitually used for locomotion and for supporting the whole weight of the body, or, as before remarked, so long as they were especially fitted for climbing trees…From these causes alone it would have been an advantage to man to become a biped, but for many actions it is indispensable that the arms and the whole upper part of the body should be free; and he must for this end stand firmly on his feet.

Only birds (and some dinosaurs) share the human bipedal gait, possibly because it is such an inefficient mode of locomotion: not even the fastest man on Earth could beat a rabbit over 100 metres. And that is not its only disadvantage. Walking upright has also brought us numerous problems and maladies that no other mammals suffer. It is a cruel fact that if we live long enough, nearly everyone will suffer the costs of being bipedal. Not just aching feet, sprained ankles, or arthritic knees and hips, but a host of conditions that are as unique to us as our peculiar way of walking. Only humans regularly endure fallen arches, fractured hips, bunions, slipped discs, shin splints, fractured vertebrae, spondylolysis, scoliosis, osteoporosis, and so on...[1]

Furthermore, in terms of energy required to move proportionately equal units of body mass over given distances, humans are not much more efficient than penguins waddling across the Antarctic icecap. Mice, squirrels, ponies, and gazelles are significantly more efficient—dogs even more so.[2] Among the apes, gorillas use relatively more energy than humans when moving about on the ground in quadruped mode; chimpanzees use 25 per cent less.[3] Apes and monkeys frequently get up on their hind legs, and can walk bipedally, but their gait lacks the mechanical efficiency of human bipedalism. Nonetheless, the apes do seem pre-adapted to bipedalism. Even when moving around on all fours they carry a large proportion of their body weight on their hind legs—about 60 per cent—which makes it relatively easy for them to stand up, whereas typical mammals such as dogs and horses carry 60 per cent of their body weight on the forelegs. Some pre-adaptation to bipedalism doubtless was a characteristic of the common ancestor of the ape and human lines, but only the human ancestor exploited its potential to the full.

The fossil evidence suggests that the evolutionary shift to habitual upright locomotion probably occurred between six and eight million years ago. Walking upright is therefore not only a unique and long-standing adaptation, it also qualifies as the 'breakthrough' adaptation that led eventually to modern humans.[4] How did it come about? From the ancestral quadruped's point of view, the advantages of walking around on two legs rather than four would have had to outweigh the disadvantages of undergoing the necessary physiological adaptation. After all, the common ancestor is unlikely to have possessed a physique that was equally suited to either quadrupedal or bipedal gait. Pre-adapted, yes, but not ready-made. The descendants opting for bipedalism underwent a number of profound changes in the structure of the skeleton and muscle function, while their cousins on the ape line remained comfortably on all fours.

The basic adaptations were concerned with taking all the weight of the body on the hind limbs and acquiring the ability to balance on a single leg as each stride is taken. The head shifted so that it was balanced on the top of the backbone, and no longer held in position by powerful neck muscles (as in the apes); the backbone developed curves in the neck and lower back, giving it an undulating structure and the function of a spring; the pelvis became broader, the arms shortened, the legs lengthened and the thighs angled inward from the hip to keep the knees under the weight of the body (rather than to the side of it, as in the apes); the feet lost their capacity to grasp and became stiff propulsive levers. All of these skeletal adaptations were accompanied by equally extensive muscular adaptations.

Textbooks and the media have created an iconic image of the ape that stood up: a dark hairy hominid standing in the shade of the forest edge, gazing out across the bare sun-burned savanna. Dubbed 'The East Side Story' in one of its most elegant presentations,[5] this scenario holds that the massive upheavals which led to the formation of the Great Rift Valley also created a 'biological barrier' between east and west. The sinking of the valley produced an upthrust of mountains to the west, disturbing atmospheric circulation and leaving regions west of the valley humid and forested, while the eastern regions were transformed into hot and dry savanna. The common ancestors of apes and humans were separated by the changing conditions, the story goes, and each of the two populations developed a lifestyle suited to the particular environment in which they found themselves. The western descendants were said to have pursued their adaptation to life in a humid, arboreal milieu: these were the Panidae (ancestor of the chimpanzee), while their cousins in the east developed a repertoire that was better adapted to life in an open savanna environment: these were the Hominidae (the human ancestor).

A nice story, but conclusively repudiated in 1994 by the discovery of fossil chimpanzees in the Rift Valley,[6] where conditions supposedly were not suitable for them, and by the analysis of fossil soils from the Tugen Hills.

Where soils are preserved in fossil beds, carbon isotope analysis offers a means of ascertaining which of two broad groups of vegetation had grown there: forest and cool wooded grassland, or tropical savanna, temperate grassland, and semi-desert. Samples were taken from across more than 800 square kilometres of the Tugen Hills, at ninety-five locations dating from 15.5 million years ago to the present day. The results showed a remarkably heterogeneous mix of vegetation throughout, with neither of the two types predominant at any time.[7]

There was no abrupt replacement of forest by savanna, as the East Side Story required. The mosaic of grassland, woodland, and patches of forest which exists there today had characterized the region for at least 15.5 million years. 'Interpretations of the origin of hominids in East Africa during the Late Miocene should be considered within the context of a heterogeneous mosaic of environments rather than an abrupt replacement of rainforests by grassland and woodland biomes,' the researchers urged. In short: if hominids adopted the bipedal gait in East Africa, they did so in an ecologically diverse setting.

Uplift associated with the formation of the Rift Valley may well have led to the establishment of broader and denser forests to the west, but it did not create challenging savanna environments to the east. In any case, the human ancestors did not have to adapt to the savanna environment; they could have retreated to the west with the forest. The Rift Valley did not form overnight—there was plenty of time. Indeed, the bipedal gait could have evolved in the forest—not out on the savanna. In any event, competition would have been the most likely provocation, not climate, nor the environment in any direct sense. Competition for resources ultimately forced a split as populations increased. Groups dispersed. Some tended to congregate along watercourses and around the Rift Valley lakes where they could exploit a variety of resources: forest, woodland, grassland, and lakes; fish, fruit, roots, seeds, and animals…All speculation, of course, with no explanation of how the transition to bipedalism came about. Do the fossils help?

Eugene Dubois was certain that the Java Man he found in 1891 had walked erect (no surprise, since his evidence was, in fact, a modern human femur), hence the name *Pithecanthropus erectus,* but believed the putative ancestor had retained the grasping feet of an ape—as is shown in his full-size reconstruction of the specimen that resides in the basement of Leiden's Natural History Museum. Similarly, in 1925 Raymond Dart deduced from the evidence of the Taung skull that *Australopithecus* was capable of erect posture and bipedal gait; and in the 1930s and 1940s Robert Broom found fossils which, he claimed, fully confirmed Dart's deduction. Peking Man and his relations from Java were eventually named *Homo erectus.* In 1960 Louis Leakey claimed that *Zinjanthropus* possibly held his head 'even more erect than in man's carriage today',[8] and in 1964 the *Homo habilis* foot bones from Olduvai Gorge were said to possess 'most of the specializations associated with the plantigrade propulsive feet of modern man'.[9]

But while these assertions reflected a common belief that the early human ancestors had been able to stand erect and move about on two legs, it was not unqualified. A curious reluctance to believe in the *perfection* of their early bipedal gait was evident. For many years the misinterpretation of Neanderthal Man's arthritis, for example, contributed to the idea that although the early ancestors may have walked upright, they could do so only in a shambling bow-legged fashion. This view was reinforced by the pronouncements of Boule and Elliot Smith, and without evidence to contradict them, such notions became points of faith among their students and followers.

Even the skeletal remains found by Robert Broom brought no complete change of attitude. The trouble with Broom's fossils was that although their overall appearance indicated an upright stance and bipedal gait, the detail was uncertain, lost in the peculiarities and the distortions of the fragmented fossils. And where the evidence was uncertain, even scientists were inclined to believe that the mode of locomotion was not entirely human. In reviewing the evidence of the South African fossils the anatomist Wilfred Le Gros Clark, for instance, concluded that erect bipedalism in the australopithecines 'had not been developed to the perfection shown in *Homo sapiens*'.[10]

The *Homo habilis* leg and foot bones were much more complete than the evidence Broom had offered, but even they were said to be less than adequate to propel their owner in a fully modern human manner. The structure of the *habilis* foot fell somewhere between that of humans and gorilla in its weight-bearing capabilities, the preliminary report said, and certain peculiarities of the ankle bone in particular suggested that 'the unique striding gait of *Homo sapiens* had not yet been achieved'.[11] The size and shape of one highly pertinent component of the Olduvai foot—its ankle bone—was compared with 131 other human, ape, and fossil ankle bones in an exhaustive study which took the measurements of seven angles and indexes of functional significance, combined them in a computer and analysed the results. This study was a notable example of the then popular canonical analysis, a multivariate statistical technique exploiting recent advances in computer technology. Its results confirmed the earlier conclusions

----

FIGURE 16.1 Eugene Dubois's full-size reconstruction of *Pithecanthropus erectus*, made in 1899. Divergent big-toes would have helped in climbing trees; a bipedal gait is not in doubt.

based solely on personal experience and contemplation of the evidence: 'whilst the Olduvai Hominid 8 foot is the foot of a biped,' the new report said, 'the striding gait of modern man had not yet been achieved'.[12]

Meanwhile, another anatomist was analysing the 'functional implications' of the *H. habilis* leg bones. The tibia and fibula (the lower leg bones) were preserved and, although the upper parts were missing, the evidence of the remainder (the 'robusticity factor' for example) indicated that the adaptation to bipedalism was well advanced at the ankle, but less so at the knee. This study also concluded that 'while the fossil form was clearly a habitually bipedal plantigrade primate, its gait may well have differed considerably from that of modern humans'.[13]

These conclusions on the bipedal status of *Homo habilis* echo views expressed by Wilfred Le Gros Clark, who believed that as the human ancestor had evolved from quadruped to biped, the adaptation would have commenced at the foot and ended at the hip,[14] so that fossils representing an intermediate stage of evolution could be expected to demonstrate an intermediate adaptation to bipedalism. And *Homo habilis*, therefore, could be expected to have stood with ankles 'somewhat flexed, suggesting a rather bent-kneed posture' as one authority surmised.[15]

But if early humans did not employ the bipedal plantigrade propulsive gait, how did they walk? The fossils themselves could not provide the answer to this question for, although measurement and comparative analysis could indicate competence in certain known functions, they could not define a completely unknown function—even where scientists may have believed the fossils were capable of performing one.

Pondering the nature of this unknown function, Sherwood Washburn suggested in 1960 that perhaps the ancestors *ran* before they were able to *walk* on two legs, and had acquired the efficient bipedal striding gait only in response to a need to cover long distances.[16] This was an idea that was pursued more than forty years later in an analysis of the difference between walking and running which invited the conclusion that the human capacity for long-distance running had indeed been a crucial factor in the evolution of the human body form.[17] The study in question shows that over very long distances a well-conditioned human runner can even outrun a horse.

In the early 1970s, Richard Leakey had envisaged that 'several methods of bipedalism' must have arisen in the course of human evolution, quite apart from the modern variety.[18] He did not define them, however, and confined them to

Australopithecus who, he believed, employed 'a locomotor pattern unique and distinctive' to themselves during the lower Pleistocene times while the true ancestors were already as fully upright and bipedal as *Homo sapiens*.[19]

But there was another, more empirical means of investigating the potential for bipedalism in ancestral primates: biomechanics, a discipline which assessed the capacity and limitations of the skeletal frame and musculature, and defined the mechanical requirements of movement and locomotion. Here the work of an American anatomist and anthropologist, Owen Lovejoy, was especially relevant.

Early in his career Lovejoy had worked on the excavation of an Amerindian (American Indian) burial site about 1,000 years old, and the study of the skeletons that were recovered there became an important component of his subsequent researches. This unique collection represented over 1,300 individuals and spanned burials during a period of between 200 and 250 years. The remains of males and females of all ages were preserved, including several foetuses, one of which was so small that it could be held in the palm of one hand. Some skeletons demonstrated unusual physical deformities, others appeared to exceed the 'normal' limits of the human form.

In all, the collection was a revealing example of the extraordinary degree to which the human skeletal frame can vary; in particular it showed very clearly that living bone is a plastic material which is often moulded to suit the demands of behaviour and anatomy. Where anatomy is normal and behaviour is not unusually demanding, the skeletal frame functions in a consistent manner, subject only to the variations of size and muscular development. But disease, broken or distorted bones may force the skeletal frame to function quite differently; and the bones may assume unusual shapes as they grow and are moulded to suit an abnormal function.

Thus, although the style and mechanics of human movement and locomotion are potentially consistent throughout the species, the detail may vary considerably. It therefore follows that morphological variations in the form of the bones are not necessarily indicative of functional variation. Nor are they necessarily indicative of taxonomic distinction. The Amerindian collection on which Lovejoy worked undoubtedly represented a population belonging to the species *Homo sapiens*, yet it included many unusual bones that probably would have been assigned to a different species, or even a different genus, if they had been discovered as individual fossils.

This apparent contradiction was at the root Lovejoy's belief that shape and form were not a sufficient basis on which to reconstruct the pattern of function. Isolated features of the components varied much more in their shape and size, he said, than the function they performed. Feet, ankles, shin bones, knees, thigh bones, hip joints, and pelvises may vary enormously, together and individually, but whether the variation actually prevented the body they supported from walking with the bipedal propulsive plantigrade gait of *Homo sapiens* was another question. And to find the answer Lovejoy and his associates sought to place the fossil evidence of the early hominids' lower limbs in their biomechanical perspective, seeking to discover not how closely they resembled the *form* of modern humans, but rather to what extent they were capable of performing the *function* of walking like them.

The answer, to summarize the published results, was that the early hominids were probably better adapted to bipedalism than we are.[20] The biomechanical pattern of their lower limb skeleton differed in one significant respect: the articular ball of the hip joint in *Australopithecus* exerted only half the pressure that was the average for the *Homo sapiens* sample. This considerable mechanical advantage resulted from the way in which body weight and the stresses of walking were distributed in the australopithecine pelvis. The distance of the hip joint from the centre of gravity was the most important feature here; in *Australopithecus* the distance was such that a smaller femoral head (the ball of the hip joint) than in *Homo* would suffice, together with a longer femoral neck (the extension at the top of the thigh bone which carries the femoral head), which in turn was a more efficient lever arm for the muscles that operated the hip joint.

Both the small femoral head and the longer femoral neck previously had been cited as evidence indicating that *Australopithecus* was not fully adapted to the upright bipedal gait. The work of Lovejoy and his team now showed that these features were integral components of a pelvic structure that was stronger and functionally more efficient than the pelvis of modern humans. But if our ancestors really were more advantageously adapted to bipedalism, how did we lose the advantage? According to Lovejoy the regression of bipedal efficiency was inevitably combined with the advance of the other most critical factor in mankind's evolution: the development of a large brain.

As the brain brought survival advantages to those who exploited its potential most fully, its enlargement over the course of successive generations was constrained only by the size of the pelvic opening, the birth canal. Clearly there would have been immediate natural selection against the combination of large-brained infant and small birth canal (both mother and child would have died during birth), and in favour of females with large birth canals through which large-brained offspring could pass into the world. For a time the progressive enlargement of the brain could have been accommodated by a progressive broadening of the hips, but there was a limit to the total pelvic breadth that could be maintained in a biped of any given stature, beyond which walking became awkward and striding efficiency was lost.[21]

So, as babies with increasingly large heads were conceived, their birth was most satisfactory—both in terms of maternal ease and species evolution—where the size of the birth canal had increased while the overall breadth of the pelvis remained unchanged. This adjustment could only be achieved by the shortening of the femoral neck, thus disturbing the structural and mechanical efficiency of the pelvis, eventually doubling the weight stress on the articular ball of the hip joint and rendering modern humans less favourably adapted to bipedalism than their ancestors.

The large brain may have become the survival tool of the species, but far from leading the way to our present status as many surmised, its development actually compromised our earlier and more fundamental evolutionary asset: the habitual upright stance and striding bipedal gait. The compromise is evident in several aspects of modern life: the greater incidence of hip joint failure in women than men demonstrates their closer proximity to the limits of pelvic structural and functional capability. By comparison with the foetal development of other mammals, the human infant is born six months earlier than it should be so that the relatively large head may pass through the birth canal. Even so, the head is severely squashed during birth, and the bones of the infant's skull overlap as it is squeezed through the pelvic opening. And of course many difficult births, especially among those achieved by Caesarean section or with the aid of forceps, are instances of the evolutionary conflict between brain size and bipedalism that natural selection would resolve more drastically in the absence of modern medical practice.

Lovejoy investigated the biomechanics of the lower limb in the early 1970s, at a time when the available fossil evidence was limited to specimens from South Africa and Olduvai Gorge. His hypothesis was essentially complete by 1973 when, in March, Richard Leakey announced the discovery at East Turkana of an almost complete fossil left leg[22] and, in October, Donald Johanson found a knee joint at Afar. The anatomical evidence of the 1.8-million-year-old East Turkana fossils and the 3-million-year-old specimen from Afar supported Lovejoy's biomechanical deductions, but did not disqualify all other interpretations. The fossils showed that hominids had walked erect 3 and 1.8 million years ago, but Richard Leakey, for instance, claimed the East Turkana specimens proved that only the ancestor of humans had 'walked erect as his normal mode of locomotion'. *Australopithecus* had walked differently, he said, its longer femoral neck implying that although the creature was capable of walking upright, it could do so only for short periods.[23]

When Mary Leakey and her son Philip found hominid fossils at Laetoli, a jolting two hour cross-country trip from her camp at Olduvai Gorge, during the 1974 Christmas holiday, she could not have known that one of them was destined to become the type specimen of a new species, *Australopithecus afarensis*, but she was certain the site merited further investigation. An expedition was arranged for 1975, and again the following year. Numerous fossils were found, including those of animals ranging in size from shrew to elephant; tortoises, and a clutch of beautifully preserved eggs matching those of the modern guinea fowl were among the finds, as well as tiny leaves identical to those that grow on trees in the acacia woodlands today. The fossil beds had been dated to between 3.59 and 3.77 million years ago—the period when the bipedal ancestors of humanity were consolidating their presence in the Rift Valley—but hominids were scarce at Laetoli: a few fragments of jaw and some isolated teeth were found in 1975, and some pieces of a juvenile skeleton in 1976. After that promising Christmas visit, it seemed that hopes of more discoveries were not to be fulfilled.

That was the state of affairs when palaeontologist Andrew Hill went for a stroll one evening with David Western, a wildlife ecologist then visiting the Laetoli sites. Their walk took them across a dry river bed in which an expanse of fine-grained volcanic tuff was exposed. Elephants had recently passed that way too, and had left a number of their cannonball-sized droppings scattered about the river bed. In equatorial Africa, a sun-dried ball of elephant dung appeals to the same instincts that snowballs awaken in northern latitudes. People fling them at one another and, unsurprisingly perhaps, wildlife ecologists tend to be more adept at this than palaeontologists. Dr Hill fell as he turned to avoid a particularly well-aimed missile from Dr Western. While on his knees, pleading for a break in hostilities, he noticed a curious spattering of tiny indentations in the surface of the grey tuff which brought to mind a picture he had once seen of raindrop prints preserved in ash at Pompeii. They were indeed raindrop prints and, having attracted his attention, they led Hill to examine the surface more closely. Amid the puzzling indentations he recognized an unmistakable series of animal tracks.[24]

People had crossed that indented tuff surface hundreds of times during the course of two seasons, but always on the way to somewhere else, with a clear picture in mind of the fossils they were looking for. By chance, an airborne ball of elephant dung introduced a fresh point of view, instantly focusing the investigators' attention on the totally different fossil information that lay at their feet—fully visible, but hidden until then by the blinkers of preconceived notion. Dr Hill's fortuitous fall redirected the thrust of the Laetoli expedition. Fossil bones were relegated to the status of secondary interest and during the final weeks of the 1976 season the identification of fossil prints became the primary endeavour.

The preservation of fossil tracks at Laetoli was due to an unusual and possibly unique combination of climatic, volcanic, and mineralogical conditions. A series of light ash eruptions from nearby Sadiman and Lemgarut volcanoes (now dormant) coincided with a series of rain showers, probably at the onset of the rainy season. The eruptions contained a significant amount of natrocarbonatite, which yielded carbonate on contact with the rain. The ash filled depressions in the landscape, and the rain transformed them into mudpans. Animals crossed the pans while they were still wet, and their tracks dried hard as cement in the sun. The next shower of ash laid a protective covering over the tracks. A succession of ash and rain showers created at least six distinct surfaces on which tracks are preserved; in total they are about fifteen centimetres thick.[25]

During the final weeks of the 1976 season, footprints of birds and mammals ranging from elephant and rhinoceros to carnivores and hares were identified. In 1977 and 1978 seven sites were found where the footprint-bearing surfaces were exposed by natural erosion and weathering. Mammal and bird prints occurred everywhere. Then, in 1978 a biochemist contributing his specialist expertise to the Laetoli investigations, Dr Paul Abell, spotted what he thought might be the impression of a hominid heel eroding from the edge of a gulley. It was a shallow indentation, such as a tennis ball would make in wet cement, exposed where the thin covering of soil and debris had eroded away from the calcrete surface. One small indentation, seen at random among the cracks and fractures of an eroding shelf, in one small section of the eighty square kilometres of deposits at Laetoli. It could so easily have been missed. The front half of the foot had already gone.

Tim White was assigned to begin excavating the area immediately surrounding the print; it was a relatively simple matter to start with, given the shallow depth of the covering soils, but complicated by the fractured nature of the surface in which the prints were set, and the entanglement of shrub and grass roots filling the cracks and depressions. About 20 centimetres behind the heel another print emerged, this time complete and clearly made by a right foot; behind that another left foot, then a right, and so on…

The Laetoli footprint trail was a once-in-a-lifetime discovery for everyone involved—and tensions developed as Tim White insisted upon a degree of caution and meticulous excavation that Mary Leakey thought was not only time-consuming and unnecessary, but also looked like an attempt to take over the operation. 'He's getting out of hand,' she said, 'and needs to be put in his place.' For his part, White let it be known that he regarded management of the excavation as decidedly less than ideal. The delicate footprint impressions were being damaged as the infill was removed, he claimed, and detailed recording of every stage was being neglected—criticisms with which other experts tended to agree.

There were frosty moments around the dinner table. Mary Leakey retired to bed early. Ultimately, though, Tim White had no choice but to acknowledge his subservient role. He stood back, as it were, observing without comment, and the danger of further confrontation was shortly averted by the discovery of a second trail, of larger prints, running next to the first. Not just one, but two trails. The team uncovered 23.5 metres of them during the 1978 season, and returned the following year to extend the excavation into an area where the covering was deeper and the footprints better preserved. The total length of the excavations amounted to 41 metres, exposing 27.5 metres of the footprint trail. Sixty-nine individual prints were uncovered; some were incomplete or eroded, leaving only indeterminate depressions to mark where the footprints had been; thirty-five were close to perfect—3.6 million years old, but little different to the footprints we might have left on a wet sandy beach five minutes ago.

Sadiman and Lemgarut have been dormant for millennia, but the Laetoli landscape is otherwise not very different today from that which its inhabitants knew

FIGURE 16.2 Track in an aerial view of the Laetoli exposures (top) leads to the site of the footprint trail. Fossilized eggs and acacia leaves date from 3.6 million years ago.

3.6 million years ago. The highland foothills are covered with dense acacia thorn-bush, and the upper slopes are swathed in grasses that turn from green to golden as the dry season takes hold. Westward, the plain extends to a distant horizon, the broad undulating expanse broken here and there by huge steep-sided outcrops of granite and gneiss that rise like islands from the plains (indeed, in geological terms they are known as *inselbergs*, island mountains). In shallow valleys, strands of woodland mark the watercourses along which the seasonal rains drain away to Olduvai Gorge, about forty kilometres from Laetoli. Elephants come down from the highlands; giraffes cross the plain, their legs blurred in the shimmering heat haze so that they appear to float rather than walk; lions lie concealed in the dun-coloured grass; herds of zebra and antelope mingle nervously; flocks of guinea fowl scatter noisily. Laetoli preserves an image of the Earth in a pristine state.

The footprint trails that were excavated, measured, and recorded during the summers of 1978 and 1979 ran parallel and about twenty-five centimetres apart, heading south, away from the volcanoes. The even depth of each print indicated that the pace had been unhurried. Noting that the prints and stride of one trail were larger than the others, Mary Leakey succumbed to the awe of the discovery, abandoned the rigour of science for a moment and wondered aloud if the prints could have been made by a family—a man and a woman and a child. The wom-an's prints were deeper than might be expected for their size, she pointed out, particularly those of the left foot, suggesting that the woman had been carrying an uneven load—perhaps a baby on her hip. At one point in the trail she appeared to have stopped, and paused, as though something had caught her attention and she had turned to glance back over her shoulder—'You can just picture it,' said Mary. Indeed, the sight of footprints left by an ancestor so long ago combines the commonplace and the miraculous in an image that words struggle to match.

The Laetoli footprints were entirely human. Unlike the form of the ape footprint, they showed a well-developed arch to the foot and no divergence of the big toe. The size of the feet and stride suggested the larger individual stood about 140 cen-timetres tall, and the smaller about 120 centimetres. They were slight figures in the ancient landscape, but there could be no doubt that the Laetoli hominids had already acquired the habitual, upright, bipedal, free-striding gait 3.6 million years ago. Sur-prisingly though, they seemed not to have acquired the talent for making stone tools, which many supposed would have been an immediate consequence of bipedalism freeing the hands to develop manipulative skills. Although hominids were bipedal at

Laetoli 3.6 million years ago not a single artefact or introduced stone of any kind was found anywhere among the deposits. The earliest known tools are about 2.6 million years old (see p. 304). Our ancestors, it seems, were walking erect with their hands free for more than a million years before they used them to make stone tools.

'Now who needs fossil bones to substantiate bipedalism?' Mary Leakey asked as the number and perfection of the Laetoli footprints became apparent. 'They're superfluous. Absolutely superfluous.'

'Well, I don't know…' Tim White equivocated in the interest of good relations, but knew full well that early hominid fossil foot bones could provide important information on the origin of human bipedality—unaware at the time, of course, that fossil foot bones discovered and analysed under his direction would be key elements of palaeoanthropology's next major breakthrough, a quarter-century later.

Meanwhile, though, the evidence of function provided by the Laetoli trail was so obvious, so unequivocal, that its sheer wonder suffused palaeoanthropology with a rare glow of fraternal agreement—it was a discovery of which the entire science could be proud. Who could argue with the Laetoli monograph's conclusion that 'in all discernible morphological features, the feet of the individuals that made the [Laetoli] trails are indistinguishable from those of modern humans'?[26] And since the hominid fossils from Laetoli had been grouped with those from Ethiopia as a new species, *Australopithecus afarensis*, was it not most likely that Lucy's foot would have fitted the Laetoli prints as easily as Cinderella's had slid into the glass slipper?[27] Thus Lucy became the hominid who had walked across the Laetoli mudpan. But if there was little or nothing more to be said about the Laetoli footprints (since they demonstrated function so clearly), there was a great deal more to be said about the fossils, despite Mary Leakey's contention, simply because their evidence of form was so random, fractured, and open to diverse interpretation. Once again, doubts and disagreements arose.

None of Lucy's foot bones had been preserved, but those from other individuals in the collection were sufficiently different from the human condition, it transpired, for some researchers to declare that *A. afarensis* could not have made the trail at Laetoli after all. The toes of *A. afarensis* were too long and curved to make footprints as modern as those at Laetoli, anthropologist Russell Tuttle (and co-authors) argued. Another species of *Australopithecus* or an anonymous genus of the Hominidae, with remarkably humanoid feet, must have been responsible, they said.[28] In other words: 'Lucy was one of the step-sisters, not Cinderella.'[29] Wrong, said another party of researchers who made a reconstruction of a female A. *afarensis* foot which they compared directly with the Laetoli tracks. Their conclusion? 'A. *afarensis* represents the best candidate for the maker of the Laetoli hominid trails.'[30]

Meanwhile, questions were being raised concerning the mode of bipedalism in A. *afarensis*. Was it wholly bipedal, or did it retain a capacity to climb trees with ease? Long arms relative to leg length, curved finger bones, shoulder blades that seemed designed to facilitate swinging through the trees all lent weight to the argument that no matter how human-like the prints at Laetoli were, A. *afarensis* was an adept tree-climber too. In a valiant (and engaging) attempt to define the parameters of the arboreal/bipedal debate,[31] anatomist Jack Stern listed the skeletal traits that distinguished A. *afarensis* from modern humans according to which of them represented an arboreal component of behaviour, and which was related to a novel form of bipedalism. Out of thirty-six discernible traits, the score was seventeen for bipedalism, fifteen for arborealism, and four tied.

Does this help to clarify the argument? Not a great deal, one feels, on reading (in the same paper) of the minute detail from which some differences of interpretation had emerged. Johanson and co-workers, for instance, reported that Lucy's first rib had a distinct double facet on its head, separated by a central ridge, whereas another author, palaeoanthropologist James C. Ohman, said the rib in question had only one facet.[32] When experts differ so fundamentally on a single tiny point, the quality of the evidence they are discussing (and the value of their conclusions) must surely be in doubt.

Then *Orrorin tugenensis* was discovered (see p. 358), dating from six million years ago and entirely different from everything else, Brigitte Senut, Martin Pickford, and their colleagues declared. *Orrorin* most definitely was not an australopithecine, they said, but most certainly was the oldest then known ancestor on the human line. Fortuitously, the collection of fossils constituting their Oldest Man, included three pieces of thighbone. Computed tomography (CT) scans of these fossils convinced Senut and her colleagues that *Orrorin's* gait had been more humanlike than that of the australopithecines who were living at Laetoli and in

FIGURE 16.3 The footprints preserved in a calcrete surface at Laetoli, Tanzania, showed that hominids had walked upright for at least 3.6 million years. The trail on the right is that of an extinct genus of horse: *Hipparion*.

Ethiopia some three million years later.[33] Their conclusion was based primarily on the fact that the bone appeared to be more dense on the bottom of the femoral neck than on the top. This and associated weight-bearing features were said to show that the hips were stabilized in a manner that matched those of modern humans. If this was true, then *Orrorin* had pushed the origin and perfection of the human bipedal gait back millions of years, dismissed the australopithecines as candidates for human ancestry, and effectively demanded that the story of human evolution—as currently understood—should be totally revised.

Predictably, the evidence was unpicked, the interpretations scrutinized, and the conclusions disputed—vehemently. After a presentation in the opulent wood-panelled *Grande Salle* of the French Academy of Sciences in 2004, where Georges Cuvier and other luminaries of science had presented their findings, Brigitte Senut was accused of adopting 'une position créationniste' in her claims that the human bipedal gait had been perfected so long ago. By way of counter-attack she implicitly accused Tim White of withholding evidence of the 4.5-million-year-old *Ardipithecus ramidus* remains, which though found between 1994 and 1996 remained unpublished. Senut was alluding to hints that *A. ramidus* offered important new insights on the origin of bipedalism which White had yet to disclose. 'Let's just say *ramidus* had a type of locomotion unlike anything living today,' he had told a journalist in 1997. 'If you want to find something that walked like it did, you might try the bar in *Star Wars*.'[34]

Pending a more authoritative assessment of the *A. ramidus* evidence for bipedalism, palaeoanthropologist Brian Richmond undertook a comparative study of the *Orrorin tugenensis* evidence.[35] Eight critical diagnostic features of the fossils were measured for comparison with those of about 300 thighbones from fossil hominids, apes, and modern humans (including small-bodied adult individuals from African Pygmy and Andaman Island populations). The results of a series of multivariate analyses showed that *Orrorin* was most closely related to the australopithecines. 'Frankly, I was surprised to see how similar it was to australopithecines, since it was twice as old,' Richmond said. He found no indications of any differences between the bipedal gait of *Orrorin* and that of the australopithecines, which suggests that this form of bipedalism must have evolved very early in the hominid line and appears to have persisted as a successful locomotor strategy for as long as 4 million years. He concluded: 'Additional lower limb fossils from the late Miocene and early Pliocene will be needed to test this hypothesis.'

CHAPTER SEVENTEEN

Ardipithecus ramidus
(1994 & 2009)

B RIGITTE SENUT'S outburst in the French Academy of Sciences in 2004, and Brian Richmond's plea for lower limb bone fossils to test his 2008 hypothesis are examples of the frustration—not to say exasperation—expressed by some in the palaeoanthropological community as they awaited authoritative descriptions of the *Ardipithecus ramidus* fossils. The 1994 and 1995 *Nature* announcements had been enough for the importance of the new hominid to be recognized (see p. 392). The fossils were around 4.4 million years old which meant they would fit comfortably in the gap between *A. afarensis* at 3.6 million years ago and the common ancestor of apes and hominids at 5-6 million years (as predicted by the molecular clock). Thus they could represent an intermediate stage in hominid evolution (an observation which inspired even *Nature* to refer to *Ardipithecus ramidus* as a potential 'Missing Link'). It was confidently expected that full descriptions of the material would clarify its status. While they waited, scientists speculated and gossiped and the years sped by.

The speculation was principally generated by the fact that the *Ar. ramidus* collection was known to include a partial skeleton. This had been announced at a press conference in early 1995, and several scientific conferences had been told that work on it was under way.[1]

The point was that a partial skeleton from 4.4 million years ago was likely to offer new and revelatory information on the origins of human bipedality, but so long as the details remained unpublished even the most erudite speculation would remain just that (and White's joke that clues to the *Ar. ramidus* style of locomotion might be found at the bar in *Star Wars* was more provocative than conciliatory).

To be fair, there was good reason for the work taking so long—both in the collection itself and in Tim White's own experience. The fossils were in very poor condition (crushed and brittle, 'like road-kill', he said), requiring the most meticulous preparation and reconstruction—which took time. On a personal level, White was a painstaking and demanding director of the work being conducted on the fossils, not one to be rushed, and well aware of the numerous instances in which premature, or ill-considered, publication has blighted the history of palaeoanthropological science. In particular, he had observed Louis Leakey's espousal of spurious evidence for the early human colonization of America at first hand, and also had been directly involved with the refutation of Richard Leakey's claims for the Oldest Man status of the 1470 fossil skull (see pp. 336 and 354)—two episodes which warned against putting any consideration before that of scientific prudence.

But even the more prudent announcement of *Australopithecus afarensis*, with which he had been involved, had not gone entirely according to plan. So, this time, with *Ardipithecus ramidus*, Dr Timothy D. White, Professor of Integrative Biology at the University of California at Berkeley, was determined to get it right. No matter how long it took. Nothing would be left to chance. Every aspect would be explored.

The ensuing announcement was a blockbuster—no other word will suffice. The key item was a special issue of *Science*,[2] wherein forty-seven scientists from ten countries contributed to eleven research articles (with online links to additional reports and extensive supplementary data) giving details and analyses of the general anatomy, skull, teeth, pelvis, limbs, feet, and hands of *Ardipithecus*, as well as reconstructions of the geology and biology of the region in which the species had lived, 4.4 million years ago. 'We've been able to put together a fantastic, high-resolution snapshot of a period that was a blank', said Tim White.

The announcements described fossils from at least 36 individuals, but the undisputed centrepiece was the partial skeleton of an adult female. 'Ardi', as the team nicknamed her, stood about 120 centimetres tall and weighed about 50 kilograms. She was thus about as big as a chimpanzee and had a brain size to match.

An astutely managed publicity campaign ensured that news of Ardi would reach the huge global non-specialist audience for whom *Science* was not customary reading. Each research article was preceded by a single-page summary written for a general audience. The day before publication, simultaneous press conferences were held in Washington DC and Addis Ababa, under the auspices of the American Association for the Advancement of Science (which publishes *Science*). Pre-recorded television interviews and discussions with Tim White and the principal researchers were made available to all media outlets; *Science* gave non-subscribers online access to the full papers and background video coverage (free of charge); there was an 'exclusive report' documentary on the Discovery Channel; an invitation to discuss *Ardipithecus ramidus* with key *Science* writers on Facebook; pod casts and blogs…

The artist Jay Matternes had played a key role in the restoration of the skeleton and his drawings of how Ardi may have looked in life were a central element of the publicity package. Within days she had appeared in newspapers and on television screens around the world (she was even the subject of a waggish pop song: '*Ardipithecus ramidus*, she's related to all of us…').[3]

Never, in all the history of palaeoanthropology, had work on a collection of fossils been so prominently published and so extensively publicized. Was the hype justified? In short—yes. If the interpretations White and his team have drawn from fossil evidence are correct, *Ardipithecus ramidus* is the most important palaeoanthropological discovery for thirty years and one of the most important ever made. In the first instance, the discovery presents a lot of new and unexpected evidence, revealing 'a vast intermediate stage in our evolution that nobody knew about,' said anatomist C. Owen Lovejoy of Kent State University, Ohio, who worked on the skeletal material, 'it changes everything'. Secondly, the *Ardipithecus* fossils refute what had become a fundamental assumption of palaeoanthropological inquiry: namely that humans had evolved from an ancestor that closely resembled the modern chimpanzee. The roots of this assumption can be traced to Thomas Huxley's hope (published in 1863)[4] that 'the fossilised bones of an Ape more anthropoid, or a Man more pithecoid, than any yet known [might be found] by some unborn palaeontologist', and to Charles Darwin's conclusion (in *The Descent of Man*, 1871) that Africa was humanity's most probable birthplace.

Darwin warned against speculating on the connection between humans and an extinct ape-like creature in the absence of fossil evidence, but his words and those of Huxley and their contemporaries effectively established the concept of a 'Missing Link', and inspired the search for it. Africa's chimpanzees were an obvious candidate for the looks, life, and behaviour of such a creature, and so the idea that our forebears passed through a stage in which they looked like proto-chimpanzees became entrenched. Subsequently, genetic research showing that living humans and chimpanzees are very closely related has strengthened the apparent validity of the model. Chimpanzee fossils would have tested it, but virtually none are known and so the model has not been challenged by hard evidence.

As previous chapters have shown, the fossil evidence of human evolution was also slow to accumulate, especially in respect of fossils that added something new to what was already known, and which therefore could qualify as major characters in the story of human evolution. There was Neanderthal Man, at the very beginning; *Homo erectus*, who introduced an Asian twist; Piltdown Man, who told a cautionary tale; the Taung child (*Australopithecus africanus*), who took the story to Africa; *Zinjanthropus* and *Homo habilis*, who pushed the beginnings back to nearly 2 million years ago; then Lucy, the Laetoli footprints, and *A. afarensis* showing that hominids had walked upright, as we do, 3.6 million ago—while their brain was still no bigger than a chimpanzee's.

Now the *Ardipithecus ramidus* evidence indicated that despite the genetic similarities, and although we shared a common ancestor, chimpanzees are not as relevant to the story of human evolution as had been supposed. The proposition here is that chimps and humans evolved from the common ancestor along very different trajectories; chimps have specialized greatly since the separation and are therefore a poor model for the last common ancestor, and for understanding human innovations such as our ability to walk.[5]

Thus, *Ardipithecus* is not a 'missing link', nor is it the 'Ape more anthropoid, or Man more pithecoid' that Thomas Huxley had hoped for. It represents, White and his co-authors say, 'a basal hominid adaptive plateau preceding the emergence of *Australopithecus* and its successor, *Homo*.'[6] Ardi is quite different from anything known (or even imagined) hitherto, with some surprising features...all in all, a most peculiar primate.[7]

FIGURE 17.1 A stereolithographic 3D printout of the *Ardipithecus ramidus* skull, with the issue of *Science* and papers on the discovery.

'Dr. White has kept this skeleton in his closet for the last fifteen years or so,' a commentator told the *New York Times*[8], 'but I think it has been worth the wait.'

The fossil remains of *Ardipithecus ramidus* came from a discrete band, or geological unit, of sedimentary deposits that winds through a western portion of the Afar Triangle—barely eighty kilometres from Hadar, where Lucy was found and Gona, known for the world's oldest stone tools (2.6 million years). The unit, which geologists have named the Lower Aramis Member, is exposed along the tributaries of the Awash River and at other points where the scant seasonal rains erode the slopes. Varying between three and six metres thick, it is sandwiched between two continuous deposits of volcanic material, both of which are dated to 4.4 million years ago, plus or minus overlapping margins of error. Thus the sediments and the fossils they contain must have been deposited during a relatively short period of time—possibly in as little as 100 years, and probably no more than 10,000 years.

The distinctive characteristics of the unit, and the volcanic deposits above and below, have enabled geologists to trace its course across a 9 km arc which therefore represents a thin transect through the landscape as it was for a brief period, 4.4 million years ago, when *Ardipithecus ramidus* lived there. Today, the landscape is one of the most inhospitable on earth—searingly hot, with an occasional squat acacia thorn tree offering only an illusion of shade; a dreary semi-desert, sparsely populated by the Afar people whose goats, sheep, and cattle somehow find enough browse to keep themselves (and their owners) alive. There are brigands too. On one occasion, tribesmen living near the *Ar. ramidus* site threatened to kill Tim White and co-director of the joint American–Ethiopian expeditions, Berhane Asfaw. Which is why the expeditions are always accompanied by Afar policemen armed with AK-47s. Apart from aggressive tribesmen, the expeditions have also had to deal with poisonous snakes, scorpions, malarial mosquitoes, lions, hyenas, flash floods, dust tornadoes, and contaminated food and water. 'Nothing in the field comes easy', White told a visiting reporter.[9]

To ensure that the biological setting of the 4.4-million-year-old landscape Ardi had inhabited could be reconstructed as fully and accurately as possible, 100 per cent collection 'crawls' were conducted at the hominid-bearing sites along the 9 km fortuitous transect. 'Literally, we crawled over every square inch', Tim White explained, 'on hands and knees, collecting every piece of bone, every piece of wood, every seed, every snail, every scrap…'. Wherever any piece of a hominid was found, the area over which other parts of the specimen might have been distributed was cleared of loose stones and rubble, then swept with a broom. The surface was then marked out and excavated very meticulously, at a rate of about 20 mm per day vertically.[10] The location of fossils was recorded, and the excavated sediment was taken away to be sieved and sifted for anything that might have been missed—and then sieved and sifted again, through a smaller mesh, so that every single piece was recovered, no matter how small.

The result of this process was that between 1994 and 2000 a total of more than 150,000 plant and animal fossils was collected from the hominid-bearing exposures.[11] At the date of the *Science* announcement (October 2009), just 110 hominid specimens had been catalogued.[12] Ninety per cent of the faunal assemblage consisted of bone splinters and tooth fragments that could not be identified below the family level, but the remaining 10 per cent included more than 6,000 identifiable mammal specimens, representing animals that ranged in size from shrews to antelopes and elephants, as well as many birds and small mammals which are highly sensitive to environmental conditions and thus particularly helpful in reconstructing the environment. Parrots and peafowl were the most numerous birds; owls, doves, swifts, and sparrows were common, while open-country birds were exceedingly rare—a distribution of species which is consistent with a mostly woodland habitat. Similarly, woodland- or forest-dwelling monkeys, mice, shrews, and such creatures were predominant among the mammals.

The woodland nature of the environment in Ardi's time was confirmed by the numerous pieces of fossil wood, seeds, and phytoliths (hard silica parts from plants) that the team recovered. These showed that fig, hackberry (*Celtis* sp.), and palm trees had been present, while an abundance of fossil insect larvae, snails, and millipedes in the assemblage indicated the presence of a damp environment— not of the tropical rainforest variety, but as is found today where groundwater supports grassy woodland with up to about 65 per cent tree cover.[13]

By collecting and classifying those thousands of vertebrate, invertebrate, and plant fossils, as well as identifying the isotopic composition of soil samples and teeth, an evocative picture of more bountiful times has been teased from the harsh and seemingly barren landscape of the Middle Awash. Ardi and her kind had inhabited a grassy woodland with patches of denser forest and freshwater springs. Shrews, hares, porcupines, and small carnivores scuttled in the shrubby undergrowth. Colobus monkeys chattered in the trees, while baboons, giraffes, kudus, hyenas roamed below. Ardi probably fed both in the trees and on the ground but, although more omnivorous than chimpanzees (who eat a lot of fruit), seems to have consumed only small amounts of open-environment resources. She died on a flat floodplain, where her corpse largely escaped the attention of scavenging carnivores and her bones were trampled into the mud by other animals. Millions of years later, erosion brought her badly crushed bones back to the surface.

At the place where Ardi's skeleton was found, an elongated cairn of heavy black cobbles has been erected as a monument to that ancient ancestor, in the style of an Afar grave.

The Middle Awash expeditions had been scouring the exposures for almost a decade before they had even a glimpse of the story that lay hidden where the cairn marking Ardi's last resting place now stands. Then, on 17 December 1992, a glint from among the pebbles caught the eye of Gen Suwa, one of Tim White's former graduate students. It was the polished surface of a tooth root, and immediately recognizable as a hominid molar.

Gen Suwa had found the tooth a few kilometres from where Ardi lay, but his discovery set in motion a programme of investigation that would eventually lead to her discovery. For the rest of that season, and again the following year, the area was subjected to total collection crawls. And while the accumulation of animal and plant fossils was beginning to reveal evidence of a wooded environment, by the end of December 1993, the expeditions had found some significant hominid fossils too—seventeen in all, including a number of isolated teeth, arm bones, and part of the lower jaw of a child with molar teeth still in place. Tim White himself found part of the base of a skull.

The particularities of the collection suggested something entirely new, not simply very old at 4.4 million years. There were similarities with Lucy's species, *Australopithecus afarensis*, such as small diamond-shaped upper canines (quite different from the apes' large dagger-like canines); but also significant differences, which, for White and his colleagues, were enough to merit the creation of a new species. In September 1994 a paper assigning them to *Australopithecus ramidus* was published in *Nature*, under a heading which claimed that the new species represented the 'long-sought potential root species for the Hominidae'. This was challenged on the grounds that leg bones and a pelvis were needed to prove that an ancestral hominid walked upright. In response, White joked that he would be delighted with more parts and, as though placing an order, specifically requested a thigh and a skull. Weeks later, in November 1994, the team delivered—and not just the skull and leg bones that White had 'ordered', but also a pelvis, ankle, hand and foot bones, and a lower jaw. By January 1995, it was clear the team had uncovered the rarest of rare finds, a partial skeleton, more than 1 million years older than Lucy. It took three seasons to uncover and extract the skeleton, but within months of its initial discovery the team had learned enough to revise the *Australopithecus ramidus* attribution. A corrigendum published in *Nature* in May 1995 raised the specimen from specific to generic distinction, and so *Ardipithecus ramidus* (from the Afar words for 'root' and 'ground'), came into being.

The skeleton was the find of a lifetime, but the team's excitement was tempered by its terrible condition. It had been trampled and the fragments scattered within an ever-enlarging excavation. Only about ten pieces were found on the surface; most were in situ and recovered during years of digging; the skull was crushed to 4 centimetres in height. The teeth, hand and foot bones were mostly undistorted, but all the larger limb bones were crushed to a variable degree and so soft they would crumble when touched. To prevent desiccation and further disintegration, the encasing sediment was dampened as the fossils were gently exposed with dental picks, porcupine quills, and slivers of bamboo. Several coats of consolidant were applied before the block containing each specimen was dug out and covered in plaster and aluminium foil jackets for transport to the National Museum of Ethiopia, where the delicate task of separating the fossils from the matrix could be best accomplished.

Over the next several years, White himself spent many months in the museum laboratory. Acetone was applied with brushes and hypodermic needles to resoften and remove small patches of consolidant-hardened encasing matrix. With the aid of binocular microscopes, 'microsurgery' was performed at the interface between softened matrix and bone, proceeding millimetre by sub millimetre, rehardening each cleaned surface with consolidant. The freed specimens were still fragile and soft, but radiographic access was excellent. To preserve the original fossils in their discovery state, most restoration and correction for distortion was accomplished with plaster replicas or micro-computed tomography digital data.[14]

Although the skull had been so badly crushed, crucial detail was preserved on many significant parts. In a previous era, anatomists probably would have attempted to reconstruct the skull manually, with glue and plaster. In this instance, the delicate pieces were flown to Japan, where Gen Suwa was now professor at the Museum of the University of Tokyo and developing techniques that would enable him to make a digital reconstruction of the skull. In December 2003, the original fossils were scanned with high-resolution micro-computed tomography (CT). More than 5,000 slices were made, from which Suwa segmented the representations of the better-preserved parts into 64 separate polygon shells.[15] On screen, Suwa positioned and aligned the individual images to create a reconstruction of the skull which was then 'printed' on a 3-D stereolithic printer. But it was no easy task. Refining the procedures took years. Suwa estimates that he spent a total of 1,000 hours assembling the digital reconstruction; it was March 2009 before he was satisfied that his latest attempt—the tenth—was an accurate representation of the *Ar. ramidus* cranium.

Suwa and palaeoanthropologist Berhane Asfaw then compared the reconstructed skull with those of fossil and living primates in museums around the world. They noted that the base of Ardi's cranium was short from front to back, indicating that her head balanced atop the spine, as with upright walkers, rather than to the front of the spine, as with the quadrupedal apes. Her face was more vertical than a chimpanzee's and her muzzle less protuberant. Her teeth, like those of all later hominids, lacked the chimpanzee's dagger-like sharpened upper canines. Realizing that this combination of traits matched those of an even older skull, the 6-million to 7-million-year-old *Sahelanthropus tchadensis* from Chad (see p. 365), the team concluded that both represent an early stage of hominid evolution, distinct from both chimpanzees and *Australopithecus*.

Meanwhile, anatomist Owen Lovejoy was collaborating with Gen Suwa to make models of the pelvic bones based on the original fossils and a suite of CT scans such as had been made of the cranium fragments. Lovejoy made 14 versions before he was satisfied that he had an accurate representation of the *Ardipithecus* pelvis. This helped him analyse the form and function of the specimen itself, a process which had begun when the fossil came out of the ground. Observations were based on the fossil, not the reconstruction. The reconstruction, in effect, illuminated features in the fossils which led Lovejoy to conclude that *Ardipithecus ramidus* 'unveils how our skeleton became progressively modified for bipedality' from one that was originally more suited to life in the trees—a heritage that has left us rather ungainly.

FIGURE 17.2 Successive views to show location of the *Ardipithecus* skeleton excavation; yellow flags mark where each piece of the skeleton was found dispersed, in plan (overhead) and profile (side) views; insets show excavation of mandible, tibia shaft and hipbone (top).

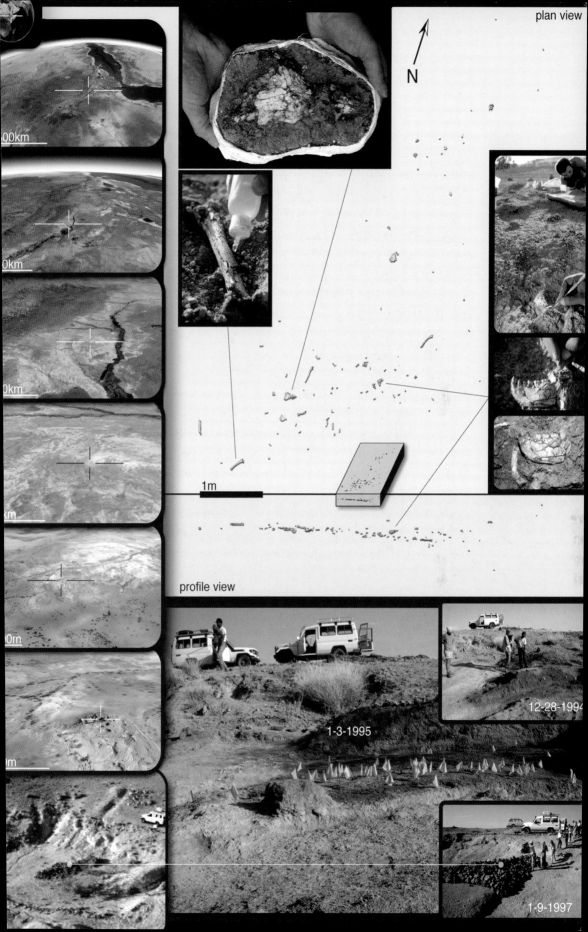

plan view

N

1m

profile view

12-28-1994

1-3-1995

1-9-1997

Our legs are massive because they continue to house almost all the muscles required for climbing, Lovejoy points out. Our hamstrings, the large muscles on the back of our thighs, must slow down the swinging limb with each step. Furthermore, when each limb leaves the ground to be swung forward, it and the pelvis are unsupported and would slump towards the ground were it not for muscles acting on the other side of the body. Chimpanzees and other primates cannot prevent such slumping when walking upright because they cannot reposition these muscles effectively. Their spine is too inflexible, and their ilia—the large pelvic bones to which the gluteals attach—are positioned and shaped differently. Modifying a chimp or gorilla pelvis to enable upright walking would require extensive structural changes, Lovejoy reports, but in *Ardipithecus* there has been enough modification to produce a mosaic pelvis that was useful for both climbing and upright walking.[16]

The ilia of Ardi's pelvis were shorter and broader than in the apes, so that she could balance on one leg at a time while walking. Lovejoy also inferred that her spine was long and curved like a human's rather than short and stiff like a chimpanzee's— changes which suggested that *Ardipithecus ramidus* had been bipedal for a very long time. He concluded that '*Ar. ramidus* thus now provides evidence on the long-sought locomotor transition from arboreal life to habitual terrestrial bipedality.'[17] But of course, walking requires that feet—as well as pelvis—are adapted to the task.

Given the importance of bipedalism, the special adaptations to the feet which enable us to walk and run obviously are crucial elements in the story of human evolution. The key feature of the modern human foot is its capacity to dissipate the considerable kinetic force which is generated when the foot strikes the ground, and then to become a rigid lever that propels the body forward for the next stride.[18] How this came about has been a point of debate for a long time, with most authorities concluding that the human foot must have evolved from one similar to that of modern African apes, but hard evidence as to how this might have happened has been lacking. There were no fossils indicating any kind of intermediate state. As we have seen, *Homo erectus* was fully bipedal, and even Lucy and her kind walked as well as we do—3.6 million years ago.

Comprehensive evidence of an ancestral hominid walking upright through the Middle Awash landscape 4.4 million years ago would be definitive. A fossil foot would be most definitive of all, but foot bones are rarely found, and the chances of finding most of a single foot even more remote. Even the 100 per cent collection crawl strategy was unlikely to produce that. But events proved otherwise—forty bones from Ardi's feet and ankles were found. 'This team seems to suck fossils out of the ground', Lovejoy told a reporter as he unveiled a cast of a tiny pea-sized sesamoid bone for effect. 'Their obsessiveness gives you—this!'[19]

Ardi's foot bones were relatively well-preserved and included sufficient elements for Lovejoy to reconstruct Ardi's foot. It was primitive, with an opposable (or divergent) big toe that could be used to grasp branches. But the bases of the four other toes were aligned so that they reinforced the forefoot into a more rigid lever as she pushed off. Because it had substantially modified four toes for upright walking, even while retaining the grasping big toe, the *Ardipithecus* foot was an odd mosaic that worked both for upright walking and climbing in trees. Thus, Ardi was a 'facultative' biped, still living in both worlds—upright on the ground (though not walking as well as Lucy) and still spending a lot of time in the trees. But she did not hang from branches like African apes, or climb vertically, says Lovejoy. Instead, she was a slow and careful climber, moving on flat hands and feet on top of branches in the mid-canopy, a form of locomotion known as palmigrady.

An important clue to the diagnosis, it transpires, was the tiny sesamoid bone mentioned above. This bone is critical for understanding the evolution of the foot, Lovejoy and his co-authors explain in a summary of the findings.[20] Technically known as the os peroneum, it facilitates the action of the muscle which controls the big toe. It is present in Old World monkeys and gibbons, but not in our more recent ape relatives. Monkeys are very accomplished at leaping between trees. To do so effectively, they must keep their feet rigid as they take off to leap across gaps in the canopy (otherwise, much of the torque from their foot muscles would be dissipated within the foot rather than transferred to the tree). The os peroneum helps them to do this.

The African apes are too large to do much leaping. They have therefore lost the features that maintain a rigid foot and have instead modified theirs for more effective grasping—almost to the point of making it difficult to distinguish their feet from their hands. Extant apes lack the os peroneum, and are able to grasp without stiffening the more flexible joints in the midfoot. The result is that they can both grasp and mould their feet around an object at the same time with considerable force. Conversely, though, their feet have become less effective as levers, making them far less useful for walking about on the ground.

The foot of *Ar. ramidus* shows that none of these ape-like changes were present in the last common ancestor of African apes and humans, Lovejoy claims. That ancestor, which many had thought to be chimpanzee-like, must have had a more monkey-like foot, he says. Not only did it have an os peroneum, it must also have had all the other characteristics associated with that critical pea-sized bone. These were retained in the hominid line, but abandoned by chimpanzees and gorillas. Our feet evolved in one direction, it seems, while those of the African apes were evolving in quite another.

And the hands? Here again, *Ardipithecus ramidus* confounds expectations—not only in that almost all of Ardi's hands were found in the excavation, but also in what those fossils have revealed.

The ability to pick up things, inspect and handle them is a defining characteristic of all primates, and has probably been a central selective force in the evolution of intelligence. As might be expected of creatures that shared a common ancestor, primate hands are all fundamentally similar, but the hands of the African apes are specialized in a number of ways that makes them dramatically different from ours. Apes must support their large body mass as they climb to feed and nest, especially in the middle and upper parts of the canopy. Their hands must therefore withstand very high forces, and this is facilitated by elongated palms and fingers. But because their thumb has not been elongated in the same way, touching thumb-to-palm and thumb-to-finger is very awkward for apes. Our palms are much shorter and our wrists more flexible; which allows us to grasp isolated objects with great dexterity and force (a 'power grip') and partly explains why humans are much more adept at making and using tools.

Furthermore, the high loads that apes bear as they move about have required them to stiffen the joints between their fingers and palms. This and other forelimb characteristics have led them to adopt an unusual form of four-legged movement, in which they support themselves on their knuckles rather than on their palms. Only African apes exhibit this 'knuckle-walking'. Other primates, such as monkeys, support themselves on their palms when moving about on the ground.

When apes are knuckle-walking, their long arms angle their bodies upwards, with some 60 per cent of their bodyweight borne by the legs. If the last common ancestor walked in similar fashion, as many authorities have surmised, this posture could have 'pre-adapted' the human line to evolve our fully upright stance

FIGURE 17.3 Owen Lovejoy (right) and Bruce Latimer discuss the *Ardipithecus* pelvis in the palaeoanthropology laboratory of the National Museum of Ethiopia, Addis Ababa.

and two-legged gait. Thus it has been proposed that bipedal hominids such as Lucy and her kin evolved from a knuckle-walking ancestor that was already partly terrestrial[21]. Here again, proposal and debate were not restrained by much in the way of fossil evidence. Even Lucy, the most complete early skeleton yet found, even that remarkable specimen had only two hand bones—far short of the number needed to interpret the structure and evolution of the hand.

The *Ardipithecus* skeleton changes that. Not only is it more than 1 million years older than Lucy, its hands are virtually complete and intact. And they show that, contrary to speculative expectation, the hands of the 4.4-million-year-old hominid were profoundly different from those of African apes. The *Ardipithecus* hand lacks the adaptations that dissipate the high-impact loads that apes experience when knuckle-walking, and has virtually none of the specializations that protect ape hands from injury as they climb and feed in trees. The *Ardipithecus* wrist joints were not as stiff, and the joints between the palms and fingers were much more flexible. Moreover, a large joint in the middle of the wrist was even more flexible than our own, enabling *Ardipithecus* to bend its hand backwards at the wrist, so that nearly all its bodyweight was supported on its palms as it moved along tree branches, and the body could lean well forward of a supporting arm before it was necessary to let go of the branch.

Ardipithecus neither resembled nor behaved like the extant African apes, and the fact that their hands, arms, and feet lacked the specialized features found in the African apes implies that the course of human evolution did not take our ancestors through any adaptive stages that relied on the suspensionary, vertical climbing, and knuckle-walking strategies that characterize modern African ape anatomy and behaviour. Hence, the locomotor strategies of the earliest hominids were less ape-like and quite different from those of any living form. This not only disqualifies the proto-chimpanzee view of human evolution once again, it also implies that chimps should be seen as adaptive cul-de-sacs rather than analogues for a stage in human emergence. Hominids and the African apes have both evolved extensively since we shared a common ancestor, and while our ancestors followed their path, the great apes became 'isolated, uniquely specialized relict species', says Lovejoy, 'surviving today only by their occupation of forest refugia.'[22]

At the end of one *Science* paper, White and his co-authors describe *Ardipithecus ramidus* as 'peculiar primates' and indeed, an artist's impressions of Ardi's skeleton and of how she would have looked in life do suggest that Tim White's reference to the denizens of the Star Wars bar was not far off the mark. A small-brained shambling biped, with arms so long she could touch her knees while standing erect at the bar (take a moment to try and do the same), who could hold a glass in her foot and walk on her hands...

'Like nothing we have seen before, or could even imagine,' is an oft-repeated description of *Ardipithecus ramidus*. But is the evidence good enough to support the far-reaching conclusions that the Middle Awash research team have drawn from it?

The findings were published in a peer-reviewed journal, which means they were approved by independent specialists, but non-specialists might still be troubled by the strength of conviction with which the conclusions and interpretations are expressed—especially given the forcefulness with which Tim White has criticized the interpretations of excessively damaged evidence in the past.[23] The non-specialist also might wonder about the difference between Gen Suwa's 9th reconstruction of the skull and the 10th, for instance; or that between Owen Lovejoy's 13th reconstruction of the pelvis and the 14th. They checked every version against the original fossil and no major conclusion was based on anything but the preserved fossil bone but, with such a severely damaged specimen and when working towards the creation of something never seen before, how could they be certain that the final version was correct, and not a fulfilment of preconceptions imposed by their anatomical knowledge and years of experience?

Of course, non-specialists must shrug off such doubts and bow to the greater knowledge of the expert. But specialists have been sceptical too. Several have challenged the team's argument that Ardi reveals the basic body plan of the common ancestor of humans and chimpanzees. Some question whether the crushed pelvis really shows the anatomical details needed to demonstrate bipedality. The pelvis is 'suggestive' of bipedality but not conclusive, says one. The skeleton does not unequivocally signal hominid status, says another, while a third believes the head is consistent with *Ardipithecus* being a hominid, 'but the rest of the body is much more questionable'.[24]

Palaeoanthropologist David Pilbeam of Harvard University summarizes the overall criticism: 'because the description and interpretation of the finds are entwined, my first reaction is to be sceptical about some of the conclusions'.

The boundary between description and interpretation is often blurred in palaeoanthropology, but the editors at Science had to be convinced that the evidence and claims were valid, so while the summaries are mostly interpretation intended for the broader audience, there is plenty of data and description in the research articles they preface. There is also a qualifying admission of palaeoanthropology's greatest need, which has not changed since the days of Huxley and Darwin: more evidence, please. By implication, the team's conclusion to their paper on the forelimbs of Ardipithecus ramidus, entitled 'Careful Climbing in the Miocene', applies to the entire work: 'Further fossil remains from the Late Miocene, including those before and after the African ape-hominid phyletic divergences, will test this hypothesis derived from our analysis of Ar. ramidus.'[25]

And so the search continues, no longer so preoccupied with Missing Links or the Oldest Man, but always confronting issues of method, exactitude, validity (and personality) as palaeoanthropologists strive to make sense of the tantalizing fossils they unearth and cherish as evidence of our evolutionary story. The pattern was set in 1863, when Thomas Huxley published Man's Place in Nature, with its anatomical description of the Engis and Neanderthal fossils establishing some ground rules for the practice of palaeoanthropology. For the first 100 years the discipline was more of a debating society than a science, with its participants more numerous than the objects on which their interest was focused, but since the 1950s more fossils and a steadily more rigorous approach have both elevated the status of palaeoanthropology and broadened its appeal.

The picture was very clear to begin with, when half a dozen or so fossils were set along a continuum with plenty of space between them for erudite speculation. Some practitioners even managed to find (or manufacture, in the case of Piltdown) specimens that filled the gaps with Missing Links, but those days are gone. The accumulating abundance of evidence (genetic as well as fossil) shows that our ancestors who lived in Africa all those millions of years ago were not alone. They were one of several (or perhaps many) primates whose evolutionary trajectories were similar to ours, and who lived at the same time. Untangling the

FIGURE 17.4 Composite photograph of the Ardipithecus ramidus skeleton shows the approximate placement of the elements recovered.

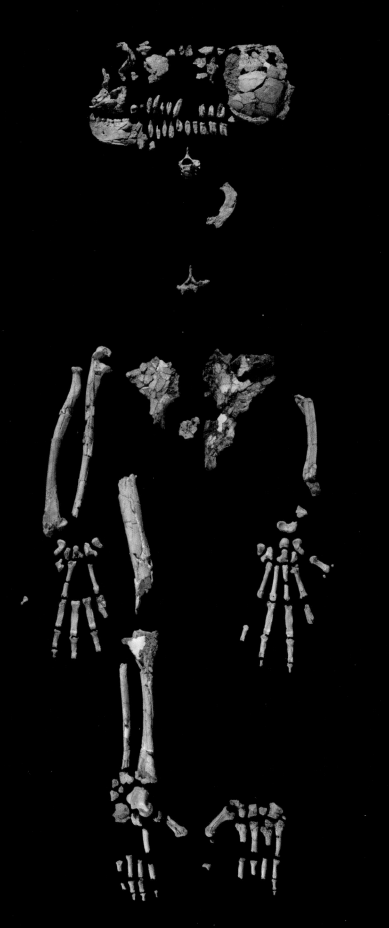

fossil evidence to reveal our single line of descent is a daunting task but, paradoxically, the confusing (not to say frustrating and occasionally exasperating) detail in which the science often appears to indulge also brings a refreshing clarity to the broader picture: where not so long ago the cognoscenti could still argue as to whether the brain, the hands, or the feet were the adaptation to which we owe our existence, hard evidence now shows that the feet led the way.

It is a humbling thought. The large and amazing brain, by which we set such store, did not begin to dominate our behavioural repertoire until several million years after our ancestors had begun walking upright. Even stone tools, once thought to have been a critical factor in the initial stages of human evolution and in use soon after bipedalism had freed the hands to develop manipulative skills, even they did not become evident until long after the advent of bipedalism. No, for the greater part of our evolutionary history the human ancestors had only the dubious advantages of a habitual bipedal gait to set them apart from other creatures as they coped with the vagaries of nature. For millions of years, through time and space, the combination of zoological inheritance and environmental circumstance was enough to ensure the survival of those small, lightly built animals. The most deeply set element of our evolutionary inheritance stems from that natural world, from the moment when those ancestors stood and walked upright. They were the pioneers of a trend that would eventually see humanity colonize the globe, create civilizations, leave footprints on the moon, and wonder about our origins...

NOTES

CHAPTER 1

1. Ussher, James, 1650/2003. *The Annals of the World*, Revised and updated by Larry and Marion Pierce, Master Books, Green Forest, Ark.

2. Fuller, John G. C. M. 2001. 'Before the hills in order stood: the beginning of the geology of time in England', pp. 15–23 in Lewis, C. L. E., and Knell, S. J. (eds.) 2001, *The Age of the Earth: From 4004 BC to AD 2002*, Geological Society, London, Special Publications, 190.

3. Hales, W. 1809. *A New Analysis of Chronology and Geography*, 3 vols., London. Cited and illustrated in Fuller, John G. C. M. 2001. 'Before the hills in order stood: the beginning of the geology of time in England' pp. 15–23 in Lewis, C. L. E., and Knell, S. J. (eds.) 2001, *The Age of the Earth: From 4004 BC to AD 2002*, Geological Society, London, Special Publications, 190, p. 20.

4. Fuller, John G. C. M. 2005. 'A date to remember: 4004 BC', *Earth Sciences History*, 24(1), 5–14. Cited in Wyse Jackson, Patrick, 2006, *The Chronologer's Quest: Episodes in the Search for the Age of the Earth*, Cambridge University Press, p. 30.

5. Fuller, John G. C. M. 2001. 'Before the hills in order stood: the beginning of the geology of time in England', pp. 15–23 in Lewis, C. L. E., and Knell, S. J. (eds.) 2001, *The Age of the Earth: From 4004 BC to AD 2002*, Geological Society, London, Special Publications, 190, p.23.

6. Leakey Richard E., and Lewin, Roger, 1977. *Origins*, Macdonald and Jane's, London, pp. 21–2.

7. Rappaport, Rhoda, 1997. *When Geologists were Historians, 1665–1750*, Cornell University Press, Ithaca and London, chapter 1.

8. Barnes, Sherman B. 1934. 'The Scientific Journal, 1665–1730', *Scientific Monthly* 38: 257–60. Cited in Rappaport, Rhoda, 1997, *When Geologists were Historians, 1665–1750*, Cornell University Press, Ithaca and London.

9. Stated without reference in Gould, Stephen Jay, 1987. *Time's Arrow Time's Cycle—Myth and Metaphor in the Discovery of Geological Time*, Harvard University Press, Cambridge, Mass., and London, p. 1.

10. These paragraphs on Descartes and his work follow the outline in Wyse Jackson, Patrick, 2006. *The Chronologer's Quest: Episodes in the Search for the Age of the Earth*, Cambridge University Press, pp. 34–6.

11. Pepys, Samuel, 1926. *Private Correspondence and Miscellaneous Papers*, edited by J. R. Tanner, 2 vols., London, vol. 1, p. 23.

12. Gould, Stephen Jay, 1987. *Time's Arrow Time's Cycle—Myth and Metaphor in the Discovery of Geological Time*, Harvard University Press, Cambridge, Mass., and London, pp. 23–4.

13. Rappaport, Rhoda, 1997. *When Geologists were Historians, 1665–1750*, Cornell University Press, Ithaca and London, p. 142.

14. Gould, Stephen Jay, 1987. *Time's Arrow Time's Cycle – Myth and Metaphor in the Discovery of Geological Time*, Harvard University Press, Cambridge, Mass., and London, pp. 38–41.

15. See Wyse Jackson, Patrick, 2006. *The Chronologer's Quest: Episodes in the Search for the Age of the Earth*, Cambridge University Press, p. 42.

16. Roger, Jacques, 1997. *Buffon: A Life in Natural History*, Cornell University Press, Ithaca, p. 356.

17. Rudwick, Martin J. S. 2005. *Bursting the Limits of Time: The Reconstruction of Geohistory in the Age of Revolution*, University of Chicago Press, Chicago and London, p. 129.

18. Quoted in Eiseley, Loren, 1961. *Darwin's Century: Evolution and the Men who Discovered it*, Anchor Books edition, New York, p. 41.

19. Rudwick, Martin J. S. 2001. 'Jean-André de Luc and nature's chronology', pp. 51–60 in Lewis, C. L. E., and Knell, S. J. (eds.) 2001, *The Age of the Earth: From 4004 BC to AD 2002*, Geological Society, London, Special Publications, 190.

20. Jones, Jean, 1985. 'Hutton's agricultural research and his life as a farmer'. *Annals of Science* 42: 537–601. Cited in Rudwick, Martin J. S. 2005: 161.

21. Quoted in: Wyse Jackson, Patrick, 2006. *The Chronologer's Quest: Episodes in the Search for the Age of the Earth*, Cambridge University Press, p. 88.

22. Geikie, A. 1905. *The Founders of Geology*, Macmillan, New York, pp. 314–15, quoted in Gould, Stephen Jay, 1987. *Time's Arrow Time's Cycle—Myth and Metaphor in the Discovery of Geological Time*, Harvard University Press, Cambridge, Mass., and London, p. 67.

23. A discussion of the revisionist view, with references, is given in Gould, Stephen Jay, 1987. *Time's Arrow Time's Cycle—Myth and Metaphor in the Discovery of Geological Time*, Harvard University Press, Cambridge, Mass., and London, chapter 3.

24. Ashworth, William B., Jr. 1984. *Theories of the Earth, 1644–1830: The History of a Genre*, Kansas City, Missouri (Linda Hall Library). Cited in Rudwick, Martin J. S. 2005. *Bursting the Limits of Time. The Reconstruction of Geohistory in the Age of Revolution*, University of Chicago Press, Chicago and London, p. 134.

25. Rudwick, Martin J. S. 1996. *Cuvier and Brongniart, William Smith and the Reconstruction of Geohistory*, Earth Sciences History 15, Tacoma, Wash., pp. 25–36, in Rudwick, Martin J. S. 2004. *The New Science of Geology: Studies in the Earth Sciences in the Age of Revolution*, Variorum Collected Studies Series CS789, Ashgate Variorum, Hampshire, England, p. VII: 7.

26. Paraphrased from Gould, Stephen Jay, 1987: 152.

27. Torrens, Hugh S. 2001. 'Timeless order: William Smith (1769–1839) and the search for raw materials 1800–1820', pp. 61–83 in Lewis, C. L. E., and Knell, S. J. (eds.) 2001, *The Age of the Earth: From 4004 BC to AD 2002*, Geological Society, London, Special Publications, 190, p. 61.

28. Eyles, Joan M. 1969. 'William Smith: Some Aspects of his Life and Work', pp. 142–58 in Schneer, Cecil J. (ed.) 1969, *Toward a History of Geology*, MIT Press, Cambridge, Mass., and London, p. 149.

29. These and other details are from: Torrens, Hugh S. 2001.

30. Baker, T. H. 1911. *Records of the Seasons, Prices of Agricultural Produce and Phenomena Observed in the British Isles*, Simpkin Marshall, London, pp. 234–5, in Torrens, Hugh S. 2001.

31. Rudwick, Martin J. S. 1996, VII: 9.

32. Rudwick, Martin J. S. 1996. VII: 10.

33. Wyse Jackson, Patrick, 2006. *The Chronologer's Quest: Episodes in the Search for the Age of the Earth*, Cambridge University Press, p. 128.

34. Eyles, Joan M. 1969. 'William Smith: Some Aspects of his Life and Work', pp. 142–58 in Schneer, Cecil J. (ed.) 1969, *Toward a History of Geology*, MIT Press, Cambridge Mass., and London, p. 157.

35. Rudwick, Martin J. S. 1996. VII: 12.

CHAPTER 2

1. The title of a splendid book: Rudwick, Martin J. S. 1972. *The Meaning of Fossils: Episodes in the History of Palaeontology*, MacDonald, London.

2. See: Duffin, Christopher J. 2005. 'The western lapidary tradition in early geological literature: medical and magical minerals', *Geology Today* 21(2): 58–63.

3. Quoted at: http://www.ucmp.berkeley.edu/history/agricola.html

4. See: Duffin, Christopher J. 2005.

5. See: Rudwick, Martin J. S. 1972: 7.

6. These paragraphs draw principally on Adams, Frank Dawson, 1954. *The Birth and Development of the Geological Sciences*, Dover, New York, pp. 176–83, and Rudwick, Martin J. S. 1972, chapter 1.

7. Cited with references in Rudwick, Martin J. S. 1972: 39–40.

8. This paragraph summarizes Rappaport, Rhoda, 1997. *When Geologists Were Historians, 1665–1750*, Cornell University Press, Ithaca and London, p. 106, and Rudwick, Martin J. S. 1972: 84.

9. Scheuchzer, Johann, 1708. Quoted in Jahn, Melvin J. 1969. 'Some notes on Dr. Scheuchzer...', pp. 193–213 in Schneer, Cecil J. (ed.) 1969, *Toward a History of Geology*, MIT Press, Cambridge, Mass., and London, p. 199.

10. See Rappaport, Rhoda, 1997 in chapter 1.

11. Quoted in Raven, Charles E. 1942. *John Ray Naturalist: His Life and Works*, Cambridge University Press, Cambridge, p. 83.

12. Quoted in Raven, Charles E. 1942: 421.

13. Rappaport, Rhoda, 1997: 109.

14. Quoted in Raven, Charles E., 1942: 437.

15. Rudwick, Martin J. S. 1972: 53–4, 66–8; see also Gian, Battista Vai, and Caldwell, W. Glen E. (eds.) 2006. *The Origins of Geology in Italy*, Geological Society of America, p. 71.

16. Rappaport, Rhoda, 1997: 112–13.

17. Leibnitz, Gottfried, 1696 at: http://www.leibnitz-translations.com/tentzel. htm AI 13, p. 204, 3/13 August 1696.

18. Quotations etc. from http://www.oum.ox.ac.uk/learning/pdfs/plot.pdf on: Plot, Robert, 1677. *The Natural History of Oxfordshire, being an essay towards the Natural History of England*, Oxford, pp. 131–9.

19. Charig, Alan, 1983. *A New Look at the Dinosaurs*, British Museum (Natural History), London, pp. 107, 44–51.

20. The following paragraphs on the Ohio fossils follow Rudwick, Martin J. S., 2005. *Bursting the Limits of Time. The Reconstruction of Geohistory in the Age of Revolution*, University of Chicago Press, Chicago and London, pp. 266–9.

21. See Hedeen, Stanley, and Faragher, John Mack, 2008. *Big Bone Lick*, University of Kentucky Press.

22. Quoted in Rudwick, Martin J. S. 2005: 269.

23. Quoted in Rudwick, Martin J. S. 2005: 270.

24. Darwin, Erasmus, 1794. *Zoonomia*, London, vol. 1, p. 572.

25. Quoted in Leakey, Richard E., and Lewin, Roger, 1977. *Origins*, Macdonald and Jane's, London, p. 28.

26. Eiseley, Loren. 1961. *Darwin's Century*, Anchor Books, New York, p. 89.

27. Quoted in Rudwick, Martin J. S. 2005: 355.

28. Quoted in Eiseley, Loren, 1961: 85.

29. Cuvier, Georges, 1837. *Edinburgh Review* 65: 23.

30. Cuvier, Georges, 1796. *Squelette trouvé au Paraguay* (skeleton found in Paraguay), translated by Martin Rudwick, in Rudwick, Martin J. S. 1997, *Georges Cuvier, Fossil Bones, and Geological Catastrophes*, University of Chicago Press, Chicago and London, pp. 27–32.

31. This paragraph follows Rudwick, Martin J. S. 2005: 360–3, where note 20 makes it clear that Cuvier's elephant lecture was given before that on *Megatherium*.

32. Rudwick, Martin J. S. 1972: 101.

33. Rudwick, Martin J. S. 2005: 368.

34. In Rudwick, Martin J. S. 1997: 53, 222.

35. Rudwick, Martin J. S. 2005: 447.

36. Cuvier, Georges, 1815. *Essay on the Theory of the Earth*, Edinburgh, p. 109.

37. Rudwick, Martin J. S. 1997: 252.

CHAPTER 3

1. Quotations and some observations in the following paragraphs on Johann Scheuchzer and his work appear with reference to sources in Jahn, Melvin J. 1969. 'Some notes on Dr. Scheuchzer…', pp. 193–213 in Schneer, Cecil J. (ed.) 1969. *Toward a History of Geology*, MIT Press, Cambridge, Mass., and London, p. 208.

2. Southey, Thomas, 1827. *Chronological History of the West Indies*, London, p. 487.

3. Cuvier, Georges, 1831 (trans.) *Discourse on the Revolutions of the Surface of the Globe*, Carey & Lea, Philadelphia, p. 81. Also at: http://www.geology.19thcenturyscience.org/books/1831-Cuvier-Revolutions/

4. Mantell, Gideon A. 1850. 'On the remains of man…' *The Archaeological Journal*, December 1850, p. 337.

5. König, Charles, 1814. 'On a fossil human skeleton from Guadaloupe', *Philosophical Transactions of the Royal Society* 34: 107–22.

6. Blake, C. C. 1862. 'On the crania of the most ancient races of men', *Geologist* vol. 5, p. 207.

7. Quatrefages, A. de, and Hamy, E. T. 1882. *Crania ethnica: Les crânes des races humaines*, pt. 1: *Races humaines fossiles*, Paris. Schmitz, Ralf W. 2006b. 'The discovery of fossil man in the 18th and 19th century', pp. 9–16 in Schmitz, Ralf W. (ed.) 2006a, *Neanderthal 1856–2006*, Verlag Philipp von Zabern, Mainz am Rhein, p. 10.

8. Anon. 1864. 'Notes on the antiquity of man', *Anthropological Review*, London, p. 71. Schlothheim, M. de. 1820. Letter, in *The Isis*, no. 8, suppl. 6; quoted in Cuvier, Georges, 1831, pp. 81–5.

9. e.g. Wendt, Herbert, 1968. *Before the Deluge*, Gollancz, London, p.116.

10. Rudwick, Martin J. S. 1997. *Georges Cuvier, Fossil Bones, and Geological Catastrophes*, U. Chicago Press, Chicago and London, p. 233.

11. Lyell, C. 1863. *The Antiquity of Man*, London, pp. 68–9.

12. Schmerling, P. C. 1833–4. *Recherches sur les Ossements Fossiles découverts dans les Cavernes de la Province de Liége*, Liége, p. 59.

13. Quoted in Boule, Marcellin, and Vallois, Henri V. 1957. *Fossil Men*, The Dryden Press, New York, pp. 12–14.

14. Quoted in Lyell, C. 1863: 68.

15. Quoted in Boule, Marcellin, and Vallois, Henri V. 1957: 12.

16. Pengelly, W. 1869. 'The Literature of Kent's Cavern', *Trans. Devon Association* 16, pp. 189–434.

17. Lyell, C. 1863: 183.

18. Schmitz, Ralf W. (ed.) 2006a: 36, 73–4.

19. Schmitz, Ralf W. (ed.) 2006a: 37, 46.

20. Schaafhausen, H. 1858. Bonn. *On the crania of the most ancient races of man*, Muller's Archiv 1858, p. 453; translated by G. Busk 1861 with remarks and original figures taken from a cast of the Neanderthal cranium, *Natural History Review*, April 1861, pp. 155–75.

CHAPTER 4

1. Quoted in Darwin, Charles (ed. Francis Darwin) 1909. *The foundations of the Origin of Species, a sketch written in 1842*, University of Cambridge Press, p. xiii.

2. Quoted in Browne, Janet, 2006. *Darwin's Origin of Species. A Biography*, Atlantic Books, London, p. 45.

3. This and the following paragraphs draw on Browne, Janet, 2006: 58–60; Lyell, Sir Charles, 1863. *The Antiquity of Man*, John Murray, London, pp. 408–9; www.archive.org/details/journalofproceedo3linn

4. Quoted in Darwin, Francis (ed.) 1958. *The Autobiography of Charles Darwin and Selected Letters (1892)*, Dover Publications, New York, p. 201.

5. Quoted in Darwin, Francis (ed.) 1958: 209.

6. Browne, Janet, 2006: 105.

7. Chambers, Robert, 1844. *Vestiges of the Natural History of Creation*, London, p. 231.

8. Chambers, Robert, 1844: 208.

9. Chambers, Robert, 1844: 281.

10. Browne, Janet., 2006: 51, 53.

11. Darwin, Charles, 1859 (1968). *The Origin of Species*. Penguin Books, London, p. 58.

12. Leakey, Richard E., and Lewin, Roger, 1977. *Origins*, Macdonald and Jane's, London, p. 21.

13. An account which Huxley described in 1861 as 'substantially correct' is given in Darwin, Francis (ed.) 1958: 250–4.

14. Radford, Tim, 2004. 'Flawed genius of Darwin's arch rival', *Guardian*, 19 July 2004, London.

15. Owen, Richard, 1860. 'Darwin on the Origin of Species', *Edinburgh Review*, 3: 487–532.

16. Owen, The Rev. Richard, 1894. *The Life of Richard Owen by his Grandson*, John Murray, London. p. 292; see Owen, Richard, 2007. *On the Nature of Limbs*, University of Chicago Press, p. xxxix.

17. Owen, Richard, 1848. *On the Archetype and Homologies of the Vertebrate Skeleton*, London.

18. Quoted in Owen, Richard, 2007. *On the Nature of Limbs*, University of Chicago Press, p. 86.

19. Owen, Richard, 1855. 'Of the anthropoid apes and their relation to Man', *Proceedings of the Royal Institution of Great Britain 1854–1858*, 3: pp. 26–41.

20. Anon. 1862, editorial, *Medical Times and Gazette*, 28 June 1862, London.

21. Schaaffhausen, H. 1858. *On the crania of the most ancient races of man*, Muller's Archiv 1858, p. 453; translated by George Busk 1861 with remarks and original figures, taken from a cast of the Neanderthal cranium, *Natural History Review*, April 1861, 155–75; Blake, C. C. 1862. 'On the crania of the most ancient races of man', *Geologist* 5, 139–57.

22. Mayer, F. 1864. 'Ueber die fossilen Ueberreste eines menschlichen Schädels und Skeletes in einer Felsenhöhle des Düssel—oder Neanderthales', *Arch. Anst. Physiol.*, Leipzig, pp. 1–26.

23. Huxley, T. H. 1864. 'Further remarks upon the human remains from the Neanderthal', *Natural History Review*, 1: 429–46.

24. Huxley, T. H. 1863. *Man's Place in Nature*, Ann Arbor Edition 1959, Michigan, p. 181.

25. King, W. 1864. 'The reputed fossil man of the Neanderthal', *Quarterly Journal of Science*, 1: 88–97.

26. Technically, a skull is the entire head, including the lower jaw (the mandible). Very few fossil specimens are so complete, but for simplicity this text follows the common practice of calling them skulls when a significant portion is present. The Neanderthal specimen consists of only a calotte (skullcap) and is referred to as such.

27. Busk, G. 1864a. 'Report on the British Association Meeting', *Bath Chronicle*, 22 September, Bath.

28. Busk, G. 1864b. Pithecoid Priscan Man from Gibraltar, *Reader*, 23 July, London.

29. Falconer, H. 1864. Letter to G. Busk of 27 August 1864, quoted by Keith, Arthur, 1911, 'The early history of the Gibraltar cranium', *Nature*, London, 87: 313.

30. Busk, G., and Falconer, H. 1865. 'On the fossil contents of the Genista cave, Gibraltar', *Quarterly Journal of the Geological Society*, London, 21: 364–70.

31. Virchow, R. 1872. 'Untersuchung des Neanderthal-Schädels', *Zoo. Ethn. Berlin* 4: 157–65.

32. Boule, M. 1921. *Les Hommes Fossiles*, Paris; 1923, *Fossil Man*, Edinburgh.

33. Boule, M. 1911–13. 'L'Homme fossile de La Chapelle-aux-Saints', *Annales de Paléontologie* 6, 7, 8. Paris.

34. Smith, G. E. 1927. *The Evolution of Man* (2nd edition), London, p. 109.

35. Cave, A. J. E., and Straus, W. L. Jnr. 1957. 'Pathology and Posture of Neanderthal Man', *Quarterly Review of Biology* 32: 348–63.

36. Harvati, Katerina, Frost, Stephen R., and McNulty, Kieran P. 2004. 'Neanderthal taxonomy reconsidered', *Proc. Nat. Acad. Sci.*: 101 (5): 1147–52.

37. Parfitt, Simon A., *et al.* 2005. 'The earliest record of human activity in northern Europe', *Nature* 438: 1008–12.

38. Stringer, Chris, 2006. *Homo Britannicus*, Allen Lane, London.

39. Parfitt, Simon A., *et al.* 2010. 'Early Pleistocene human occupation at the edge of the boreal zone in northwest Europe', *Nature* 466: 229–33.

40. www.amnh.org/exhibitions/atapuerca/caves/first.php

41. Bermúdez, J. M., *et al.* 2004. 'The Atapuerca sites and their contributions to the Knowledge of Human Evolution in Europe'. *Evolutionary Anthropology*, 13: 25–41.

42. Bermúdez, J. M., *et al.* 1997. 'A Hominid from the Lower Pleistocene of Atapuerca, Spain: Possible Ancestor to Neanderthals and Modern Humans', *Science* 276: 1392–5.

43. Arsuaga, Jean-Luis, *et al.* 1997. *Journal of Human Evolution* 33: 109–27.

44. Aiello, Leslie C., and Wheeler, Peter, 2003. 'Neanderthal Thermoregulation and the Glacial Climate', pp. 147–66 in Van Andel, Tjeerd H., and Davies, William (eds.) *Neanderthals and Modern Humans in the European Landscape During the Last Glaciation*, McDonald Institute for Archaeological Research, Cambridge, p. 156.

45. Kittler, Ralf, Kayser, Manfred, and Stoneking, Mark, 2003. 'Molecular evolution of *Pediculus humanus* and the origin of clothing', *Current Biology* 13: 1414–17.

46. Churchill, S. E. 2006. 'Bioenergetic perspectives on Neanderthal thermoregulatory and activity budgets', pp. 113–34 in Harvati, K., and Harrison, T. (eds.) 2006, *Neanderthals Revisited: New Approaches and Perspectives*, Springer, Dordrecht.

47. Richards, Michael P., *et al.* 2000. 'Neanderthal diet at Vindija and Neanderthal predation', *Proc. Nat. Acad. Sci.* 97 (13): 7663–6.

48. Bocherens, Hervé, *et al.* 2005. 'Isotopic evidence for diet and subsistence pattern of the Saint-Césaire I Neanderthal', *Journal of Human Evolution*, 49: 71–87.

49. Hockett, Bryan, and Haws, Jonathan A. 2005. 'Nutritional ecology and the human demography of Neanderthal extinction', *Quaternary International*, 137: 21–34.

50. Thieme, Hartmut, 1997. 'Lower Palaeolithic hunting spears from Germany', *Nature* 385: 807–10.

51. Thieme, Hartmut, 2000. 'Lower Palaeolithic Hunting Weapons from Schöningen, Germany—the Oldest Spears in the World', *Acta Anthropologica Sinica* 19: 140–7.

52. This paragraph summarizes papers cited in Hockett, Bryan, and Haws, Jonathan A. 2005, pp. 29, 24.

53. Henry, Amanda G., Brooks, Alison S., and Piperno, Dolores R., 2010. 'Microfossils in calculus demonstrate consumption of plants and cooked foods in Neanderthal diets', *Proc. Nat. Acad. Sci.*, Early Edition at: www.pnas.org/cgi/doi/10.101073/pnas.1016868108

54. Richards, M. P., and Trinkaus, E. 2009. 'Isotopic evidence for the diets of European Neanderthals and early modern humans'. *Proc. Nat. Acad. Sci.* 106: 16034–9.

55. Quoted in Sample, Ian, 2010c. 'Meat and two veg: the cooked diet of Neanderthals', *Guardian*, 28 December, p. 14.

56. Ibid.

57. Lalueza-Fox, Carles, *et al.* 2011. 'Genetic evidence for patrilocal mating behavior among Neandertal groups', *Proc. Nat. Acad. Sci.* 108: 250–53.

58. Ibid.

59. Finlayson, Clive, *et al.* 2006. 'Late survival of Neanderthals at the southernmost extreme of Europe', *Nature* 443: 850–3.

60. Quoted in Hall, Stephen S. 2008. 'Last of the Neanderthals', *National Geographic*, October 2008, 214 (4): p. 58.

61. Quoted in *Guardian*, 14 September 2006, p. 9.

CHAPTER 5

1. Daniel, Glyn, 1975. *A Hundred and Fifty Years of Archaeology*. Duckworth, p. 40.

2. Ellesmere, Lord, 1849. *A Guide to Northern Antiquities*. London.

3. Lubbock, John 1865. *Prehistoric Times*. London.

4. Lartet, L. 1869. 'Une sépultre des troglodytes du Périgord', *Annales des Sciences naturelles*, 5th series, vol. 10. Lartet, L., and Chaplain-Duparc, H. 1874. 'Une sépultre des anciens troglodytes des Pyrénées', *Matériaux* 9.

5. Rivière, E. 1887. *De l'Antiquité de l'Homme dans les Alpes-Maritimes*, Paris.

6. Daniel, Glyn, 1975: 96–7.

7. Gorjanovic-Kramberger, K. 1906. *Der diluviale Mensch von Krapina in Kroatien*, Wiesbaden.

8. Schwalbe, G. 1906. *Studien zur Vorgeschichte des Menschen*, Stuttgart.

9. Boule, M., and Vallois, H. V. 1957. *Fossil Men*, New York, p. 256.

10. Boule, M., 1913, quoted in Spencer, F. 1984, 'The Neanderthals and their evolutionary significance: A brief historical survey', pp. 1–49 in Smith, F. H., and Spencer, F. (eds.) 1984. *The Origin of Modern Humans*, New York, p. 21.

11. Quoted in Spencer 1984: 25.

12. Hrdlicka, A. 1927. 'The Neanderthal phase of man', *J. Roy. Anthrop. Inst.* 57: 249–74.

13. Marston, A. 1937. 'The Swanscombe Skull', *Journal of the Royal Anthropological Institute*, London, 67; 394. Stringer, C., and Hublin, J.-J. 1999. 'A new age determination for the Swanscombe skull and its implications for human evolution', *Journal of Human Evolution*, 37: 873–7.

14. Vallois, H. V. 1949. 'The Fontéchevade fossil men', *American Journal of Physical Anthropology*, NS 7: 339–62.

15. Garrod, D. A. E., and Bate, D. M. A. 1937. *The Stone Age of Mount Carmel*, Oxford.

16. Vallois, H. V. 1954. 'Neanderthals and Praesapiens', *J. Roy. Anthrop. Ins.* London, 84: 111–30, p. 112.

17. Vallois, H. V. 1954: 128.

18. Solecki, R. S. 1975. 'Shanidar IV, a Neanderthal flower burial in northern Iraq,' *Science* 190: 880–1.

19. Gargett, R. H. 1989. 'Grave shortcomings: the evidence for Neanderthal burial,' *Current Anthropology* 32: 157–90.

20. Brace, C. L. 1964. 'The fate of the "classic" Neanderthals: a consideration of hominid catastrophism', *Current Anthropology*, vol. 5. Wolpoff, M. H. 1980. *Paleoanthropology*, New York.

21. Constable, G. 1973, *The Neanderthals*, Time-Life Books, New York, p. 28.

22. Howells, W. W. 1976. 'Explaining modern man: evolutionists versus migrationists', *Journal of Human Evolution*, 5: 477–95.

23. Léveque, F., and Vandermeersch, B. 1980. 'Les découvertes de restes humains dans un horizon Castelperronien de Saint-Césaire (Charente-Maritime)', *Bull. Soc. Préhist. Fr.*, 77: 35.

24. Stringer, C. B., Hublin, J.-J., and Vandermeersch, B. 1984. 'The origin of anatomically modern humans in Western Europe', pp. 51–136 in Smith, F. H., and Spencer, F. (eds.) 1984, *The Origin of Modern Humans*, New York.

25. Stringer, C. B., and Kruszynski, R. G. 1981. 'Allez Neanderthal', *Nature*, 289: 823–4.

26. Bräuer, G. 1984. 'The Afro-European *sapiens* hypothesis, and hominid evolution in Asia during the late Middle and Upper Pleistocene', pp. 145–66 in Andrews, P., and Franzen, J. L. (eds.) 1984, *The Early Evolution of Man, with Special Emphasis on Southeast Asia and Africa*, Courier Forschungsinstitut Senckenberg 69, p. 145.

27. Nuttall, G. H. F. 1904. *Blood Immunity and Blood Relationships*, Cambridge.

28. Sarich, V. M., and Wilson, A. C. 1967. 'Immunological time scale for hominid evolution', *Science* 158: 1200–3.

29. Simons, E. L., 1965. 'New fossil apes from Egypt and the initial differentiation of the Hominoidea', *Nature* 205: 135–9. Pilbeam, David, 1972. *The Ascent of Man*, Macmillan, New York.

30. Pilbeam, D., *et al.* 1982. 'New hominoid skull material from the Miocene of Pakistan', *Nature* 295: 232–4. Andrews, P., and Cronin, J. 1982. 'The relationships of *Sivapithecus* and *Rampithecus* and the evolution of the orang-utan', *Nature* 297: 541.

31. Wilson, A. C., *et al.* 1985. 'Mitochondrial DNA and two perspectives of evolutionary genetics', *Biological Journal of the Linnaean Society* 26: 375–400.

32. Wilson, A. C., *et al.* 1985: 379.

33. Stoneking, M., Bhatia, K., and Wilson, A. C. 1986. 'Rate of sequence divergence estimated from restriction maps of mitochondrial DNA from Papua New Guinea', *Cold Spring Harbor Symposia in Quantitative Biology* 51: 433–49.

34. Cann, R. L., Stoneking, M., and Wilson, A. C. 1987. 'Mitochondrial DNA and human evolution', *Nature* 325: 31–6.

35. Poulton, J. 1987. 'All about Eve', *New Scientist*, 14 May, pp. 51–3.

36. Wilson, A. C., *et al.* 1986. 'Mitochondrial clans and the age of our common mother', *Proceedings of the 7th International Congress of Human Genetics*, Berlin.

37. For a review of the issue see: Mirazon, Marta, and Foley, Robert, 1994. 'Multiple dispersals and modern human origins', *Evolutionary Anthropology* 3: 48–60.

38. Cavalli-Sforza, Luigi Luca, 1991. 'Genes, people and languages', *Scientific American*, November, pp. 71–8.

39. Pääbo, Svante, 1985. 'Molecular cloning of Ancient Egyptian mummy DNA', *Nature* 314: 644–5.

40. Krings, Matthias, Stone, Anne, Schmitz, Ralf W., Krainitzki, Heike, Stoneking, Mark, and Pääbo, Svante, 1997. 'Neanderthal DNA Sequences and the Origin of Modern Humans'. *Cell* 90: 19–30. Press reports: *Guardian*, 11 July 1997, p. 3; *New Scientist*, 19 July 1997, p. 5.

41. Green, R. E., *et al.* 2010. 'A draft sequence of the Neanderthal genome', *Science* 328: 710–22; DattonyRet, 2009. 'Neanderthal genome to be unveiled', *Nature* 457: 645.

42. Sample, Ian, 2010*a*. 'Most humans have DNA link to Neanderthals', *Guardian* 7 May, p. 21.

43. Quoted in Sample, Ian, 2010. 'Most humans have DNA link to Neanderthals', *Guardian* 7 May, p. 21.

44. Quoted in Dalton, Rex, 2010. 'Fossil finger points to new human species', *Nature* 464: 472–3.

45. Reich, David, *et al.* 2010. 'Genetic history of an archaic hominin group from Denisova Cave in Siberia', *Nature* 468: 1053–60.

46. Quoted in Sample, Ian, 2010*b*. 'Fossil finger points to previously unknown group of human relatives', *Guardian*, 22 December.

47. Ibid.

48. White, Tim D., *et al.* 2003. 'Pleistocene *Homo sapiens* from the Middle Awash, Ethiopia', *Nature* 423: 742–7. McDougall, I., Brown, F. H., and Fleagle, J. G. 2005. 'Stratigraphic placement and age of modern humans from Kibish, Ethiopia', *Nature* 433: 733–6.

CHAPTER 6

1. Darwin, Charles, 1871. *The Descent of Man* (2nd edition), London, p. 3.

2. Haeckel, Ernst, 1876. *The History of Creation*, 2 vols. London, vol. 2, p. 278.

3. Haeckel, 1876 (2): 33.

4. Haeckel, 1876 (1): 307.

5. Haeckel, 1876 (2): 293.

6. Haeckel, 1876 (2): 326–7.

7. Haeckel, 1876 (2): 325.

8. Haeckel, Ernst, 1906. *Last Words on Evolution*, London, p. 77.

9. Haeckel, Ernst, 1899. *The Last Link*, London, p. 77.

10. Dubois, E. 1891. 'Paleontologische onderzoekingen op Java', *Verslagen van het Mijnwezen*, Batavia, fourth quarter.

11. Dubois, E. 1891. 'Paleontologische onderzoekingen op Java', *Verslagen van het Mijnwezen*, Batavia, fourth quarter, p. 13.

12. Dubois, E. 1892. *Verslagen van het Mijnwezen*, Batavia, third quarter, p. 11.

13. Dubois, E. 1894. *Pithecanthropus erectus, eine menschenähnliche Uebergangsform aus Java*, Batavia.

14. Dubois, J. M. F. Unpublished manuscript, Trinil: 'A Biography of Professor Dr Eugene Dubois, the discoverer of *Pithecanthropus erectus*'.

15. Haeckel, Ernst, 1899. *The Last Link*, London, p. 22.

16. Keith, Arthur, 1942. *The Rationalist Annual*, London.

17. Dubois, E. 1898. 'The brain-cast of Pithecanthropus erectus', *Proceedings of the International Congress of Zoology*, Cambridge, pp. 79–96.

18. Dubois, E. 1920. 'The proto-Australian fossil man of Wadjak, Java', *Koninklijke Akademie van Wetenschappen*; proceedings 13, Amsterdam, pp. 1013–51.

19. Dubois, E. 1935. 'On the Gibbon-like appearance of Pithecanthropus erectus', *Koninklijke Akademie van Wetenschappen*; proceedings 38, Amsterdam, pp. 578–85.

20. Dubois, E. 1933. 'The shape and size of the brain in Sinanthropus and in Pithecanthropus', *Koninklijke Akademie van Wetenschappen*; proceedings 36, Amsterdam, pp. 415–23.

21. Dubois, E. 1935. 'On the gibbon-like appearance of Pithecanthropus erectus', *Koninklijke Akademie van Wetenschappen*; proceedings 38, Amsterdam, pp. 578−85.

22. Dubois, E. 1940. 'The fossil human remains discovered in Java…', *Koninklijke Akademie van Wetenschappen*; proceedings 43, Amsterdam, pp. 494−6, 842−51, 1268−75.

23. Koenigswald, G. H. R. von, and Weidenreich, F., 1939. 'The relationship between Pithecanthropus and Sinanthropus', *Nature* 144: 926−9.

24. Mayr, E. 1951. 'Taxonomic categories in fossil hominids', *Cold Spring Harbor Symposia on Quantitative Biology* 15: 108−18.

25. Dubois, E. 1940. 'The fossil human remains discovered in Java…', *Koninklijke Akademie van Wetenschappen*; proceedings 43, Amsterdam, p. 1275.

26. Keith, Arthur, 1942. *The Rationalist Annual*, London.

27. Campbell, B. 1965. 'The nomenclature of the Hominidae', *Occasional Paper of the Royal Anthropological Institute* 23.

28. Mayr, E. 1976. *Evolution and the Diversity of Life*, London, p. 530.

29. Mayr, E. 1944. 'On the concept and terminology of vertical subspecies and species', *National Research Council Bulletin*, 2, pp.11−16; Mayr, E. 1951. 'Taxonomic categories in fossil hominids', *Cold Spring Harbor Symposia on Quantitative Biology* 15: 108−18.

30. Brace, C. L. 1967. *The Stages of Human Evolution*, Englewood Cliffs, NJ: Prentice-Hall; Wolpoff, M. H. 1971. 'Competitive exclusion among Lower Pleistocene hominids: the single species hypothesis', *Man*, 6: 601−14.

31. Hennig, W. 1966. *Phylo-genetic Systematics*, Urbana.

32. Halstead, L. B. 1978. 'The cladistic revolution—can it make the grade?' *Nature* 276: 759−60; Patterson, C., *et al.* 1979. 'The salmon, the lungfish and the cow: a reply'. *Nature*, vol. 277: 175−6.

33. Wood, B. A. 1984. 'The origin of *Homo erectus*', pp. 99−111 in Andrews, P., and Franzen, J. L. (eds.) 1984, *The Early Evolution of Man, with special emphasis on Southeast Asia and Africa*, Courier Forschungsinstitut Senckenberg 69, p. 109.

34. Quoted in Walker, Alan, and Shipman, Pat, 1996. *The Wisdom of Bones*, Weidenfeld & Nicolson, London, p. 22.

35. Schoetensack, O. 1908. *Der Unterkiefer des Homo heidelbergensis aus den Sanden von Mauer bei Heidelberg*. Leipzig.

36. Quoted in Johanson, Donald, and Edgar, Blake, 1996. *From Lucy to Language*, Simon & Schuster, New York, p. 196.

37. Woodward, A. S. 1921. 'A new cave man from Rhodesia, South Africa', *Nature* 108: 371–2.

38. This summary follows: Klein, Richard G. 1999. *The Human Career* (2nd edition), University of Chicago Press, Chicago and London, pp. 316–17.

39. Wood, B. A. 2000. 'The history of the genus *Homo*'. *Human Evolution* 15: 39–49, p. 47.

40. Walker, Alan, and Shipman, Pat, 1996. *The Wisdom of Bones*, Weidenfeld & Nicolson, London, p. 118.

41. Walker, Alan, and Shipman, Pat, 1996, p. 20.

42. Simpson, Scott W., *et al.* 2008. 'A Female *Homo erectus* Pelvis from Gona, Ethiopia', *Science* 322: 1089–92.

43. Butzer, K. W., and Isaac, G. L. 1975. *After the Australopithecines*, Mouton, The Hague.

44. Rightmire, G. Philip, 1998. 'Human evolution in the Middle Pleistocene: the role of *Homo heidelbergensis*', *Evolutionary Anthropology*, vol. 6, pp. 218–27, p. 221.

45. The following paragraphs are drawn principally from: Aiello, Leslie C. 2010. 'Five Years of *Homo floresiensis*', *American Journal of Physical Anthropology*, 142: 167–179, in which references to sources will be found.

46. Hopkin, Michael. 2005. Hirst's hobbit. *Nature* 434: 702.

47. See Dawkins, Richard, 2004. 'One giant step for our sense of wonder'. *Sunday Times*, London, October 31, 2004, p.6.

48. A special edition of the Journal of Human Evolution published in 2009 covers all aspects: Morwood, M. J. & Jungers, W. L. 2009. *J Hum Evol* 57: 437–648.

49. Cited in Lahr, M. M. & Foley. R. 2004. 'Human evolution writ small'. *Nature* 431: 1044.

50. Robert Martin, quoted in the *Los Angeles Times*, 20 May 2006.

51. *See* Aiello, Leslie C. 2010. 'Five Years of *Homo floresiensis*', *American Journal of Physical Anthropology*, 142: 171.

52. Aiello, Leslie C. 2010. 'Five Years of *Homo floresiensis*', *American Journal of Physical Anthropology*, 142:167–179.

CHAPTER 7

1. Keith, A. 1950. *An Autobiography*, London, p. 122.

2. Keith, A. 1894. *Journal of Anatomy* 28: 149–335.

3. Keith, A. 1950: 170.

4. Keith, A. 1950: 317.

5. Keith, A. 1912*a*. *The Human Body*, London, p. 78.

6. Smith, G. E. 1912. 'Presidential Address, Anthropology Section', *Report of the British Association*, 1912, Dundee, pp. 575–98.

7. Woodward, A. S. 1885. 'Modern ideas of the Creation', *Macclesfield Courier and Herald*, Macclesfield, 28 March 1885.

8. Woodward, A. S. 1913. 'Missing links among extinct animals'. *Report of the British Association*, Birmingham, p. 783.

9. Mortillet, G. de, 1883. *Le Préhistorique*, Paris, pp. 301–2.

10. Quoted in Spencer, Frank, 1990*a*. *Piltdown. A Scientific forgery*, Natural History Museum Publications, Oxford University Press, London, Oxford, and New York, p. 14.

11. Harrison, E. R. 1928. *Harrison of Ightham*, London, p. 84.

12. Quoted in Spencer, Frank, 1990: 24.

13. Newton, E. T. 1895. 'On a human skull and limb bones found in the Palaeolithic terrace-gravel at Galley Hill, Kent', *Quart. J. Geol. Soc. Lond.* 51: 505–27.

14. Keith, A. 1925*a*. *The Antiquity of Man* (2nd edition), p. 258.

15. Moir, J. Reid, 1912. 'The occurrence of a human skeleton in a glacial deposit at Ipswich', *Proceedings of the Prehistory Society of East Anglia*, 1. Keith, A. 1915. *The Antiquity of Man*, London. Anon. 1912. 'The earliest known Englishman', *Illustrated London News* 140: 442, 446–7.

16. Keith, A. 1912*b*. 'Modern problems relating to the antiquity of man'. *Report of the British Association*, Dundee, p. 758.

17. Smith, G. E. 1912: 577.

18. Woodward, A. S. 1916. 'Charles Dawson—an obituary', *Geological Magazine* (6) 3: 477–9.

19. Dawson, C., and Woodward, A. S. 1913. 'On the discovery of a Palaeolithic human skull and mandible in a flint-bearing gravel overlying the Wealden (Hastings Beds) at Piltdown, Fletchling, Sussex', *Quarterly Journal of the Geological Society*, 69: 117–44.

20. Woodward, Sir Arthur Smith, 1948. *The Earliest Englishman*. Watts & Co., London, p. 11.

21. Weiner, J. S. 1955. *The Piltdown Forgery*, Oxford University Press, London, p. 120.

22. Smith, G. E. 1913*a*. 'Preliminary report on the cranial cast [Piltdown skull]', *Quarterly Journal of the Geological Society*, 69: 145–7.

23. Quoted in: Spencer, Frank, 1990*a*: 49.

24. Ibid.

25. Dawson and Woodward, 1913: 134–5.

26. Smith, G. E. 1913*a*: 147.

27. Keith, A. 1950: 324.

28. Keith, A. 1913*a*. 'The human skull etc. from Piltdown', *Quarterly Journal of the Geological Society* 69: 148.

29. Keith, A. 1913*b*. Report in *The Times*, 11 August.

30. Woodward, A. S. 1913. 'Missing links among extinct animals', *Report of the British Association*, Birmingham, p. 786.

31. Keith, A. 1913*c*. 'The Piltdown skull and brain cast', *Nature*, 92: 197.

32. Smith, G. E. 1913*b*. 'The Piltdown skull and braincast', *Nature*, 92: 267.

33. Smith, G. E. 1927. *The Evolution of Man* (2nd edition), London, p. 184.

34. Keith, A. 1913*c*. 'The Piltdown skull and brain cast', Nature, 92: 97.

35. Keith, A. 1950: 327.

36. Keith, A. 1914. 'The reconstruction of fossil human skulls', *Journal of the Royal Anthropological Institute*, London, 44: 12. Keith, A. 1915: 537–78.

37. Woodward, A. S. 1917. 'Fourth note on the Piltdown gravel, with evidence of a second skull of *Eoanthropus dawsoni*', *Quarterly Journal of the Geological Society*, 73: 1–10.

38. In Woodward, A. S. 1917.

39. Ibid.

40. Waterston, D. 1913. 'The Piltdown mandible', *Nature*, 92: 319.

41. Boule, M. 1923, *Fossil Men*, Edinburgh, p. 472.

42. Miller, G. S. 1915. 'The jaw of Piltdown Man'. *Smithsonian Miscellaneous Collections* 65: 1–31.

43. MacCurdy, G. G. 1916. 'The revision of *Eoanthropus dawsoni*'. *Science*, 43: 228–31.

44. Quoted in Spencer, F. 1990*a*: 103.

45. Smith, G. E. 1927: 73.

46. Boule, M. 1923: 472.

47. Osborn, H. F. 1927. *Man rises to Parnassus*, Princeton, NJ, p. 53.

48. Keith, A., in Woodward, A. S. 1948. *The Earliest Englishman*, Watts, London, p. xi.

49. Leakey, L. S. B. 1934. *Adam's Ancestors*, London, p. 221.

50. White, H. J. O. 1926. 'The geology of the country near Lewes, with map by F. H. Edmunds', *Memoir Geological Survey of England and Wales*, Expl. Sheet 319.

51. Marston, A. T. 1937. 'The Swanscombe skull'. *Journal of the Royal Anthropological Institute*, 67: 394.

52. Middleton, J. 1844. 'On fluorine in bones, its source, and its application in the determination of the geological age of fossil bones'. *Proceedings of the Geological Society*, 4: 431–3.

53. Carnot, A. 1893. 'Recherches sur le composition générale et le teneur en fluor des os modernes et des os fossiles de differents âges', *Ann. Min.* (9, Mem.) 3: 155–95.

54. Oakley, K. P., and Montagu, M. F. A. 1949. 'A reconsideration of the Galley Hill skeleton'. *Bulletin of the British Museum (Natural History), Geology*, 1,(2): 27–46.

55. Oakley, K. P., and Hoskins, C. R. 1950. 'New evidence on the antiquity of Piltdown Man'. *Nature*, 165: 379–82.

56. Weiner, J. S. 1955. *The Piltdown Forgery*, Oxford University Press, London, pp. 26–35.

57. Lyne, C. W. 1916. 'The significance of the radiographs of the Piltdown teeth'. *Proceedings of the Royal Society of Medicine* 9 (3 Odont. Sect.): 33–62.

58. Anon. 1953. Parliamentary report comment on Piltdown in *The Times*, 27 November.

59. Kramer, L. M. J. 1953. Letter to *The Times*, 28 November.

60. Quoted in Spencer, F. 1990a: 188.

61. Miller, G. S. 1929. 'The controversy over human "missing links"', *Smithsonian Report for 1928*, Washington, DC, pp. 413–65, p. 441.

62. Tobias, Phillip V. 1990. 'Introduction to a forgery', in Spencer, F. 1990a: xii.

63. Walsh, John Evangelist, 1998. *Unravelling Piltdown*, Random House Value Publishing gives an excellent review of the cases for and against the suspects; supplementing the more academic volumes of Frank Spencer, 1990.

64. Gardiner, Brian G. 2003. 'The Piltdown Forgery: a re-statement of the case against Hinton'. *Zoological Journal of the Linnaean Society*, 139: 315–35.

65. Gee, Henry, 1996. 'Box of bones "clinches" identity of Piltdown palaeontology hoaxer', *Nature*, 381: 261–2.

66. Quoted in Spencer, Frank. 1990b. *The Piltdown Papers 1908–1955*. Natural History Museum Publications, Oxford University Press, London, p. 243.

67. Gardiner, Brian G. 2003: 323.

CHAPTER 8

1. Dart, Raymond A. 1978. Interview with author, Johannesburg.

2. Haughton, S. H. 1920. 'On the occurrence of a species of baboon in deposits near Taungs', Abstract in *Transactions of the Royal Society of South Africa* 12, 1925: lxviii.

3. Partridge, T. C., 1973. 'Geomorphological dating of cave opening at Makapansgat, Sterkfontein, Swartkrans and Taung', *Nature* 246: 75–9. Brain, C. K. 1975. 'An introduction to the South African Australopithecine bone accumulations', *Archaeozoological Studies* (ed. A. T. Clason), Amsterdam, pp. 109–19.

4. Terry, R. 1974. *Raymond A. Dart: Taung 1924–1974*, The Museum of Man and Science, Johannesburg.

5. Young, R. B. 1925. Quoted in *The Star*, Johannesburg. News report, 4 February.

6. Dart, Raymond A. 1959. *Adventures with the Missing Link*, Hamish Hamilton, London, p. 6.

7. Dart, Raymond A. 1959: 16.

8. Dart, Raymond A. 1925. 'Australopithecus africanus: the Man-Ape of South Africa', *Nature* 115: 195–9.

9. Keith, A., Smith, G. E., Woodward, A. S., and Duckworth, W. L. H. 1925. 'The fossil anthropoid from Taungs', *Nature* 115: 234–6.

10. see: http://www.law.umkc.edu/faculty/projects/FTrials/scopes/scopes.htm

11. Dart, Raymond A. 1959: 43.

12. Dart, Raymond A. 1959: 40.

13. Clark, Wilfred Le Gros, 1967b. *Man-Apes or Ape-Men?* New York, p. 26.

14. Keith, A. 1925b. 'The Taungs skull', *Nature* 116: 11.

15. Dart, R., and Keith, A. 1925. 'On the Taungs skull, an exchange of letters', *Nature* 116: 462.

16. Dart, Raymond A. 1959: 62.

17. Abel, W., 1931. 'Kritische Untersuchungen über *Australopithecus africanus* Dart', *Morphol. Jahrb.* 65 (4): 539–640.

18. Dart, Raymond A. 1959: 56.

19. Dart, Raymond A. 1978. Interview with author, Johannesburg.

CHAPTER 9

1. Andersson, J. Gunnar, 1934. *Children of the Yellow Earth*, Kegan Paul, London, p. xx.

2. Zdansky, Otto, 1978. Personal communication, interview with author, Uppsala.

3. Andersson, 1934: 101.

4. Zdansky, Otto, 1978. Personal communication, interview with author, Uppsala.

5. Andrews, R. C. 1932. *Natural History of Central Asia. A narrative of the explorations of the Central Asiatic expeditions in Mongolia and China, 1921–1930*, vol. 1: *The New Conquest of China*, introduction.

6. Andrews, R. C. 1932: 572.

7. Andrews, R. C. 1932: 453.

8. Andrews, R. C. 1932: 208.

9. Zdansky, O. 1978.

10. Zdansky, Otto, 1923. 'Über ein Saungerknockenlager in Chou K'ou Tien', *Geological Survey of China Bulletin* 5: 83–9, Peking.

11. Zdansky, Otto, 1928. *Die Saugetiere der Quartarfauna von Chou K'ou Tien*, Palaeontologica Sinica, Series C, 5 (4), Peking.

12. Anon. 1926. News report on Peking Man, *Manchester Guardian*, 17 November.

13. Andersson, J. Gunnar, 1934: 106.

14. Black, D. 1926. 'Tertiary Man in Asia: The Chou K'ou Tien discovery', *Nature*, 118: 733–4; *Science*, 64: 586–7.

15. Zdansky, O. 1927. 'Preliminary notice on two teeth of a hominid from a cave in Chihli (China)', *Geological Survey of China Bulletin* 5: 281–4, Peking.

16. Bohlin, Birger, 1978. Personal communication, interview with author, Uppsala.

17. Black, D. 1927. *On a lower molar hominid tooth from the Chou K'ou deposit*, Palaeontologica Sinica, Ser. D, vol. 7, fascicule 1 (November) pp. 1–29. 'Further hominid remains of Lower Quaternary age from the Chou Kou Tien deposit', *Nature* 120: 954; *Science* 67: 135–6.

18. Osborn, H. F. 1922. Quoted in '*Hesperopithicus*, the first anthropoid ape found in America', *American Museum Novitiates* (1925), 37: 1–5.

19. Woodward, A. S. 1922. Letter to *The Times*, London, 22 May.

20. Osborn, H. F. 1925. *American Museum of Natural History Bulletin*, February 1925, quoted in *The Times*, London, 25 February 1928.

21. Anon. 1928. Leader comment on *Hesperopithecus* in *The Times*, 25 February, London.

22. Smith, G. E. 1929. Report in the *Manchester Guardian*, 16 September.

23. Hood, D. 1964. *Davidson Black—A Biography*, University of Toronto Press, p. 93.

24. Quoted in Hood, D. 1964: 100.

25. Boaz, Noel T., and Ciochon, Russell L. 2004. *Dragon Bone Hill. An Ice-Age Saga of Homo erectus*, Oxford University Press, New York, p. 24.

26. Pei, W. C. 1929. 'An account of the discovery of an adult *Sinanthropus* skull in the Chou K'ou Tien deposit', *Geological Survey of China Bulletin* 8 (3).

27. Koenigswald, G. H. R. von, and Weidenreich, F. 1939. 'The relationship between *Pithecanthropus* and *Sinanthropus*', *Nature* 144: 926–9.

28. Gregory, W. K. 1949. 'Franz Weidenreich, 1873–1949', *American Anthropologist* 51: 85–90.

29. Day, Michael H. 1986. *Guide to Fossil Man* (4th edition), Cassel, London, p. 371.

30. This paragraph follows Boaz and Ciochon 2004: 33–5, where references to original sources are given.

31. Weidenreich, F. 1936. *The mandibles of Sinanthropus pekinensis: a comparative study*, Palaeontologica Sinica, Ser. D, III: 1–163. Weidenreich, F. 1937. *The dentition of Sinanthropus pekinensis: a comparative odontography of the hominids*, Palaeontologica Sinica, NS. D, 1: 1–180. Weidenreich, F. 1941. *The extremity bones of Sinanthropus pekinensis*, Palaeontologica Sinica, Ser. D, 5: 1–150. Weidenreich, F. 1943. *The skull of Sinanthropus pekinensis: a comparative study on a primitive hominid skull*, Palaeontologica Sinica, Ser. D, 10: 1–291.

32. Shapiro, Harry L. 1974. *Peking Man*, George Allen & Unwin, London.

33. Shapiro, 1974.

34. Quoted in Boaz and Ciochon, 2004: 41. See also Jia, Lanpo, and Huang, Wei-wen, 1990. *The Story of Peking Man: From Archaeology to Mystery*, Oxford University Press, New York.

35. Quoted in Boaz and Ciochon, 2004: 49–50.

36. Boaz and Ciochon, 2004: 54.

37. Wu, R., and Olsen, J. W. (eds.) 1985. *Palaeoanthropology and Palaeolithic Archaeology in the People's Republic of China*, Orlando, p. 6.

38. Wu, Xinzhi, and Poirier, Frank E. 1995. *Human Evolution in China: A Metric Description of the Fossils and a Review of the Sites*, Oxford University Press, New York.

39. Woo, J. K., and Peng, R. C. 1959. 'Fossil human skull of Early Palaeoanthropic stage found at Mapa, Shaoquan, Kwantung Province', *Vert. Palasiat.* 3: 176–82.

40. Woo, J. K. 1966. 'The skull of Lantian Man', *Current Anthropology* 7: 83–6.

41. Wang, Y., *et al.* 1979. 'Discovery of Dali fossil man and its preliminary study', *Sci. Sin.* 24: 303–6. Wu, X., and Poirier, F. E. 1995. 'Dali, a skull of Archaic *Homo sapiens* from China', in Wu, Xinzhi, and Poirier, Frank E. 1995.

42. Wu, R. 1982. 'Recent advances of Chinese palaeoanthropology', *Occ. Pap.* Ser. Ii, University of Hong Kong.

43. Wu, R. K., *et al.* 1985. *Multi-disciplinary Study of the Peking Man Site at Zhoukoudian* [in Chinese], Science Press, Beijing.

44. Wu, R. 1983. 'Peking Man', *Scientific American* 248 (6): 78–86.

45. Shen, Guanjun, *et al.* 2009. 'Age of Zhoukoudian *Homo erectus*…' *Nature* 458: 198–200.

46. Zhu, R. X., *et al.* 2004. 'New evidence on the Earliest Human Presence at High Northern Latitudes in Northeast Asia', *Nature* 431: 559–62.

47. Zhu, R. X., *et al.* 2008. 'Early evidence of the genus *Homo* in East Asia', *J. Human Evolution* 55: 1075–85.

48. Ciochon, Russell L., and Arthur Bettis III, E. 2009. 'Asia *Homo erectus* converges in time', *Nature* 458: 153–4.

49. Gittings, John, 1998. 'Chinese balk at "Out of Africa" theory', *Guardian*, 3 October, London.

50. Jia, Lanpo, 1980. *Early Man in China*, Beijing, p. 3.

51. Wu, R., and Lin, S. 1985. 'Chinese Palaeoanthropology: Retrospect and Prospect', in Wu, R., and Olsen, J. W. (eds.) 1985: 1–17.

52. Jia, Lanpo, and Huang, Weiwen, 1990: 243.

53. Chu, J. Y., *et al.* 1998. 'Genetic relationship of populations in China', *Proc. Natl. Acad. Sci.*, USA, 95: 11763–8.

54. Cavalli-Sforza, L. Luca, 1998. 'The Chinese Human Genome Diversity Project', *Proc. Natl. Acad. Sci.*, USA, 95; 11501–3.

55. Gittings, John, 1998.

56. http://www.chinadaily.com.cn/opinion/2008-01/28/content_6424452.htm

CHAPTER 10

1. Quoted in Terry, R. 1974. *Raymond A. Dart: Taung 1924–1974*, Museum of Man and Science, Johannesburg.

2. Findlay, G. H. 1972. *Dr Robert Broom, F.R.S. A.A.*, Balkema, Cape Town, p. 101.

3. Findlay, G. H. 1972: 43.

4. Findlay, G. H. 1972: 50–1.

5. Broom, Robert, 1933. *The Coming of Man: Was it Accident or Design?* Witherby, London. Broom, Robert, 1950. *Finding the Missing Link*, Watts, London, pp. 91–100.

6. Broom, Robert, 1939. 'On evolution', *Star*, 18 August, Johannesburg.

7. In Findlay, G. H. 1972: 133–53.

8. Broom, Robert, 1915. 'On the organ of Jacobson and its relations in the Insectivora', *Proceedings of the Zoological Society of London*, pp. 157–62, 347–54.

9. Findlay, G. H. 1972: 57.

10. Broom, Robert, 1925*a*, quoted in Findlay, G. H. 1972: 52.

11. Dart, Raymond A. 1959. *Adventures with the Missing Link*, Watts, London, p. 37.

12. Broom, Robert, 1925*b*. 'Some notes on the Taungs skull', *Nature* 115: 569–71.

13. Broom, Robert, 1950: 39.

14. Broom, Robert, 1946. Quoted in Wells, L. H. 1966, 'The Robert Broom Memorial Lecture', *South Africa Journal of Science*, September 1967, p. 365.

15. Findlay, G. H. 1972: 54.

16. Jones, T. 1978. Personal communication, interview with author, Pretoria.

17. Wells, L. H. 1966.

18. Broom, Robert, 1936*a*. 'A new fossil anthropoid skull from South Africa', *Nature* 138: 486–8.

19. Broom, Robert, 1936*b*. 'On an ancestral link between ape and man', *Illustrated London News* 189; 476–7.

20. Broom, Robert, 1950: 50.

21. Broom, Robert, 1938a. 'More discoveries of *Australopithecus*', *Nature* 141: 828−89; 1938b. 'The Missing Link is no longer missing', *Illustrated London News* 193; 513−14.

22. Broom, Robert, 1950: 50.

23. Broom, Robert, 1942a. 'The hand of the ape-man *Paranthropus robustus*', *Nature* 149: 513−14; 1942b. 'An ankle-bone of the ape-man *Paranthropus robustus*', *Nature* 152: 689−90.

24. Broom, Robert, and Schepers, G. W. H. 1946. *The South African fossil ape-men. The Australopithecinae*, Part 1. *The occurrence and general structure of the South African ape-men*, Transvaal Museum Memoir 2.

25. Broom and Schepers 1946: 142.

26. Clark, W. E. Le Gros, 1946. *Nature* 157: 863−5.

27. Broom, Robert, 1950: 63.

28. Keith, Sir Arthur. 1948. *A New Theory of Human Evolution*, Watts & Co., London, pp. 210, 159, 234.

29. Keith, 1948: 206.

30. Keith, 1948: 229.

31. Broom, R., Robinson, J. T., and Schepers, G. W. H. 1950. *Sterkfontein ape-man, Plesianthropus*, Transvaal Museum Memoir 2, Pretoria.

32. Ashton, E. H., and Zuckerman, S. 1950. 'Some quantitative dental characteristics of fossil anthropoids', *Philosophical Transactions of the Royal Society*, B. 234: 485.

33. Quoted in Findlay, F. 1972: 86.

34. Clark, W. E. Le Gros, 1967a. 'Hominid characters of the australopithecine dentition', *Journal of the Royal Anthropological Institute*, 80: p. 37; 1967b. *Man-Apes or Ape-Men?*, New York, p. 35.

35. Yates, F., and Healy, M. J. R. 1951. 'Statistical methods in anthropology', *Nature* 168: 1116.

36. Zuckerman, S. 1966. 'Myths and methods in anatomy', *Journal of the Royal College of Surgeons of Edinburgh*, 11: 87−114.

37. Ardrey, Robert, 1961. *African Genesis*, Fontana/Collins, London, p. 324.

38. In fact, *Paranthropus* has become the preferred generic attribution for species that were previously described as 'robust' Australopithecines, i.e. *A. Robustus, A. boisei, A. aethiopicus* (described in 1985).

39. Tobias, P. V. 1978. Personal communication, interview with author, Johannesburg.

40. Dart, R. 1959: 100.

41. Dart, R. A. 1948. 'The Makapansgat proto-human *Australopithecus prometheus*', *American Journal of Physical Anthropology*, NS 7, 259–84.

42. Dart, R. A. 1953. 'The predatory transition from ape to man', *International Anthropological and Linguistic Review* 1: 201–18.

43. Dart, R. A. 1953: 204, 209.

44. Dart, R. A. 1953: 208–7.

45. For example: Lorenz, Konrad, 1966. *On Aggression*, translated by Marjorie Latzke, Methuen, London.

46. Tobias, Phillip V. 1992. Letter to the author, 13 February.

47. Washburn. S. L., and Lancaster, J. 1968. 'The evolution of hunting', pp. 293–303 in Lee, R. B., and DeVore, I. (eds.) 1968, *Man the Hunter*, Aldine Press, New York.

48. Washburn, S. L. (ed.) 1963. *Social Life of Early Man*, Chicago.

49. Isaac, G. Ll. 1978. 'The food-sharing behavior of proto-human hominids', *Scientific American*, vol. 238 (4): 90–106.

50. Teleki, G. 1981. 'The omnivorous diet and eclectic feeding habits of chimpanzees in Gombe National Park, Tanzania', pp. 303–43 in Harding R., and Teleki, G. (eds.) 1981, *Omnivorous Primates*, New York, p. 327.

51. Lee, R. B. 1968. 'What hunters do for a living, or, how to make out on scarce resources', pp. 30–48 in Lee, R. B., and DeVore, I. (eds.) 1968, *Man the Hunter*, Aldine Press, New York.

52. Brain, C. K. 1981. *The Hunters or the Hunted? An Introduction to African Cave Taphonomy*, University of Chicago Press, Chicago.

53. Berger, L. R., and Clarke, R. J. 1995. 'Eagle involvement in accumulation of the Taung child fauna', *Journal of Human Evolution*, 29; 275–99.

54. Clarke, Ronald J., and Tobias, Phillip V. 1995. 'Sterkfontein Member 2 Foot Bones of the Oldest South African Hominid', *Science* 269: 521–4.

55. Clarke, R. J. 1998. 'First ever discovery of a well-preserved skull and associated skeleton of *Australopithecus*', *South African Journal of Science* 94: 460–4.

56. Clarke, R. J. 2002. 'Newly revealed information on the Sterkfontein Member 2 *Australopithecus* skeleton', *South African Journal of Science* 98; 523–6.

57. Potts, R. 1998, quoted at: www.washingtonpost.com/wpsrv/national/daily/dec98/safrica10.htm

CHAPTER 11

1. Leakey, L. S. B. 1969*b*. Public lecture, California. Recording in possession of Leakey estate.

2. Leakey, L. S. B. 1937. *White African*, Ballantine Books, New York (1973) p. 55.

3. Leakey, L. S. B. 1937: 132–3.

4. Reck, H. 1914. Quoted in 'A Man of 150,000 years ago?' *Illustrated London News*, 4 April, p. 563.

5. Leakey, M. D. 1979*a*. Interview with author, Olduvai.

6. Leakey, L. S. B. 1937: 252.

7. Leakey, L. S. B., Hopwood, A. T., and Reck, H. 1931. 'Age of the Oldoway bone beds, Tanganyika', *Nature* 128: 724.

8. Leakey, L. S. B. 1932*a*. Article in *The Times*, London, 9 March.

9. Leakey, L. S. B. 1932*b*. Article in *The Times*, London, 19 April.

10. Keith, Arthur. 1931. *New Discoveries Relating to the Antiquity of Man*, Norton, New York, p. 158.

11. Royal Anthropological Institute, Proceedings. 1933. 'Early human remains in East Africa', *Man* 33: 68.

12. Woodward, A. S. 1933. 'Early human remains in East Africa', *Man* 33: 210.

13. Leakey, L. S. B., *et al.* 1933. 'The Oldoway human skeleton', *Nature* 131: 397–8.

14. Boswell, P. G. H. 1935. 'Human remains from Kanam and Kanjera, Kenya Colony', *Nature* 135: 371.

15. Leakey, L. S. B. 1936. 'Fossil human remains from Kanam and Kanjera, Kenya Colony', *Nature* 138 : 643.

16. Bishop, L. C., *et al.* 2006. 'Recent Research into Oldowan Hominin Activities at Kanjera South, Western Kenya', *African Archaeological Review* 23: 31–40.

17. Plummer, Thomas W., Kinyua, A. Muriithi, and Potts, Richard, 1994. 'Provenancing of Hominid and Mammalian Fossils from Kanjera, Kenya, using EDXRF', *J. of Archaeological Science* 21: 553–63.

18. Leakey, L. S. B. 1951. *Olduvai Gorge: A Report on the Evolution of the Hand-Axe Culture in Beds I–IV*, Cambridge University Press, Cambridge.

19. Cole, S. 1975. *Leakey's Luck*, Collins, London, pp. 117–25.

20. Leakey, M. D. 1971. *Olduvai Gorge*, vol. 3: *Excavations in Beds I and II*, Cambridge University Press, Cambridge, p. 199.

21. Leakey, L. S. B. 1965. *Olduvai Gorge, 1951–1961*. vol. 1, Cambridge University Press, Cambridge, p. 76.

22. Leakey, L. S. B. 1954. 'The giant animals of prehistoric Tanganyika, and the hunting grounds of Chellean man…', *Illustrated London News* 244: 1047–51.

23. Leakey, L. S. B. 1958b. 'Recent discoveries at Olduvai Gorge, Tanganyika', *Nature* 181: 1099–1103.

24. Leakey, L. S. B. 1958a. 'A giant child among the giant animals of Olduvai?', *Illustrated London News* 232: 1104–5.

25. Robinson, J. T. 1959. 'An alternative interpretation of the supposed giant deciduous hominid tooth from Olduvai', *Nature* 185: 407.

26. Leakey, L. S. B. 1959b. Reply to Robinson, J. T. 1959, *Nature* 185: 408.

27. Leakey, M. D. 1979b. *Olduvai Gorge: My Search for Early Man*, Collins, London, p. 75. Leakey, M. D. 1984. *Disclosing the Past*, Doubleday, New York, p. 121.

28. Oakley, K. P. 1956. 'The earliest toolmakers', *Antiquity* 30: 4–8.

29. Dart, R. A. 1955. 'The first australopithecine fragment from the Makapansgat pebble culture stratum', *Nature* 176: 170.

30. Robinson, J. T., and Mason, R. 1957. 'Occurrence of stone artifacts with *Australopithecus* at Sterkfontein', *Nature* 180: 521. Robinson, J. T. 1961. 'Australopithecines and the origin of Man', *Ann. Rep. Smithsonian Institution*, 1961: 479–500.

31. Leakey, L. S. B. 1958*b*. 'Recent discoveries at Olduvai Gorge, Tanganyika', *Nature* 181: 1099–1103.

32. Leakey, L. S. B. 1959*a*. 'A new fossil skull from Olduvai', *Nature* 184: 491–3.

33. I am grateful to Andrew Hill for bringing this to my attention.

34. Leakey, L. S. B. 1960*b*. 'From the Taung skull to "Nutcracker Man"', *Illustrated London News* 236: 44.

35. Leakey, L. S. B. 1960*a*. 'Finding the world's earliest man', *National Geographic* 118: 420–35.

36. Robinson, J. T. 1960. 'The affinities of the new Olduvai australopithecine', *Nature* 186: 456–7.

37. Washburn, S. L. 1960. 'Tools and human evolution', *Scientific American* 203 (3): 3–15.

38. Leakey, L. S. B. 1959*b*. Quoted in *The Times*, London, 4 September 1959.

39. Leakey, M. D., 1979*a*. Interview with author, Olduvai.

40. Leakey, L. S. B., Everden, J. F., and Curtis, G. H. 1961. 'Age of Bed 1, Olduvai Gorge, Tanganyika', *Nature* 191: 478–9.

41. Payne, M. 1978. Interview with author, Washington.

42. Day, M. H., and Stringer, C. B. 1982. 'A Reconsideration of the Omo-Kibish Remains and the *erectus–sapiens* transition', in Ciochon, R.L., and Fleagle, J. G. (ed.) 2006, *The Human Evolution Source Book*, (2nd edition), Pearson, New Jersey, pp. 528–37.

43. Howell, F. C., and Coppens, Y. 1976. 'An overview of hominidae from the Omo Succession, Ethiopia', pp. 522–32 in Coppens, Y., Howell, F. C., Isaac, G. Ll., and Leakey, R. E. F. (ed.) 1976. *Earliest Man and Environments in the Lake Rudolf Basin*, Chicago, p. 530.

44. Leakey, R. E. F. 1970*a*. 'In search of man's past at Lake Rudolf', *National Geographic* 137: 712–33, p. 719.

45. Leakey, R. E. F. 1977. Quoted in 'Puzzling out man's ascent', *Time*, 7 November.

46. Aiello, L. C., and Andrews, P. 2000. 'The Australopithecines in Review', *Human Evolution* 15: 17–38.

47. Rak, Y. 1983. *The Australopithecine Face*, Academic Press, New York.

48. Walker, A., Leakey, R. E. F., Harris, J. M. and Brown, F. H. 1986. '2.5-Myr *Australopithecus boisei* from west of Lake Turkana, Kenya', *Nature* 322: 517–22.

49. Delson, E. 1987. 'Evolution and palaeobiology of robust *Australopithecus*', *Nature* 327: 654–5.

50. Lewin, R. 1986. 'New fossil upsets human family', *Science* 233: 123–4.

51. Hill, Andrew, 2009. Comment: '*Paranthropus* has become the preferred generic attribution for species that were previously described as "robust" australopithecines, i.e. *A. robustus, A. boisei, A. aethiopicus*' (described in 1985).

52. Delson, E. 1987. 'Evolution and palaeobiology of robust *Australopithecus*', *Nature* 654–5.

53. Klein, Richard G. 1999. *The Human Career* (2nd edition), University of Chicago Press, Chicago, pp. 226–27.

CHAPTER 12

1. Frere, John, 1797. Letter to the Society of Antiquaries, *Archaeologia* 13: 204.

2. Oakley, K. P., and Leakey, M. D. 1937. 'Report on excavations at Jaywick Sands, Essex (1934)', *Proceedings of the Prehistoric Society* 3: 217–60.

3. Leakey, M. D., 1971. *Olduvai Gorge*, vol. 3: *Excavations in Beds I and II*, Cambridge University Press, Cambridge.

4. Hay, R. L. 1976. *Geology of Olduvai Gorge*, University of California Press, Berkeley.

5. Blumenschine, Robert J., *et al.* 2003. 'Late Pliocene *Homo* and Hominid Land Use from Western Olduvai Gorge, Tanzania', *Science* 299: 1217–21.

6. Blumenschine, R. J., *et al.* 2008. 'Effects of distance from stone source on landscape-scale variation in Oldowan artifact assemblages', *Journal of Archaeological Science*, 35: 76–86.

7. Leakey, M. D. 1979b. *Olduvai Gorge: My Search for Early Man*, Collins, London, p. 86.

8. Potts, Richard, 1986. 'Temporal Span of Bone Accumulations at Olduvai Gorge and Implications for Early Hominid Foraging Behavior', *Paleobiology*, 12 (winter), pp. 25–31.

9. Leakey M. D. 1979b: 51.

10. Leakey, M. D. 1967. 'Preliminary survey of the cultural material from Beds I and II Olduvai Gorge, Tanzania', in Bishop, W. W., and Clark, J. D. (eds.) 1967, *Background to Evolution in Africa*, University of Chicago Press, Chicago, p. 417.

11. Leakey, M. D. 1979*b*: 55.

12. Washburn, S. L., and Lancaster, J. 1968. 'The evolution of hunting', pp. 293–303 in Lee, R. B., and DeVore, I. (eds.) 1968, *Man the Hunter*, Aldine, New York.

13. Isaac, G. Ll. 1978. 'The food-sharing behavior of protohuman hominids', *Scientific American* 238(4): pp. 90–106.

14. Bunn, H. T. 1982. 'Meat-eating and human evolution', Ph.D. diss. Univ. of California, Berkeley. Potts, R. 1984. 'Home bases and early hominids', *American Scientist* 72: 338–47. Toth, N. 1982. 'The stone technologies of early hominids at Koobi Fora, Kenya', Ph.D. diss. University of California, Berkeley.

15. Isaac, G. Ll. 1981. 'Emergence of human behaviour patterns', pp. 177–88 in Young, J. Z., Jope, M. E., and Oakley, K. P. (eds.) 1981, *The Emergence of Man*, Phil. Trans. R. Soc. B. 292: 3–5.

16. Potts, R. 1984. 'Home bases and early hominids', *American Scientist* 72: 338–47.

17. Bunn, H. T. 1981. 'Archaeological evidence for meat-eating by Plio-Pleistocene hominids from Koobi Fora and Olduvai Gorge', *Nature* 291: 574–6. Potts, R., and Shipman, P. 1981. 'Cutmarks made by stone tools on bones from Olduvai Gorge, Tanzania', *Nature* 291: 577–80.

18. Shipman, P. 1984*a*. 'The earliest bone tools: re-assessing the evidence from Olduvai Gorge', *Anthroquest* 29: 9–10.

19. Shipman, P. 1981. Quoted in Lewin, R. 1981. 'Protohuman activity etched in fossil bones', *Science* 213: 123–4.

20. Lewin, R. 1984. 'Man the scavenger', *Science* 224: 720–1. Bower, B. 1985. 'Hunting ancient scavengers', *Science News* 127: 155–7.

21. Shipman, P. 1984*b*. 'Ancestors: scavenger hunt', *Natural History* 93 (4): 20–7.

22. Andrews, P., and Cook, J. 1985. 'Natural modifications to bones in a temperate setting', *Man NS* 20: 675–91.

23. Behrensmeyer, A. K., *et al.* 1986. 'Trampling as a cause of bone surface damage and pseudo-cutmarks', *Nature* 319: pp. 768–71.

24. Tryon, Christian A. 2008. 'Reinvestigating Early Human Behavior at Olduvai Gorge', Review of Dominguez-Rodrigo, Manuel, Barba, Rebecca, and Egeland, Charles P. 2007. *Deconstructing Olduvai: A Taphonomic Study of the Bed I Sites*, Springer, New York.

25. Leakey, L. S. B. 1951. *Olduvai Gorge: A Report on the Evolution of the Hand-Axe Culture in Beds I – IV*, Cambridge University Press, p. 34.

26. Leakey, M. D. 1979*b*: 110–22.

27. Toth, N. 1985. 'The Oldowan re-assessed: a close look at early stone artifacts', *Journal of Archaeological Science* 12: 101–20.

28. Plummer, Thomas, 2004. 'Flaked Stones and Old Bones: Biological and Cultural Evolution at the Dawn of Technology', *Yearbook of Physical Anthropology* 47: 118–64.

29. Semaw, S., *et al.* 1997. '2.5-million-year-old stone tools from Gona, Ethiopia', *Nature* 385: 333–6.

30. Semaw, S., *et al.* 1997: 336.

31. Quoted at http://www.stoneageinstitute.org/c_home.shtml

32. Quoted in Isaac, G. Ll., and McCown, Elizabeth R. (eds.) 1976. *Human Origins— Louis Leakey and the East African Evidence*, W. A. Benjamin, California, p. 495.

33. Dominguez-Rodrigo, M., *et al.* 2001. 'Woodworking activities by early humans: a plant residue analysis on Acheulian stone tools from Peninj (Tanzania)', *Journal of Human Evolution* 40: 289–99.

34. Clark, J. Desmond, 1989. 'The origin and spread of modern humans: a broad perspective on the African evidence', pp. 565–88 in Mellars, Paul, and Stringer, Chris (eds.) 1989, *The Human Revolution – Behavioural and Biological Perspectives on the Origins of Modern Humans*, Edinburgh University Press, Edinburgh, p. 570.

35. Gibbons, Ann, 2009*c*. 'Oldest Stone Blades Uncovered', *ScienceNOW Daily News*, 2 April.

36. The following summary draws upon a review paper which gives references to the specific facts and observations mentioned: McBrearty, Sally, and

Brooks, Alison S. 2000. 'The revolution that wasn't: a new interpretation of the origin of modern human behavior', *Journal of Human Evolution* 39: 453–563, p. 495.

37. Yellen, John E., *et al.* 1995. 'A Middle Stone Age Worked Bone Industry from Katanda, Upper Semliki Valley, Zaire', *Science* 268: 553–5.

38. Quoting from paper referred to in McBrearty and Brooks, 2000: 511.

39. Deacon, H. J. 1989. 'Late Pleistocene palaeoecology and archaeology in the southern Cape, South Africa', pp. 547–64 in Mellars and Stringer, 1989: 557–8.

40. Parkington, John, 2001. 'Milestones: The Impact of the Systematic Exploitation of Marine Foods on Human Evolution', pp. 327–36 in Tobias, Phillip V., Raath, Michael A., Moggi-Cecchi, Jacopo, and Doyle, Gerald A. (eds.), 2001, *Humanity from African Naissance to Coming Millennia*, Florence University Press and Witwatersrand University Press, Florence and Johannesburg.

41. McBrearty and Brooks, 2000: 30.

42. Ambrose, S. H. 1998. *Journal of Archaeological Science* 28: 377.

43. Wurz, Sarah, 1999. 'The Howiesons Poort backed artefacts from Klasies River: an argument for symbolic behaviour', *South African Archaeological Bulletin* 54: 38–50. Wurz, Sarah, 2002. 'Variability in the Middle Stone Age Lithic Sequence 115,000–60,000 Years Ago at Klasies River, South Africa', *Journal of Archaeological Science* 29: 1001–15.

44. Henshilwood, Christopher, *et al.*, 2004. Middle Stone Age Shell Beads from South Africa. *Science*, 304: 404. D'Errico, Francesco, *et al.*, 2005. '*Nassarius kraussianus* Shell Beads from Blombos Cave: Evidence for Symbolic Behavior in the Middle Stone Age', *Journal of Human Evolution*, vol. 48 (1): 3–24.

45. Henshilwood, C. 2004. Quoted in *The Guardian*, London, 16 April 2004.

46. McBrearty, Sally and Brooks, Alison S., 2000. 'The revolution that wasn't: a new interpretation of the origin of modern human behaviour', *Journal of Human Evolution*, 39: 453–563.

CHAPTER 13

1. Leakey, L. S. B., Tobias, P. V., and Napier, J. R. 1964. 'A new species of the genus *Homo* from Olduvai Gorge', *Nature* 202: 7–9.

2. Napier, J. R. 1962. 'Fossil hand bones from Olduvai Gorge', *Nature* 196: 409–11.

3. Day, M. H., and Napier, J. R. 1964. 'Fossil foot bones from Olduvai Gorge', *Nature* 201: 969–70.

4. Davis, P. R. 1964. 'Hominid fossils from Bed I, Olduvai Gorge, Tanganyika', *Nature* 201: 967–70.

5. Leakey, L. S. B. 1961. 'New finds at Olduvai Gorge', *Nature* 189: 649–50.

6. Tobias, P. V. 1964. 'The Olduvai Bed I hominine with special reference to its cranial capacity', *Nature* 202: 3–4.

7. Leakey, L. S. B., Tobias, P. V., and Napier, J. R. 1964: 7–9.

8. Leakey, M. D. 1984. *Disclosing the Past*, Doubleday, New York, p. 128.

9. Clark, W. E. Le Gros, 1964. *The Fossil Evidence for Human Evolution*, Chicago University Press, Chicago, p. 86.

10. Oxnard, C. E., 1972. 'Functional morphology in primates: some mathematical and physical methods', in Tuttle, R. (ed.) 1972, *The Functional and Evolutionary Biology of Primates*, Chicago University Press. Day, M. H. 'Hominid postcranial material from Bed I, Olduvai Gorge', in Isaac, G. Ll., and McCown, E. R. (eds.), 1976, *Human Origins: Louis Leakey and the East African Evidence*, W. A. Benjamin Inc., California, p. 366.

11. Campbell, B. 1964. 'Just another "man-ape"?', *Discovery* 25 (June): 37–8.

12. Clark, W. E. le Gros, 1964.

13. Robinson, J. T. 1965. '*Homo habilis* and the australopithecines', *Nature* 205: 121–4.

14. Campbell, B. 1964.

15. Tobias, P. V., and Napier, J. R. 1964. Letter to *The Times*, London, 29 May.

16. Oakley, K. P. 1964. 'The evolution of man', *Discovery* 25 (August): 49.

17. Pilbeam, D. 1972. *The Ascent of Man*, MacMillan, New York, p. 135.

18. Tobias, P. V. 1991. *Olduvai Gorge*, vol. 4: *The skulls, endocasts and teeth of Homo habilis*, Cambridge University Press, Cambridge, p. 30.

19. Leakey, M. D. 1984: 127–8.

20. Tobias, P. V. 1991: 21–3.

21. Tobias. P. V. 1991: 616.

22. Tobias, P. V. 1991: 845.

23. Tobias, P. V. 1991: 49.

24. Susman, R. L., and Stern, J. T. 1982. 'Functional morphology of *Homo habilis*', *Science* 217: 931–4.

25. Leakey, M. D. 1984: 210.

26. Johanson, D. C., *et al.*, 1987. 'New partial skeleton of *Homo habilis* from Olduvai Gorge, Tanzania', *Nature* 327: 205–9.

27. Johanson, D. C. 1987. Quoted in Lewin, R. 1987*a*. 'The earliest "humans" were more like apes', *Science* 236: 1061–3.

28. White, T. D. 1987. Quoted in Lewin, R. 1987*a*. 'The earliest "humans" were more like apes', *Science* 236: 1061–3.

29. Clark, F. C. 1991. '*Homo habilis* in Detail', *Science* 253: 1294–7.

30. Wood, Bernard, 1987. 'Who is the "real" *Homo habilis?*' *Nature* 327: 187–8.

31. Wood, B. A., 2000. 'The History of the Genus *Homo*', *Human Evolution* 15: 39–49.

CHAPTER 14

1. Hill, Andrew, and Ward, Steven, 1988. 'Origin of the Hominidae: the record of African large hominoid evolution between 14 My and 4 My', *Yearbook of Physical Anthropology* 31: 52.

2. Walker, A. C., and Leakey, R. E. F. 1978. 'The hominids of East Turkana', *Scientific American* 238 (8): 54–66, p. 62.

3. Cole, Sonia, 1975. *Leakey's Luck: The Life of Louis Seymour Bazett Leakey 1903–1972*, Collins, London, p. 351. The following paragraphs on the Calico episode are drawn primarily from chapter 13 of Cole's biography.

4. Leakey, L. S. B., Simpson, Ruth De Ette, and Clements, Thomas, 1968. 'Archaeological Excavations in the Calico Mountains, California: Preliminary Report', *Science* 160: 1022–3.

5. Leakey, M. D. 1984. *Disclosing the Past*, Doubleday & Co., New York, p. 142.

6. http://www.meetup.com/Friends-of-Calico-Early-Man-Site/

7. Leakey, M. D. 1984: 159.

8. *Time*, 1977. 'Puzzling out man's ancestor', 7 November, p. 54.

9. Leakey, R. E. F. 1970*a*. 'In search of man's past at Lake Rudolf', *National Geographic* 137: 712–33.

10. Leakey, R. E. F. 1970*a*: 725.

11. Fitch, F. J., and Miller, J. A. 1970. 'Radioisotopic age determinations of Lake Rudolf artefact site', *Nature* 226: 226–8.

12. Leakey, R. E. F. 1970*b*. 'Fauna and artefacts from a new Plio-Pleistocene locality near Lake Rudolf in Kenya', *Nature* 226: 223–4. Leakey, R. E. F. 1970*a*: 731–2.

13. Leakey, R. E. F. 1971. 'Further evidence of Lower Pleistocene hominids from Lake Rudolf, North Kenya', *Nature* 231: 241–5. Leakey, R. E. F., 1972*a*. 'Further evidence of Lower Pleistocene hominids from Lake Rudolf, North Kenya, 1971', *Nature* 237: 264–9.

14. Leakey, R. E. F. 1972*b*. 'New evidence for the evolution of man', *Social Biology* 19: 99–114.

15. Walker, A. C. 1978. Personal communication, interview with author, Cambridge, Mass.

16. Leakey, R. E. F., 1973*a*. 'Skull 1470', *National Geographic* 143: 819–29.

17. Leakey, R. E. F. 1977. Quoted in 'Puzzling out man's ascent', *Time*, 7 November.

18. See Walker, A. C. 1976. 'Remains attributable to *Australopithecus* in the East Rudolf succession', pp. 484–9 in Coppens, Y., Howell, F. C., Isaac, G. Ll., and Leakey, R. E. F. (eds.) 1976, *Earliest Man and Environments in the Lake Rudolf Basin*, University of Chicago Press, Chicago.

19. Day, M. H., Leakey, R. E. F., Walker, A. C., and Wood, B. A. 1975. 'New hominids from East Rudolf, Kenya, I', *American Journal of Physical Anthropology* 42: 461–76.

20. Wood, B. A. 1991. *Koobi Fora Research Project*, vol. 4: *Hominid cranial remains*, Clarendon Press, Oxford.

21. Cooke, H. B. S. 1976. 'Suidae from Plio-Pleistocene strata of the Rudolf Basin', in Coppens, Y., *et al.* (eds.) 1976: 251–63.

22. Fitch, F. J., and Miller, J. A. 1976. 'Conventional potassium-argon and argon-40/argon-39 dating of volcanic rocks of East Rudolf', in Coppens, Y., *et al.* (eds.) 1976: 132.

23. Hall, E. T. 1974. 'Old bones—but how old?' *Sunday Telegraph*, 3 September.

24. Fitch F. J., and Miller, J. A. 1970. 'Radioisotopic age determinations of Lake Rudolf artefact site', *Nature* 226: 226–8.

25. Brock, A., and Isaac, G. Ll. 1974. 'Palaeomagnetic stratigraphy and chronology of the hominid-bearing sediments east of Lake Turkana, Kenya', *Nature* 247: 344–8.

26. Cooke, H. B. S. 1976.

27. Cooke, H. B. S. 1976: 261.

28. Isaac, G. Ll. 1976. Coppens, Y., *et al.* (eds.) 1976: 6.

29. Curtis, G. H., Drake, R., Cerling, T. E., and Hampel, J. E. 1975. 'Age of KBS tuff in Koobi Fora Formation, East Rudolf, Kenya', *Nature* 358: 395–8.

30. Leakey, R. E. F. 1979*a*. Personal communication, interview with author.

31. White, T. D., and Harris, J. M. 1977. 'Suid evolution and correlation of African hominid localities', *Science* 198: 13–21.

32. Leakey R. E. F. 1979*a*.

33. Fitch, F. J. 1979. Personal communication, interview with author.

34. Brown, F. H., McDougall, I., Davies, T., and Maier, R. 1985. 'An integrated Plio-Pleistocene chronology for the Turkana Basin', pp. 82–90 in Delson, E. (ed.) 1985, *Ancestors: The Hard Evidence*, Alan R. Liss, New York. Brown, F. H. 1994. 'Development of Pliocene and Pleistocene chronology of the Turkana Basin, east Africa, and its relation to other sites', pp. 285–312 in Corruccini, R. S., and Ciochon, R. L. (eds.) 1995, *Integrative paths to the past: Palaeoanthopological advances in honor of F. Clark Howell*, Prentice Hall, Englewood Cliffs, NJ.

35. McDougall, I. 1985. 'K-Ar and ^{40}Ar/^{39}Ar dating of the hominid-bearing Plio-Pleistocene of Koobi-Fora, Lake Turkana, northern Kenya', *Geol. Soc. Am. Bull.* 96: 792–4.

36. Patterson, B., Behrensmeyer, A. K., and Sill, W. D. 1970. 'Geology of a new Pliocene locality in northwestern Kenya', *Nature* 256: 279–84.

37. Hill, Andrew, Ward, Steven, and Brown, Barbara, 1992. 'Anatomy and age of the Lothagam mandible', *Journal of Human Evolution* 22: 439–51.

38. Ward, Steven, and Hill, Andrew, 1987. 'Pliocene Hominid Partial Mandible from Tabarin, Baringo, Kenya', *American Journal of Physical Anthropology* 72: 21–37.

39. Leakey, R. E. F. 1969. 'New cercopithecidae from the Chemeron Beds of Lake Baringo, Kenya', pp. 53–69 in Leakey, L. S. B. (ed.) 1969, *Fossil Vertebrates of Africa*, vol. 1, Academic Press, London.

40. Hill, Andrew, 2002. 'Paleoanthropological research in the Tugen Hills, Kenya', *Journal of Human Evolution* 42: 1–10.

41. Hill, Andrew, 1985. 'Early hominid from Baringo, Kenya', *Nature* 315: 222–4.

42. Deino, Alan L., *et al.* 2002. '…geochronology and paleomagnetic stratigraphy of the Lukeino and lower Chemeron Formations at Tabarin and Kapcheberek, Tugen Hills, Kenya', *J. Human Evolution* 42: 117–40.

43. Senut, B., Pickford, M., Gommery, D., Mein, P., Cheboi, K., and Coppens, Y. 2001. 'First hominid from the Miocene (Lukeino Formation, Kenya)', *Comptes Rendus de l'Acadèmie des Sciences, Sciences de la Terre et des Planètes* 332: 137–44.

44. Ward, Steven, and Hill, Andrew, 1987: 35.

45. Lichfield, J., and Connor, S. 2001. 'How 14 pieces of bone and six million years could rewrite the story of human evolution', *Independent*, London, 7 February, p. 3.

46. Senut, B., *et al.* 2001: 138 and 143.

47. See *Science*, 2000 vol. 290, p. 2065, and *Science*, 2001, vol. 291, p. 986.

48. Butler, Decan, 2001. 'The battle of Tugen Hills', *Nature* 410: 508–9.

49. Aiello, Leslie C., and Collard, Mark, 2001. 'Our newest oldest ancestor?' *Nature*, 410: 526–7.

50. Michel Brunet's career and events surrounding the discovery of and controversies concerning *Sahelanthropus* are covered with references to sources in Gibbons, Ann, 2006. *The First Human*, Doubleday, New York.

51. Brunet, Michel, 2002. 'Dreams of the past', *Nature* 423: 121. Gibbons, Ann, 2006. *The First Human*, Doubleday, New York.

52. Brunet, Michel, *et al.* 2002. 'A new hominid from the Upper Miocene of Chad, Central Africa', *Nature*, 418: 145–55.

53. Reported in McKie, Robin, 2002. 'Fossil find of the century…', *Observer* (London), 14 July, p. 6.

54. Wood, Bernard, 2002. 'Hominid revelations from Chad', *Nature* 418: 134.

55. Quoted in Gibbons, Ann, 2002. 'One scientist's quest for the origin of our species', *Science* 298: 1709.

56. Wolpoff, Milford H., Senut, Brigitte, Pickford, Martin, and Hawks, John, 2002. 'Sahelanthropus or Sahelpithecus?' Nature 419: 581–2.

57. Lebatard, Anne-Marie, et al. 2008. 'Cosmogenic nuclide dating…', PNAS 105 (9): 3226–31.

58. Zollikofer, Christoph P. E., et al. 2005. 'Virtual reconstruction of Sahelanthropus tchadensis', Nature 434: 755–9.

59. Wolpoff, Milford H., et al. 2006. 'An Ape or the Ape:…', PaleoAnthropology 2006: 36–50.

60. Bulletin de la Société Géologique de Normandie et des Amis du Muséum du Havre, 2009, vol. 96, part 1.

61. http://johnhawks.net/weblog/fossils/sahelanthropus/was-toumai-buried-facing-mecca-2009.html

62. Constans, Nicholas, 2009. 'Le fémur de Toumaï', La Recherche, July.

CHAPTER 15

1. Kern, E. P. H. 1981. 'Battle of the Bones', Life 4(12): 109–20.

2. Quoted in Lewin, Roger, 1987b. Bones of Contention, Simon & Schuster, New York, p. 14.

3. Johanson, D. C., and Taieb, M. 1976. 'Plio-Pleistocene hominid discoveries in Hadar, Ethiopia', Nature 260: 293–7.

4. Johanson, D. C., Splingaer, M., and Boaz, N. T. 1976. 'Paleontological excavations in the Shungura Formation, Lower Omo Basin, 1969–73', pp. 402–20 in Coppens, Y., Howell, F. C., Isaac, G. Ll., and Leakey, R. E. F (eds.) 1976, Earliest Man and Environments in the Lake Rudolf Basin, University of Chicago Press, Chicago.

5. Johanson, D. C. 1976. 'Ethiopia yields first "Family" of early man', National Geographic, December, p. 801.

6. Johanson, D. C., 1974, Addis Ababa, quoted in Ottoway, D. B. 1974a. '3-million-year-old human fossils found', Herald Tribune, Paris, 28 October.

7. Johanson 1976: 793.

8. Ottoway, D. B. 1974*b*. 'Oldest partial skeleton of "Man" is found', *Herald Tribune*, Paris, 27 December.

9. Johanson, D. C. 1976: 801.

10. Johanson, D. C., 1979. 'Our roots go deeper', in *Science Year 1979*, Worldbook Childcraft International Inc., Chicago. Johanson, D. C., and Edey, M. A. 1981. *Lucy: The Beginnings of Humankind*, Simon & Schuster, New York.

11. Leakey, R. E. F., and Lewin, R. 1977. *Origins*, Macdonald and Jane's, London, p. 90.

12. Walker, A. C. 1978. Interview with author, Cambridge, Mass.

13. Johanson, D. C. 1976: 809.

14. Leakey, M. D., *et al.* 1976. 'Fossil hominids from the Laetoli Beds', *Nature* 262: 460–6.

15. Johanson, D. C., White, T. D., and Coppens, Y. 1978. 'A new species of the genus *Australopithecus* (Primates: Hominidae) from the Pliocene of Eastern Africa', *Kirtlandia* 28: 1–14.

16. Johanson, D. C. 1979, 'Our roots go deeper', in *Science Year 1979*, Worldbook Childcraft International Inc., Chicago.

17. Reader, J. A. 1978. 'Tim White presents *Australopithecus afarensis*', Notes on seminar and discussion, 28 June, Nairobi.

18. Johanson, D. C., White, T. D., and Coppens, Y. 1978: 1–14.

19. White, T. D. 1977. 'New fossil hominids from Laetoli, Tanzania', *American Journal of Physical Anthropology* 46: 197–230.

20. Johanson, D. C., and Edey, M. A. 1981. *Lucy, The Beginnings of Humankind*, Simon & Schuster, New York, p. 290.

21. Hinrichsen, D. 1978. 'How old are our ancestors?' *New Scientist*, London, vol. 78, p. 571.

22. Day, M. H., Leakey, M. D., and Olson, T. R. 1980. 'On the status of *Australopithecus afarensis*', *Science* 207: 1102–3.

23. Quoted in Johanson and Edey, 1981: 295.

24. Quoted in Johanson and Edey, 1981: 295.

25. Tobias, P. V. T. 1981. 'The emergence of man in Africa and beyond', pp. 43–57 in Young, J. Z., Jope, E. M., and Oakley, K. P. (eds.) 1981, *The Emergence of Man*, Phil. Trans. Roy. Soc. B. 292.

26. Tobias 1981: 47.

27. Leakey, Mary, 1984. *Disclosing the Past*, Doubleday, New York, pp. 180–4.

28. Johanson and Edey, 1981: 290.

29. Leakey, M. D. 1981. 'Tracks and Tools', pp. 95–102 in Young, J. Z., Jope, E. M., and Oakley, K. P. (eds.) 1981, *The Emergence of Man*, Phil. Trans. Roy. Soc. B. 292, p. 102.

30. Leakey R. E. F. and Walker, A. C. 1980. 'On the status of *Australopithecus afarensis*', *Science*, 207: 1103.

31. Leakey, R. E. F. 1979*b*. Quoted in Rensberger, B. 1979. 'Rival anthropologists divide on "re-human" find', *New York Times*, 18 February.

32. Leakey, R. E. F. 1979*a*. Interview with author, Nairobi.

33. Johanson, D. C. 1978. Interview with author, Cleveland, Ohio.

34. White, T. D. 1985. 'The hominids of Hadar and Laetoli: an element by element comparison of the dental samples', pp. 138–52 in Delson, E. (ed.) 1985, *Ancestors: The Hard Evidence*, New York.

35. Johanson and Edey, 1981: 183–5.

36. Johanson and Edey, 1981: 156–9.

37. Dalton, Rex, 2006. 'The History Man', *Nature* 443: 268–9.

38. Wood, Bernard, 1994. 'The oldest hominid yet', *Nature* 371: 280–1.

39. White, Tim D., Suwa, Gen, and Asfaw, Berhane, 1994. '*Australopithecus ramidus*, a new species of early hominid from Aramis, Ethiopia', *Nature* 371: 306–12.

40. White, Tim D., Suwa, Gen, and Asfaw, Berhane, 1995. '*Australopithecus ramidus*, a new species of early hominid from Aramis, Ethiopia—a corrigendum', *Nature* 375: 88.

41. Haile-Selassie, Y., Safaw, B., and White, T. D. 2004. 'Hominid cranial remains from Upper Pleistocene deposits at Aduma, Middle Awash, Ethiopia', *Am. J. Phys. Anthropol.* 123: 1–10.

42. Wood, Bernard, and Lonergan, Nicholas, 2008. 'The hominin fossil record: taxa, grades and clades', *Journal of Anatomy* 212: 354–76.

43. White, Tim D. 2002. 'Earliest hominids', pp. 407–16 in Hartwig, Walter Carl (ed.) 2002, *The Primate Fossil Record*, Cambridge University Press, Cambridge.

44. Wood, B. 2006. 'A precious little bundle', *Nature* 443: 278–80.

45. Wynn, Jonathan G. *et al.* 2006. 'Geological and palaeontological context of a Pliocene juvenile hominin at Dikika, Ethiopia', *Nature* 443: 332–6.

46. Alemseged, Zeresenay, *et al.* 2006. 'A juvenile early hominin skeleton from Dikika, Ethiopia', *Nature* 443: 296–301.

CHAPTER 16

1. These issues are covered in Latimer, Bruce, 2005. 'The Perils of Being Bipedal', *Annals of Biomechanical Engineering* 33 (1): 3–6.

2. Alexander, R. McNeill, 1992. 'Human Locomotion', pp. 80–5 in *Cambridge Encyclopaedia of Human Evolution*, p. 84.

3. Steudel, Karen L. 1994. 'Locomotor energetics and hominid evolution', *Evolutionary Anthropology* 3 (2): 42–7.

4. Latimer, Bruce, 2005: 3.

5. Coppens, Yves, 1994. 'The east side story: the origin of humankind', *Scientific American* 270 (5): 62–9.

6. McBrearty, Sally, and Jablonski, Nina G. 2005. 'First fossil chimpanzee', *Nature* 437: 105–8.

7. Kingston, J. D., Marino, D. D., and Hill, A. 1994. 'Isotopic evidence for Neogene hominid paleoenvironments in the Kenya Rift Valley', *Science* 264: 955–9.

8. Leakey, L. S. B. 1960a. 'Finding the world's earliest man', *National Geographic* 118: 420–35, p. 434.

9. Leakey, L. S. B., Tobias, P. V., and Napier, J. R. 1964. 'A new species of the genus *Homo* from Olduvai Gorge', *Nature* 202: 7–9.

10. Clark, W. E. Le Gros, 1964. *The Fossil Evidence for Human Evolution*, Chicago, p. 162.

11. Day, M. H., and Napier, J. R. 1964. 'Fossil foot bones from Olduvai Gorge', *Nature* 201: 969–70.

12. Day, M. H., and Wood, B. A. 1968. 'Functional affinities of the Olduvai Hominid 8 talus', *Man*, NS 3: 440–55.

13. Davis, P. R., 1964. 'Hominid fossils from Bed I, Olduvai Gorge, Tanganyika', *Nature* 201: 967–70.

14. Clark, W. E. Le Gros, 1967*b*. *Man-Apes or Ape-Men?* New York, p. 43.

15. Pilbeam, D. 1972. *The Ascent of Man*, Macmillan, New York, p. 140.

16. Washburn, S. 1960. 'Tools and human evolution', *Scientific American* 203 (3): 3–15.

17. Bramble, Dennis M., and Lieberman, Daniel E. 2004. 'Endurance running and the evolution of *Homo*', *Nature* 432: 345–52.

18. Leakey, R. E. F. 1978. Interview with author, Nairobi.

19. Leakey, R. E. F. 1972*c*. 'Man and sub-Men on Lake Rudolf', *New Scientist* 56: 385–7, p. 387.

20. Lovejoy, C. O. 1973. 'The gait of australopithecines', *Yearbook of Physical Anthropology* 17: 147–61; Lovejoy, C. O. 1975. 'Biomechanical perspectives on the lower limb of early hominids', pp. 291–326 in Tuttle, R. H. (ed.) 1976, *Primate Morphology and Evolution*, The Hague. Lovejoy, C. O. 1988. 'Evolution of Human Walking', *Scientific American* 259: 118–25. Lovejoy, C. O., Heiple, K. G., and Burnstein, A. H. 1973. 'The gait of Australopithecus', *American Journal of Physical Anthropology* 38: 757–80.

21. Lovejoy, *et al.* 1973: 777.

22. Leakey, R. E. F. 1973*b*. 'Further evidence of Lower Pleistocene hominids from East Rudolf, North Kenya', *Nature* 242: 170–3.

23. Leakey R. E. F. 1973*a*. 'Skull 1470', *National Geographic* 143: 819–29, p. 828.

24. Hill, Andrew, 1976. Personal communication, Nairobi.

25. Leakey, M. D., and Hay, R. L. 1979. 'Pliocene footprints in the Laetoli beds at Laetoli, northern Tanzania', *Nature* 278: 317–23. Leakey, M. D., and Harris, J. M. (eds.) 1987. *Laetoli: A Pliocene Site in Northern Tanzania*, Clarendon Press, Oxford.

26. Tuttle, R. H. 1987. 'Kinesiological inferences and evolutionary implications from Laetoli bipedal trails', pp. 503–23 in Leakey, M. D., and Harris, J. M. (eds.) 1987, *Laetoli: A Pliocene Site in Northern Tanzania*, Clarendon Press, Oxford, p. 508.

27. Quoted p. 80 in Gore, Rick, 1997. 'The First Steps', *National Geographic*, February 1997, pp. 72–99.

28. Tuttle, R. H., Webb, D. M., and Baksh, M. 1991. 'Laetoli toes and *Australopithecus afarensis*', *Human Evolution* 6 (3): 193–200.

29. Quoted in Gore, Rick, 1997: 80.

30. White, Tim D., and Suwa, Gen, 1987. 'Hominid Footprints at Laetoli: Facts and Interpretations', *American Journal of Physical Anthropology* 72: 485–514.

31. Stern, J. T., Jr. 2000. 'Climbing to the Top. A Personal Memoir of *Australopithecus afarensis*', *Evolutionary Anthropology* 9: 113–33, p. 115.

32. Stern, J. T., Jr. 2000: 121.

33. Galik, K., *et al.* 2004. 'External and internal morphology of the *Orrorin tugenensis* femur', *Science* 305: 1450.

34. Quoted in Gore, Rick, 1997: 88.

35. Richmond, Brian, and Jungers, William L. 2008. '*Orrorin tugenensis* Femoral Morphology and the Evolution of Hominin Bipedalism', *Science* 319: 1662–5.

CHAPTER 17

1. White, Tim, 2010. Email to author, 16 Sept. 2010.

2. *Science*, 2 October 2009, vol. 326, issue 5949.

3. Mann, J. *Ardipithecus ramidus*. http://www.youtube.com/watch?v=S-DCcr-LIcL4

4. Huxley, T. H. 1863. *Evidence as to Man's Place in Nature*, London, p. 50.

5. Hanson, B. 2009. 'Light on the Origin of Man', *Science* 326: 60.

6. White, Tim D., *et al.* 2009. '*Ardipithecus ramidus* and the Paleobiology of Early Hominids', *Science* 326: 75.

7. White, Tim D., *et al.* 2009d. 'Macrovertebrate Paleontology and the Pliocene Habitat of *Ardipithecus ramidus* and the Paleobiology of Early Hominids', *Science* 326: 92.

8. Wilford, J. N. 2009. *New York Times*, 1 October.

9. Gibbons, Ann, 2009b. 'The View From Afar', *Science* 326: 41–3.

10. White, Tim D., *et al.* 2009. '*Ardipithecus ramidus* and the Paleobiology of Early Hominids', *Science* 326: 77.

11. Louchart, Antoine, *et al.* 2009. 'Taphonomic, Avian, and Small-Vertebrate Indicators of the *Ardipithecus ramidus* Habitat', *Science* 326: 66 and online DOI 10.1126/science1175823

12. Gibbons, Ann. 2009a. 'A New Kind of Ancestor: *Ardipithecus* Unveiled', *Science* 326: 38.

13. WoldeGabriel, Giday, *et al.*, 2009. 'The Geological, Isotopic, Botanical, Invertebrate, and Lower Vertebrate Surroundings of *Ardipithecus ramidus*', *Science* 326: 66 and online DOI 10.1126/science1175817

14. White, Tim D., *et al.* 2009. '*Ardipithecus ramidus* and the Paleobiology of Early Hominids', *Science* 326: 78.

15. Suwa, Gen, *et al.* 2009. 'The *Ardipithecus ramidus* Skull and its Implications for Hominid Origins', *Science* 326: 68 and online DOI 10.1126/science1175825

16. Lovejoy, C. Owen, *et al.* 2009b. 'The Pelvis and Femur of *Ardipithecus ramidus*: The Emergence of Upright Walking', *Science* 326: 71.

17. Lovejoy, C. Owen, *et al.* 2009b. *Science* 326: 71 and online DOI 10.1126/-science1175831

18. Lovejoy, C. Owen, *et al.* 2009a. 'Combining Prehension and Propulsion: The Foot of *Ardipithecus ramidus*'. *Science* 326: 72 and online DOI 10.1126/science 1175832

19. Quoted in Gibbons, Ann. 2009a. 'A New Kind of Ancestor: *Ardipithecus* Unveiled', *Science* 326: 38.

20. Lovejoy, C. Owen, *et al.* 2009a.

21. Richmond, Brian G., and Strait, David S. 2000. 'Evidence that humans evolved from a knuckle-walking ancestor', *Nature* 404: 382–5.

22. Lovejoy, C. Owen, 2009d. 'Reexamining Human Origins in the Light of *Ardipithecus ramidus*', *Science* 326: 74 and online DOI 10.1126/science117834

23. White, Tim, 2003. 'Early Hominids—Diversity or Distortion?' *Science* 299: 1994.

24. Gibbons, Ann. 2009a. 'A New Kind of Ancestor: *Ardipithecus* Unveiled', *Science* 326: 39.

25. Lovejoy, C. Owen, *et al.* 2009c. 'Careful Climbing in the Miocene: The Forelimbs of *Ardipithecus ramidus* and Humans are Primitive', *Science* 326 and online DOI 10.1126/science117827

ILLUSTRATION SOURCES

The author and publishers wish to thank the following institutions and individuals for their assistance in facilitating the photography, and for their kind permission to reproduce the illustrations; all photographs are by the author, except where otherwise stated.

1.1 The Manuscripts section of Trinity College Library, Dublin. Photograph by Dr D. P. McCarthy.

1.2 The Wellcome Library, London.

1.3 Top and middle: from G. Y. Craig and C. D. Waterston, 1978. *James Hutton's Theory of the Earth—the Lost Drawings*, Scottish Academic Press, Edinburgh; the Wellcome Library, London. Bottom left: Science Photo Library, London; bottom right: photograph by Dr Keith Montgomery, University of Wisconsin.

1.4 http://cartographia.files.worldpress.com/2008/05smith-main.jpg

2.1 From Conrad Gesner's *De Rerum Fossilium, Lapidum et Gemmarum* 1565, the Wellcome Library, London. Portrait: Museum zu Allerheiligen, Schaffhausen.

2.2 Specimens: the University Museum, Oxford. Lhywd portrait: the Ashmolean Library, Oxford.

2.3 From Robert Plot's *Natural History of Oxfordshire*, 1686; The Wellcome Library, London.

2.4 The University Museum, Oxford, and the London Library.

3.1 Bert Sliggers, Teylers Museum, Haarlem; photograph by Martijn Zegel.

3.2 From Georges Cuvier's *Recherches sur les ossemens fossiles òu l'on rétablit les caractéres de plusieurs animaux dont les révolutions du globe ont détruit les espèces*, 1824, vol. 5, pt 2; The Wellcome Library, London.

4.1 Rheinisches Landesmuseum, Bonn.

4.2 Facilities: the Charles Darwin Museum, Downe, courtesy of the Royal
     College of Surgeons. Paintings by John Gould from *The Natural History of
     the Voyage of the Beagle*, The London Library.

4.3 Photograph by Javier Trueba, Madrid Scientific Films, Science Photo
     Library; courtesy Juan-Luis Arsuaga.

4.4 Specimen: Natural History Museum, London. Engraving: The Royal
     Society, London.

4.5 Musée de l'Homme, Paris.

4.6 Photograph by Javier Trueba, Madrid Scientific Films, Science Photo
     Library; courtesy Juan-Luis Arsuaga.

5.1 Top left: Peabody Museum of Archaeology and Ethnology, Harvard
     University. Top right and bottom: Musée de l'Homme, Paris.

5.2 Musée de l'Homme, Paris.

5.3 South African Museum, Cape Town.

5.4 Journal: Macmillan Publishers Ltd: Nature 423, 6941 © 2003. Specimen:
     photograph © Tim D. White 2010, courtesy National Museum of
     Ethiopia.

6.1 From Ernst Haeckel, *History of Creation*, 1876, p. 28.

6.2 Dubois Collection, Rijkmuseum von Natuurlijke Historie, Leiden.

6.3 Geologisch-Paläontologisches Institut der Universität, Heidelberg.

6.4 The Swedish Museum of Natural History; reconstruction by Atelier
     Daynes, Paris; photograph by Staffan Wearndt.

6.5 Photo © 2009 S. Plailly; reconstruction by Atelier Daynes, Paris.

7.1 Natural History Museum, London.

7.2 Natural History Museum, London.

7.3 Illustrated London News Picture Library; Natural History Museum,
     London.

7.4 Natural History Museum, London.

8.1 Department of Anatomy, University of the Witwatersrand Medical
     School, Johannesburg.

8.2 Raymond Dart personal papers.

8.3 Specimen: Department of Anatomy, University of the Witwatersrand
     Medical School, Johannesburg; publication: Bernard Price Institute,
     Johannesburg.

9.1 The late Professor G. H. R. von Koenigswald; Senckenberg-Museum, Frankfurt am Main.

9.2 Palaeontogical Institute, Uppsala.

9.3 The late Professor Birger Bohlin.

9.4 American Museum of Natural History, New York, and the Weidenreich family archive.

10.1 Robert Broom Collection, Transvaal Museum, Pretoria.

10.2 Transvaal Museum, Pretoria.

10.3 Transvaal Museum, Pretoria.

10.4 C. K. Brain, Swartkrans Project and the Transvaal Museum, Pretoria.

10.5 Ron Clarke and Sterkfontein Research Project.

11.1 The late Dr M. D. Leakey and the Olduvai Gorge Research Project.

11.2 Photograph: the late Dr M. D. Leakey; specimens: Natural History Museum, London.

11.3 National Museum, Dar es Salaam.

11.4 Koobi Fora Research Project, National Museums of Kenya.

12.1 Olduvai Gorge Research Project.

12.2 Olduvai Gorge Research Project, and Peter Jones.

12.3 Olduvai Gorge Research Project.

12.4 Professor Chris Henshilwood, Blombos Cave Project; South African Museum, Cape Town.

12.5 Professor Chris Henshilwood, Blombos Cave Project; South African Museum, Cape Town.

13.1 Louis Leakey papers; National Museums of Kenya.

13.2 Professor Phillip Tobias.

13.3 Photograph by Tim D. White.

14.1 Photograph by Tim D. White; HERC Howell Library.

14.2 Richard Leakey; Koobi Fora Research Project; National Museums of Kenya.

14.3 National Museums of Kenya.

14.4 Photographs courtesy of Michel Brunet and the Mission Paléoanthropologique Franco-Tchadienne.

14.5 Photographs by Alain Beauvilain.

15.1 Dr D. C. Johanson, Cleveland Museum of Natural History on behalf of The National Museum of Ethiopia.

15.2   Cleveland Museum of Natural History on behalf of The National Museum of Ethiopia.

15.3   Cleveland Museum of Natural History on behalf of The National Museum of Ethiopia.

15.4   Photograph courtesy of Dr Zeray Alemseged and the Dikika Research Project.

16.1   Dubois Collection, Rijkmuseum von Natuurlijke Historie, Leiden.

16.2   Laetoli Research Project.

16.3   Laetoli Research Project.

17.1   Journal: American Association for the Advancement of Science, *Science* © 2009. Specimen photograph by Dr Tim D. White.

17.2   From *Science* © 2009, photographs courtesy of Tim White and National Museum of Ethiopia.

17.3   Photograph (c) 1995 David L. Brill / Brill Atlanta, courtesy of the National Museum of Ethiopia.

17.4   Image © Tim White, 2008.

BIBLIOGRAPHY

ABEL, W. 1931. 'Kritische Untersuchungen über *Australopithecus africanus* Dart', *Morphol. Jahrb.* 65 (4): 539–640.

ADAMS, F. D. 1954. *The Birth and Development of the Geological Sciences.* Dover, New York.

AIELLO, L. C. 2010. 'Five Years of *Homo floresiensis*', *American Journal of Physical Anthropology* 142: 167–79.

——, and ANDREWS, P. 2000. 'The Australopithecines in Review', *Human Evolution* 15: 17–38.

——, and COLLARD, M. 2001. 'Our newest oldest ancestor?' *Nature* 410: 526–7.

——, and WHEELER, P. 2003. 'Neanderthal Thermoregulation and the Glacial Climate', pp. 147–66 in Van Andel, T. H., and Davies W. (eds.) *Neanderthals and Modern Humans in the European Landscape During the Last Glaciation*, McDonald Institute for Archaeological Research, Cambridge.

ALEMSEGED, Z., *et al.* 2006. 'A juvenile early hominin skeleton from Dikika, Ethiopia', *Nature* 443: 296–301.

ALEXANDER, R. M. 1992. 'Human Locomotion', pp. 80–5 in *Cambridge Encyclopedia of Human Evolution*, p. 84.

AMBROSE, S. H. 1998. *Journal of Archaeological Science* 28: 377.

ANDERSSON, J. G. 1934. *Children of the Yellow Earth*, Kegan Paul, London.

ANDREWS, P., and COOK, J. 1985. 'Natural modifications to bones in a temperate setting', *Man*, NS 20: 675–91.

——, and CRONIN, J. 1982. 'The relationships of *Sivapithecus* and *Rampithecus* and the evolution of the orang-utan', *Nature* 297: 541.

——, and FRANZEN, J. L. (eds.) 1984. *The Early Evolution of Man, with special emphasis on Southeast Asia and Africa*, Courier Forschungsinstitut Senckenberg 69.

ANDREWS, R. C. 1932. *Natural History of Central Asia. A narrative of the explorations of the Central Asiatic expeditions in Mongolia and China, 1921–1930*, vol. 1: *The New Conquest of China*, New York.

ANON. 1862. editorial, *Medical Times and Gazette*, 28 June, London.

—— 1864. 'Notes on the antiquity of man', *Anthropological Review*, London, p. 71.

—— 1912. 'The earliest known Englishman', *Illustrated London News* 140: 442, 446–7.

—— 1926. News report on Peking Man, *Manchester Guardian*, 17 November.

—— 1928. Leader comment on *Hesperopithecus* in *The Times*, 25 February, London.

—— 1953. Parliamentary report comment on Piltdown in *The Times*, 27 November.

ARDREY, R. 1961. *African Genesis*, Fontana/Collins, London.

ARSUAGA, J.-L., *et al.* 1997. 'Sima de los Huesos (Sierra de Atapuerca, Spain). The site', *Journal of Human Evolution* 33: 109–27.

ASHTON, E. H., and ZUCKERMAN, S. 1950. 'Some quantitative dental characteristics of fossil anthropoids', *Philosophical Transactions of the Royal Society*, B. 234: 485.

ASHWORTH, W. B., Jr. 1984. *Theories of the Earth, 1644–1830: The History of a Genre*, Kansas City, Mo. (Linda Hall Library).

BAKER, T. H. 1911. *Records of the Seasons, Prices of Agricultural Produce and Phenomena Observed in the British Isles*, Simpkin Marshall, London, pp. 234–5, in Torrens, H. S. 2001.

BARNES, S. B. 1934. 'The Scientific Journal, 1665–1730', *Scientific Monthly* 38: 257–60.

BEHRENSMEYER, A. K., *et al.* 1986. 'Trampling as a cause of bone surface damage and pseudo-cutmarks', *Nature* 319: 768–71.

BERGER, L. R., and CLARKE, R. J. 1995. 'Eagle involvement in accumulation of the Taung child fauna', *Journal of Human Evolution* 29: 275–99.

BERMÚDEZ, J. M., *et al.* 1997. 'A Hominid from the Lower Pleistocene of Atapuerca, Spain: Possible Ancestor to Neandertals and Modern Humans', *Science* 276: 1392–5.

BERMÚDEZ, J. M., *et al.* 2004. 'The Atapuerca sites and their contributions to the Knowledge of Human Evolution in Europe', *Evolutionary Anthropology* 13: 25–41.

BISHOP, L. C., *et al.* 2006. 'Recent Research into Oldowan Hominin Activities at Kanjera South, Western Kenya', *African Archaeological Review* 23: 31–40.

BLACK, D. 1926. 'Tertiary Man in Asia: The Chou K'ou Tiew discovery', *Nature* 118: 733–4; *Science* 64: 586–7.

—— 1927a. *On a lower molar hominid tooth from the Chou K'ou Tien deposit*, Palaeontologica Sinica, Ser. D, vol. 7, fascicule 1 (November) pp. 1–29.

—— 1927b. 'Further hominid remains of Lower Quaternary age from the Chou Kou Tien deposit', *Nature* 120: 954; *Science* 67: 135–6.

BLAKE, C. C. 1862. 'On the crania of the most ancient races of man', *Geologist* 5: 139–57.

BLUMENSCHINE, R. J., *et al.* 2003. 'Late Pliocene *Homo* and Hominid Land Use from Western Olduvai Gorge, Tanzania', *Science* 299: 1217–21.

—— 2008. 'Effects of distance from stone source on landscape-scale variation in Oldowan artifact assemblages', *Journal of Archaeological Science* 35: 76–86.

BOAZ, N. T., and CIOCHON, R. L. 2004. *Dragon Bone Hill: An Ice-Age Saga of Homo erectus*, Oxford University Press, New York.

BOCHERENS, H., *et al.* 2005. 'Isotopic evidence for diet and subsistence pattern of the Saint-Césaire I Neanderthal'. *Journal of Human Evolution* 49: 71–87.

BOHLIN, B. 1978. Personal communication, interview with author, Uppsala.

BOSWELL, P. G. H. 1935. 'Human remains from Kanam and Kanjera, Kenya Colony', *Nature* 135: 371.

BOULE, M. 1911–13. 'L'Homme fossile de La Chapelle-aux-Saints', *Annales de Paléontologie* 6, 7, 8. Paris.

—— 1913, quoted in Spencer, F. 1984 'The Neanderthals and their evolutionary significance: A brief historical survey', pp. 1–49 in Smith, F. H., and Spencer, F. (eds.) 1984, *The Origin of Modern Humans: A World Survey of the Fossil Evidence*. New York.

—— 1921. *Les Hommes fossiles*, Paris.

—— 1923. *Fossil Man*, Edinburgh.

——, and VALLOIS, H. V. 1957. *Fossil Men*, The Dryden Press, New York.

BOWER, B. 1985. 'Hunting ancient scavengers', *Science News* 127: 155–7.

BRACE, C. L. 1964. 'The fate of the "classic" Neanderthals: a consideration of hominid catastrophism', *Current Anthropology*, 5.

—— 1967. *The Stages of Human Evolution*, Prentice Hall, Englewood Cliffs, NJ.

BRAIN, C. K. 1975. 'An introduction to the South African Australopithecine bone accumulations', *Archaeozoological Studies* (ed. A. T. Clason), Amsterdam, pp. 109–19.

—— 1981. *The Hunters or the Hunted? An Introduction to African Cave Taphonomy*, University of Chicago Press, Chicago.

BRAMBLE, D. M., and LIEBERMAN, D. E. 2004. 'Endurance running and the evolution of *Homo*', *Nature* 432: 345–52.

BRÄUER, G. 1984. 'The Afro-European *sapiens* hypothesis, and hominid evolution in Asia during the late Middle and Upper Pleistocene', pp. 145–66 in Andrews, P., and Franzen, J. L., (eds.) 1984, *The Early Evolution of Man, with Special Emphasis on Southeast Asia and Africa*, Courier Forschungsinstitut Senckenberg 69.

BROCK, A., and ISAAC, G. Ll. 1974. 'Palaeomagnetic stratigraphy and chronology of the hominid-bearing sediments east of Lake Turkana, Kenya', *Nature* 247: 344–8.

BROOM, R. 1915. 'On the organ of Jacobson and its relations in the Insectivora', *Proceedings of the Zoological Society of London*, pp. 157–62, 347–54.

—— 1925a, quoted in Findlay, G. H. 1972: 52.

—— 1925b. 'Some notes on the Taungs skull', *Nature* 115: 569–71.

—— 1933. *The Coming of Man: Was it Accident or Design?* Witherby, London.

—— 1936a. 'A new fossil anthropoid skull from South Africa', *Nature* 138: 486–8.

—— 1936b. 'On an ancestral link between ape and man', *Illustrated London News* 189: 476–7.

—— 1938a. 'More discoveries of *Australopithecus*', *Nature* 141: 828–89.

BROOM, R. 1938b. 'The Missing Link is no longer missing', *Illustrated London News* 193: 513–14.

—— 1939. 'On evolution'. *Star*, 18 August, Johannesburg.

—— 1942a. 'The hand of the ape-man *Paranthropus robustus*', *Nature* 149: 513–14.

—— 1942b. 'An ankle-bone of the ape-man *Paranthropus robustus*', *Nature* 152: 689–90.

—— 1950. *Finding the Missing Link*, Watts, London.

——, and SCHEPERS, G. W. H. 1946. *The South African fossil ape-men. The Australopithecinae*, Part 1: *The occurrence and general structure of the South African ape-men*, Transvaal Museum Memoir 2.

——, ROBINSON, J. T., and SCHEPERS, G. W. H. 1950. *Sterkfontein ape-man, Plesianthropus*, Transvaal Museum Memoir 2, Pretoria.

BROWN, F. H. 1994. 'Development of Pliocene and Pleistocene chronology of the Turkana Basin, east Africa, and its relation to other sites', pp. 285–312 in Corruccini, R. S., and Ciochon, R. L. (eds.) 1995, *Integrative paths to the past: Palaeoanthopological advances in honor of F. Clark Howell*, Prentice Hall, Englewood Cliffs, NJ.

BROWN, F. H., McDOUGALL, I., DAVIES, T., and MAIER, R. 1985. 'An integrated Plio-Pleistocene chronology for the Turkana Basin', pp. 82–90 in Delson, E. (ed.) 1985, *Ancestors: The Hard Evidence*, Alan R. Liss, New York.

BROWN, P., *et al.* 2004. 'A New Small-Bodied Hominin from the Late Pleistocene of Flores, Indonesia', *Nature* 431: 1055–61.

BROWNE, J., 2006. *Darwin's Origin of Species: A Biography*, Atlantic Books, London

BRUNET, M. 2002. 'Dreams of the past', *Nature* 423: 121.

——, *et al.* 2002. 'A new hominid from the Upper Miocene of Chad, Central Africa', *Nature* 418: 145–55.

Bulletin de la Société Géologique de Normandie et des Amis du Muséum du Havre 2009, vol. 96, part 1.

BUNN, H. T. 1981. 'Archaeological evidence for meat-eating by Plio-Pleistocene hominids from Koobi Fora and Olduvai Gorge', *Nature* 291: 574–6.

—— 1982. 'Meat-eating and human evolution', Ph.D. diss. Univ. of California, Berkeley.

BUSK, G. 1864a. 'Report on the British Association Meeting'. *Bath Chronicle*, 22 September, Bath.

—— 1864b. 'Pithecoid Priscan Man from Gibraltar'. *Reader* 23 July 1864, London.

——, and FALCONER, H. 1865. 'On the fossil contents of the Genista cave, Gibraltar'. *Quarterly Journal of the Geological Society*, London, 21: 364–70.

BUTLER, D. 2001. 'The battle of Tugen Hills', *Nature* 410: 508–9.

BUTZER, K. W., and ISAAC, G. L. 1975. *After the Australopithecines*, Mouton, The Hague.

Cambridge Encyclopaedia of Human Evolution, 1992. Cambridge University Press, Cambridge.

CAMPBELL, B. 1964. 'Just another "man-ape"?', *Discovery* 25 (June): 37–8.

—— 1965. 'The nomenclature of the Hominidae', *Occasional Paper of the Royal Anthropological Institute* 23.

CANN, R. L., STONEKING, M., and WILSON, A. C. 1987. 'Mitochondrial DNA and human evolution', *Nature* 325: 31–6.

CARNOT, A. 1893. 'Recherches sur le composition générale et le teneur en fluor des os modernes et des os fossiles de differents âges', *Ann. Min.* (9, Mem.) 3: 155–95.

CAVALLI-SFORZA, L. L. 1991. 'Genes, people and languages', *Scientific American*, November, pp. 71–8.

—— 1998. 'The Chinese Human Genome Diversity Project', *Proc. Nat. Acad. Sci.*, USA, 95: 11501–3.

CAVE, A. J. E., and STRAUS, W. L. Jr. 1957. 'Pathology and Posture of Neanderthal Man'. *Quarterly Review of Biology* 32: 348–63.

CHAMBERS, R. 1844. *Vestiges of the Natural History of Creation*, London.

CHARIG, A. 1983. *A New Look at the Dinosaurs*, British Museum (Natural History), London.

CHU, J. Y., *et al.* 1998. 'Genetic relationship of populations in China', *Proc. Nat. Acad. Sci.*, USA, 95: 11763–8.

CHURCHILL, S. E. 2006. 'Bioenergetic perspectives on Neanderthal thermoregulatory and activity budgets', pp. 113–34 in Harvati, K., and Harrison, T. (eds.) 2006, *Neanderthals Revisited: New Approaches and Perspectives*, Springer, Dordrecht.

CIOCHON, R. L., and BETTIS, E. A. III. 2009. 'Asia *Homo erectus* converges in time', *Nature* 458: 153–4.

——, and FLEAGLE, J. G. (eds.) 2006. *The Human Evolution Source Book* (2nd edition), Pearson, New Jersey.

CLARK, A., *et al.* 2008. 'Genome sequences from extinct relatives', *Cell* 134: pp. 388–9.

CLARK, F. C. 1991. '*Homo habilis* in Detail', *Science*, 253: 1294–7.

CLARK, J. D. 1989. 'The origin and spread of modern humans: a broad perspective on the African evidence', pp. 565–88 in Mellars, P., and Stringer, C. (eds.) 1989, *The Human Revolution — Behavioural and Biological Perspectives on the Origins of Modern Humans*, Edinburgh University Press, Edinburgh.

CLARK, W. E. Le Gros, 1946. *Nature* 157: 863–5.

—— 1964. *The Fossil Evidence for Human Evolution*, Chicago University Press, Chicago.

—— 1967a. 'Hominid characters of the australopithecine dentition', *Journal of the Royal Anthropological Institute* 80: 37.

—— 1967b. *Man-Apes or Ape-Men?* New York.

CLARKE, R. J. 1998. 'First ever discovery of a well-preserved skull and associated skeleton of *Australopithecus*'. *South African Journal of Science* 94: 460–4.

—— 2002. 'Newly revealed information on the Sterkfontein Member 2 *Australopithecus* skeleton', *South African Journal of Science* 98: 523–6.

——, and TOBIAS, P. V. 1995. 'Sterkfontein Member 2 Foot Bones of the Oldest South African Hominid', *Science* 269: 521–4.

COLE, S. 1975. *Leakey's Luck: The Life of Louis Seymour Bazett Leakey 1903–1972*, Collins, London.

CONSTABLE, G. 1973. *The Neanderthals*, Time-Life Books, New York.

CONSTANS, N. 2009. 'Le fémur de Toumaï', *La Recherche*, July.

COOKE, H. B. S. 1976. 'Suidae from Plio-Pleistocene strata of the Rudolf Basin', in Coppens, Y., *et al.* (eds.) 1976: 251–63.

COPPENS, Y. 1994. 'The east side story: the origin of humankind', *Scientific American* 270 (5): 62–9.

——, HOWELL, F. C., ISAAC, G. Ll., and LEAKEY, R. E. F. (eds.) 1976. *Earliest Man and Environments in the Lake Rudolf Basin*, University of Chicago Press, Chicago.

CORRUCCINI, R. S., and CIOCHON, R. L. (eds.) 1995. *Integrative paths to the past: Palaeoanthopological advances in honor of F. Clark Howell*, Prentice Hall, Englewood Cliffs, NJ.

CURTIS, G. H., DRAKE, R., CERLING, T. E., and HAMPEL, J. E. 1975. 'Age of KBS tuff in Koobi Fora Formation, East Rudolf, Kenya', *Nature* 358: 395–8.

CUVIER, G. 1796. *Squelette trouvé au Paraguay* (skeleton found in Paraguay), translated by Martin Rudwick, in: Rudwick, M. J. S. 1997, *Georges Cuvier, Fossil Bones, and Geological Catastrophes*, University of Chicago Press, Chicago and London, pp. 27–32.

—— 1815. *Essay on the Theory of the Earth*, Edinburgh.

—— 1831 (trans.) *Discourse on the Revolutions of the Surface of the Globe*, Carey & Lea, Philadelphia.

—— 1837. *Edinburgh Review*, vol. 65.

DALTON, R. 2006. 'The History Man', *Nature* 443: 268–9.

—— 2009, 'Neanderthal genome to be unveiled', *Nature* 457: 645.

—— 2010. 'Fossil finger points to new human species', *Nature* 464: 472–3.

DANIEL, G. 1975. *A Hundred and Fifty Years of Archaeology*. Duckworth

DART, R. A. 1925. 'Australopithecus africanus: the Man-Ape of South Africa', *Nature* 115: 195–9.

—— 1948. 'The Makapansgat proto-human *Australopithecus prometheus*', *American Journal of Physical Anthropology*, NS 7: 259–84.

—— 1953. 'The predatory transition from ape to man', *International Anthropological and Linguistic Review* 1: 201–18.

—— 1955. 'The first australopithecine fragment from the Makapansgat pebble culture stratum', *Nature* 176: 170.

—— 1959. *Adventures with the Missing Link*, Watts, London.

DART, R. A. 1978. Interview with author, Johannesburg.

——, and KEITH, A. 1925. 'On the Taungs skull, an exchange of letters', *Nature* 116: 462.

DARWIN, CHARLES, (ed. Francis Darwin) 1909. *The Foundations of the Origin of Species, a sketch written in 1842*, University of Cambridge Press.

—— 1859 (1968). *The Origin of Species*, Penguin Books, London.

—— 1871. *The Descent of Man* (2nd edition), London.

DARWIN, E. 1794. *Zoonomia*, London, vol. 1.

DARWIN, F. (ed.) 1958. *The Autobiography of Charles Darwin and Selected Letters* (1892), Dover Publications, New York.

DAVIS, P. R. 1964. 'Hominid fossils from Bed I, Olduvai Gorge, Tanganyika', *Nature* 201: 967–70.

DAWKINS, R. 2004. 'One giant step for our sense of wonder', *The Sunday Times*, London, 31 October, p. 6.

DAWSON, C., and WOODWARD, A. S. 1913. 'On the discovery of a Palaeolithic human skull and mandible in a flint-bearing gravel overlying the Wealden (Hastings Beds) at Piltdown, Fletchling, Sussex', *Quarterly Journal of the Geological Society* 69: 117–44.

DAY, M. H. 1976. 'Hominid postcranial material from Bed I, Olduvai Gorge', in Isaac, G. Ll., and McCown, E. R. (eds.) 1976, *Human Origins: Louis Leakey and the East African Evidence*, W. A. Benjamin Inc., California.

—— 1986. *Guide to Fossil Man* (4th edition), Cassel, London.

——, and NAPIER, J. R. 1964. 'Fossil foot bones from Olduvai Gorge', *Nature* 201: 969–70.

——, and STRINGER, C. B. 1982. 'A Reconsideration of the Omo-Kibish Remains and the *erectus–sapiens* transition', in Ciochon, R. I., and Fleagle, J. G. (eds.) 2006, *The Human Evolution Source Book* (2nd edition), Pearson, New Jersey, pp. 528–37.

——, and WOOD, B. A. 1968. 'Functional affinities of the Olduvai Hominid 8 talus', *Man*, NS 3: 440–55.

——, LEAKEY, M. D., and OLSON, T. R. 1980. 'On the status of *Australopithecus afarensis*', *Science* 207: 1102–3.

——, LEAKEY, R. E. F., WALKER, A. C., and WOOD, B. A. 1975. 'New hominids from East Rudolf, Kenya, I', *American Journal of Physical Anthropology* 42: 461–76.

DEACON, H. J. 1989. 'Late Pleistocene palaeoecology and archaeology in the southern Cape, South Africa', pp. 547–64 in Mellars and Stringer, 1989.

DEINO, Alan L., *et al.* 2002. '…geochronology and paleomagnetic stratigraphy of the Lukeino and lower Chemeron Formations at Tabarin and Kapcheberek, Tugen Hills, Kenya', *J. Human Evolution* 42: 117–40.

DELSON, E. (ed.) 1985. *Ancestors: The Hard Evidence*, Alan R. Liss, New York.

—— 1987. 'Evolution and palaeobiology of robust *Australopithecus*', *Nature* 327: 654–5.

D'ERRICO, F., *et al.* 2005. '*Nassarius kraussianus* Shell Beads from Blombos Cave: Evidence for Symbolic Behavior in the Middle Stone Age', *Journal of Human Evolution* 48 (1): 3–24.

DOMINGUEZ-RODRIGO, M., *et al.* 2001. 'Woodworking activities by early humans: a plant residue analysis on Acheulian stone tools from Peninj (Tanzania)', *Journal of Human Evolution* 40: 289–99.

DUBOIS, E. 1891. 'Paleontologische onderzoekingen op Java', *Verslagen van het Mijnwezen*, Batavia, fourth quarter.

—— 1892. *Verslagen van het Mijnwezen*, Batavia, third quarter.

—— 1894. *Pithecanthropus erectus, eine menschenähnliche Uebergangsform aus Java*, Batavia.

—— 1898. 'The brain-cast of Pithecanthropus erectus', *Proceedings of the International Congress of Zoology*, Cambridge, pp. 79–96.

—— 1920. 'The proto-Australian fossil man of Wadjak, Java', *Koninklijke Akademie van Wetenschappen*; proceedings 13, Amsterdam, pp. 1013–51.

—— 1933. 'The shape and size of the brain in Sinanthropus and in Pithecanthropus', *Koninklijke Akademie van Wetenschappen*; proceedings 36, Amsterdam, pp. 415–23.

—— 1935. 'On the Gibbon-like appearance of Pithecanthropus erectus', *Koninklijke Akademie van Wetenschappen*; proceedings 38, Amsterdam, pp. 578–85.

DUBOIS, E. 1940. 'The fossil human remains discovered in Java...', *Koninklijke Akademie van Wetenschappen; proceedings* 43, Amsterdam, pp. 494–6, 842–51, 1268–75.

DUBOIS, J. M. F. Unpublished manuscript, Trinil: 'A Biography of Professor Dr Eugene Dubois, the discoverer of *Pithecanthropus erectus*'.

DUFFIN, C. J. 2005. 'The western lapidary tradition in early geological literature: medical and magical minerals', *Geology Today* 21 (2): 58–63.

EISELEY, L. 1961. *Darwin's Century: Evolution and the Men who Discovered it*, Anchor Books edition, New York.

ELLESMERE, Lord, 1849. *A Guide to Northern Antiquities*, London.

EYLES, JOAN M. 1969. 'William Smith: Some Aspects of his Life and Work', pp 142–58 in C. J. Schneer, (ed.) 1969, *Toward a History of Geology*, MIT Press, Cambridge, Mass., and London.

FALCONER, H. 1864. Letter to G. Busk of 27 August 1864, quoted by Keith, Arthur, 1911, 'The early history of the Gibraltar cranium', *Nature*, London 87: 313.

FINDLAY, G. H. 1972. *Dr Robert Broom, F.R.S. A.A.* Balkema, Cape Town.

FINLAYSON, C., *et al.* 2006. 'Late survival of Neanderthals at the southernmost extreme of Europe'. *Nature* 443: 850–3.

FITCH, F. J. 1979. Personal communication, interview with author.

FITCH F. J., and MILLER, J. A. 1970. 'Radioisotopic age determinations of Lake Rudolf artefact site', *Nature* 226: 226–8.

———— 1976. 'Conventional potassium-argon and argon-40/argon-39 dating of volcanic rocks of East Rudolf', in Coppens, Y., *et al.* (eds.) 1976: 132.

FRERE, J. 1797. Letter to the Society of Antiquaries, *Archaeologia* 13: 204.

FULLER, J. G. C. M. 2001. 'Before the hills in order stood: the beginning of the geology of time in England', pp. 15–23 in Lewis, C. L. E. and Knell, S. J. (eds.) 2001, *The Age of the Earth: From 4004 BC to AD 2002*, Geological Society, London, Special Publications, 190.

—— 2005. 'A date to remember: 4004 BC', *Earth Sciences History*, 24, part 1, 5–14. Cited in Wyse Jackson, P. 2006. *The Chronologer's Quest: Episodes in the Search for the Age of the Earth*, Cambridge University Press.

GALIK, K., *et al.* 2004. 'External and internal morphology of the *Orrorin tugenensis* femur', *Science* 305: 1450.

GARDINER, B. G. 2003. 'The Piltdown Forgery: a re-statement of the case against Hinton', *Zoological Journal of the Linnaean Society* 139: 315–35.

GARGETT, R. H. 1989. 'Grave shortcomings: the evidence for Neanderthal burial', *Current Anthropology* 32: 157–90.

GARROD, D. A. E., and BATE, D. M. A. 1937. *The Stone Age of Mount Carmel*, Oxford.

GEE, H. 1996. 'Box of bones "clinches" identity of Piltdown palaeontology hoaxer', *Nature* 381: 261–2.

GEIKIE, A. 1905. *The Founders of Geology*, Macmillan, New York.

GIAN, B. V., and CALDWELL, W. G. E. (eds.) 2006. *The Origins of Geology in Italy*, Geological Society of America.

GIBBONS, A. 2002. 'One scientist's quest for the origin of our species', *Science* 298: 1709.

—— 2006. *The First Human*, Doubleday, New York.

—— 2009a. 'A New Kind of Ancestor: *Ardipithecus* Unveiled', *Science* 326: 36–40.

—— 2009b. 'The View From Afar', *Science* 326: 41–3.

—— 2009c. 'Oldest Stone Blades Uncovered', *Science Now Daily News*, 2 April.

GITTINGS, J. 1998. 'Chinese balk at "Out of Africa" theory', *Guardian*, 3 October, London.

GORE, R. 1997. 'The First Steps', *National Geographic*, February, pp. 72–99.

GORJANOVIC-KRAMBERGER, K. 1906. *Der diluviale Mensch von Krapina in Kroatien*, Wiesbaden.

GOULD, S. J. 1987. *Time's Arrow Time's Cycle — Myth and Metaphor in the Discovery of Geological Time*, Harvard University Press, Cambridge, Mass., and London.

GREEN, R. E., *et al.* 2010. 'A draft sequence of the Neanderthal genome', *Science* 328: 710–22.

GREGORY, W. K. 1949. 'Franz Weidenreich, 1873–1949', *American Anthropologist* 51: 85–90.

HAECKEL, E. 1876. *The History of Creation*, 2 vols. London.

—— 1899. *The Last Link*, London.

—— 1906. *Last Words on Evolution*, London.

HAILE-SELASSIE, Y., SAFAW, B., and WHITE, T. D. 2004. 'Hominid cranial remains from Upper Pleistocene deposits at Aduma, Middle Awash, Ethiopia', *Am. J. Phys. Anthropol.* 123: 1–10.

HALES, W. 1809. *A New Analysis of Chronology and Geography*, 3 vols. London.

HALL, E. T. 1974. 'Old bones — but how old?', *Sunday Telegraph*, 3 September.

HALL, S. S. 2008. 'Last of the Neanderthals', *National Geographic*, October, 214 (4): 34–59.

HALSTEAD, L. B. 1978. 'The cladistic revolution — can it make the grade?' *Nature* 276: 759–60.

HANSON, B. 2009. 'Light on the Origin of Man', *Science* 326: 60.

HARDING, R., and TELEKI, G. (eds.) 1978. *Omnivorous Primates*, New York.

HARRISON, E. R. 1928. *Harrison of Ightham*, London.

HARTWIG, W. C. (ed.) 2002. *The Primate Fossil Record*, Cambridge University Press, Cambridge.

HARVATI, K., and HARRISON, T. (eds.) 2006. *Neanderthals Revisited: New Approaches and Perspectives*, Springer, Dordrecht.

——, FROST, S. R., and McNULTY, K. P. 2004. 'Neanderthal taxonomy reconsidered', *Proc. Nat. Acad. Sci.* 101 (5): 1147–52.

HAUGHTON, S. H. 1920. 'On the occurrence of a species of baboon in deposits near Taungs', Abstract in *Transactions of the Royal Society of South Africa*, 12, 1925: lxviii.

HAWKS, J. 2009. http://johnhawks.net/weblog/fossils/sahelanthropus/was-toumai-bergeret-recherche-2009.html

HAY, R. L. 1976. *Geology of Olduvai Gorge*, University of California Press, Berkeley.

HEDEEN, S., and FARAGHER, J. M. 2008. *Big Bone Lick*, University of Kentucky Press.

HENNIG, W. 1966. *Phylo-genetic Systematics*, Urbana.

HENRY, A. G., BROOKS, A. S., and PIPERNO, D. R. 2010. 'Microfossils in calculus demonstrate consumption of plants and cooked foods in Neanderthal diets', *Proc. Nat. Acad. Sci.*, Early Edition at: www.onas.org/cqi/doi/10.101073/pnas.1016868108

HENSHILWOOD, C. 2004. Quoted in *Guardian*, London, 16 April.

——, et al. 2004. 'Middle Stone Age Shell Beads from South Africa', *Science* 304: 404.

HILL, A. 1976. Personal communication, Nairobi.

—— 1985. 'Early hominid from Baringo, Kenya', *Nature* 315: 222–4.

—— 2002. 'Paleoanthropological research in the Tugen Hills, Kenya', *Journal of Human Evolution* 42: 1–10.

——, and WARD, S. 1988. 'Origin of the Hominidae: the record of African large hominoid evolution between 14 My and 4 My', *Yearbook of Physical Anthropology*, vol. 31.

————, and BROWN, B. 1992. 'Anatomy and age of the Lothagam mandible', *Journal of Human Evolution*, 22: 439–51.

HINRICHSEN, D. 1978. 'How old are our ancestors?' *New Scientist*, London, 78: 571.

HOCKETT, B., and HAWS, J. A. 2005. 'Nutritional ecology and the human demography of Neandertal extinction', *Quaternary International* 137: 21–34.

HOOD, D. 1964. *Davidson Black—A Biography*, University of Toronto Press.

HOPKIN, M. 2005. 'Hirst's hobbit', *Nature* 434: 702.

HOWELL, F. C., and COPPENS, Y. 1976. 'An overview of Hominidae from the Omo Succession, Ethiopia', pp. 522–32 in Coppens, Y., Howell, F. C., Isaac, G. Ll., and Leakey, R. E. F. (eds.) 1976, *Earliest Man and Environments in the Lake Rudolf Basin*, Chicago.

HOWELLS, W. W. 1976. 'Explaining modern man: evolutionists versus migrationists', *Journal of Human Evolution* 5: 477–95.

HRDLICKA, A. 1927. 'The Neanderthal phase of man', *J. Roy. Anthrop. Inst.* 57: 249–74.

HUXLEY, T. H. 1863. *Evidence as to Man's Place in Nature*, London.

—— 1863. *Man's Place in Nature*, Ann Arbor edition 1959, Michigan.

HUXLEY, T. H. 1864. 'Further remarks upon the human remains from the Neanderthal', *Natural History Review* 1: 429–46.

ISAAC, G. Ll. 1976. Introduction. Coppens, Y., *et al.* (eds.) 1976: 3–7.

——1978. 'The food-sharing behavior of protohuman hominids', *Scientific American* 238 (4): 90–106.

—— 1981. 'Emergence of human behaviour patterns', pp. 177–88 in Young, J. Z., Jope, E. M., and Oakley, K. P. (eds.) 1981, *The Emergence of Man*, Phil. Trans. R. Soc. B. 292: 3–5.

——, and McCOWN, E. R. (eds.) 1976. *Human Origins: Louis Leakey and the East African Evidence*, W. A. Benjamin Inc., California.

JAHN, M. J. 1969. 'Some notes on Dr. Scheuchzer...', pp. 193–213 in Schneer, C. J. (ed.) 1969, *Toward a History of Geology*, MIT Press, Cambridge, Mass. and London.

JIA, Lanpo, 1980. *Early Man in China*, Beijing.

——, and HUANG, WEIWEN, 1990. *The Story of Peking Man: From Archaeology to Mystery*, Oxford University Press, New York.

JOHANSON, D. C. 1974. Quoted in Ottoway, D. B. 1974a. '3-million-year-old human fossils found', *Herald Tribune*, Paris, 28 October.

——1976. 'Ethiopia yields first "Family" of early man', *National Geographic*, December, 150: 790–811.

——1978. Interview with author, Cleveland, Ohio.

——1979. 'Our roots go deeper', in *Science Year 1979*, Worldbook Childcraft International Inc., Chicago.

—— 1987. Quoted in Lewin, R. 1987a. 'The earliest "humans" were more like apes', *Science* 236: 1061–3.

——, and EDEY, M. A. 1981. *Lucy: The Beginnings of Humankind*, Simon & Schuster, New York.

——, and EDGAR, BLAKE, 1996. *From Lucy to Language*, Simon & Schuster, New York.

——, and TAIEB, M. 1976. 'Plio-Pleistocene hominid discoveries in Hadar, Ethiopia', *Nature* 260: 293–7.

——, SPLINGAER, M., and BOAZ, N. T. 1976. 'Paleontological excavations in the Shungura Formation, Lower Omo Basin, 1969–73', pp. 402–20 in Coppens, Y., Howell, F. C., Isaac, G. Ll., and Leakey, R. E. F (eds.) 1976, *Earliest Man and Environments in the Lake Rudolf Basin*, University of Chicago Press, Chicago.

——, WHITE, T. D., and COPPENS, Y. 1978. 'A new species of the genus *Australopithecus* (Primates: Hominidae) from the Pliocene of Eastern Africa', *Kirtlandia* 28: 1–14.

——, *et al.* 1987. 'New partial skeleton of *Homo habilis* from Olduvai Gorge, Tanzania', *Nature* 327: 205–9.

JONES, J. 1985. 'Hutton's agricultural research and his life as a farmer', *Annals of Science* 42: 537–601.

—— 1978. Personal communication, interview with author, Pretoria.

KEITH, A. 1894. *Journal of Anatomy* 28: 149–335.

—— 1912*a*. *The Human Body*, London.

—— 1912*b*. 'Modern problems relating to the antiquity of man', *Report of the British Association*, Dundee, p. 758.

—— 1913*a*. 'The human skull etc. from Piltdown', *Quarterly Journal of the Geological Society* 69.

—— 1913*b*. Report in *The Times*, 11 August.

—— 1913*c*. 'The Piltdown skull and brain cast', *Nature* 92: 197.

—— 1914. 'The reconstruction of fossil human skulls', *Journal of the Royal Anthropological Institute*, London, 44: 12.

—— 1915. *The Antiquity of Man*, London.

—— 1925*a*. *The Antiquity of Man* (2nd edition), London.

—— 1925*b*. 'The Taungs skull', *Nature* 116: 11.

—— 1931. *New Discoveries Relating to the Antiquity of Man*, Norton, New York.

—— 1942. *The Rationalist Annual*, London.

—— 1948. *A New Theory of Human Evolution*, Watts & Co., London.

—— 1950. *An Autobiography*, London.

KEITH, A., and DART, R. 1925. 'On the Taungs skull, an exchange of letters', *Nature* 116: 462.

——, SMITH, G. E., WOODWARD, A. S., and DUCKWORTH, W. L. H. 1925. 'The fossil anthropoid from Taungs', *Nature* 115: 234–6.

KERN, E. P. H. 1981. 'Battle of the Bones', *Life* 4 (12): 109–20.

KING, W. 1864. 'The reputed fossil man of the Neanderthal', *Quarterly Journal of Science* 1: 88–97.

KINGSTON, J. D., MARINO, D. D., and HILL, A. 1994. 'Isotopic evidence for Neogene hominid paleoenvironments in the Kenya Rift Valley', *Science* 264: 955–9.

KITTLER, R., KAYSER, M., and STONEKING, M. 2003. 'Molecular evolution of *Pediculus humanus* and the origin of clothing', *Current Biology* 13: 1414–17.

KLEIN, R. G. 1999. *The Human Career* (2nd edition), University of Chicago Press, Chicago and London.

KOENIGSWALD, G. H. R. von, and WEIDENREICH, F. 1939. 'The relationship between Pithecanthropus and Sinanthropus', *Nature* 144: 926–9.

KÖNIG, C. 1814. 'On a fossil human skeleton from Guadeloupe', *Philosophical Transactions of the Royal Society* 34: 107–22.

KRAMER, L. M. J. 1953. Letter to *The Times*, 28 November.

KRINGS, M., CAPELLI, C., and TSCHENTSCHER, F. 2006. 'Human evolution: Clues from Neanderthal mtDNA control region sequences — What's next?' pp. 320–8 in Schmitz, R. W. (ed.) 2006, *Neanderthal 1856–2006*, Verlag Philipp von Zabern, Mainz.

——, STONE, A., SCHMITZ, R. W., KRAINITZKI, H., STONEKING, M., and PÄÄBO, S. 1997. 'Neanderthal DNA Sequences and the Origin of Modern Humans', *Cell* 90: 19–30.

LAHR, M. M., and FOLEY, R. 2004. 'Human evolution writ small', *Nature* 431: 1044.

LALUEZA-FOX, C., et al. 2011. 'Genetic evidence for patrilocal mating behaviour among Neanderthal groups', *Proc. Nat. Acad. Sci.* 108: 250–3.

LARTET, L. 1869. 'Une sépultre des troglodytes du Périgord', *Annales des Sciences naturelles*, 5th series, vol. 10.

—— and CHAPLAIN-DUPARC, H. 1874. 'Une sépultre des anciens troglodytes des Pyrénées', *Matériaux* 9.

LATIMER, B. 2005. 'The Perils of Being Bipedal', *Annals of Biomechanical Engineering* 33 (1): 3–6.

LEAKEY, L. S. B. 1932*a*. Article in *The Times*, London, 9 March.

—— 1932*b*. Article in *The Times*, London, 19 April.

—— 1934. *Adam's Ancestors*, London.

—— 1936. 'Fossil human remains from Kanam and Kanjera, Kenya Colony', *Nature* 138: 643.

—— 1937 (1973). *White African*, Ballantine Books, New York.

—— 1951. *Olduvai Gorge: A Report on the Evolution of the Hand-Axe Culture in Beds I–IV*, Cambridge University Press, Cambridge.

—— 1954. 'The giant animals of prehistoric Tanganyika, and the hunting grounds of Chellean man…', *Illustrated London News* 244: 1047–51.

—— 1958*a*. 'A giant child among the giant animals of Olduvai?' *Illustrated London News* 232: 1104–5.

—— 1958*b*. 'Recent discoveries at Olduvai Gorge, Tanganyika', *Nature*, 181: 1099–1103.

—— 1959*a*. 'A new fossil skull from Olduvai', *Nature* 184: 491–3.

—— 1959*b*. Reply to Robinson, J. T. 1959, *Nature* 185: 408.

—— 1959*c*. Quoted in *The Times*, London, 4 September.

—— 1960*a*. 'Finding the world's earliest man', *National Geographic* 118: 420–35.

—— 1960*b*. 'From the Taung skull to "Nutcracker Man"', *Illustrated London News*, 236:44.

—— 1961. 'New finds at Olduvai Gorge', *Nature* 189: 649–50.

—— 1965. *Olduvai Gorge, 1951–1961*. vol. 1, Cambridge University Press, Cambridge.

—— (ed.) 1969*a*. *Fossil Vertebrates of Africa*, vol. 1, Academic Press, London.

—— 1969*b*. Public lecture, California. Recording in possession of Leakey estate.

LEAKEY, L. S. B., *et al.* 1933. 'The Oldoway human skeleton', *Nature* 131: 397–8.

——, EVERDEN, J. F., and CURTIS, G. H. 1961. 'Age of Bed 1, Olduvai Gorge, Tanganyika', *Nature* 191: 478–9.

——, HOPWOOD, A. T., and RECK, H. 1931. 'Age of the Oldoway bone beds, Tanganyika', *Nature* 128: 724.

——, SIMPSON, R. DE ETTE, and CLEMENTS, T. 1968. 'Archaeological Excavations in the Calico Mountains, California: Preliminary Report', *Science* 160: 1022–3.

——, TOBIAS, P. V., and NAPIER, J. R. 1964. 'A new species of the genus *Homo* from Olduvai Gorge', *Nature* 202: 7–9.

LEAKEY, M. D. 1967. 'Preliminary survey of the cultural material from Beds I and II Olduvai Gorge, Tanzania', in Bishop, W. W., and Clark, J. D. (eds.) 1967, *Background to Evolution in Africa*, University of Chicago Press, Chicago, p. 417.

—— 1971. *Olduvai Gorge*, vol. 3, *Excavations in Beds I and II*, Cambridge University Press, Cambridge.

—— 1979*a*. Interview with author, Olduvai Gorge.

—— 1979*b*. *Olduvai Gorge: My Search for Early Man*, Collins, London.

—— 1981. 'Tracks and Tools', pp. 95–102 in Young, J. Z., Jope, E. M., and Oakley, K. P. (eds.) 1981, *The Emergence of Man*, Phil. Trans. Roy. Soc. B. 292.

—— 1984. *Disclosing the Past*, Doubleday & Co., New York.

——, and HARRIS, J. M. (eds.) 1987. *Laetoli: A Pliocene Site in Northern Tanzania*, Clarendon Press, Oxford.

——, and HAY, R. L. 1979. 'Pliocene footprints in the Laetoli beds at Laetoli, northern Tanzania', *Nature* 278: 317–23.

——, *et al.* 1976. 'Fossil hominids from the Laetoli Beds', *Nature* 262: 460–6.

LEAKEY, R. E. F. 1969. 'New cercopithecidae from the Chemeron Beds of Lake Baringo, Kenya', pp. 53–69 in Leakey, L. S. B. (ed.), 1969*a*, *Fossil Vertebrates of Africa*, vol. 1, Academic Press, London.

—— 1970*a*. 'In search of man's past at Lake Rudolf', *National Geographic* 137: 712–33.

—— 1970b. 'Fauna and artefacts from a new Plio-Pleistocene locality near Lake Rudolf in Kenya', *Nature* 226: 223–4.

—— 1971. 'Further evidence of Lower Pleistocene hominids from Lake Rudolf, North Kenya', *Nature* 231: 241–5.

—— 1972a. 'Further evidence of Lower Pleistocene hominids from Lake Rudolf, North Kenya, 1971', *Nature* 237: 264–9.

—— 1972b. 'New evidence for the evolution of man', *Socisl Biology* 19: 99–114.

—— 1972c. 'Man and sub-Men on Lake Rudolf', *New Scientist* 56: 385–7.

—— 1973a. 'Skull 1470', *National Geographic* 143: 819–29.

—— 1973b. 'Further evidence of Lower Pleistocene hominids from East Rudolf, North Kenya', *Nature* 242: 170–3.

—— 1977. Quoted in 'Puzzling out man's ascent', *Time*, 7 November.

—— 1978. Interview with author, Nairobi.

—— 1979a. Personal communication, interview with author.

—— 1979b. Quoted in Rensberger, B. 1979. 'Rival anthropologists divide on "Pre-human" find', *New York Times*, 18 February.

——, and LEWIN, R. 1977. *Origins*, Macdonald and Jane's, London.

——, and WALKER, A. C. 1980. 'On the status of *Australopithecus afarensis*', *Science*, 207: 1103.

LEBATARD, A.-M., *et al.* 2008. 'Cosmogenic nuclide dating…', *PNAS*, 105 (9): 3226–31.

LEE, R. B. 1968. 'What hunters do for a living, or, how to make out on scarce resources', pp. 30–48 in Lee, R. B., and DeVore, I. (eds.), 1968, *Man the Hunter*, Aldine Press, New York.

——, and DEVORE, I. (eds.) 1968. *Man the Hunter*, Aldine Press, New York.

LÉVEQUE, F., and VANDERMEERSCH, B. 1980. 'Les Découvertes de restes humains dans un horizon Castelperronien de Saint-Césaire (Charrente-Maritime)', *Bull. Soc. Préhist. Fr.* 77: 35.

LEWIN, R. 1984. 'Man the scavenger', *Science* 224: 720–1.

—— 1986. 'New fossil upsets human family', *Science* 233: 123–4.

LEWIN, R. 1987a. 'The earliest "humans" were more like apes', *Science* 236: 1061–3.

—— 1987b. *Bones of Contention*. Simon & Schuster, New York.

LEWIS, C. L. E., and KNELL, S. J. (eds.) 2001. *The Age of the Earth: from 4004 BC to AD 2002*, Geological Society, London, Special Publications, 190.

LICHFIELD, J., and CONNOR, S. 2001. 'How 14 pieces of bone and six million years could rewrite the story of human evolution', *Independent*, London, 7 February, p. 3.

LEIBNITZ, G. 1696 at: http://www.leibnitz-translations.com/tentzel.htm AI 13, p.204, 3/13 August 1696

LORDKIPANIDZE, D., *et al.* 2005. 'The earliest toothless hominin skull', *Nature* 434: 717–18.

LORENZ, K. 1966. *On Aggression*, translated by Marjorie Latzke, Methuen, London.

LOUCHART, A., *et al.* 2009. 'Taphonomic, Avian, and Small-Vertebrate Indicators of the *Ardipithecus ramidus* Habitat', *Science* 326: 20; and online 66e1–66e4.

LOVEJOY, C. O. 1973. 'The gait of australopithecines', *Yearbook of Physical Anthropology* 17: 147–61.

—— 1975. 'Biomechanical perspectives on the lower limb of early hominids', pp. 291–326 in Tuttle, R. H. (ed.) 1976, *Primate Morphology and Evolution*, The Hague.

—— 1988. 'Evolution of Human Walking', *Scientific American* 259: 118–25.

——, *et al.* 2009a. 'Combining Prehension and Propulsion: The Foot of *Ardipithecus ramidus*', *Science* 326: 26; and online p. 72e1 – 72e8.

——, *et al.* 2009b. 'The Pelvis and Femur of *Ardipithecus ramidus*: The Emergence of Upright Walking', *Science* 326: 25; online p. 71e5.

——, *et al.* 2009c. 'Careful Climbing in the Miocene: The Forelimbs of *Ardipithecus ramidus* and Humans are Primitive', *Science* 326, online p. 70e7.

—— 2009d. 'Reexamining Human Origins in the Light of *Ardipithecus ramidus*', *Science* 326; online p. 74e1.

——, HEIPLE, K. G., and BURNSTEIN, A. H. 1973. 'The gait of *Australopithecus*', *American Journal of Physical Anthropology*, 38: 757–80.

LUBBOCK, J. 1865. *Prehistoric Times*, London.

LYELL, C. 1863. *The Antiquity of Man*, John Murray, London.

LYNE, C. W. 1916. 'The significance of the radiographs of the Piltdown teeth', *Proceedings of the Royal Society of Medicine* 9 (3 Odont. Sect.): 33–62.

McBREARTY, S., and BROOKS, A. S. 2000. 'The revolution that wasn't: a new interpretation of the origin of modern human behavior', *Journal of Human Evolution* 39: 453–563.

——, and JABLONSKI, N. G. 2005. 'First fossil chimpanzee', *Nature* 437: 105–8.

MacCURDY, G. G. 1916. 'The revision of *Eoanthropus dawsoni*', *Science* 43: 228–31.

McDOUGALL, I. 1985. 'K-Ar and ^{40}Ar/^{39}Ar dating of the hominid-bearing Plio-Pleistocene of Koobi-Fora, Lake Turkana, northern Kenya', *Geol. Soc. Am. Bull.* 96: 792–4.

——, BROWN, F. H., and FLEAGLE, J. G., 2005. 'Stratigraphic placement and age of modern humans from Kibish, Ethiopia', *Nature* 433: 733–6.

McKIE, R. 2002. 'Fossil find of the century…', *Observer* (London), 14 July, p. 6.

MANN, J. 2010. *Ardipithecus ramidus*. http://www.youtube.com/watch?v=S-DCcrLlcL4

MANTELL, G. A. 1850. 'On the remains of man…', *Archaeological Journal*, December, p. 337.

MARSTON, A. 1937. 'The Swanscombe Skull', *Journal of the Royal Anthropological Institute*, London, 67: 394.

MARTIN, R. 2006. Quoted in the *Los Angeles Times*, 20 May.

MAYER, F. 1864. 'Ueber die fossilen Ueberreste eines menschlichen Schädels und Skeletes in einer Felsenhöhle des Düssel — oder Neanderthales', *Arch. Anst. Physiol.*, Leipzig, pp. 1–26.

MAYR, E. 1944. 'On the concept and terminology of vertical subspecies and species', *National Research Council Bulletin*, 2: 11–16.

—— 1951. 'Taxonomic categories in fossil hominids', *Cold Spring Harbor Symposia on Quantitative Biology* 15: 108–18.

—— 1976. *Evolution and the Diversity of Life*, London.

MELLARS, P., and STRINGER, C. (eds.) 1989. *The Human Revolution — Behavioural and Biological Perspectives on the Origins of Modern Humans*, Edinburgh University Press, Edinburgh.

MIDDLETON, J. 1844. 'On fluorine in bones, its source, and its application in the determination of the geological age of fossil bones', *Proceedings of the Geological Society* 4: 431–3.

MILLER, G. S. 1915. 'The jaw of Piltdown Man', *Smithsonian Miscellaneous Collections* 65: 1–31.

—— 1929. 'The controversy over human "missing links"', *Smithsonian Report for 1928*. Washington, DC, pp. 413–65.

MIRAZON, M., and FOLEY, R. 1994. 'Multiple dispersals and modern human origins', *Evolutionary Anthropology* 3: 48–60.

MOIR, J. R. 1912. 'The occurrence of a human skeleton in a glacial deposit at Ipswich', *Proceedings of the Prehistory Society of East Anglia*, 1.

MORTILLET, G. de, 1883. *Le Préhistorique*, Paris.

MORWOOD, M. J., and JUNGERS, W. L. 2009. 'Paleoanthropological research at Liang Bua, Flores, Indonesia', *J. Hum. Evol.* 57: 437–648.

NAPIER, J. R. 1962. 'Fossil hand bones from Olduvai Gorge', *Nature* 196: 409–11.

NEWTON, E. T. 1895. 'On a human skull and limb bones found in the Palaeolithic terrace-gravel at Galley Hill, Kent', *Quart. J. Geol. Soc. Lond.* 51: 505–27.

NUTTALL, G. H. F. 1904. *Blood Immunity and Blood Relationships*, Cambridge.

OAKLEY, K. P. 1956. 'The earliest toolmakers', *Antiquity* 30: 4–8.

—— 1964. 'The evolution of man', *Discovery* 25 (August): 49.

——, and HOSKINS, C. R. 1950. 'New evidence on the antiquity of Piltdown Man', *Nature* 165: 379–82.

——, and LEAKEY, M. D. 1937. 'Report on excavations at Jaywick Sands, Essex (1934)', *Proceedings of the Prehistoric Society* 3: 217–60.

——, and MONTAGU, M. F. A., 1949. 'A reconsideration of the Galley Hill skeleton', *Bulletin of the British Museum (Natural History), Geology* 1 (2): 27–46.

OSBORN, H. F. 1922. Quoted in '*Hesperopithecus*, the first anthropoid ape found in America', *American Museum Novitiates* (1925), 37: 1–5.

—— 1925. *American Museum of Natural History Bulletin*, February 1925, quoted in *The Times*, London, 25 February 1928.

—— 1927. *Man rises to Parnassus*, Princeton, NJ.

OTTOWAY, D. B. 1974*a*. '3-million-year-old human fossils found', *Herald Tribune*, Paris, 28 October.

—— 1974*b*. 'Oldest partial skeleton of "Man" is found', *Herald Tribune*, Paris, 27 December.

OWEN, R. 1848. *On the Archetype and Homologies of the Vertebrate Skeleton*, London.

—— 1855. 'Of the anthropoid apes and their relation to Man', *Proceedings of the Royal Institution of Great Britain 1854–1858*, 3: 26–41.

—— 1860. 'Darwin on the Origin of Species', *Edinburgh Review* 3: 487–532.

—— 1894. *The Life of Richard Owen by his Grandson*, John Murray, London.

—— 2007. *On the Nature of Limbs*, University of Chicago Press.

OXNARD, C. E. 1972. 'Functional morphology in primates: some mathematical and physical methods', in Tuttle, R. (ed.) 1972, *The Functional and Evolutionary Biology of Primates*, Chicago University Press.

PÄÄBO, S. 1985. 'Molecular cloning of Ancient Egyptian mummy DNA', *Nature* 314: 644–5.

—— 1997. Quoted in the *Guardian*, 11 July, p. 3; *New Scientist*, 19 July 1997, p. 5.

PARFITT, S. A., *et al.* 2005. 'The earliest record of human activity in northern Europe', *Nature* 438: 1008–12.

——, *et al.* 2010. 'Early Pleistocene human occupation at the edge of the boreal zone in northwest Europe', *Nature* 466: 229–33.

PARKINGTON, J. 2001. 'Milestones: The Impact of the Systematic Exploitation of Marine Foods on Human Evolution', pp. 327–36 in Tobias, P. V., Raath, M. A., Moggi-Cecchi, J., and Doyle, G. A. (eds.) 2001, *Humanity from African Naissance to Coming Millennia*. Florence University Press and Witwatersrand University Press, Florence and Johannesburg.

PARTRIDGE, T. C. 1973. 'Geomorphological dating of cave opening at Makapansgat, Sterkfontein, Swartkrans and Taung', *Nature* 246: 75–9.

PATTERSON, B., BEHRENSMEYER, A. K., and SILL, W. D. 1970. 'Geology of a new Pliocene locality in northwestern Kenya', *Nature* 256: 279–84.

PATTERSON, C., *et al.* 1979. 'The salmon, the lungfish and the cow: a reply', *Nature* 277: 175–6.

PAYNE, M. 1978. Interview with author, Washington.

PEI, W. C. 1929. 'An account of the discovery of an adult *Sinanthropus* skull in the Chou K'ou tien deposit', *Geological Survey of China Bulletin* 8 (3).

PENGELLY, W. 1869. 'The Literature of Kent's Cavern', *Trans. Devon Association* 16: 189–434.

PEPYS, SAMUEL, 1926. *Private Correspondence and Miscellaneous Papers.* Edited by J. R. Tanner, 2 vols., London, vol. 1, p. 23.

PILBEAM, D. 1972. *The Ascent of Man*, Macmillan, New York.

PILBEAM, D., *et al.* 1982. 'New hominoid skull material from the Miocene of Pakistan', *Nature* 295: 232–4.

PLOT, R. 1677. *The Natural History of Oxfordshire, being an essay towards the Natural History of England.* Oxford, pp.131–9 at: http://www.oum.ox.ac.uk/learning/pdfs/plot.pdf

PLUMMER, T. 2004. 'Flaked Stones and Old Bones: Biological and Cultural Evolution at the Dawn of Technology', *Yearbook of Physical Anthropology* 47: 118–64.

——, KINYUA, A. M., and POTTS, R. 1994. 'Provenancing of Hominid and Mammalian Fossils from Kanjera, Kenya, using EDXRF', *J. of Archaeological Science* 21: 553–63.

POIRIER, F. E. 1995. 'Dali, a skull of Archaic *Homo sapiens* from China', in Wu, X., and Poirier, F. E. 1995.

POTTS, R. 1984. 'Home bases and early hominids', *American Scientist* 72: 338–47.

—— 1986. 'Temporal Span of Bone Accumulations at Olduvai Gorge and Implications for Early Hominid Foraging Behavior', *Paleobiology* 12 (winter): 25–31.

—— 1998, quoted at : www.washingtonpost.com/wpsrv/national/daily/dec98/safrica10.htm

——, and SHIPMAN, P. 1981. 'Cutmarks made by stone tools on bones from Olduvai Gorge, Tanzania', *Nature* 291: 577–80.

POULTON, J. 1987. 'All about Eve', *New Scientist*, 14 May, pp. 51–3.

QUATREFAGES, A. de, and HAMY, E. T. 1882. *Crania ethnica: Les Crânes des races humaines*, pt. 1: *Races humaines fossiles*, Paris.

RADFORD, T. 2004. 'Flawed genius of Darwin's arch rival', *Guardian*, 19 July, London.

RAK, Y. 1983. *The Australopithecine Face*, Academic Press, New York.

RAPPAPORT, R. 1997. *When Geologists were Historians, 1665–1750*, Cornell University Press, Ithaca and London.

RAVEN, C. E. 1942. *John Ray Naturalist: His Life and Works*, Cambridge University Press, Cambridge.

READER, J. A. 1978. 'Tim White presents *Australopithecus afarensis*', Notes on seminar and discussion, 28 June, Nairobi.

RECK, H. 1914. Quoted in 'A Man of 150,000 years ago?' *Illustrated London News*, 4 April, p. 563.

REICH, D., *et al.* 2010. 'Genetic history of an archaic hominin group from Denisova Cave in Siberia', *Nature* 468: 1053–60.

RENSBERGER, B. 1979. 'Rival anthropologists divide on "pre-human" find', *New York Times*, 18 February.

RICHARDS, M. P., and TRINKAUS, E. 2009. 'Isotopic evidence for the diets of European Neanderthals and early modern humans', *Proc. Nat. Acad. Sci.* 106: 16034–9.

——, *et al.* 2000. 'Neanderthal diet at Vindija and Neanderthal predation'. *Proc. Nat. Acad. Sci.* 97 (13): 7663–6.

RICHMOND, B., and JUNGERS, W. L. 2008. '*Orrorin tugenensis* Femoral Morphology and the Evolution of Hominin Bipedalism', *Science* 319: 1662–5.

——, and STRAIT, D. S. 2000. 'Evidence that humans evolved from a knuckle-walking ancestor', *Nature* 404: 382–5.

RIGHTMIRE, G. P. 1998. 'Human evolution in the Middle Pleistocene: the role of *Homo heidelbergensis*', *Evolutionary Anthropology* 6: 218–27.

RIVIÈRE, E. 1887. *De l'Antiquité de l'Homme dans les Alpes-Maritimes*, Paris.

ROBINSON, J. T. 1959. 'An alternative interpretation of the supposed giant deciduous hominid tooth from Olduvai', *Nature* 185: 407.

—— 1960. 'The affinities of the new Olduvai australopithecine', *Nature* 186: 456–7.

ROBINSON, J. T. 1961. 'Australopithecines and the origin of Man', *Ann. Rep. Smithsonian Institution*, 1961: 479–500.

—— 1965. '*Homo habilis* and the australopithecines', *Nature* 205: 121–4.

——, and MASON, R. 1957. 'Occurrence of stone artifacts with *Australopithecus* at Sterkfontein', *Nature* 180: 521.

ROGER, J. 1997. *Buffon: A Life in Natural History*, Cornell University Press, Ithaca.

Royal Anthropological Institute, Proceedings, 1933. 'Early human remains in East Africa', *Man* 33: 65–8.

RUDWICK, M. J. S. 1972. *The Meaning of Fossils: Episodes in the History of Palaeontology*, MacDonald, London.

—— 1996. *Cuvier and Brongniart, William Smith and the Reconstruction of Geohistory*, Earth Sciences History 15, Tacoma, Wash.

—— 1997. *Georges Cuvier, Fossil Bones, and Geological Catastrophes*, University of Chicago Press, Chicago and London.

—— 2001. 'Jean-André de Luc and nature's chronology', pp. 51–60 in Lewis, C. L. E. and Knell, S. J. (eds.) 2001, *The Age of the Earth: From 4004 BC to AD 2002*, Geological Society, London, Special Publications, 190.

—— 2004. *The New Science of Geology: Studies in the Earth Sciences in the Age of Revolution*, Variorum Collected Studies Series CS789, Ashgate Variorum, Hampshire, England.

—— 2005. *Bursting the Limits of Time: The Reconstruction of Geohistory in the Age of Revolution*, University of Chicago Press, Chicago and London.

SAMPLE, I. 2010*a*. 'Most humans have DNA link to Neanderthals', *Guardian*, 7 May, p. 21.

—— 2010*b*. 'Fossil finger points to previously unknown group of human relatives', *Guardian*, 22 December.

—— 2010*c*. 'Meat and two veg: the cooked diet of Neanderthals', *Guardian*, 28 December, p. 14.

SARICH, V. M., and WILSON, A. C. 1967. 'Immunological time scale for hominid evolution', *Science* 158: 1200–3.

SCHAAFFHAUSEN, H. 1858. *On the crania of the most ancient races of man*, Muller's Archiv 1858, p. 453; translated by George Busk 1861 with remarks and original figures, taken from a cast of the Neanderthal cranium, *Natural History Review*, April 1861, 155–75.

SCHEUCHZER, J. 1708. Quoted in Jahn, M. J. 1969. 'Some notes on Dr. Scheuchzer…', pp.193–213 in Schneer, C. J. (ed.) 1969, *Toward a History of Geology*, MIT Press, Cambridge, Mass., and London.

SCHLOTHHEIM, M. de. 1820. Letter in *The Isis*, no. 8, suppl. 6; quoted in Cuvier, G. 1831 pp. 81–5.

SCHMERLING, P. C. 1833–4. *Recherches sur les Ossements Fossiles découverts dans les Cavernes de la Province de Liége*, Liége.

SCHMITZ, R. W. (ed.) 2006a. *Neanderthal 1856–2006*, Verlag Philipp von Zabern, Mainz am Rhein.

—— 2006b. 'The discovery of fossil man in the 18th and 19th century', pp. 9–16 in Schmitz, R. W. (ed.) 2006a, *Neanderthal 1856–2006*, Verlag Philipp von Zabern, Mainz am Rhein.

SCHNEER, C. J. (ed.) 1969. *Toward a History of Geology*, MIT Press, Cambridge, Mass., and London.

SCHOETENSACK, O. 1908. *Der Unterkiefer des Homo heidelbergensis aus den Sanden von Mauer bei Heidelberg*, Leipzig.

SCHWALBE, G. 1906. *Studien zur Vorgeschichte des Menschen*, Stuttgart.

SEMAW, S., *et al.* 1997. '2.5-million-year-old stone tools from Gona, Ethiopia', *Nature* 385: 333–6.

SENUT, B., PICKFORD, M., GOMMERY, D., MEIN, P., CHEBOI, K., and COPPENS, Y. 2001. 'First hominid from the Miocene (Lukeino Formation, Kenya)', *Comptes Rendus de l'Acadèmie des Sciences, Sciences de la Terre et des Planètes* 332: 137–44.

SERRE, DAVID, *et al.* 2004. 'No Evidence of Neanderthal mtDNA Contribution to Early Modern Humans', *PloS Biology* 2: 313–17.

SHAPIRO, H. L. 1974. *Peking Man*, George Allen & Unwin, London.

SHEN, G., *et al.* 2009. 'Age of Zhoukoudian *Homo erectus*…', *Nature* 458: 198–200.

SHIPMAN, P. 1981. Quoted in Lewin, R. 1981. 'Protohuman activity etched in fossil bones', *Science* 213: 123–4.

—— 1984a. 'The earliest bone tools: re-assessing the evidence from Olduvai Gorge', *Anthroquest* 29: 9–10.

SHIPMAN, P. 1984b. 'Ancestors: scavenger hunt', *Natural History* 93 (4): 20–7.

SIMONS, E. L. 1965. 'New fossil apes from Egypt and the initial differentiation of the Hominoidea', *Nature* 205: 135–9.

SIMPSON, S. W., *et al.* 2008. 'A Female *Homo erectus* Pelvis from Gona, Ethiopia', *Science* 322: 1089–92.

SMITH, F. H., and SPENCER, F. (eds.) 1984. *The Origin of Modern Humans*, New York.

SMITH, G. E. 1912. 'Presidential Address, Anthropology Section', *Report of the British Association*, 1912, Dundee, pp. 575–98.

—— 1913a. 'Preliminary report on the cranial cast [Piltdown skull]', *Quarterly Journal of the Geological Society* 69: 145–7.

—— 1913b. 'The Piltdown skull and braincast', *Nature* 92: 267.

—— 1927. *The Evolution of Man* (2nd edition), London.

—— 1929. Report in the *Manchester Guardian*, 16 September.

SOLECKI, R. S. 1975. 'Shanidar IV, a Neanderthal flower burial in northern Iraq', *Science* 190: 880–1.

SOUTHEY, T. 1827. *Chronological History of the West Indies*, London, p. 487.

SPENCER, F. 1984. 'The Neanderthals and their evolutionary significance: A brief historical survey', pp. 1–49 in Smith, F. H., and Spencer, F. (eds.) 1984, *The Origins of Modern Humans*, New York.

—— 1990a. *Piltdown: A Scientific forgery*, Natural History Museum Publications, Oxford University Press, London, Oxford, and New York.

—— 1990b. *The Piltdown Papers 1908–1955*, Natural History Museum Publications, Oxford University Press, London.

STERN, J. T., Jr. 2000. 'Climbing to the Top. A Personal Memoir of *Australopithecus afarensis*', *Evolutionary Anthropology* 9: 113–33.

STEUDEL, K. L. 1994. 'Locomotor energetics and hominid evolution', *Evolutionary Anthropology* 3 (2): 42–7.

STONEKING, M., BHATIA, K., and WILSON, A. C. 1986. 'Rate of sequence divergence estimated from restriction maps of mitochondrial DNA from Papua New Guinea', *Cold Spring Harbor Symposia in Quantitative Biology* 51: 433–49.

STRINGER, C. B., and HUBLIN, J.-J. 1999. 'A new age determination for the Swanscombe skull and its implications for human evolution', *Journal of Human Evolution* 37: 873–7.

—— 2006. *Homo Britannicus*, Allen Lane, London.

——, and KRUSZYNSKI, R. G. 1981. 'Allez Neanderthal', *Nature* 289: 823–4.

——, HUBLIN, J.-J., and VANDERMEERSCH, B. 1984. 'The origin of anatomically modern humans in Western Europe', pp. 51–136 in Smith, F. H., and Spencer, F. (eds.) 1984, *The Origin of Modern Humans*, New York.

SUSMAN, R. L., and STERN, J. T. 1982. 'Functional morphology of *Homo habilis*', *Science* 217: 931–4.

SUWA, G., *et al.* 2009. 'The *Ardipithecus ramidus* Skull and its Implications for Hominid Origins', *Science* 326: 22; and online 68e2.

TEAFORD, M. F., and UNGAR, P. S. 2000. 'Diet and the Evolution of the Earliest Human Ancestors'. *Proceedings of the National Academy of Sciences* 97: 13506–11.

TELEKI, G. 1981. 'The omnivorous diet and eclectic feeding habits of chimpanzees in Gombe National Park, Tanzania', pp. 303–43 in Harding, R., and Teleki, G. (eds.) 1981, *Omnivorous Primates*, New York.

TERRY, R. 1974. *Raymond A. Dart: Taung 1924–1974*, Museum of Man and Science, Johannesburg.

THIEME, H. 1997. 'Lower Palaeolithic hunting spears from Germany', *Nature* 385: 807–10.

—— 2000. 'Lower Palaeolithic Hunting Weapons from Schöningen, Germany— the Oldest Spears in the World', *Acta Anthropologica Sinica* 19: 140–7.

Time, 1977. 'Puzzling out man's ancestor', 7 November, p. 54.

TOBIAS, P. V. 1964. 'The Olduvai Bed I hominine with special reference to its cranial capacity', *Nature* 202: 3–4.

—— 1978. Personal communication, interview with author, Johannesburg.

—— 1981. 'The emergence of man in Africa and beyond', pp. 43–57 in Young, J. Z., Jope, E. M., and Oakley, K. P. (eds.) 1981, *The Emergence of Man*, Phil. Trans. Roy. Soc. B.292.

TOBIAS, P. V. 1990. 'Introduction to a forgery', in Spencer, F. 1990a.

—— 1991. *Olduvai Gorge*, vol. 4: *The skulls, endocasts and teeth of Homo habilis*, Cambridge University Press, Cambridge.

—— 1992. Letter to the author, 13 February.

——, and NAPIER, J. R. 1964. Letter to *The Times*, London, 29 May.

——, RAATH M. A., MOGGI-CECCHI, J., and DOYLE, G. A. (eds.), 2001. *Humanity from African Naissance to Coming Millennia*, Florence University Press and Witwatersrand University Press, Florence and Johannesburg.

TORRENS, H. S. 2001. 'Timeless order: William Smith (1769–1839) and the search for raw materials 1800–1820', pp. 61–83 in Lewis, C. L. E. and Knell, S. J. (eds.) 2001, *The Age of the Earth: From 4004 BC to AD 2002*, Geological Society, London, Special Publications, 190.

TOTH, N. 1982. 'The stone technologies of early hominids at Koobi Fora, Kenya', Ph.D. diss. University of California, Berkeley.

—— 1985. 'The Oldowan re-assessed: a close look at early stone artifacts', *Journal of Archaeological Science* 12: 101–20.

TRYON, C. A. 2008. 'Reinvestigating Early Human Behavior at Olduvai Gorge', Review of Dominguez-Rodrigo, M., Barba, R., and Egeland, C. P. 2007, *Deconstructing Olduvai: A Taphonomic Study of the Bed I Sites*, Springer, New York.

TUTTLE, R. H. (ed.) 1976. *Primate Morphology and Evolution*, The Hague.

—— 1987. 'Kinesiological inferences and evolutionary implications from Laetoli bipedal trails', pp. 503–23 in Leakey, M. D., and Harris, J. M. (eds.) 1987, *Laetoli: A Pliocene Site in Northern Tanzania*, Clarendon Press, Oxford.

——, WEBB, D. M., and BAKSH, M. 1991. 'Laetoli toes and *Australopithecus afarensis*', *Human Evolution* 6. (3): 193–200.

USSHER, J., 1650/2003. *The Annals of the World*. Revised and updated by Larry and Marion Pierce, Master Books, Green Forest, Ark.

VALLOIS, H. V. 1949. 'The Fontéchevade fossil men', *American Journal of Physical Anthropology*, NS 7: 339–62.

—— 1954. 'Neanderthals and Praesapiens', *Journal of the Royal Anthropological Institute*, London, 84: 111–30.

VAN ANDEL, T. H., and DAVIES, W. (eds.) 2003. *Neanderthals and Modern Humans in the European Landscape During the Last Glaciation*, McDonald Institute for Archaeological Research, Cambridge.

VIRCHOW, R. 1872. 'Untersuchung des Neanderthal-Schädels', *Zoo. Ethn. Berlin* 4: 157–65.

WALKER, A. C. 1976. 'Remains attributable to *Australopithecus* in the East Rudolf succession', pp. 484–9 in Coppens, Y., Howell, F. C., Isaac, G. Ll., and Leakey, R. E. F. (eds.) 1976, *Earliest Man and Environments in the Lake Rudolf Basin*, University of Chicago Press, Chicago.

—— 1978. Personal communication, interview with author, Cambridge, Mass.

——, and LEAKEY, R. E. F. 1978. 'The hominids of East Turkana', *Scientific American*, 238 (8): 54–66.

————, HARRIS, J. M., and BROWN, F. H. 1986. '2.5-Myr *Australopithecus boisei* from west of Lake Turkana, Kenya', *Nature* 322: 517–22.

——, and SHIPMAN, P. 1996. *The Wisdom of Bones*, Weidenfeld & Nicolson, London.

WALSH, J. E. 1998. *Unravelling Piltdown*, Random House Value Publishing, New York.

WANG, Y. *et al.* 1979. 'Discovery of Dali fossil man and its preliminary study', *Sci. Sin.* 24: 303–6.

WARD, S., and HILL, A. 1987. 'Pliocene Hominid Partial Mandible from Tabarin, Baringo, Kenya', *American Journal of Physical Anthropology* 72: 21–37.

WASHBURN, S. L. 1960. 'Tools and human evolution', *Scientific American* 203 (3): 3–15.

—— (ed.) 1963. *Social Life of Early Man*, Chicago.

——, and LANCASTER, J. 1968. 'The evolution of hunting', pp. 293–303 in Lee, R. B., and DeVore, I. (eds.) 1968, *Man the Hunter*, Aldine, New York.

WATERSTON, D. 1913. 'The Piltdown mandible', *Nature* 92: 319.

WEIDENREICH, F. 1936. *The mandibles of Sinanthropus pekinensis: a comparative study*, Palaeontologica Sinica, Ser. D, III: 1–163.

WEIDENREICH, F. 1937. *The dentition of Sinanthropus pekinensis: a comparative odontography of the hominids*, Palaeontologica Sinica, NS D, 1: 1–180.

—— 1941. *The extremity bones of Sinanthropus pekinensis*, Palaeontologica Sinica, Ser. D, 5: 1–150.

—— 1943. *The skull of Sinanthropus pekinensis: a comparative study on a primitive hominid skull*, Palaeontologica Sinica, Ser. D, 10: 1–291.

WEINER, J. S. 1955. *The Piltdown Forgery*, Oxford University Press, London.

WELLS, L. H. 1966. 'The Robert Broom Memorial Lecture', *South Africa Journal of Science*, September 1967.

WENDT, H. 1968. *Before the Deluge*, Gollancz, London.

WHITE, H. J. O. 1926. 'The geology of the country near Lewes, with map by F. H. Edmunds', *Memoir Geological Survey of England and Wales*, Expl. Sheet 319.

WHITE, T. D. 1977. 'New fossil hominids from Laetoli, Tanzania', *American Journal of Physical Anthropology* 46: 197–230.

—— 1985. 'The hominids of Hadar and Laetoli: an element by element comparison of the dental samples', pp. 138–52 in Delson, E. (ed.) 1985, *Ancestors: The Hard Evidence*, New York.

—— 1987. Quoted in Lewin, R. 1987a. 'The earliest "humans" were more like apes', *Science* 236: 1061–3.

—— 2002. 'Earliest hominids', pp. 407–16 in Hartwig, W. C. (ed.) 2002, *The Primate Fossil Record*, Cambridge University Press, Cambridge.

—— 2003. 'Early Hominids—Diversity or Distortion?' *Science* 299: 1994.

——, and HARRIS, J. M. 1977. 'Suid evolution and correlation of African hominid Localities', *Science* 198: 13–21.

——, and SUWA, G. 1987. 'Hominid Footprints at Laetoli: Facts and Interpretations', *American Journal of Physical Anthropology* 72: 485–514.

——, SUWA, G., and ASFAW, B., 1994. '*Australopithecus ramidus*, a new species of early hominid from Aramis, Ethiopia', *Nature* 371: 306–12.

————, and ASFAW, B. 1995. '*Australopithecus ramidus*, a new species of early hominid from Aramis, Ethiopia – a corrigendum', *Nature* 375: 88.

——, *et al.* 2003. 'Pleistocene *Homo sapiens* from the Middle Awash, Ethiopia', *Nature* 423: 742–7.

————, *et al.* 2009*a*. '*Ardipithecus ramidus* and the Paleobiology of Early Hominids', *Science* 326: 75–86.

————, *et al.* 2009*b*. Macrovertebrate Paleontology and the Pliocene Habitat of *Ardipithecus ramidus* and the Paleobiology of Early Hominids, *Science* 326: 92.

WILSON, A. C., *et al.* 1985. 'Mitochondrial DNA and two perspectives of evolutionary genetics', *Biological Journal of the Linnaean Society* 26: 375–400.

———— 1986. 'Mitochondrial clans and the age of our common mother', *Proceedings of the 7th International Congress of Human Genetics*, Berlin.

WOLDEGABRIEL, G., *et al.* 2009. 'The Geological, Isotopic, Botanical, Invertebrate, and Lower Vertebrate Surroundings of *Ardipithecus ramidus*', *Science* 326: 19, and online 65e1–65e5.

WOLPOFF, M. H. 1971. 'Competitive exclusion among Lower Pleistocene hominids: the single species hypothesis', *Man* 6: 601–14.

—— 1980. *Paleoanthropology*, New York.

——, *et al.* 2006. 'An Ape or *the* Ape:…', *PaleoAnthropology* 2006: 36–50.

——, SENUT, B. PICKFORD, M., and HAWKS, J. 2002. '*Sahelanthropus* or *Sahelpithecus?*' *Nature* 419: 581–2.

WOO, J. K. 1966. 'The skull of Lantian Man', *Current Anthropology* 7: 83–6.

——, and PENG, R. C. 1959. 'Fossil human skull of Early Palaeoanthropic stage found at Mapa, Shaoquan, Kwantung Province', *Vert. Palasiat.* 3: 176–82.

WOOD, B. A. 1984. 'The origin of *Homo erectus*', pp. 99–111 in Andrews, P., and Franzen, J. L. (eds.) 1984, *The Early Evolution of Man, with special emphasis on Southeast Asia and Africa*, Courier Forschungsinstitut Senckenberg 69.

—— 1987. 'Who is the "real" *Homo habilis?*' *Nature* 327: 187–8.

—— 1991. *Koobi Fora Research Project*, vol. 4: *Hominid cranial remains*, Clarendon Press, Oxford.

—— 1994. 'The oldest hominid yet', *Nature* 371: 280–1.

—— 2000. 'The history of the genus *Homo*', *Human Evolution* 15: 39–49.

WOOD, B. A. 2002. 'Hominid revelations from Chad', *Nature* 418: 134.

—— 2006. 'A precious little bundle', *Nature* 443: 278–80.

——, and LONERGAN, N. 2008. 'The hominin fossil record: taxa, grades and clades', *Journal of Anatomy* 212: 354–76.

WOODWARD, A. S. 1885. 'Modern ideas of the Creation', *Macclesfield Courier and Herald*, Macclesfield, 28 March 1885.

—— 1913. 'Missing links among extinct animals', *Report of the British Association*, Birmingham.

—— 1916. 'Charles Dawson—an obituary', *Geological Magazine* (6) 3, pp. 477–9.

—— 1917. 'Fourth note on the Piltdown gravel, with evidence of a second skull of *Eoanthropus dawsoni*', *Quarterly Journal of the Geological Society* 73: 1–10.

—— 1921. 'A new cave man from Rhodesia, South Africa', *Nature* 108: 371–2.

—— 1922. Letter to *The Times*, London, 22 May.

—— 1933. 'Early human remains in East Africa', *Man* 33: 210.

—— 1948. *The Earliest Englishman*, Watts, London.

WU, R. 1982. 'Recent advances of Chinese palaeoanthropology', *Occ. Pap. Ser. Ii*, University of Hong Kong.

—— 1983. 'Peking Man'. *Scientific American* 248 (6): 78–86.

——, and LIN, S. 1985. 'Chinese Palaeoanthropology: Retrospect and Prospect', pp. 1–17 in Wu, R., and Olsen, J. W. (eds.) 1985 *Palaeoanthropology and Palaeolithic Archaeology in the People's Republic of China*, Orlando.

——, and OLSEN, J. W. (eds.) 1985. *Palaeoanthropology and Palaeolithic Archaeology in the People's Republic of China*, Orlando.

WU, R. K., *et al.* 1985. *Multi-disciplinary Study of the Peking Man Site at Zhoukoudian* [in Chinese], Science Press, Beijing.

WU, X., and POIRIER, F. E. 1995. *Human Evolution in China: A Metric Description of the Fossils and a Review of the Sites*, Oxford University Press, New York.

WURZ, S. 1999. 'The Howiesons Poort backed artefacts from Klasies River: an argument for symbolic behaviour', *South African Archaeological Bulletin* 54: 38–50.

—— 2002. 'Variability in the Middle Stone Age Lithic Sequence 115,000–60,000 Years Ago at Klasies River, South Africa', *Journal of Archaeological Science* 29: 1001–15.

WYNN, J. G., *et al.* 2006. 'Geological and palaeontological context of a Pliocene juvenile hominin at Dikika, Ethiopia', *Nature* 443: 332–6.

WYSE JACKSON, P. 2006. *The Chronologer's Quest: Episodes in the Search for the Age of the Earth*, Cambridge University Press.

YATES, F., and HEALY, M. J. R. 1951. 'Statistical methods in anthropology', *Nature* 168: 1116.

YELLEN, J. E., *et al.* 1995. 'A Middle Stone Age Worked Bone Industry from Katanda, Upper Semliki Valley, Zaire', *Science* 268: 553–5.

YOUNG, J. Z., JOPE, E. M., and OAKLEY, K. P. (eds.) 1981. *The Emergence of Man*, Phil. Trans. Roy. Soc. B. 292.

YOUNG, R. B. 1925. Quoted in *The Star*, Johannesburg. News report, 4 February.

ZDANSKY, O. 1923. 'Über ein Saungerknockenlager in Chou K'ou Tien', *Geological Survey of China Bulletin* 5: 83–9, Peking.

—— 1927. 'Preliminary notice on two teeth of a hominid from a cave in Chihli (China)', *Geological Survey of China Bulletin* 5: 281–4, Peking.

—— 1928. *Die Saugetiere der Quartarfauna von Chou K'ou Tien*, Palaeontologica Sinica, Series C, 5 (4), Peking.

—— 1978. Personal communication, interview with author, Uppsala.

ZHU, R. X., *et al.* 2004. 'New evidence on the Earliest Human Presence at High Northern Latitudes in Northeast Asia', *Nature* 431: 559–62.

——, *et al.* 2008. 'Early evidence of the genus *Homo* in East Asia', *J. Human Evolution* 55: 1075–85.

ZOLLIKOFER, C. P. E., *et al.* 2005. 'Virtual reconstruction of *Sahelanthropus tchadensis*', *Nature* 434: 755–9.

ZUCKERMAN, S. 1966. 'Myths and methods in anatomy', *Journal of the Royal College of Surgeons of Edinburgh* 11: 87–114.

INDEX